Sociology

Exploring the Architecture of Everyday Life

THIRD EDITION

READINGS

Excellence and Innovation for Teaching Introductory Sociology...

THE EDITOR'S PURPOSE

"I am a sociology teacher first and foremost. So I set out to write a book that is as helpful to the craft of teaching sociology as possible. You will not find a gargantuan summary of every sociological concept, topic, and theory here. Instead, I chose to limit the focus, allowing for a deeper, more thorough, and hopefully more useful analysis of key ideas in the discipline. The book revolves around a sustained theme—the reciprocal relationship between the individual and society—and continually shows the reader his or her active role as creator and shaper of society. I examine the crucial links between people's common, everyday experiences and the broader structural features of their social worlds. Along the way I use a personal style of writing that I think will appeal to students and instructors alike."

David M. Newman
DePauw University

This companion anthology to the text, *Sociology: Exploring the Architecture of Everyday Life*, Third Edition, provides provocative, eye-opening examples of the practice of sociology in a well-edited, well-designed, affordable format. If you adopt both the text and the anthology, a special "two-for-one" price is available from us to your bookstore! Call or e-mail Pine Forge Press for details.

ALSO AVAILABLE

Teaching Resources and an Annotated Bibliography for Teaching Sociology, superbly researched and crafted, is available for use with the third edition of David Newman's text and companion anthology. Test materials, synopses of articles, additional suggested exercises, literary and visual resources, and entries for the unique annotated bibliography were created with input and suggestions from a nationwide group of dedicated introductory teachers.

PINE FORGE PRESS, 2455 Teller Road, Thousand Oaks, CA 91320
tel: (805) 499-4224 ■ fax: (805) 499-7881 ■ E-mail: sales@pfp.sagepub.com
http://www.pineforge.com

Newman's *Sociology*
Exploring the Architecture of Everyday Life
THIRD EDITION

Features of this wonderful new third edition include the following:

- Using more cross-cultural examples, Newman effectively shows students how their lives are linked to, and affected by, our increasingly global society.

- Additional research illustrations, visual essays, micro-macro connections, and examples have been added, making the book even more meaningful to today's students.

- Statistics, examples and graphics have been updated and refreshed throughout the book, keeping it current and accessible.

- An Internet component has been incorporated into several of the "Your Turn" exercises.

Visit our web site at http://www.pineforge.com **to view the** *new* **study site for David Newman's book!** Included are do-it-yourself reviews and tests for students, web activities designed to enhance learning, a bulletin board where students and teachers can post messages, and a resource file containing web sites and additional helpful information!

"The greatest challenge for me in teaching has been to find ways of engaging students in the curriculum; to encourage them to use their sociological imagination and to recognize the intersection between their own lives and the larger social/historical forces and institutions existing all around them. Newman's text has been a close to perfect tool in this endeavor. Students told me it was the best introductory textbook they'd ever seen. They claim to 'recognize' themselves in his examples. What is important about this is that the examples persuasively dispel the notion that sociology is about 'other people but not me.'"

—Kelly Murphy, University of Pittsburgh

A companion text entitled

Sociology: Exploring the Architecture of Everyday Life
Third Edition

accompanies this anthology and is available from
your instructor and college bookstore.

Sociology

Exploring the Architecture of Everyday Life

THIRD EDITION

READINGS

David M. Newman

Department of Sociology and Anthropology
DePauw University

Pine Forge Press

Thousand Oaks, California ■ London ■ New Delhi

Cover photograph by Helen Levitt. Printed by arrangement with Knox Burger Associates Ltd. Reprinted from *In the Street,* published by Duke University Press, © 1987, Helen Levitt.

Copyright © 1995, 1997, 2000 by Pine Forge Press

For information, address:

Pine Forge Press
A Sage Publications Company
2455 Teller Road
Thousand Oaks, California 91320
(805) 499-4224
E-mail: sales@pfp.sagepub.com

Sage Publications Ltd.
6 Bonhill Street
London EC2A 4PU
United Kingdom

Sage Publications India Pvt. Ltd.
M-32 Market
Greater Kailash I
New Delhi 110 048 India

Production Management: Scratchgravel Publishing Services
Copy Editor: Susan Pendleton
Typesetter: Scratchgravel Publishing Services
Cover Designer: Ravi Balasuriya

Printed in the United States of America
99 00 01 02 03 10 9 8 7 6 5 4 3 2 1

Library of Congress Cataloging-in-Publication Data
Newman, David M., 1958–
    Sociology : exploring the architecture of everyday life :
readings / David M. Newman. — 3rd ed.
    p.   cm.
    ISBN 0-7619-8655-3
    1. Sociology.   I. Title.
HM586 .N48   2000
    301—dc21
                                                    99-6793
                                                      CIP

This book is printed on acid-free paper that meets Environmental Protection Agency standards for recycled paper.

About the Editor

David M. Newman (Ph.D., University of Washington) is an Associate Professor of Sociology at DePauw University. In addition to the introductory course, he teaches courses in research methods, family, social psychology, and deviance. He has won teaching awards at both the University of Washington and DePauw University.

About the Publisher

Pine Forge Press is a new educational publisher, dedicated to publishing innovative books and software throughout the social sciences. On this and any other of our publications, we welcome your comments. Please call or write us at:

Pine Forge Press
A Sage Publications Company
2455 Teller Road
Thousand Oaks, CA 91320
(805)499-4224
E-mail: sales@pfp.sagepub.com

Visit our World Wide Web site, your direct link to a multitude of on-line resources:

http://www.pineforge.com

PINE FORGE PRESS TITLES OF RELATED INTEREST

Adventures in Social Research: Data Analysis Using SPSS® for Windows™ by Earl Babbie and Fred Halley

Media/Society: Industries, Images, and Audiences by David Croteau and William Hoynes

Exploring Social Issues Using SPSS® for Windows 95™ Versions 7.5, 8.0, or Higher by Joseph F. Healey, John Boli, Earl Babbie, and Fred Halley

Race, Ethnicity, Gender, and Class: The Sociology of Group Conflict and Change, 2nd Ed., by Joseph F. Healey

Race, Ethnicity, and Gender in the United States: Inequality, Group Conflict, and Power by Joseph F. Healey

Sociological Snapshots: Seeing Social Structure and Change in Everyday Life, 2nd Ed., by Jack Levin

Sociology: Exploring the Architecture of Everyday Life, 3rd Ed., by David M. Newman

Building Community: Social Science in Action edited by Philip Nyden, Anne Figert, Mark Shibley, and Darryl Burrows

The Production of Reality: Essays and Readings on Social Interaction, 2nd Ed., by Jodi O'Brien and Peter Kollock

The McDonaldization of Society, Rev. Ed., by George Ritzer

Second Thoughts: Seeing Conventional Wisdom through the Sociological Eye by Janet M. Ruane and Karen A. Cerulo

Shifts in the Social Contract: Understanding Change in American Society by Beth Rubin

The Pine Forge Press Series in Research Methods and Statistics

Edited by Kathleen S. Crittenden

Social Statistics for a Diverse Society, **2nd Ed.,** by Chava Frankfort-Nachmias and Anna Leon-Guerrero

Experimental Design and the Analysis of Variance by Robert Leik

How Sampling Works by Richard Maisel and Caroline Hodges Persell

Program Evaluation by George McCall

Investigating the Social World: The Process and Practice of Research, **2nd Ed.,** by Russell K. Schutt

Multiple Regression: A Primer by Paul Allison

A Guide to Field Research by Carol A. Bailey

Designing Surveys: A Guide to Decisions and Procedures by Ronald Czaja and Johnny Blair

Sociology for a New Century

A Pine Forge Press Series edited by Charles Ragin, Wendy Griswold, and Larry Griffin

Global Inequalities by York W. Bradshaw and Michael Wallace

Schools and Societies by Steven Brint

How Societies Change by Daniel Chirot

Constructing Identities: Race and Ethnicity in the Modern World by Stephen Cornell and Douglas Hartmann

Cultures and Societies in a Changing World by Wendy Griswold

Crime and Disrepute by John Hagan

Gods in the Global Village: The World's Religions in Sociological Perspective by Lester Kurtz

Waves of Democracy: Social Movements and Political Change by John Markoff

Development and Social Change: A Global Perspective by Philip McMichael

Constructing Social Research by Charles C. Ragin

Women and Men at Work by Barbara Reskin and Irene Padavic

Cities in a World Economy by Saskia Sassen

Gender, Family, and Social Movements by Suzanne Staggenborg

CONTENTS

15   Architects of Change: Reconstructing Society   386

One of the greatest challenges I face as a teacher of sociology is trying to get my students to see the relevance of the course material to their own lives and to appreciate fully its connection to the larger society. I teach my students to see that sociology is all around us. It's in our families, our careers, our media, our goals, our interests, our desires, even our minds. Sociology can be found at the neighborhood pub or in the maintenance bay at the local gas station. It's with us when we're alone and when we're in a mob of people. Sociology can answer questions of global as well as private significance—from how some countries create and maintain dominance over others to why we find some people attractive and not others; from why poverty, discrimination, crime, and homelessness exist to why Americans eat scrambled eggs rather than rice for breakfast.

With these ideas in mind I set out to compile this collection of short articles, chapters, and excerpts designed to help introduce you to sociology. Instructors and students alike responded quite positively to the readings in the first two editions of this book. It would have been easy simply to include those same readings in this third edition. But I very much wanted the book to be fresh and contemporary. Hence, seventeen of the thirty-one readings are new additions, most of which were written within the past five years.

As in the first two editions, these selections don't provide a lot of dry factual information, concept definitions, or reviews of past research. Instead, they are vivid, provocative, and eye-opening *examples* of the practice of sociology. Many of the readings are drawn from carefully conducted social research. They provide important illustrations of how sociologists support their theories, insights, and ideas with empirical evidence.

In addition to accurately representing the sociological perspective and providing rigorous coverage of the discipline, the selections are all enjoyable to read. I hope that each of them stimulates thoughtful reflection as you examine what society is, how it works, and, most important, your place in it.

The readings represent a variety of styles. Some use common, everyday experiences and phenomena (such as sadness, sports, marriage, childbirth, fast-food restaurants, perceptions of time) to illustrate the relationship between the individual and society. Others focus on important social issues or problems (crime, race relations, poverty, educational inequalities, immigration, global economics, political extremism) or on historical events (massacres during war time, drug scares, peace movements). Furthermore, they are written by people from a variety of professions. You need not be a trained sociologist to see the world sociologically. So this book includes articles written by psychologists, anthropologists, social commentators, and journalists as well as by sociologists.

To help you get the most out of these selections I've written brief introductions to each chapter that provide the sociological context for the readings. For those of you who are also reading the accompanying textbook, these introductions will furnish a quick intellectual link between the readings and the textbook. After each selection you will find a set of discussion questions to ponder. These items are not examlike information questions to determine whether you absorbed all the details in a given reading. Instead the questions make you think about the meaning and relevance of each reading. They frequently ask you to apply a specific author's conclusions to some contemporary issue in society or to your own life experiences. It is my hope that these questions will generate a lot of classroom debate and help you see the sociological merit of the readings.

A new World Wide Web site established for this third edition includes do-it-yourself reviews and tests for students, web-based activities designed to enhance learning, and a chat room where students and teachers can post messages and debate matters of sociological significance. The site can be accessed via the Pine Forge web site at www.pineforge.com.

Books like these are enormous projects. As with the first two editions, I would like to thank Steve Rutter, Sherith Pankratz, Becky Smith, and the rest of the staff at Pine Forge Press for their useful advice and assistance in putting this reader together. I am grateful to Anne and Greg Draus at Scratchgravel Publishing for producing a high-quality book under extreme time pressure and to Sheri Gilbert for securing all the copyright permissions. I would also like to thank Bizz Steele for magically and promptly acquiring many of the books and articles I desperately needed.

Enjoy!

David M. Newman
Department of Sociology/Anthropology
DePauw University
Greencastle, IN 46135
E-Mail: DNEWMAN@DEPAUW.EDU

ACKNOWLEDGMENTS

I appreciate the many helpful comments offered by the reviewers of the three editions of this book:

Deborah Abowitz, Bucknell University
Stephen Adair, Central Connecticut State University
Rebecca Adams, University of North Carolina, Greensboro
Ron Aminzade, University of Minnesota
Afroza Anwary, Carleton College
George Arquitt, Oklahoma State University
Carol Auster, Franklin and Marshall College
David Bogen, Emerson College
Todd Campbell, Loyola University, Chicago
Doug Currivan, University of Massachusetts, Boston
Jeff Davidson, University of Delaware
Kimberly Davies, Augusta State University
James J. Dowd, University of Georgia
Charlotte Chorn Dunham, Texas Tech University
Charles Edgley, Oklahoma State University
Rachel Einwohner, Purdue University
Shalom Endleman, Quinnipiac College
Rebecca Erickson, University of Akron
Kimberly Faust, Fitchburg State University
Patrick Fontane, St. Louis College of Pharmacy
Barry Goetz, University of Dayton
Valerie Gunter, University of New Orleans
Charles Harper, Creighton University
Doug Harper, Duquesne University
Peter Hennen, University of Minnesota
Susan Hoerbelt, University of South Florida
Valerie Jenness, University of California, Irvine
Kathryn Johnson, Barat College
Richard Jones, Marquette University
Tom Kando, California State University, Sacramento
Steve Keto, Kent State University
Peter Kivisto, Augustana College
Marc LaFountain, State University of West Georgia

Melissa Latimer, West Virginia University

Joseph Lengermann, University of Maryland, College Park

Fred Maher

Kristen Marcussen, University of Iowa

Benjamin Mariante, Stonehill College

Joseph Marolla, Virginia Commonwealth University

James R. McIntosh, Lehigh University

Jerome McKibben, Fitchburg State University

Ted P. McNeilsmith, Adams State College

Melinda Milligan, University of California, Davis

Susannne Monahan, Montana State University

Kelly Murphy, University of Pittsburgh

Elizabeth Ehrhardt Mustaine, University of Central Florida

Toska Olson, University of Washington

Larry Perkins

Bernice Pescosolido, Indiana University, Bloomington

Mike Plummer, Boston College

Edward Ponczek, William Rainey Harper College

Judith Richlin-Klonsky, University of California, Los Angeles

Robert Robinson, Indiana University, Bloomington

Mary Rogers, University of West Florida

Sally S. Rogers, Montgomery College

Michael Ryan, Upper Iowa University

Mark Shibley, Southern Oregon University

Thomas Shriver, Oklahoma State University

Katherine Slevin, College of William and Mary

Nicholas Sofios, Providence College

Kandi Stinson, Xavier University

Robert Tellander, Sonoma State University

Kathleen Tiemann, University of North Dakota

Steven Vallas, Georgia Institute of Technology

John Walsh, University of Illinois, Chicago

Gregory Weiss, Roanoke College

Marty Wenglinsky, Quinnipiac College

Stephan Werba, Catonsville Community College

Norma Williams, University of North Texas

Janelle Wilson, University of Minnesota, Duluth

Mark Winton, University of Central Florida

Cynthia A. Woolever, Lexington Theological Seminary

Ashraf Zahedi, Santa Clara University

Stephen Zehr, University of Southern Indiana

We gratefully acknowledge the following for permission to reprint the selections in this anthology:

Excerpts from "The Mundanity of Excellence: An Ethnographic Report on Stratification and Olympic Swimmers" by Daniel F. Chambliss. *Sociological Theory,* Vol. 7, No. 1, Spring 1989, pp. 70–86. Washington, DC: American Sociological Association. Copyright © 1989 by the American Sociological Association. Reprinted by permission.

"The My Lai Massacre: A Military Crime of Obedience" in *Crimes of Obedience* (pp. 1–20), ed. Herbert Kelman and V. Lee Hamilton. Copyright © 1989 by Yale University Press. Reprinted by permission.

From *Speaking of Sadness: Depression, Disconnection, and the Meanings of Illness* (pp. 3–11, 165–185) by David A. Karp. Copyright © 1996 by Oxford University Press, Inc. Used by permission of Oxford University Press, Inc.

Excerpts from "The Crack Attack: Politics and Media in the Crack Scare" from *Crack in America: Demon Drugs and Social Justice* (pp. 18–51), ed. Craig Reinarman and Harry G. Levine, Berkeley: University of California Press. Copyright © 1997 by the Regents of the University of California. Reprinted by permission.

"Researching Dealers and Smugglers," republished with permission of the Columbia University Press, 562 W. 113th St., New York, NY 10025. Excerpts from *Wheeling and Dealing* (pp. 11–28), by Patricia A. Adler, 1985. Reproduced by permission of the publisher via Copyright Clearance Center, Inc.

From *A Geography of Time* (pp. 81–100) by Robert Levine. Copyright © 1997 by Robert Levine. Reprinted by permission of Basic Books, a member of Perseus Books, L.L.C.

"Fashions in Childbirth" from *American Way of Birth* (pp. 51–73) by Jessica Mitford. Copyright © 1992 by Jessica Mitford. Used by permission of Dutton, a division of Penguin Putnam, Inc.

Excerpts from "The Gloried Self: The Aggrandizement and the Constriction of Self" by Patricia A. Adler and Peter Adler. *Social Psychology Quarterly,* 1985, 52:4, pp. 299–310. Washington, DC: American Sociological Association. Copyright © 1985 by the American Sociological Association. Reprinted by permission.

Excerpts from "Transsexuals' Narrative Construction of the 'True Self'" by Douglas Mason-Schrock. *Social Psychology Quarterly,* 1996, 59:3, pp. 176–192. Washington, DC: American Sociological Association. Copyright © 1996 by the American Sociological Association. Reprinted by permission.

Excerpts from "Making It by Faking It" by Robert Granfield. *Journal of Contemporary Ethnology,* Vol. 20, No. 3, October 1991, pp. 331–351. Copyright © 1991 by Sage Publications. Reprinted by permission of Sage Publications, Inc.

Reprinted from "Suspended Identity: Identity Transformation in a Maximum Security Prison" by Thomas J. Schmid and Richard S. Jones, *Symbolic Interaction,* 14(4): pp. 415–432. Copyright © 1991 by JAI Press, Inc. With permission from Elsevier Science.

Reprinted by permission of Transaction Publishers. "The Saints and the Rough-necks" by William Chambliss. *Society,* 11:1, Nov./Dec., pp. 24–31. Copyright © 1973 by Transaction Publishers; all rights reserved.

From Jeffrey Reiman, "A Crime by Any Other Name . . ." in *The Rich Get Richer and the Poor Get Prison,* 5th Ed. (pp. 59–96). Copyright © 1997 by Allyn & Bacon. Reprinted/adapted by permission.

Excerpts from "Exiles from Kinship" republished with permission of the Columbia University Press, 562 W. 113th St., New York, NY 10025. From *Families We Choose: Lesbians, Gays, Kinship* (excerpts from pp. 21–41) by Kath Weston, 1991. Reprinted by permission of the publisher via Copyright Clearance Center, Inc.

Excerpts from *The Time Bind: When Work Becomes Home and Home Becomes Work* (pp. 6–9, 25–30, 35–46, 198–201, 211–218, 244–249) by Arlie Russell Hochschild. Copyright © 1997 by Arlie Russell Hochschild. Published by Metropolitan Books, Henry Holt and Company, Inc.

Excerpts from *Fast Food, Fast Talk: Service Work and the Routinization of Everyday Life* (pp. 1–3, 15, 72–76, 105–117, 179–195, 211–213) by Robin Leidner. Berkeley: University of California Press. Copyright © 1993 by the Regents of the University of California. Reprinted by permission.

From John Van Maanen, "The Smile Factory: Work at Disneyland" in *Reframing Organizational Culture* (pp. 58–75), ed. Peter Frost, 1991. Copyright © 1991 by Sage Publications, Inc. Reprinted by permission of Sage Publications, Inc.

"The Bohemian Grove." Excerpts of approximately 18 pages from *The Bohemian Grove and Other Retreats: A Study in Ruling-Class Cohesiveness* by G. William Domhoff. Copyright © 1974 by G. William Domhoff. Reprinted by permission of the author.

"These Dark Satanic Mills" reprinted with the permission of Simon & Schuster, Inc. from *One World, Ready or Not: The Manic Logic of Global Capitalism* (pp. 333–359) by William Greider. Copyright © 1997 by William Greider.

"Savage Inequalities in America's Schools: Life on the Mississippi" excerpts from *Savage Inequalities: Children in America's Schools* (pp. 7–8, 10–14, 20–21, 23–25, 27–30, 34–35, 124–130) by Jonathan Kozol. Copyright © 1991 by Jonathan Kozol. Reprinted by permission of Crown Publishers, Inc.

Excerpts from *Making Ends Meet: How Single Mothers Survive Welfare and Low-Wage Work* (pp. 1–9, 61–87) by Kathryn Edin and Laura Lein. Copyright © 1997 by Russell Sage Foundation, New York, New York. Reprinted by permission.

"The Code of the Streets" by Elijah Anderson, *The Atlantic Monthly,* May 1994, pp. 81–94. From *The Code of the Streets* by Elijah Anderson. Copyright © 1999 by Elijah Anderson. Reprinted by permission of W. W. Norton & Company, Inc.

Excerpts from *The Agony of Education: Black Students at White Colleges and Universities* (28 pages excerpted from pp. 1–13, 83–114) by Joe R. Feagin, Hernan Vera, and Nikitah Imani. Copyright © 1996. Reproduced by permission of Routledge, Inc.

I

The Individual and Society

CHAPTER 1

Taking a New Look at a Familiar World

The primary theme of sociology is that our everyday thoughts and actions are the product of a complex interplay between massive social forces and personal characteristics. We can't understand the relationship between individuals and their societies without understanding both. The *sociological imagination* is the ability to see the impact of social forces on our private lives. It is an awareness that our lives lie at the intersection of personal biography and societal history. The sociological imagination encourages us to move beyond individualistic explanations of human experiences to an understanding of the mutual influence that individuals and society have on one another. So, rather than study what goes on *within* people, sociologists study what goes on *between* and *among* people, as individuals, groups, organizations, or entire societies. Sociology forces us to look outside the tight confines of our individual personalities to understand the social phenomena that shape us.

Consider athletic performance. I'm sure you've seen televised coverage of the Olympics. If you're like me, you probably sat in awe of those remarkable athletes—the elite of their respective sports—competing at a level far beyond the reach of most "normal" people. As we watch them perform, it's easy to conclude that such athletes are a different breed, that they have some inborn, personal quality—call it "talent"—that propels them to world-class achievements. But Daniel Chambliss, in "The Mundanity of Excellence," argues that, as much as we'd like to believe otherwise, these world-class athletes are not that different from the rest of us. Their excellence comes from fundamentally ordinary activities that take place within identifiable social worlds that have their own unique values, attitudes, and behavior patterns. By explaining athletic excellence in such a way, Chambliss helps introduce us to the sociological perspective on understanding social life: Behavior commonly attributed to innate qualities can be better understood by examining the broader social context within which it takes place.

The Mundanity of Excellence

An Ethnographic Report on Stratification and Olympic Swimmers

Daniel F. Chambliss

Olympic sports and competitive swimming in particular provide an unusually clear opportunity for studying the nature of excellence. In other fields, it may be less clear who are the outstanding performers: the best painter or pianist, the best businessperson, the finest waitress or the best father. But in sport (and this is one of its attractions) success is defined more exactly, by success in competition. There are medals and ribbons and plaques for first place, second, and third; competitions are arranged for the head-to-head meeting of the best competitors in the world; in swimming and track, times are electronically recorded to the hundredth of a second; there are statistics published and rankings announced, every month or every week. By the end of the Olympic Games every four years, it is completely clear who won and who lost, who made the finals, who participated in the Games, and who never participated in the sport at all.

Within competitive swimming in particular, clear stratification exists not only between individuals but also between defined levels of the sport as well. At the lowest level, we see the country club teams, operating in the summertime as a loosely run, mildly competitive league, with volunteer, part-time coaches. Above that there are teams that represent entire cities and compete with other teams from other cities around the state or region; then a "Junior Nationals" level of competition, featuring the best younger (under 18 years old) athletes; then the Senior Nationals level (any age, the best in the nation); and finally, we could speak of world- or Olympic-class competitors. At each such level, we find, predictably, certain people competing: one athlete swims in a summer league, never seeing swimmers from another town; one swimmer may consistently qualify for the Junior Nationals, but not for Seniors; a third may swim at the Olympics and never return to Junior Nationals. The levels of the sport are remarkably distinct from one another.

. . . Because success in swimming is so definable, . . . we can clearly see, by comparing levels and studying individuals as they move between and within levels, what exactly produces excellence. In addition, careers in swimming are relatively short; one can achieve tremendous success in a brief period of time. Rowdy Gaines, beginning in the sport when 17 years old, jumped from a country club league to a world record in the 100 meter freestyle event in only three years. This allows the researcher to conduct true longitudinal research in a few short years. . . .

. . . This report draws on extended experience with swimmers at every level of ability, over some half a dozen years. Observation has covered the span of careers, and I have had the chance to compare not just athletes within a certain level (the view that most coaches have), but between the most discrepant levels as well. Thus these findings avoid the usual . . . problem of an observer's being familiar mainly with athletes at one level. . . .

The Nature of Excellence

By "excellence" I mean "consistent superiority of performance." The excellent athlete regularly, even routinely, performs better than his or her competitors. Consistency of superior performances tells us that one athlete is indeed better than another, and that the difference between them is not merely the product of chance. This definition can apply at any level of the sport, differentiating athletes. The superiority discussed here may be that of one swimmer over another, or of all athletes at one level (say, the Olympic class) over another. By this definition, we need not judge performance against an absolute criterion, but only against other performances. There are acknowledged leaders on every team, as well as teams widely recognized as dominant.

To introduce what are sources of excellence for Olympic athletes, I should first suggest—saving the demonstration for later—what *does not* produce excellence.

(1) Excellence is not, I find, the product of socially deviant personalities. These swimmers don't appear to be "oddballs," nor are they loners ("kids who have given up the normal teenage life").[1] If their achievements result from a personality characteristic, that characteristic is not obvious. Perhaps it is true, as the mythology of sports has it, that the best athletes are more self-confident (although that is debatable); but such confidence could be an effect of achievement, not the cause of it.[2]

(2) Excellence does *not* result from quantitative changes in behavior. Increased training time, *per se,* does not make one swim fast; nor does increased "psyching up," nor does moving the arms faster. Simply doing more of the same will not lead to moving up a level in the sport.

(3) Excellence does *not* result from some special inner quality of the athlete. "Talent" is one common name for this quality; sometimes we talk of a "gift," or of "natural ability." These terms are generally used to mystify the essentially mundane processes of achievement in sports, keeping us away from a realistic analysis of the actual factors creating superlative performances, and protecting us from a sense of responsibility for our own outcomes.

So where does excellence—consistent superiority of performance—come from?

I. Excellence Requires Qualitative Differentiation

Excellence in competitive swimming is achieved through qualitative differentiation from other swimmers, not through quantitative increases in activity. . . .

. . . I should clarify what is meant here by "quantitative" and "qualitative." By quantity, we mean the number or amount of something. Quantitative improvement entails an increase in the number of some one thing one does. An athlete who practices 2 hours a day and increases that activity to 4 hours a day has made a quantitative change in behavior. Or, one who swims 5 miles and changes to 7 miles has made a quantitative change. She does more of the same thing; there is an increase in quantity. Or again, a freestyle swimmer who, while maintaining the same stroke technique, moves his arms at an increased number of strokes per minute has made a quantitative change in behavior. Quantitative improvements, then, involve doing *more of the same thing.*

By quality, though, we mean the character or nature of the thing itself. A qualitative change involves modifying what is actually being done, not simply doing more of it. For a swimmer doing the breaststroke, a qualitative change might be a change from pulling straight back with the arms to sculling them outwards, to the sides; or from lifting oneself up out of the water at the turn to staying low near the water. Other qualitative changes might include competing in a regional meet instead of local meets; eating vegetables and complex carbohydrates rather than fats and sugars; entering one's weaker events instead of only one's stronger events; learning to do a flip turn with freestyle, instead of merely turning around and pushing off; or training at near-competition levels of intensity, rather than casually. Each of these involves doing things differently than before, not necessarily doing more. Qualitative improvements involve doing *different kinds of things.*

Now we can consider how qualitative differentiation is manifested:

Different levels of the sport are qualitatively distinct. Olympic champions don't just do much more of the same things that summer-league country club swimmers do. They don't just swim more hours, or move their arms faster, or attend more workouts. What makes them faster cannot be quantitatively compared with lower-level swimmers, because while there may be quantitative differences—and certainly there are, for instance in the number of hours spent in workouts—these are not, I think, the decisive factors at all.[3]

Instead, they do things differently. Their strokes are different, their attitudes are different, their groups of friends are different, their parents treat the sport differently, the swimmers prepare differently for their races, and they enter different kinds of meets and events. There are numerous discontinuities of this sort between, say, the swimmer who competes in a local City League meet and one who enters the Olympic Trials. Consider three dimensions of difference:

(1) Technique: The styles of strokes, dives and turns are dramatically different at different levels. A "C" (the lowest rank in United States Swimming's ranking system) breaststroke swimmer tends to pull her arms far back beneath her, kick the legs out very wide without bringing them together at the finish, lift herself high out of the water on the turn, fail to take a long pull underwater after the turn, and touch at the finish with one hand, on her side. By comparison, an "AAAA" (the highest rank) swimmer, sculls the arms out to the side and sweeps back in (never actually pulling backwards), kicks narrowly with the feet finishing together, stays low on the turns, takes a long underwater pull after the turn, and touches at the finish with both hands. Not only are the strokes different, they are so different that the "C" swimmer may be amazed to see how the "AAAA" swimmer looks when swimming. The appearance alone is dramatically different, as is the speed with which they swim. . . .

(2) Discipline: The best swimmers are more likely to be strict with their training, coming to workouts on time, carefully doing the competitive strokes legally (i.e., without violating the technical rules of the sport),[4] watch what they eat, sleep regular hours, do proper warmups before a meet, and the like. Their energy is carefully channeled. Diver Greg Louganis, who won two Olympic gold medals in 1984, practices only three hours each day—not a long time—divided into two or three sessions. But during each session, he tries to do every dive perfectly. Louganis is never sloppy in practice, and so is never sloppy in meets.[5]

(3) Attitude: At the higher levels of competitive swimming, something like an inversion of attitude takes place. The very features of the sport that the "C" swimmer finds unpleasant, the top-level swimmer enjoys. What others see as boring—swimming back and forth over a black line for two hours, say—they find peaceful, even meditative,[6] often challenging, or therapeutic. They enjoy hard practices, look forward to difficult competitions, try to set difficult goals. Coming into the 5:30 A.M. practices at Mission Viejo, many of the swimmers were lively, laughing, talking, enjoying themselves, perhaps appreciating the fact that most people would positively hate doing it. It is incorrect to believe that top athletes suffer great sacrifices to achieve their goals. Often, they don't see what they do as sacrificial at all. They like it.

These qualitative differences are what distinguish levels of the sport. They are very noticeable, while the quantitative differences between levels, both in training and in competition, may be surprisingly small indeed. . . . Yet very small quantitative differences in performance may be coupled with huge qualitative differences: In the finals of the men's 100-meter freestyle swimming event at the 1984 Olympics, Rowdy Gaines, the gold medalist, finished ahead of second-place Mark Stockwell by .44 seconds, a gap of only 8/10 of 1%. Between Gaines and the 8th place finisher (a virtual unknown named Dirk Korthals, from West Germany), there was only a 2.2% difference in time. Indeed, between Rowdy Gaines, the fastest swimmer in the world that year, and a respectable 10-year-old, the quantitative difference in speed would only be about 30%.

Yet here, as in many cases, a rather small *quantitative* difference produces an enormous *qualitative difference:* Gaines was consistently a winner in major international meets, holder of the world record, and the Olympic Gold Medalist in three events.

Stratification in the sport is discrete, not continuous. There are significant, qualitative breaks— discontinuities—between levels of the sport. These include differences in attitude, discipline, and technique which in turn lead to small but consistent quantitative differences in speed. Entire teams show such differences in attitude, discipline, and technique, and consequently certain teams are easily seen to be "stuck" at certain levels.[7] Some teams always do well at the National Championships, others do well at the Regionals, others at the County Meet. And certainly swimmers typically remain within a certain level for most of their careers, maintaining throughout their careers the habits with which they began. Within levels, competitive improvements for such swimmers are typically marginal, reflecting only differential growth rates (early onset of puberty, for instance) or the jockeying for position within the relatively limited sphere of their own level. . . .

. . . Athletes move up to the top ranks through *qualitative jumps:* noticeable changes in their techniques, discipline, and attitude, accomplished usually through a change in settings, e.g., joining a new team with a new coach, new friends, etc., who work at a higher level. Without such qualitative jumps, no major improvements (movements through levels) will take place. . . .

This is really several worlds, each with its own patterns of conduct. . . . If, as I have suggested, there really are qualitative breaks between levels of the sport, and if people really don't "work their way up" in any simple additive sense, perhaps our very conception of a single swimming world is inaccurate. I have spoken of the "top" of the sport, and of "levels" within the sport. But these words suggest that all swimmers are, so to speak, climbing a single ladder, aiming towards the same goals, sharing the same values, swimming the same strokes, all looking upwards towards an Olympic gold medal. But they aren't.[8] Some want gold medals, some want to make the team, some want to exercise, or have fun with friends, or be out in the sunshine and water. Some are trying to escape their parents. The images of the "top" and the "levels" of swimming which I have used until now may simply reflect the dominance of a certain faction of swimmers and coaches in the sport: top is what *they* regard as the top, and their definitions of success have the broadest political currency in United States Swimming. Fast swimmers take as given that faster is better—instead of, say, that more beautiful is better; or that parental involvement is better; or that "well-rounded" children (whatever that may mean) are better. . . .

So we should envision not a swimming world, but multiple worlds[9] (and changing worlds is a major step toward excellence), a horizontal rather than vertical differentiation of the sport. What I have called "levels" are better described as "worlds" or "spheres." In one such world, parents are loosely in charge, coaches are teenagers employed as lifeguards, practices are held a few times a week, competitions are scheduled perhaps a week in advance, the season lasts for a few weeks in the summertime, and athletes who are much faster than the others may be discouraged by social pressure even from competing, for they take the fun out of it.[10] The big event of the season is the City Championship, when children from the metropolitan area will spend two days racing each other in many events, and the rest of the time sitting under huge tents playing cards, reading, listening to music, and gossiping. In another world, coaches are very powerful, parents seen only occasionally (and never on the pool deck), swimmers travel thousands of miles to attend meets, they swim 6 days a week for years at a time, and the fastest among them are objects of respect and praise. The big event of the season may be the National Championships, where the athletes may spend much time—sitting under huge tents, playing cards, reading, listening to music and gossiping.[11]

Each such world has its own distinctive types of powerful people and dominant athletes, and being prominent in one world is no guarantee of being prominent in another.[12] At lower levels, the parents of swimmers are in charge; at the higher levels, the coaches; perhaps in the Masters teams which are made up only of swimmers over 25 years old, the swimmers themselves. Each world, too, has its distinctive goals: going to the Olympics, doing well at the National Junior Olympics, winning the City Meet, having a good time for a few weeks. In each world the techniques are at least somewhat distinct (as with the breaststroke, discussed above), and certain demands are made on family and friends. In all of these ways, and many more, each so-called "level" of competitive swimming is qualitatively different than others. The differences are not simply quantifiable steps along a one-dimensional path leading to the Olympic Games. Goals are varied, participants have competing commitments, and techniques are jumbled.

II. Why "Talent" Does Not Lead to Excellence

. . . "Talent" is perhaps the most pervasive lay explanation we have for athletic success. Great athletes, we seem to believe, are born with a special gift, almost a "thing" inside of them, denied to the rest of us—perhaps physical, genetic, psychological, or physiological. Some have "it," and some don't. Some are "natural athletes," and some aren't. While an athlete, we acknowledge, may require many years of training and dedication to develop and use that talent, it is always "in there," only waiting for an opportunity to come out. When children perform well, they are said to "have" talent; if performance declines, they may be said to have "wasted their talent." We believe it is that talent, conceived as a substance behind the surface reality of performance, which finally distinguishes the best among our athletes.

But talent fails as an explanation for athletic success, on conceptual grounds. It mystifies excellence, subsuming a complex set of discrete actions behind a single undifferentiated concept. To understand these actions and the excellence

which they constitute, then, we should first debunk this concept of talent and see where it fails. On at least three points, I believe, "talent" is inadequate.

Factors other than talent explain athletic success more precisely. We can, with a little effort, see what these factors are in swimming: geographical location, particularly living in southern California where the sun shines year round and everybody swims; fairly high family income, which allows for the travel to meets and payments of the fees entailed in the sport, not to mention sheer access to swimming pools when one is young; one's height, weight, and proportions; the luck or choice of having a good coach, who can teach the skills required; inherited muscle structure—it certainly helps to be both strong and flexible; parents who are interested in sports. Some swimmers, too, enjoy more the physical pleasures of swimming; some have better coordination; some even have a higher percentage of fast-twitch muscle fiber. Such factors are clearly definable, and their effects can be clearly demonstrated. To subsume all of them, willynilly, under the rubric of "talent" obscures rather than illuminates the sources of athletic excellence.

It's easy to do this, especially if one's only exposure to top athletes comes once every four years while watching the Olympics on television, or if one only sees them in performances rather than in day-to-day training. Say, for instance, that one day I turn on the television set and there witness a magnificent figure skating performance by Scott Hamilton. What I see is grace and power and skill all flowing together, seemingly without effort; a single moving picture, rapid and sure, far beyond what I could myself do. . . . "His skating," I may say, referring to his actions as a single thing, "is spectacular." With that quick shorthand, I have captured (I believe) at a stroke the wealth of tiny details that Hamilton, over years and years, has fitted together into a performance so smoothly that they become invisible to the untrained eye.[13] Perhaps, with concentration, Hamilton himself can feel the details in his movements; certainly a great coach can see them, and pick out the single fault or mistake in an otherwise flawless routine. But to me, the performance is a thing entire.

Afterwards, my friends and I sit and talk about Hamilton's life as a "career of excellence," or as showing "incredible dedication," "tremendous motivation"—again, as if his excellence, his dedication, his motivation somehow exist all-at-once. His excellence becomes a thing inside of him which he periodically reveals to us, which comes out now and then; his life and habits become reified. "Talent" is merely the word we use to label this reification.

But that is no explanation of success.

Talent is indistinguishable from its effects. One cannot see that talent exists until after its effects become obvious. Kalinowski's research on Olympic swimmers demonstrates this clearly.

> One of the more startling discoveries of our study has been that it takes a while to recognize swimming talent. Indeed, it usually takes being successful at a regional level, and more often, at a national level (in AAU swimming) before the child is identified as talented. (p. 173)

> "They didn't say I had talent until I started to get really good [and made Senior Nationals at sixteen]; then they started to say I had talent . . ." (p. 174)

> . . . despite the physical capabilities he was born with, it took Peter several years (six by our estimate) to appear gifted. This is the predominant, though not exclusive, pattern found in our data on swimmers. Most of them are said to be "natural" or "gifted" after they had already devoted a great deal of time and hard work to the field. (p. 194)

> . . . whatever superior qualities were attributed to him as he grew older and more successful, they were not apparent then [before he was thirteen]. (p. 200)

The above quotations suggest that talent is *discovered* later in one's career, the implication being that while the athlete's ability *existed* all along, we were unaware of it until late. Kalinowski, like many of us, holds to the belief

that there must be this thing inside the athlete which precedes and determines success, only later to be discovered. But the recurring evidence he finds suggests a different interpretation: perhaps there is no such thing as "talent," there is only the outstanding performance itself. He sees success and immediately infers behind it a cause, a cause *for which he has no evidence other than the success itself*. Here, as elsewhere, talent (our name for this cause) cannot be measured, or seen, or felt in any form other than the success to which it supposedly gives rise. . . .

The "amount" of talent needed for athletic success seems to be strikingly low. It seems initially plausible that one must have a certain level of natural ability in order to succeed in sports (or music or academics). But upon empirical examination, it becomes very difficult to say exactly what that physical minimum is. Indeed, much of the mythology of sport is built around people who lack natural ability who went on to succeed fabulously. An entire genre of inspirational literature is built on the theme of the person whose even normal natural abilities have been destroyed: Wilma Rudolph had polio as a child, then came back to win the Olympic 100-Meter Dash. Glenn Cunningham had his legs badly burned in a fire, then broke the world record in the mile. Such stories are grist for the sportswriter's mill.

More than merely common, these stories are almost routine. Most Olympic champions, when their history is studied, seem to have overcome sharp adversity in their pursuit of success. Automobile accidents, shin splints, twisted ankles, shoulder surgery are common in such tales. In fact, they are common in life generally. While some necessary minimum of physical strength, heart/lung capacity, or nerve density may well be required for athletic achievement (again, I am *not* denying differential advantages), that minimum seems both difficult to define and markedly low, at least in many cases. Perhaps the crucial factor is not natural ability at all, but the willingness to overcome natural or unnatural disabilities of the sort that most of us face, ranging from minor inconveniences in getting up and going to work, to accidents and injuries, to gross physical impairments.

And if the basic level of talent needed, then, seems so low as to be nearly universally available, perhaps the very concept of talent itself—no longer differentiating among performers—is better discarded altogether. It simply doesn't explain the differences in outcomes. Rather than talk about talent and ability, we do better to look at what people actually do that creates outstanding performance.

The concept of talent hinders a clear understanding of excellence. By providing a quick . . . "explanation" of athletic success, it satisfies our casual curiosity while requiring neither an empirical analysis nor a critical questioning of our tacit assumptions about top athletes. At best, it is an easy way of admitting that we don't know the answer. . . . But the attempt at explanation fails. . . . Through the notion of talent, we transform particular actions that a human being does into an object possessed, held in trust for the day when it will be revealed for all to see.

This line of thought leads to one more step. Since talent can be viewed only indirectly in the effects that it supposedly produces, its very existence is a matter of faith. The basic dogma of "talent" says that what people do in this world has a cause lying behind them, that there is a kind of backstage reality where the real things happen, and what we—you and I—see here in our lives (say, the winning of a gold medal) is really a reflection of that true reality back there. Those of us who are not admitted to the company of the elect—the talented—can never see what that other world of fabulous success is really like, and can never share those experiences. And accepting this faith in talent, I suggest, we relinquish our chance of accurately understanding excellence. . . .

III. The Mundanity of Excellence

"People don't know how ordinary success is," said Mary T. Meagher, winner of 3 gold medals in the Los Angeles Olympics, when asked what the public least understands about her sport. She then spoke of starting her career in a sum-

mer league country club team, of working her way to AAU meets, to faster and faster competitions, of learning new techniques, practicing new habits, meeting new challenges.[14] What Meagher said—that success is ordinary—in some sense applies, I believe, to other fields of endeavor as well: to business, to politics, to professions of all kinds, including academics. In what follows I will try to elaborate on this point, drawing some examples from the swimming research, and some from other fields, to indicate the scope of this conception.

Excellence is mundane. Superlative performance is really a confluence of dozens of small skills or activities, each one learned or stumbled upon, which have been carefully drilled into habit and then are fitted together in a synthesized whole. There is nothing extraordinary or superhuman in any one of those actions; only the fact that they are done consistently and correctly, and all together, produce excellence. When a swimmer learns a proper flip turn in the freestyle races, she will swim the race a bit faster; then a streamlined push off from the wall, with the arms squeezed together over the head, and a little faster; then how to place the hands in the water so no air is cupped in them; then how to lift them over the water; then how to lift weights to properly build strength, and how to eat the right foods, and to wear the best suits for racing, and on and on.[15] Each of those tasks seems small in itself, but each allows the athlete to swim a bit faster. And having learned and consistently practiced all of them together, and many more besides, the swimmer may compete in the Olympic Games. The winning of a gold medal is nothing more than the synthesis of a countless number of such little things—even if some of them are done unwittingly or by others, and thus called "luck."

So the "little things" really do count. We have already seen how a very small (in quantitative terms) difference can produce a noticeable success. Even apparent flukes can lead to gold medal performances:

In the 100-Meter Freestyle event in Los Angeles, Rowdy Gaines, knowing that the starter for the race tended to fire the gun fast, anticipated the start; while not actually jumping the gun, it seems from video replays of the race that Gaines knew exactly when to go, and others were left on the blocks as he took off. But the starter turned his back, and the protests filed afterwards by competitors were ignored. Gaines had spent years watching starters, and had talked with his coach (Richard Quick) before the race about this starter in particular. (Field notes; see Chambliss, 1988, for full description)

Gaines was not noticeably faster than several of the other swimmers in the race, but with this one extra tactic, he gained enough of an advantage to win the race. And he seemed in almost all of his races to find such an advantage; hence the gold medal. Looking at such subtleties, we can say that not only are the little things important; in some ways, the little things are the only things. . . .

In swimming, or elsewhere, these practices might at first glance seem very minimal indeed:

When Mary T. Meagher was 13 years old and had qualified for the National Championships, she decided to try to break the world record in the 200-Meter Butterfly race. She made two immediate qualitative changes in her routine: first, she began coming on time to all practices. She recalls now, years later, being picked up at school by her mother and driving (rather quickly) through the streets of Louisville, Kentucky, trying desperately to make it to the pool on time. That habit, that discipline, she now says, gave her the sense that every minute of practice time counted. And second, she began doing all of her turns, during those practices, correctly, in strict accordance with the competitive rules. Most swimmers don't do this; they turn rather casually, and tend to touch with one hand instead of two (in the butterfly, Meagher's stroke). This, she says, accustomed her to doing things one step better than those around her—always. Those are the two major changes she made in her training, as she remembers it.[16]

Meagher made two quite mundane changes in her habits, either one of which anyone could do, if he or she wanted. Within a year Meagher had broken the world record in the butterfly. . . .

Motivation is mundane, too. Swimmers go to practice to see their friends, to exercise, to feel strong afterwards, to impress the coach, to work towards bettering a time they swam in the last meet. Sometimes, the older ones, with a longer view of the future, will aim towards a meet that is still several months away. But even given the longer-term goals, the daily satisfactions need to be there. The mundane social rewards really are crucial (see Chambliss, 1988, Chapter 6). By comparison, the big, dramatic motivations— winning an Olympic gold medal, setting a world record—seem to be ineffective unless translated into shorter-term tasks. Viewing "Rocky" or "Chariots of Fire" may inspire one for several days, but the excitement stirred by a film wears off rather quickly when confronted with the day-to-day reality of climbing out of bed to go and jump in cold water. If, on the other hand, that day-to-day reality is itself fun, rewarding, challenging; if the water is nice and friends are supportive, the longer-term goals may well be achieved almost in spite of themselves. Again, Mary T. Meagher:

I never looked beyond the next year, and I never looked beyond the next level. I never thought about the Olympics when I was ten; at that time I was thinking about the State Championships. When I made cuts for Regionals [the next higher level of competition], I started thinking about Regionals; when I made cuts for National Junior Olympics, I started thinking about National Junior Olympics . . . I can't even think about the [1988] Olympics right now. . . . Things can overwhelm you if you think too far ahead. (Interview notes)

This statement was echoed by many of the swimmers I interviewed. While many of them were working towards the Olympic Games, they divided the work along the way into achievable steps, no one of which was too big. They found their challenges in small things: working on a better start this week, polishing up their backstroke technique next week, focusing on better sleep habits, planning how to pace their swim. . . .

. . . Many top swimmers are accustomed to winning races in practice, day after day. Steve Lundquist, who won two gold medals in Los Angeles, sees his success as resulting from an early decision that he wanted to win every swim, every day, in every practice. That was the immediate goal he faced at workouts; just try to win every swim, every lap, in every stroke, no matter what. Lundquist gained a reputation in swimming for being a ferocious workout swimmer, one who competed all the time, even in the warmup. He became so accustomed to winning that he entered meets knowing that he could beat these people—he had developed the habit, every day, of never losing. The short-term goal of winning this swim, in this workout, translated into his ability to win bigger and bigger races. Competition, when the day arrived for a meet, was not a shock to him, nothing at all out of the ordinary.[17]

This leads to a third and final point.

In the pursuit of excellence, maintaining mundanity is the key psychological challenge. In common parlance, winners don't choke. Faced with what seems to be a tremendous challenge or a strikingly unusual event, such as the Olympic Games, the better athletes take it as a normal, manageable situation[18] ("It's just another swim meet," is a phrase sometimes used by top swimmers at a major event such as the Games) and do what is necessary to deal with it. Standard rituals (such as the warmup, the psych, the visualization of the race, the taking off of sweats, and the like) are ways of importing one's daily habits into the novel situation, to make it as normal an event as possible. Swimmers like Lundquist, who train at competition-level intensity, therefore have an advantage: arriving at a meet, they are already accustomed to doing turns correctly, taking legal starts, doing a proper warmup, and being aggressive from the outset of the competition. If each day of the season is approached with a seriousness of purpose, then the big meet will not come as a shock. The

athlete will believe "I belong here, this is my world"—and not be paralyzed by fear or self-consciousness. The task then is to have training closely approximate competition conditions. . . .

The mundanity of excellence is typically unrecognized. I think the reason is fairly simple. Usually we see great athletes only after they have become great—after the years of learning the new methods, gaining the habits of competitiveness and consistency, after becoming comfortable in their world. They have long since perfected the myriad of techniques that together constitute excellence. Ignorant of all of the specific steps that have led to the performance and to the confidence, we think that somehow excellence sprang full grown from this person, and we say he or she "has talent" or "is gifted." Even when seen close up, the mundanity of excellence is often not believed:

> Every week at the Mission Viejo training pool, where the National Champion Nadadores team practiced, coaches from around the world would be on the deck visiting, watching as the team did their workouts, swimming back and forth for hours. The visiting coaches would be excited at first, just to be here; then soon—within an hour or so usually—they grew bored, walking back and forth looking at the deck, glancing around at the hills around the town, reading the bulletin boards, glancing down at their watches, wondering, after the long flight out to California, when something dramatic was going to happen. "They all have to come to Mecca, and see what we do," coach Mark Schubert said. "They think we have some big secret." (Field notes)

But of course there is no secret; there is only the doing of all those little things, each one done correctly, time and again, until excellence in every detail becomes a firmly ingrained habit, an ordinary part of one's everyday life.

Conclusions

The foregoing analysis suggests that we have overlooked a fundamental fact about Olympic-class athletes; and the argument may apply far more widely than swimming, or sports. I suggest that it applies to success in business, politics, and academics, in dentistry, bookkeeping, food service, speechmaking, electrical engineering, selling insurance (when the clients are upset, you climb in the car and go out there to talk with them), and perhaps even in the arts.[19] Consider again the major points:

(1) *Excellence is a qualitative phenomenon.* Doing more does not equal doing better. High performers focus on qualitative, not quantitative, improvements; it is qualitative improvements which produce significant changes in level of achievement; different levels of achievement really are distinct, and in fact reflect vastly different habits, values, and goals.

(2) *Talent is a useless concept.* Varying conceptions of natural ability ("talent," e.g.) tend to mystify excellence, treating it as the inherent possession of a few; they mask the concrete actions that create outstanding performance; they avoid the work of empirical analysis and logical explanations (clear definitions, separable independent and dependent variables, and at least an attempt at establishing the temporal priority of the cause); and finally, such conceptions perpetuate the sense of innate psychological differences between high performers and other people.

(3) *Excellence is mundane.* Excellence is accomplished through the doing of actions, ordinary in themselves, performed consistently and carefully, habitualized, compounded together, added up over time. While these actions are "qualitatively different" from those of performers at other levels, these differences are neither unmanageable nor, taken one step at a time, terribly difficult. Mary T. Meagher came to practice on time; some writers always work for three hours each morning, before beginning anything else; a businessperson may go ahead and make that tough phone call; a job applicant writes one more letter; a runner decides, against the odds, to enter the race; a county commissioner submits a petition to run for Congress; a teenager asks for a date; an actor attends one more audition. Every time a decision comes up, the qualitatively "correct" choice will be made. The action,

in itself, is nothing special; the care and consistency with which it is made is.

Howard Becker has presented a similar argument about the ordinariness of apparently unusual people in his book *Outsiders* (1961). But where he speaks of deviance, I would speak of excellence. Becker says, and I concur:

> We ought not to view it as something special, as depraved or in some magical way better than other kinds of behavior. We ought to see it simply as a kind of behavior some disapprove of and others value, studying the processes by which either or both perspectives are built up and maintained. Perhaps the best surety against either extreme is close contact with the people we study. (Becker, p. 176)

After three years of field work with world-class swimmers, having the kind of close contact that Becker recommends, I wrote a draft of some book chapters, full of stories about swimmers, and I showed it to a friend. "You need to jazz it up," he said. "You need to make these people more interesting. The analysis is nice, but except for the fact that these are good swimmers, there isn't much else exciting to say about them as individuals." He was right, of course. What these athletes do was rather interesting, but the people themselves were only fast swimmers, who did the particular things one does to swim fast. It is all very mundane. When my friend said that they weren't exciting, my best answer could only be, simply put: *That's the point.*

NOTES

The author wishes to thank Randall Collins and Gary Alan Fine for their comments on an earlier draft of this paper.

1. In fact, if anything they are more socially bonded and adept than their peers. The process by which this happens fits well with Durkheim's (1965) description of the sources of social cohesion.

2. These issues are addressed at length in "The Social World of Olympic Swimmers." Daniel F. Chambliss, in preparation.

3. True, the top teams work long hours, and swim very long distances, but (1) such workouts often begin

after a swimmer achieves national status, not before, and (2) the positive impact of increased yardage seems to come with huge increases, e.g., the doubling of workout distances—in which case one could argue that a *qualitative* jump has been made. The whole question of "how much yardage to swim" is widely discussed within the sport itself.

Compare the (specious, I think) notion that a longer school day/term/year will produce educational improvements.

4. One day at Mission Viejo, with some sixty swimmers going back and forth the length of a 50-meter pool, coach Mark Schubert took one boy out of the water and had him do twenty pushups before continuing the workout. The boy had touched the wall with one hand at the end of a breaststroke swim. The rules require a two-handed touch.

One hundred and twenty hands should have touched, one hundred and nineteen *did* touch, and this made Schubert angry. He pays attention to details.

5. From an interview with his coach, Ron O'Brien.

6. Distance swimmers frequently compare swimming to meditation.

7. For example: several well-known teams consistently do well at the National Junior Olympics ("Junior Nationals," as it is called informally), and yet never place high in the team standings at the National Championships ("Senior Nationals"), the next higher meet.

These teams actually prevent their swimmers from going to the better meet, holding them in store for the easier meet so that the team will do better at that lesser event. In this way, and in many others, teams choose their own level of success.

8. March and Olsen make a similar point with regard to educational institutions and organizations in general: organizations include a variety of constituents with differing goals, plans, motivations, and values. Unity of purpose, even with organizations, cannot simply be assumed. Coherence, not diversity, is what needs explaining. March and Olsen, 1976.

9. See Shibutani in Rose, 1962, on "social worlds." Blumer, 1969.

10. These fast swimmers who come to slow meets are called hot dogs, showoffs, or even jerks. (Personal observations.)

11. Again, personal observations from a large number of cases. While there are significant differences between swimmers of the Olympic class and a country club league, the basic sociability of their worlds is not one of them.

12. "Indeed, prestige ladders in the various worlds are so different that a man who reaches the pinnacle of success in one may be completely unknown elsewhere." Shibutani in Rose, 1962.

Similarly in academia: one may be a successful professor at the national level and yet find it difficult to gain employment at a minor regional university. Professors at the regional school may suspect his/her motives, be jealous, feel that he/she "wouldn't fit in," "won't stay anyway," etc. Many top-school graduate students discover upon entering the markets that no-name colleges have no interest in them; indeed, by attending a Chicago or Harvard Ph.D. program one may limit oneself to the top ranks of employment opportunities.

13. "Now, no one can see in an artist's work how it evolved: that is its advantage, for wherever we can see the evolution, we grow somewhat cooler. The complete art of representation wards off all thought of its solution; it tyrannizes as present perfection" (Nietzsche, 1984, p. 111).

14. Meagher's entire career is described in detail in Chambliss, 1988.

15. Such techniques are thoroughly explained in Maglischo (1982) and Troup and Reese (1983).

16. Interview notes.

17. Interview notes.

18. An interesting parallel: some of the most successful generals have no trouble sleeping before and after major battles. For details on Ulysses Grant and the Duke of Wellington, see Keegan, p. 207.

19. Professor Margaret Bates, an opera enthusiast, tells me that this "mundanity of excellence" argument applies nicely to Enrico Caruso, the great singer, who carefully perfected each ordinary detail of his performance in an effort to overcome a recognized lack of "natural ability."

REFERENCES

Blumer, Herbert. 1969. *Symbolic Interactionism.* Englewood Cliffs: Prentice Hall.

Chambliss, Daniel F. 1988. *Champions: The Making of Olympic Swimmers.* New York: Morrow.

Durkheim, Emile. 1965. *The Elementary Forms of the Religious Life.* New York: Free Press.

Kalinowsky, Anthony G. "The Development of Olympic Swimmers," and "One Olympic Swimmer," in Bloom (1985), pp. 139–210.

Keegan, John. 1987. *The Mask of Command.* New York: Viking.

Maglischo, Ernest W. 1982. *Swimming Faster.* Palo Alto: Mayfield.

March, James G. and Olsen, Johan P. 1976. *Ambiguity and Choice in Organizations.* Bergen, Norway: Universitetsforlaget.

Nietzsche, Friedrich. 1984. *Human, All Too Human.* Lincoln.: University of Nebraska Press.

Shibutani, T. "Reference Groups and Social Control," in Rose, Arnold M. 1962. *Human Behavior and Social Process.* Boston: Houghton Mifflin, pp. 128–147.

Troup, John and Reese, Randy. 1983. *A Scientific Approach to the Sport of Swimming.* Gainesville, FL: Scientific Sports.

THINKING ABOUT THE READING

Why does Chambliss feel that "talent" is a useless concept in explaining success among world-class swimmers? Where, instead, does he think that athletic excellence comes from? Why do you suppose we have such a strong tendency to focus on "talent" or "natural ability" in explaining superior performances? If it's true, as Chambliss suggests, that factors such as geographical location, high family income and interest, and the luck of having a good coach can all play important roles in creating world-class swimmers, then there are probably many potentially successful athletes who don't have the opportunity to excel in certain sports because of their social circumstances. Relatively few inner-city kids grow up to succeed in "wealthy" sports such as swimming, tennis, and golf. However, the inner city produces many of the world's best basketball, football, and track stars. What kinds of social circumstances encourage success in these sports? Can you identify other areas of life (other than sports) where achievement might similarly be affected by the kinds of social circumstances described in this article?

CHAPTER 2

Seeing and Thinking Sociologically

Although society exists as an objective entity, it is also a social construction that is created, reaffirmed, and altered through the day-to-day interactions of the very people it influences and controls. Humans are social beings. We constantly look to others to help define and interpret the situations in which we find ourselves. Other people can influence what we see, feel, think, and do. But it's not just other people that influence us. We also live in a *society*, which consists of socially recognizable combinations of individuals—relationships, groups, and organizations—as well as the products of human action—statuses, roles, culture, and institutions.

The influence of social structure on our personal actions is often felt most forcefully when we are compelled to obey the commands of someone who is in a position of authority. In "The My Lai Massacre: A Military Crime of Obedience," Herbert Kelman and Lee Hamilton describe a specific example of a crime in which the individuals involved attempted to deny responsibility for their actions by claiming that they were following the orders of a military officer who had the legitimate right to command them. This incident occurred in the midst of the Vietnam war. Arguably, people do things under such trying conditions that they wouldn't ordinarily do, even—as in this case—kill defenseless people. Kelman and Hamilton make a key sociological point by showing that these soldiers were not necessarily psychological misfits who were especially mean or violent. Instead, the researchers argue, they were ordinary people caught up in tense circumstances that made obeying the brutal commands of an authority seem like the normatively and morally acceptable thing to do.

The influence society has on our everyday lives is often obscured by our culture's tendency to see people's problems in individualistic terms. In his article, "Speaking of Sadness," David Karp shows us how the private experience of depression is shaped by social processes and cultural expectations. Karp, a sufferer of clinical depression himself, observes that our society's emphasis on individual achievement and self-fulfillment, not to mention Americans' ever-increasing sense of social isolation, conspires to create an environment in which more and more people suffer from debilitating depression. Karp's observations illustrate the profound power of the sociological imagination by showing that even such an apparently private "illness" as depression cannot be fully understood without seeing its relationship to the culture and the economy.

The My Lai Massacre

A Military Crime of Obedience

Herbert Kelman and V. Lee Hamilton

March 16, 1968, was a busy day in U.S. history. Stateside, Robert F. Kennedy announced his presidential candidacy, challenging a sitting president from his own party—in part out of opposition to an undeclared and disastrous war. In Vietnam, the war continued. In many ways, March 16 may have been a typical day in that war. We will probably never know. But we do know that on that day a typical company went on a mission—which may or may not have been typical—to a village called Son (or Song) My. Most of what is remembered from that mission occurred in the subhamlet known to Americans as My Lai 4.

The My Lai massacre was investigated and charges were brought in 1969 and 1970. Trials and disciplinary actions lasted into 1971. Entire books have been written about the army's year-long cover-up of the massacre (for example, Hersh, 1972), and the cover-up was a major focus of the army's own investigation of the incident. Our central concern here is the massacre itself—a crime of obedience—and public reactions to such crimes, rather than the lengths to which many went to deny the event. Therefore this account concentrates on one day: March 16, 1968.

Many verbal testimonials to the horrors that occurred at My Lai were available. More unusual was the fact that an army photographer, Ronald Haeberle, was assigned the task of documenting the anticipated military engagement at My Lai—and documented a massacre instead. Later, as the story of the massacre emerged, his photographs were widely distributed and seared the public conscience. What might have been dismissed as unreal or exaggerated was depicted in photographs of demonstrable authenticity. The domi-nant image appeared on the cover of *Life:* piles of bodies jumbled together in a ditch along a trail—the dead all apparently unarmed. All were Oriental, and all appeared to be children, women, or old men. Clearly there had been a mass execution, one whose image would not quickly fade.

So many bodies (over twenty in the cover photo alone) are hard to imagine as the handiwork of one killer. These were not. They were the product of what we call a crime of obedience. Crimes of obedience begin with orders. But orders are often vague and rarely survive with any clarity the transition from one authority down a chain of subordinates to the ultimate actors. The operation at Son My was no exception.

"Charlie" Company, Company C, under Lt. Col. Frank Barker's command, arrived in Vietnam in December 1967. As the army's investigative unit, directed by Lt. Gen. William R. Peers, characterized the personnel, they "contained no significant deviation from the average" for the time. Seymour S. Hersh (1970) described the "average" more explicitly: "Most of the men in Charlie Company had volunteered for the draft; only a few had gone to college for even one year. Nearly half were black, with a few Mexican-Americans. Most were eighteen to twenty-two years old. The favorite reading matter of Charlie Company, like that of other line infantry units in Vietnam, was comic books" (p. 18). The action at My Lai, like that throughout Vietnam, was fought by a cross-section of those Americans who either believed in the war or lacked the social resources to avoid participating in it. Charlie Company was indeed average for that time, that place, and that war.

Two key figures in Charlie Company were more unusual. The company's commander, Capt. Ernest Medina, was an upwardly mobile Mexican-American who wanted to make the army his career, although he feared that he might never advance beyond captain because of his lack of formal education. His eagerness had earned him a nickname among his men: "Mad Dog Medina." One of his admirers was the platoon leader Second Lt. William L. Calley, Jr., an undistinguished, five-foot-three-inch junior-college dropout who had failed four of the seven courses in which he had enrolled his first year. Many viewed him as one of those "instant officers" made possible only by the army's then-desperate need for manpower. Whatever the cause, he was an insecure leader whose frequent claim was "I'm the boss." His nickname among some of the troops was "Surfside 5½," a reference to the swashbuckling heroes of a popular television show, "Surfside 6."

The Son My operation was planned by Lieutenant Colonel Barker and his staff as a search-and-destroy mission with the objective of rooting out the Forty-eighth Viet Cong Battalion from their base area of Son My village. Apparently no written orders were ever issued. Barker's superior, Col. Oran Henderson, arrived at the staging point the day before. Among the issues he reviewed with the assembled officers were some of the weaknesses of prior operations by their units, including their failure to be appropriately aggressive in pursuit of the enemy. Later briefings by Lieutenant Colonel Barker and his staff asserted that no one except Viet Cong was expected to be in the village after 7 A.M. on the following day. The "innocent" would all be at the market. Those present at the briefings gave conflicting accounts of Barker's exact orders, but he conveyed at least a strong suggestion that the Son My area was to be obliterated. As the army's inquiry reported: "While there is some conflict in the testimony as to whether LTC Barker ordered the destruction of houses, dwellings, livestock, and other foodstuffs in the Song My area, the preponderance of the evidence indicates that such destruction was implied, if not specifically directed, by his orders of 15 March" (Peers Report, in Goldstein et al., 1976, p. 94).

Evidence that Barker ordered the killing of civilians is even more murky. What does seem clear, however, is that—having asserted that civilians would be away at the market—he did not specify what was to be done with any who might nevertheless be found on the scene. The Peers Report therefore considered it "reasonable to conclude that LTC Barker's minimal or nonexistent instructions concerning the handling of noncombatants created the potential for grave misunderstandings as to his intentions and for interpretation of his orders as authority to fire, without restriction, on all persons found in target area" (Goldstein et al., 1976, p. 95). Since Barker was killed in action in June 1968, his own formal version of the truth was never available.

Charlie Company's Captain Medina was briefed for the operation by Barker and his staff. He then transmitted the already vague orders to his own men. Charlie Company was spoiling for a fight, having been totally frustrated during its months in Vietnam—first by waiting for battles that never came, then by incompetent forays led by inexperienced commanders, and finally by mines and booby traps. In fact, the emotion-laden funeral of a sergeant killed by a booby trap was held on March 15, the day before My Lai. Captain Medina gave the orders for the next day's action at the close of that funeral. Many were in a mood for revenge.

It is again unclear what was ordered. Although all participants were alive by the time of the trials for the massacre, they were either on trial or probably felt under threat of trial. Memories are often flawed and self-serving at such times. It is apparent that Medina relayed to the men at least some of Barker's general message—to expect Viet Cong resistance, to burn, and to kill livestock. It is not clear that he ordered the slaughter of the inhabitants, but some of the men who heard him thought he had. One of those who claimed to have heard such orders was Lt. William Calley.

As March 16 dawned, much was expected of the operation by those who had set it into motion. Therefore a full complement of "brass" was present in helicopters overhead, including Barker, Colonel Henderson, and their superior,

Major General Koster (who went on to become commandant of West Point before the story of My Lai broke). On the ground, the troops were to carry with them one reporter and one photographer to immortalize the anticipated battle.

The action for Company C began at 7:30 as their first wave of helicopters touched down near the subhamlet of My Lai 4. By 7:47 all of Company C was present and set to fight. But instead of the Viet Cong Forty-eighth Battalion, My Lai was filled with the old men, women, and children who were supposed to have gone to market. By this time, in their version of the war, and with whatever orders they thought they had heard, the men from Company C were nevertheless ready to find Viet Cong everywhere. By nightfall, the official tally was 128 VC killed and three weapons captured, although later, unofficial body counts ran as high as 500. The operation at Son My was over. And by nightfall, as Hersh reported: "the Viet Cong were back in My Lai 4, helping the survivors bury the dead. It took five days. Most of the funeral speeches were made by the Communist guerrillas. Nguyen Bat was not a Communist at the time of the massacre, but the incident changed his mind. 'After the shooting,' he said, 'all the villagers became Communists'" (1970, p. 74). To this day, the memory of the massacre is kept alive by markers and plaques designating the spots where groups of villagers were killed, by a large statue, and by the My Lai Museum, established in 1975 (Williams, 1985).

But what could have happened to leave American troops reporting a victory over Viet Cong when in fact they had killed hundreds of noncombatants? It is not hard to explain the report of victory; that is the essence of a cover-up. It is harder to understand how the killings came to be committed in the first place, making a cover-up necessary.

Mass Executions and the Defense of Superior Orders

Some of the atrocities on March 16, 1968, were evidently unofficial, spontaneous acts: rapes, tortures, killings. For example, Hersh (1970) describes Charlie Company's Second Platoon as entering "My Lai 4 with guns blazing" (p. 50); more graphically, Lieutenant "Brooks and his men in the second platoon to the north had begun to systematically ransack the hamlet and slaughter the people, kill the livestock, and destroy the crops. Men poured rifle and machine-gun fire into huts without knowing—or seemingly caring—who was inside" (pp. 49–50).

Some atrocities toward the end of the action were part of an almost casual "mopping-up," much of which was the responsibility of Lieutenant LaCross's Third Platoon of Charlie Company. The Peers Report states: "The entire 3rd Platoon then began moving into the western edge of My Lai (4), for the mop-up operation. . . . The squad . . . began to burn the houses in the southwestern portion of the hamlet" (Goldstein et al., 1976, p. 133). They became mingled with other platoons during a series of rapes and killings of survivors for which it was impossible to fix responsibility. Certainly to a Vietnamese all GIs would by this point look alike: "Nineteen-year-old Nguyen Thi Ngoc Tuyet watched a baby trying to open her slain mother's blouse to nurse. A soldier shot the infant while it was struggling with the blouse, and then slashed it with his bayonet." Tuyet also said she saw another baby hacked to death by GIs wielding their bayonets. "Le Tong, a twenty-eight-year-old rice farmer, reported seeing one woman raped after GIs killed her children. Nguyen Khoa, a thirty-seven-year-old peasant, told of a thirteen-year-old girl who was raped before being killed. GIs then attacked Khoa's wife, tearing off her clothes. Before they could rape her, however, Khoa said, their six-year-old son, riddled with bullets, fell and saturated her with blood. The GIs left her alone" (Hersh, 1970, p. 72). All of Company C was implicated in a pattern of death and destruction throughout the hamlet, much of which seemingly lacked rhyme or reason.

But a substantial amount of the killing was *organized* and traceable to one authority: the First Platoon's Lt. William Calley. Calley was originally charged with 109 killings, almost all of them mass executions at the trail and other locations. He stood trial for 102 of these killings, was convicted of 22 in 1971, and at first received a life sentence.

Though others—both superior and subordinate to Calley—were brought to trial, he was the only one convicted for the My Lai crimes. Thus, the only actions of My Lai for which *anyone* was ever convicted were mass executions, ordered and committed. We suspect that there are common-sense reasons why this one type of killing was singled out. In the midst of rapidly moving events with people running about, an execution of stationary targets is literally a still life that stands out and whose participants are clearly visible. It can be proven that specific people committed specific deeds. An execution, in contrast to the shooting of someone on the run, is also more likely to meet the legal definition of an act resulting from intent—with malice aforethought. Moreover, American military law specifically forbids the killing of unarmed civilians or military prisoners, as does the Geneva Convention between nations. Thus common sense, legal standards, and explicit doctrine all made such actions the likeliest target for prosecution.

When Lieutenant Calley was charged under military law it was for violation of the Uniform Code of Military Justice (UCMJ) Article 118 (murder). This article is similar to civilian codes in that it provides for conviction if an accused:

> without justification or excuse, unlawfully kills a human being, when he—
>
> 1. has a premeditated design to kill;
> 2. intends to kill or inflict great bodily harm;
> 3. is engaged in an act which is inherently dangerous to others and evinces a wanton disregard of human life; or
> 4. is engaged in the perpetration or attempted perpetration of burglary, sodomy, rape, robbery, or aggravated arson. (Goldstein et al., 1976, p. 507)

For a soldier, one legal justification for killing is warfare; but warfare is subject to many legal limits and restrictions, including, of course, the inadmissibility of killing unarmed noncombatants or prisoners whom one has disarmed. The pictures of the trail victims at My Lai certainly portrayed one or the other of these. Such an action would be illegal under military law; ordering another to commit such an action would be illegal; and following such an order would be illegal.

But following an order may provide a second and pivotal justification for an act that would be murder when committed by a civilian. American military law assumes that the subordinate is inclined to follow orders, as that is the normal obligation of the role. Hence, legally, obedient subordinates are protected from unreasonable expectations regarding their capacity to evaluate those orders:

> An order requiring the performance of a military duty may be inferred to be legal. An act performed manifestly beyond the scope of authority, or pursuant to an order that a man of ordinary sense and understanding would know to be illegal, or in a wanton manner in the discharge of a lawful duty, is not excusable. (Par. 216, Subpar. *d*, Manual for Courts Martial, United States, 1969 Rev.)

Thus what *may* be excusable is the good-faith carrying out of an order, as long as that order appears to the ordinary soldier to be a legal one. In military law, invoking superior orders moves the question from one of the action's consequences—the body count—to one of evaluating the actor's motives and good sense.

In sum, if anyone is to be brought to justice for a massacre, common sense and legal codes decree that the most appropriate targets are those who make themselves executioners. This is the kind of target the government selected in prosecuting Lieutenant Calley with the greatest fervor. And in a military context, the most promising way in which one can redefine one's undeniable deeds into acceptability is to invoke superior orders. This is what Calley did in attempting to avoid conviction. Since the core legal issues involved points of mass execution—the ditches and trail where America's image of My Lai was formed—we review these events in greater detail.

The day's quiet beginning has already been noted. Troops landed and swept unopposed into the village. The three weapons eventually reported as the haul from the operation were picked up from three apparent Viet Cong who fled the village when the troops arrived and were pursued and killed by helicopter gunships. Obviously the Viet Cong did frequent the area. But it appears that by about 8:00 A.M. no one who met the troops was aggressive, and no one was armed. By the laws of war Charlie Company had no argument with such people.

As they moved into the village, the soldiers began to gather its inhabitants together. Shortly after 8:00 a.m. Lieutenant Calley told Pfc. Paul Meadlo that "you know what to do with" a group of villagers Meadlo was guarding. Estimates of the numbers in the group ranged as high as eighty women, children, and old men, and Meadlo's own estimate under oath was thirty to fifty people. As Meadlo later testified, Calley returned after ten or fifteen minutes: "He [Calley] said, 'How come they're not dead?' I said, 'I didn't know we were supposed to kill them.' He said, 'I want them dead.' He backed off twenty or thirty feet and started shooting into the people— the Viet Cong—shooting automatic. He was beside me. He burned four or five magazines. I burned off a few, about three. I helped shoot 'em" (Hammer, 1971, p. 155). Meadlo himself and others testified that Meadlo cried as he fired; others reported him later to be sobbing and "all broke up." It would appear that to Lieutenant Calley's subordinates something was unusual, and stressful, in these orders.

At the trial, the first specification in the murder charge against Calley was for this incident; he was accused of premeditated murder of "an unknown number, not less than 30, Oriental human beings, males and females of various ages, whose names are unknown, occupants of the village of My Lai 4, by means of shooting them with a rifle" (Goldstein et al., 1976, p. 497).

Among the helicopters flying reconnaissance above Son My was that of CWO Hugh Thompson. By 9:00 or soon after, Thompson had noticed some horrifying events from his perch. As he spotted wounded civilians, he sent down smoke markers so that soldiers on the ground could treat them. They killed them instead. He reported to headquarters, trying to persuade someone to stop

what was going on. Barker, hearing the message, called down to Captain Medina. Medina, in turn, later claimed to have told Calley that it was "enough for today." But it was not yet enough.

At Calley's orders, his men began gathering the remaining villagers—roughly seventy-five individuals, mostly women and children—and herding them toward a drainage ditch. Accompanied by three or four enlisted men, Lieutenant Calley executed several batches of civilians who had been gathered into ditches. Some of the details of the process were entered into testimony in such accounts as Pfc. Dennis Conti's: "A lot of them, the people, were trying to get up and mostly they was just screaming and pretty bad shot up. . . . I seen a woman tried to get up. I seen Lieutenant Calley fire. He hit the side of her head and blew it off" (Hammer, 1971, p. 125).

Testimony by other soldiers presented the shooting's aftermath. Specialist Four Charles Hall, asked by Prosecutor Aubrey Daniel how he knew the people in the ditch were dead, said: "There was blood coming from them. They were just scattered all over the ground in the ditch, some in piles and some scattered out 20, 25 meters perhaps up the ditch. . . . They were very old people, very young children, and mothers. . . . There was blood all over them" (Goldstein et al., 1976, pp. 501–502). And Pfc. Gregory Olsen corroborated the general picture of the victims: "They were—the majority were women and children, some babies. I distinctly remember one middle-aged Vietnamese male dressed in white right at my feet as I crossed. None of the bodies were mangled in any way. There was blood. Some appeared to be dead, others followed me with their eyes as I walked across the ditch" (Goldstein et al., 1976, p. 502).

The second specification in the murder charge stated that Calley did "with premeditation, murder an unknown number of Oriental human beings, not less than seventy, males and females of various ages, whose names are unknown, occupants of the village of My Lai 4, by means of shooting them with a rifle" (Goldstein et al., 1976, p. 497). Calley was also charged with and tried for shootings of individuals (an old man and a child);

these charges were clearly supplemental to the main issue at trial—the mass killings and how they came about.

It is noteworthy that during these executions more than one enlisted man avoided carrying out Calley's orders, and more than one, by sworn oath, directly refused to obey them. For example, Pfc. James Joseph Dursi testified, when asked if he fired when Lieutenant Calley ordered him to: "No I just stood there. Meadlo turned to me after a couple of minutes and said 'Shoot! Why don't you shoot! Why don't you fire!' He was crying and yelling. I said, 'I can't! I won't!' And the people were screaming and crying and yelling. They kept firing for a couple of minutes, mostly automatic and semi-automatic" (Hammer, 1971, p. 143)....

Disobedience of Lieutenant Calley's own orders to kill represented a serious legal and moral threat to a defense *based* on superior orders, such as Calley was attempting. This defense had to assert that the orders seemed reasonable enough to carry out; that they appeared to be legal orders. Even if the orders in question were not legal, the defense had to assert that an ordinary individual could not and should not be expected to see the distinction. In short, if what happened was "business as usual," even though it might be bad business, then the defendant stood a chance of acquittal. But under direct command from "Surfside 5½," some ordinary enlisted men managed to refuse, to avoid, or at least to stop doing what they were ordered to do. As "reasonable men" of "ordinary sense and understanding," they had apparently found something awry that morning; and it would have been hard for an officer to plead successfully that he was more ordinary than his men in his capacity to evaluate the reasonableness of orders.

Even those who obeyed Calley's orders showed great stress. For example, Meadlo eventually began to argue and cry directly in front of Calley. Pfc. Herbert Carter shot himself in the foot, possibly because he could no longer take what he was doing. We were not destined to hear a sworn version of the incident, since neither side at the Calley trial called him to testify.

The most unusual instance of resistance to authority came from the skies. CWO Hugh Thompson, who had protested the apparent carnage of civilians, was Calley's inferior in rank but was not in his line of command. He was also watching the ditch from his helicopter and noticed some people moving after the first round of slaughter—chiefly children who had been shielded by their mothers' bodies. Landing to rescue the wounded, he also found some villagers hiding in a nearby bunker. Protecting the Vietnamese with his own body, Thompson ordered his men to train their guns on the Americans and to open fire if the Americans fired on the Vietnamese. He then radioed for additional rescue helicopters and stood between the Vietnamese and the Americans under Calley's command until the Vietnamese could be evacuated. He later returned to the ditch to unearth a child buried, unharmed, beneath layers of bodies. In October 1969, Thompson was awarded the Distinguished Flying Cross for heroism at My Lai, specifically (albeit inaccurately) for the rescue of children hiding in a bunker "between Viet Cong forces and advancing friendly forces" and for the rescue of a wounded child "caught in the intense crossfire" (Hersh, 1970, p. 119). Four months earlier, at the Pentagon, Thompson had identified Calley as having been at the ditch.

By about 10:00 A.M., the massacre was winding down. The remaining actions consisted largely of isolated rapes and killings, "clean-up" shootings of the wounded, and the destruction of the village by fire. We have already seen some examples of these more indiscriminate and possibly less premeditated acts. By the 11:00 A.M. lunch break, when the exhausted men of Company C were relaxing, two young girls wandered back from a hiding place only to be invited to share lunch. This surrealist touch illustrates the extent to which the soldiers' action had become dissociated from its meaning. An hour earlier, some of these men were making sure that not even a child would escape the executioner's bullet. But now the job was done and it was time for lunch—and in this new context it seemed only natural to ask the children who had managed to escape execution to join them. The massacre had ended. It remained only for the Viet Cong to reap the political rewards among the survivors in hiding.

The army command in the area knew that something had gone wrong. Direct commanders, including Lieutenant Colonel Barker, had firsthand reports, such as Thompson's complaints. Others had such odd bits of evidence as the claim of 128 Viet Cong dead with a booty of only three weapons. But the cover-up of My Lai began at once. The operation was reported as a victory over a stronghold of the Viet Cong Forty-eighth. . . .

William Calley was not the only man tried for the event at My Lai. The actions of over thirty soldiers and civilians were scrutinized by investigators; over half of these had to face charges or disciplinary action of some sort. Targets of investigation included Captain Medina, who was tried, and various higher-ups, including General Koster. But Lieutenant Calley was the only person convicted, the only person to serve time.

The core of Lieutenant Calley's defense was superior orders. What this meant to him—in contrast to what it meant to the judge and jury—can be gleaned from his responses to a series of questions from his defense attorney, George Latimer, in which Calley sketched out his understanding of the laws of war and the actions that constitute doing one's duty within those laws:

Latimer: Did you receive any training which had to do with the obedience to orders?

Calley: Yes, sir.

Latimer: . . . what were you informed [were] the principles involved in that field?

Calley: That all orders were to be assumed legal, that the soldier's job was to carry out any order given him to the best of his ability.

Latimer: . . . what might occur if you disobeyed an order by a senior officer?

Calley: You could be court-martialed for refusing an order and refusing an order in the face of the enemy, you could be sent to death, sir.

Latimer: [I am asking] whether you were required in any way, shape or form to make a determination of the legality or illegality of an order?

Calley: No, sir. I was never told that I had the choice, sir.

Latimer: If you had a doubt about the order, what were you supposed to do?

Calley: . . . I was supposed to carry the order out and then come back and make my complaint. (Hammer, 1971, pp. 240–241)

Lieutenant Calley steadfastly maintained that his actions within My Lai had constituted, in his mind, carrying out orders from Captain Medina. Both his own actions and the orders he gave to others (such as the instruction to Meadlo to "waste 'em") were entirely in response to superior orders. He denied any intent to kill individuals and any but the most passing awareness of distinctions among the individuals: "I was ordered to go in there and destroy the enemy. That was my job on that day. That was the mission I was given. I did not sit down and think in terms of men, women, and children. They were all classified the same, and that was the classification that we dealt with, just as enemy soldiers." When Latimer asked if in his own opinion Calley had acted "rightly and according to your understanding of your directions and orders," Calley replied, "I felt then and I still do that I acted as I was directed, and I carried out the orders that I was given, and I do not feel wrong in doing so, sir" (Hammer, 1971, p. 257).

His court-martial did not accept Calley's defense of superior orders and clearly did not share his interpretation of his duty. The jury evidently reasoned that, even if there had been orders to destroy everything in sight and to "waste the Vietnamese," any reasonable person would have realized that such orders were illegal and should have refused to carry them out. The defense of superior orders under such conditions is inadmissible under international and military law. The U.S. Army's *Law of Land Warfare* (Dept. of the Army, 1956), for example, states that "the fact that the law of war has been violated pursuant to an order of a superior authority, whether military or civil, does not deprive the act in question of its character of a war crime, nor does it constitute a defense in the trial of an accused individual, unless he did not know and could not reasonably have been expected to know that the act was unlawful" and that "members of the armed forces are bound to obey only lawful orders" (in Falk et al., 1971, pp. 71–72).

The disagreement between Calley and the court-martial seems to have revolved around the definition of the responsibilities of a subordinate to obey, on the one hand, and to evaluate, on the other. This tension . . . can best be captured via the charge to the jury in the Calley court-martial, made by the trial judge, Col. Reid Kennedy. The forty-one pages of the charge include the following:

> Both combatants captured by and noncombatants detained by the opposing force . . . have the right to be treated as prisoners. . . . Summary execution of detainees or prisoners is forbidden by law. . . . I therefore instruct you . . . that if unresisting human beings were killed at My Lai (4) while within the effective custody and control of our military forces, their deaths cannot be considered justified. . . . Thus if you find that Lieutenant Calley received an order directing him to kill unresisting Vietnamese within his control or within the control of his troops, *that order would be an illegal order.*
>
> A determination that an order is illegal does not, of itself, assign criminal responsibility to the person following the order for acts done in compliance with it. Soldiers are taught to follow orders, and special attention is given to obedience of orders on the battlefield. Military effectiveness depends on obedience to orders. On the other hand, the obedience of a soldier is not the obedience of an automaton. A soldier is a reasoning agent, obliged to respond, not as a machine, but as a person. The law takes these factors into account in assessing criminal responsibility for acts done in compliance with illegal orders.

> The acts of a subordinate done in compliance with an unlawful order given him by his superior are excused and impose no criminal liability upon him unless the superior's order is one which a man of *ordinary sense and understanding* would, under the circumstances, know to be unlawful, or if the order in question is actually known to the accused to be unlawful. (Goldstein et al., 1976, pp. 525–526; emphasis added)

By this definition, subordinates take part in a balancing act, one tipped toward obedience but tempered by "ordinary sense and understanding."

A jury of combat veterans proceeded to convict William Calley of the premeditated murder of no less than twenty-two human beings. (The army, realizing some unfortunate connotations in referring to the victims as "Oriental human beings," eventually referred to them as "human beings.") Regarding the first specification in the murder charge, the bodies on the trail, [Calley] was convicted of premeditated murder of not less than one person. (Medical testimony had been able to pinpoint only one person whose wounds as revealed in Haeberle's photos were sure to be immediately fatal.) Regarding the second specification, the bodies in the ditch, Calley was convicted of the premeditated murder of not less than twenty human beings. Regarding additional specifications that he had killed an old man and a child, Calley was convicted of premeditated murder in the first case and of assault with intent to commit murder in the second.

Lieutenant Calley was initially sentenced to life imprisonment. That sentence was reduced: first to twenty years, eventually to ten (the latter by Secretary of Defense Callaway in 1974). Calley served three years before being released on bond. The time was spent under house arrest in his apartment, where he was able to receive visits from his girlfriend. He was granted parole on September 10, 1975.

Sanctioned Massacres

The slaughter at My Lai is an instance of a class of violent acts that can be described as sanctioned massacres (Kelman, 1973): acts of indiscriminate, ruthless, and often systematic mass violence, carried out by military or paramilitary personnel while engaged in officially sanctioned campaigns, the victims of which are defenseless and unresisting civilians, including old men, women, and children. Sanctioned massacres have occurred throughout history. Within American history, My Lai had its precursors in the Philippine war around the turn of the century (Schirmer, 1971) and in the massacres of American Indians. Elsewhere in the world, one recalls the Nazis' "final solution" for European Jews, the massacres and deportations of Armenians by Turks, the liquidation of the kulaks and the great purges in the Soviet Union, and more recently the massacres in Indonesia and Bangladesh, in Biafra and Burundi, in South Africa and Mozambique, in Cambodia and Afghanistan, in Syria and Lebanon. . . .

The occurrence of sanctioned massacres cannot be adequately explained by the existence of psychological forces—whether these be characterological dispositions to engage in murderous violence or profound hostility against the target—so powerful that they must find expression in violent acts unhampered by moral restraints. Instead, the major instigators for this class of violence derive from the policy process. The question that really calls for psychological analysis is why so many people are willing to formulate, participate in, and condone policies that call for the mass killings of defenseless civilians. Thus it is more instructive to look not at the motives for violence but at the conditions under which the usual moral inhibitions against violence become weakened. Three social processes that tend to create such conditions can be identified: authorization, routinization, and dehumanization. Through authorization, the situation becomes so defined that the individual is absolved of the responsibility to make personal moral choices. Through routinization, the action becomes so organized that there is no opportunity for raising moral questions. Through dehumanization, the actors' attitudes toward the target and toward themselves be-

come so structured that it is neither necessary nor possible for them to view the relationship in moral terms.

Authorization

Sanctioned massacres by definition occur in the context of an authority situation, a situation in which, at least for many of the participants, the moral principles that generally govern human relationships do not apply. Thus, when acts of violence are explicitly ordered, implicitly encouraged, tacitly approved, or at least permitted by legitimate authorities, people's readiness to commit or condone them is enhanced. That such acts are authorized seems to carry automatic justification for them. Behaviorally, authorization obviates the necessity of making judgments or choices. Not only do normal moral principles become inoperative, but—particularly when the actions are explicitly ordered—a different kind of morality, linked to the duty to obey superior orders, tends to take over.

In an authority situation, individuals characteristically feel obligated to obey the orders of the authorities, whether or not these correspond with their personal preferences. They see themselves as having no choice as long as they accept the legitimacy of the orders and of the authorities who give them. Individuals differ considerably in the degree to which—and the conditions under which—they are prepared to challenge the legitimacy of an order on the grounds that the order itself is illegal, or that those giving it have overstepped their authority, or that it stems from a policy that violates fundamental societal values. Regardless of such individual differences, however, the basic structure of a situation of legitimate authority requires subordinates to respond in terms of their role obligations rather than their personal preferences; they can openly disobey only by challenging the legitimacy of the authority. Often people obey without question even though the behavior they engage in may entail great personal sacrifice or great harm to others.

An important corollary of the basic structure of the authority situation is that actors often do not see themselves as personally responsible for the consequences of their actions. Again, there are individual differences, depending on actors' capacity and readiness to evaluate the legitimacy of orders received. Insofar as they see themselves as having had no choice in their actions, however, they do not feel personally responsible for them. They were not personal agents, but merely extensions of the authority. Thus, when their actions cause harm to others, they can feel relatively free of guilt. A similar mechanism operates when a person engages in antisocial behavior that was not ordered by the authorities but was tacitly encouraged and approved by them—even if only by making it clear that such behavior will not be punished. In this situation, behavior that was formerly illegitimate is legitimized by the authorities' acquiescence.

In the My Lai massacre, it is likely that the structure of the authority situation contributed to the massive violence in both ways—that is, by conveying the message that acts of violence against Vietnamese villagers were *required*, as well as the message that such acts, even if not ordered, were *permitted* by the authorities in charge. The actions at My Lai represented, at least in some respects, responses to explicit or implicit orders. Lieutenant Calley indicated, by orders and by example, that he wanted large numbers of villagers killed. Whether Calley himself had been ordered by his superiors to "waste" the whole area, as he claimed, remains a matter of controversy. Even if we assume, however, that he was not explicitly ordered to wipe out the village, he had reason to believe that such actions were expected by his superior officers. Indeed, the very nature of the war conveyed this expectation. The principal measure of military success was the "body count"—the number of enemy soldiers killed—and any Vietnamese killed by the U.S. military was commonly defined as a "Viet Cong." Thus, it was not totally bizarre for Calley to believe that what he was doing at My Lai was to increase his body count, as any good officer was expected to do.

Even to the extent that the actions at My Lai occurred spontaneously, without reference to superior orders, those committing them had reason to assume that such actions might be tacitly

approved of by the military authorities. Not only had they failed to punish such acts in most cases, but the very strategies and tactics that the authorities consistently devised were based on the proposition that the civilian population of South Vietnam—whether "hostile" or "friendly"—was expendable. Such policies as search-and-destroy missions, the establishment of free-shooting zones, the use of antipersonnel weapons, the bombing of entire villages if they were suspected of harboring guerrillas, the forced migration of masses of the rural population, and the defoliation of vast forest areas helped legitimize acts of massive violence of the kind occurring at My Lai.

Some of the actions at My Lai suggest an orientation to authority based on unquestioning obedience to superior orders, no matter how destructive the actions these orders call for. Such obedience is specifically fostered in the course of military training and reinforced by the structure of the military authority situation. It also reflects, however, an ideological orientation that may be more widespread in the general population. . . .

Routinization

Authorization processes create a situation in which people become involved in an action without considering its implications and without really making a decision. Once they have taken the initial step, they are in a new psychological and social situation in which the pressures to continue are powerful. As Lewin (1947) has pointed out, many forces that might originally have kept people out of a situation reverse direction once they have made a commitment (once they have gone through the "gate region") and now serve to keep them in the situation. For example, concern about the criminal nature of an action, which might originally have inhibited a person from becoming involved, may now lead to deeper involvement in efforts to justify the action and to avoid negative consequences.

Despite these forces, however, given the nature of the actions involved in sanctioned massacres, one might still expect moral scruples to intervene; but the likelihood of moral resistance is greatly reduced by transforming the action into routine, mechanical, highly programmed operations.

Routinization fulfills two functions. First, it reduces the necessity of making decisions, thus minimizing the occasions in which moral questions may arise. Second, it makes it easier to avoid the implications of the action, since the actor focuses on the details of the job rather than on its meaning. The latter effect is more readily achieved among those who participate in sanctioned massacres from a distance—from their desks or even from the cockpits of their bombers.

Routinization operates both at the level of the individual actor and at the organizational level. Individual job performance is broken down into a series of discrete steps, most of them carried out in automatic, regularized fashion. It becomes easy to forget the nature of the product that emerges from this process. When Lieutenant Calley said of My Lai that it was "no great deal," he probably implied that it was all in a day's work. Organizationally, the task is divided among different offices, each of which has responsibility for a small portion of it. This arrangement diffuses responsibility and limits the amount and scope of decision making that is necessary. There is no expectation that the moral implications will be considered at any of these points, nor is there any opportunity to do so. The organizational processes also help further legitimize the actions of each participant. By proceeding in routine fashion—processing papers, exchanging memos, diligently carrying out their assigned tasks—the different units mutually reinforce each other in the view that what is going on must be perfectly normal, correct, and legitimate. The shared illusion that they are engaged in a legitimate enterprise helps the participants assimilate their activities to other purposes, such as the efficiency of their performance, the productivity of their unit, or the cohesiveness of their group (see Janis, 1972).

Normalization of atrocities is more difficult to the extent that there are constant reminders of the true meaning of the enterprise. Bureaucratic inventiveness in the use of language helps to cover up such meaning. For example, the SS had a set of *Sprachregelungen,* or "language rules," to govern descriptions of their extermination program. As Arendt (1964) points out, the term *lan-*

guage rule in itself was "a code name; it meant what in ordinary language would be called a lie" (p. 85). The code names for killing and liquidation were "final solution," "evacuation," and "special treatment." The war in Indochina produced its own set of euphemisms, such as "protective reaction," "pacification," and "forced-draft urbanization and modernization." The use of euphemisms allows participants in sanctioned massacres to differentiate their actions from ordinary killing and destruction and thus to avoid confronting their true meaning.

Dehumanization

Authorization processes override standard moral considerations; routinization processes reduce the likelihood that such considerations will arise. Still, the inhibitions against murdering one's fellow human beings are generally so strong that the victims must also be stripped of their human status if they are to be subjected to systematic killing. Insofar as they are dehumanized, the usual principles of morality no longer apply to them.

Sanctioned massacres become possible to the extent that the victims are deprived in the perpetrators' eyes of the two qualities essential to being perceived as fully human and included in the moral compact that governs human relationships: *identity*—standing as independent, distinctive individuals, capable of making choices and entitled to live their own lives—and *community*—fellow membership in an interconnected network of individuals who care for each other and respect each other's individuality and rights (Kelman, 1973; see also Bakan, 1966, for a related distinction between "agency" and "communion"). Thus, when a group of people is defined entirely in terms of a category to which they belong, and when this category is excluded from the human family, moral restraints against killing them are more readily overcome.

Dehumanization of the enemy is a common phenomenon in any war situation. Sanctioned massacres, however, presuppose a more extreme degree of dehumanization, insofar as the killing is not in direct response to the target's threats or provocations. It is not what they have done that marks such victims for death but who they are—the category to which they happen to belong. They are the victims of policies that regard their systematic destruction as a desirable end or an acceptable means. Such extreme dehumanization becomes possible when the target group can readily be identified as a separate category of people who have historically been stigmatized and excluded by the victimizers; often the victims belong to a distinct racial, religious, ethnic, or political group regarded as inferior or sinister. The traditions, the habits, the images, and the vocabularies for dehumanizing such groups are already well established and can be drawn upon when the groups are selected for massacre. Labels help deprive the victims of identity and community, as in the epithet "gooks" that was commonly used to refer to Vietnamese and other Indochinese peoples.

The dynamics of the massacre process itself further increase the participants' tendency to dehumanize their victims. Those who participate as part of the bureaucratic apparatus increasingly come to see their victims as bodies to be counted and entered into their reports, as faceless figures that will determine their productivity rates and promotions. Those who participate in the massacre directly—in the field, as it were—are reinforced in their perception of the victims as less than human by observing their very victimization. The only way they can justify what is being done to these people—both by others and by themselves—and the only way they can extract some degree of meaning out of the absurd events in which they find themselves participating (see Lifton, 1971, 1973) is by coming to believe that the victims are subhuman and deserve to be rooted out. And thus the process of dehumanization feeds on itself.

REFERENCES

Arendt, H. (1964). *Eichmann in Jerusalem: A report on the banality of evil.* New York: Viking Press.

Bakan, D. (1966). *The duality of human existence.* Chicago: Rand McNally.

Department of the Army. (1956). *The law of land warfare* (Field Manual, No. 27-10). Washington, DC: U.S. Government Printing Office.

Falk, R. A.; Kolko, G.; & Lifton, R. J. (Eds.). (1971). *Crimes of war.* New York: Vintage Books.

French, P. (Ed.). (1972). *Individual and collective responsibility: The massacre at My Lai.* Cambridge, MA: Schenkman.

Goldstein, J.; Marshall, B.; & Schwartz, J. (Eds.). (1976). *The My Lai massacre and its cover-up: Beyond the reach of law?* (The Peers report with a supplement and introductory essay on the limits of law). New York: Free Press.

Hammer, R. (1971). *The court-martial of Lt. Calley.* New York: Coward, McCann, & Geoghegan.

Hersh, S. (1970). *My Lai 4: A report on the massacre and its aftermath.* New York: Vintage Books.

————. (1972). *Cover-up.* New York: Random House.

Janis, I. L. (1972). *Victims of groupthink: A psychological study of foreign-policy decisions and fiascoes.* Boston: Houghton Mifflin.

Kelman, H. C. (1973). Violence without moral restraint: Reflections on the dehumanization of victims and victimizers. *Journal of Social Issues,* 29(4), 25–61.

Lewin, K. (1947). Group decision and social change. In T. M. Newcomb & E. L. Hartley (Eds.), *Readings in social psychology.* New York: Holt.

Lifton, R. J. (1971). Existential evil. In N. Sanford, C. Comstock, & Associates, *Sanctions for evil: Sources of social destructiveness.* San Francisco: Jossey-Bass.

————. (1973). *Home from the war—Vietnam veterans: Neither victims nor executioners.* New York: Simon & Schuster.

Manual for courts martial, United States (rev. ed.). (1969). Washington, DC: U.S. Government Printing Office.

Schirmer, D. B. (1971, April 24). My Lai was not the first time. *New Republic,* pp. 18–21.

Williams, B. (1985, April 14–15). "I will never forgive," says My Lai survivor. *Jordan Times* (Amman), p. 4.

THINKING ABOUT THE READING

According to Kelman and Hamilton, what social processes create conditions under which restraints against violence are weakened? The incident they describe provides us with an uncomfortable picture of human nature. Do you think most people would have reacted the way the soldiers at My Lai did? Are we all potential massacrers? Does the phenomenon of obedience to authority go beyond the tightly structured environment of the military? Can you think of incidents in your own life when you've done something—perhaps harmed or humiliated another person—because of the powerful influence of others?

Speaking of Sadness

Depression, Disconnection, and the Meanings of Illness

David A. Karp

Living with Depression

In greater or lesser degree I have grappled with depression for almost 20 years. I suppose that even as a child my experience of life was as much characterized by anxiety as by joy and pleasure. And as I look back, there were lots of tip-offs that things weren't right. I find it difficult to remember much of my early years, but throughout high school and college I felt uncertain of myself, feared that I could not accomplish what was expected of me, and had plenty of sleepless nights. At college one of my roommates nicknamed me "weak heart," after a character-type in Dostoyevsky novels, because I often seemed a bit of a lost soul. During all those years, though, I had no real baseline for evaluating the "normalcy" of my feelings. At most, I had defined myself as more anxious than other people and as a "worrier." None of this seemed to warrant treatment of any sort. Even though I was muddling along emotionally, probably like having a constant low-grade fever, I was achieving well enough in school to presume that underneath it all I was okay. It wasn't until my early thirties that I was forced to conclude that something was "really wrong" with me.

People who have lived with depression can often vividly remember the situations that forced them to have a new consciousness as a troubled person. One such occasion for me was a 1974 professional meeting of sociologists in Montreal. By any objective standards I should have been feeling pretty good. I had a solid academic job at Boston College, had just signed my first book contract, and I had a great wife, beautiful son, and a new baby daughter at home. From the outside my life looked pretty good.

During the week I was in Montreal I got virtually no sleep. It's true, I was staying in a strange city and in a borrowed apartment—maybe this was the problem. But I had done a fair amount of traveling and never had sleeping difficulties quite as bad. Then, I thought, "Maybe I'm physically ill. It must be the flu." But again, it was unlike any flu I'd ever had. I wasn't just tired and achy. Each sleepless night my head was filled with disturbing ruminations and during the day I felt a sense of intolerable grief as though somebody close to me had died. I was agitated and sensed a melancholy qualitatively different from anything in the past. I couldn't concentrate because the top of my head felt as if it would blow off, and the excitement of having received the book contract was replaced by the dread and certainty that I wasn't up to the task of writing it. It truly was a miserable week and the start of what I now know was an extended episode of depression. It was also the beginning of a long pilgrimage to figure out what was wrong with me, what to name it, what to do about it, and how to live with it. It has been a bewildering, frustrating, often deeply painful journey.

Despite a progressive worsening of the feelings I first experienced in Montreal, it took me quite a while before I fully connected the word depression to my situation. Being depressed was not yet part of my self-description or identity. It was another prolonged and even more debilitating period of insomnia, compounded with anxiety and sadness, that pushed me to a doctor's office (an internist, not a psychiatrist). For the first time, I heard someone tell me that I was clinically depressed and that I needed "antidepressant medications." This too was a decisive moment in my growing self-definition as a troubled person....

Like everyone who suffers with depression, I [have] spent a lot of time ... considering its causes. Throughout the early 1970s I thought I had a pretty good explanation. I was a young assistant professor struggling to do enough publishing so that I would not lose my job. As they say in the academic business, 1977 was to be my "up or out year"; I would either be promoted or "terminated." In short, I was under enormous pressure for six years, juggling the tasks of teaching, counseling students, serving on departmental and university committees, presenting papers at professional meetings, and writing two books that had to be done before I was evaluated for tenure.

I thought for sure that my depression was rooted in these situational demands and that once I got tenure it would go away. I was promoted in 1977 and found that the depression actually deepened. Of course, this meant that my "tenure theory" was wrong and I needed to construct a new one. However, discarding it was no easy thing. The theory's failure suggested a wholly new and more frightening interpretation of depression's locus. Now I had to confront the possibility that my sickness might not arise from social situations, but somehow from my self.

By 1980 my sleeping, which has always been the key barometer of my psychic state, had become just awful.... Sometimes I might get to sleep, but even on my best nights I was up every hour or so. On my worst nights I got no sleep. I remember those nights especially well because they were so distinctly horrible....

The two central feelings typifying my depression were frantic anxiety and a sense of grief. These feelings coupled to generate a sort of catastrophic thinking about events in my life as concrete as the next day's lecture and as amorphous as the quality of my relationships. None of these thoughts were productive. They were just insistently there, looping endlessly in my brain. Sometimes, as though God were serving up a particularly ironic punishment, I would drift off to sleep only shortly before I had to begin my day. The day did follow, filled with obligations

that seemed burdensome and often impossible. Each day was spent struggling to appear competent, constantly feeling amazed that I had gotten through the last test and that I would certainly "shut down" in the face of the next....

During all of this I felt deeply alone. Everyone else seemed to be moving through their days peacefully, laughing and having fun. I resented them because they were experiencing such an easy time of it; I felt utterly cut off from them emotionally. I was angry because there was no way they could understand what I was going through. Their very presence seemed to magnify my sense of isolation. I never felt seriously suicidal, but the combination of those days and nights often led me to feel that my life was not worth living. Although some days were far better than others, raising the elusive hope that I might be emerging from my difficulty, I basically dragged along, feeling barely alive....

Given the pervasiveness of depression, it is not surprising that both medical and social scientists have tried to understand its causes and suggest ways of dealing with it. When I first considered writing about depression I did a computer search that turned up nearly 500 social science studies done in just the last few years. Researchers have tried to link the incidence of depression to every imaginable social factor. For example, since the rate of depression is twice as great for women than for men, studies have been conducted seeking to relate depression with gender roles, family structure, powerlessness, child rearing, and the like. Studies can also be found trying to link depression with, among other things, age (especially during adolescence and old age), unemployment, physical illness, disability, child abuse, ethnicity, race, and social class....

Sickness, Self, and Society

... All human beings ... think about the world in causal terms. All of us use cause and effect inferences in trying to understand important features of our lives.... Efforts to come to grips with depression turn on its presumed causes.... In this way, everyone suffering from depression inevitably becomes a theorist as they try to give order and coherence to their situation. With rare exceptions, the theories they generate locate the cause(s) of depression somewhere either in their biographies or their biologies. Occasionally, [people] spin out more complex theories that see depression as resulting from the subtle interplay of personal history, recent life events, and chemical imbalances. However, even those who name situational causes for their emotional problems typically restrict their conceptual vision to the immediate and local circumstances of their lives. Only rarely do sufferers of depression relate their condition to the kinds of broad cultural trends that, I believe, influence our consciousness about everything.

The reach of sociological thinking extends well beyond the immediate milieus of daily life. In fact, exercise of the sociological imagination *requires* analysis of the connections between daily life and larger cultural arrangements. . . . The abiding theoretical questions of sociology flow from consideration of the individual-society connection. Sociologists presume an ongoing intersection of personal biographies and the larger arenas of history and social structure. A sociological angle of vision sees an inseparability between the character of culture and even our innermost thoughts and feelings, including, of course, the deeply troubling thoughts and feelings we label as depression. As George Herbert Mead expressed it with the title of his famous book, an adequate *social* psychology of human experience must consider the ways in which *Mind, Self and Society*[1] mutually transform each other. [Next I will focus] on how the structure of contemporary American society may be implicated in the production of increasingly larger numbers of people who complain of and are diagnosed as having diseased minds and selves.

Like many sociologists, one of my favorite examples to illustrate the cultural roots of what initially appears to be an exclusively personal disorder is Émile Durkheim's classic study of suicide[2] that is generally seen as a sociological *tour de force*. Aside from the intrinsic importance of the topic, Durkheim presumably chose to study suicide because, at first glance, it appears explicable *only* in individualistic, psychological terms. However, by testing a series of logically produced, deductive hypotheses linking suicide to such variables as religion, marital status, and membership in the military, Durkheim convincingly demonstrated the connection between suicide *rates* and degrees of *social integration*. Specifically, he argued that modernizing societies, like his own nineteenth century France, were less successful than earlier agrarian societies in providing sources of integration for their members. Such societies were characterized by what Durkheim termed *anomie*—a state of relative normlessness. His brilliant work verified that anomic societies that fail to integrate their members adequately also fail to insulate them from suicide. Suicide, in short, is as much a social as it is a psychological phenomenon.

Another first-rate sociologist, Kai Erikson, provides a valuable example for illustrating how a sociological perspective is necessary to see social patterns that would be missed if we only look at things "up close and personal," as they say on *Wide World of Sports*.[3] He has us imagine that we are walking along 42nd Street near Times Square. At the street level we can clearly see the faces of the thousands of people who pass us. We can see their individual expressions, their particular body idioms, their apparent ages, and so on. At this range, they normally seem to take no notice of anyone around them. Each stranger appears as a solitary atom, buzzing along in a wholly independent way.

Were we, however, to climb to the roof of a nearby 12-story building and look down on the flow of sidewalk traffic, we would see an extraordinary thing. It is true that from this vantage point we miss the particularities of each individual. However, we would instead witness a miraculous pattern—thousands of people moving along the street in an incredibly well-organized, efficient, and cooperative fashion. Moreover, each person on the street would likely be wholly unaware of their contribution to the web of behavior necessary to sustain such an enormously complex social order. It is as if each pedestrian is guided by an invisible social force, a kind of social gravity, about which they have only the vaguest awareness. I am proposing that most people suffering from depression, like street pedestrians, are only dimly aware of how the constitution of culture might be contributing to their depressed condition.

Although estimates of the number of Americans suffering from depression vary, there is general consensus that the number is in the vicinity of 11 million people and that economic losses from poor productivity, lost work days, hospitalization, outpatient care, and so on, is a staggering $43.7 billion dollars a year.[4] More important to my concerns are the data from a range of studies showing tremendous increases in the rates of depression. For example: (1) The incidence of depression among those born after World War II is much higher and the age of onset much earlier than in earlier population cohorts.[5] (2) In recent decades, there has been a continuing rise in depression among young women, but a disproportionate increase of depression among men has been closing the depression gender gap.[6] (3) There has been an absolute explosion of depression among "baby boomers."[7] These and similar findings warrant the conclusion that America is in the grip of a depression epidemic; that we have entered an "age of melancholy."[8]

. . . While any search for patterns necessarily suggests cause, I prefer to think about the link between cultural dimensions and depression in probabilistic terms. Epidemiologists, for example, describe poverty as a "risk factor" for a range of health problems. Poverty provides a context that makes individuals more vulnerable to disease. The notion of risk factors implies likelihoods rather than direct causal relationships. In Durkheimian fashion, [I will detail] the cultural dimensions of contemporary American society that provide the context for our collective vulnerability to emotional distress.[9] In particular, my thesis can be expressed as a theoretical equation. It is:

MEDICALIZATION + DISCONNECTION
+ POSTMODERNIZATION
= PERSONAL DISLOCATION

. . . I will define what I have in mind as each is discussed. Immediately, though, my argument is best advanced by showing how fundamentally the idea of depression is connected to culture. If the features of a particular culture truly influence what is even recognized as an illness, we should expect wide cultural variation in the labeling of particular physical and emotional experiences as health or illness.

Culture, Health, and Emotion

In a classic article written [over] 50 years ago, the medical historian Erwin H. Ackerknecht argued against the view that disease is a strictly physical phenomenon. Citing the important role played by social factors in the definition and treatment of illness, Ackerknecht maintained that "medicine's practical goal is not primarily a biological one, but that of social adjustment in a given society. . . . Even the notion of disease depends rather on the decisions of society than on objective facts."[10] As the following examples illustrate, societies differ dramatically in their response to the same physical symptoms:

> Pinto (dyschromic spirochetosis), a skin disease, is so common among many South American tribes that the few *healthy* men that *are not* suffering from pinto are regarded as *pathological* to the point of being excluded from marriage. The crippled feet of the traditional Chinese woman, diseased to us, were, of course, normal to the Chinese. Intestinal worms among the African Thongas are not at all regarded as pathological. They are thought to be necessary for digestion.[11]

Not only is the definition of what constitutes an illness or pathological condition subject to cultural variations, but, in an even more far-reaching sense, one's *experience* of bodily symptoms is shaped by social processes and expectations as well. In a now famous study, Mark

Zborowski illustrated how responses to pain varied by the respondent's ethnicity.[12] Jewish-American patients, for example, evidenced substantial philosophical concern and anxiety about their condition and were pessimistic about the future course of their illness. Protestant patients felt optimistic about their prospects for recovery while viewing doctors as experts to whom one went for "mending," much like bringing a car to an auto mechanic for repairs. Italian-Americans, by contrast, wanted immediate pain relief, and, unlike Jewish respondents, had little concern about the larger "meanings" of the pain.

We should expect that the same principles apply to emotional pain and there is, indeed, substantial evidence that depression carries quite different meanings in different cultures. In a series of books and articles,[13] Arthur Kleinman, who is both an anthropologist and a physician, has written with eloquence and power on the value of looking at a range of emotional disorders cross culturally. Although he does not posit a particular theory as underlying his inquiries, Kleinman's analysis bears a striking resemblance to "symbolic interaction." . . . I say this because the underlying motif of his work is the *socially generated meanings of illness,* the importance of appreciating the dialectics of body and culture, symptom and society. In fact, Kleinman's mission seems nothing short of reforming the teaching and practice of medicine. By dismissing how illness carries very different symbolic meanings in different cultural settings, Western medicine, based nearly exclusively on a biomedical model, falls short in both its modes of diagnosis and treatment.

Like other medical anthropologists, Kleinman's thinking rests on the fundamental distinction between *illness* and *disease.* . . . Distinguishing the two words helps to make plain the difference between the subjective experience of bodily or emotional distress (illness) and the presumed biological cause of the distress (disease).

When first becoming sick we begin an interpretive process about the meaning of symptoms. We make assessments about the severity of our discomfort, and, usually in consultation with family and friends, assess the significance of our trouble, deciding what to name it and how to respond to it. The point here is that these interpretations can be rooted in widely varying normative orders and cultural symbol systems. Such culturally induced interpretations, moreover, "orient us to how to act when ill, how to communicate distress, how to diagnose and treat, how to regard and manage the life problems illness creates, how to negotiate this social reality and interpret its meaning for ourselves and for others."[14] Disease, in contrast to illness, is "what the practitioner creates in the recasting of illness in terms of theories of disorder."[15] In Western medicine this typically means identifying the biological dysfunction presumably giving rise to the symptoms described by the patient.

Once we recognize the critical importance of cultural meanings in how symptoms are experienced and dealt with, we can also pinpoint a fundamental difficulty with the practice of Western medicine. American medicine is primarily concerned with disease and pays little attention to the patient's illness. The nearly single-minded efforts of physicians to quickly locate the presumed biological dysfunctions associated with symptoms leads to a problematic disjunction between what patients want from doctors and what they get. Evidence from a recent poll on dissatisfaction with conventional medicine[16] suggests that patients want to be heard by physicians and feel alienated when the full context of their illness experience is defined as irrelevant to their treatment. As a result, patients are seeking treatment from "alternative" healers in ever increasing numbers. Not incidentally, anxiety and depression rank one and two among the problems for which alternative help is sought.

Because of bureaucratic time imperatives[17] and physicians' felt need to quickly diagnose the patient's disease, most doctor/patient encounters in the United States are very short. While initial visits to a doctor might range up to 30 minutes, the average length of doctor/patient encounters is typically between 5 and 10 minutes. In a recent *Newsweek* story,[18] it was reported that patients' average time spent with psychiatrists in some clinics is an astonishing 3 minutes! Whether the figure is as low as 3 or as high as the 17 minutes reported in another study,[19] one thing is plain: Doctors are normally uninterested in hearing patients' illness experience—they listen only insofar as the information provided helps them to make a diagnosis. In fact, to let the patient "go on" about their symptoms and feelings is often seen as an obstacle to "good" medicine.[20] . . .

An anthropologically informed view sees diagnosis and treatment in very different terms. Illness narratives are deemed critical for appreciating precisely what physicians typically leave out of the picture—namely, how culturally prescribed meanings shape illness realities and, therefore, patients' likely responses to different modes of treatment. just as patients' experiences of symptoms arise out of particular symbol systems, so also must the likely efficacy of treatments be understood in cultural context. Nowhere is this line of thinking more apparently true than in psychiatry where emotional feelings define the problem and where the discovery of a clear disease entity is most elusive. Kleinman and his colleague Byron Good state with wonderful clarity what a cross-cultural perspective on depression teaches us. Based on a range of investigations, they say

> It is simply not tenable . . . to argue that dysphoric emotion and depressive illness are invariant across cultures. When culture is treated as a constant . . . it is relatively easy to view depression as [exclusively] a biological disorder. . . . From this perspective, culture appears epiphenomenal; cultural differences may exist, but they are not considered essential to the phenomenon itself. However, when culture is treated as a significant variable . . . many of our assumptions about the nature of emotions and illness are cast into sharp relief. Dramatic differences are found across cultures in the social organization, personal experience, and consequences of such emotions as sadness, grief, and anger, of behaviors such as withdrawal or aggression, and of psychological characteristics such as passivity and helpless-

ness. . . . Dysphoria, even the pervasive loss of pleasure . . . is associated with quite different symptoms of distress and has widely varied consequences for the sufferer. . . . Depressive illness and dysphoria are thus not only interpreted differently in non-Western societies and across cultures; they are constituted as fundamentally different forms of social reality.[21]

The essential finding of Kleinman's work and a number of other anthropologically oriented investigations on depression is that biological, psychological, and social processes are intricately woven together in creating the depression phenomenon. While there does appear to be a core syndrome of depression that can be observed universally across cultures, the equally clear findings of comparative research show wide variation in the experience of depression. Depressive disorders, in other words, display both universal and culture-specific properties.

Psychiatric medicine in the United States, with its heavily scientific bias, largely presumes biochemical pathology as the ultimate source of depressive disorders everywhere. Such a view is sustained despite the existence of "impressive data that there is no such thing as depression that occurs solely from biological causes."[22] To be sure, it would be equally plausible to say that real-world experiences produce depression by altering biochemistry and thus stand first in the hierarchy of depression's causes. Right now, though, it would be as presumptuous to make this claim as it is of American medicine to claim biology as the absolute foundation of depressive disorders. The truth is that there is no way to untangle the intersection of cultural and biological factors and, consequently, no sure way to claim the greater significance of either nature or nurture in causing depression. Despite this epistemological problem, the role of culture and the contributions of social science in understanding the course of illness remain very much at the margins of American medical training and practice.

This discussion asserts wide cultural variation in the incidence, meaning, and experience of psychiatric disorders, but is not grounded with concrete examples. To get specific, I can report that historically the best predictor of rates of admission to mental hospitals and suicides in North America is the health of the economy (the worse the economy the greater the rates); that the incidence and course of schizophrenia is tied to a society's level of technology (the more modernized a society the greater is the incidence of intractable schizophrenia); that a diagnostic category such as "narcissistic personality disorder," increasingly common in the United States, is virtually unheard of elsewhere; that in certain Asian societies "semen loss" resulting from nocturnal discharge is viewed with great alarm and anguish because sperm contains "qi" (vital energy), seen as absolutely necessary for health; that eating disorders such as anorexia and bulimia are most thoroughly characteristic of capitalist economies; that lack of joy, a central criterion for defining someone as depressed in the United States, would never be mentioned as a problem in Buddhist cultures such as Sri Lanka; that it is considered perfectly normal for American Indians grieving the loss of a spouse literally to hear the voices of the dead, and that the linguistic equivalents of anxiety and depression simply do not exist in many languages.[23]

In several of his books, Kleinman singles out China to illustrate how cultural sentiments influence the way doctors and their patients respond to the complex of feelings American doctors would unmistakably call depression. In contrast to the United States, depression is an infrequent diagnosis in China. Instead, patients suffering from a combination of such symptoms as anxiety, general debility, headaches, backaches, sadness, irritability, insomnia, poor appetite, and sexual dysfunction are diagnosed as suffering from "neurasthenia." Ironically, neurasthenia as a diagnostic category originated in the United States and was once thought of as "the American disease." Now, it is virtually never used in this country, just as the depression diagnosis is very rarely used in China. The choice of the neurasthenia diagnosis turns on cultural preferences. In China, where mental illness is deeply stigmatizing for both sick individuals and their families,

doctors and patients find congenial a diagnosis—neurasthenia—that traces the disease to a neurological weakness rather than a mental disorder. In other words, the same symptoms are labeled, interpreted, responded to, and experienced quite differently in the two cultures. It would be proper to say that, although suffering from nominally the same symptoms, the illness realities of Chinese and Americans are truly worlds apart.

Medicalization

The foregoing discussion implies that a necessary condition for widespread depressive illness is a culturally induced readiness to view emotional pain as a disease requiring medical intervention. The grounds for interpreting pain as an abnormal medical condition have been largely established through the increasing incursion of medical and other therapeutic experts into literally every aspect of our lives. Doctors in particular have become explorers, discovering every conceivable aspect of the human condition as potentially problematic and warranting their intervention. Such a "medicalization" process[24] has dramatically increased the number of uncomfortable or disliked feelings and behaviors that we now see as illnesses.

The so-called medical model is based on two apparently unassailable premises: (1) Normalcy is preferable to abnormalcy, and (2) normalcy is a synonym for health and abnormalcy a synonym for pathology. Definitions of health and pathology, in turn, are derived from laboratory research that is presumed to be thoroughly objective. In this way, medical definitions of health gain the status of scientific facts instead of merely collectively agreed on cultural designations.

Because it is better to be healthy than to be sick, the medical model legitimizes physicians' intervention, whether requested or not, to determine one's health status. No other profession provides for the extensive access to a person's body, mind, and self as do physical and psychiatric medicine. By defining certain features of the human condition as illnesses to be cured, physicians give themselves the right to explore every part of the human anatomy, to prescribe a myriad of curative agents, and even to compel treatment.

The term *healthy,* as used in the medical model, can be equated with *conformity.* In societies where it predominates, the medical model often supersedes legal or religious commandments in regulating behavior. "Peculiar" individuals who were once viewed as possessed or as agents of the devil are now classified as emotionally ill. In the name of science, the advice of medical experts is used in the courts to determine whether certain actions should be defined as crimes. Medicine, especially psychiatric medicine, is often used to "treat" individuals whose behaviors do not conform to the expectations of the powerful or impinge on their moral sensitivities.

There can be little dispute that behavior in today's "postindustrial" society is dominated by "experts." Experts follow us through the life course, advising us on virtually every aspect of existence. They are there when we are born and accompany us each step along the way until we die. Among other things, we rely on experts to tell us how to maintain health, how to become educated, how to make love, how to raise children, and how to age correctly. Most relevant here is that experts now tell us when our "selves" need repair and the proper procedures for doing it. . . .

You might also understand that this dependence on therapeutic experts arises out of the distinctive problems posed by modern life. Every generation, because of its unique historical situation, experiences the world differently than its predecessors. Whatever the historical conditions into which people are born, however, one problem remains constant: Human beings need a coherent framework for comprehending life and death. In some historical periods the traditional meanings transmitted from one generation to the next adequately perform this function. In other epochs, meaning coherence is not so easily established. As Peter Berger and Thomas Luckmann note, the current moment in the Western world appears to be one in which many individuals experience particular difficulty in understanding themselves. They say that "In societies

with a very simple division of labor . . . there is . . . no problem of identity. The question 'Who am I?' is unlikely to arise in consciousness, since the socially defined answer is massively real subjectively and consistently confirmed in all significant social interaction."[25]

When people come together and collectively act on their definitions of injustice, a social movement is born. In Ralph Turner's words, "The phenomenon of a man crying out with indignation because his society has not supplied him with a sense of personal worth and identity is the distinctive new feature of our era. The idea that a man who does not feel worthy and cannot find his proper place in life is to be pitied is an old one. The notion that he is indeed a victim of injustice is the new idea."[26] Today, alienation, previously seen as only a work-related phenomenon, has a much broader connotation. In the present era, alienation refers to a psychological condition in which people are unable to locate a clear conception of self and feel a sense of wholeness. In the context of such alienation, the "therapeutic state" has triumphed.[27]

As a more personalized conception of alienation has been taking root in American society, popular writings by psychiatrists, psychologists, and advice columnists have become increasingly influential. Television appearances have made "mind-tinkerers" such as Leo Buscaglia, "Dr. Ruth," Marianne Williamson, and John Bradshaw national celebrities. Their appeal attests to a pervasive anxiety about questions of identity and psychological well-being in the society. Such experts are constantly dispensing prescriptions for happiness, sexual fulfillment, and mental health.

The movement toward an all-embracing concern with psychological health and personal identity has been accompanied by a corresponding transformation in our explanations of human behavior. When people act in a way we consider deviant, our first impulse is to question their mental health and to probe their psychological makeup. Are they normal? Why are they doing that? What is wrong with them? Because of the medicalization process, such behaviors as alcoholism that years ago were viewed as evidence of sinfulness or moral degeneracy are now explained as illness. A "sickness vocabulary" has replaced a "sin vocabulary." For instance, the so-called "abuse excuse" as used in the celebrated trials of Erik and Lyle Menendez for murdering their parents has resulted in two hung juries. I would guess the same result would be virtually impossible had the Menendez brothers committed their crime 20 years ago.

Preoccupied with their dis-ease, huge numbers of Americans purchase the time and expertise of professionals in order to discover more about themselves. . . . We are in an era that has been characterized as the *age of narcissism*[28] and Americans are said to have constructed a "me, myself, and I" society. The availability of thousands of self-help books alone suggests that ours is a culture intensively absorbed with questions of self-fulfillment and self-realization.

The transformation in our self-conceptions has not been accomplished by mental health experts alone. Their orientation toward life is complemented by other self-oriented, self-discovery groups and movements. For example, large numbers of Americans continue to be involved in various fundamentalist and Eastern religious groups, as well as quasi-religious "personal growth" movements like Scientology and Transcendental Meditation.[29] Groups of this sort provide guidance for self-searching pilgrims, often by supplying absolutely definitive answers to the questions "Who am I and where do I fit in?" "New" religions thrive by providing world views alternative to the kind of scientific and bureaucratic rationality that insinuates even the innermost preserves of our everyday lives. The widespread interest in astrology, dianetics, and the paranormal is explicable as a reaction to a world in which science and technology have portrayed the universe as barren and bereft of meaning.

Yet another "revolution" directed toward the search for and repair of broken selves has been occurring in the last decade or so. In many ways, the springing up of self-help and support groups for dealing with almost every imaginable human trouble represents a combination of many of the elements I have been describing. The self-help revolution reflects the full flowering of a therapeutic culture in America. In self-help groups people turn to others afflicted with the same personal troubles and try, through conversation, to "heal" themselves of what they perceive to be their shared illness. An illness rhetoric (often implying biological causation) is sometimes joined with a spiritual vocabulary (as in programs like Alcoholics Anonymous) positing that "recovery" requires surrendering to a higher power. The self-help phenomenon thus derives its allure by combining elements of therapy with elements of religion and science. It is a powerful brew that has drawn the faith of millions.[30]

. . . As might be expected, the response of mental health professionals to the self-help phenomenon has been lukewarm.[31] While many mental health professionals are legitimately concerned about the wisdom of laypersons treating themselves, we should not miss the point that the self-help idea threatens their own claim to exclusive expertise about a number of mental health problems.

Recently a self-help backlash has developed. While people may individually feel better through participation in them, critics say that their collective effect may be the production of a national mentality in which virtually everyone perceives themselves as suffering from some sort of illness and as the "victim" of circumstances beyond their control. Dissidents wonder whether claims such as the one made by John Bradshaw, a leader of the "recovery movement," that 96 percent of American families are "dysfunctional," trivializes such real abuses as incest by grouping them with an enormous range of experiences that are somehow deemed as damaging people. Critics worry that the underlying illness ideology of support groups furthers the view—distinctly a product of the modern world—that individuals do not bear ultimate responsibility for their life problems and personal behaviors. Along these lines, the sociologist Edwin Shur pointed out several years ago that increased personal consciousness is too often achieved at the expense of a diminished social consciousness.[32]

As a final observation about the emergence of a therapeutic culture, I would add that self-absorption is consistent with the emphasis on self-satisfaction fostered by capitalism in general and advertising in particular. In the industrial age, society was primarily organized around the world of work. A person who did not work, for any reason other than physical disability, was defined as immoral, lazy, and worthless. This perspective on work was beautifully captured in Max Weber's notion of the Protestant Ethic which defines work as intrinsically valuable.[33] It appears, however, that the moral restraints of the work ethic have fundamentally been undermined by a consumption ethic. If workers imbued with the Protestant Ethic lived to work, now most of us work to consume.

The shift toward the social production of consumer-oriented selves has had far-reaching consequences. Since material possessions alone cannot ensure feelings of meaningfulness and satisfaction, many today find themselves caught up in an endless quest for personal significance; a quest made even more illusive by the built-in obsolescence of the products produced. There is always a "better" product in the works, and so the flames of advertising are always nearby heating the cauldron of contemporary anxiety.[34] In advanced capitalist societies virtually anything can be made into a commodity for sale, including our selves. . . .

. . . The experience of depression occurs within a cultural context that has enormously expanded the range of emotions defined as abnormal. Authors like Martin Gross have been skeptical about the legitimacy of such redefinitions. He comments, for example, that "what the psychological society has done is to redefine normality. It has taken the painful reactions to the normal vicissitudes of life . . . despair, anger, frustration—and labeled them as maladjustments. The semantic trick is in equating happiness with normality. By permitting this, we have given up our simple right to be normal and suffering at the same time."[35] While my sense is that such brush stroke observations about the "diseasing of America"[36] are unfair to millions of people whose suffering far exceeds what human beings ought to endure, they do properly sensitize us to an enormously increased readiness to interpret emotional discomfort as disease. Such a cultural mind-set has made it possible for medicine to "discover" depression and for millions of Americans to realize that they suffer from it.

The underlying metaphor . . . is of a cultural chemistry that catalyzes depression. Thus far I have outlined one piece of the mix that foments depression, a culturally induced readiness to interpret emotional pain as illness. Like any chemical mix, the elements involved cannot create a particular reaction until they are brought together. A second factor that really gets the depression reaction going is the increasing disconnection that appears to characterize Americans' relations with each other and with society. An elaboration of the social forces diminishing human connection extends my argument . . . that depression, at its root, is a disease of disconnection.

Disconnection

Sigmund Freud was once asked what people needed to be happy. The questioner no doubt expected a long, complicated answer reflecting Freud's years of deep reflection on the matter. His simple response, however, was "arbeiten und lieben,"—work and love. Happy people feel connected to others at work and through their intimate relationships. When those connections are threatened, diminished, or broken, people suffer. Today, millions of Americans are suffering from what my colleague Charles Derber calls "double trouble."[37] Those in double trouble have neither meaningful work nor sustaining intimate ties. The withering of community life in both domains fosters a rootlessness and social disintegration that unquestionably contributes to the growth of emotional disorders.[38]

. . . These ideas have a rich history. Classical sociological theorists (such as Émile Durkheim, Max Weber, and Ferdinand Toennies) fundamentally agreed that the bond between individuals and society had been dangerously weakened in "modern" society.[39] They were unanimous in their view that people were less morally constrained in urban societies because their relationships and commitments to communities of all sorts had become far more tenuous. These nineteenth century writers feared that the eclipse of community would foreshadow the demise of the family and would, in turn, precipitate an increase in all sorts of human pathologies—from crime to suicide.

Although these sociologists could not have had America in mind when they wrote, their analysis appears prophetic. Even the most optimistic among us must acknowledge that America has extraordinary problems. Each day the newspaper assails us with more bad news about rates of homelessness, poverty, suicide, drug addiction, AIDS, teenage pregnancy, illiteracy, and unemployment. In the midst of great wealth we are increasingly becoming two nations, the haves and the have nots, one nation black and the other white, one comfortable and the other destitute.[40] Racism, sexism, and ageism characterize ever-increasing antagonisms between groups that perceive each other only as adversaries. The focus here is more limited, however. My analysis turns on the question: "How do the increasingly loose human connections at work and at home contribute to the staggering and growing number of Americans who have fallen sick with depression?" Although any analytical separation of work and home is artificial since these life areas extensively affect each other,[41] I choose for simplicity's sake to discuss them one at a time.

The Work Disconnection. A well-established tradition of sociological literature illustrates the centrality of work to personal identity.[42] Occupational status may be the central yardstick by which we assess our own and others' "social value." In a very fundamental way, we *are* what we *do.* Our feelings of self-esteem and personal well-being are wrapped up in our work. Therefore, it is perfectly predictable that a legion of studies demonstrate how unemployment deprives individuals of much more than a regular paycheck. Loss of work bears a consistent relationship with serious family and psychiatric problems.[43] Our mental health unquestionably depends on being able to provide a satisfactory answer to the ubiquitous question "What kind of work do you do?" Without work, people feel lifeless, rootless, and marginal.

The disastrous consequences of joblessness for those at the bottom of the American class structure is an old story. If there is any news here it is, unfortunately, that things have gotten worse for the poorest and most marginalized populations in America's dying inner cities. Perhaps the outstanding fact bearing on this issue is the increasing concentration of nonwhites in central city areas. While there has been some modest movement of blacks to the suburbs since 1970, it has largely been the middle-class segment of the black population that has moved, leaving behind an increasing concentration of poor blacks within urban ghettoes. Blacks have been greatly overrepresented in inner-city areas since their initial migration from the rural South to the urban North beginning in the 1950s. However, according to William Julius Wilson,[44] poor blacks are experiencing ever increasing *social isolation* within central cities.

Such profoundly important demographic transformations in American society cannot be understood apart from the imperatives of corporate capitalism. We have entered into a new round of capitalist accumulation in which older, industrial cities are no longer favorable sites for the accumulation of profit. Corporations, free to move wherever there is cheaper labor and fewer legal restrictions, have largely fled the rustbelt cities of the midwest and the frostbelt cities of the northeast in favor of cities in the south and southwest. In yet another round of moves, corporations are now leaving the country altogether to "exploit" the cheap labor in Third World countries. These processes are part of the general "deindustrialization of America"[45] that has removed almost all meaningful job opportunities for the hyperghettoized minorities trapped in America's once great cities.

Without work, black men become less desirable marriage partners and are unable to support the families they do have. Poor black families are then increasingly headed by young women dependent on welfare or the few available jobs that provide less than bare subsistence wages. As a result, "children are being raised in an institutionless community, where everyone is poor, instability is the norm, and the social and psychological role of fatherhood is nonexistent.[46] Such a situation breeds depression that spreads easily from one generation to the next. The mechanism of transmission acts like this: (1) Unemployed women caring for children at home suffer from rates of depression as high as 40 percent.[47] (2) Depressed mothers simply cannot provide the care, nurturance, and empathy that is necessary for children to grow up with good emotional health. Understandably, (3) children whose primary caretaker is depressed are themselves at enormously high risk for becoming depressed.[48] (4) Depressed children become depressed adults who pass on their disease to their own children. And so on and on. So, we have another of the vicious cycles associated with depression. This one, however, is pushed along by an obviously dysfunctional *social* rather than biological system.[49]

The poor in America have always lived with occupational instability and its fallout. In contrast, middle-class workers have historically been immune from occupational insecurity. Indeed, achieving the American Dream of middle-class life has until recently been synonymous with tremendous occupational stability. In decades past, middle- to upper-middle-class workers in large organizations could count on being taken care of from "Womb to tomb." No more. Today, the catch-words "downsizing" and "reengineering" keep the fear of job loss at the forefront of middle-class workers' collective consciousness. Once again the logic of capitalist accumulation is creating a revolution. This one is qualitatively different than earlier economic restructurings because it directly touches the middle classes in hurtful ways. Instead of the strong bond of commitment and loyalty that organizations and middle-class workers previously felt toward each other, the new economic rules of corporate life emphasize efficiency, whatever the human cost. Knowing that they could be here today, but gone

tomorrow, middle-class workers are constantly in "fear of falling.[50]

Along with those middle-class workers who continue to hold full-time jobs, however tenuously, is a growing army of well-educated "contingent workers" who are occupational nomads often working for "temp agencies." By 1988 one quarter of the American workforce worked on a contingent basis and the numbers are growing so rapidly that they will likely outnumber full-time workers by the turn of the century.[51] . . . Middle-class contingent workers *feel* contingent for good reason. They are disconnected from work in a way never before witnessed in the United States.

All social life involves a tension between freedom and constraint. Living in a society inevitably involves a trade-off between personal liberty and commitment to others. We judge some societies as immoral because they allow virtually no personal freedoms and others because they seem unable to constrain their members. For much of its history, the glory of American democracy seemed to be that it provided a healthy balance between commitment and freedom. For a long time, the pursuit of personal happiness and individual goals seemed compatible with a set of cultural values that Americans willingly embraced and held them together as a nation.

In the world of work, at least for "white collar" workers, there has been, until recently, a kind of *quid pro quo*. Organizations provided long-term security and received, in turn, worker loyalty, commitment, and responsibility. Loyalty, responsibility, security, commitment. These are the binding features of social systems, the glue that sustains the bond between individuals and social institutions. Unhappily, America's emerging "post-industrial" economy seems to have fundamentally altered the meaning of work for many by eroding loyalty, commitment, and mutual responsibility between organizations and workers.[52] Because emotional well-being is so unquestionably related to social attachment, the millions of Americans who are becoming occupationally marginal are at increasingly greater risk for being victimized by diseases of disconnection.

This section has sustained attention on how work is being reshaped in America's post-industrial, advanced capitalist society. Critics of capitalism, however, would maintain that the negative effects of capitalism on human relationships are far more inclusive than those in the workplace. In a more general way, the values underpinning capitalism are evident in a large variety of face-to-face encounters.

Competition, for example, is one of the cornerstones of capitalism. Advocates of capitalism maintain that competition is a necessary ingredient in both maintaining organizational efficiency and motivating individuals. On the negative side, however, competition pits individuals against each other, diminishes trust, and generally dehumanizes relationships. As the earlier discussion of advertising also intimates, capitalism contributes to a culture of inauthenticity. In a society where everything and everyone is evaluated by their profit potential, individuals are aware that they are constantly being manipulated, seduced, and conned by those who want to sell them or "take them." In a world held together by appearances and a tissue of illusions and deceptions, everyone becomes an enemy of sorts whose motives cannot be accepted at face value. In short, the abstract values of capitalism "trickle down" to everyday consciousness in a way that induces human beings to distrust and withdraw from each other. Withdrawal and increased isolation . . . are important features of the social dialectics of depression.

The Love Disconnection. Another underlying theme of nineteenth-century theory was the parallel development of capitalism and unbridled individualism. Although each of the classical theorists focused on somewhat different features of the social order, they agreed that while the central unit of earlier societies had been the larger collectivities of family and community, the central unit in their contemporary society had become the individual. Further, as the pursuit of financial gain and personal mobility became ascendant social values, relationships became more rational, impersonal, and contractual. Whereas people in earlier agrarian societies related to each other emotionally, with their hearts, those in the new social order related rationally, with their heads.

While the sociological analysis of individualism extends to the origins of the discipline, the conversation about its significance in understanding American character and social structure has recently been reinvigorated through the writings of Robert Bellah and his colleagues.[53] In 1985 they published a book entitled *Habits of the Heart* that details how individualism fosters self-absorption and guarantees a collective sense of strangeness, isolation, and loneliness. This book has been widely praised as providing lucid, penetrating insights into our current cultural condition and has stimulated multiple responses to its ideas.

Bellah and his co-authors distinguish two forms of individualism, *instrumental individualism* and *expressive individualism*. Instrumental individualism refers to the freedom to pursue financial and career success. This is the kind of individualism celebrated in the maxims of Ben Franklin's "Poor Richard" and in the Horatio Alger "rags to riches" stories. Expressive individualism, in contrast, refers to the deep and abiding concerns that Americans have with personal self-fulfillment, with the idea that one of life's missions is to maximize personal happiness by discovering who you "really" are. This second form of individualism is thoroughly consistent with the "therapeutic culture" described earlier.

The essential problem posed by "excessive" individualism is that it privatizes the goals and pursuits of persons and thereby erodes the social attachments that provide society's moral anchor. Individualism undermines commitment to community since membership in any community (from the family to local community to nation) implies behavioral constraints that people perceive as inconsistent with personal fulfillment. The dilemma posed by the need both for attachment and freedom is beautifully captured in Bellah's analysis of romantic love in America. Americans believe deeply in romantic love as a necessary requirement for self satisfaction. At the same time, love and marriage, which are based on the free giving of self to another, pose the problem that in sharing too completely with an-other one might lose oneself. The difficulties that Americans have in maintaining intimate rela-tionships stems in part from the uneasy balance between sharing and being separate. . . .

Among the many groups that have emerged as part of the self-help phenomenon, one deserves special mention in the context of this discussion. Across the country these days thousands flock to a group called "Co-Dependents Anonymous," a relatively new "12-stepper." Co-dependency is "a popular new disease, blamed for such diverse disorders as drug abuse, alcoholism, anorexia, child abuse, compulsive gambling, chronic late-ness, fear of intimacy, and low self esteem."[54] I find the idea of co-dependence interesting be-cause this newly discovered disorder arises out of widespread confusion about the permissible lim-its of human closeness. Members come to these groups because they see themselves as unable to sustain reasonable intimacy boundaries and feel overwhelmed by certain relationships. As previ-ously, it would be unfair to minimize the real pain that pushes individuals to cure themselves of overinvolvement. It nevertheless seems clear that codependency can arise as a pathological condition only in a society that fosters deep am-bivalence about the value of extensive ties.

That Americans have problems with intimacy and commitment is surely reflected in the failure of half the marriages made in the country. Of course, marital problems and failures cannot be linked exclusively to patterns of self-absorption intrinsic to a cultural ethic of individualism. Failed relationships, as I indicated earlier, are also a result of the long-term, institutionalized poverty of some groups and the declining economic for-tunes of others. Such difficult circumstances are hardly conducive to maintaining strong family and communal ties. Still, the passionate belief in individualism itself takes its toll. Americans feel incredibly ambivalent about all forms of social at-tachments. Like moths to the proverbial flame, they are drawn to sources of connection for the comfort they provide, but equally fear what they perceive as the stifling features of all sorts of inti-macies. Many are afraid that supportive social

bonds will evolve into bondage. They continu-ously flirt with intimacy and commitment, but in the end often choose a life style that maximizes both freedom and loneliness.

For a time the prevailing wisdom in America was that, on balance, children were better off when poor marriages split up. Yes, certainly there is substantial trauma when a marriage first ends, but children, the thinking went, are enormously resilient and eventually adapt in an emotionally healthy way. Whatever lingering problems they might have would surely have been worse if they too had to endure the bad marriage. Since the di-vorce revolution did not really begin until the 1970s, only now are we able to learn about the long-term emotional effects of broken marriages on children.

Immediately, let's recognize that children most usually live with their mothers after a di-vorce. This fact, coupled with compelling data on the "feminization of poverty"[55] post divorce, suggest the possible initiation of the same type of depression cycle earlier described as existing among poor inner-city, female-headed house-holds. In addition, recent data on the long-term effects of divorce debunk the notion that the negative emotional effects of divorce on children are short-lived. The 50 percent divorce rate seems instead to have produced an adult popula-tion with persistent and severe emotional prob-lems, depression among them.[56] Among the few issues that political conservatives and liberals agree on these days is that the disintegration of the traditional family across all social classes may be producing just the kinds of problems nine-teenth-century theorists presciently imagined.

It is said that when people on their death beds review their lives they rarely say they should have worked harder in order to own even more things than they do. Presumably, most regrets center on relationships that could have been better nur-tured and more fulfilling. However, as Bellah's analysis maintains, to live a life that truly centers on the quality of relations with others is exceed-ingly difficult for many, maybe most, Americans. The cultural pull away from others is often too powerful to resist. A culture that prizes individual self-realization above all else becomes a world held together by only the barest and most tenuous social connections. More and more Americans, identifying individual achievement as the primary medium for personal fulfillment, join the "lonely crowd" identified years ago by David Riesman.[57] To be part of the lonely crowd means being connected to many in general and few in particular. Having opted for loose intimate connections, increasing numbers of people then wonder why they feel the stirrings of emotional discontent that often evolves into the more dramatic malaise of depression.

NOTES

1. George Herbert Mead, *Mind, Self and Society* (Chicago: University of Chicago, 1934).

2. E. Durkheim, *Suicide* (New York: The Free Press, 1951).

3. K. Erikson, "On sociological prose," *The Yale Review* 78 (1989): 525–538.

4. M. Miller, "Dark days, the staggering cost of depression," *The Wall Street Journal,* Thursday, December 2, 1993, pp. B1, 6.

5. G. Klerman, "Evidence for increases in rates of depression in North America and Western Europe in recent decades." In H. Hippius, G. Klerman, and N. Matusssek (eds.), *New Results in Depression Research* (Berlin, Germany: Springer Verlag, 1986).

6. J. Brody, "Recognizing demons of depression, in either sex," *New York Times,* Wednesday, December 18,1991, p. C21.

7. See, G. Klerman, et. al., *Interpersonal Psychotherapy of Depression* (New York: Basic Books, 1984); B. Felton, "Cohort variation in happiness," *International Journal of Aging and Human Development* 25 (1987): 27–42; D. Regier, et al., "One month prevalence of mental disorders in the United States," *Archives of General Psychiatry* 45 (1988): 977–986.

8. T. Maher, "The withering of community life and the growth of emotional disorders." *Journal of Sociology and Social Welfare* 19 (1992), p. 138.

9. Although the context of the discussion here, as throughout the book, is on the ways social context shapes the depression experience, the broad social and cultural arrangements described in this chapter do not relate exclusively to depression. As indicated in the text, to pin generic features of American culture to depression alone would be like relating poverty in America to one social problem only. Just as poverty bears a strong relationship to a whole host of human difficulties, the features of American society that foster loneliness, depersonalization, distrust, inauthenticity, mutual indifference, and social disconnection are associated with multiple emotional illnesses. A whole range of disorders from anxiety to depression to paranoia to schizophrenia flourish in societies and situations that maximize the kinds of personal dislocations arising out of social disattachment.

10. E. Ackernecht, 'The role of medical history in medical education," *Bulletin of the History of Medicine* 21 (1947): 142–143.

11. Ibid., p. 143.

12. M. Zborowski, "Cultural components in responses to pain." In C. Clark and H. Robboy (eds.), *Social Interaction* (New York: St. Martin's, 1992).

13. Among his work demonstrating cross-cultural variation in the meanings of affective disorders, see A. Kleinman and B. Good (eds.), *Culture and Depression* (Berkeley: University of California Press, 1986), *Social Origins of Distress and Disease* (New Haven, CT: Yale University Press, 1986), *Rethinking Psychiatry* (New York: Free Press, 1988), and *The Illness Narratives* (New York: Basic Books, 1988).

14. A. Kleinman, *Social Origins of Distress and Disease,* op. cit., p. 145.

15. A. Kleinman, *The Illness Narratives,* op. cit., p. 5.

16. The results of this survey were reported in the *Boston Globe* on Thursday, January 28, 1993, p. 11.

17. See W. Yoels and J. Clair, 1994. "Never enough time: How medical residents manage a scarce resource," *The Journal of Contemporary Ethnography* 23 (1994): 185–213.

18. *Newsweek* (February 1, 1994).

19. H. Waitzkin, *The Politics of Medical Encounters: How Patients and Doctors Deal with Social Problem* (New Haven, CT: Yale University Press, 1991).

20. W. Yoels and W. Clair, op. cit.

21. A. Kleinman, *The Illness Narratives* (New York, Basic Books, 1988, p. 5).

22. A. Kleinman, *Rethinking Psychiatry,* op. cit., p. 73.

23. These and similar examples are found throughout the works of Arthur Kleinman noted above.

24. For a complete discussion of the medicalization process and particularly the medicalization of devi-

ance, see P. Conrad and J. Schneider, *Deviance and Medicalization* (St. Louis: C. V. Mosby, 1980).

25. P. Berger and T. Luckmann, *The Social Construction of Reality* (New York: Doubleday Anchor, 1967), p. 164.

26. R. Turner, "The theme of contemporary social movements," *British Journal of Sociology* 20 (1969), p. 395.

27. See P. Rieff, *Triumph of the Therapeutic State* (New York: Harper & Row, 1966).

28. C. Lasch, *The Culture of Narcissism* (New York: W. W. Norton, 1978).

29. For a broadly based discussion of such groups, see R. Wuthnow, "Religious movements and countermovements in North America." In J. Beckford (ed.), *New Religious Movements and Rapid Social Change* (London: Sage, 1986).

30. In his recent book entitled *Sharing the Journey Together: Support Groups and America's New Quest for Community* (New York: The Free Press, 1994), Robert Wuthnow argues that the ever-proliferating range of support groups now constitute the primary mechanism through which Americans achieve a sense of community and connection.

31. See T. Powell, *Self Help Organizations and Professional Practice* (Silver Spring, MD: National Association of Social Workers, 1987) and T. Powell (ed.), *Working with Self Help* (Silver Spring, MD: National Association of Social Workers, 1990).

32. E. Schur, *The Awareness Trap* (New York: McGraw-Hill, 1976).

33. M. Weber, *The Protestant Ethic and the Spirit of Capitalism,* translated by T. Parsons (New York: Scribner's, 1930).

34. Among those who have written about the relationship between capitalism and advertising, the work of Stewart Ewen is particularly cogent. See Ewen's two books entitled *Captains of Consciousness* (New York: McGraw-Hill, 1976) and *All Consuming Images* (New York: Basic Books, 1988).

35. M. Gross, *The Psychological Society* (New York: Random House, 1978), p. 6.

36. S. Peele, *Diseasing of America: Addiction Treatment Out of Control* (Lexington, MA: Lexington Books, 1989).

37. Personal conversation.

38. See T. Maher, "The withering of community life and the growth of emotional disorders," *Journal of Sociology and Social Welfare* 19 (1992): 125–143.

39. For a discussion of how nineteenth-century theorists considered the changing nature of the social bond with the advent of urban industrialization, see D. Karp, G. Stone, and W. Yoels, *Being Urban: A Sociology of City Life* (New York: Praeger, 1991).

40. A. Hacker, *Two Nations: Black and White, Separate, Hostile, Unequal* (New York: Scribner's, 1992).

41. R. Sennett and J. Cobb demonstrate, as an example, how the powerlessness of working-class men on their jobs helps to explain the widely observed pattern of male authoritarianism in working-class homes. This analysis is found in their book *The Hidden Injuries of Class* (New York: Random House, 1973).

42. See, for example, H. Becker and A. Strauss, "Careers, personality, and adult socialization," *American Journal of Sociology* 62 (1956): 253–263, and E. Hughes, *Men and Their Work* (New York: The Free Press, 1958).

43. See, R. Cohn, "The effects of employment status change on self attitudes," *Social Psychology* 41 (1978): 81–93; R. Coles, "Work and self respect." In E. Erikson (ed.), *Adulthood* (New York: W. W. Norton, 1978); R. Rothman, *Working: Sociological Perspectives* (Englewood Cliffs, NJ: Prentice Hall, 1987).

44. W. Wilson, *The Truly Disadvantaged* (Chicago: University of Chicago Press, 1987).

45. B. Bluestone and B. Harrison, *The Deindustrialization of America* (New York: Basic Books, 1982).

46. T. Maher, op. cit., p. 134

47. Reported in T. Maher, op. cit.

48. Reported in T. Maher, op. cit.

49. If anything, the rate of severe depression among America's underclass is probably underestimated since this population segment is the most invisible, has the least access to information about depression, and has effectively been abandoned by the health care system.

50. B. Ehrenreich, *Fear of Falling: The Inner Life of the Middle Class* (New York: HarperCollins, 1989).

51. *Time,* "The temping of America," March 29, 1993.

52. See, for example, C. Davies, "The throwaway culture: Job detachment and depression," *The Gerontologist* 25 (1985): 228–231.

53. R. Bellah, R. Madson, W. M. Sullivan, A. Swidler, and S. M. Tipton, *Habits of the Heart: Individualism and Commitment in American Life* (Berkeley: University of California Press, 1985).

54. W. Kaminer, "Chances are you're co-dependent too," *New York Times Book Review* (February, 11, 1990): 1, 26ff.

55. L. Weitzman, *The Divorce Revolution: The Unexpected Social and Economic Consequences in America* (New York: Free Press, 1985).

56. J. Wallerstein and S. Blakeulee, *Second Chances: Men, Women and Children: A Decade After Divorce* (New York: Ticknor and Fields, 1989).

57. D. Riesman, *The Lonely Crowd* (New Haven, CT: Yale University Press, 1950).

THINKING ABOUT THE READING

What does Karp mean when he says that depression is not an exclusively personal, biochemical disorder? What evidence does he provide to support his argument that this ailment is shaped by cultural and social processes? Why is depression so pervasive in technologically complex, postindustrial societies? Pay particular attention to the impact of individualism, occupational instability, and economic competition on people's emotions. If we take this argument one step further, it would imply that simple, preindustrial societies are somewhat inoculated against depression. Do you agree? Using Karp's argument as a starting point, discuss the effectiveness of drug therapy as the dominant treatment for depression. If it's true that people in different cultures experience depression differently, can the same antidepressant drug have similar effects across cultures?

II

The Construction of Self and Society

CHAPTER 3

Building Reality:
The Construction of Social Knowledge

Sociologists often talk about reality as a *social construction*. What they mean is that truth, knowledge, and so on, are discovered, made known, reinforced, and changed by members of society. As social beings, we respond to our interpretations and definitions of situations, not to the situations themselves, thereby shaping reality. How we distinguish fact from fantasy, truth from fiction, myth from reality are not merely abstract philosophical questions but are very much tied to interpersonal interaction, group membership, culture, history, power, economics, and politics. But not all of us possess the same ability to define reality. Individuals and groups in positions of power have the ability to control information, define values, create myths, manipulate events, and ultimately influence what others take for granted. The mass media are especially influential in shaping perceptions of reality.

In "The Crack Attack," Craig Reinarman and Harry Levine show us how the news media function to *create* a reality that the public comes to take for granted. They focus, in particular, on the emergence of "the crack problem" in American society. In the late 1980s, crack, a cocaine derivative, came to be seen as one of the most evil scourges on the social landscape. Even today we hear it described with terms like *plague* and *epidemic*. We hear horror stories about crack babies— children born addicted to the drug—whose lives are marked by emotional, intellectual, and behavioral suffering. But Reinarman and Levine point out that the terrified public concern over crack—the reality of the crack problem—is as much a function of media publicity, political opportunism, and the class, race, and ethnicity of crack users as it is a consequence of the actual chemical power and physical danger of the substance itself. In this sense, media representations don't merely *reflect* some "objective" reality, they actually help create it.

Discovering truth and amassing useful knowledge lay at the heart of any academic discipline. The purpose of a field such as sociology is to provide the public with useful and accurate information about how society works. This is typically accomplished through systematic social research—experiments, field research, unobtrusive research, and surveys. But gathering trustworthy data from people is a difficult task. People sometimes lie or have difficulty recalling past events in their lives. Sometimes the simple fact of observing people's behavior changes that behavior. And sometimes the information needed to answer questions about important, controversial issues is hard to obtain without raising ethical issues.

Patricia Adler provides an interesting example of how sociologists do research on controversial topics in "Researching Dealers and Smugglers." To many people, the sellers and users of illegal drugs are a dangerous scourge on American society. Adler was interested in understanding the upper echelons of the illicit drug trade—a small, secretive group of people condemned by most in society but understood by few. Given the illegal and potentially dangerous activities involved, it is unlikely that drug smugglers would willingly answer questions about their trade on a survey or in an interview. So Adler and her husband established close friendships with dealers and smugglers and used a research technique called participant observation to collect inside information about their activities. Putting oneself in the world of one's research subjects can provide rich information, but it can also cause serious potential dangers.

The Crack Attack

Politics and Media in the Crack Scare

Craig Reinarman and Harry G. Levine

America discovered crack and overdosed on oratory.
—*New York Times* (Editorial, October 4, 1988)

This *New York Times* editorial had a certain unintended irony, for "America's paper of record" itself had long been one of the leading orators, supplying a steady stream of the stuff on which the nation had, as they put it, "overdosed." Irony aside, the editorial hit the mark. The use of powder cocaine by affluent people in music, film, sports, and business had been common since the 1970s. According to surveys by the National Institute on Drug Abuse (NIDA), by 1985, more than twenty-two million Americans in all social classes and occupations had reported at least trying cocaine. Cocaine smoking originated with "freebasing," which began increasing by the late 1970s (see Inciardi, 1987; Siegel, 1982). Then (as now) most cocaine users bought cocaine hydrochloride (powder) for intranasal use (snorting). But by the end of the 1970s, some users had begun to "cook" powder cocaine down to crystalline or "base" form for smoking. All phases of freebasing, from selling to smoking, took place most often in the privacy of homes and offices of middle-class or well-to-do users. They typically purchased cocaine in units of a gram or more costing $80 to $100 a gram. These relatively affluent "basers" had been discovering the intense rush of smoking cocaine, as well as the risks, for a number of years before the term "crack" was coined. But most such users had a stake in conventional life. Therefore, when they felt their cocaine use was too heavy or out of control, they had the incentives and resources to cut down, quit, or get private treatment.

There was no orgy of media and political attention in the late 1970s when the prevalence of cocaine use jumped sharply, or even after middle-class and upper-class users began to use heavily, especially when freebasing. Like the crack users who followed them, basers had found that this mode of ingesting cocaine produced a much more intense and far shorter "high" because it delivered more pure cocaine into the brain far more directly and rapidly than by snorting. Many basers had found that crack's intense, brutally brief rush, combined with the painful "low" or "down" that immediately followed, produced a powerful desire immediately to repeat use—to binge (Waldorf et al., 1991).

Crack's pharmacological power alone does not explain the attention it received. In 1986, politicians and the media focused on crack—and the drug scare began—when cocaine smoking became visible among a "dangerous" group. Crack attracted the attention of politicians and the media because of its downward mobility to and increased visibility in ghettos and barrios. The new users were a different social class, race, and status (Duster, 1970; Washton and Gold, 1987). Crack was sold in smaller, cheaper, precooked units, on ghetto streets, to poorer, younger buyers who were already seen as a threat (*e.g., New York Times,* August 30, 1987; *Newsweek,* November 23, 1987; *Boston Globe,* May 18, 1988). Crack spread cocaine smoking into poor populations already beset with a cornucopia of troubles (Wilson, 1987). These people tended to

51

have fewer bonds to conventional society, less to lose, and far fewer resources to cope with or shield themselves from drug-related problems.

The earliest mass media reference to the new form of cocaine may have been a *Los Angeles Times* article in late 1984 (November 25, p. cc1) on the use of cocaine "rocks" in ghettos and barrios in Los Angeles. By late 1985, the *New York Times* made the national media's first specific reference to "crack" in a story about three teenagers seeking treatment for cocaine abuse (November 17, p. B12). At the start of 1986, crack was known only in a few impoverished neighborhoods in Los Angeles, New York, Miami, and perhaps a few other large cities. . . .

The Frenzy: Cocaine and Crack in the Public Eye

When two celebrity athletes died in what news stories called "crack-related deaths" in the spring of 1986, the media seemed to sense a potential bonanza. Coverage skyrocketed and crack became widely known. "Dramatic footage" of black and Latino men being carted off in chains, or of police breaking down crack house doors, became a near nightly news event. In July 1986 alone, the three major TV networks offered seventy-four evening news segments on drugs, half of these about crack (Diamond et al., 1987; Reeves and Campbell, 1994). In the months leading up to the November elections, a handful of national newspapers and magazines produced roughly a thousand stories discussing crack (Inciardi, 1987, p. 481; Trebach, 1987, pp. 6–16). Like the TV networks, leading news magazines such as *Time* and *Newsweek* seemed determined not to be outdone; each devoted five cover stories to crack and the "drug crisis" in 1986 alone.

In the fall of 1986, the CBS news show *48 Hours* aired a heavily promoted documentary called "48 Hours on Crack Street," which Dan Rather previewed on his evening news show: "Tonight, CBS News takes you to the streets, to the war zone, for an unusual two hours of hands-on horror." Among many shots from hidden cameras was one of New York Senator Alphonse D'Amato

and then-U.S. Attorney Rudolf Guiliani, *in cognito,* purchasing crack to dramatize the brazenness of street corner sales in the ghetto. All this was good business for CBS: the program earned the highest Nielsen rating of any similar news show in the previous five years—fifteen million viewers (Diamond et al., 1987, p. 10). Three years later, after poor ratings nearly killed *48 Hours,* the show kicked off its season with a three-hour special, "Return to Crack Street."

The intense media competition for audience shares and advertising dollars spawned many similar shows. Three days after "48 Hours on Crack Street," NBC ran its own prime-time special, "Cocaine Country," which suggested that cocaine and crack use had become pandemic. This was one of dozens of separate stories on crack and cocaine produced by NBC alone—an unprecedented fifteen hours of air time—in the seven months leading up to the 1986 elections (Diamond et al., 1987; Hoffman, 1987). By mid-1986, *Newsweek* claimed that crack was the biggest story since Vietnam and Watergate (June 15, p. 15), and *Time* soon followed by calling crack "the Issue of the Year" (September 22, 1986, p. 25). The words "plague," "epidemic," and "crisis" had become routine. The *New York Times,* for example, did a three-part, front-page series called "The Crack Plague" (June 24, 1988, p. A1).

The crack scare began in 1986, but it waned somewhat in 1987 (a nonelection year). In 1988, drugs returned to the national stage as stories about the "crack epidemic" again appeared regularly on front pages and TV screens (Reeves and Campbell, 1994). One politician after another reenlisted in the War on Drugs. In that election year, as in 1986, overwhelming majorities of both houses of Congress voted for new antidrug laws with long mandatory prison terms, death sentences, and large increases in funding for police and prisons. The annual federal budget for antidrug efforts surged from less than $2 billion in 1981 to more than $12 billion in 1993. The budget for the Drug Enforcement Administration (DEA) quadrupled between 1981 and 1992 (Massing, 1993). The Bush administration alone spent $45 billion—more than all other presidents since Nixon combined—mostly for law enforcement (Horgan, 1993; Office of National Drug Control Policy, 1992)....

An April 1988 ABC News special report termed crack "a plague" that was "eating away at the fabric of America." According to this documentary, Americans spend "$20 billion a year on cocaine," American businesses lose "$60 billion" a year in productivity because their workers use drugs, "the educational system is being undermined" by student drug use, and "the family" is "disintegrating" in the face of this "epidemic." This program did not give its millions of viewers any evidence to support such dramatic claims, but it did give them a powerful *vocabulary of attribution*: "drugs," especially crack, threatened all the central institutions in American life—families, communities, schools, businesses, law enforcement, even national sovereignty.

This media frenzy continued into 1989. Between October 1988 and October 1989, for example, the *Washington Post* alone ran 1565 stories—28,476 column inches—about the drug crisis. Even Richard Harwood (1989), the *Post's* own ombudsman, editorialized against what he called the loss of "a proper sense of perspective" due to such a "hyperbole epidemic." He said that "politicians are doing a number on people's heads." In the fall of 1989, another major new federal antidrug bill to further increase drug war funding (S-1233) began winding its way through Congress. In September, President Bush's "drug czar," William Bennett, unveiled his comprehensive battle plan, the *National Drug Control Strategy*. His introduction asks, "What . . . accounts for the intensifying drug-related chaos that we see every day in our newspapers and on television? One word explains much of it. That word is *crack*. . . . Crack is responsible for the fact that vast patches of the American urban landscape are rapidly deteriorating" (The White House, 1989, p. 3, original emphasis)....

On September 5, 1989, President Bush, speaking from the presidential desk in the Oval Office, announced his plan for achieving "victory over drugs" in his first major prime-time address to the nation, broadcast on all three national televi-

sion networks. We want to focus on this incident as an example of the way politicians and the media systematically misinformed and deceived the public in order to promote the War on Drugs. During the address, Bush held up to the cameras a clear plastic bag of crack labeled "EVIDENCE." He announced that it was "seized a few days ago in a park across the street from the White House" (*Washington Post*, September 22, 1989, p. A1). Its contents, Bush said, were "turning our cities into battle zones and murdering our children." The president proclaimed that, because of crack and other drugs, he would "more than double" federal assistance to state and local law enforcement (*New York Times*, September 6, 1989, p. A11). The next morning the picture of the president holding a bag of crack was on the front pages of newspapers across America.

About two weeks later, the *Washington Post*, and then National Public Radio and other newspapers, discovered how the president of the United States had obtained his bag of crack. According to White House and DEA officials, "the idea of the President holding up crack was [first] included in some drafts" of his speech. Bush enthusiastically approved. A White House aide told the *Post* that the president "liked the prop. . . . It drove the point home." Bush and his advisors also decided that the crack should be seized in Lafayette Park across from the White House so the president could say that crack had become so pervasive that it was being sold "in front of the White House" (Isikoff, 1989).

This decision set up a complex chain of events. White House Communications Director David Demarst asked Cabinet Affairs Secretary David Bates to instruct the Justice Department "to find some crack that fit the description in the speech." Bates called Richard Weatherbee, special assistant to Attorney General Dick Thornburgh, who then called James Milford, executive assistant to the DEA chief. Finally, Milford phoned William McMullen, special agent in charge of the DEA's Washington office, and told him to arrange an undercover crack buy near the White House because "evidently, the President wants to show it could be bought anywhere" (Isikoff, 1989).

Despite their best efforts, the top federal drug agents were not able to find anyone selling crack (or any other drug) in Lafayette Park, or anywhere else in the vicinity of the White House. Therefore, in order to carry out their assignment, DEA agents had to entice someone to come to the park to make the sale. Apparently, the only person the DEA could convince was Keith Jackson, an eighteen-year-old African-American high school senior. McMullan reported that it was difficult because Jackson "did not even know where the White House was." The DEA's secret tape recording of the conversation revealed that the teenager seemed baffled by the request: "Where the [expletive deleted] is the White House?" he asked. Therefore, McMullan told the *Post*, "we had to manipulate him to get him down there. It wasn't easy" (Isikoff, 1989).

The undesirability of selling crack in Lafayette Park was confirmed by men from Washington, D.C., imprisoned for drug selling, and interviewed by National Public Radio. All agreed that nobody would sell crack there because, among other reasons, there would be no customers. The crack-using population was in Washington's poor African-American neighborhoods some distance from the White House. The *Washington Post* and other papers also reported that the undercover DEA agents had not, after all, actually seized the crack, as Bush had claimed in his speech. Rather, the DEA agents purchased it from Jackson for $2400 and then let him go.

This incident illustrates how a drug scare distorts and perverts public knowledge and policy. The claim that crack was threatening every neighborhood in America was not based on evidence; after three years of the scare, crack remained predominantly in the inner cities where it began. Instead, this claim appears to have been based on the symbolic political value seen by Bush's speech writers. When they sought, after the fact, to purchase their own crack to prove this point, they found that reality did not match their script. Instead of changing the script to reflect reality, a series of high-level officials instructed federal drug agents to *create* a reality that would fit the script. Finally, the president of the United States displayed the procured prop on national television. Yet, when all this was revealed, neither politicians nor the media were led to question the president's policies or his claims about crack's pervasiveness.

As a result of Bush's performance and all the other antidrug publicity and propaganda, in 1988 and 1989, the drug war commanded more public attention than any other issue. The media and politicians' antidrug crusade succeeded in making many Americans even more fearful of crack and other illicit drugs. A *New York Times/ CBS News* poll has periodically asked Americans to identify "the most important problem facing this country today." In January 1985, 23% answered war or nuclear war; less than 1% believed the most important problem was drugs. In September 1989, shortly after the president's speech and the blizzard of drug stories that followed, 64% of those polled believed that drugs were now the most important problem, and only 1% thought that war or nuclear war was most important. Even the *New York Times* declared in a lead editorial that this reversal was "incredible" and then gently suggested that problems like war, "homelessness and the need to give poor children a chance in life" should perhaps be given more attention (September 28, 1989, p. A26).

A year later, during a lull in antidrug speeches and coverage, the percentage citing "drugs" as the nation's top problem had dropped to 10%. Noting this "precipitous fall from a remarkable height," the *Times* observed that an "alliance of Presidents and news directors" shaped public opinion about drugs. Indeed, once the White House let it be known that the president would be giving a prime-time address on the subject, all three networks tripled their coverage of drugs in the two weeks prior to his speech and quadrupled it for a week afterward (*New York Times*, September 6, 1990, p. A11; see also Reeves and Campbell, 1994). All this occurred while nearly every index of drug use was dropping.

The crack scare continued in 1990 and 1991, although with somewhat less media and political attention. By the beginning of 1992—the last year of the Bush administration—the War on Drugs in general, and the crack scare in particular, had begun to decline significantly in prominence and importance. However, even as the drug war was receiving less notice from politicians and the media, it remained institutionalized, bureaucratically powerful, and extremely well funded (especially police, military, and education/propaganda activities).

From the opening shots in 1986 to President Bush's national address in 1989, and through all the stories about "crack babies" in 1990 and 1991, politicians and the media depicted crack as supremely evil—*the* most important cause of America's problems. As recently as February of 1994, a prominent *New York Times* journalist repeated the claim that "An entire generation is being sacrificed to [crack]" (Staples, 1994). As in all drug scares since the nineteenth-century crusade against alcohol, a core feature of drug war discourse is the *routinization of caricature*—worst cases framed as typical cases, the episodic rhetorically recrafted into the epidemic.

Official Government Evidence

On those rare occasions when politicians and journalists cited statistical evidence to support their claims about the prevalence of crack and other drug use, they usually relied on two basic sources, both funded by the National Institute on Drug Abuse. One was the Drug Abuse Warning Network (DAWN), a monitoring project set up to survey a sample of hospitals, crisis and treatment centers, and coroners across the country about drug-related emergencies and deaths. The other was the National Household Survey on Drug Abuse among general population households and among young people. Other data sources existed, but these usually were either anecdotal, specific to a particular location, or based on a skewed sample. Therefore, we review what these two NIDA data sources had to say about crack because they were the only national data and because they are still considered by experts and claims makers to be the most reliable form of evidence available.

The Drug Abuse Warning Network

DAWN collects data on a whole series of drugs—from amphetamine to aspirin—that might be present in emergencies or fatalities. These data take the form of "mentions." A drug mention is produced when a patient, or someone with a patient, tells attending medical personnel that the patient recently used the drug, or occasionally, if a blood test shows the presence of the drug. These data provided perhaps the only piece of statistical support for the crack scare. They indicated that cocaine was "mentioned" in an increasing number of emergency room episodes in the 1980s. During 1986, as the scare moved into full swing, there were an estimated 51,600 emergency room episodes in which cocaine was mentioned (NIDA, 1993a). In subsequent years, the estimated number of such mentions continued to rise, providing clear cause for concern. By 1989, for example, the estimated number of emergency room episodes in which cocaine was mentioned had more than doubled to 110,000. Although the estimate dropped sharply in 1990 to 80,400, by 1992, it had risen again to 119,800 (NIDA, 1993a).

Unfortunately, the meaning of a mention is ambiguous. In many of these cases, cocaine was probably incidental to the emergency room visit. Such episodes included routine cases in which people went to emergency rooms, for example, after being injured as passengers in auto accidents and in home accidents. Moreover, in most cases, cocaine was only one of the drugs in the person's system; most people had also been drinking alcohol. Finally, the DAWN data do not include information about preexisting medical or mental health conditions that make any drug use, legal or illegal, more risky. For all these reasons, one cannot properly infer direct cause from the estimates of emergency room mentions. Cocaine did play a causal role in many of these emergency cases, but no one knows how many or what proportion of the total they were.

The DAWN data on deaths in which cocaine was mentioned by medical examiners also must be closely examined. When the crack scare got under way in 1986, coroners coded 1092 deaths as "cocaine related" (NIDA, 1986a), and as crack spread, this number, too, increased substantially. In 1989, the secretary of health and human services reported a 20% decline in both deaths and emergency room episodes in which cocaine was mentioned, but both indices rose again in 1991 and 1992. The 1992 DAWN figures showed 3020 deaths in which cocaine was mentioned (NIDA, 1992).

But cocaine *alone* was mentioned in only a fraction of these deaths; in 1986, for example, in less than one in five (NIDA, 1986a). In most of these cases, cocaine had been used with other drugs, again, most often alcohol. Although any death is tragic, cocaine's role in such fatalities remains ambiguous. "Cocaine related" is not the same as "cocaine caused," and "cocaine-related deaths" does not mean "deaths *due to* cocaine." There is little doubt that cocaine contributes to some significant (but unknown) percentage of such deaths. But journalists, politicians, and most of the experts on whom they relied never acknowledged the ambiguities in the data. Nor did they commonly provide any comparative perspective. For example, for every *one* cocaine-related death in the U.S., there have been approximately two hundred tobacco-related deaths and at least fifty alcohol-related deaths. Seen in this light, cocaine's role in mortality and morbidity was substantially less than media accounts and political rhetoric implied.

More serious interpretive and empirical difficulties appeared when the DAWN data were used to support claims about crack. Despite all the attention paid to the crack "plague" in 1986, when crack was allegedly "killing a whole generation," the DAWN data contained *no specific information on crack* as distinct from cocaine. In fact, the DAWN data show that in the vast majority of both emergencies and deaths in which cocaine received a mention, the mode of ingestion of cocaine was *not* "smoking" and therefore could not have been caused by crack. Thus, although it is likely that crack played a role in some of the emergencies and deaths in which cocaine was "mentioned," the data necessary to attribute them accurately to crack did not exist.

NIDA Surveys

The NIDA-sponsored surveys of drug use produce the data that are the statistical basis of all estimates of the prevalence of cocaine and other drug use. One of the core claims in the crack scare was that drug use among teenagers and young adults was already high and that it was growing at an alarming rate. Although politicians and the media often referred to teen drug use as an "epidemic" or "plague," the best official evidence available at the time did not support such claims. The National Household Survey on Drug Abuse surveys over eight thousand randomly selected households each year. These surveys show that the number of Americans who had used any illegal drug in the previous month began to decline in 1979, and in the early years of the crack scare, use of drugs, including cocaine, continued to decline (*New York Times*, September 24, 1989, p. A1; *Newsweek*, February 19, 1990, p. 74). Lifetime prevalence of cocaine use among young people (the percentage of those twelve through twenty-five years old who had "ever" tried it) peaked in 1982, *four years before the scare began*, and continued to decline after that (NIDA, 1991, p. 14). The sharpest rise in lifetime prevalence among young adults had taken place between 1972 and 1979; it produced no claims of an epidemic or plague by politicians and journalists (Johnston et al., 1988; NIDA, 1986b).

In February 1987, NIDA released the results of its 1986 annual survey of high school seniors. The *New York Times* handling of the story shows how even the most respectable media institutions sometimes skew facts about drug use to fit a story line. In the article's "lead," the *Times* announced a rise in the percentage of high school seniors reporting "daily" use of cocaine. Only later did one learn that this had risen very slightly and, more important for evaluating claims of a "plague," that daily use among seniors had now reached 0.4%. Daily crack use, even by this fraction of 1% of high school seniors, is surely troubling, but it hardly constituted a new drug epidemic or plague. Still later in the story, the *Times* presented a table showing other declines in cocaine use by young adults and high school seniors. Indeed, as the *Times* noted toward the end of its piece, virtually all forms of teenage drug use (including marijuana, LSD, and heroin) had declined—as they had in previous years (*New York Times,* February 24, 1987, p. A21; cf. Johnston et al., 1988; NIDA, 1991).

Two leading NIDA scholars, reporting in 1986 on the results of the household survey in *Science* magazine, wrote that "both annual prevalence and current prevalence [of all drug use] among college students and the total sample up to four years after high school has been relatively stable between 1980 and 1985" (Kozel and Adams, 1986, p. 973). The director of NIDA's high school surveys, Dr. Lloyd Johnston, made a similar point in 1987: "To some degree the fad quality of drugs has worn off" (*New York Times,* February 24, 1987, p. A21). When the findings of the high school senior survey for 1987 were released, the survey's director reported that "the most important" finding was that cocaine had again "showed a significant drop in use." He even reported a decline in the use of crack (Johnston et al., 1988).

These reported declines were in keeping with the general downward trend in drug use. In the early 1980s, according to the NIDA surveys, about one in six young Americans had tried cocaine powder. But between 1986 and 1987, the proportion of both high school seniors and young adults who had used cocaine in any form in the previous year dropped by 20% (Johnston et al., 1988). Further, two-thirds of those who had ever tried cocaine had not used it in the previous month. Although a significant minority of young people had tried cocaine powder at some point, the great majority of them did not continue to use it.

There had been a few signs of increasing cocaine use. The proportion of youngsters who reported using cocaine at least once in the previous month had increased slightly over the years, although it never exceeded 2% of all teens in the seven national household surveys between 1972 and 1985. The 1988 NIDA household survey found an increase in the number of adult daily users of cocaine, presumably the group that included crack addicts. But this group constituted

only about 1.3% of those adults who had ever used cocaine. NIDA also estimated that about 0.5% of the total U.S. adult population had used cocaine in the week prior to the survey (NIDA, 1988).

But aside from these few slight increases, almost all other measures showed that the trends in official drug use statistics had been down even before the scare began. . . . The figures for cocaine use in particular were dropping just as crisis claims were reaching a crescendo, and had dropped still further precisely when the Bush/Bennett battle plan was being announced with such fanfare in 1989. Indeed, as White House officials anonymously admitted a few weeks after the president's "bag of crack" speech, the new plan's "true goals" were far more modest than its rhetoric: the Bush plan was "simply to move the nation 'a little bit' beyond where current trends would put it anyway" (*New York Times,* September 24, 1989, p. A1).

National Survey Data on Crack

Tom Brokaw reported on *NBC Nightly News* in 1986 (May 23) that crack was "flooding America" and that it had become "America's drug of choice." His colleagues at the other networks and in the print media had made similar claims. An ordinarily competent news consumer might well have gathered the impression that crack could be found in the lockers of most high school students. Yet, at the time of these press reports, *there were no prevalence statistics at all on crack* and no evidence of any sort showing that smoking crack had become the preferred mode even of cocaine use, much less of drug use.

When NIDA released the first official data on crack a few months later, they still did not support claims about widespread crack use. On the contrary, the NIDA survey found that most cocaine use could not have been crack because the preferred mode of use for 90% of cocaine users was "sniffing" rather than smoking (NIDA, 1986a; see also Inciardi, 1987). An all-but-ignored Drug Enforcement Administration press release issued in August 1986, during the first hysterical summer of the crack scare, sought to correct the misperception that crack use was now the major drug problem in America. The DEA said, "Crack is currently the subject of considerable media attention.... The result has been a distortion of the public perception of the extent of crack use as compared to the use of other drugs.... [Crack] presently appears to be a secondary rather than primary problem in most areas" (Drug Enforcement Administration, cited in Diamond et al., 1987, p. 10; Inciardi, 1987, p. 482).

The first official measures of the prevalence of teenage crack use began with NIDA's 1986 high school survey. It found that 4.1% of high school seniors reported having *tried* crack (at least once) in the previous year. This figure dropped to 3.9% in 1987 and to 3.1% in 1988, a 25% decline (Johnston et al., 1988; *National Report on Substance Abuse*, 1994, p. 3). This means that at the peak of crack use, 96% of America's high school seniors had never tried crack, much less gone on to more regular use, abuse, or addiction. Any drug use among the young is certainly worrisome, particularly when in such an intense form as crack. However, at the start of the crusade to save "a whole generation" of children from death by crack in the spring of 1986, the latest official data showed a national total of eight "cocaine-related" deaths of young people age eighteen and under for the preceding year (Trebach, 1987, p. 11). There was no way to determine whether any of these deaths involved crack use or even if cocaine was in fact the direct cause.

In general, the government's national surveys indicate that a substantial minority of teenagers and young adults experiment with illicit drugs. But as with other forms of youthful deviance, most tend to abandon such behavior as they assume adult roles. Politicians, the media, and antidrug advertisements often claimed that cocaine is inevitably addicting but that crack is still worse because it is "instantaneously addicting." However, according to the official national surveys, two-thirds of Americans of all ages who had ever tried cocaine had not used it in the month prior to the surveys. It is clear that the vast majority of the more than twenty-two million Americans who have tried cocaine do not use it in crack form, do not escalate to regular use, and do not end up addicted....

In sum, the official evidence on cocaine and crack available during the crack scare gave a rather different picture than Americans received from the media and politicians. The sharp rise in mentions of cocaine in emergency room episodes and coroners' reports did offer cause for concern. But the best official evidence of drug use never supported the claims about an "epidemic" or "plague" throughout America or about "instantaneous addiction." Moreover, as media attention to crack was burgeoning, the actual extent of crack use was virtually unknown, and most other official measures of cocaine use were actually decreasing. Once crack use was actually measured, its prevalence turned out to be low to start with and to have declined throughout the scare (*National Report on Substance Abuse*, 1994, p. 3).

Crack as an Epidemic and Plague

The empirical evidence on crack use suggests that politicians and journalists have routinely used the words "epidemic" and "plague" imprecisely and rhetorically as words of warning, alarm, and danger. Therefore, on the basis of press reports, it is difficult to determine if there was any legitimacy at all in the description of crack use as an epidemic or plague. Like most other drug researchers and epidemiologists, we have concluded that crack addiction has never been anything but relatively rare across the great middle strata of the U.S. population. If the word "epidemic" is used to mean a disease or disease-like condition that is "widespread" or "prevalent," then there has never been an epidemic of crack addiction (or even crack use) among the vast majority of Americans. Among the urban poor, however, especially African-American and Latino youth, heavy crack use has been more common. An "epidemic of crack *use*" might be a description of what happened among a distinct minority of teenagers and young adults from impoverished urban neighborhoods in the mid to late 1980s. However, many more people use tobacco and alcohol heavily than use cocaine in any form. Alcohol drinking and tobacco smoking each kills far more people than all forms of cocaine and heroin use combined. Therefore, "epidemic" would be more appropriate to describe tobacco and alcohol use. But politicians and the media have not talked about tobacco and alcohol use as epidemics or plagues. The word "epidemic" also can mean a rapidly spreading disease. In this precise sense as well, in inner-city neighborhoods, crack use may have been epidemic (spreading rapidly) for a few years among impoverished young African-Americans and Latinos. However, crack use was never spreading fast or far enough among the general population to be termed an epidemic there.

"Plague" is even a stronger word than epidemic. Plague can mean a "deadly contagious disease," an epidemic "with great mortality," or it can refer to a "pestilence," an "infestation of a pest, [e.g.,] a plague of caterpillars." Crack is a central nervous system stimulant. Continuous and frequent use of crack often burns people out and does them substantial psychological and physical harm. But even very heavy use does not usually directly kill users. In this sense, crack use is not a plague. One could say that drug dealers were "infesting" some blocks of some poor neighborhoods in some cities, that there were pockets of plague in some specific areas; but that was not how "crack plague" was used.

When evaluating whether the extent and dangers of crack use match the claims of politicians and the media, it is instructive to compare how other drug use patterns are discussed. For example, an unusually balanced New York Times story (October 7, 1989, p. 26) compared crack and alcohol use among suburban teenagers and focused on the middle class. The Times reported that, except for a few "urban pockets" in suburban counties, "crack and other narcotics are rarely seen in the suburbs, whether modest or wealthy." ...

The Times also reported that high school seniors were outdrinking the general adult population. Compared to the 64% of teenagers, only 55% of adults had consumed alcohol in the last

month. Furthermore, teenagers have been drinking more than adults since at least 1972, when the surveys began. Even more significant is the kind of drinking teenagers do—what the Times called "excessive 'binge' drinking": "More than a third of the high school seniors had said that in the last two weeks they had had five or more drinks in a row." Drinking is, of course, the most widespread form of illicit drug use among high school students. As the Times explained, on the weekend, "practically every town has at least one underage party, indoors or out" and that "fake identification cards, older siblings, friends, and even parents all help teenagers obtain" alcohol.

The point we wish to emphasize is that even though illicit alcohol use was far more prevalent than cocaine or crack use, and even though it held substantial risk for alcohol dependence, addiction, drinking-driving deaths, and other alcohol-related problems, the media and politicians have not campaigned against teen drunkenness. Used as a descriptive term meaning "prevalent," the word "epidemic" fits teenage drinking far better than it does teenage crack use. Although many organizations have campaigned against drinking and driving by teenagers, the politicians and media have not used terms like "epidemic" or "plague" to call attention to illicit teenage drinking and drunkenness. Unlike the Times articles on crack, often on the front page, this article on teen drunkenness was placed in the second section on a Saturday.

It is also worth noting the unintentionally ironic mixing of metaphors, or of diagnoses and remedies, when advocates for the War on Drugs described crack use as an epidemic or plague. Although such disease terminology was used to call attention to the consequences of crack use, most of the federal government's domestic responses have centered on using police to arrest users. Treatment and prevention have always received a far smaller proportion of total federal antidrug funding than police and prisons do as a means of handling the "epidemic." If crack use is primarily a crime problem, then terms like "wave" (as in crime wave) would be more fitting. But if this truly is an "epidemic"—a widespread disease—

then police and prisons are the wrong remedy, and the victims of the epidemic should be offered treatment, public health programs, and social services. . . .

The Political Context of the "Crack Crisis"

If the many claims about an "epidemic" or "plague" endangering "a whole generation" of youth were at odds with the best official data, then what else was animating the new War on Drugs? In fact, even if all the exaggerated claims about crack had been true, it would not explain all the attention crack received. Poverty, homelessness, auto accidents, handgun deaths, and environmental hazards are also widespread, costly, even deadly, but most politicians and journalists never speak of them in terms of crisis or plague. Indeed, far more people were (and still are) injured and killed every year by domestic violence than by illicit drugs, but one would never know this from media reports or political speeches. The existence of government studies suggesting that crack contributed to the deaths of a small proportion of its users, that an unknown but somewhat larger minority of users became addicted to it, that its use was related to some forms of crime, and so on were neither necessary nor sufficient conditions for all the attention crack received (Spector and Kitsuse, 1977).

Like other sociologists, historians, and students of drug law and public policy, we suggest that understanding antidrug campaigns requires more than evidence of drug abuse and drug-related problems, which can be found in almost any period. It requires analyzing these crusades and scares as phenomena in their own right and understanding the broader social, political, and economic circumstances under which they occur (see, *e.g.,* Bakalar and Grinspoon, 1984; Brecher, 1972; Duster, 1970; Gusfield, 1963, 1981; Lindesmith, 1965; Morgan, 1978; Musto, 1973; Rumbarger, 1989). The crack scare also must be understood in terms of its political context and its appeal to important groups within American society. The mass media and politicians, however,

did not talk about drugs this way. Rather, they decontextualized the drama, making it appear as if the story had no authors aside from dealers and addicts. Their writing of the crack drama kept abusers, dealers, crimes, and casualties under spotlights while hiding other important factors in the shadows. We suggest that over and above the very real problems some users suffered with crack, the rise of the New Right and the competition between political parties in a conservative context contributed significantly to the making of the crack scare.

The New Right and Its Moral Ideology

During the post-Watergate rebuilding of the Republican Party, far right wing political organizations and fundamentalist Christian groups set about to impose what they called "traditional family values" on public policy. This self-proclaimed "New Right" felt increasingly threatened by the diffusion of modernist values, behaviors, and cultural practices—particularly by what they saw as the interconnected forms of 1960s hedonism involved in sex outside (heterosexual) marriage and consciousness alteration with (illicit) drugs. The New Right formed a core constituency for Ronald Reagan, an extreme conservative who had come to prominence as governor of California in part by taking a hard line against the new political movements and cultural practices of the 1960s.

Once he became president in 1981, Reagan and his appointees attempted to restructure public policy according to a radically conservative ideology. Through the lens of this ideology, most social problems appeared to be simply the consequences of *individual moral choices* (Ryan, 1976). Programs and research that had for many years been directed at the social and structural sources of social problems were systematically defunded in budgets and delegitimated in discourse. Unemployment, poverty, urban decay, school crises, crime, and all their attendant forms of human troubles were spoken of and acted upon as if they were the result of *individual* deviance, immorality, or weakness. The most basic premise of social science—that individual choices are influenced by social circumstances—was rejected as left-wing ideology. Reagan and the New Right constricted the aperture of attribution for America's ills so that only the lone deviant came into focus. They conceptualized people *in* trouble as people who *make* trouble (Gusfield, 1985); they made social control rather than social welfare the organizing axis of public policy (Reinarman, 1988).

With regard to drug problems, this conservative ideology is a form of *sociological denial.* For the New Right, people did not so much abuse drugs because they were jobless, homeless, poor, depressed, or alienated; they were jobless, homeless, poor, depressed, or alienated because they were weak, immoral, or foolish enough to use illicit drugs. For the right wing, American business productivity was not lagging because investors spent their capital on mergers and stock speculation instead of on new plants and equipment, or for any number of other economic reasons routinely mentioned in the *Wall Street Journal* or *Business Week.* Rather, conservatives claimed that businesses had difficulty competing partly because many workers were using drugs. In this view, U.S. education was in trouble not because it had suffered demoralizing budget cuts, but because a "generation" of students was "on drugs" and their teachers did not "get tough" with them. The new drug warriors did not see crime plaguing the ghettos and barrios for all the reasons it always has, but because of the influence of a new chemical bogeyman. Crack was a godsend to the Right. They used it and the drug issue as an ideological fig leaf to place over the unsightly urban ills that had increased markedly under Reagan administration social and economic policies. "The drug problem" served conservative politicians as an all-purpose scapegoat. They could blame an array of problems on the deviant individuals and then expand the nets of social control to imprison those people for causing the problems.

The crack crisis had other, more specific political uses. Nancy Reagan was a highly visible antidrug crusader, crisscrossing the nation to urge schoolchildren to "Just Say No" to drugs. Mrs. Reagan's crusade began in 1983 (before crack came into existence) when her "p.r.-conscious operatives," as *Time* magazine called them, convinced her that "serious-minded displays" of "social consciousness" would "make her appear more caring and less frivolous." Such a public relations strategy was important to Mrs. Reagan. The press had often criticized her for spending hundreds of thousands of dollars on new china for the White House, lavish galas for wealthy friends, and high-fashion evening gowns at a time when her husband's economic policies had induced a sharp recession, raised joblessness to near Depression-era levels, and cut funding for virtually all programs for the poor. *Time* explained that "the timing and destinations of her antidrug excursions last year were coordinated with the Reagan-Bush campaign officials to satisfy their particular political needs" (*Time,* January 14, 1985, p. 30). . . .

Political Party Competition

The primary political task facing liberals in the 1980s was to recapture some of the electorate that had gone over to the Right. Reagan's shrewdness in symbolically colonizing "middle American" fears put Democrats on the defensive. Most Democrats responded by moving to the right and pouncing upon the drug issue. Part of the early energy for the drug scare in the spring and summer of 1986 came from Democratic candidates trading charges with their Republican opponents about being "soft on drugs." Many candidates challenged each other to take urine tests as a symbol of their commitment to a "drug-free America." One Southern politician even proposed that candidates' spouses be tested. A California senatorial candidate charged his opponent with being "a noncombatant in the war on drugs" (*San Francisco Chronicle,* August 12, 1986, p. 9). By the fall of 1986, increasingly strident calls for a drug war became so much a part of candidates' standard stump speeches that even conservative columnist William Safire complained of antidrug "hysteria" and "narcomania"

(*New York Times,* September 11, 1986, p. A27). Politicians demanded everything from death penalties in North America to bombing raids in South America.

Crack could not have appeared at a more opportune political moment. After years of dull debates on budget balancing, a "hot" issue had arrived just in time for a crucial election. In an age of fiscal constraint, when most problems were seen as intractable and most solutions costly, the crack crisis was the one "safe" issue on which all politicians could take "tough stands" without losing a single vote or campaign contribution. The legislative results of the competition to "get tough" included a $2 billion law in 1986, the so-called "Drug-Free America Act," which whizzed through the House (392 to 16) just in time for members of Congress to go home and tell their constituents about it. In the heat of the preelection, antidrug hysteria, the symbolic value of such spending seemed to dwarf the deficit worries that had hamstrung other legislation. According to *Newsweek,* what occurred was "a can-you-top-this competition" among "election-bound members of both parties" seeking tough antidrug amendments. The 1986 drug bill, as Representative David McCurdy (D-Okla) put it, was "out of control," adding through a wry smile, "but of course I'm for it" (September 22, 1986, p. 39).

The prominence of the drug issue dropped sharply in both political speeches and media coverage after the 1986 election, but returned during the 1988 primaries. Once again the crack issue had political utility. One common observation about the 1988 presidential election campaigns was that there were no domestic or foreign policy crises looming on which the two parties could differentiate themselves. As a *New York Times* headline put it: "Drugs as 1988 Issue: Filling a Vacuum" (May 24, 1988, p. A14). In the 1988 primary season, candidates of both parties moved to fill this vacuum in part by drug-baiting their opponents and attacking them as "soft on drugs." In the fall, both Democrats Dukakis and Bentsen and Republicans Bush and Quayle claimed that their opponents were soft on drugs while asserting that their side would wage a "*real*

War on Drugs." And, just as they did before the 1986 election, members of Congress from both parties overwhelmingly passed a new, even more strict and costly antidrug bill.

The antidrug speeches favoring such expenditures became increasingly transparent as posturing, even to many of the speakers. For example, Senator Christopher Dodd (D-Conn) called the flurry of antidrug amendments a "feeding frenzy" (*New York Times,* May 22, 1988, p. E4). An aide to another senator admitted that "everybody was scrambling to get a piece of the action" (*New York Times,* May 24, 1988, p. A14). Even President Reagan's spokesperson, Marlin Fitzwater, told the White House press corps that "everybody wants to out-drug each other in terms of political rhetoric" (*Boston Globe,* May 18, 1988, p. 4). But however transparent, such election-year posturing—magnified by a media hungry for the readers and ratings that dramatic drug stories bring—enhanced the viability of claims about the menace of crack far more than any available empirical evidence could. In the fall of 1989, Congress finalized yet another major antidrug bill costing more than the other two combined. According to research by the Government Accounting Office, the federal government spent more than $23 billion on the drug war during the Reagan era, three-fourths of it for law enforcement (*Alcoholism and Drug Abuse Week,* 1989, p. 3). . . .

Politicians and the media were *forging,* not following, public opinion. The speeches and stories *led* the oft-cited poll results, not the other way around. In 1987, between elections—when drug problems persisted in the ghettos and barrios but when the drug scare was not so enflamed by election rhetoric and media coverage—only 3 to 5% of those surveyed picked drugs as our most important problem (*New York Times,* May 24, 1988, p. A14). But then again in 1989, immediately following President Bush's speech escalating the drug war, nearly two-thirds of the people polled identified drugs as America's most important problem. When the media and politicians invoked "public opinion" as the driving force behind their actions against crack, they inverted the actual causal sequence (Edelman, 1964, p. 172).

We argued in the previous section that the New Right and other conservatives found ideological utility in the crack scare. In this section, we have suggested that conservatives were not the only political group in America to help foment the scare and to benefit from it. Liberals and Democrats, too, found in crack and drugs a means of recapturing Democratic defectors by appearing more conservative. And they too found drugs to be a convenient scapegoat for the worsening conditions in the inner cities. All this happened at a historical moment when the Right successfully stigmatized the liberals' traditional solutions to the problems of the poor as ineffective and costly. Thus, in addition to the political capital to be gained by waging the war, the new chemical bogeyman afforded politicians across the ideological spectrum both an explanation for pressing public problems and an excuse for not proposing the unpopular taxing, spending, or redistributing needed to do something about them.

The End of the Crack Scare

In the 1980s, the conservative drive to reduce social spending exacerbated the enduring problems of impoverished African-American and Latino city residents. Partly in response, a minority of the young urban poor turned either to crack sales as their best shot at the American Dream and/or to the crack high as their best shot at a fleeting moment of pleasure. Inner-city churches, community organizations, and parent groups then tried to defend their children and neighborhoods from drug dealing and use on the one hand and to lobby for services and jobs on the other hand. But the crack scare did not inspire politicians of either party to address the worsening conditions and growing needs of the inner-city poor and working class or to launch a "Marshall Plan for cities." In the meantime, the white middle-class majority viewed with alarm the growing numbers, visibility, and desperation of the urban poor. And for years many Americans believed the central fiction of the crack scare: that drug use was not a symptom of urban decay but one of its most important causes.

All this gave federal and local authorities justification for widening the nets of social control. Of course, the new drug squads did not reduce the dangerousness of impoverished urban neighborhoods. But the crack scare did increase criminal justice system supervision of the underclass. By 1992, one in four young African-American males was in jail or prison or on probation or parole—more than were in higher education. . . . During the crack scare, the prison population more than doubled, largely because of the arrests of drug users and small dealers. This gave the U.S. the highest incarceration rate in the world (Currie, 1985; Irwin and Austin, 1994).

By the end of 1992, however, the crack scare seemed spent. There are a number of overlapping reasons for this. Most important was the failure of the War on Drugs itself. Democrats as well as Republicans supported the War on Drugs, but the Reagan and Bush administrations initiated and led it, and the drug war required support from the White House. George Bush appointed William Bennett to be a "tough" and extremely high profile "drug czar" to lead the campaign against drugs. But Bennett, criticized for his bombastic style, quit after only eighteen months (some press accounts referred to it as the "czar's abdication"). After that, the Bush administration downplayed the drug war, and it hardly figured at all in the presidential primaries or campaign in 1992. Bill Clinton said during the campaign that there were no easy solutions to drug problems and that programs that work only on reducing supply were doomed to fail. The Clinton administration eschewed the phrase "War on Drugs," and Lee Brown, Clinton's first top drug official, explicitly rejected the title of drug czar (Reinarman, 1994). After billions of tax dollars had been spent and millions of young Americans had been imprisoned, hard-core drug problems remained. With so little to show for years of drug war, politicians seemed to discover the limits of the drug issue as a political weapon. Moreover, with both parties firmly in favor of the "get tough" approach, there was no longer any partisan political advantage to be had.

The news media probably would have written dramatic stories about the appearance of smokeable cocaine in poor neighborhoods at any time. Television producers have found that drug stories, especially timely, well-advertised, dramatic ones, often receive high ratings. But the context of the Reagan-led drug war encouraged the media to write such pieces. Conservatives had long complained that the media had a liberal bias; in the mid-1980s, drug coverage allowed the media to rebut such criticism and to establish conservative credentials (Reeves and Campbell, 1994). As we have suggested, news coverage of drugs rose and fell with political initiatives, especially those coming from the president. Therefore, as the White House withdrew from the drug issue, so did the press.

After about 1989, it became increasingly difficult to sustain the exaggerated claims of the beginning of the crack scare. The mainstream media began to publish stories critical of earlier news coverage (though usually not their own). . . . *Newsweek* finally admitted in 1990 what it called the "dirty little secret" about crack that it had concealed in all of its earlier scare stories: "A lot of people use it without getting addicted," and that the anonymous "media" had "hyped instant and total addiction" (February 19, 1990, pp. 74–75). As early as 1988, it was clear that crack was not "destroying a whole generation"; it was not even spreading beyond the same poverty context that had long given rise to hard-core heroin addiction. Moreover, because of the obvious destructive effects of heavy use, people in ghettos and barrios had come to view "crack heads" as even lower in status than winos or junkies. Even crack dealers preferred powder cocaine and routinely disparaged crack heads (Williams, 1989). All of this meant that drugs in general, and crack in particular, declined in newsworthiness. Media competition had fueled the crack scare in its early years, and the same scramble for dramatic stories guaranteed that the media would move on to other stories. By 1992, the crack scare had faded beyond the media's horizon of hot new issues.

Finally, the crack scare could recede into the background partly because it had been *institu-*

tionalized. Between 1986 and 1992, Congress passed and two presidents signed a series of increasingly harsh antidrug laws. Federal antidrug funding increased for seven successive years, and an array of prison and police programs was established or expanded. All levels of government, from schools to cities, counties, and states, established agencies to warn about crack and other drug problems. And multimillion-dollar, corporate-sponsored, private organizations such as the Partnership for a Drug-Free America had been established to continue the crusade.

Conclusion

Smoking crack *is* a risky way to use an already potent drug. Despite all the exaggerations, heavy use of it *has* made life more difficult for many people—most of them from impoverished urban neighborhoods. If we agree that too many families have been touched by drug-related tragedies, why have we bothered criticizing the crack scare and the War on Drugs? If even a few people are saved from crack addiction, why should anyone care if this latest drug scare was in some measure concocted by the press, politicians, and moral entrepreneurs to serve their other agendas? Given the damage that drug abuse can do, what's the harm in a little hysteria? . . .

First, we suspect that drug scares do not work very well to reduce drug problems and that they may well promote the behavior they claim to be preventing. For all the repression successive drug wars have wrought (primarily upon the poor and the powerless), they have yet to make a measurable dent in our drug *problems.* For example, prompted by the crack crisis and inspired by the success of patriotic propaganda in World War II, the Partnership for a Drug-Free America ran a massive advertising campaign to "unsell drugs." From 1987 to 1993, the Partnership placed over $1 billion worth of advertising donated by corporations and the advertising industry. The Partnership claims to have had a "measurable impact" by "accelerating intolerance" to drugs and drug users. The Partnership claims it "can legitimately take some of the credit for the 25% decline in illicit drug usage since our program was launched" (Hedrick, 1990). However, the association between the Partnership's antidrug advertising and the declines in drug use appears to be spurious. Drug use was declining well before the Partnership's founding; taking credit for what was already happening is a bit like jumping in front of a parade and then claiming to have been leading it all along. More important, drug *use* increased in the mid 1990s among precisely those age groups that had been targeted by Partnership ads, while drug *problems* continued throughout their campaign. Furthermore, Partnership ads scrupulously avoided any mention of the two forms of drug use most prevalent among youth: smoking and drinking. This may have something to do with the fact that the Partnership for a Drug-Free America is a partnership between the media and advertising industries, which make millions from alcohol and tobacco advertising each year, and with the fact that alcohol and tobacco companies contribute financially to the Partnership's campaign against illicit drugs. Surely public health education is important, but there is no evidence that selective antidrug propaganda and scare tactics have significantly reduced drug problems.

Indeed, hysterical and exaggerated antidrug campaigns may have increased drug-related harm in the U.S. There is the risk that all of the exaggerated claims made to mobilize the population for war actually arouse interest in drug use. In 1986, the *New England Journal of Medicine* reported that the frequency of teenage suicides increases after lurid news reports and TV shows about them (Gould and Shaffer, 1986; Phillips and Carstensen, 1986). Reports about drugs, especially of new and exotic drugs like crack, may work the same way. In his classic chapter, "How To Launch a Nation Wide Drug Menace," Brecher (1972) shows how exaggerated newspaper reports of dramatic police raids in 1960 functioned as advertising for glue sniffing. The arrests of a handful of sniffers led to anti–glue sniffing hysteria that actually spread this hitherto unknown practice across the U.S. In 1986, the media's desire for dramatic drug sto-

ries interacted with politicians' desire for partisan advantage and safe election-year issues, so news about crack spread to every nook and cranny of the nation far faster than dealers could have spread word on the street. When the media and politicians claimed that crack is "the most addictive substance known to man," there was some commonsense obligation to explain why. Therefore, alongside all the statements about "instant addiction," the media also reported some very intriguing things about crack: "whole body orgasm," "better than sex," and "cheaper than cocaine." For TV-raised young people in the inner city, faced with a dismal social environment and little economic opportunity, news about such a substance in their neighborhoods may have functioned as a massive advertising campaign for crack.

Further, advocates of the crack scare and the War on Drugs explicitly rejected public health approaches to drug problems that conflicted with their ideology. The most striking and devastating example of this was the total rejection of syringe distribution programs by the Reagan and Bush administrations and by drug warriors such as Congressman Charles Rangel. People can and do recover from drug addiction, but no one recovers from AIDS. By the end of the 1980s, the fastest growing AIDS population was intravenous drug users. Because syringes were hard to get, or their possession criminalized, injectors shared their syringes and infected each other and their sexual partners with AIDS. In the early 1980s, activists in a number of other Western countries had developed syringe distribution and exchange programs to prevent AIDS, and there is by now an enormous body of evidence that such programs are effective. But the U.S. government has consistently rejected such "harm reduction" programs on the grounds that they conflict with the policy of "zero tolerance" for drug use or "send the wrong message." As a result, cities such as Amsterdam, Liverpool, and Sydney, which have needle exchange programs, have very low or almost no transmission of AIDS by intravenous drug users. In New York City, however, roughly half the hundreds of thousands of injection drug users are HIV positive or already have AIDS. In short, the crack scare and the drug war policies it fueled will ultimately contribute to the deaths of tens of thousands of Americans, including the families, children, and sexual partners of the infected drug users.

Another important harm resulting from American drug scares is they have routinely blamed individual immorality and personal behavior for endemic social and structural problems. In so doing, they diverted attention and resources away from the underlying sources of drug abuse and the array of other social ills of which they are part. One necessary condition for the emergence of the crack scare (as in previous drug scares) was the linking of drug use with the problems faced by racial minorities, the poor, and youth. In the logic of the scare, whatever economic and social troubles these people have suffered were due largely to their drug use. Obscured or forgotten during the crack scare were all the social and economic problems that underlie crack abuse—and that are much more widespread—especially poverty, unemployment, racism, and the prospects of life in the permanent underclass.

Democrats denounced the Reagan and Bush administrations' hypocrisy in proclaiming "War on Drugs" while cutting the budgets for drug treatment, prevention, and research. However, the Democrats often neglected to mention an equally important but more politically popular development: the "Just Say No To Drugs" administrations had, with the help of many Democrats in Congress, also "just said no" to virtually every social program aimed at creating alternatives for and improving the lawful life chances of inner-city youth. These black and Latino young people were and are the group with the highest rate of crack abuse. Although, most inner-city youth have always steered clear of drug abuse, they could not "just say no" to poverty and unemployment. Dealing drugs, after all, was (and still is) accurately perceived by many poor city kids as the highest-paying job—straight or criminal—that they are likely to get.

The crack scare, like previous drug scares and antidrug campaigns, promoted misunderstandings of drug use and abuse, blinded people to the social sources of many social problems (including drug problems), and constrained the social policies that might reduce those problems. It routinely used inflated, misleading rhetoric and falsehoods such as Bush's televised account of how he came into possession of a bag of crack. At best, the crack scare was not good for public health. At worst, by manipulating and misinforming citizens about drug use and effects, it perverted social policy and political democracy.

REFERENCES

Alcoholism and Drug Abuse Week, "$23 Billion Spent on Federal Drug Effort Since 1981." July 5, 1989, pp. 3–4.

Anderson, Jack, and Michael Binstein, "Drug Informants Beating the System." *Washington Post,* September 10, 1992, p. D23.

Bakalar, James B., and Lester Grinspoon, *Drug Control in a Free Society.* Cambridge: Cambridge University Press, 1984.

Belenko, Steven, and Jeffrey Fagan, "Crack and the Criminal Justice System." New York: New York City Criminal Justice Agency, 1987.

Brecher, Edward M., *Licit and Illicit Drugs.* Boston: Little, Brown, 1972.

Chin K.-L, "Special Event Codes for Crack Arrests." Internal memorandum, New York City Criminal Justice Agency, 1988.

Currie, Elliott, *Confronting Crime.* New York: Pantheon, 1985.

Diamond, Edwin, Frank Accosta, and Leslie-Jean Thornton, "Is TV News Hyping America's Cocaine Problem?" *TV Guide,* February 7, 1987, pp. 4–10.

Drug Enforcement Administration, "Special Report: The Crack Situation in the U.S." Unpublished, Strategic Intelligence Section. Washington, DC: DEA, August 22, 1986.

Duster, Troy, *The Legislation of Morality.* New York: Free Press, 1970.

Edelman, Murray, *The Symbolic Uses of Politics.* Urbana: University of Illinois Press, 1964.

Gould, Madelyn S., and David Shaffer, "The Impact of Suicide in Television Movies: Evidence of Imitation." *New England Journal of Medicine* 315:690–694 (1986).

Grinspoon, Lester, and James B. Bakalar, *Cocaine: A Drug and Its Social Evolution*. New York: Basic Books, 1976.

Gusfield, Joseph R., *Symbolic Crusade*. Urbana: University of Illinois Press, 1963.

———, *The Culture of Public Problems*. Chicago: University of Chicago Press, 1981.

———, "Alcohol Problems—An Interactionist View," in J. P. von Wartburg et al., eds., *Currents in Alcohol Research and the Prevention of Alcohol Problems*. Berne, Switzerland: Hans Huber, 1985.

Harwood, Richard, "Hyperbole Epidemic." *Washington Post*, October 1, 1989, p. D6.

Hedrick, Thomas A., Jr., "Pro Bono Anti-Drug Ad Campaign Is Working." *Advertising Age*, June 25, 1990, p. 22.

Himmelstein, Jerome, *The Strange Career of Marijuana*. Westport, CT: Greenwood Press, 1983.

Hoffman, Abbie, *Steal This Urine Test: Fighting Drug Hysteria in America*. New York: Penguin Books, 1987.

Horgan, John, "A Kinder War." *Scientific American*, July 25, 1993, p. 6.

Inciardi, James, "Beyond Cocaine: Basuco, Crack, and Other Coca Products." *Contemporary Drug Problems* 14:461–492 (1987).

Irwin, John, and James Austin, *It's About Time: America's Imprisonment Binge*. Belmont, CA: Wadsworth, 1994.

Isikoff, Michael, "Drug Buy Set Up for Bush Speech: DEA Lured Seller to Lafayette Park." *Washington Post*, September 22, 1989, p. A1.

Johnson, Bruce D., et al., *Taking Care of Business: The Economics of Crime by Heroin Abusers*. Lexington, MA: Lexington Books, 1985.

Johnston, Lloyd D., Patrick M. O'Malley, and Jerald G. Bachman, *Illicit Drug Use, Smoking, and Drinking by America's High School Students, College Students, and Young Adults, 1975–1987*. Washington, DC: National Institute on Drug Abuse, 1988.

Kitsuse, John I., and Aaron V. Cicourel, "A Note on the Use of Official Statistics." *Social Problems* 11:131–139 (1963).

Kozel, Nicholas, and Edgar Adams, "Epidemiology of Drug Abuse: An Overview." *Science* 234:970–974 (1986).

Lindesmith, Alfred R., *The Addict and the Law*. Bloomington: Indiana University Press, 1965.

Massing, Michael, Review essay on "Swordfish," *New York Review of Books*, July 15, 1993, pp. 30–32.

Morgan, Patricia, "The Legislation of Drug Law: Economic Crisis and Social Control," *Journal of Drug Issues* 8:53–62 (1978).

Musto, David, *The American Disease: Origins of Narcotic Control*. New Haven, CT: Yale University Press, 1973.

National Institute on Drug Abuse, *Data from the Drug Abuse Warning Network: Annual Data 1985*. Statistical Series 1, #5. Washington, DC: National Institute on Drug Abuse, 1986a.

———, *National Household Survey on Drug Abuse, 1985*. Washington, DC: Division of Epidemiology and Statistical Analysis, National Institute on Drug Abuse, 1986b.

———, *National Household Survey on Drug Abuse: 1988 Population Estimates*. Washington, DC: Division of Epidemiology and Prevention Research, National Institute on Drug Abuse, 1988.

———, *National Household Survey on Drug Abuse: Main Findings 1990*. Washington, DC: Epidemiology and Prevention Research, National Institute on Drug Abuse, 1990.

———, *Annual Medical Examiner Data, 1991: Data from the Drug Abuse Warning Network*. Washington, DC: Division of Epidemiology and Prevention Research, National Institute on Drug Abuse, 1992.

———, *Estimates from the Drug Abuse Warning Network: 1992 Estimates of Drug-Related Emergency Room Episodes*. Washington, DC: Substance Abuse and Mental Health Services Administration, U.S. Dept. of Health and Human Services, 1993a.

———, *National Household Survey on Drug Abuse: Population Estimates 1992*. Washington, DC: Substance Abuse and Mental Health Services Administration, U.S. Dept. of Health and Human Services, 1993b.

National Report on Substance Abuse, "Federal Officials Express Alarm at Youth's Rising Illicit Drug Use." February 11, 1994, p. 2.

New York Times, "No Change in Basics: Bush Rejects Any Fundamental Shift, Instead Vowing Unprecedented Vigor." September 6, 1989, p. A11.

Office of National Drug Control Policy, *National Drug Control Strategy: Budget Summary*. Washington, DC: U.S. Government Printing Office, 1992.

Phillips, David P., and Lundie L. Carstensen, "Clustering of Teenage Suicides After Television News

Stories About Suicide." *New England Journal of Medicine* 315:685–689 (1986).

Reeves, Jimmie L., and Richard Campbell, *Cracked Coverage: Television News, the Anti-Cocaine Crusade, and the Reagan Legacy.* Durham, NC: Duke University Press, 1994.

Reinarman, Craig, "The Social Construction of an Alcohol Problem: The Case of Mothers Against Drunk Drivers and Social Control in the 1980s." *Theory and Society* 17:91–119 (1988).

———, "Glasnost in U.S. Drug Policy?: Clinton Constrained." *International Journal of Drug Policy* 5:42–49 (1994).

Rogin, Michael Paul, *Ronald Reagan, the Movie: and Other Episodes in Political Demonology.* Berkeley: University of California Press, 1987.

Rumbarger, John, *Profits, Power, and Prohibition,* Albany: State University of New York Press, 1989.

Ryan, William, *Blaming the Victim.* New York: Vintage, 1976.

Schneider, Joseph, and John I. Kitsuse, eds., *Studies in the Sociology of Social Problems.* Norwood, NJ: Ablex, 1984.

Siegel, Ronald, "Cocaine Smoking." *Journal of Psychoactive Drugs* 14:271–359 (1982).

Spector, Malcolm, and John Kitsuse, *Constructing Social Problems.* Menlo Park, CA: Cummings, 1977.

Staples, Brent, "Coke Wars." *New York Times Book Review,* February 6, 1994, p. 11.

Trebach, Arnold, *The Great Drug War.* New York: Macmillan, 1987.

University of Michigan, "Drug Use Rises Among American Teen-Agers." News and Information Services, January 27, 1994.

Waldorf, Dan, Craig Reinarman, and Sheigla Murphy, *Cocaine Changes.* Philadelphia: Temple University Press, 1991.

Washton, Arnold, and Mark Gold, "Recent Trends in Cocaine Abuse," *Advances in Alcohol and Substance Abuse* 6:31–47 (1987).

The White House, *National Drug Control Strategy.* Washington, DC: U.S. Government Printing Office, 1989.

Williams, Terry, *The Cocaine Kids.* Reading, MA: Addison-Wesley, 1989.

Wilson, William Julius, *The Truly Disadvantaged.* Chicago: University of Chicago Press, 1987.

Zinberg, Norman E., *Drug, Set, and Setting: The Basis for Controlled Drug Use.* New Haven, CT: Yale University Press, 1984.

THINKING ABOUT THE READING

How does Reinarman and Levine's article support the contention that reality is a social construction? Consider the broader implications of their argument: The use of certain substances becomes a serious social problem *not* because it is an objectively dangerous activity but because it receives sufficient media and political attention. What does this contention suggest about the way social problems and public fears are created and maintained in society? What does it tell us about our collective need to identify a scapegoat for our social problems? Why are there such vastly different public attitudes and legal responses to crack cocaine versus powder cocaine? Can you think of other situations in which heightened media coverage and political attention have created widespread public concern and moral outrage where none was warranted? How has this article affected your views about the "War on Drugs" and the decriminalization of illegal drugs?

Researching Dealers and Smugglers

Patricia A. Adler

I strongly believe that investigative field research (Douglas 1976), with emphasis on direct personal observation, interaction, and experience, is the only way to acquire accurate knowledge about deviant behavior. Investigative techniques are especially necessary for studying groups such as drug dealers and smugglers because the highly illegal nature of their occupation makes them secretive, deceitful, mistrustful, and paranoid. To insulate themselves from the straight world, they construct multiple false fronts, offer lies and misinformation, and withdraw into their group. In fact, detailed, scientific information about upper-level drug dealers and smugglers is lacking precisely because of the difficulty sociological researchers have had in penetrating into their midst. As a result, the only way I could possibly get close enough to these individuals to discover what they were doing and to understand their world from their perspectives (Blumer 1969) was to take a membership role in the setting. While my different values and goals precluded my becoming converted to complete membership in the sub-culture, and my fears prevented my ever becoming "actively" involved in their trafficking activities, I was able to assume a "peripheral" membership role. I became a member of the dealers' and smugglers' social world and participated in their daily activities on that basis. . . .

Getting In

When I moved to Southwest County [California] in the summer of 1974, I had no idea that I would soon be swept up in a subculture of vast drug trafficking and unending partying, mixed with occasional cloak-and-dagger subterfuge. I had moved to California with my husband, Peter, to attend graduate school in sociology. We rented a condominium townhouse near the beach and started taking classes in the fall. We had always felt that socializing exclusively with academicians left us nowhere to escape from our work, so we tried to meet people in the nearby community. One of the first friends we made was our closest neighbor, a fellow in his late twenties with a tall, hulking frame and gentle expression. Dave, as he introduced himself, was always dressed rather casually, if not sloppily, in T-shirts and jeans. He spent most of his time hanging out or walking on the beach with a variety of friends who visited his house, and taking care of his two young boys, who lived alternately with him and his estranged wife. He also went out of town a lot. We started spending much of our free time over at his house, talking, playing board games late into the night, and smoking marijuana together. We were glad to find someone from whom we could buy marijuana in this new place, since we did not know too many people. He also began treating us to a fairly regular supply of cocaine, which was a thrill because this was a drug we could rarely afford on our student budgets. We noticed right away, however, that there was something unusual about his use and knowledge of drugs: while he always had a plentiful supply and was fairly expert about marijuana and cocaine, when we tried to buy a small bag of marijuana from him he had little idea of the going price. This incongruity piqued our curiosity and raised suspicion. We wondered if he might be dealing in larger quantities. Keeping our suspicions to ourselves, we began observing Dave's activities a little more closely. Most of his friends were in their late twenties and early thirties and, judging by their lifestyles and automobiles, rather wealthy. They came and left his house at all hours, occasionally extending their parties through the night and the next day into the following night. Yet throughout this time we never saw Dave or any of his friends engage in any activity that resembled a legitimate job. In most places this might have evoked community suspicion, but few of the people we encountered in Southwest County seemed to hold traditionally structured jobs. Dave, in fact, had no visible means of financial support. When we asked him what he did for a living, he said something vague about being a real estate speculator, and we let it go at that. We never voiced our suspicions directly since he chose not to broach the subject with us.

We did discuss the subject with our mentor, Jack Douglas, however. He was excited by the prospect that we might be living among a group of big dealers, and urged us to follow our instincts and develop leads into the group. He knew that the local area was rife with drug trafficking, since he had begun a life history case study of two drug dealers with another graduate student several years previously. That earlier study was aborted when the graduate student quit school, but Jack still had many hours of taped interviews he had conducted with them, as well as an interview that he had done with an undergraduate student who had known the two dealers independently, to serve as a cross-check on their accounts. He therefore encouraged us to become friendlier with Dave and his friends. We decided that if anything did develop out of our observations of Dave, it might make a nice paper for a field methods class or independent study. . . .

We thus watched Dave and continued to develop our friendship with him. We also watched his friends and got to know a few of his more regular visitors. We continued to build friendly relations by doing, quite naturally, what Becker (1963), Polsky (1969), and Douglas (1972) had advocated for the early stages of field research: we gave them a chance to know us and form judgments about our trustworthiness by jointly pursuing those interests and activities which we had in common.

Then one day something happened which forced a breakthrough in the research. Dave had two guys visiting him from out of town and, after snorting quite a bit of cocaine, they turned their conversation to a trip they had just made from Mexico, where they piloted a load of marijuana back across the border in a small plane. Dave made a few efforts to shift the conversation to another subject, telling them to "button their lips," but they apparently thought that he was joking. They thought that anybody as close to Dave as we seemed to be undoubtedly knew the nature of his business. They made further allusions to his involvement in the operation and discussed the outcome of the sale. We could feel the wave of tension and awkwardness from Dave when this conversation began, as he looked toward us to see if we understood the implications of what was being said, but then he just shrugged it off as done. Later, after the two guys left, he discussed with us what happened. He admitted to us that he was a member of a smuggling crew and a major marijuana dealer on the side. He said that he knew he could trust us, but that it was his practice to say as little as possible to outsiders about his activities. This inadvertent slip, and Dave's subsequent opening up, were highly significant in forging our entry into Southwest County's drug world. From then on he was open in discussing the nature of his dealing and smuggling activities with us.

He was, it turned out, a member of a smuggling crew that was importing a ton of marijuana weekly and 40 kilos of cocaine every few months. During that first winter and spring, we observed Dave at work and also got to know the other members of his crew, including Ben, the smuggler himself. Ben was also very tall and broad shouldered, but his long black hair, now flecked with gray, bespoke his earlier membership in the hippie subculture. A large physical stature, we observed, was common to most of the male participants involved in this drug community. The women also had a unifying physical trait: they were extremely attractive and stylishly dressed. This included Dave's ex-wife, Jean, with whom he reconciled during the spring. We therefore became friendly with Jean and through her met a number of women ("dope chicks") who hung around the dealers and smugglers. As we continued to gain the friendship of Dave and Jean's associates we were progressively admitted into their inner circle and apprised of each person's dealing or smuggling role.

Once we realized the scope of Ben's and his associates' activities, we saw the enormous research potential in studying them. This scene was different from any analysis of drug trafficking that we had read in the sociological literature because of the amounts they were dealing and the fact that they were importing it themselves. We decided that, if it was at all possible, we would capitalize on this situation, to "opportunistically" (Riemer 1977) take advantage of our prior expertise and of the knowledge, entree, and rapport we had already developed with several key people in this setting. We therefore discussed the idea of doing a study of the general subculture with Dave and several of his closest friends (now becoming our friends). We assured them of the anonymity, confidentiality, and innocuousness of our work. They were happy to reciprocate our friendship by being of help to our professional careers. In fact, they basked in the subsequent attention we gave their lives.

We began by turning first Dave, then others, into key informants and collecting their life histories in detail. We conducted a series of taped, depth interviews with an unstructured, open-ended format. We questioned them about such topics as their backgrounds, their recruitment into the occupation, the stages of their dealing careers, their relations with others, their motivations, their lifestyle, and their general impressions about the community as a whole.

We continued to do taped interviews with key informants for the next six years until 1980, when we moved away from the area. After that, we occasionally did follow-up interviews when we returned for vacation visits. These later interviews focused on recording the continuing unfolding of events and included detailed probing into specific conceptual areas, such as dealing networks, types of dealers, secrecy, trust, paranoia, reputation, the law, occupational mobility, and occupational stratification. The number of taped interviews we did with each key informant varied, ranging between 10 and 30 hours of discussion.

Our relationship with Dave and the others thus took on an added dimension—the research relationship. As Douglas (1976), Henslin (1972), and Wax (1952) have noted, research relationships involve some form of mutual exchange. In our case, we offered everything that friendship could entail. We did routine favors for them in the course of our everyday lives, offered them insights and advice about their lives from the perspective of our more respectable position, wrote letters on their behalf to the authorities when they got in trouble, testified as character witnesses at their non-drug-related trials, and loaned them money when they were down and out. When Dave was arrested and brought to trial for check-kiting, we helped Jean organize his defense and raise the money to pay his fines. We spelled her in taking care of the children so that she could work on his behalf. When he was eventually sent to the state prison we maintained close ties with her and discussed our mutual efforts to buoy Dave up and secure his release. We also visited him in jail. During Dave's incarceration, however, Jean was courted by an old boyfriend and gave up her reconciliation with Dave. This proved to be another significant turning point in our research because, desperate for money, Jean looked up Dave's old dealing connections and went into the business herself. She did not stay with these marijuana dealers and smugglers for long, but soon moved into the cocaine business. Over the next several years her experiences in the world of cocaine dealing brought us into contact with a different group of people. While these people knew Dave and his associates (this was very common in the Southwest County dealing and smuggling community), they did not deal with them directly. We were thus able to gain access to a much wider and more diverse range of subjects than we would have had she not branched out on her own.

Dave's eventual release from prison three months later brought our involvement in the research to an even deeper level. He was broke and had nowhere to go. When he showed up on our doorstep, we took him in. We offered to let him stay with us until he was back on his feet again and could afford a place of his own. He lived with us for seven months, intimately sharing his daily experiences with us. During this time we witnessed, firsthand, his transformation from a scared ex-con who would never break the law again to a hard-working legitimate employee who only dealt to get money for his children's Christmas presents, to a full-time dealer with no pretensions at legitimate work. Both his process of changing attitudes and the community's gradual reacceptance of him proved very revealing.

We socialized with Dave, Jean, and other members of Southwest County's dealing and smuggling community on a near-daily basis, especially during the first four years of the research (before we had a child). We worked in their legitimate businesses, vacationed together, attended their weddings, and cared for their children. Throughout their relationship with us, several participants became co-opted to the researcher's perspective and actively sought out instances of behavior which filled holes in the conceptualizations we were developing. Dave, for one, became so intrigued by our conceptual dilemmas that he undertook a "natural experiment" entirely on his own, offering an unlimited supply of drugs to a lower-level dealer to see if he could work up to higher levels of dealing, and what factors would enhance or impinge upon his upward mobility.

In addition to helping us directly through their own experiences, our key informants aided us in widening our circle of contacts. For instance, they let us know when someone in whom we might be interested was planning on dropping by, vouching for our trustworthiness and reliability as friends who could be included in business conversations. Several times we were even awakened in the night by phone calls informing us that someone had dropped by for a visit, should we want to "casually" drop over too. We rubbed the sleep from our eyes, dressed, and walked or drove over, feeling like sleuths out of a television series. We thus were able to snowball, through the active efforts of our key informants, into an expanded study population. This was supplemented by our own efforts to cast a research net and befriend other dealers, moving from contact to contact slowly and carefully through the domino effect.

The Covert Role

The highly illegal nature of dealing in illicit drugs and dealers' and smugglers' general level of suspicion made the adoption of an overt research role highly sensitive and problematic. In discussing this issue with our key informants, they all agreed that we should be extremely discreet (for both our sakes and theirs). We carefully approached new individuals before we admitted that we were studying them. With many of these people, then, we took a covert posture in the research setting. As nonparticipants in the business activities which bound members together into the group, it was difficult to become fully accepted as peers. We therefore tried to establish some sort of peripheral, social membership in the general crowd, where we could be accepted as "wise" (Goffman 1963) individuals and granted a courtesy membership. This seemed an attainable goal, since we had begun our involvement by forming such relationships with our key informants. By being introduced to others in this wise rather than overt role, we were able to interact with people who would otherwise have shied away from us. Adopting a courtesy membership caused us to bear a courtesy stigma however, and we suffered since we, at times, had to disguise the nature of our research from both lay outsiders and academicians.

In our overt posture we showed interest in dealers' and smugglers' activities, encouraged them to talk about themselves (within limits, so as to avoid acting like narcs), and ran home to write field notes. This role offered us the advantage of gaining access to unapproachable people while avoiding researcher effects, but it prevented us from asking some necessary, probing questions and from tape recording conversations. We therefore sought, at all times, to build toward a conversion to the overt role. We did this by working to develop their trust.

Developing Trust

Like achieving entree, the process of developing trust with members of unorganized deviant groups can be slow and difficult. In the absence of a formal structure separating members from outsiders, each individual must form his or her own judgment about whether new persons can be admitted to their confidence. No gatekeeper existed to smooth our path to being trusted, although our key informants acted in this role whenever they could by providing introductions and references. In addition, the unorganized nature of this group meant that we met people at different times and were constantly at different levels in our developing relationships with them. We were thus trusted more by some people than by others, in part because of their greater familiarity with us. But as Douglas (1976) has noted, just because someone knew us or even liked us did not automatically guarantee that they would trust us.

We actively tried to cultivate the trust of our respondents by tying them to us with favors. Small things, like offering the use of our phone, were followed with bigger favors, like offering the use of our car, and finally really meaningful favors, like offering the use of our home. Here we often trod a thin line, trying to ensure our personal safety while putting ourselves in enough of a risk position, along with our research subjects, so that they would trust us. While we were able to build a "web of trust" (Douglas 1976) with some members, we found that trust, in large part, was not a simple status to attain in the drug world. Johnson (1975) has pointed out that trust is not a one-time phenomenon, but an ongoing developmental process. From my experiences in this research I would add that it cannot be simply assumed to be a one-way process either, for it can be diminished, withdrawn, reinstated to varying degrees, and requestioned at any point. Carey (1972) and Douglas (1972) have remarked on this waxing and waning process, but it was especially pronounced for us because our subjects used large amounts of cocaine over an extended period of time. This tended to make them alternately warm and cold to us. We thus lived through a series of ups and downs with the people we were trying to cultivate as research informants.

The Overt Role

After this initial covert phase, we began to feel that some new people trusted us. We tried to intuitively feel when the time was right to approach them and go overt. We used two means of approaching people to inform them that we were involved in a study of dealing and smuggling: direct and indirect. In some cases our key informants approached their friends or connections and, after vouching for our absolute trustworthiness, convinced these associates to talk to us. In other instances, we approached people directly, asking for their help with our project. We worked our way through a progression with these secondary contacts, first discussing the dealing scene overtly and later moving to taped life history interviews. Some people reacted well to us, but others responded skittishly, making appointments to do taped interviews only to break them as the day drew near, and going through fluctuating stages of being honest with us or putting up fronts about their dealing activities. This varied, for some, with their degree of active involvement in the business. During the times when they had quit dealing, they would tell us about their present and past activities, but when they became actively involved again, they would hide it from us.

This progression of covert to overt roles generated a number of tactical difficulties. The first was the problem of *coming on too fast* and blowing it. Early in the research we had a dealer's old lady (we thought) all set up for the direct approach. We knew many dealers in common and had discussed many things tangential to dealing with her without actually mentioning the subject. When we asked her to do a taped interview of her bohemian lifestyle, she agreed without hesitation. When the interview began, though, and she found out why we were interested in her, she balked, gave us a lot of incoherent jumble, and ended the session as quickly as possible.

Even though she lived only three houses away we never saw her again. We tried to move more slowly after that.

A second problem involved simultaneously *juggling our overt and covert roles* with different people. This created the danger of getting our cover blown with people who did not know about our research (Henslin 1972). It was very confusing to separate the people who knew about our study from those who did not, especially in the minds of our informants. They would make occasional veiled references in front of people, especially when loosened by intoxicants, that made us extremely uncomfortable. We also frequently worried that our snooping would someday be mistaken for police tactics. Fortunately, this never happened. . . .

Problems and Issues

Reflecting on the research process, I have isolated a number of issues which I believe merit additional discussion. These are rooted in experiences which have the potential for greater generic applicability.

The first is the *effect of drugs on the data-gathering process.* Carey (1972) has elaborated on some of the problems he encountered when trying to interview respondents who used amphetamines, while Wax (1952, 1957) has mentioned the difficulty of trying to record field notes while drinking sake. I found that marijuana and cocaine had nearly opposite effects from each other. The latter helped the interview process, while the former hindered it. Our attempts to interview respondents who were stoned on marijuana were unproductive for a number of reasons. The primary obstacle was the effects of the drug. Often, people became confused, sleepy, or involved in eating to varying degrees. This distracted them from our purpose. At times, people even simulated overreactions to marijuana to hide behind the drug's supposed disorienting influence and thereby avoid divulging information. Cocaine, in contrast, proved to be a research aid. The drug's warming and sociable influence opened people up, diminished their inhibitions,

and generally increased their enthusiasm for both the interview experience and us.

A second problem I encountered involved *assuming risks while doing research.* As I noted earlier, dangerous situations are often generic to research on deviant behavior. We were most afraid of the people we studied. As Carey (1972), Henslin (1972), and Whyte (1955) have stated, members of deviant groups can become hostile toward a researcher if they think that they are being treated wrongfully. This could have happened at any time from a simple occurrence, such as a misunderstanding, or from something more serious, such as our covert posture being exposed. Because of the inordinate amount of drugs they consumed, drug dealers and smugglers were particularly volatile, capable of becoming malicious toward each other or us with little warning. They were also likely to behave erratically owing to the great risks they faced from the police and other dealers. These factors made them moody, and they vacillated between trusting us and being suspicious of us.

At various times we also had to protect our research tapes. We encountered several threats to our collection of taped interviews from people who had granted us these interviews. This made us anxious, since we had taken great pains to acquire these tapes and felt strongly about maintaining confidences entrusted to us by our informants. When threatened, we became extremely frightened and shifted the tapes between different hiding places. We even ventured forth one rainy night with our tapes packed in a suitcase to meet a person who was uninvolved in the research at a secret rendezvous so that he could guard the tapes for us.

We were fearful, lastly, of the police. We often worried about local police or drug agents discovering the nature of our study and confiscating or subpoenaing our tapes and field notes. Sociologists have no privileged relationship with their subjects that would enable us legally to withhold evidence from the authorities should they subpoena it. For this reason we studiously avoided any publicity about the research, even holding back on publishing articles in scholarly journals until we were nearly ready to move out of the setting. The closest we came to being publicly exposed as drug researchers came when a former sociology graduate student (turned dealer, we had heard from inside sources) was arrested at the scene of a cocaine deal. His lawyer wanted us to testify about the dangers of doing drug-related research, since he was using his research status as his defense. Fortunately, the crisis was averted when his lawyer succeeded in suppressing evidence and had the case dismissed before the trial was to have begun. Had we been exposed, however, our respondents would have acquired guilt by association through their friendship with us.

Our fear of the police went beyond our concern for protecting our research subjects, however. We risked the danger of arrest ourselves through our own violations of the law. Many sociologists (Becker 1963; Carey 1972; Polsky 1969; Whyte 1955) have remarked that field researchers studying deviance must inevitably break the law in order to acquire valid participant observation data. This occurs in its most innocuous form from having "guilty knowledge": information about crimes that are committed. Being aware of major dealing and smuggling operations made us an accessory to their commission, since we failed to notify the police. We broke the law, secondly, through our "guilty observations," by being present at the scene of a crime and witnessing its occurrence (see also Carey 1972). We knew it was possible to get caught in a bust involving others, yet buying and selling was so pervasive that to leave every time it occurred would have been unnatural and highly suspicious. Sometimes drug transactions even occurred in our home, especially when Dave was living there, but we finally had to put a stop to that because we could not handle the anxiety. Lastly, we broke the law through our "guilty actions," by taking part in illegal behavior ourselves. Although we never dealt drugs (we were too scared to be seriously tempted), we consumed drugs and possessed them in small quantities. Quite frankly, it would have been impossible for a nonuser to have gained access to this group to gather the data presented here. This was the minimum involvement necessary to obtain even the courtesy membership we achieved. Some kind of illegal action was also found to be a necessary or helpful component of the research by Becker (1963), Carey (1972), Johnson (1975), Polsky (1969), and Whyte (1955).

Another methodological issue arose from the *cultural clash between our research subjects and ourselves.* While other sociologists have alluded to these kinds of differences (Humphreys 1970, Whyte 1955), few have discussed how the research relationships affected them. Relationships with research subjects are unique because they involve a bond of intimacy between persons who might not ordinarily associate together, or who might otherwise be no more than casual friends. When fieldworkers undertake a major project, they commit themselves to maintaining a long-term relationship with the people they study. However, as researchers try to get depth involvement, they are apt to come across fundamental differences in character, values, and attitudes between their subjects and themselves. In our case, we were most strongly confronted by differences in present versus future orientations, a desire for risk versus security, and feelings of spontaneity versus self-discipline. These differences often caused us great frustration. We repeatedly saw dealers act irrationally, setting themselves up for failure. We wrestled with our desire to point out their patterns of foolhardy behavior and offer advice, feeling competing pulls between our detached, observer role which advised us not to influence the natural setting, and our involved, participant role which called for us to offer friendly help whenever possible. . . .

The final issue I will discuss involved the various *ethical problems* which arose during this research. Many fieldworkers have encountered ethical dilemmas or pangs of guilt during the course of their research experiences (Carey 1972; Douglas 1976; Humphreys 1970; Johnson 1975; Klockars 1977, 1979; Rochford 1985). The researchers' role in the field makes this necessary because they can never fully align themselves with their subjects while maintaining their identity and personal commitment to the scientific community. Ethical dilemmas, then, are directly related to the amount of deception researchers use in gathering the data, and the degree to which they have accepted such acts as necessary and therefore neutralized them.

Throughout the research, we suffered from the burden of intimacies and confidences. Guarding secrets which had been told to us during taped interviews was not always easy or pleasant. Dealers occasionally revealed things about themselves or others that we had to pretend not to know when interacting with their close associates. This sometimes meant that we had to lie or build elaborate stories to cover for some people. Their fronts therefore became our fronts, and we had to weave our own web of deception to guard their performances. This became especially disturbing during the writing of the research report, as I was torn by conflicts between using details to enrich the data and glossing over description to guard confidences.

Using the covert research role generated feelings of guilt, despite the fact that our key informants deemed it necessary, and thereby condoned it. Their own covert experiences were far more deeply entrenched than ours, being a part of their daily existence with non-drug world members. Despite the universal presence of covert behavior throughout the setting, we still felt a sense of betrayal every time we ran home to write research notes on observations we had made under the guise of innocent participants. . . .

Conclusions

The aggressive research strategy I employed was vital to this study. I could not just walk up to strangers and start hanging out with them as Liebow (1967) did, or be sponsored to a member of this group by a social service or reform organization as Whyte (1955) was, and expect to be accepted, let alone welcomed. Perhaps such a strategy might have worked with a group that had nothing to hide, but I doubt it. Our modern, pluralistic society is so filled with diverse subcultures whose interests compete or conflict with

each other that each subculture has a set of knowledge which is reserved exclusively for insiders. In order to survive and prosper, they do not ordinarily show this side to just anyone. To obtain the kind of depth insight and information I needed, I had to become like the members in certain ways. They dealt only with people they knew and trusted, so l had to become known and trusted before I could reveal my true self and my research interests. Confronted with secrecy, danger, hidden alliances, misrepresentations, and unpredictable changes of intent, I had to use a delicate combination of overt and covert roles. Throughout, my deliberate cultivation of the norm of reciprocal exchange enabled me to trade my friendship for their knowledge, rather than waiting for the highly unlikely event that information would be delivered into my lap. I thus actively built a web of research contacts, used them to obtain highly sensitive data, and carefully checked them out to ensure validity. . . .

Finally, I feel strongly that to ensure accuracy, research on deviant groups must be conducted in the settings where it naturally occurs. As Polsky (1969:115–16) has forcefully asserted:

> This means—there is no getting away from it—the study of career criminals *au natural,* in the field, the study of such criminals as they normally go about their work and play, the study of "uncaught" criminals and the study of others who in the past have been caught but are not caught at the time you study them. . . . Obviously we can no longer afford the convenient fiction that in studying criminals in their natural habitat, we would discover nothing really important that could not be discovered from criminals behind bars.

By studying criminals in their natural habitat I was able to see them in the full variability and complexity of their surrounding subculture, rather than within the artificial environment of a prison. I was thus able to learn about otherwise inaccessible dimensions of their lives, observing and analyzing firsthand the nature of their social organization, social stratification, lifestyle, and motivation.

REFERENCES

Becker, Howard. 1963. *Outsiders.* New York: Free Press.

Blumer, Herbert. 1969. *Symbolic Interactionism.* Englewood Cliffs, NJ: Prentice-Hall.

Carey, James T. 1972. "Problems of access and risk in observing drug scenes." In Jack D. Douglas, ed., *Research on Deviance*, pp. 71–92. New York: Random House.

Douglas, Jack D. 1972. "Observing deviance." In Jack D. Douglas, ed., *Research on Deviance*, pp. 3–34. New York: Random House.

———. 1976. *Investigative Social Research.* Beverly Hills, CA: Sage.

Goffman, Erving. 1963. *Stigma.* Englewood Cliffs, NJ: Prentice-Hall.

Henslin, James M. 1972. "Studying deviance in four settings: research experiences with cabbies, suicides, drug users and abortionees." In Jack D. Douglas, ed., *Research on Deviance*, pp. 35–70. New York: Random House.

Humphreys, Laud. 1970. *Tearoom Trade.* Chicago: Aldine.

Johnson, John M. 1975. *Doing Field Research.* New York: Free Press.

Klockars, Carl B. 1977. "Field ethics for the life history." In Robert Weppner, ed., *Street Ethnography*, pp. 201–26. Beverly Hills, CA: Sage.

———. 1979. "Dirty hands and deviant subjects." In Carl B. Klockars and Finnbarr W. O'Connor, eds., *Deviance and Decency*, pp. 261–82. Beverly Hills, CA: Sage.

Liebow, Elliot. 1967. *Tally's Corner.* Boston: Little, Brown.

Polsky, Ned. 1969. *Hustlers, Beats, and Others.* New York: Doubleday.

Riemer, Jeffrey W. 1977. "Varieties of opportunistic research." *Urban Life* 5:467–77.

Rochford, E. Burke, Jr. 1985. *Hare Krishna in America.* New Brunswick, NJ: Rutgers University Press.

Wax, Rosalie. 1952. "Reciprocity as a field technique." *Human Organization* 11:34–37.

———. 1957. "Twelve years later: an analysis of a field experience." *American Journal of Sociology* 63: 133–42.

Whyte, William F. 1955. *Street Corner Society.* Chicago: University of Chicago Press.

THINKING ABOUT THE READING

Many of the issues sociologists try to understand are phenomena that occur under highly secretive circumstances. Patricia Adler chose a research method that brought her and her husband face to face with people involved in serious criminal activities. Only from this vantage point could they fully understand the social forces at play. Do you think their tactic was ethically justifiable? Should social researchers be obligated to report criminal activity to the proper authorities, or is it appropriate to conceal such information in the name of scientific inquiry? Can you think of a better way to acquire accurate information about drug dealers and smugglers?

CHAPTER 4

Building Order: Culture and History

Culture provides members of a society with a common bond, a sense that they see certain facets of society in similar ways. That members of a society can live together at all depends on the fact that they share a certain amount of cultural knowledge. Social norms—the rules and standards that govern all social encounters—provide order in our day-to-day lives. Norms reflect commonly held assumptions about conventional behavior. They tell us what to expect from others and what others can expect from us. Violations of norms mark the boundaries of acceptable behavior and symbolically reaffirm what a particular society defines as right and wrong. Norms, of course, vary greatly across cultures. Indeed, the more ethnically and culturally diverse a society is, the greater the likelihood of normative clashes between groups.

We can see clear evidence of the power of cultural norms when we examine how members of a different society handle some taken-for-granted aspect of everyday life. Take, for instance, the experience of time. If you've ever traveled abroad you know that people perceive the importance of time differently. In some places everyday life is incredibly fast-paced; in others it seems slow and lethargic. In the industrialized world, events are often meticulously timed and scheduled. But in less developed parts of the world, time is much less restrictive and events occur more spontaneously. In "A Geography of Time," Robert Levine uses his own travel experiences and anthropological observations to examine the impact of culture on the perception and use of time. He shows us how conflicts can result from clashes between people operating on different conceptions of time (what he calls *clock time* and *event time*). His comparison of the way time is experienced in other cultures versus our own reminds us that the time norms we consider to be normal and superior are in the end arbitrary and not shared worldwide. This is a humbling but important lesson for people who assume that their cultural way of life is natural and normal.

Even within the same society we can see normative variation. Over the span of a few years, most cultures present an image of stability and agreement regarding normative boundaries. But this agreement is illusory. Over a generation or even a decade, that sense of order is replaced by a sense of change. As Jessica Mitford shows in "Fashions in Childbirth," even our most fundamental biological experiences are touched by culture and history. Mitford points out that something so utterly natural and universal as giving birth can be affected by broader historical changes. She describes how the normal, healthy childbirth practices of one era can seem disastrous, dangerous, even barbaric, by another. Technological advances in childbirth practices are always the result of the standard practices and problems of the times. Hence what is considered an improvement for one age often turns out to be a problem for the next.

A Geography of Time

Robert Levine

Living on Event Time

Anyone who has traveled abroad—or waited in a doctor's office, for that matter—knows that the clock, or even the calendar, is sometimes no more than an ornament. The event at hand, on these occasions, often begins and ends with complete disregard for the technicalities of a timepiece. We in the industrialized world expect punctuality. But life on clock time is clearly out of line with virtually all of recorded history. And it is not only from a historical perspective that these temporal customs are so deviant. Still today, the idea of living by the clock remains absolutely foreign to much of the world.

One of the most significant differences in the pace of life is whether people use the hour on the clock to schedule the beginning and ending of activities, or whether the activities are allowed to transpire according to their own spontaneous schedule. These two approaches are known, respectively, as living by clock time and living by event time. The difference between clock and event time is more than a difference in speed, although life certainly does tend to be faster for people on clock time. Let me again turn to a personal example.

A few years after my stay in Brazil I became eligible for a sabbatical leave from my university. I decided to invest my term of "rest and renewal" in a study of international differences in the pace of life. I also chose to use the opportunity to live out a childhood dream—to travel around the world.

Precisely where I would go wasn't altogether clear. The phrase "travel around the world" had a lovely ring to it, but I must admit that I wasn't certain just what it entailed. Never having done very well in geography, I had very little grasp of how the nations of the world are arranged and even less notion of their innards. Not knowing what I'd encounter, it was impossible to plan exactly where to visit or how long I would stay in each country. I decided, instead, to let the trip evolve its own form. Fortunately, the research I had designed allowed me the flexibility to decide where and when to collect data along the way.

I bought a map of the world and marked the locations of the four most exotic sights I could invoke: The Great Wall of China, Mount Everest, the Taj Mahal and the Great Pyramids of Egypt. I drew a line connecting the marks. Although I was uncertain how many of these wonders I'd actually see, they gave my trip a rough outline. I decided to fly to the edge of Western Asia and then make my way by land, moving in a rough westerly direction, around the globe. Searching the map for Asia's outside edge, my finger landed on Indonesia.

I purchased a one-way plane ticket to Jakarta, with stops along the way in Japan, Taiwan, and Hong Kong. Beyond that, I had no tickets. From Indonesia I would travel up the Malaysian peninsula toward Thailand, and then west across Asia toward home. My only rules would be to travel no better than second class and to stay on the ground as much as possible. I gave up my house lease, loaned out my car, put my possessions in storage, and told everyone who needed to know I'd be gone for the semester. (Professors don't think in terms of months. Our unit of time is the semester.) The semester stretched into two semesters (one year, tossing in a summer vacation).

The trip began with a flight from San Francisco to Tokyo. Settling in for the long ride, I tried to focus on what I was beginning. My first thought was that I had no keys in my pocket. Next, that in place of an appointment calendar, I was carrying, for the first time in my life, a journal. Then came the realization that I had no commitments. There was nothing, other than carrying out my very flexible research plans, that needed to be done. I didn't have to be any place at any specific time for six whole months. There were no plans or schedules to interfere with whatever might come along. I could let my opportunities come forth on their own and I would choose those I wished to follow. I was free, free, free!

My joy lasted nearly half a minute. Then the terror: What in the world would I do for a whole semester without a schedule or plans? I looked ahead and saw layers and layers of nothing. How would I fill my time? I have never in my life so yearned for an appointment—with anyone for anything. It really was pitiful. Here I was freer and more mobile than most people in the world could ever dream of being. I was Marlon Brando on his motorcycle—with a passport, a Ph.D., and a steady paycheck. And I responded with an anxiety attack.

When I dozed off a little later on the flight, I dreamed about a passage from William Faulkner's *Light in August*. It is when the character named Christmas, hungry and fleeing from the sheriff, becomes obsessed with time. I later looked up the actual quotation:

> . . . *I have not eaten since I have not eaten since* trying to remember how many days it had been since Friday in Jefferson, in the restaurant where he had eaten his supper, until after a while, in the lying still with waiting until the men should have eaten and gone to the field, the name of the day of the week seemed more important than the food. Because when the men were gone at last and he descended, emerged, into the level, jonquil-colored sun and went to the kitchen door, he didn't ask for food at all . . . he heard his mouth saying "Can you tell me what day this is? I just want to know what day this is."

"What day it is?" Her face was gaunt as his, her body as gaunt and as tireless and as driven. She said: "You get away from here! It's Tuesday! You get away from here! I'll call my man!"

He said, "Thank you," as the door banged.

After finally arriving in Tokyo, I checked into a hotel room an ex-student had reserved for me. This was the only room reservation I had for the next six months (twelve months, actually—but, mercifully, I didn't know that then). After unpacking, I put on the robe and slippers provided by the hotel. The bottom of the robe showed considerably more thigh than its maker had intended and the slippers only fit over three of my toes. But I liked the image and, coupled with a dip in the hot tub and a very large bottle of Sapporo beer, I went to sleep with some iota of hope for my immediate future.

The next morning I awoke to a view of green tiled roofs, banyan trees, and an enormous reclining Buddha. At the sight of my little robe and slippers my anticipation returned. I was ready to let events take their own course. What to do first? I loved my hot tub the night before, so decided to start my day with another long dip. Then I found a tea shop next door. The waiter spoke a little English, the food was good, and there was even a *Herald Tribune* to keep me company. After breakfast I explored my neighborhood reclining Buddha, who turned out to be resting in a large temple surrounded by a lovely park. I took out a book to read, stretched my legs and watched life in Tokyo parade by.

Next? A friend had given me a list of gardens he thought I'd enjoy seeing. Why not? I randomly chose one, and thoroughly enjoyed the visit. That evening I had a nice dinner at a restaurant near my hotel. I ended my day with a hot tub, my robe and slippers, and a Sapporo.

The following morning I shot out of bed with an adrenalin charge. What might this new day have in store? How to begin? A hot bath first, of course. Then, recalling the pleasant morning before, I returned to my tea shop for breakfast. After that I could think of no place on earth I would rather be than sitting beside my local

Buddha. That afternoon I tried another garden. In the evening I returned to the same restaurant. And, of course, I took a hot bath and nursed my Sapporo before turning in. Another lovely day.

Day three went something like: hot tub/breakfast at the tea shop/Buddha/gardens/dinner/hot tub/Sapporo. The next day was the same. As was the next. And the next.

Looking back at that first week, I see you could have set a clock by my activities. What time is it, you ask? "He's reading his book in the park, so it must be 10 o'clock." "Now he's leaving the hot tub, so that must mean a little after eight." Without intending it, I'd created the structure I so craved on my plane trip. Ironically, one of the very reasons I chose a career in academia in the first place was because it, more than other professions, allowed me to arrange my own time. But when confronted with no limits, I had bounced to the other extreme. To my surprise as well as humbling disappointment, I had built a tighter schedule than the one I lived at work.

Drowning in Event Time

My behavior, I now recognize, was a textbook struggle between the forces of clock time, on the one hand, and event time on the other. Under clock time, the hour on the timepiece governs the beginning and ending of activities. When event time predominates, scheduling is determined by activities. Events begin and end when, by mutual consensus, participants "feel" the time is right. The distinction between clock and event time is profound. The sociologist Robert Lauer conducted in his book *Temporal Man* an intensive review of the literature concerning the meaning of time throughout history. The most fundamental difference, he found, has been between people operating by the clock versus those who measure time by social events.[1]

Many countries extoll event time as a philosophy of life. In Mexico, for example, there is a popular adage to "Give time to time" (*Darle tiempo al tiempo*). Across the globe in Africa, it is said that "Even the time takes its time." Psychologist Kris Eysell, while a Peace Corps volunteer in Liberia, was confronted by a variation on this African expression. She describes how every day, as she made her eight-mile walk from home to work, complete strangers would call out to her along the way: "Take time, Missy."

My experiences in Japan were those of a clock time addict floundering in situations where programming by the clock had lost its effectiveness. I was, I have since come to learn, drowning in good company. The social psychologist James Jones had even more complicated temporal challenges during his stay in Trinidad. Jones, an African-American, is quite familiar with the casualness of what used to be called "colored people's time" (CPT). But he was unprepared for the quagmire of life on event time. Jones first confronted the popular motto "Anytime is Trinidad time" soon after arriving, and said he spent the rest of his stay trying to understand just what it meant:

> CPT simply implied that coming late to things was the norm and contrasted with the Anglo-European penchant for punctuality and timeliness. Over the course of my year in Trinidad, though, I came to understand that Trinidadians had personal control over time. They more or less came and went as they wanted or felt. "I didn't feel to go to work today," was a standard way of expressing that choice. Time was reckoned more by behavior than the clock. Things started when people arrived and ended when they left, not when the clock struck 8:00 or 1:00.[2]

To visitors from the world of clocks, life conducted on event time often appears, in James Jones's words, to be "chronometric anarchy."

Where are the Cows?: Measuring Time in Burundi

When event time people do listen to the clock, it is often nature's clock they hear. Salvatore Niyonzima, one of my former graduate students, describes his home country of Burundi as a classic example of this.

As in most of Central Africa, Niyonzima says, life in Burundi is guided by the seasons. More than 80 percent of the population of Burundi are farmers. As a result, "people still rely on the phases of nature," he explains. "When the dry season begins it is time for harvesting. And when the rainy season comes back—then, of course, it's time to return to the fields and plant and grow things, because this is the cycle."

Appointment times in Burundi are also often regulated by natural cycles. "Appointments are not necessarily in terms of a precise hour of the day. People who grew up in rural areas, and who haven't had very much education, might make an early appointment by saying, 'Okay, I'll see you tomorrow morning when the cows are going out for grazing.'" If they want to meet in the middle of the day, "they set their appointment for the time 'when the cows are going to drink in the stream,' which is where they are led at midday." In order to prevent the youngest cows from drinking too much, Niyonzima explains, farmers typically spend two or three hours with them back in a sheltered place, while their elders are still drinking from the stream. "Then in the afternoon, let's say somewhere around three o'clock, it's time again to get the young cows outside for the evening graze. So if we want to make a late appointment we might say 'I'll see you when the young cows go out.'"

Being any more precise—to say, for example, "I'll meet you in the latter part of the time when the cows are out drinking"—would be, Niyonzima says, "just too much. If you arrange to come to my place when the cows are going to drink water, then it means it's around the middle of the day. If it's an hour earlier or an hour later, it doesn't matter. He knows that he made an appointment and that he'll be there." Precision is difficult and mostly irrelevant because it is hard to know exactly at what time people will be leading the cows out in the first place. "I might decide to lead them to the river one hour later because I either got them out of the home later or it didn't look like they really had that much to eat because the place where they were grazing didn't have very much pasture."

People in Burundi use similarly tangible images to mark the nighttime. "We refer to a very

dark night as a 'Who are you?' night," Niyonzima explains. "This means that it was so dark that you couldn't recognize anybody without hearing their voice. You know that somebody is there but can't see them because it is so dark, so you say 'Who are you?' as a greeting. They speak and I hear their voice and now I recognize who they are. 'Who are you?'–time is one way to describe when it gets dark. We might refer back to an occasion as having occurred on a 'Who are you?' night."

Specifying precise nighttime appointments, Niyonzima says, "gets difficult. 'Who are you?' simply refers to the physical condition of darkness. I certainly wouldn't give a time like 8 P.M. or 9 P.M. When people want to name a particular time of the night, they might use references to aspects of sleep. They may, for example, say something occurred at a time 'When nobody was awake' or, if they wanted to be a little more specific, at the time 'When people were beginning the first period of their sleep.' Later in the night might be called 'Almost the morning light' or the time 'When the rooster sings'; or, to get really specific, 'When the rooster sings for the first time' or the second time, and so on. And then we're ready for the cows again."

Contrast the natural clocks of Burundi to the clock time scheduling that prevails in the dominant Anglo culture of the United States. Our watches dictate when it is time to work and when to play; when each encounter must begin and end.

Even biological events are typically scheduled by the clock. It is normal to talk about it being "too early to go to sleep" or "not yet dinner time," or too late to take a nap or eat a snack. The hour on the clock, rather than the signal from our bodies, usually dictates when it is time to begin and stop. We learn these habits at a very early age. A newborn is fully capable of recognizing when he or she is hungry or sleepy. But it is not long before parents either adjust their baby's routine to fit their own or, in response to whatever may be the prevailing cultural standards (often defined by popular Dr. Spock–type advice manuals), train the child to eat and sleep to more "healthy" rhythms. The baby then learns when to be hungry and when to be sleepy.

As adults, some people are particularly susceptible to the control of the clock. Several years ago, in a series of classic studies, social psychologist Stanley Schachter and his colleagues observed the eating behaviors of obese and normal-weight people. Schachter theorized that a major factor in obesity is a tendency for eating to be governed by external cues from the surrounding environment. People of normal weight, he believed, are more responsive to their internal hunger pangs. One powerful external cue, Schachter hypothesized, is the clock.

To test his theory, Columbia University dormitory students were brought into a room in which the experimenters had doctored the clocks so that some subjects thought it was earlier than their usual dinner time and others thought it was later than their usual dinner time. Participants were told to help themselves to a bowl of crackers in front of them. As Schachter predicted, the obese people ate more crackers when they thought it was after their dinner time than when they were made to believe that it was not yet time for dinner. The time on the clock had no bearing on how many crackers the normal-weight subjects ate. They ate when they were hungry. The overweight people ate when the time on the clock said it was appropriate.[3] As my over-three-hundred-pound uncle replied when I once asked him if he was hungry, "I haven't been hungry in 45 years."

Is Time Money?

When the clock predominates, time becomes a valuable commodity. Clock time cultures take for granted the reality of time as fixed, linear, and measurable. As Ben Franklin once advised, "Remember that time is money." But to event time cultures, for whom time is considerably more flexible and ambiguous, time and money are very separate entities.

The clash between these attitudes can be jarring. When, on my sabbatical trip, I moved out of my hot tub/breakfast/Buddha routine and made a trip to the Taj Mahal, for example, the most frequent comments I heard spoken by first-world visitors referred to the amount of work that went into the building—variations on the question, "How long must that have taken?" Perhaps the second most frequent comment I heard from tourists in India went something like: "That embroidery must have taken forever. Can you imagine how much that would cost back home?" Finding bargains on foreigners' time is, in fact, a favorite vacation activity of many Westerners. But these comments wouldn't mean much to the Indian artist who spent months embroidering a fabric or to their ancestors who'd built the Taj Mahal. When event time predominates, the economic model of clock time makes little sense. Time and money are independent entities. You need to give time to time, as they say in Mexico.

In my travels in South America and Asia I have repeatedly been confused, and sometimes even harassed, by comments such as: "Unlike you Americans, time is not money for us." My usual response is something like: "But our time is all we have. It's our most valuable, our only really valuable, possession. How can you waste it like that?" Their typical retort—usually in a less frantic tone than my own—begins with unqualified agreement that time is, indeed, our most valuable commodity. But it is for exactly this reason, event timers argue, that time shouldn't be wasted by carving it into inorganic monetary units.

Burundi again provides a case in point. "Central Africans," Salvatore Niyonzima says, "generally disregard the fact that time is always money. When I want the time to wait for me, it does. And when I don't want to do something today—for any reason, whatever reason—I can just decide to do it tomorrow and it will be as good as today. If I lose some time I'm not losing something very important because, after all, I have so much of it."

Jean Traore, an exchange student from Burkina Faso in Eastern Africa, finds the concept of "wasting time" confusing. "There's no such thing as wasting time where I live," he observes. "How can you waste time? If you're not doing one thing, you're doing something else. Even if you're just talking to a friend, or sitting around, that's what you're doing." A responsible Burkina Faso citizen is expected to understand and accept this view of time, and to recognize that what is truly wasteful—sinful, to some—is to not make sufficient time available for the people in your life.

Mexico is another example. Frustrated U.S. business people often complain that Mexicans are *plagued* by a lack of attachment to time. But as writer Jorge Castaneda points out, "they are simply different . . . Letting and watching time go by, being late (an hour, a day, a week), are not grievous offenses. They simply indicate a lower rung on the ladder of priorities. It is more important to see a friend of the family than to keep an appointment or to make it to work, especially when work consists of hawking wares on street corners." There is also an economic explanation: "There is a severe lack of incentives for being on time, delivering on time, or working overtime. Since most people are paid little for what they do, the prize for punctuality and formality can be meaningless: time is often not money in Mexico."

Event time and clock time are not totally unrelated. But event time encompasses considerably more than the clock. It is a product of the larger gestalt; a result of social, economic, and environmental cues, and, of course, of cultural values. Consequently, clock time and event time often constitute worlds of their own. As Jorge Castaneda observes about Mexico and the United States, "time divides our two countries as much as any other single factor."[4]

Other Event Time Cultures

Life in industrialized society is so enmeshed with the clock that its inhabitants are often oblivious to how eccentric their temporal beliefs can appear to others. But many people in the world aren't as "civilized" as us. (Psychologist Julian Jaynes defines civilization as "the art of living in towns of such size that everyone does not know everyone else.") Even today, organic clocks like Burundi's time of the cows are often the only standard that insiders are willing to accept. For many, if not most, people in the world, living by mechanical clocks would feel as abnormal and confusing as living without a concrete schedule would to a Type A Westerner.

Anthropologists have chronicled many examples of contemporary event time cultures. Philip Bock, for example, analyzed the temporal sequence of a wake conducted by the Micmac Indians of Eastern Canada. He found that the wake can be clearly divided into gathering time, prayer time, singing time, intermission, and mealtime. But it turns out that none of these times are directly related to clock time. The mourners simply move from one time to another by mutual consensus. When do they begin and end each episode? When the time is ripe and no sooner.[5]

Robert Lauer tells of the Nuers from the Sudan, whose calendars are based on the seasonal changes in their environment. They construct their fishing dams and cattle camps, for example, in the month of *kur*. How do they know when it is *kur*? It's *kur* when they're building their dams and camps. They break camp and return to their villages in the months of *dwat*. When is it *dwat*? When people are on the move.[6] There's an old joke about an American on a whirlwind tour of Europe who is asked where he is. "If it's Tuesday," he responds, "this must be Belgium." If Nuers were asked the same question they might answer: "If it's Belgium, this must be Tuesday."

Many people use their social activities to mark time rather than the other way around. In parts of Madagascar, for example, questions about how long something takes might receive an answer like "the time of a rice-cooking" (about half an hour) or "the frying of a locust" (a quick moment). Similarly, natives of the Cross River in Nigeria have been quoted as saying "the man died in less than the time in which maize is not yet completely roasted" (less than fifteen minutes). Closer to home, not too many years ago the *New English Dictionary* included a listing for the term "pissing while"—not a particularly exact measurement, perhaps, but one with a certain cross-cultural translatability.

Most societies have some type of week, but it turns out it's not always seven days long. The Incas had a ten-day week. Their neighbors, the

Muysca of Bogota, had a three-day week. Some weeks are as long as sixteen days. Often the length of the week reflects cycles of activities, rather than the other way around. For many people, their markets are the main activity requiring group coordination. The Khasis of Assam, Pitirim Sorokin reports, hold their market every eighth day. Being practical people, they've made their week eight days long and named the days of the week after the places where the main markets occur.[7]

Natives of the Andaman jungle in India are another people with little need to buy calendars. The Andamanese have constructed a complex annual calendar built around the sequence of dominant smells of trees and flowers in their environment. When they want to check the time of year, the Andamanese simply smell the odors outside their door.[8]

The monks in Burma have developed a fool-proof alarm clock. They know it is time to rise at daybreak "when there is light enough to see the veins in their hand."[9]

There are groups who, even though they have wristwatches, prefer to measure time imprecisely. The anthropologist Douglas Raybeck, for example, has studied the Kelantese peasants of the Malay Peninsula, a group he refers to as the "coconut-clock" people. The Kelantese approach to time is typified by their coconut clocks—an invention they use as a timer for sporting competitions. This clock consists of a half coconut shell with a small hole in its center that sits in a pail of water. Intervals are measured by the time it takes the shell to fill with water and then sink—usually about three to five minutes. The Kelantese recognize that the clock is inexact, but they choose it over the wristwatches they own.[10]

Some people don't even have a single-word equivalent of "time." E. R. Leach has studied the Kachin people of North Burma. The Kachin use the word *ahkying* to refer to the time of the clock. The word *na* refers to a long time, and *tawng* to a short time. The word *ta* refers to springtime and *asak* to the time of a person's life. A Kachin wouldn't regard any of these words as synonymous with another. Whereas time for most Westerners is treated as an objective entity—it is a

noun in the English language—the Kachin words for time are treated more like adverbs. Time has no tangible reality for the Kachin.[11]

Many North American Indian cultures also treat time only indirectly in their language. The Sioux, for example, have no single word in their language for "time," "late," or "waiting." The Hopi, observes Edward Hall, have no verb tenses for past, present, and future. Like the Kachin people, the Hopi treat temporal concepts more like adverbs than nouns. When discussing the seasons, for example, "the Hopi cannot talk about summer being hot, because summer is the quality hot, just as an apple has the quality red," Hall reports. "Summer and hot are the same! Summer is a *condition:* hot." It is difficult for the Kachin and the Hopi to conceive of time as a quantity. Certainly, it is not equated with money and the clock. Time only exists in the eternal present.

Many Mediterranean Arab cultures define only three sets of time: no time at all, now (which is of varying duration), and forever (too long). As a result, American businessmen have often encountered frustrating communication breakdowns when trying to get Arabs to distinguish between different waiting periods—between, say, a long time and a very long time.[12]

I ran into similar dictionary problems once when trying to translate a time survey into Spanish for a Mexican sample. Three of my original English questions asked people when they would "expect" a person to arrive for a certain appointment, what time they "hoped" that person would arrive, and how long they would "wait" for them to arrive. It turns out that the three English verbs "to expect," "to hope," and "to wait" all translate into the single Spanish verb "*esperar.*" (The same verb is used in Portuguese.) I eventually had to use roundabout terms to get the distinctions across.

There is an old Yiddish proverb that says, "It's good to hope, it's the waiting that spoils it." Compare this to a culture whose language does not routinely distinguish between expecting, hoping, and waiting, and you have a pretty clear picture of how the latter feels about the clock. At first, I was frustrated by the inability to translate my questionnaires. Later, though, I came to see that my translation failures were telling me as much about Latin American concepts of time as were their responses to my formal questions. The silent and verbal languages of time feed upon each other.

Keeping Everything from Happening at Once

The primary function of clock time, it may be argued, is to prevent simultaneously occurring events from running into one another. "Time is nature's way of keeping everything from happening at once," observes a contemporary item of graffiti. The more complex our network of activities, the greater the need to formalize scheduling. A shared commitment to abide by clock time serves to coordinate traffic. The Khasis and Nuers are able to avoid governance by the clock because the demands on their time are relatively distinct and uncomplicated.

But we don't have to cross continents to see groups still operating on event time. Even in clock-time-dominated cultures, there are people whose temporal demands more closely resemble the sparsity of Asian villagers than that of the surrounding clock-coordinated society. In these subcultures, life takes on the cadence of event time.

Alex Gonzalez, a fellow social psychologist raised in a Mexican-American barrio in Los Angeles, has described the attitude toward time among his childhood friends who remain in his old neighborhood. Many of these people are unemployed, have little prospect of employment, and, he observes, almost no future time perspective. His old neighborhood, Gonzalez says, is filled with people who congregate loosely each day and wait for something to capture their interest. Their problem is not so much finding time for their activities as it is to find activities to fill their time. They stay with the event until, by mutual consent, it feels like time to move on. Time is flat. Watches are mostly ornaments and symbols of status. They're rarely for telling time.[13]

How would these people react if you gave them a Day Runner? Probably like Jonathan Swifts's Lilliputians did to Gulliver, who looked at his watch before doing anything. He called it his oracle. The Lilliputians he met in his travels decided that Gulliver's watch must be his God. In other words, they thought he was crazy.

The Advantage of Temporal Flexibility

Clock time cultures tend to be less flexible in how they schedule activities. They are more likely to be what anthropologist Edward Hall calls monochronic or M-time schedulers: people who like to focus on one activity at a time. Event time people, on the other hand, tend to prefer polychronic or P-time scheduling: doing several things at once.[14] M-time people like to work from start to finish in linear sequence: the first task is begun and completed before turning to another, which is then begun and completed. In polychronic time, however, one project goes on until there is an inclination or inspiration to turn to another, which may lead to an idea for another, then back to the first, with intermittent and unpredictable pauses and resumptions of one task or another. Progress on P-time occurs a little at a time on each task.

P-time cultures are characterized by a strong involvement with people. They emphasize the completion of human transactions rather than keeping to schedules. Two Burundians deep in conversation, for example, will typically choose to arrive late for their next appointment rather than cut into the flow of their discussion. Both would be insulted, in fact, if their partner were to abruptly terminate the conversation before it came to a spontaneous conclusion. "If you value people," Hall explains about the sensibility of P-time cultures, "you must hear them out and cannot cut them off simply because of a schedule."

P-time and M-time don't mix well. Allen Bluedorn, a professor of management at the University of Missouri, and his colleagues have found that M-time individuals are happier and more productive in M-time organizations while polychronic people do better in polychronic ones. These findings are applicable not only to foreign cultures, but also to different organizational cultures in the United States.[15]

Both M-time and clock time thinking tend to be concentrated in achievement-oriented, industrialized societies like the United States. P-time and event time are more common in third-world economies. In general, people who live on P-time are less productive—by Western economic standards, at least—than are M-time people. But there are occasions when polychronicity is not only more people-oriented, but also more productive. Rigid adherence to schedules can cut things short just when they are beginning to move forward. And as the invention of the word processor has taught even the most rigid of M-time people, working in nonlinear progression, spontaneously shifting attention from one section of a project to another, making connections from back to front as well as vice versa, can be both liberating and productive.

The most fruitful approach of all, however, is one that moves flexibly between the worlds of P-time and M-time, event time and clock time, as suits the situation. Some of the newer entrants into the economics of industrialization have managed monetary success without wholesale sacrifice of their traditional commitment to social obligations. Once again, the Japanese, with their blend of traditional Eastern and modern Western cultures, provide a noteworthy example.

A few years ago, I received a letter from Kiyoshi Yoneda, a businessman from Tokyo who has spent more than five years living in the West. My research on cross-national differences in the pace of life, which found that the Japanese had the fastest pace of life in the world, had just been reported in the international press. Mr. Yoneda wrote because he was concerned (with good reason, I might add) about the superficiality of my understanding of Japanese attitudes toward time. He wanted me to understand that the Japanese may be fast, but that doesn't mean that they treat the clock with the same reverence as people in the West.

Meetings in Japan, he pointed out, start less punctually and end much more "sluggishly" than they do in the United States. "In the Japanese company I work for," he wrote, "meetings go all the way until some agreement is made, or until everybody is tired; and the end is not sharply predefined by a scheduled time. The agreement is often not clearly stated. Perhaps in order to compensate [for] the unpredictability of the closing time of a meeting, you are not blamed if you [go] away before the meeting is over. Also, it's quite all right to sleep during the meeting. For instance, if you are an engineer and not interested in the money-counting aspects of a project, nobody expects you to stay wide awake paying attention to discussions concerning details of accounting. You may fall asleep, do your reading or writing, or stand up to get some coffee or tea."

Monochronic and polychronic organizations each have their weaknesses. Monochronic systems are prone to undervaluing the humanity of their members. Polychronic ones tend toward unproductive chaos. It would seem that the most healthy approach to P-time and M-time is to hone skills for both, and to execute mixtures of each to suit the situation. The Japanese blend offers one provocative example of how people take control of their time, rather than the other way around.

More Time Wars

Because cultural norms are so widely shared by the surrounding society, people often forget that their own rules are arbitrary. It is easy to confuse cultural normalcy with ethnocentric superiority. When people of different cultures interact, the potential for misunderstanding exists on many levels. For example, members of Arab and Latin cultures usually stand much closer when they're speaking to people than we do in the United States, a fact we frequently misinterpret as aggression or disrespect. Similarly, we often misconstrue the intentions of people with temporal customs different from our own. Such are the difficulties of communicating the silent languages of culture.

Nearly every traveler has experienced these blunders, in the forms of their own misunderstanding of the motives of the surrounding culture as well as others' misinterpretations of theirs. A particularly frequent source of mishaps involves clashes between clock time and event time. Fortunately, most of our stumblings are limited to unpleasant miscommunications. When misunderstandings occur at a higher level, however, they can be serious business.

An example of this occurred in 1985, when a group of Shiite Muslim terrorists hijacked a TWA jetliner and held 40 Americans hostage, demanding that Israel release 764 Lebanese Shiite prisoners being held in prison. Shortly after, the terrorists handed the American hostages over to Shiite Muslim leaders, who assured everybody that nothing would happen if the Israelis met their demands.

At one point during the delicate negotiations Ghassan Sablini, the number-three man in the Shiite militia Amal (who had assumed the role of militant authorities), announced that the hostages would be handed back to the hijackers in two days if no action was taken on their demand that Israel release its Shiite prisoners. This created a very dangerous situation. The U.S. negotiators knew that neither they nor the Israelis could submit to these terrorist demands without working out a face-saving compromise. But by setting a limit of "two days" the Shiite leaders made a compromise unlikely and had elevated the crisis to a very dangerous level. People held their breath. At the last minute, however, Sablini was made to understand how his statement was being interpreted. To everyone's relief, he explained: "We said a couple of days but we were not necessarily specifying 48 hours."[16]

Forty deaths and a possible war were nearly caused by a miscommunication over the meaning of the word "day." To the U.S. negotiators, the word referred to a technical aspect of time: 24 hours. For the Muslim leader, a day was merely a figure of speech meaning "a while." The U.S. negotiators were thinking on clock time. Sablini was on event time.

NOTES

1. Lauer, R. (1981). *Temporal Man: The Meaning and Uses of Social Time.* New York: Praeger.

2. Jones, J. (1993). An exploration of temporality in human behavior. In Schank, R., and Langer, E. (eds.), *Beliefs, Reasoning, and Decision-Making: Psycho-Logic in Honor of Bob Abelson.* Hillsdale, NJ: Lawrence Erlbaum.

3. Schachter, S., and Gross, L. (1968). Manipulated time and eating behavior. *Journal of Personality and Social Psychology* 10, 93–106.

4. Castaneda, J. (1995, July). Ferocious differences. *The Atlantic Monthly,* 68–76, 73, 74.

5. Bock, P. (1964). Social structure and language structure. *Southwestern Journal of Anthropology* 20, 393–403.

6. Lauer, R. H. (1981). *Temporal Man: The Meaning and Uses of Social Time.* New York: Praeger.

7. Sorokin, P. (1964). *Sociocultural Causality, Space, Time.* New York: Russel and Russel.

8. Rifkin, J. (1987, September/October). Time wars: A new dimension shaping our future. *Utne Reader,* 46–57.

9. Thompson, E. P. (1967). Time, work-discipline, and industrial capitalism. *Past and Present* 38, 56–97.

10. Raybeck, D. (1992). The coconut-shell clock: Time and cultural identity. *Time and Society* 1 (3), 323–40.

11. Leach, E. R. (1961). *Rethinking Anthropology.* London: Athlone Press.

12. Hall, E. (1983). *The Dance of Life.* Garden City, NY: Doubleday.

13. Gonzalez has also done important research on the subject of time. See Gonzalez, A., and Zimbardo, P. (1985, March). Time in perspective. *Psychology Today,* 20–26.

14. Hall, E. (1983). *The Dance of Life.* Garden City, NY: Doubleday.

15. Bluedorn, A., Kaufman, C., and Lane, P. (1992). How many things do you like to do at once? An introduction to monochronic and polychronic time. *Academy of Management Executive* 6, 17–26.

16. UPI (1985, June 23). Ships with 1,800 Marines off Lebanon. Reprinted in *The Fresno Bee,* A1.

THINKING ABOUT THE READING

What is the difference between *clock time* and *event time?* How are these different types of time related to the level of development of a particular culture? Levine seems to be arguing that event time is a less stressful, more healthy way for people to live their lives than clock time, even though clock time is a characteristic of more advanced societies. Do you think an achievement-oriented, technologically complex society like the United States could ever exist on event time? If not, are there ways that society could reduce the stressful effects of clock time? As you ponder this question, make sure you address how other institutions (economy, family, politics, education, and so on) would be affected. What lessons can you draw from this article about Americans' strong tendency to view societies that aren't as "sophisticated" as theirs as somehow inferior?

Fashions in Childbirth

Jessica Mitford

In childbirth, as in other human endeavors, fashions start with the rich, are then adopted by the aspirant middle class with an assist from the ever-watchful media, and may or may not eventually filter down to the poor.

Beginning in the early years of the twentieth century, more and more well-to-do American women chose hospitals as the site of their lying-in. This was much encouraged by the medical profession, for several reasons: it relieved the family doctor of long hours at the patient's bedside waiting for the birth to happen; it gave impetus to the development of obstetrics as a medical specialty; it allowed for bringing into play the ever-proliferating technological improvements that were only available in a hospital setting; and it mandated complete control of parturition by doctors to the exclusion of midwives, marking another step in the passing of power over the birth process from traditional female to professional male. (There has been something of a parallel development in England, except that there, the really rich never have adjusted to the idea of turning out of their commodious, well-staffed houses into the sterile and regimented atmosphere of a hospital. In the 1980s it was still a matter of surprise and comment when Princess Diana decided to have her firstborn in a hospital.)

For the expectant mother, an overriding consideration in choice of hospital over home birth was the promise held out by the former of alleviation of pain, via ever more up-to-date anesthetics for those who could afford them.

Looking over the literature on pain in childbirth, beginning with the Bible (as God said to Eve in one of His bad moods, "In sorrow shalt thou bring forth children"), one can readily appreciate the terror that assailed women at the prospect. Actually God's injunction to Eve was mild compared to the horrendous description in the Church of England's *Book of Common Prayer* for "The Thanksgiving of Women After Child-Birth": "The snares of death compassed me round about; and the pains of hell gat hold upon me." As a small child, wishing—like most children—to know precisely what was in store for me when I grew up, I remember reading and re-reading this awful warning each Sunday morning in church, while the clergyman droned on with his dull sermon. My mother, asked what it felt like to have a baby, was hardly reassuring: "Like an orange being stuffed up your nostril," she said.

In view of these dire predictions, it's little wonder that a principal factor determining fashions in childbirth involved the whole matter of avoidance of pain, initially centered on the quest for the best available anesthetic.

Shortly before World War I, numerous rich American women made pilgrimages to Germany for their accouchements, there to savor the delights of a new discovery, "Twilight Sleep." Having partaken of this miracle, they couldn't praise it enough; not only was delivery completely painless, they said, but their babies turned out amazingly healthy, beautiful, and intelligent. Arbiters of fashion, society leaders like Mrs. John Jacob Astor, joined forces with feminists in a campaign to end once and for all the scourge of suffering in childbirth. Newspapers and magazines took up the cause. In 1915, the Twilight Sleep Maternity Hospital was established in Boston under the leadership of Dr. Eliza Taylor Ransom, founder of the New England Twilight Sleep Association.[1]

Confronted by this deluge of influential female demand, doctors and hospitals soon fell into line, and by the late 1930s Twilight Sleep had become the anesthetic of choice, routinely administered in the more go-ahead hospitals along the Eastern seaboard. Obstetricians welcomed it because it gave them more control over the laboring woman than the chloroform/ether routine. Furthermore, the procedure resulted in an influx of paying patients, for whom the hospitals provided luxurious, tastefully decorated private wards, far from the cluttered institutional quarters of the charity patients.

The ingredients that produced the miracle of Twilight Sleep are akin to those used in the "truth serum" we read about in sensational accounts of interrogations of prisoners of war and other captives at the mercy of their jailers. In 1940, Dr. Joseph B. De Lee described the procedure as applied to the captive patient at the mercy of her obstetrician. "Naturally," he wrote, "the profession eagerly grasped this opportunity to relieve women of the pain of childbirth, and these drugs soon were extensively employed here and abroad."[2]

In Twilight Sleep, hypodermic injections of morphine combined with scopalomine (a powerful hallucinogenic and amnesiac) and pentobarbitol sodium were given every hour:

> The object is to maintain the patient in a state of amnesia, and this is determined by testing her memory.... Shortly after the second injection, the patient is asked if she remembers what has gone before, has she seen the nurse or intern? If she remembers, another dose is given. If not, nothing is done for an hour, when, if the mind seems to be clearer, 1/300 grain of scopalomine is given. Care must be exercised that the woman does not attain full consciousness....
>
> During the pains she moves about restlessly, or turns from one side to the other, or grunts a little, and occasionally opens her eyes. She will respond to questions, but incoherently. As the second stage [movement of baby out of the cervix into the birth canal] draws near its end she bears down and becomes very restless.

> Occasionally this becomes extreme, and several nurses are required to hold her.... A few whiffs of ether are often needed as the head passes through the vulva.

A graphic description of Twilight Sleep as witnessed by a father appeared in *They All Hold Swords*, a memoir of pre–World War II days by Cedric Belfrage. Cedric and his wife, Molly Castle, both young, adventurous British journalists, somehow ended up in Southern California for the birth of their baby in 1936. Thinking it would surely be a boy, they named the unborn child Fred. They chose a small bungalow hospital, a unique feature of which was that Cedric was allowed to be present throughout the entire procedure—unheard of in those days.

The doctor explained that he would be giving Molly the first of several dopes which would blot out her memory. "Soon, she began to moan.... Between two pains she said, 'I hope you don't mind me crying out a bit now, darling. I could control my will before but now after the drugs I can't control it anymore.'" As hours went by the doctor called the nurse to administer more injections. "'She will continue to show apparent signs of consciousness during the pains,' he said. 'But tomorrow she won't remember anything about it.'"

Later, Molly was wheeled into the delivery room, where the doctor strapped her onto a table.

> The nurse put the nose-cap over Molly's face and began sprinkling ether on it from a perforated can.... Suddenly Molly seemed to come alive; she fought out wildly. Three of us were holding her, but she managed to wrench a hand free to claw frantically at the cap over her nose. She opened her eyes wide and gave a shrill, terrified scream. It was nearly a quarter of an hour before she was completely quiet again. The doctor remained calm, washing his hands over and over again in the corner. He said it was the dope she had had before that made her react this way to ether. She would remember nothing about it afterwards.
>
> She was snoring now, her body limp, her face almost covered by the ether cap. The doctor

began probing with his great forceps. A lot of blood came. . . .

He grasped something between the long, invisible arms of the forceps. He pulled hard. . . . He took a pair of scissors in one hand and in a careful, matter-of-fact way cut a slit to make the opening wider. A minute later the round object was almost out. . . . Everything was a mass of blood and I thought Fred must be dead already.

To Cedric Belfrage's untrained eye the newborn "was exactly, in color and texture and size, like a large rabbit freshly skinned. . . . I could see that Fred was a girl." The doctor slapped her; she yelped. Some hours later, when Molly woke up, "I told her she had had a fine rabbit. She remembered nothing since the second shot in the arm, she said, except a vague nightmare memory of seeing people in gas-masks leaning over her, which made her think the war had started."

So much for a father's viewpoint. Some observations by health professionals, beginning with Sheila Kitzinger, author of *The Complete Book of Pregnancy and Childbirth*:

Many women have described it as "twilight nightmare" because of its side effects. The usual amnesiac scopalomine (also known as "scope" or "the bomb") can cause total disorientation which may not end when the labor ends, thus its nightmarish quality. It is supposed to make women forget their labor but, in fact, most women report hazy memories of having felt like an animal howling in pain.[3]

It was my impression from my own birth experiences in California, and those of various friends whose babies were born after 1940, that Twilight Sleep had vanished from the scene around the outbreak of World War II—presumably because of the potential dangers to mother and child of the massive amounts of anesthetic required.

I was surprised to learn that this was not so. For decades after it was forsaken by the cognoscenti, Twilight Sleep was still used in out-of-the-way places, mainly for clinic patients, indigents or the uninsured.

In 1989 Dr. Arlan Cohn, an internist in Berkeley, California, told me about "a form of outrageous anesthesia used at times during labor in the mid-fifties when I took my internship in St. Louis. The mixture of scopalomine and Demerol or morphine injected into the mother resulted in an acute psychotic reaction during which the mother would scream out the darkest secrets of her life in a stream-of-consciousness babble that would have made James Joyce blush. The mother would then awake from this nightmare with total amnesia for her wild behavior. God only knows what this crazy injection did to the fetal brain."

Mary Welcome, a certified nurse-midwife practicing in Atlanta, saw Twilight Sleep administered as late as 1974, when she was doing her nurse's training. In 1989 she told me, "I can recall we would have hordes of laboring women—the doctors would knock them out, you know, with scopalomine, an amnesia drug, heavy-duty narcotics and sedatives. The women would be thrashing about in bed and yelling—but totally unaware of any of this. You had to put the rails up to keep them safe. Our nursing instructors told us you should be listening to the heartbeat every fifteen minutes, but the nurses would do this maybe twice in an eight-hour shift. And you'd look at their nursing records and realize that those women were left alone in there for hours. They were drugged up and knocked out. And the babies were often born unconscious themselves. You'd have to give them drugs to reverse the narcotics the mother had, and they'd stay sleepy for days."

In 1990, in a belated effort to discover the precise nature of the anesthetic I had endured in 1941 (hot air pumped up the rectum), I consulted numerous local physicians, but none of them had ever heard of such a thing. They tactfully suggested that I might have been hallucinating after the inhalation of gas. One wrote, "I'll bet my career that it was inhaled gas and not an enema that put you under. Gas anesthesia tends to scramble the mind of mother (and newborn) temporarily." He added that the use of inhaled gas is now "uniformly recognized as potentially very dangerous to mother and newborn."

Eventually the mystery was solved, again by a passage from Joseph De Lee's *The Principles and Practice of Obstetrics.* He set forth the formula for "rectal ether instillation" followed by a soothingly sophomoric lullaby presumably meant to be memorized by the attending obstetrician:

Early in the labor the patient is addressed as follows: "Mrs. _____, we are desirous of making your labor as painless as possible, and are prepared to do so without danger to you or your baby. Our success in relieving you will depend somewhat upon your cooperation. Therefore, when your pains become uncomfortable let the nurse know and she will give you two, or perhaps three, capsules (pentobarbital sodium, each $1\frac{1}{2}$ grains) to relieve you.

"When your pains again become uncomfortable notify her as before and she will give you another capsule or two (pentobarbital sodium), or maybe a hypodermic (morphine sulfate, $\frac{1}{6}$ or $\frac{1}{4}$ grain).

"Later, when this medicine begins to lose its effect, let her know and she will inject a solution into your rectum (ether-oil or ether-paraldehyde oil)."[4]

Dr. De Lee was an articulate and extremely influential early proponent of the notion that *all* births, including those designated "low-risk," are inherently pathogenic and should be treated as such. "It always strikes physicians as well as laymen as bizarre," he wrote, "to call labor an abnormal function, a disease, and yet it is a decidedly pathological process."

His theories were sprung upon a waiting world—of obstetricians, that is—in his exhaustive *Principles and Practice,* a 1,200-page tome first published in 1913 and thereafter reprinted many times until 1940. A sampling of the De Lee philosophy, following his description of scientific advances in obstetrics:

This knowledge will raise the level and the dignity of our profession. Why is this process so slow? I believe, because, up to within a few years, the profession, and the public, considered childbirth to be a normal function, one

requiring little medical supervision and hardly worth the attention of an expert surgeon. . . .

It must be evident to anyone who will give the matter unbiased thought that, if we can invest obstetrics with the dignity of a great science, which it deserves, if we will acknowledge the pathogenic nature of this function, improvement will follow in every field of practice, and that anachronism, the midwife, will spontaneously disappear.[5]

These concepts, incorporating as they did the twin aspirations of enhanced professional prestige and assured monopoly of their chosen field, were quickly embraced by De Lee's fellow practitioners. The fourfold remedy for the disease of childbirth, adapted from De Lee's teachings, continued to be standard practice in obstetrical wards for at least two generations. These were to be uniformly applied to all births, without distinction—forget about high risk/low risk. To summarize:

1. The patient should be placed in the "lithotomy position." (Incidentally, this expression was one I had not heard until I started consorting with childbirth professionals, who told me it means lying supine with legs in air, bent and wide apart, supported by stirrups. However, the *Oxford English Dictionary* gives but one definition: "Lithotomy: The operation or art of cutting for stone in the bladder.")

2. She should be sedated from the first stage of labor.

3. The physician should perform an episiotomy, a cut of several inches through the skin and muscles between the vagina and anus to enlarge the space through which the baby must pass.

4. The physician should use forceps to effectuate delivery.

These measures, De Lee emphasized, could offset the dangers of unaided birth, in which "only a small minority of women escape damage by the direct action of the natural process itself. So frequent are these bad effects, that I have often wondered whether Nature did not deliberately intend women to be used up in the process of reproduction, in a manner analogous to that of the salmon, which dies after spawning."

The opening shot in defense of the spawning salmon, heretofore voiceless sufferers caught in a net of obstetrical procedures, came from a most unlikely quarter: *The Ladies' Home Journal,* which in 1957 and 1958 ran a series of hair-raising letters on the subject.

To put this in context: The *LHJ* was then, is now, and ever shall be one of those multimillion-circulation women's mags whose essential loyalty is to their advertisers, their contents generally consisting of short, exhortative text pieces on how to be a better wife/mother, how to dress better for less, how to cook for a crowd of teenagers, etc., surrounded by lovely huge color ads bearing approximately the same message. In *The Feminine Mystique,* published in 1963, Betty Friedan plunged into a devastating analysis and critique of the insipid outpourings of these magazines, one of her examples being the *LHJ.* Combing through issue after issue of the late 1950s, she turned up some marvelous plums for her chapter titled "The Happy Housewife Heroine." Yet buried somewhere in those issues was a remarkable correspondence starkly headlined "Cruelty in the Maternity Wards."

Why—and how—the ultrarespectable, superbland *LHJ* got involved in a head-on confrontation with the American medical establishment remains a mystery. In 1990, I wrote to the present editor asking for enlightenment; she did not answer my letter. I can only conclude that it was one of those unpredictable moments in the life of a nation, an individual, or in this case a magazine, when a steamroller of pent-up anger may have overridden normal editorial caution.

In any event, in November 1957 *The Ladies' Home Journal* published a brief letter in its reader-mail column from a registered nurse (name withheld at her request, as she feared reprisals from the medical community) asking for an investigation of "the tortures that go on in modern delivery rooms":

I have seen doctors who have charming examination-room manners show traces of sadism in the delivery room. One I know does cutting and suturing without anesthetic. He has nurses use a mask to stifle the patient's outcry.

Great strides have been made in maternal care, but some doctors still say, "Tie them down so they won't give us any trouble."

Six months later, the *LHJ* editor reported a flood of letters' relating childbirth experiences "so shocking that they deserve national attention." The May 1958 issue devoted many pages to excerpts from this outpouring of complaints, adding the requisite sententious disclaimer that "the *Journal* does not question that the overwhelming majority of obstetricians and maternity hospitals resent such practices."

A few quotations from the *LHJ*'s letters to the editor of May 1958 convey the general feeling. A mother of three, all born in different hospitals with different doctors, seemed dismayed at the yawning chasm between promise and reality:

The practice of obstetrics is the most modern and medieval, the kindest to mothers and the cruelest. I know of many instances of cruelty, stupidity and harm done to mothers by obstetricians who are callous or completely indifferent. . . . Women are herded like sheep through an obstetrical assembly line, are drugged and strapped on tables while their babies are forceps-delivered. Obstetricians today are businessmen who run baby factories.

Another wrote:

I was immediately rushed into the labor room. A nurse prepared me. Then, with leather cuffs strapped around my wrists and legs, I was left alone for nearly eight hours, until the actual delivery.

Recurrent complaints concerned the strapping down of the laboring mother; the prohibition of the father's presence during labor and delivery; and the general assembly-line atmosphere.

The May issue gave rise to yet another ava-lanche of letters, many of which were printed in the issue of December 1958:

> Far too many doctors, nurses and hospitals seem to assume that just because a woman is about to give birth she becomes a nitwit, an incompetent, reduced to the status of a cow (and not too valuable a cow, at that). . . .
>
> I was strapped to the delivery table on Saturday morning and lay there until I was delivered on Sunday afternoon. When I slipped my hand from the strap to wipe sweat from my face I was severely reprimanded by the nurse. . . . For thirty-six hours my husband didn't know whether I was living or dead. I would have given anything if I could just have held his hand.

Some reported babies born dead, or hope-lessly brain-damaged, victims (the writers sus-pected) of obstetrician-mandated delayed deliv-ery and too much anesthetic.

With few exceptions, the doctors who re-sponded to these allegations against the profes-sion issued blanket denials; nothing of the kind ever happened in *their* hospitals. An obstetri-cian's wife wrote indignantly of the many sacri-fices she had made: "I have broken many an en-gagement, kept many dinners warm, and cut vacations short because of my husband's con-cern for his patients." Well, really! Aren't these minor inconveniences supposed to be a normal part of any conscientious doctor's way of life?

Nurses, also, had their say. Like the registered nurse whose letter originally stirred up the hornet's nest, these asked for protective anonym-ity. Most came down squarely on the side of the complaining mothers, and deplored the mental-ity of the profession:

> Because of what is politely termed "medical ethics," the truth of much bad practice is kept from the public. Personally I feel it is compa-rable to the "ethics" which keeps criminals from telling on their accomplices. . . . What makes me angry is that the incompetent and unscrupu-lous people get away with so much.

Whether or not these *cris de coeur* had any di-rect effect on the development of a feminist birth philosophy as a feature of the women's liberation movement, then some years in the future, is at this late stage a matter of conjecture.*

In any event, predating the women's move-ment of the sixties and seventies there arose a new phenomenon: "natural childbirth," originat-ing with the 1933 publication of *Natural Child-birth* (later called *Childbirth Without Fear*) by an English obstetrician, Dr. Grantly Dick-Read. This was superseded in the 1950s by the work of Dr. Fernand Lamaze, a French physician whose methods derived from Pavlovian theories he had studied in the Soviet Union. Thus, as in the case of Twilight Sleep, the innovators were foreign male physicians, and the first Americans to ex-plore the possibilities offered by the new tech-niques were well-to-do women who traveled to Europe for the purpose.

On the face of it, the two systems seem simi-lar. Dr. Dick-Read's view was that the pains of childbirth are largely caused by fear-induced ten-sion, which could be greatly ameliorated by in-struction ahead of time about the childbearing process combined with classes in relaxation, ex-ercises to keep the body supple, and training in deep breathing. Lamaze's method, which he called *"accouchement sans douleur"* (labor with-out pain),[6] also required prenatal instruction in the physiology of pregnancy and labor, limber-ing-up exercises and breathing techniques—he favored rapid, shallow panting over Dr. Dick-Read's deep breathing.

Be that as it may—whether one is a deep breather or a shallow panter—the medical estab-lishment after some initial resistance adopted (and modified for its convenience) the concept of natural childbirth and its concomitant, prena-tal classes in which a lecturer trained in the method explains how it's done. Beginning in the

---

The Ladies' Home Journal series is, however, mentioned in several of the books I consulted, including Wertz and Wertz's *Lying-In* and Margot Edwards and Mary Waldorf's *Reclaim-ing Birth*.

1970s as a response to the women's movement, these classes are now routinely offered in the posher U.S. hospitals under the umbrella term "prepared childbirth." Fathers, married or unmarried (discreetly termed "partners" in the promotional lit) are cordially invited to come and breathe along in class, and if inclined are welcome to stay in the hospital throughout the labor and delivery.

(Incidentally, the "prepared childbirth" sessions are not to be confused with prenatal care, in which from the earliest stages of pregnancy the expectant mother goes for regularly scheduled visits to her midwife or to her obstetrician for physical examination, advice on nutrition, and the ubiquitous tests of urine, blood, etc. Prenatal care is universally thought to be an essential preamble to a successful outcome: midwives, obstetricians, experts here and abroad, are united in its advocacy.)

Also-rans in the natural-birth sweeps—but nevertheless influential voices—were Robert Bradley of Denver and a French physician, Frédérick Leboyer. While each had his share of enthusiastic supporters, both to some extent eventually fell afoul of the feminist movement.

Dr. Bradley, a pioneer of "husband-coached childbirth" (the title of his book published in 1965 by Harper & Row), was implacably opposed to the use of drugs in childbirth, and himself presided over some thirteen thousand drug-free births in which the husband-coach was a full participant. But he used unfortunate terminology, referring to the uterus as the "baby box" and the clitoris as the "passion button." It seemed to some women that Bradley was enlisting husbands in a male power alliance in which husband and obstetrician became the benign custodians of the little woman's physiology and behavior. Bradley's reputation was not enhanced when he remarked to a father, "Let's face a fact: they [pregnant women] are nuttier than a fruitcake."

Unlike others of his contemporaries—Lamaze, Dick-Read, Bradley, *et al.*—who had embraced the cause of natural childbirth, Leboyer had scant sympathy for the laboring mother. On the con-

trary, his pity was all for the struggling fetus trying desperately to make its way through the rigid birth canal into an alien environment.

To help it recover from this horrible experience, he advocated "gentle birth," described in his book *Birth Without Violence* (New York: Knopf, 1975). The delivery room should be dimly lighted and all present very quiet—Leboyer didn't much like having fathers around, as they are apt to exclaim loudly at the first sight of the newborn. As soon as the babe emerged, Leboyer lowered it into a lukewarm bath, simulating its former watery home. For a soft and kindly introduction to its fellow human beings, Leboyer—*not* the mother—would give the baby a gentle, reassuring massage; only then would the mother be given it to hold.

As for the mother, Leboyer surmised that for the baby she must appear to be a monster incarnate. At the onset of labor it finds itself being crushed, stifled, assaulted:

> With its heart bursting, the infant sinks into hell . . . the mother is driving it out. At the same time she is holding it in, preventing its passage. It is she who is the enemy. She who stands between the child and life. Only one of them can prevail. It is mortal combat . . . not satisfied with crushing, the monster twists it in a refinement of cruelty.[7]

Women who welcome Leboyer's advocacy of softly lit, quiet labor rooms in contrast to the bright lights and constant banging about encountered in many hospitals—and may also favor a nice warm bath for the newborn—can hardly be expected to choke down the rest of his strangely misogynistic views of motherhood.

The dramatic transformation of the father's role from the 1960s to the late 1980s is described by Warren Hinckle III, who sampled both. "Hink Three," as I call him for short, was one of the trio of *Ramparts* editors, all under thirty, who in the 1960s tweaked the noses of President Johnson, the CIA, and the military with stunning exposés that contributed in no small measure to LBJ's downfall and the eventual ending of the Vietnam War. "Never trust anybody over thirty!" was the slogan of Hink III and his editorial colleagues, Robert Scheer and Dugald Stermer.

Hinckle's account of fatherhood in the sixties:

In Irish San Francisco, birthing was a simple division of labor: The woman went to the hospital, and the man went to the bar. The intimate details of birth were left to the mother and the mother-in-law on the reasonable ground that they had experience in such matters.

I waited for the birth of my first two children in the yellow half-light of Cookie Picetti's Star Cafe on Kearny Street. They were born three years apart but the theater of nativity remained the same: The phone rang in the bar. Cookie picked up the receiver and listened intently. A smile as broad as a barge crossed his face. "Ya godda goil," said Cookie. He hung up the phone. I bought drinks for the house. The house bought drinks back.[8]

Onward to 1989. The goils are grown up and Warren Hinckle is remarried, his wife, Susan Cheever, expecting some time in November. They are living in New York; although Hink III is now in his fifties, his description of the Blessed Event seems perfectly trustworthy:

On the night of the earthquake [October 17, 1989] I was dragooned in a Lamaze class on the fifth floor of a grotty office building on New York's upper East Side, seated next to a Dentyne-popping yuppie.

"Now, everyone take off their shoes and get on the floor and the men can practice being human labor tables," said the instructor. She had a computer voice with a programmed smile.

When the men had been human labor tables long enough, there was a lot of huff-and-puff practice pain control breathing—"Let's take a deep, cleansing breath," said the computer voice. I excused myself to go to the bathroom and raced downstairs to a bar across the street and watched San Francisco burn on the television.

Back upstairs at the pain factory the ladies had finished breathing and the men were

putting their penny loafers back on and there was the smell of socks in the air.

"Now you guys just remember that you're glued in the labor room with your partner— you can't move an inch, you can wait to pee until after the baby is born," the instructor said, giggling girlishly.[9]

A couple of weeks later, the scene shifts to Mount Sinai hospital, where Dr. Herbert Jaffin decides to try for vaginal delivery, although Susan, age forty-six, had had a previous cesarean. Jaffin recommends the posture of "*Sitzfleisch*, loosely translated as sitting on your butt." Later, he proceeds "to violate the scripture of the more puritanical 'natural birth' advocates" by administering Pitocin and an epidural.

At the moment of birth, Dr. Jaffin "waved his tools [forceps] like a matador and proceeded to his art.

"Suddenly the baby was there all red, white and blue—blue of skin and red with blood and the goop of birth, with the whites of his eyes flashing, arms waving and flapping in the air."[10]

Thus the triumphal entry of Warren Hinckle IV, also known by me as Hink Four but called Quad by his proud parents and their friends; clearly an occasion of exhilaration for his doting papa.

Autre temps, autres moeurs. John Kenneth Galbraith in June 1989, answering a letter in which I had mentioned that I was writing this book, observed:

Alas, it is a subject to which I had not previously given more than three minutes' thought. Kitty and I had, over the years, discussed the circumstances which caused her, while in perfect health, to be confined to the hospital for a full 10 days when Alan was born, now close on to 50 years ago. Our offspring handled the whole situation in approximately two days. Anyhow, quite clearly this is something to be explored.

Yes, but also worth exploring is Professor Galbraith's not previously having given more than three minutes' thought to the subject. This conjures up the picture of his wife, Kitty, struggling bravely, solo, with the pangs of labor while JKG, busy man that he always was (and is), occupies himself with vital problems of national and international import.

If the scene could be reenacted today, we might visualize Galbraith being dragged by a giant hook, like those used in French theaters to remove unpopular performers, off the world stage and into his wife's delivery chamber. There his attention would be concentrated for a lot more than three minutes, as he breathes and strains, à la Dick-Read or Lamaze, in unison with Kitty until the great moment when he is called upon to himself cut the umbilical cord.

In the wake of these developments, new inventions mushroomed, some eminently sensible, others wild enough to qualify for Ripley's *Believe It Or Not*.

Item: Birthing stool, advertised in Ina May Gaskin's quarterly publication *The Birth Gazette*.[11] The stool is adapted from that used by centuries of midwives, whose kit included a wooden contraption that looks something like a toilet seat (minus, obviously, a watery flush), for squatting on during labor. The modern version is (according to the ad) "finely handcrafted of pine, leather and 4" foam," and looks quite comfy for the purpose.

Item: Another *sitzfleisch* gadget, the birth cushion, invented by Jason Gardosi of St. Mary's Hospital in London. Like the birthing stool, it is designed to support the thighs and allow for squatting deliveries. According to the London *Independent*, this method had "almost halved forceps deliveries of first babies, shortened second stage labor and resulted in less injury to the mother." At least sixty National Health Service hospitals were offering British maternity patients the option of using the cushion.[12]

Item: Underwater birth. I went to see a documentary film on this called *Water Baby*, produced and introduced by Karil Daniels of Point of View Productions. The movie shows practitioners delivering babies underwater in three countries: in the Soviet Union, Igor Charkovsky, who first promulgated the idea in the 1960s ("He's not a doctor, he's a boat builder," I was told by

Sheila Kitzinger, who is something less than a fan); in France, Dr. Michel Odent of the Centre Hospitalier Général de Pithiviers, who in *The Lancet* of December 24, 1983, reported the 100th birth underwater in his hospital, almost all without subsequent complications; and in the United States, Dr. Michael Rosenthal, obstetrician of the Family Birthing Center in Upland, California.

Underwater labor, viz., lying in a warm bath to ease the discomfort of contractions in the early stages, allowing as it does for freedom of movement absent the pull of gravity, has long been an option offered by midwives and other home-birth advocates. But in *Water Baby* we see the infant's head, body, and legs slowly emerging in a small birthing pool, sometimes with the enthusiastic "partner" alongside the mom. Having been accustomed to a watery environment for nine months, the commentator explains, the babe rather likes this. It doesn't need to breathe until the cord is cut, as it still gets oxygen from that source.

"Do many babies drown?" I asked nervously. Hardly any, Karil Daniels said; she had only heard of one case, rumored but never authenticated, in which the parents did it all by themselves in the family bathtub without a trained birth attendant.

Rather to my surprise—and relief—Ina May Gaskin, that birth innovator *par excellence . . .*, voiced the same misgivings. She didn't know how many documented cases of fetal deaths had been attributable to underwater births; but she did feel that two of the births shown in Karil Daniels's film "came dangerously near the edge." She also questioned the hygienic precautions, especially when other people—birth assistants and those ever-present "partners"—plunge full of enthusiasm into the tub along with mom and the unborn babe.

Ms. Gaskin's main, eminently commonsensical observation is that since our ancestors from time immemorial were born into air, along with all other mammals—puppies, kittens, giraffes, elephants, etc.—why disturb the natural order?

Item: Heading into the Twilight Zone, we learn of the Empathy Belly, designed by Linda

Ware, a "prenatal educator" in Redmond, Washington. The belly, consisting of a huge womb-like structure with large breasts, priced at $595, is designed to be worn by the male partner so that he can appreciate the discomfort of the later stages of pregnancy. It weighs thirty-five pounds, is guaranteed to cause backache, shortness of breath, and fatigue, and comes with a special pouch that presses on the wearer's bladder, creating an uncomfortable desire to urinate at inappropriate moments. According to its inventor, "a half hour in the Empathy Belly teaches a man more about what goes on during pregnancy. He ends up being more understanding and supportive about what a woman goes through. For most men, it opens up a new world of feelings. It's something they think about and enjoy." In short, the perfect Father's Day gift for the likes of Hink III or J. K. Galbraith.

Item: The Uterine University. In a development of the notion that one is never too young to learn, prenatal educators from Florida to Washington state are promoting devices for the in utero education of the fetus.

Offerings include Fetal Teaching Systems, cassettes to be worn by the mother-to-be on a body-belt, available from Mr. Shannon Thomas of Orlando, Florida; the "Listen Baby" fabric belt with two speakers and a little microphone, from Roger Hurst of Infant Technology in Denver; and the Pregaphone, invented by Dr. Rene Van de Carr of Santa Barbara, California.

Whether the fetus, swimming about in its amniotic fluid, enjoys the lessons—or whether it is bored by the whole idea—has not yet been fully researched, although Dr. Brent Logan of the Washington Institute of Prenatal Education in Snohomish does record a baby saying "Gogo" three times shortly after delivery. "The nurses were amazed," he said. (The newborn's utterance is, it seems to me, subject to at least two interpretations: was it saying "Go! Go!" meaning "Leave me alone!" or simply burping like any illiterate?)

Item: In what must be one of the most imaginative lawsuits of recent years, attorney Michael Box filed suit in Jefferson City, Missouri, contending that the state is illegally imprisoning an inmate's fetus. Box cited Missouri's antiabortion law, which says life begins at conception. If that is so, he said, "then fetuses are supposed to be like anyone else—they're a person, and they have constitutional rights."

He contends that key provisions of the Missouri law, upheld by the U.S. Supreme Court in its July 1989 ruling on the abortion issue, extend to the unborn "all the rights, privileges and immunities available to other persons." Hence the fetus (whose mother-to-be is serving a three-year sentence for forgery and stealing) has been illegally imprisoned—having itself never been charged with a crime, allowed to consult an attorney, convicted, or sentenced.

If this legal theory should prevail, will the courts be bombarded with Writs of Habeas Fetus?[13]

Aside from some of the zanier products of the ever-fertile American entrepreneurial imagination, there seems to be no doubt that for the affluent, and those with large, inclusive health insurance policies, hospital birth today can be a highly enjoyable experience.

Vying to capture the carriage trade, hospitals outdo each other in advertising birth à la mode, which, they assure us, offers all the cozy benefits of home birth in a safe hospital setting. Latching on to the popularity and publicity surrounding the home-birth movement of the 1970s, a typical ad like one from Eden Hospital in Castro Valley, California, shows a couple and baby with the headline "Having My Baby at Eden Was So Comforting, Almost Like Delivering at Home." At HCA West Paces Ferry Hospital in Atlanta, "Birthing suites feature early American furniture complete with a four-poster bed and a charming cradle." (Cost: $7,000 minimum.) Most offer rooming-in with the mother for the baby and the father, who—perhaps in deference to the shade of Dr. Semmelweis—is asked to wash his hands. Not only fathers, but siblings and anyone else the mother wants to invite are welcome to attend the birth. A champagne dinner for two served in the mother's room concludes this magnificent birthday treat.

In Alexandria, Virginia, in April 1990, I went to see the Alexandria Hospital, which, I was told, is the preferred place for yuppie births. This offers all the above-described advantages plus a pink dining room called "Le Bébé" with fresh flowers on each table for two, where the new parents can choose among filet mignon, "catch of the day," and chicken Kiev.

I can visualize a TV miniseries segment showing the delighted parents as they depart from these charming surroundings, clasping their pink bébé (there would be few of darker hue) and its brand-new Vuitton diaper carrier. In the final scene, they enter their comfortable dwelling, a bower of flowers sent by well-wishers, all to the background music of the Brahms Lullaby.

NOTES

1. "Twilight Sleep Association"
Again I am indebted to Wertz and Wertz, pp. 150–52.

2. "extensively employed here and abroad"
Joseph B. DeLee, *The Principles and Practice of Obstetrics* (Philadelphia: W. B. Saunders, 1940).

3. "an animal howling in pain"
Sheila Kitzinger, *The Complete Book of Pregnancy and Childbirth* (New York: Alfred A. Knopf, 1985) p. 241.

4. "ether-paraldehyde oil"
DeLee, op. cit.

5. "will spontaneously disappear"
DeLee, op. cit.

6. "labor without pain"
Fernand Lamaze, Painless Childbirth (Chicago: Henry Regnery, 1970).

7. "a refinement of cruelty"
Leboyer quotations are from *The New Our Bodies, Ourselves* (Boston Women's Health Book Collective, 1984). Other books consulted for accounts of Bradley and Leboyer are Margot Edwards and Mary Waldorf, *Reclaiming Birth;* Kitzinger, *The Complete Book of Pregnancy and Childbirth,* and Wertz and Wertz, *Lying-In.*

8. "The house bought drinks back"
Warren Hinckle, "Fifty-something," *San Francisco Examiner,* December 3, 1989.

9. "giggling girlishly"
Hinkle, op. cit.

10. "waving and flapping in the air"
Hinckle, op. cit.

11. *"The Birth Gazette"*
Quarterly publication, The Farm, Summertown, Tennessee, 38483.

12. "the option of using the cushion"
The Independent, London, July 7, 1989.

13. "Writs of Habeas Fetus"
San Francisco Chronicle, August 4, 1989.

THINKING ABOUT THE READING

Describe how contemporary methods of childbirth compare to those used in the early part of the 20th century. How does the history of childbirth conform to our conceptions of "progress"? At one point Mitford writes, ". . . for the affluent and those with large, inclusive health insurance policies, hospital birth today can be a highly enjoyable experience." But what about those who are less affluent? Describe how popular childbirth practices reflect dominant class values and maintain class differences. Also, how do these practices reflect the status of women at a given point in time?

CHAPTER 5

Building Identity:
The Social Construction of Self

Sociology reminds us that humans don't develop in a social vacuum. Other people, historical events, and social institutions can determine not only what we do and say but what we value and who we become. Our self-concept, identity, and sense of self-worth are derived from the reactions, real or imagined, of other people.

The fundamental task of any society is to reproduce itself—to create members whose behaviors, desires, and goals correspond to those defined as appropriate by that particular society. *Socialization* is the process by which individuals learn their culture and learn to live according to the norms of their society. It is how we learn to perceive our world, gain a sense of our own racial or ethnic identity, and interact appropriately with others. This learning process occurs within the context of several social institutions—schools, religious institutions, the mass media, and the family—and it extends beyond childhood. Adults must be resocialized into a new galaxy of norms, values, and expectations each time they leave or abandon old roles and enter new ones.

One of the most important outcomes of socialization, both for the individual and for society as a whole, is the development of a sense of self. The ability to modify our behavior to meet the expectations of other people and society in general rests on the development of the self. But sociologists tell us that our selves can change from situation to situation. In "The Gloried Self," Patricia and Peter Adler show how entry into a world of celebrity and glory can dramatically alter people's self-concepts. The authors focus on the experiences of varsity basketball players at a medium-sized university that has a tradition of basketball excellence. Although very few of us will ever become famous, idolized celebrities, this article nicely shows how self-concepts are derived from the reflected appraisals of others.

Socialization also teaches us what it means to be a man or a woman, and what we should and should not do across a range of situations. Whereas "sex" refers to biological characteristics, "gender" designates the psychological, social, and cultural aspects of maleness and femaleness. We learn to identify our sex and act in accordance with the gendered social expectations that go with it. Although such a process seems clear-cut, sociological evidence shows that it can sometimes be quite complex. Even the notion that there are two and only two sexes is sometimes called into question.

Transsexuals—people who believe they were born in the wrong-sexed bodies and seek to remedy the mistake through altering their physical appearance or undergoing surgery—provide an interesting example of the complexities of gender socialization. Through interviews and observations, Douglas Mason-Schrock, in "Transsexuals' Narrative Construction of the 'True Self,'" examines the process through which transsexuals construct their self-concepts. In a social world where the vast majority of people take their gender identities for granted, transsexuals face considerable cultural resistance. Mason-Schrock found that most transsexuals collaborate with others who serve as their models, guides, and sources of affirmation in creating a differently gendered true self. He also found that whereas transsexuals challenge some cultural ideas about sex (for instance, that it is biological and permanent), they also reinforce others (for instance, that there are only two sexes and an individual must be one or the other, even if that means "correcting" a mistake through surgery).

The Gloried Self

The Aggrandizement and the Constriction of Self

Patricia A. Adler and Peter Adler

. . . In this paper we describe and analyze a previously unarticulated form of self-identity: the "gloried" self, which arises when individuals become the focus of intense interpersonal and media attention, leading to their achieving celebrity. The articulation of the gloried self not only adds a new concept to our self repertoire but also furthers our insight into self-concept formation in two ways: it illustrates one process whereby dynamic contradictions between internal and external pressures become resolved, and it highlights the ascendance of an unintended self-identity in the face of considerable resistance.

The development of the gloried self is an outgrowth of individuals' becoming imbued with celebrity. It does not matter whether that celebrity is positive or negative; in our society we accord status and recognition for both fame and notoriety (Goldsmith 1983). Development of a gloried self is caused in part by the treatment of individuals' selves as objects by others. A "public persona" is created, usually by the media, which differs from individuals' private personas. These public images are rarely as intricate or as complex as individuals' real selves; often they draw on stereotypes or portray individuals in extreme fashion to accentuate their point. Yet the power of these media portrayals, reinforced by face-to-face encounters with people who hold these images, often causes indi-

viduals to objectify their selves to themselves. Individuals thus become initially alienated from themselves through the separation of their self-concept from the conception of their selves held by others. Ultimately they resolve this disparity and reduce their alienation by changing their self-images to bridge the gap created by others' perceptions of them, even though they may fight this development as it occurs.

Characteristically, the gloried self is a greedy self, seeking to ascend in importance and to cast aside other self-dimensions as it grows. It is an intoxicating and riveting self, which overpowers other aspects of the individual and seeks increasing reinforcement to fuel its growth. Yet at the same time, its surge and display violate societal mores of modesty in both self-conception and self-presentation. Individuals thus become embroiled in inner conflict between their desire for recognition, flattery, and importance and the inclination to keep feeding this self-affirming element, and the socialization that urges them to fight such feelings and behavioral impulses. That the gloried self succeeds in flourishing, in spite of individuals' struggle against it, testifies to its inherent power and its drive to eclipse other self-dimensions. . . .

Setting and Methods

Over a five-year period (1980–1985) we conducted a participant-observation study of a major college basketball program. . . .

The research was conducted at a medium-sized (6,000 students) private university (hereafter referred to as "the University") in the mid-south central portion of the United States, with a

We would like to thank Paul Colomy, Stanford Lyman, and Ralph Turner for comments on earlier versions of this manuscript, which is a modified version of a paper presented at the 1988 annual meeting of the American Sociological Association in Atlanta. Please address all correspondence to Dr. Peter Adler, Department of Sociology, University of Denver, Denver, CO 80208.

predominantly white, suburban, middle-class student body. The basketball program was ranked in the top 40 of Division I NCAA schools throughout our research, and in the top 20 for most of two seasons. The team played in post-season tournaments every year, and in four complete seasons won approximately four times as many games as it lost. Players generally were recruited from the surrounding area; they were predominantly black (70%) and ranged from lower to middle class. In general, the basketball program was fairly representative of what Coakley (1986) and Frey (1982) term "big-time" college athletics. Although it could not compare to programs at the largest athletic universities, its recent success compensated for its size and lack of tradition. The basketball program's national ranking and its success (along with that of other athletic teams) in sending graduating members into the professional leagues further imbued the entire athletic milieu with a sense of seriousness and purpose.

The Experience of Glory

Experiencing glory was exciting, intoxicating, and riveting. Two self-dimensions were either created or expanded in the athletes we studied: the reflected self and the media self.

The Reflected Self

As a result of the face-to-face interactions between team members and people they encountered through their role as college athletes, the athletes' impressions of themselves were modified and changed. As Cooley (1902) and Mead (1934) were the first to propose, individuals engage in role-taking; their self-conceptions are products of social interaction, affected by the reflected impressions of others. According to Cooley (1902), these "looking glass" selves are formed through a combination of cognitive and affective forces; although individuals react intellectually to the impressions they perceive others forming about them, they also develop emotional reactions about these judgments. Together

these reactions are instrumental in shaping their self-images. Thus individuals use what Rosenberg (1979) and Sullivan (1953) call "reflected appraisals" in forging a new sense of self.

The forging and modification of reflected selves began as team members perceived how people *treated* them; subsequently they formed *reactions* to that treatment. One of the first things they all noticed was that they were sought intensely by strangers. Large numbers of people, individually and in groups, wanted to be near them, to get their autographs, to touch them, and to talk to them. People treated them with awe and respect. One day, for example, the head coach walked out of his office and found a woman waiting for him. As he turned towards her she threw herself in front of him and began to kiss his feet, all the while telling him what a great man he was. More commonly, fans who were curious about team matters approached players, trying to engage them in conversation. These conversations sometimes made the players feel awkward because although they wanted to be polite to their fans, they had little to say to them. Carrying on an interaction was often difficult. As one player said:

> People come walking up to you, and whether they're timid or pushy, they still want to talk. It's like, here's their hero walking face-to-face with them and they want to say anything just so they can have a conversation with them. It's *hero worshipping*. But what do you actually say to your hero when you see him?

These interactions, then, often took the form of ritualized pseudo-conversations, in which players and their fans offered each other stylized but empty words.

Many fans accorded players "cognitive recognition" (Goffman 1963), identifying them socially and expecting them to respond in kind. Players found themselves thrust into a "pseudo-intimacy" (Bensman and Lilienfeld 1979) with these fans, who had seen them so often at games and on television. Yet although their relationship with players was one-sided, fans often expected players to reciprocate their feelings of intimacy. As a result of their celebrity, team members found themselves in "exposed positions" (Goffman 1963), where they were open to engagement in personal interaction with individuals whom they did not know at all.

Players also found themselves highly prized in interacting with boosters (financial supporters of the team). Boosters showered all players with invitations to their houses for team meetings or dinner. They fought jealously to have players seen with them or gossiped about as having been in their houses. It soon became apparent to players that boosters derived social status from associating with them; boosters "basked in the reflected glory" (Burger 1985; Cialdini et al. 1976; Sigelman 1986) of the players. This situation caused players to recognize that they were "glory bearers," so filled with glory that they could confer it on anyone by their mere presence. They experienced a sense of the "Midas touch": they had an attribute (fame) that everybody wanted and which could be transmitted. Their ability to cast glory onto others and their desirability to others because of this ability became an important dimension of their new, reflected self-identity.

The Media Self

A second dimension of the self created from the glory experience was influenced largely by media portrayals. Altheide (1984) discusses the effect of the media as a fulcrum between self-feelings and the impressions, expectations, and behavior of others. He argues that modern life is characterized increasingly by media attention, leading to the creation of a "media self" whereby the self is raised to the level of self-consciousness, the focus of the individual's own attention. Fenigstein, Scheier, and Buss (1975) call this state "public self-consciousness," in which the self comes to be perceived as a social actor who serves as a stimulus for others' behavior. Most of the athletes who came to the University had received some media publicity in high school (68%), but the national level of the print and video coverage they received after arriving, coupled with the intensity of the constant focus, caused them to develop more compelling and more salient media selves than they had possessed previously.

Radio, television, and newspaper reporters covering the team often sought out athletes for "human interest" stories. These features presented media-framed angles that cast athletes into particular roles and tended to create new dimensions of their selves. Images were created from a combination of individuals' actual behavior and reporters' ideas of what made good copy. Thus through media coverage, athletes were cast into molds that frequently were distorted or exaggerated reflections of their behavior and self-conceptions.

Team members, for whom the media had created roles, felt as if they had to live up to these portrayals. For instance, two players were depicted as "good students"—shy, quiet, religious, and diligent. Special news features emphasized their outstanding traits, illustrating how they went regularly to class, were humanitarian, and cared about graduating. Yet one of them lamented:

> Other kids our age, they go to the fair and they walk around with a beer in their hand, or a cigarette, but if me and Dan were to do that, then people would talk about that. We can't go over to the clubs, or hang around, without it relaying back to Coach. We can't even do things around our teammates, because they expect us to be a certain way. The media has created this image of us as the "good boys," and now we have to live up to it.

Other players (about 20%) were embraced for their charismatic qualities; they had naturally outgoing personalities and the ability to excite a crowd. These players capitalized on the media coverage, exaggerating their antics to gain attention and fame. Yet the more they followed the media portrayal, the more likely it was to turn into a caricature of their selves. One player described how he felt when trapped by his braggart media self:

> I used to like getting in the paper. When reporters came around I would make those Mohammed Ali type outbursts—I'm gonna do

this, I'm gonna do that. And they come around again, stick a microphone in your face, 'cause they figure somewhere Washington will have another outburst. But playing that role died out in me. I think sometimes the paper pulled out a little too much from me that wasn't me. But people seen me as what the paper said, and I had to play that role.

Particular roles notwithstanding, all the players shared the media-conferred sense of self as celebrity. Raised to the status of stars, larger than life, they regularly read their names and statements in the newspaper, saw their faces on television, or heard themselves whispered about on campus. One team member described the consequences of this celebrity:

> We didn't always necessarily agree with the way they wrote about us in the paper, but people who saw us expected us to be like what they read there. A lot of times it made us feel uncomfortable, acting like that, but we had to act like they expected us to, for the team's sake. We had to act like this was what we was really like.

Ironically, however, the more they interacted with people through their dramaturgically induced media selves, the more many of the team members felt familiar and comfortable with those selves ("We know what to do, we don't have to think about it no more"). The media presented the selves and the public believed in them, so the athletes continued to portray them. Even though they attempted to moderate these selves, part of them pressed for their legitimacy and acceptance. Over time the athletes believed these portrayals increasingly. . . . Athletes thus went through a gradual process of abandoning their "role distance" (Goffman 1961) and becoming more engrossed or more deeply involved in their media selves. The recurrent social situations of their everyday lives served as the foils against which both their public and their private selves developed. The net effect of having these selves placed upon them and of interacting through them with others was that athletes integrated them into their core selves.

Self-Aggrandizement

Athletes were affected profoundly by encounters with the self-images reflected onto them by others, both in person and through the media. It was exciting and gratifying to be cast as heroes. Being presented with these images and feeling obligated to interact with people through them, athletes added a new self to their repertoire: a glorified self. This self had a greater degree of aggrandizement than their previous identities. The athletes may have dreamed of glory, but until now they had never formed a structured set of relationships with people who accorded it to them. . . .

One result of receiving such intense personal interest and media attention was that players developed "big heads." They were admired openly by so many people and their exploits were regarded as so important that they began to feel more notable. Although they tried to remain modest, all of the players found that their celebrity caused them to lose control over their sense of self-importance. As one player observed:

> You try not to let it get away from you. You feel it coming all around you. People building you up. You say to yourself that you're the same guy you always were and that nothing has changed. But what's happening to you is so unbelievable. Even when you were sitting at home in high school imagining what college ball would be like, you could not imagine this. All the media, all the fans, all the pressure. And all so suddenly, with no time to prepare or ease into it. Doc, it got to go to your head. You try to fight it, and you think you do, but you got to be affected by it, you got to get a big head.

Although the players fought to normalize and diminish their feelings of self-aggrandizement, they were swept away in spite of themselves by the allure of glory, to varying degrees. Their sense of glory fed their egos, exciting them beyond their ability to manage or control it. They had never before been such glory-generating figures, had never felt the power that was now invested in them by the crowds or worshipful fans. They developed deep, powerful feelings affirming how important they had become and how good it felt.

All the members of the University's basketball program developed gloried selves, although the degree varied according to several factors. To some extent, their aggrandizement and glorification were affected by the level of attention they received. Individuals with more talent, who held central roles as team stars, were the focus of much media and fan attention. Others, who possessed the social and interpersonal attributes that made them good subjects for reporters, fruitful topics of conversation for boosters, and charismatic crowd pleasers, also received considerable notice. In addition, those who were more deeply invested in the athletic role were more likely to develop stronger gloried selves. They looked to this arena for their greatest rewards and were the most susceptible to its aggrandizing influence. Finally, individuals resisted or yielded to the gloried self depending on personal attributes. Those who were naturally more modest and more self-effacing tried harder to neutralize the effects and had more difficulty in forging grandiose self-conceptions than those who were boastful or pretentious.

The Price of Glory

Athletes' self-aggrandizement, as we have seen, was a clear consequence of the glory experience. Self-diminishment was a corresponding and concomitant effect. Athletes paid a price for becoming gloried in the form of self-narrowing or self-erosion. They sacrificed both the multidimensionality of their current selves and the potential breadth of their future selves; various dimensions of their identities were either diminished, detached, or somehow changed as a result of their increasing investment in their gloried selves.

Self-Immediacy

One of the first consequences of the ascent of the gloried self was a loss of future orientation. In all their lives, from the most celebrated player to the least, these individuals had never experienced

such a level of excitement, adulation, intensity, and importance. These sensations were immediate and real, flooding all team members' daily lives and overwhelming them. As a result, their focus turned toward their present situation and became fixed on it.

This reaction was caused largely by the absorbing quality of the moment. During the intensity of the season (and to a lesser extent during the off-season), their basketball obligations and involvements were prominent. When they were lying exhausted in their hotel rooms, hundreds of miles from campus, or on their beds after a grueling practice, the responsibilities of school seemed remote and distant. One player described his state of preoccupation:

> I've got two finals tomorrow and one the next day. I should be up in the room studying right now. But how can I get my mind on that when I know I've got to guard Michael Jordan tomorrow night?

Their basketball affairs were so much more pressing, not only in the abstract but also because other people made specific demands on them, that it was easy to relegate all other activities to a position of lesser importance.

Many players who had entered college expecting to prepare themselves for professional or business careers were distracted from those plans and relinquished them (71%). The demands of the basketball schedule became the central focus of their lives; the associated physical, social, and professional dimensions took precedence over all other concerns. Despite their knowledge that only two percent of major-college players eventually play in the NBA (Coakley 1986; Leonard and Reyman 1988), they all clung to the hope that they would be the ones to succeed. . . .

Diminished Awareness

Locked into a focus on the present and stuck with a vision of themselves that grew from their celebrity status, all team members, to varying degrees, became desensitized to the concerns of their old selves. They experienced a heightened sensitivity and reflectivity toward the gloried self and a loss of awareness of the self-dimensions unrelated to glory. Nearly everyone they encountered interacted with them, at least in part, through their gloried selves. As this self-identity was fed and expanded, their other selves tended to atrophy. At times the athletes seemed to be so blinded by their glory that they would not look beyond it. As Goffman (1967, p. 43) observed, "Whatever his position in society, the person insulates himself by blindnesses, half-truths, illusions, and rationalizations." . . .

Discussion

As we have shown, high school graduates entered the world of college athletics and underwent a fundamental transformation. Thrust into a whirlwind of adulation and celebrity, they reacted to the situation through a process of simultaneous self-aggrandizement and self-diminishment. The gloried self expanded, overpowering all of their other statuses and self-dimensions; it became the aspect of self in which they lived and invested. They immersed themselves single-mindedly in this portion of their selves, and the feedback and gratification they derived from this identity dwarfed their other identities. They had not anticipated this situation, but gradually, as they were drawn into the arena of glory, they were swept away by stardom and fame. Their commitment to the athletic self grew beyond anything they had ever imagined or intended. Once they had experienced the associated power and centrality, they were reluctant to give them up. They discarded their other aspirations, lost touch with other dimensions of their selves (even to the point of detachment), and plunged themselves into the gloried self.

Athletes' gloried selves arose originally as dramaturgical constructions. Other people, through the media or face to face, conferred these identities on athletes through their expectations of them. Athletes responded by playing the corresponding roles because of organizational loyalty, interactional obligations, and enjoyment. Yet in contrast to other roles, which can be played casually and without consequence,

athletes' actions in these roles increased their commitment and their self-involvement in them and made the athletes "more or less unavailable for alternative lines of action" (Kornhauser 1962, p. 321). The gloried self not only influenced athletes' future behavior but also transformed their self-conceptions and identities. . . .

. . . Athletes' engulfment by the glorified self was fueled both internally and externally. They developed gloried selves as new, more powerful, and more alluring identities were set before them. Then they chose to diminish the salience of other self-dimensions (see Adler and Adler 1987) in order to seek fulfillment from the new, intoxicating identity. In doing so they shunted aside significant others associated with their former identities and sought the company of those who would reinforce the gloried self. . . .

REFERENCES

Adler, Patricia and Peter Adler. 1987. "The Reconstruction of Role Identity Salience: College Athletes and the Academic Role." *Social Science Journal* 24:443–55.

Altheide, David L. 1984. "The Media Self." Pp. 177–95 in *The Existential Self in Society,* edited by J. A. Kotarba and A. Fontana. Chicago: University of Chicago Press.

Bensman, Joseph and Robert Lilienfeld. 1979. *Between Public and Private.* New York: Free Press.

Burger, Jerry M. 1985. "Temporal Effects on Attributions for Academic Performances and Reflected-Glory Basking." *Social Psychology Quarterly* 48:330–36.

Cialdini, Robert B., Richard J. Borden, Avril Thorne, Marcus Randall Walker, Stephen Freeman, and Lloyd Reynolds Sloan. 1976. "Basking in Reflected Glory: Three (Football) Field Studies." *Journal of Personality and Social Psychology* 34:366–75.

Coakley, Jay J. 1986. *Sport in Society.* 3d. ed. St. Louis: Mosby.

Cooley, Charles H. 1902. *Human Nature and Social Order.* New York: Scribners.

Fenigstein, Allan, Michael F. Scheier, and Arnold H. Buss. 1975. "Public and Private Self-Consciousness: Assessment and Theory." *Journal of Consulting and Clinical Psychology* 43:522–27.

Frey, James H. 1982. "Boosterism, Scarce Resources and Institutional Control: The Future of American Intercollegiate Athletics." *International Review of Sport Sociology* 17:53–70.

Goffman, Erving. 1961. *Encounters.* Indianapolis: Bobbs-Merrill.

———. 1963. *Behavior in Public Places.* New York: Free Press.

———. 1967. *Interaction Ritual.* New York: Anchor Doubleday.

Goldsmith, Barbara. 1983. "The Meaning of Celebrity." *New York Times Magazine,* December 4, pp. 75–82, 120.

Kornhauser, William. 1962. "Social Bases of Political Commitment: A Study of Liberals and Radicals." Pp. 321–39 in *Human Behavior and Social Processes,* edited by A. M. Rose. Boston: Houghton Mifflin.

Leonard, Wilbert M. and Jonathon E. Reyman. 1988. "The Odds of Attaining Professional Athlete Status: Refining the Computations." *Sociology of Sport Journal* 5:162–69.

Mead, George Herbert. 1934. *Mind, Self and Society.* Chicago: University of Chicago Press.

Rosenberg, Morris. 1979. *Conceiving the Self.* New York: Basic.

Sigelman, Lee. 1986. "Basking in Reflected Glory: An Attempt at Replication." *Social Psychology Quarterly* 49:90–92.

Sullivan, Harry S. 1953. *The Interpersonal Theory of Psychiatry.* New York: Norton.

THINKING ABOUT THE READING

According to Adler and Adler, how do fame and celebrity alter people's self-concepts? What do they mean when they say that self-concepts are formed from the "reflected appraisals" of others? Have you ever known someone who suddenly became famous? How did this person change? Did he or she become a "completely different" person, or were some elements of his or her past self retained? What do such changes tell us about the social nature of the self? What are the personal and social costs of the gloried self?

Transsexuals' Narrative Construction of the "True Self"

Douglas Mason-Schrock

Stories are like containers that hold us together; they give us a sense of coherence and continuity. By telling what happened to us once upon a time, we make sense of who we are today. To fashion a biographical story imposes a comforting order on our experience, but how do we arrive at stories that feel right, that point to authentic selfhood? One way to find out is to examine how people create new self-narratives to support a radical change in identity. We might find, as Gergen and Gergen (1983:266) have suggested, that stories are not simply told about a preexisting self but that stories, and their collective creation, bring phenomenologically real "true selves" into being.

Transsexuals provide an intriguing opportunity to study this process of self-construction. The desired identity change is indeed radical: from one gender to another. Typically transsexuals . . . believe they were born in wrong-sexed bodies and want to remedy the mistake, eventually through surgery. The process entails relearning how to do gender, down to the smallest details of self-presentation. The process is also anguishing, in that transsexuals often face rejection from family and friends. In addition, there are the problems of finding ways to pay for therapy, electrolysis, hormone treatments, and surgery. To be willing to endure this process, one must believe firmly that the "true self" demands it.

We already know a great deal about how transsexuals manage stigma (Feinbloom 1976; Kando 1973) and how they learn to do gender differently (Garfinkel 1967; Kessler and McKenna 1978). We have many hypotheses about the causes of transsexualism, including theories that emphasize biology (Benjamin 1966), socialization (Stoller 1968), labeling (Risman 1982), patriarchy (Raymond [1979] 1994), and capitalism (Billings and Urban 1982). More difficult to penetrate, however, is the *process* whereby transsexuals themselves fashion a new sense of self after the old self begins to unravel. Transsexuals face a peculiar difficulty in this regard because their bodies, as signifiers, belie the new gender identities they want to claim. Moreover, in Western cultures the body is taken to be an unequivocal sign of gender; thus it is not easy for those born with penises to define themselves as "female inside."[1] The implication is that transsexuals must look elsewhere, beyond their natural bodies, for signs of the gendered character of their "true selves."

One place where they learn to look is the past. Through participating in the so-called "transgender community," they learn how to scan their biographies for evidence of a differently gendered "true self." In this paper I focus on how transsexuals learn to do this—that is, how they learn, from others in the transgender community, to find biographical evidence of a differently gendered "true self" and to fashion this information into a story that leads inexorably to the identity "transsexual." . . .

I would like to thank Michael Schwalbe, Marcy Mason-Schrock, Sherryl Kleinman, and Brian Powell for helpful comments on previous drafts of this paper. I would also like to thank members of the NCSU Qualitative Research and Writing Group for their encouragement and guidance throughout this project.

The Transgender Community

My involvement in the transgender community[2] began after I found an advertisement for a therapist who specialized in "transgender issues." When I called her and explained my research interests, she said that she co-led a transgender support group and invited me to the next meeting.

I attended eight (of a possible 12) of these meetings over a 15-month period. Each meeting lasted about three hours. Between 10 and 26 cross-dressers, transsexuals, and sometimes their significant others were present at each meeting. During the first half of each meeting, members discussed and sought advice on personal issues. The second half of the meeting usually consisted of an instructional program—for example, a makeup seminar, a video lecture on voice alteration, or a presentation on the legal rights of transgenderists. Beside the regular meetings, I also attended the group's annual Christmas party and went to a hockey game with a born male dressed as a woman. I wrote field notes as soon as possible after each meeting.

I also read magazines, pamphlets, and short articles written and distributed by various transgender organizations. In addition, I found an Internet community of transgenderists and consistently read two Internet newsgroups, subscribed to a "semi-private" e-mail list, and lurked on a weekly real-time support group for transgenderists on America Online. Sometimes I took notes off the screen; at other times I downloaded relevant public documents. I interviewed three transsexuals via e-mail, and conducted one face-to-face interview with an erotic transvestite I met over the Internet.

Other data derived from interviews with 10 transsexuals whom I met at support group meetings. The interviews lasted 2 to $3^{1}/_{2}$ hours; I recorded and transcribed them in full. I used an interview guide that consisted of a list of orienting questions; the interviews were otherwise unstructured. Nine of the interviewees were biologically born males; one was born female. None of the interviewees had undergone sex reassignment surgery, although all but one expressed a desire to do so. In regard to sexual orientation, the born female saw herself as a heterosexual man. Three of the born males viewed themselves as lesbian women, three as heterosexual women, and three others said they would try out both orientations. All of the people I interviewed were white and ranged in age from 31 to 47. Eight of the 10 held middle-class jobs in professional or technical fields or were working on graduate degrees.

Throughout this study I wrote numerous analytic memos in an attempt to make sense of the data (Lofland and Lofland 1984). At the beginning of data collection, I used these memos to try to answer the question "What is going on here?" This helped to jump-start the process of analytic induction (Manning 1991). As I wrote these memos, the significance of storytelling began to emerge. Toward the end of data collection I began to categorize and sort the data, following the techniques described by Strauss (1987). For example, I categorized the stories by theme and then generated subcategories. I also coded the data in terms of process—that is, by searching my field notes to learn how storytelling unfolded during interaction. Through these procedures I came to understand the "how" and the "what" of transsexuals' self-narratives.

Making the Differently Gendered "True Self"

"A girl brain in a boy body," said one interviewee when I asked her what it meant to be transsexual. Transsexuals believed they were *born* into the wrong-sexed bodies. Through biological miswiring, they felt they had been given a body signifying a gender different from that of their "true self." This biological view of gender implied that transsexuals' differently gendered "true selves" had existed from birth. Consequently, to be secure in their new self-definitions, they had to find evidence that they had *always* been different. Together they found such evidence in their biographies. That is, they collectively reinterpreted certain past events as evidence of transsexuality. This reinterpretation took place while presenting their self-narratives to each other. Transsexuals most often told stories of childhood events. This was where the remaking of the self began.

Childhood Stories

During an interview, one male-to-female transsexual had difficulty defining transsexualism. She said that nobody had ever asked her to do that before, and added:

> I guess that it would be whatever the medical term or psychological term is. I'm not exactly sure. But it always has been there since I can remember; probably at four years old I felt more female than . . . male.

During support group meetings and interviews, and on computer networks, transgenderists often said, "I've felt different *as long as I can remember.*" Early memories of feeling ambivalent about gender, or memories of doing gender unconventionally, were regarded as key pieces of evidence for transsexuality. Transsexuals viewed childhood as a time when their authentic impulses had not yet been stifled by restrictive gender boundaries. At that time, the "true self" reigned. To construct their new identity, transsexuals most often told childhood stories about (1) actual or fantasized cross-dressing experiences, and (2) getting caught cross-dressing. . . . What mattered was how these stories were interpreted.

Early cross-dressing stories. Children learn early to attribute their own and others' gender on the basis of clothing (Cahill 1989), and as adults they take this cultural sign of gender for granted. Male-to-female transsexuals viewed early cross-dressing experiences as evidence of always having possessed a differently gendered "true self."[3] . . .

. . . Most stories of early cross-dressing suggested that at first it was undertaken almost on a whim. This account by a 40-year-old was typical:

> I was five years old. We lived in town, but there was an old family homeplace that nobody was living in at the time. . . . I was just exploring in the attic one day and found a black dress hanging from a nail in the rafters. I just tried it

> on and it felt good. I started going through all the drawers, finding other things to try on. And over the years following that—the house had no closets; they used wardrobes—I emptied out one of the wardrobes and turned that into my wardrobe. As I found bits and pieces of clothing that appealed to me, I just added them to my wardrobe.

This person remembered cross-dressing at the homeplace until she went to college. When she told a similar version of this story at a support group meeting, several members smiled and nodded. These responses not only affirmed the individual narrator's transsexual identity, but also conveyed the message that telling stories of early cross-dressing was an acceptable way to show that the identity fit.

Remembering the *feelings* associated with these experiences was crucial because support group members, like most people, took them as signs of the "true self" (Gordon 1989; Hochschild 1983). Discussing feelings when telling self-narratives can help storytellers reexperience these feelings; which, in turn, makes the feelings seem intimately connected with one's sense of self (Barclay 1994; Shotter 1990). . . . At support group meetings, revealing these "true feelings" indicated to newcomers that childhood cross-dressing wasn't undertaken for mere amusement, but was the expression of a deeper self. . . .

The most commonly accepted evidence of transsexualism in the transgender community was cross-dressing or fantasizing about cross-dressing *as a child*. The age at which one began such activities was significant, because transsexuals believed that the "true self" was most likely to express itself at an early age. One person I interviewed said she remembered beginning to cross-dress at age 3. Transsexuals believed that the "true self" was more likely to govern one's actions in childhood because its impulses had not yet been constrained by parents, teachers, and peers.

The age at which a person began cross-dressing was also viewed as a way to distinguish transsexuals from both erotic transvestites and cross-dressers. By emphasizing the early age of actual or fantasized cross-dressing, transsexuals dissociated themselves from transvestites, who usually told of beginning to cross-dress during adolescence for erotic purposes. By stressing that their early feelings and activities reflected an *exclusively* gendered "true self," rather merely an *aspect* of self, transsexuals distanced themselves from cross-dressers, who often talked about cross-dressing as if it were a hobby. By emphasizing differences, support group members policed the boundaries (see Schwalbe and Mason-Schrock 1996) between the three closely related identities: transvestite, cross-dresser, and transsexual.

It was especially important to make such distinctions because most transsexuals formally had defined themselves as cross-dressers. Policing also took place when support group members told stories about dressing in women's clothing as adults. At one meeting several *cross-dressers* exchanged detailed accounts of dressing up as women for Halloween, with emphasis on humorous aspects of fooling friends or restroom episodes. No transsexuals joined in with similar stories. A construction worker—a newcomer who hadn't yet publicly labeled herself a cross-dresser or a transsexual—was asked by a cross-dresser if she had ever "dressed up" for Halloween. She replied:

> Halloween is for dressing in costumes, and this is not a costume. It is part of who I am, part of me. If I dressed at Halloween it would be like saying that this is false, but it isn't, it's real. Femininity is an art form. I practice the art of femininity.

. . .

Getting caught cross-dressing. One meeting, which was called "Family Issues Night," started with an exchange of stories about coming out to family members. During a lull in the conversation, the group leader asked a longtime member to talk about her family situation. She told the group about cross-dressing as a child and gave a detailed account of getting caught cross-dressed. Her parents sent her regularly to a psychiatrist for several months, until she learned to tell the

man "what he wanted to hear." This experience, she said, led her to question for many years the normality of cross-dressing. Other transsexuals responded by telling their own stories about getting caught; often they emphasized that it made them ashamed.

Overall these stories helped to create the notion that the "true self" was constrained by forces *outside* the individual. Because the transsexuals felt that their differently gendered "true self" had always existed, the stories helped to explain why they had denied its existence for 30 to 40 years. By stressing the negative social consequences in telling each other these stories, getting caught became a "turning point" in transsexuals' self-narratives (see Mishler 1992). The turning point, however, did not bring them closer to self-actualization; rather, it estranged them from the "true self." Any periodic cessation of cross-dressing thus could be attributed to pressure from others. . . .

One born male in her mid-thirties (who started to live full-time as a woman about five months after the interview) felt that being prohibited from cross-dressing squelched the natural development of her differently gendered "true self." In an interview she said:

> I knew it was antisocial behavior [but] . . . looking back on it, I wish it had been different. I wish I would have been like the kid in school that was beat up because he was a sissy, just because maybe now I'd be much farther along. . . . I have about two or three years before I can get the surgery. I feel that had I been more honest with my feelings at an earlier age, or allowed myself to express myself the way I wanted to at an earlier age, that I'd be different—more of a complete person now. About that age I started to internalize my feelings and my tendencies, and bury it.

Negative social reactions to cross-dressing or other "cross-gendered" activities such as little boys acting feminine, were seen as building up barriers to the expression of the differently gendered "true self." Transsexuals regarded such negative responses as the foundation for full-blown denial (which I will discuss in detail below). Stories about getting caught thus linked childhood cross-dressing stories with denial narratives. Weaving these stories together made them appear, at least on the surface, to be seamless constructions of self-meaning. . . .

Stories of Denial

Interpreting early cross-dressing . . . experiences as signs of a differently gendered "true self" helped the transsexuals define themselves as having been born in the wrong-sexed body. Yet they also had to *explain away* prior involvement in activities that signified their *un*wanted gender identity. If a male-to-female transsexual had . . . signified conventional masculinity most of her life, this history had to be reinterpreted to support her new gender identity. If it was not reinterpreted, she might doubt that she was really a transsexual. If the transsexuals had been trying to present a virtual identity to others, they simply could have avoided giving discrediting information (Goffman 1963:95). But because they were doing identity work to create a phenomenologically real "true self," they had to find a way to reconcile discrepant biographical data.

To resolve this identity dilemma, transsexuals gave accounts of being "in denial" before they came to terms with transsexuality. Denial narratives were perhaps the most powerful identity-making resource shared in the transgender community. These narratives were fashioned from psychological rhetoric and thus had scientific legitimacy. To transsexuals, denial meant repressing their "true selves" and thus denying who they really were. This allowed male-to-female transsexuals to interpret the past expression of masculinity as the presentation of a false self (and vice versa for born females). Thus denial narratives helped them explain away things that might have undermined their claims to possessing differently gendered "true selves."

Presenting a denial narrative could facilitate a complete change in identity over a short period, as in the following example. A born male who had been attending meetings for several months consistently introduced herself as a cross-dresser

until one meeting, when she introduced herself as "just myself." She explained that she wasn't sure anymore what it meant to be a cross-dresser. As I wrote in my field notes, she

> talked about a story that happened earlier in the week. She got a catalog in the mail and said, "I was flipping through the catalog and got to the lingerie section. They have live models who model the bras and panties and I was looking at a bra and you could see a significant portion of her breast and I sort of wondered if that was for sale also."

This story expressed the narrator's desire to change her *body*, not only her clothing, and primed the group for her identity transition. At the following meeting she introduced herself, with some hesitation, by saying, "I'm coming to realize that I'm a transsexual." She went on to explain that it was difficult to say this in front of the others because she had been "*struggling to get through denial.*" Group members offered her support; some said she was brave and courageous for taking such a big step. By invoking the denial narrative she completed her identity change in the eyes of the group. No one dared ask whether she really had been in denial because so many others relied on denial narratives to sustain their own claims to transsexuality.

Like other stories considered acceptable for transsexual identity-making, allusions to denial were constantly worked into group discussions. Denial was often mentioned in brief but significant ways during support group meetings. Transsexuals got the most mileage from denial narratives, however, when telling their complete life histories. These accounts of denial referred to three principal kinds of experiences: (1) self-distractions, (2) masculinity/femininity pursuits, and (3) self-mislabeling.

Self-distractions.   Tales of denial emphasizing self-distractions were accounts of life events that diverted transsexuals' attention from seeing their "true selves." Interviewees said they turned to drugs or sources of bliss to hide their transsexuality. Many said that awareness of the social consequences of stigmatization caused them to find ways to suppress their unconventional "true feelings" . . .

Transsexuals felt that denial, although often strong enough to shut out the "true self" for many years, was always at risk of collapsing. When transsexuals presented denial narratives, they split the self in two: (1) the protagonist or "true self," who worked relentlessly to tear down the barriers of denial, and (2) the antagonist or socially aware "self," who struggled to make repairs. Eventually, they felt, the "true self" proved to have more stamina and the barriers could not withstand the pressure; the "true self" thus won out in this "romance narrative" (see Gergen and Gergen 1988; Murray 1985).

Although stories of substance abuse were most common, self-distraction narratives included a variety of preoccupations. For example, the born female said he had so many other problems in his life, including health difficulties and family problems, that he wasn't able to focus on gender-related issues until very recently. Transsexuals could search their biographies for virtually any event in their lives that demanded a great deal of time or emotional energy, and could reinterpret it as a period of denial.

Masculinity/femininity pursuits.   Whereas self-distraction narratives focused on doing things or being in situations that inhibited self-reflection, masculinity/femininity pursuits were stories about trying to conform to conventional notions of gender. By defining as *denial* the behavior stereotypically associated with the gender category they were leaving behind, transsexuals were able to gloss over these biographical contradictions. For instance, one born male had been a successful football player in high school. Later, as an adult man, this person had won a community award for organizing and coaching Little League sports. At the time of the interview, she viewed what others called "successes" as efforts to sustain denial. . . .

Besides the display of physical signs of masculinity, sometimes the main theme of masculinity pursuits was overconformity to traditional gen-

der norms. During one interview a transsexual—who, as a man, had had three unsuccessful marriages to women—explained that she had signified a particularly abusive aspect of masculinity in sustaining denial:

> When it came to women, I was a son-of-a-bitch. . . . I really was. I treated women like dirt. [I'd tell them], "You don't know what you're talking about. Let me just do everything, you just sit back and go with the flow. You're not smart enough. You don't know what's going on in the world." . . . to quote it on your tape, it may not seem right, but "Finger them, fuck them, and forget them" . . . was my attitude: Let's see how many women I could lay in the course of a week, or in the course of a month. It was like a game, but even when all of this was going on, inside I was hating what I was doing. [I'd think,] "I don't know this person; the real person is in here." And when I am seeing the woman that I am with, I am thinking, "I would love to *be* you." I would love to be them. . . . it was like I was a different person. It was almost like standing back and watching somebody else do these things. Even now, especially now, when I look back it's like I don't believe all that. (C: And you were doing those things to—) To compensate for—I thought that if I'm real macho, if I'm a real "*man man*" or "*boy boy*" or teenager, or whatever it is, then people aren't going to notice this little feminine side in me that's wanting to come out and just touch somebody or be real gentle.

Ironically, this person wanted to be the kind of person he treated so badly. She said she didn't like the things she had done, but did them because she was trying to be a man. This guilt (about treating women badly) helped solidify the interpretation of denial because it was interpreted as signaling that *something* was wrong with how she had acted as a man.

Masculinity/femininity pursuits also took the form of hobbies. When I walked into the living room of one interviewee's townhouse, the first thing I noticed, with some unease, was a collection of large hunting knives, a few pieces of which were on display on a coffee table. This born male said she had collected these knifes in an attempt to conform to traditional masculinity. In addition, this 44-year-old newly self-defined transsexual told the following story of denial:

> Then I started, over a period of a couple years, going through these cycles of really getting into [cross-dressing] and saying "I'm going to go forward," and then stopping and saying, "No, this is out of hand" and engage[ing] in some hobby or activity that would serve as a vehicle for repression. I went through a bit of collecting guns, going to gun shows, and doing a lot of shooting, 'cause that was a really *manly* thing to do. I went through a bit of wearing Redman hats and driving around in pickup trucks and going to mud bog races and those kinds of things 'cause that's the *manly* thing to do. I bought a Harley and went down to Daytona for bike week with half a million Harley riders. Did that for several years because that's the manly thing to do. Of course, the last time I did it I wore a pink lace camisole and stockings and garter belt underneath my leather jacket and my jeans.

. . .

Self-mislabeling. Beside attempting to align the narrator with gender-appropriate activities, some transsexuals' stories of denial emphasized "self-mislabeling." These accounts most often involved defining oneself as a transvestite or cross-dresser, although labeling oneself homosexual, androgynous, or even a sensitive male was not infrequent. After becoming active in the transgender subculture, transsexuals learned to interpret their experiments with these identities as denial. One born male, who recently had begun living full-time as a woman, said in an interview:

> At one point I thought, . . . "I like dressing like a girl but the only thing I know is there are gay people and straight people, [so] I must be a gay person," and that pushed me into that life for a while and I stayed there before I realized that I didn't quite identify [with them].

In this person's account of self-mislabeling, she implied that a limited knowledge about alternative identities, specifically *transsexual*, led her to falsely identify as homosexual, thus denying her "true self."

Eight of the nine male-to-female transsexuals I interviewed had previously labeled themselves transvestites or cross-dressers. Unlike other stories of denial, these accounts were often brief and vague. Interviewees often tried to gloss this prior identity confusion by making statements such as, "When I was in denial I thought I might be a transvestite." At the support group meetings, no one was ever asked to clarify such statements. One possible reason why they avoided moving beyond surface details was that doing so could raise a potentially embarrassing question: How could they be sure that the label *transsexual* was correct and not just another mistake? Honoring vague accounts at strategic moments thus helped maintain the power of denial narratives and sanctioned the identity *transsexual*. . . .

Self-Narratives as Collective Creations

Although an isolated individual who felt inauthentic doing gender conventionally could have invented stories similar to those discussed above (because they relied heavily on stereotypical views of gender), they would have been much less powerful without group affirmation. It was the transgender *community* that cemented the interpretation of gender nonconformity as evidence of transsexuality rather than homosexuality.[4] In this community in the United States, with its over 200 local support groups and national and regional conferences, the templates for self-narratives were made and used. These narrative forms also were maintained and transmitted through community publications, computer networks, and television talk shows. The community functioned in four key ways to help individuals fashion their own self-narratives: (1) modeling, (2) guiding, (3) affirming, and (4) tactful blindness.

Modeling

At support group meetings, the narratives were maintained and transferred to new members largely through *modeling*. In this process, first of all, those transsexuals who were adept at telling self-narratives did so voluntarily. In telling their stories, they gave the new members clues about the types of significant events to look for in their own biographies. If the newcomers listened closely, they could find the rhetorical tools that could be used, with some slight alterations, to signify their own differently gendered "true self."

One way in which established members did this was by tagging on relevant identity slogans while ostensibly talking about something else. At several of the meetings, transsexuals introduced themselves as "transsexual" and added something like "and I've been cross-dressing since I was five years old." This was somewhat of a ritual; if one person started it, most of the other transsexuals followed with similar introductions. Referencing acceptable self-narratives in this way alerted new members that talking about childhood cross-dressing was linked somehow to transsexualism. In addition, the modeling, or ritualistic repeating of the introduction by those already "in the know," helped to legitimate and sustain childhood cross-dressing stories as an acceptable way to claim a differently gendered "true self."

To make modeling work, it was particularly important for transsexuals well versed in their self-narratives to publicly declare themselves as *transsexuals,* because both cross-dressers and transsexuals attended the meetings. This allowed newcomers who weren't sure what identity to choose to distinguish between the self-narratives of transsexuals and those of cross-dressers. Then they could examine their own biographies to see which kind of story fit them better. For instance, when one transsexual went to her first support group meeting, told her story, and then heard other stories, she said she was "amazed" and felt as though she had "come home." Despite her uncertainty about her identity before the meeting, hearing transsexuals tell stories similar to hers helped convince her that she was a transsexual. . . .

The identity "transsexual," although stigmatized, is becoming culturally viable (Garber 1992), largely because of the legitimating power of the medical community (Raymond [1979]1994) and the work of activist organizations (MacKenzie 1994). As a result, transsexuals' self-narratives can be heard on television talk shows and, recently, in feature films. One interviewee said she first heard transsexuals' stories on the *Sally Jessy Raphael Show.* She saw parts of her life in their stories, called the "expert doctor" who had appeared on the show, and then drove across four states to see him. The doctor "diagnosed" her as transsexual (or affirmed her narrative) and helped her find a support group.

Guiding

Whereas modeling concerned studying others' stories and figuring out how to apply them to one's self, guiding was more interactive. Established members often asked newcomers questions about their pasts, which drew out stories that fit the subculture's acceptable narrative forms. This process was like the collective opening up of a person's biography to highlight life events that the group perceived as evidence of transsexuality. The new member then could tell stories about these highlighted biographical passages at this and future gatherings, and his or her differently gendered "true self" thus could be affirmed by others.

For example, when a new member voluntarily revealed a little about himself or herself (showing willingness to self-disclose) but didn't use an acceptable self-narrative, a regular member sometimes asked, "So when did you *first* cross-dress?" After introducing myself at the first meeting I attended, I was asked if I had ever dressed or been dressed in "female clothes." After I said that my older sister once might have dressed me as a girl, one member uttered a conspicuously satisfied "Hmmm."[5] If my agenda had been to look for my "true self" rather than to conduct research, I might have seen this early life event as a sign of "who I really am."

Guiding was sometimes more overt. At two of the eight meetings I attended—each of which included several first-timers—the coleader/therapist asked if anyone had ever "purged their feminine clothing." Almost everyone raised a hand. On both occasions, a longtime member explained that she had conducted more than 10 purges in the past 20 years, and added that she had only recently realized that her feelings were not going to fade. Similarly, on one of these occasions a member in her sixties told the group:

> I went through phases of purging for close to fifty years. I've burned enough clothes to fill this entire room. I'm really serious, this entire room. I just don't do it anymore because I know I'll regret it later.

These exchanges helped newcomers to define past purges as futile attempts to deny "who they really are." In addition, they helped preserve purging stories as identity-making tools for everyone. Because these occasions were initiated and guided by the therapist, who "specialized in transgender issues," the self-narratives seemed all the more legitimate means of claiming a differently gendered "true self."

Guiding and modeling pointed to pieces of biography that were crucial parts of the transsexual narrative. Newcomers who learned what these were could then use them in assembling the puzzling pieces of their differently gendered "true selves." The passing down of the narratives to newcomers not only aided in the newcomers' own quest for personal meaning, but also preserved the rhetorical tools as they became old-timers themselves. Eventually they would become the givers, rather than the receivers, of identity-making clues.

Affirming

Modeling and guiding worked, especially in interactions, because of the audience members' reactions to the stories. Identities, like all things, become meaningful through the responses of others (Stone 1981). At support group meetings, when someone talked about recent events in his or her life, he or she might touch on one of the acceptable self-narratives. After mentioning a significant piece of biographical evidence, others reacted in subtle ways—usually with "um-hums," nods, smiles, or sometimes sighs or "ahs." These "murmurings" (Goffman 1974:541) validated the story as well as the narrator's identity.

At one meeting, for example, a participant described being tormented by the question of whether she wanted to tell a friend, who knew her as a man, about her desire to become a woman. When asked why she wanted to tell, she explained that it was becoming difficult to continue presenting an inauthentic self to someone who was close to her. She added that she had been in denial for a long time and did not want to deny her "true self" to a good friend. When denial of the "true self" was brought up, some members nodded or smiled. The speaker had touched on an acceptable community narrative for self-construction. The listeners' responses delicately but unmistakably reinforced the speaker's differently gendered "true self," and also marked denial narratives as a resource on which transsexuals could draw to fashion a new identity.

Tactful Blindness

Beside making overt responses, transsexuals sometimes affirmed self-narratives by *not* questioning their validity or logical coherence. Self-narratives always have loose ends and can be unraveled by anyone who wishes to do so. Transsexuals thus practiced "tact" (Goffman 1967:29) when they ignored discrepancies and implausibilities in each other's stories. By doing so, the support group members nurtured the fragile new identities they were trying to acquire. This collective "looking the other way" also shielded the practice of using self-narratives to create evidence of a "true self" that did not yet exist.

Thus a certain tactful blindness allowed people with diverse biographies to see themselves as possessing similar "true selves." At one meeting, for example, a born male who had been a competitive cyclist and remembered (under hypnosis) cross-dressing just once as a child was sitting next to a born male who had never participated in sports and had cross-dressed throughout childhood. Both identified as transsexual; this identity was affirmed and supported by group members when they told their contrasting stories. No one ever questioned how such different experiences could be unequivocal evidence of the same kind of "true self."

Overall the creation and maintenance of acceptable narratives was a community effort. The transgender community created the culture, which in turn provided resources for identity work. The resources available to transgenderists often fed on each other. For example, transgender support groups, including the one I attended, often had libraries of publications to help newcomers understand what they were experiencing. National publications listed local support groups, Internet groups, and places offering therapeutic and medical help. People I interviewed passed all sorts of information about transgender issues between themselves and (on a few occasions) to me. The narrative construction of "true selves" required a great deal of cooperation.

Conclusion

Transsexuals used self-narratives to convincingly invent a differently gendered "true self," but they didn't invent or use self-narratives in isolation. Subcultural involvement, at some level, was essential. My analysis shows that not only frameworks for interpreting identities (e.g., Becker 1963) but also symbolic resources for making those identities are created subculturally. Through modeling, guiding, affirming, and tactful blindness, transsexuals created and learned the narrative forms that sustained an identity which their physical bodies could not. . . .

. . . The problem faced by the transsexuals stemmed from contradictions between gender ideology (in this case, "sex determines gender") and self-definitions of gender (whereby gender identity doesn't correspond to sex). In other words, the transgender community arose from a conflict between a desire for authenticity and a highly-constraining gender order. Transsexuals used narratives to construct and affirm an identity that most people regard as morally suspect and as less real than "normal" gender identities.

In their support groups and other forums, they did "oppositional identity work" (Schwalbe and Mason-Schrock 1996); that is, they deflected the stigma imposed by, and subverted (at least partially), the identity codes of mainstream culture.

Although the transsexuals challenged some cultural ideas about gender (namely that sex equals gender), their self-narratives reinforced others. Because most people believe in gender difference and assume they are biologically based (Epstein 1988), transsexuals used these essentialist ideas to give plausibility to their stories. Their self-narratives thus supported gender polarization (Bem 1993) and the naturalization of gender (Connell 1987). Thus, even while they sought radical change as individuals, their self-narratives actually reinforced a highly conservative view of gender. . . .

NOTES

1. As Young (1989:152) puts it, "For us, the body is the locus of the self, indistinguishable from it and expressive of it."

2. This community includes *transsexuals*, who believe they were born in wrong-sexed bodies and who often seek surgery to correct the problem, and *cross-dressers* who wear gender-discrepant clothing in order to express themselves more authentically. People who cross-dress for erotic reasons, referred to as *transvestites* by members of the subculture, are generally *not* accepted as legitimate members of the transgender community. *Transgenderism* refers to the community's legitimate members, namely transsexuals and cross-dressers.

3. Cross-dressing stories were not central to female-to-male transsexuals' self-narratives, probably because our culture accepts girls wearing boys' clothing, but not the reverse. Boys and men endanger their privileged status by wearing women's clothing; thus the act is viewed as more consequential and is not undertaken lightly. When girls and women dress in men's clothing, perhaps it is more likely to be seen as merely "playing with fashion."

4. Lesbians and gay men often tell stories like those told by the transsexuals (for example, see Sears 1991); the main difference is that transsexuals rarely talk

about same-sex attractions. I suspect that this is not because transsexuals never experienced such attractions, but because the transgender community discourages overt discussion of sexuality as a way to avoid being stigmatized as "perverts." This in turn helps reinforce the notion that gender nonconformity has everything to do with *gender* identities and little to do with *sexual* identities.

5. I suspect that some members of the support group thought I was in denial. At my fourth meeting, after introducing myself, a longtime member said to newcomers, "Doug's job is to figure us out, and our job is to get him in a dress." Thinking about how I might deny this allegation led me to see the paradoxical nature of denial: there is no logical way to deny not being in denial.

REFERENCES

Barclay, Craig R. 1994. "Composing Protoselves through Improvisation." Pp. 55–77 in *The Remembering Self: Construction and Accuracy in the Self-Narrative,* edited by Ulric Neisser and Robyn Fivush. New York: Cambridge University Press.

Becker, Howard S. 1963. *Outsiders.* New York: Free Press.

Bem, Sandra L. 1993. *The Lenses of Gender: Transforming the Debate on Sexual Inequality.* New Haven: Yale University Press.

Benjamin, Harry. 1996. *The Transsexual Phenomenon.* New York: Julian Press.

Billings, Dwight and Thomas Urban. 1982. "The Socio-Medical Construction of Transsexualism: An Interpretation and Critique." *Social Problems* 3:266–282.

Connell, R. W. 1987. *Gender and Power.* Stanford: Stanford University Press.

Epstein, Cynthia Fuchs. 1988. *Deceptive Distinctions: Sex, Gender, and the Social Order.* New Haven: Yale University Press.

Feinbloom, Deborah Heller. 1976. *Transvestites and Transsexuals.* New York: Delta.

Garber, Marjorie. 1992. *Vested Interests: Cross-Dressing and Cultural Anxiety.* New York: Routledge.

Garfinkel, Harold. 1967. *Studies in Ethnomethodology.* Englewood Cliffs, NJ: Prentice-Hall.

Gergen, Kenneth J. and Mary M. Gergen. 1983. "Narratives of the Self." Pp. 254–323 in *Studies in Social Identity,* edited by Theodore R. Sarbin and Karl E. Scheibe. New York: Praeger.

Goffman, Erving. 1963. *Stigma: Notes on the Management of Spoiled Identity.* Englewood Cliffs, NJ: Prentice-Hall.

———. 1967. *Interaction Ritual.* New York: Pantheon.

———. 1974. *Frame Analysis.* New York: Harper.

Gordon, Steven L. 1989. "Institutional and Impulsive Orientations in Selectively Appropriating Emotions to Self." Pp. 115–135 in *The Sociology of Emotions: Original Essays and Research Papers,* edited by David D. Franks and E. Doyle McCarthy. Greenwich, CT: JAI.

Hochschild, Arlie Russell. 1983. *The Managed Heart: Commercialization of Human Feeling.* Berkeley: University of California Press.

Kando, Thomas. 1973. *Sex Change.* Springfield, IL: Thomas.

Kessler, Suzanne and Wendy McKenna. 1978. *Gender: An Ethnomethodological Approach.* New York: Wiley.

Lofland, John and Lyn H. Lofland. 1984. *Anaylzing Social Settings: A Guide to Qualitative Observation and Analysis.* Belmont, CA: Wadsworth.

MacKenzie, G.O. 1994. *Transgender Nation.* Bowling Green, OH: Bowling Green State University Popular Press.

Manning, Peter K. 1991. "Analytic Induction." Pp. 401–431 in *Symbolic Interactionism: Contemporary Issues,* Vol. 2, edited by Kenneth Plummer. Brookfield, VT: Edward Elgar.

Mishler, Elliot G. 1992. "Work, Identity, and Narrative: An Artist-Craftsman's Story." Pp. 21–40 in *Storied Lives: The Cultural Politics of Self-Understanding,* edited by George C. Rosenwald and Richard L. Ochberg. New Haven: Yale University Press.

Murray, Kevin. 1985. "Life as Fiction." *Journal of the Theory of Social Behaviour* 15:172–185.

Raymond, Janice G. [1979] 1994. *The Transsexual Empire: The Making of the She-Male.* New York: Teachers College Press.

Risman, Barbara J. 1982. "The (Mis)Acquisition of Gender Identity among Transsexuals." *Qualitative Sociology* 4:312–325.

Schwalbe, Michael L. and Douglas Mason-Schrock. 1996. "Identity Work as Group Process." Pp. 113–147 in *Advances in Group Processes,* Vol. 13, edited by Barry Markovsky, Michael J. Lovaglia, and Robin Simon. Greenwich, CT: JAI.

Sears, James T. 1991. *Growing Up Gay in the South: Race, Gender, and Journeys of the Spirit.* New York: Harrington Park Press.

Schotter, John. 1984. *Social Accountability and Selfhood.* Oxford: Basil Blackwell.

Stoller, Robert. 1968. *Sex and Gender.* New York: Science House.

Stone, Gregory P. 1981. "Appearance and the Self: A Slightly Revised Version." Pp. 87–102 in *Social Psychology though Symbolic Interaction,* edited by Gregory P. Stone and Harvey A. Farberman. Waltham, MA: Ginn.

Strauss, Anselm. 1987. *Qualitative Analysis for Social Scientists.* Cambridge. UK: Cambridge University Press.

Young, Katharine, 1989. "Narrative Embodiments: Enclaves of the Self in the Realm of Medicine." Pp. 152–166 in *Texts of Identity,* edited by John Schotter and Kenneth J. Gergen. London: Sage.

THINKING ABOUT THE READING

Gender is an element of our self-concepts that most people take for granted. But sociologists tell us that gender is socially constructed. Hence there are situations where it is not nearly as unambiguous as we'd like to believe. Describe the process by which preoperative transsexuals redefine their gender identity. What sorts of patterns emerge in the autobiographical stories transsexuals tell about their early years? What role do other transsexuals play in this self-constructive process? What do you think this article tells us about the nature of sex and gender? Mason-Schrock shows us that these individuals, radical though they may be with regard to their desire to surgically alter their sex, actually hold rather traditional ideas about sex and gender. But what would happen if, say, instead of wanting to change from one sex to "the other," they collectively decided to create a third sex category? How would society have to change in order to adapt to such a dramatic shift in our taken-for-granted beliefs about the category of sex?

CHAPTER 6

Building Image: Individual and Organizational Identities

A significant portion of social life is influenced by the images we form of others. We typically form impressions of people based on an initial assessment of their social group membership (race, age, gender, and so on), their personal attributes (for example, physical attractiveness), and the verbal and nonverbal messages they provide. Such assessments are usually accompanied by a set of expectations we've learned to associate with members of certain social groups or people with certain attributes. Such judgments allow us to place people in broad categories and provide a degree of predictability to forthcoming interactions.

But while we are gathering information about others to form impressions of them, we are fully aware that they are doing the same thing with us. Early in life, most of us learn that it is to our advantage to have people think highly of us. Hence, through a process called *impression management*, we attempt to control and manipulate information about ourselves to influence the impressions others form of us. Impression management provides the link between the way we perceive ourselves and the way we want others to perceive us. We've all been in situations—a first date, a job interview, meeting a girlfriend's or boyfriend's family for the first time—in which we've felt compelled to "make a good impression." What we often fail to realize, however, is that personal impression management can often be influenced by larger organizational and institutional forces.

In "Making It by Faking It," Robert Granfield describes some of the impression management tactics used by working-class students in an elite law school. Upon arriving on campus, these students quickly realize that their class background distinguishes them from the majority of students who come from affluent, upper-class families. They come to believe that this part of their identity is a hindrance to their future success in the field of law. Some conclude that their chances of "making it" increase if they hide their class background and consciously alter the way they speak and dress. But such impression management does not come without some costs as these students experience significant ambivalence and guilt over abandoning their family heritage.

Survival is also the theme of Thomas Schmid & Richard Jones's article, "Suspended Identity." Whereas Granfield's law students attempted to present an image of themselves as likable and sophisticated when they entered a different social environment, Schmid and Jones show us that some identity transformations require more drastic impression management techniques. Through participant observation in a maximum security prison—one of the researchers was an inmate serving a year-long felony sentence—the authors show how inmates must suspend their preprison identities and construct an inauthentic and often fearsome prison identity to survive the rigors of prison life. Most inmates discover that they can never fully recover their preprison identity upon release. They cannot return to being the same person they were before imprisonment. Here, too, we see how institutional demands can dictate the types of impressions we want others to form of us.

Making It by Faking It

Working-Class Students in an Elite Academic Environment

Robert Granfield

Research on stigma has generated significant insights into the complex relationship between self and society. The legacy of Goffman's (1963) seminal work on the subject can be found in studies on alcoholism, mental illness, homosexuality, physical deformities, and juvenile delinquency. Even the literature on gender and racial inequality has benefited from an emphasis on stigma. Goffman's attention to the social processes of devaluation and the emerging self-concepts of discredited individuals not only created research opportunities for generations of sociologists but contributed to a humanistic ideology that viewed stigma assignment and its effects as unjust.

One of the most vibrant research programs that emerged from Goffman's classic work has been in the area of stigma management. A host of conceptual terms have been employed to describe the process through which discreditable individuals control information about themselves so as to manage their social identity. Concepts such as passing, deviance disavowal, accounts, disclaimers, and covering have often been used in analyzing accommodations and adjustments to deviance, as Pfuhl's (1986) review shows. These tactics, while offering rewards associated with being seen as normal, frequently contribute to psychological stress. Possessing what Goffman (1963) referred to as "undesired differentness" (p. 5) often has significant consequences for one's personal identity as well as for available life chances. . . .

In this article, I focus on class stigma by examining a group of highly successful, upwardly mobile, working-class students who gained admission to a prestigious Ivy League law school in the East. While upward mobility from the working class occurs far less often within elite branches of the legal profession (Smigel 1969; Heinz and Laumann 1982) or corporate management (Useem and Karabel 1986), a certain amount of this type of mobility does take place. Working-class aspirants to the social elite, however, must accumulate cultural capital (Bourdieu and Passeron 1990; Cookson and Persell 1985) before they are able to transcend their status boundaries.

First, this article examines the ways in which working-class students experience a sense of differentness and marginality within the law school's elite environment. Next, I explore how these students react to their emerging class stigma by managing information about their backgrounds. I then demonstrate that these management strategies contribute to identity ambivalence and consider the secondary forms of adjustment students use to resolve this tension. Finally, I discuss why an analysis of social class can benefit from the insights forged by Goffman's work on stigma.

Setting and Methodology

The data analyzed for this article were collected as part of a much larger project associated with law school socialization (Granfield 1989). The subjects consist of students attending a prestigious, national law school in the eastern part of the United States. The school has had a long reputation of training lawyers who have become partners in major Wall Street law firms, Supreme Court judges, United States presidents and other politicians, heads of foundations, and an array of other eminent leadership positions. Throughout

125

the school's history, it has drawn mostly on the talents of high-status males. It was not until the second half of the 20th century that women, minorities, and members of the lower classes were allowed admission into this esteemed institution (Abel 1989).

Most of the students attending the university at the time the study was being conducted were White and middle class. The overwhelming majority are the sons and daughters of the professional-managerial class. Over 70% of those returning questionnaires had Ivy League or other highly prestigious educational credentials. As one would expect, fewer working-class students possessed such credentials.

A triangulated research design (Fielding and Fielding 1986) was used to collect the data. The first phase consisted of extensive fieldwork at the law school from 1985 to 1988, during which time I became a "peripheral member" (Adler and Adler 1987) in selected student groups. My activities while in the field consisted of attending classes with students, participating in their Moot Court preparations, studying with students on campus, and at times, in their apartments, lunching with them, becoming involved in student demonstrations over job recruiting and faculty hiring, attending extracurricular lectures presented on campus, and participating in orientation exercises for first-year students. Throughout the entire fieldwork phase, I assumed both overt and covert roles. During the observation periods in classrooms, I recorded teacher-student interactions that occurred.

To supplement these observations, I conducted in-depth interviews with 103 law students at various stages in their training. Both personal interviews and small-group interviews with three or four students were recorded. The interviews lasted approximately 2 hours each and sought to identify the lived process through which law students experience legal training.

Finally, I administered a survey to 50% of the 1,540 students attending the law school. The survey examined their backgrounds, motives for attending law school, subjective perceptions of personal change, expectations about future practice, and evaluations of various substantive areas of practice. Over half (391) of the questionnaires were returned—a high rate of response for a survey of six pages requiring approximately 30 minutes of the respondent's time.

For this article, a subset of working-class students was selected for extensive analysis. Of the 103 students interviewed for the larger study, 23 came from working-class backgrounds, none of these from either the labor aristocracy or the unstable sectors of the working class. Typical parental occupations include postal worker, house painter, factory worker, fireman, dock worker, and carpenter. Many of these students were interviewed several times during their law school career. . . .

Feeling Out of Place

Working-class students entered this elite educational institution with a great deal of class pride. This sense of class pride is reflected in the fact that a significantly larger proportion of working-class students reported entering law school for the purposes of contributing to social change than their non-working-class counterparts (see Granfield and Koenig 1990). That these students entered law school with the desire to help the down-trodden suggests that they identified with their working-class kin. In fact, students often credited their class background as being a motivating factor in their decision to pursue a career in social justice. One third-year student, whose father worked as a postal worker, recalled her parental influence:

> I wanted a career in social justice. It seemed to me to be a good value for someone who wanted to leave this world a little better than they found it. My parents raised me with a sense that there are right things and wrong things and that maybe you ought to try to do some right things with your life.

A second-year student said that he was influenced by the oppressive experiences that his father endured as a factory laborer. Coming to law school to pursue a career in a labor union, this student explained, "I was affected by my father who had a job as a machinist. My father believes that corporations have no decency. I would term it differently but we're talking about the same thing." Identifying with their working-class heritage produced not only a sense of pride but a system of values and ideals that greatly influenced their initial career objectives.

However, identification with the working class began to diminish soon after these students entered law school. Not long after arriving, most working-class law students encountered an entirely new moral career. Although initially proud of their accomplishments, they soon came to define themselves as different and their backgrounds a burden. Lacking the appropriate cultural capital (Bourdieu 1984) associated with their more privileged counterparts, working-class students began to experience a crisis in competency. Phrases such as "the first semester makes you feel extremely incompetent," "the first year is like eating humble pie," and "I felt very small, powerless and dumb" were almost universal among these working-class students. Some students felt embarrassed by their difficulty in using the elaborated speech codes (Bernstein 1977) associated with the middle class. One working-class woman said that she was very aware of using "proper" English, adding that "it makes me self-conscious when I use the wrong word or tense. I feel that if I had grown up in the middle class, I wouldn't have lapses. I have difficulty expressing thoughts while most other people here don't."

The recognition of their apparent differentness is perhaps best noted by examining the students' perception of stress associated with the first year of studies. Incoming working-class students reported significantly higher levels of personal stress than did their counterparts with more elite backgrounds. Much of this anxiety came from fears of academic inadequacy. Despite generally excellent college grades and their success in gaining admission to a nationally ranked law school, these students often worried that they did not measure up to the school's high standards. Nearly 62% of the first-year working-

class students reported experiencing excessive grade pressure, compared to only 35% of those students from higher social class backgrounds.

... While most students experience some degree of uncertainty and competency crisis during their first year, working-class students face the additional pressure of being cultural outsiders. Lacking manners of speech, attire, values, and experiences associated with their more privileged counterparts, even the most capable working-class student felt out of place:

> I had a real problem my first year because law and legal education are based on upper-middle-class values. The class debates had to do with profit maximization, law and economics, atomistic individualism. I remember in class we were talking about landlords' responsibility to maintain decent housing in rental apartments. Some people were saying that there were good reasons not to do this. Well, I think that's bullshit because I grew up with people who lived in apartments with rats, leaks, and roaches. I feel really different because I didn't grow up in suburbia.

... Such experiences contributed to a student's sense of living in an alien world. The social distance these students experienced early in their law school career produced considerable discomfort.

This discomfort grew more intense as they became increasingly immersed into this new elite world. Within a short span of time these students began to experience a credential gap vis-à-vis other students who possessed more prestigious academic credentials. A first-year male student who attended a state school in the Midwest explained:

> I'm not like most people here. I didn't go to prestigious schools. I'm a bit of a minority here because of that. When I got here I was really intimidated by the fact of how many Yale and Harvard people there were here.

... In general, then, as working-class students progressed through law school, they began to adopt a view of themselves as different. The recognition of this difference subsequently led them to develop techniques of adjusting to their perceived secondary status.

Faking It

The management of identity has critical strategic importance not only for group affiliation and acceptance but for life chances. Stigma limits one's opportunities to participate in social life as a complete citizen, particularly so for those possessing gender or racial stigmas. However, because of the visibility of these stigmas, a person's adjustment to second-class citizenship is accomplished typically through either role engulfment in which a person accepts a spoiled identity (Schur 1971) or through direct confrontation where assignment of secondary status is itself challenged (Schur 1980). Rarely are these groups able to employ the concealment tactics typical among those groups whose stigma is not overtly visible.

Unlike gender or racial stigma, however, individuals often adjust to class stigma by learning to conceal their uniqueness. The practice of concealing one's class background, for instance, is not unusual. Certainly, members of the elite frequently learn that it is in "bad taste" to flaunt their privileged background and that it is more gracious to conceal their eminent social status (Baltzell 1958). Similarly, individuals who experience downward mobility often attempt to maintain their predecline image by concealing loss of status. Camouflaging unemployment in the world of management by using such terms as "consultant" and by doctoring resumés are ways that downwardly mobile executives "cover" their spoiled status (Newman 1988). Concealing one's social class circumstances and the stigma that may be associated with it assist individuals in dealing with any rejection and ostracism that may be forthcoming were the person's actual status known.

Initially, students who took pride in having accomplished upward mobility openly displayed a working-class presentation of self. Many went out of their way to maintain this presentation. One first-year student who grew up in a labor union family in New York explained that "I have consciously maintained my working class image. I wear work shirts or old flannel shirts and blue jeans every day." During his first year, this student flaunted his working-class background, frequently also donning an old army jacket, hiking boots, and a wool hat. Identifying himself as part of the "proletarian left," he tried to remain isolated from what he referred to as the "elitist" law school community.

This attempt to remain situated in the working class, however, not only separated these students from the entire law school community but alienated them from groups that shared their ideological convictions. While much of the clothing worn by non-working-class law students suggests resistance to being identified as a member of the elite, working-class students become increasingly aware of their differentness. Although these students identify with the working class, others, despite their appearance, possess traits and life-styles that are often associated with more privileged groups (see Lurie 1983, Stone 1970). One first-year woman who described herself as "radical" complained that the other law school radicals were really "a bunch of upper-class White men." Subsequently, working-class students must disengage from their backgrounds if they desire to escape feeling discredited.

Working-class students disengaged from their previous identity by concealing their class backgrounds. . . . Concealment allowed students to better participate in the culture of eminence that exists within the law school and reap available rewards.

This concealment meant, for instance, that students needed to acquire new dress codes. As Stone (1970) illustrated, appearance signifies identity and exercises a regulatory function over the responses of others. Such cultural codes pertaining to appearance often are used to exclude individuals from elite social positions (Bourdieu 1984; Jackall 1988; Lamont and Lareau 1988). Although working-class students lacked the cultural capital of higher social classes, they began to realize that they could successfully mimic their more privileged counterparts. Like undistinguished prep school students (Cookson and Persell 1985), working-class law students learned how to behave in an upper-class world, including how to dress for a new audience whose favorable appraisal they must cultivate. One second-year male discussed this process:

> I remember going to buy suits here. I went to Brooks Brothers for two reasons. One, I don't own a suit. My father owns one suit, and it's not that good. Second, I think it's important to look good. A lot of my friends went to Brooks Brothers, and I feel it's worth it to do it right and not to have another hurdle to walk in and have the wrong thing on. It's all a big play act. . . . During my first year, I had no luck with interviews. I was in my own little world when I came here. I wished I had paid more attention to the dressing habits of second- and third-year students.

Being in their own "working-class world" forced these students to begin recognizing the importance of different interpersonal skills. A second-year woman commented that

> I have really begun to see the value of having good social skills. I think that this is one of the ways that law firms weed out people. In order to get jobs you have to have those social skills. I'm real conscious of that when I go out on interviews now.

The recognition among working-class students that they were able to imitate upper-class students increasingly encouraged them to conceal their backgrounds. One second-year student, whose father worked as a house painter, boasted of his mastery of "passing":

> I generally don't tell people what my father does or what my mother does. I notice that I'm different, but it's not something other people here notice because I can fake it. They don't notice that I come from a blue-collar background.

Paying attention to the impression that one presents becomes extremely important for the upwardly mobile working-class student.

These students were sometimes assisted in their performances by professional career counselors employed by the law school. These professionals gave students instructions on how to present themselves as full-fledged members of this elite community. Students were taught that unless they downplayed their social class background, the most lucrative opportunities would be denied them. A third-year woman from a working-class area in Boston recalled learning this new norm of presentation:

> I'm sort of proud that I'm from South Boston and come from a working-class background. During my second year, however, I wasn't having much luck with my first interviews. I went to talk with my adviser about how to change my resumé a bit or how to present myself better. I told my adviser that on the interviews I was presenting myself as a slightly unusual person with a different background. We talked about that, and he told me that it probably wasn't a good idea to present myself as being a little unusual. I decided that he was right and began to play up that I was just like them. After that, the interviews and offers began rolling in. I began to realize that they [interviewers] really like people who are like themselves.

Recognizing that job recruiters seek homogeneity is an important lesson that upwardly mobile working-class students must learn if they are to gain admission into high status and financially rewarding occupations. Kanter (1977) demonstrated, for instance, that managers come to reward those who resemble themselves. More recently, Jackall (1988) documented how the failure of managers to "fit in" resulted in suspicion and subsequent exclusion from advancement. Fitting in is partially important in prestigious law firms which tend to resemble the high-status clients they represent (Abel 1989). During interviews, however, working-class law students faced a distinct disadvantage, as the interviewers who actively pursued new recruits rarely posed questions about the student's knowledge of law. Most seemed intent on finding students who fit into the law firm's corporate culture. The entire recruitment process itself, from the initial interview to "fly out," represents ceremonial affirmation of these students' elite status in which they need only demonstrate their "social" competence. Working-class students typically found such interactions stressful. . . .

. . . Some of the most successful working-class students enjoyed the accolades bestowed on them because of their hard work and natural abilities. . . . However, such success comes at a price, particularly for working-class students of color. Although having achieved success, many of these students continued to feel like outsiders. One such student, a third-year Black male, reflected on what he considered the unfortunate aspects of affirmative action programs:

> I have mixed feelings about the law review because of its affirmative action policies. On the one hand, I think it's good that minorities are represented on the law review. On the other hand, there's a real stigma attached to it. Before law school, I achieved by my own abilities. On law review, I don't feel I get respect. I find myself working very hard and getting no respect. Other students don't work as hard. I spend a lot of time at the review because I don't want to turn in a bad assignment. I don't want them [other law review members] to think that I don't have what it takes.

Students who perceived themselves as outsiders frequently overcompensated for their failings because they felt judged by the "master status" associated with their social identity. This reaction to class stigma is typical among working-class students in educational institutions. In addition to developing their educational skills, working-class students are confronted with learning social skills as well. This makes succeeding particularly difficult for these students and is a task fraught with the fear of being discovered as incompetent (Sennett and Cobb 1973).

Ambivalence

Despite their maneuvers, these working-class students had difficulty transcending their previous identity. The attempt by these students to manage their stigma resulted in what Goffman (1963) termed "identity ambivalence" (p. 107). Working-class students who sought to exit their class background could neither embrace their group nor let it go. This ambivalence is often felt by working-class individuals who attain upward mobility into the professional-managerial class (Steinitz and Solomon 1986). Many experience the "stranger in paradise" syndrome, in which working-class individuals feel like virtual outsiders in middle-class occupations (Ryan and Sackrey 1984). Such experiences frequently lead to considerable identity conflict among working-class individuals who attempt to align themselves with the middle class.

The working-class law students in my sample typically experienced identity conflicts on their upward climb. Not only did they feel deceptive in their adjustment strategies, but many felt the additional burden of believing they had "sold out" their own class and were letting their group down. Like other stigmatized individuals who gain acceptance among dominant groups (Goffman 1963), these students often felt they were letting down their own group by representing elite interests. One third-year female student ruefully explained:

> My brother keeps asking me whether I'm a Republican yet. He thought that after I finished law school I would go to work to help people, not work for one of those firms that do business. In a way, he's my conscience. Maybe he's right. I've got a conflict with what I'm doing. I came from the working class and wanted to do public interest law. I have decided not to do that. It's been a difficult decision for me. I'm not completely comfortable about working at a large firm.

. . . This student experienced a form of self-alienation as a result of . . . identity ambivalence. Students often experience a sense of guilt as they transcend their working-class backgrounds. Such guilt, however, needs to be abated if these students are to successfully adjust to their new reference group and reduce the status conflict they experience. For these working-class students, making the primary adjustment to upward mobility required strategies of accommodation in personal attitudes regarding their relationship to members of less privileged social classes. Secondary identity adjustments were therefore critical in helping students mitigate the ambivalence they experienced over their own success and subsequent separation from the working class.

Resolving Ambivalence

. . . Working-class students . . . sought to manage their ambivalence by remaining "ideologically" distanced from the very social class their elite law school credential had facilitated alignment with. Many of these students became deliberate role models, unreservedly immersing themselves in higher social classes for that specific purpose. Such adjustments might be thought of as political since they were intended to directly challenge the domination of social elites. A Black working-class student described how his actions would benefit the less fortunate:

> I get slammed for being a corporate tool. People feel that I have sold out. I'm irritated by that. For years, Blacks have been treated as slaves, sharecroppers, or porters. So I think that whether I want to be a partner at Cravath or to be a NAACP defense attorney, either of these positions are politically correct. We need Black people with money and power. I think that I can make significant contributions to Black causes.

For many students who experienced ambivalence, working in elite law firms was seen as the best way to help those they left behind. Other students redefined the value of large corporate law firms for the opportunities that such positions offered in contributing to social change. One third-year student suggested:

> I used to think that social change would come about by being an activist. That's why I originally wanted to do public interest law. But you really can't accomplish much by doing this. The hiring partner at [a major New York law firm] convinced me that this is the only way to get things done. He served as the Undersecretary of State in the [former president's] administration. He made sense when he told me that if I wanted to contribute to social change I had to become an important person.

Students became less convinced that directly serving the less privileged social classes would effectively resolve the problems that concerned them. A third-year student explained how disenchanted she had become with public interest law:

> I used to think that you could do good things for people . . . . I don't think that anymore. I'm no longer troubled by the idea of being a corporate lawyer as opposed to a public interest one. I'm still concerned about social problems like poverty or poor housing, but I'm not sure that being a public interest attorney is the way to resolve those things. The needs of the people that public interest lawyers serve are just beyond what I can do as an attorney. I think I can do more good for people if I commit myself to working with community groups or activities in the bar during my spare time.

The offering of such accounts helps students resolve the contradiction they experience by choosing a large law firm practice, as does the practical planning to use one's spare time (e.g., to do community activities). Unfortunately, given the structure of contemporary large law firms, spare time is a rarity (Nelson 1988; Spangler 1986). Adopting these new definitions regarding the pursuit of effective social change means that working-class students need not feel penitent over their upward mobility. Such strategies, of course, are attractive, as they suggest that the student is becoming elite not solely because he or she is striving for personal reward and success but as a means to best pursue the noble ideals of public service and social activism.

A more drastic accommodation involved avoidance of those who reminded working-class students of their social obligations toward helping the less fortunate. Just associating with individuals whose career path was geared toward helping the down-trodden caused considerable uneasiness in working-class students who had decided to enter large law firms. One third-year student said that he had begun to avoid law students who had retained their commitment to work with the poor:

> It's taken for granted here that you can work for a large firm and still be a good person. The people who don't reinforce that message make me uncomfortable now. Frankly, that's why I'm not hanging out with the public interest people. They remind me of my own guilt.

In some cases, avoidance turned into open hostility. Another third-year student described how she now saw other students who remained committed to their ideals of helping the less fortunate: "They're so single-minded at times and I think a little naïve. They've really pushed me away from wanting to do public interest work as a full-time occupation." Condemning her condemners helped this student neutralize the guilt she felt over working for a corporate law firm.

Conclusion

This article has demonstrated that a focus on stigma holds considerable promise in analyzing social class relations and particularly the difficulties that upwardly mobile working-class youths face as they ascend the status hierarchy. Research that sought to explain the formation of identity as it intersects with social class has generated important insights into understanding stratification as a lived experience (Newman 1988; Steinitz and Solomon 1986; Connell et al. 1982; Willis 1977, 1983; Sennett and Cobb 1973). Much of this work presents a less rigid and monolithic view of social class as causing behavior and instead sees class as a social construction. According to Steinitz and Solomon (1986), "Individual members of a class construct their inter-

pretations of social class through their actions in specific contexts and times" (p. 3). Understanding how individuals interpret and experience social class as well as grasping how situational vicissitudes alter these constructions is important to gaining greater awareness of the relationship between class and identity.

The recognition that social class is an "experienced" and constructed reality offers insights into responses to stigma. Over the years, various stigmatized groups have directly combated attempts to relegate them to a secondary status within society. Certainly, women, racial minorities, gays, and those with disabilities have fought against the unjust system of devaluation which restricted their opportunities, reduced their humanity, and forced them to make adjustments, such as covering, passing, and careful disclosure, for the benefit of dominant groups. The willingness of these groups to confront critical social typifications came directly from their growing realization of the arbitrariness of such evaluations.

However, in regard to social class, the ideology of meritocracy serves to legitimate devaluation of the lower classes. Because social class position is frequently seen as the outcome of individual talent and effort, the assignment of stigma to lower socioeconomic groups is not seen as being based on arbitrary evaluation. Given the legitimacy of the meritocratic ideology, is it any wonder that upwardly mobile working-class students choose not to directly confront the devaluation they experience but rather to forge a new identity which effectively divorces them from the working class? It is not surprising to find, for example, that the movements to reform law and make it more accessible to persons of lower economic status emanated not from working-class intellectuals but from elites who were sympathetic to their plight (Katz 1984).

Upwardly mobile working-class students in this study, as well as in others, interpret and experience their social class from the perspective of stigma. However, since the stigma of being a member of the lower classes is thought to be just, upwardly mobile working-class students frequently construct identities in which they seek to escape the taint associated with their affiliation. Overcoming this stigma is therefore considered an individual rather than a collective effort. As was demonstrated in this study, such efforts often involve managing one's identity in the ways that Goffman outlined. Research that explores identity struggles as they relate to class could offer further extensions of Goffman's comments on stigma. Such research also has potential value in contributing to our understanding of working-class movements in the United States. Indeed, exploring the experience of class from the perspective of stigma and its management could offer great insight into the social psychology of working-class disempowerment.

REFERENCES

Abel, R. 1989. *American lawyers.* New York: Oxford University Press.

Adler, P., and P. Adler. 1987. *Membership roles in field research.* Newbury Park, CA: Sage.

Baltzell, E. D. 1958. *Philadelphia gentlemen.* New York: Free Press.

Bernstein, B. 1977. *Class codes and control, vol. 3: Towards a theory of educational transmission.* London: Routledge & Kegan Paul.

Bourdieu, P. 1984. *Distinction: A social critique of the judgment of taste.* Cambridge, MA: Harvard University Press.

Connell, R., D. Ashenden, S. Kessler, and G. W. Dowsett. 1982. *Making the difference.* Sydney, Australia: Allen & Unwin.

Cookson, P., and C. Persell. 1985. *Preparing for power. American's elite boarding schools.* New York: Basic Books.

Fielding, N., and J. Fielding. 1986. *Linking data.* Beverly Hills, CA: Sage.

Goffman, E. 1963. *Stigma: Notes on the management of spoiled identity.* Englewood Cliffs, NJ: Prentice Hall.

———. 1967. *Interaction ritual: Essays on face to face behavior.* New York: Pantheon.

———. 1983. The interaction order. *American Sociological Review* 48:1–17.

Granfield, R. 1989. Making the elite lawyer: Culture and ideology in legal education. Ph.d. diss., Northeastern University, Boston.

Granfield, R., and T. Koenig. 1990. From activism to pro bono: The redirection of working class altruism at Harvard Law School. *Critical Sociology* 17:57–80.

Heinz, J., and E. Laumann. 1982. *Chicago lawyers: The social structure of the bar.* New York: Russell Sage.

Jackall, R. 1988. *Moral mazes: The world of the corporate manager.* New York: Oxford University Press.

Kanter, R. 1977. *Men and women of the corporation.* New York: Basic Books.

Katz, J. 1984. *Poor people's lawyers in transition.* New Brunswick, NJ: Rutgers University Press.

Lamont, M., and A. Lareau. 1988. Cultural capital: Allusions, gaps and glissandos in recent theoretical development. *Sociological Theory* 6:153–168.

Lurie, A. 1983. *The language of clothes.* New York: Vintage.

Nelson, R. 1988. *Partners with power: The social transformation of the large law firm.* Berkeley: University of California Press.

Newman, K. 1988. *Falling from grace: The experience of downward mobility in the American middle class.* New York: Free Press.

Pfuhl, E. 1986. *The deviance process.* Belmont, CA: Wadsworth.

Ryan, J., and C. Sackrey. 1984. *Strangers in paradise: Academics from the working class.* Boston: South End Press.

Schur, E. 1971. *Labeling deviant behavior.* New York: Harper & Row.

———. 1980. *The politics of deviance.* Englewood Cliffs, NJ: Prentice Hall.

Sennett, R., and R. Cobb. 1973. *The hidden injuries of class.* New York: Random House.

Smigel, E. 1969. *The Wall Street lawyer.* Bloomington: Indiana University Press.

Spangler, E. 1986. *Lawyers for hire: Salaried professionals at work.* New Haven, CT: Yale University Press.

Steinitz, V., and E. Solomon. 1986. *Starting out: Class and community in the lives of working class youth.* Philadelphia: Temple University Press.

Stone, G. 1970. Appearance and the self. In *Social psychology through symbolic interaction,* edited by G. Stone and H. Farberman, pp. 394–414. New York: Wiley.

Useem, M., and J. Karabel. 1986. Paths to corporate management. *American Sociological Review* 51: 184–200.

THINKING ABOUT THE READING

How do working-class students learn to manage their identities and backgrounds in elite law schools? What are the long-term negative consequences of their impression management tactics? How can you account for the tendency for students' attitudes toward their working-class backgrounds to turn from ambivalent to hostile? What can law schools, as well as other institutions that typically have an "elite" clientele, do to reduce the class stigma felt by members of the lower classes? In other words, what can these institutions do to empower working-class individuals? In a society like the United States, where everyone is expected to be upwardly mobile, is class stigma inevitable in these types of situations?

Suspended Identity

Identity Transformation in a Maximum Security Prison

Thomas J. Schmid and Richard S. Jones

The extent to which people hide behind the masks of impression management in everyday life is a point of theoretical controversy (Goffman 1959; Gross and Stone 1964; Irwin 1977; Douglas et al. 1980; Douglas and Johnson 1977; Messinger et al. 1962; Blumer 1972, 1969). A variety of problematic circumstances can be identified, however, in which individuals find it necessary to accommodate a sudden but encompassing shift in social situations by establishing temporary identities. These circumstances, which can range from meteoric fame (Adler and Adler 1989) to confinement in total institutions, place new identity demands on the individual, while seriously challenging his or her prior identity bases.

A prison sentence constitutes a "massive assault" on the identity of those imprisoned (Berger 1963: 100–101). This assault is especially severe on first-time inmates, and we might expect radical identity changes to ensue from their imprisonment At the same time, a prisoner's awareness of the challenge to his identity affords some measure of protection against it. . . .

Data for the study are derived principally from ten months of participant observation at a maximum security prison for men in the upper midwest of the United States. One of the authors was an inmate serving a felony sentence for one year and one day, while the other participated in the study as an outside observer. Relying on traditional ethnographic data collection and analysis techniques, this approach offered us general observations of hundreds of prisoners, and extensive fieldnotes that were based on repeated, often daily, contacts with about fifty inmates, as well as on personal relationships established with a smaller number of inmates. We subsequently returned to the prison to conduct focused interviews with other prisoners; using information provided by prison officials, we were able to identify and interview twenty additional first-time inmates who were serving sentences of two years or less. . . .

Three interrelated research questions guided our analysis: How do first-time, short-term inmates define the prison world, and how do their definitions change during their prison careers? How do these inmates adapt to the prison world, and how do their adaptation strategies change during their prison careers? How do their self-definitions, change during their prison careers? . . .

Preprison Identity

Our data suggest that the inmates we studied have little in common before their arrival at prison, except their conventionality. Although convicted of felonies, most do not possess "criminal" identities (cf. Irwin 1970: 29–34). They begin their sentences with only a vague, incomplete image (Boulding 1961) of what prison is like, but an image that nonetheless stands in contrast to how they view their own social worlds. Their prison image is dominated by the theme of violence: they see prison inmates as violent, hostile, alien human beings, with whom they have nothing in common. They have several specific fears about what will happen to them in prison, including fears of assault, rape, and death. They are also concerned about their identities, fearing that—if they survive prison at all—they are in danger of changing in prison, either through the intentional efforts of rehabilitation personnel or through the unavoidable hardening effects of the prison environment Acting on this imagery (Blumer 1969)—or, more precisely, on the inconsonance of their self-images with this prison image—they develop an anticipatory survival strategy . . . that consists primarily of protective resolutions: a resolve to avoid all hostilities; a resolve to avoid all nonessential contacts with inmates and guards; a resolve to defend themselves in any way possible; and a resolve not to change, or to be changed, in prison.

A felon's image and strategy are formulated through a running self-dialogue, a heightened state of reflexive awareness (Lewis 1979) through which he ruminates about his past behavior and motives, and imaginatively projects himself into the prison world. This self-dialogue begins shortly after his arrest, continues intermittently during his trial or court hearings, and becomes especially intense at the time of his transfer to prison. . . .

> My first night in the joint was spent mainly on kicking myself in the butt for putting myself in the joint. It was a very emotional evening. I thought a lot about all my friends and family, the good-byes, the things we did the last couple of months, how good they had been to me, sticking by me. I also thought about my fears: Am I going to go crazy? Will I end up fighting for my life? How am I going to survive in here for a year? Will I change? Will things be the same when I get out?

His self-dialogue is also typically the most extensive self-assessment he has ever conducted; thus, at the same time that he is resolving not to change, he is also initiating the kind of introspective analysis that is essential to any identity transformation process.

Self-Insulation

A felon's self-dialogue continues during the initial weeks and months of his sentence, and it remains a solitary activity, each inmate struggling to come to grips with the inconsonance of his established (preprison) identity and his present predicament. Despite the differences in their preprison identities, however, inmates now share a common situation that affects their identities. With few exceptions, their self-dialogues involve feelings of vulnerability, discontinuity, and differentiation from other inmates, emotions that reflect both the degradations and deprivations of institutional life (cf. Goffman 1961; Sykes 1958; and Garfinkel 1956) and their continuing outsiders' perspective on the prison world. These feelings are obviously the result of everything that has happened to the inmates, but they are something else as well: they are the conditions in which every first-time, short-term inmate finds himself. They might even be called the common attributes of the inmates' selves-in-prison, for the irrelevance of their preprison identities within the prison world reduces their self-definitions, temporarily, to the level of pure emotion. These feelings, and a consequent emphasis on the "physical self" (Zurcher 1977: 176), also constitute the essential motivation for the inmates' self-insulation strategies.

An inmate cannot remain wholly insulated within the prison world, for a number of reasons. He simply spends too much of his time in the presence of others to avoid all interaction with them. He also recognizes that his prison image is based on incomplete and inadequate information, and that he must interact with others in order to acquire first-hand information about the prison world. His behavior in prison, moreover, is guided not only by his prison image but by a fundamental ambivalence he feels about his situation, resulting from his marginality between the prison and outside social worlds (Schmid and Jones 1987). His ambivalence has several manifestations throughout his prison career, but the most important is his conflicting desires for self-insulation and for human communication.

Managing a Dualistic Self

An inmate is able to express both directions of his ambivalence (and to address his need for more information about the prison) by drawing a distinction between his "true" identity (i.e., his outside, preprison identity) and a "false" identity he creates for the prison world. For most of a new inmate's prison career, his preprison identity remains a "subjective" or "personal" identity while his prison identity serves as his "objective" or "social" basis for interaction in prison (see Weigert 1986; Goffman 1963). This bifurcation of his self . . . is not a conscious decision made at a single point in time, but it does represent two conscious and interdependent identity-preservation tactics, formulated through self-dialogue and refined through tentative interaction with others.

First, after coming to believe that he cannot "be himself" in prison because he would be too vulnerable, he decides to "suspend" his preprison identity for the duration of his sentence. He retains his resolve not to let prison change him, protecting himself by choosing not to reveal himself (his "true" self) to others. . . . An inmate's decision to suspend his preprison identity emanates directly from his feelings of vulnerability, discontinuity and differentiation from other inmates. These emotions foster something like a "proto-sociological attitude" (Weigert 1986: 173; see also Zurcher 1977), in which new inmates find it necessary to step outside their taken-for-granted preprison identities. Rather than viewing these identities and the everyday life experience in which they are grounded as social constructions, however, inmates see the *prison* world as an artificial construction, and judge their "naturally occurring" preprison identities to be out of place within this construction. By attempting to suspend his preprison identity for the time that he spends in prison an inmate believes that he will again "be his old self" after his release.

While he is in confinement, an inmate's decision to suspend his identity leaves him with little or no basis for interaction. His second identity tactic, then, is the creation of an identity that allows him to interact, however cautiously, with others. This tactic consists of his increasingly sophisticated impression management skills (Goffman 1959; Schlenker 1980), which are ini-

tially designed simply to hide his vulnerability, but which gradually evolve into an alternative identity felt to be more suitable to the prison world. The character of the presented identity is remarkably similar from inmate to inmate:

> Well, I learned that you can't act like—you can't get the attitude where you are better than they are. Even where you might be better than them, you can't strut around like you are. Basically, you can't stick out. You don't stare at people and things like that. I knew a lot of these things from talking to people and I figured them out by myself. I sat down and figured out just what kind of attitude I'm going to have to take.

> Most people out here learn to be tough, whether they can back it up or not. If you don't learn to be tough, you will definitely pay for it. This toughness can be demonstrated through a mean look, tough language, or an extremely big build. . . . One important thing is never to let your guard down.

An inmate's prison identity, as an inauthentic presentation of self, is not in itself a form of identity transformation but is rather a form of identity construction. His prison identity is simply who he must pretend to be while he is in prison. It is a false identity created for survival in an artificial world. But this identity nonetheless emerges in the same manner as any other identity: it is learned from others, and it must be presented to, negotiated with, and validated by others. A new inmate arrives at prison with a general image of what prisoners are like, and he begins to flesh out this image from the day of his arrival, warily observing others just as they are observing him. Through watching others, through eavesdropping, through cautious conversation and selective interaction, a new inmate refines his understanding of what maximum security prisoners look like, how they talk, how they move, how they act. Despite his belief that he is different from these other prisoners, he knows that he cannot appear to be too different from them, if he is to hide his vulnerability. His initial image of other prisoners, his early observations, and his concern over how he appears to others thus provide a foundation for the identity he gradually creates through impression management.

Impression management skills, of course, are not exclusive to the prison world; a new inmate, like anyone else, has had experience in presenting a "front" to others, and he draws upon his experience in the creation of his prison identity. He has undoubtedly even had experience in projecting the very attributes—strength, stoicism, aplomb—required by his prison identity. Impression management in prison differs, however, in the totality with which it governs interactions and in the perceived costs of failure: humiliation, assault, or death. For these reasons the entire impression management process becomes a more highly conscious endeavor. When presenting himself before others, a new inmate pays close attention to such minute details of his front as eye contact, posture, and manner of walking:

. . .

The way you look seems to be very important. The feeling is you shouldn't smile, that a frown is much more appropriate. The eyes are very important. You should never look away; it is considered a sign of weakness. Either stare straight ahead, look around, or look the person dead in the eyes. The way you walk is important. You shouldn't walk too fast; they might think you were scared and in a hurry to get away.

To create an appropriate embodiment (Weigert 1986; Stone 1962) of their prison identities, some new intimates devote long hours to weightlifting or other body-building exercises, and virtually all of them relinquish their civilian clothes—which might express their preprison identities—in favor of the standard issue clothing that most inmates wear. Whenever a new inmate is open to the view of other inmates, in fact, he is likely to relinquish most overt symbols of his individuality, in favor of a standard issue "prison inmate" appearance.

By acting self-consciously, of course, a new inmate runs the risk of exposing the fact that he *is* acting. But he sees no alternative to playing his

part better; he cannot "not act" because that too would expose the vulnerability of his "true" identity. He thus sees every new prison experience, every new territory that he is allowed to explore, as a test of his impression management skills. Every nonconfrontive encounter with another inmate symbolizes his success at these skills, but it is also a social validation of his prison identity. Eventually he comes to see that many, perhaps most, inmates are engaging in the same kind of inauthentic presentations of self (cf. Glaser and Strauss 1964). Their identities are as "false" as his, and their validations of his identity may be equally false. But he realizes that he is powerless to change this state of affairs, and that he must continue to present his prison identity for as long as he remains in prison. . . .

By the middle of his sentence, a new inmate comes to adopt what is essentially an insider's perspective on the prison world. His prison image has evolved to the point where it is dominated by the theme of boredom rather than violence. (The possibility of violence is still acknowledged and feared, but those violent incidents that do occur have been redefined as the consequences of prison norm violations rather than as random predatory acts; see Schmid and Jones 1990.) His survival strategy, although still extant, has been supplemented by such general adaptation techniques as legal and illegal diversionary activities and conscious efforts to suppress his thoughts about the outside world. . . . His impression management tactics have become second nature rather than self-conscious, as he routinely interacts with others in terms of his prison identity.

An inmate's suspension of his preprison identity, of course, is never absolute, and the separation between his suspended identity and his prison identity is never complete. He continues to interact with his visitors at least partially in terms of his preprison identity, and he is likely to have acquired at least one inmate "partner" with whom he interacts in terms of his preprison as well as his prison identity. During times of introspection, however—which take place less frequently but do not disappear—he generally continues to think of himself as being the same person he was before he came to prison. But it is also during these periods of self-dialogue that he begins to have doubts about his ability to revive his suspended identity. . . . At this point, both the inmate's suspended preprison identity and his created prison identity are part of his "performance consciousness" (Schechner 1985), although they are not given equal value. His preprison identity is grounded primarily in the memory of his biography (Weigert 1986) rather than in self-performance. His concern, during the middle of his sentence, is that he has become so accustomed to dealing with others in terms of his prison identity—that he has been presenting and receiving affirmation of this identity for so long—that it is becoming his "true" identity.

An inmate's fear that he is becoming the character he has been presenting is not unfounded. All of his interactions within the prison world indicate the strong likelihood of a "role-person merger" (Turner 1978). An inmate views his presentation of his prison identity as a necessary expression of his inmate status. Unlike situational identities presented through impression management in the outside world, performance of the inmate role is transsituational and continuous. For a new inmate, prison consists almost exclusively of front regions, in which he must remain in character. As long as he is in the maximum security institution, he remains in at least partial view of the audience for which his prison identity is intended: other prison inmates. Moreover, because the stakes of his performance are so high, there is little room for self-mockery or other forms of role distance (Ungar 1984; Coser 1966) from his prison identity, and there is little possibility that an inmate's performance will be "punctured" (Adler and Adler 1989) by his partner or other prison acquaintances. And because his presentation of his prison identity is continuous, he also receives continuous affirmation of this identity from others—affirmation that becomes more significant in light of the fact that he also remains removed from day-to-day reaffirmation of his preprison identity by his associates in the outside world. The inauthenticity

of the process is beside the point. Stone's (1962: 93) observation that "one's identity is established when others *place* him as a social object by assigning him the same words of identity that he appropriates for himself or *announces*" remains sound even when both the announcements and the placements are recognized as false. . . .

Identity Dialectic

When an inmate's concerns about his identity first emerge, there is little that he can do about them. He recognizes that he has no choice but to present his prison identity so, following the insider's perspective he has now adopted, he consciously attempts to suppress his concerns. Eventually, however, he must begin to consider seriously his capacity to revive his suspended identity; his identity concerns, and his belief that he must deal with them, become particularly acute if he is transferred to the minimum security unit of the prison for the final months of his sentence. At the conclusion of his prison career, an inmate shifts back toward an outsider's perspective on the prison world . . . ; this shift involves the dissipation of his maximum security adaptation strategy, further revision of his prison image, reconstruction of an image of the outside world, and the initial development of an outside plan. The inmate's efforts to revive his suspended identity are part of this shift in perspectives.

It is primarily through a renewed self-dialogue that the inmate struggles to revive his suspended identity—a struggle that amounts to a dialectic between his suspended identity and his prison identity. Through self-dialogue he recognizes, and tries to confront, the extent to which these two identities really do differ. He again tries to differentiate himself from maximum security inmates.

> There seems to be a concern with the inmates here to be able to distinguish . . . themselves from the other inmates. That is—they feel they are above the others. . . . Although they may associate with each other, it still seems important to degrade the majority here.

And he does have some success in freeing himself from his prison identity.

> Well, I think I am starting to soften up a little bit. I believe the identity I picked up in the prison is starting to leave me now that I have left the world of the [maximum security] joint. I find myself becoming more and more involved with the happenings of the outside world. I am even getting anxious to go out and see the sights, just to get away from this place.

But he recognizes that he *has* changed in prison, and that these changes run deeper than the mask he has been presenting to others. He has not returned to his "old self" simply because his impression management skills are used less frequently in minimum security. He raises the question—though he cannot answer it—of how permanent these changes are. He wonders how much his family and friends will see him as having changed. As stated by one of our interview respondents:

> I know I've changed a little bit. I just want to realize how the people I know are going to see it, because they [will] be able to see it more than I can see it. . . . Sometimes I just want to go somewhere and hide.

He speculates about how much the outside world—especially his own network of outside relationships—has changed in his absence. (It is his life, not those of his family and friends, that has been suspended during his prison sentence; he knows that changes have occurred in the outside world, and he suspects that some of these changes may have been withheld from him, intentionally or otherwise.) He has questions, if not serious doubts, about his ability to "make it" on the outside, especially concerning his relationships with others; he knows, in any case, that he cannot simply return to the outside world as if nothing has happened. Above all, he repeatedly confronts the question of who he is, and who he will be in the outside world.

An inmate's struggle with these questions, like his self-dialogue at the beginning of his prison career, is necessarily a solitary activity. The identity he claims at the time of his release, in contrast to his prison identity, cannot be learned from other inmates. Also like his earlier periods of self-dialogue, the questions he considers are not approached in a rational, systematic manner. The process is more one of rumination—of pondering one question until another replaces it, and then contemplating the new question until it is replaced by still another, or suppressed from his thoughts. There is, then, no final resolution to any of the inmate's identity questions. Each inmate confronts these questions in his own way, and each arrives at his own understanding of who he is, based on this unfinished, unresolved self-dialogue. In every case, however, an inmate's release identity is a synthesis of his suspended preprison identity and his prison identity.

Postprison Identity

Because each inmate's release identity is the outcome of his own identity dialectic, we cannot provide a profile of the "typical" release identity. But our data do allow us to specify some of the conditions that affect this outcome. Reaffirmations of his preprison identity by outsiders—visits and furloughs during which others interact with him as if he has not changed—provide powerful support for his efforts to revive his suspended identity. These efforts are also promoted by an inmate's recollection of his preprison identity (i.e., his attempts, through self-dialogue, to assess who he was before he came to prison), by his desire to abandon his prison identity, and by his general shift back toward an outsider's perspective. But there are also several factors that favor his prison identity, including his continued use of diversionary activities; his continued periodic efforts to suppress thoughts about the outside world; his continued ability to use prison impression management skills; and his continuing sense of injustice about the treatment he has received. Strained or cautious interactions with outsiders, or unfulfilled furlough expectations, inhibit the revival of his preprison identity. And he faces direct, experiential evidence that he has changed: when a minimum security resident recognizes that he is now completely unaffected by reports of violent incidents in maximum security, he acknowledges that he is no longer the same person that he was when he entered prison. . . .

Just as we cannot define a typical release identity, we cannot predict these inmates' future, postprison identities, not only because we have restricted our analysis to their prison experiences but because each inmate's future identity is inherently unpredictable. What effect an ex-inmate's prison experience has on his identity depends on how he, in interaction with others, defines this experience. Some of the men we have studied will be returned to prison in the future; others will not. But all will have been changed by their prison experiences. They entered the prison world fearing for their lives; they depart with the knowledge that they have survived. On the one hand, these men are undoubtedly stronger persons by virtue of this accomplishment. On the other hand, the same tactics that enabled them to survive the prison world can be called upon, appropriately or not, in difficult situations in the outside world. To the extent that these men draw upon their prison survival tactics to cope with the hardships of the outside world—to the extent that their prison behavior becomes a meaningful part of their "role repertoire" (Turner 1978) in their everyday lives—their prison identities will have become inseparable from their "true" identities.

The Suspended Identity Model

As identity preservation tactics, an inmate's suspension of his preprison identity and development of a false prison identity are not, and cannot be, entirely successful. At the conclusion of his sentence, no inmate can ever fully revive his suspended identity; he cannot remain the same person he was before he came to prison. But his tactics do not fail entirely either. An inmate's resolve not to change, his decision to suspend his preprison identity, his belief that he will be able to revive this identity, and his subsequent struggle to revive this identity undoubtedly

minimize the identity change that would otherwise have taken place. The inmate's tactics, leading up to his suspended identity dialectic, constitute an identity transformation process . . . that differs from both the gradual, sequential model of identity transformation and models of radical identity transformation (Strauss 1959). It also shares some characteristics with each of these models.

As in cases of brainwashing and conversion, there is an external change agency involved, the inmate does learn a new perspective (an insider's perspective) for evaluating himself and the world around him, and he does develop new group loyalties while his old loyalties are reduced. But unlike a radical identity transformation, the inmate does not interpret the changes that take place as changes in a *central* identity; the insider's perspective he learns and the new person he becomes in prison are viewed as a false front that he must present to others, but a front that does not affect who he really is. And while suspending his preprison identity necessarily entails a weakening of his outside loyalties, it does not, in most cases, destroy them. Because he never achieves more than a marginal status in the prison world, the inmate's ambivalence prevents him from accepting an insider's perspective too fully, and thus prevents him from fully severing his loyalties to the outside world (Schmid and Jones 1987). He retains a fundamental, if ambivalent, commitment to his outside world throughout his sentence, and he expects to reestablish his outside relationships (just as he expects to revive his suspended identity) when his sentence is over.

Like a religious convert who later loses his faith, an inmate cannot simply return to his old self. The liminal conditions (Turner 1977) of the prison world have removed him, for too long, from his accustomed identity bearings in everyday life. He does change in prison, but his attempts to suspend and subsequently revive his preprison identity maintain a general sense of identity continuity for most of his prison career. As in the gradual identity transformation process delineated by Strauss (1959), he recognizes changes in his identity only at periodic "turning points," especially his mid-career doubts about his ability to revive his suspended identity and his self-dialogue at the end of his sentence. Also like a gradual identity transformation, the extent of his identity change depends on a balance between the situational adjustments he has made in prison and his continuing commitments to the outside world (Becker 1960, 1964). His identity depends, in other words, on the outcome of the dialectic between his prison identity and his suspended preprison identity.

The suspended identity model is one component of a holistic analysis of the experiences of first-time, short-term inmates at a specific maximum security prison. Like any holistic analysis, its usefulness lies primarily in its capacity to explain the particular case under study (Deising 1971). We nonetheless expect similar identity transformation processes to occur under similar circumstances: among individuals who desire to preserve their identities despite finding themselves involved in temporary but encompassing social worlds or social situations that subject them to new and disparate identity demands and render their prior identities inappropriate. The suspended identity model presented here provides a basis for further exploration of these circumstances.

REFERENCES

Adler, Patricia A. and Peter Adler. 1989. "The Gloried Self: The Aggrandizement and the Constriction of Self." *Social Psychology Quarterly* 52:299–310.

Becker, Howard S. 1960. "Notes on the Concept of Commitment." *American Journal of Sociology* 66:32–40.

———. "Personal Change in Adult Life." 1964. *Sociometry* 27:40–53.

Berger, Peter L. 1963. *Invitation to Sociology. A Humanistic Perspective.* Garden City, NY: Doubleday/Anchor Books.

Blumer, Herbert. 1972. "Action vs. Interaction: Review of *Relations in Public* by Erving Goffman." *Transaction* 9:50–53.

———. 1969. *Symbolic Interactionism: Perspective and Method.* Englewood Cliffs, NJ: Prentice Hall.

Boulding, Kenneth. 1961. *The Image.* Ann Arbor: University of Michigan Press.

Coser, R. 1966. "Role Distance, Sociological Ambivalence and Traditional Status Systems." *American Journal of Sociology* 72:173–187.

Deising, Paul. 1971. *Patterns of Discovery in the Social Sciences.* Chicago: Aldine-Atherton.

Douglas, Jack D., Patricia A. Adler, Peter Adler, Andrea Fontana, Robert C. Freeman, and Joseph A. Kotarba. 1980. *Introduction to the Sociologies of Everyday Life.* Boston: Allyn & Bacon.

Douglas, Jack D. and John M. Johnson. 1977. *Existential Sociology.* Cambridge: Cambridge University Press.

Garfinkel, Harold. 1956. "Conditions of Successful Degradation Ceremonies." *American Journal of Sociology* 61:420–424.

Glaser, Barney G. and Anselm L. Strauss. 1964. "Awareness Contexts and Social Interaction." *American Sociological Review* 29:269–279.

Goffman, Erving. 1961. *Asylums.* Garden City, NY: Doubleday/Anchor Books.

———. 1959. The *Presentation of Self in Everyday Life.* Garden City, NY: Doubleday/Anchor Books.

———. 1963. *Stigma: Notes on the Management of Spoiled Identity.* Englewood Cliffs, NJ: Prentice Hall.

Gross, Edward and Gregory P. Stone. 1964. "Embarrassment and the Analysis of Role Requirements." *American Journal of Sociology* 70:1–15.

Irwin, John. 1970. *The Felon.* Englewood Cliffs, NJ: Prentice Hall.

———. 1977. *Scenes.* Beverly Hills: Sage.

Lewis, David J. 1979. "A Social Behaviorist Interpretation of the Median I." *American Journal of Sociology* 84:261–287.

Messinger, Sheldon E., Harold Sampson, and Robert D. Towne. 1962. "Life as Theater: Some Notes on the Dramaturgic Approach to Social Reality." *Sociometry* 25: 98–111.

Schechner, Richard. 1985. *Between Theater and Anthropology.* Philadelphia. University of Pennsylvania Press.

Schlenker, B. 1980. *Impression Management. The Self Concept, Social Identity and Interpersonal Relations.* Belmont, CA: Wadsworth.

Schmid, Thomas and Richard Jones. 1987. "Ambivalent Actions: Prison Adaptation Strategies of New

Inmates." American Society of Criminology, annual meetings, Montreal, Quebec.

Schmid, Thomas and Richard Jones. 1990. "Experiential Orientations to the Prison Experience: The Case of First-Time, Short-Term Inmates." Pp. 189–210 in *Perspectives on Social Problems,* edited by Gale Miller and James A. Holstein. Greenwich, CT: JAI Press.

Stone, Gregory P. 1962. "Appearance and the Self." Pp. 86–118 in *Human Behavior and Social Processes,* edited by Arnold Rose. Boston: Houghton Mifflin.

Strauss, Anselm L. 1959. *Mirrors and Masks: The Search for Identity,* Glencoe: Free Press.

Sykes, Gresham. 1958. *The Society of Captives: A Study of a Maximum Security Prison.* Princeton: Princeton University Press.

Turner, Ralph H. 1978. "The Role and the Person." *American Journal of Sociology* 84:1–23.

Turner, Victor. 1977. *The Ritual Process: Structure and Anti-Structure.* Ithaca, NY: Cornell University Press.

Ungar, Sheldon. 1984. "Self-Mockery: An Alternative Form of Self-Presentation." *Symbolic Interaction* 7:121–133.

Weigert, Andrew J. 1986. "The Social Production of Identity: Metatheoretical Foundations." *Sociological Quarterly* 27:165–183.

Zurcher, Louis A. 1977. *The Mutable Self.* Beverly Hills: Sage.

THINKING ABOUT THE READING

What happens to inmates' self-concepts in prison? Given the stigmatizing effects of being identified as an "ex-con," do you think it is ever possible for people to reclaim their normal, law-abiding identities once they get out of prison? How would the identity transformations described by Schmid and Jones differ for female prisoners? Consider another environment (for instance, military boot camp, a violent street gang, a religious cult) where such a dramatic shift in public identity must take place. How would the experiences of people in these situations differ and/or resemble those of the inmates described by Schmid and Jones? What does the process of identity transformation imply about the strength and permanence of identity?

CHAPTER 7

Constructing Difference: Social Deviance

According to most sociologists, deviance is not an inherent feature of certain behaviors. Instead, it is a consequence of a definitional process. Like beauty, it is in the eye of the beholder. Deviant labels can impede everyday social life by forming expectations in the minds of others. Some sociologists argue that the definition of deviance is a form of social control exerted by more powerful people and groups over less powerful ones.

William Chambliss, in "The Saints and the Roughnecks," shows that deviant labels can have serious negative consequences and can determine future opportunities, especially for young people. What makes this idea important, sociologically, is that the application of these labels is not just a function of lawbreaking behavior but is affected by the social characteristics of the people engaging in such behavior. Most of us participate in some form of deviant activity when we are young: minor shoplifting, underage drinking, illegal drug use, driving over the speed limit, wearing bizarre clothes, skipping school, and so on. For most of us, these acts don't have any lasting impact on our identities, but for some they do.

The most obvious structural mechanism that deals with deviance is the criminal justice system. Contrary to popular belief, the police, courts, and prisons aren't simply institutional reactions to deviance. Instead, the criminal justice system has a great deal of influence in defining, explaining, and controlling deviant behavior and in shaping public perceptions of deviance.

Jeffrey Reiman, a conflict sociologist, is interested in how definitions of deviance reflect the interests of the powerful in society. In his article, "A Crime by Any Other Name...," the focus is on crime—more specifically, why certain acts are considered crimes whereas others, equally dangerous or costly, are not. He argues that "we have a greater chance ... of being killed or disabled ... by an occupational injury or disease, by unnecessary surgery, by shoddy emergency medical services than by aggravated assault or even homicide." In other words, those actions that are the most costly or pose the greatest harm are not necessarily labeled as crimes.

The Saints and the Roughnecks

William J. Chambliss

Eight promising young men—children of good, stable, white upper-middle-class families, active in school affairs, good pre-college students—were some of the most delinquent boys at Hanibal High School. While community residents and parents knew that these boys occasionally sowed a few wild oats, they were totally unaware that sowing wild oats completely occupied the daily routine of these young men. The Saints were constantly occupied with truancy, drinking, wild driving, petty theft and vandalism. Yet not one was officially arrested for any misdeed during the two years I observed them.

This record was particularly surprising in light of my observations during the same two years of another gang of Hanibal High School students, six lower-class white boys known as the Roughnecks. The Roughnecks were constantly in trouble with police and community even though their rate of delinquency was about equal with that of the Saints. What was the cause of this disparity? the result? The following consideration of the activities, social class and community perceptions of both gangs may provide some answers.

The Saints from Monday to Friday

The Saints' principal daily concern was with getting out of school as early as possible. The boys managed to get out of school with minimum danger that they would be accused of playing hookey through an elaborate procedure for obtaining "legitimate" release from class. The most common procedure was for one boy to obtain the release of another by fabricating a meeting of some committee, program or recognized club. Charles might raise his hand in his 9:00 chemis-

try class and ask to be excused—a euphemism—for going to the bathroom. Charles would go to Ed's math class and inform the teacher that Ed was needed for a 9:30 rehearsal of the drama club play. The math teacher would recognize Ed and Charles as "good students" involved in numerous school activities and would permit Ed to leave at 9:30. Charles would return to his class, and Ed would go to Tom's English class to obtain his release. Tom would engineer Charles' escape. The strategy would continue until as many of the Saints as possible were freed. After a stealthy trip to the car (which had been parked in a strategic spot), the boys were off for a day of fun.

Over the two years I observed the Saints, this pattern was repeated nearly every day. There were variations on the theme, but in one form or another, the boys used this procedure for getting out of class and then off the school grounds. Rarely did all eight of the Saints manage to leave school at the same time. The average number avoiding school on the days I observed them was five.

Having escaped from the concrete corridors the boys usually went either to a pool hall on the other (lower-class) side of town or to a cafe in the suburbs. Both places were out of the way of people the boys were likely to know (family or school officials), and both provided a source of entertainment. The pool hall entertainment was the generally rough atmosphere, the occasional hustler, the sometimes drunk proprietor and, of course, the game of pool. The cafe's entertainment was provided by the owner. The boys would "accidentally" knock a glass on the floor or spill cola on the counter—not all the time, but enough to be sporting. They would also bend spoons, put salt in sugar bowls and generally

145

tease whoever was working in the cafe. The owner had opened the cafe recently and was dependent on the boys' business which was, in fact, substantial since between the horsing around and the teasing they bought food and drinks.

The Saints on Weekends

On weekends the automobile was even more critical than during the week, for on weekends the Saints went to Big Town—a large city with a population of over a million 25 miles from Hanibal. Every Friday and Saturday night most of the Saints would meet between 8:00 and 8:30 and would go into Big Town. Big Town activities included drinking heavily in taverns or nightclubs, driving drunkenly through the streets, and committing acts of vandalism and playing pranks.

By midnight on Fridays and Saturdays the Saints were usually thoroughly high, and one or two of them were often so drunk they had to be carried to the cars. Then the boys drove around town, calling obscenities to women and girls; occasionally trying (unsuccessfully so far as I could tell) to pick girls up; and driving recklessly through red lights and at high speeds with their lights out. Occasionally they played "chicken." One boy would climb out the back window of the car and across the roof to the driver's side of the car while the car was moving at high speed (between 40 and 50 miles an hour); then the driver would move over and the boy who had just crawled across the car roof would take the driver's seat.

Searching for "fair game" for a prank was the boys' principal activity after they left the tavern. The boys would drive alongside a foot patrolman and ask directions to some street. If the policeman leaned on the car in the course of answering the question, the driver would speed away, causing him to lose his balance. The Saints were careful to play this prank only in an area where they were not going to spend much time and where they could quickly disappear around a corner to avoid having their license plate number taken.

Construction sites and road repair areas were the special province of the Saints' mischief. A

soon-to-be-repaired hole in the road inevitably invited the Saints to remove lanterns and wooden barricades and put them in the car, leaving the hole unprotected. The boys would find a safe vantage point and wait for an unsuspecting motorist to drive into the hole. Often, though not always, the boys would go up to the motorist and commiserate with him about the dreadful way the city protected its citizenry.

Leaving the scene of the open hole and the motorist, the boys would then go searching for an appropriate place to erect the stolen barricade. An "appropriate place" was often a spot on a highway near a curve in the road where the barricade would not be seen by an oncoming motorist. The boys would wait to watch an unsuspecting motorist attempt to stop and (usually) crash into the wooden barricade. With saintly bearing, the boys might offer help and understanding.

A stolen lantern might well find its way onto the back of a police car or hang from a street lamp. Once a lantern served as a prop for a reenactment of the "midnight ride of Paul Revere" until the "play," which was taking place at 2:00 A.M. in the center of a main street of Big Town, was interrupted by a police car several blocks away. The boys ran, leaving the lanterns on the street, and managed to avoid being apprehended.

Abandoned houses, especially if they were located in out-of-the-way places, were fair game for destruction and spontaneous vandalism. The boys would break windows, remove furniture to the yard and tear it apart, urinate on the walls and scrawl obscenities inside.

Through all the pranks, drinking and reckless driving the boys managed miraculously to avoid being stopped by police. Only twice in two years was I aware that they had been stopped by a Big Town policeman. Once was for speeding (which they did every time they drove whether they were drunk or sober), and the driver managed to convince the policeman that it was simply an error. The second time they were stopped they had just left a nightclub and were walking through an alley. Aaron stopped to urinate and the boys began making obscene remarks. A foot patrolman came into the alley, lectured the boys and sent them home. Before the boys got to the car one began talking in a loud voice again. The policeman, who had followed them down the alley, arrested this boy for disturbing the peace and took him to the police station where the other Saints gathered. After paying a $5.00 fine and with the assurance that there would be no permanent record of the arrest, the boy was released.

The boys had a spirit of frivolity and fun about their escapades. They did not view what they were engaged in as "delinquency," though it surely was, by any reasonable definition of that word. They simply viewed themselves as having a little fun and who, they would ask, was really hurt by it? The answer had to be no one, although this fact remains one of the most difficult things to explain about the gang's behavior. Unlikely though it seems, in two years of drinking, driving, carousing and vandalism no one was seriously injured as a result of the Saints' activities.

The Saints in School

The Saints were highly successful in school. The average grade for the group was "B," with two of the boys having close to a straight "A" average. Almost all of the boys were popular and many of them held offices in the school. One of the boys was vice-president of the student body one year. Six of the boys played on athletic teams.

At the end of their senior year, the student body selected ten seniors for special recognition as the "school wheels"; four of the ten were Saints. Teachers and school officials saw no problem with any of these boys and anticipated that they would all "make something of themselves."

How the boys managed to maintain this impression is surprising in view of their actual behavior while in school. Their technique for covering truancy was so successful that teachers did not even realize that the boys were absent from school much of the time. Occasionally, of course, the system would backfire and then the boy was on his own. A boy who was caught would be most contrite, would plead guilty and ask for mercy. He inevitably got the mercy he sought.

Cheating on examinations was rampant, even to the point of orally communicating answers to exams as well as looking at one another's papers. Since none of the group studied, and since they were primarily dependent on one another for help, it is surprising that grades were so high. Teachers contributed to the deception in their admitted inclination to give these boys (and presumably others like them) the benefit of the doubt. When asked how the boys did in school, and when pressed on specific examinations, teachers might admit that they were disappointed in John's performance, but would quickly add that they "knew that he was capable of doing better," so John was given a higher grade than he had actually earned. How often this happened is impossible to know. During the time that I observed the group, I never saw any of the boys take homework home. Teachers may have been "understanding" very regularly.

One exception to the gang's generally good performance was Jerry, who had a "C" average in his junior year, experienced disaster the next year and failed to graduate. Jerry had always been a little more nonchalant than the others about the liberties he took in school. Rather than wait for someone to come get him from class, he would offer his own excuse and leave. Although he probably did not miss any more classes than most of the others in the group, he did not take the requisite pains to cover his absences. Jerry was the only Saint whom I ever heard talk back to a teacher. Although teachers often called him a "cut up" or a "smart kid," they never referred to him as a troublemaker or as a kid headed for trouble. It seems likely, then, that Jerry's failure his senior year and his mediocre performance his junior year were consequences of his not playing the game the proper way (possibly because he was disturbed by his parents' divorce). His teachers regarded him as "immature" and not quite ready to get out of high school.

The Police and the Saints

The local police saw the Saints as good boys who were among the leaders of the youth in the community. Rarely, the boys might be stopped in town for speeding or for running a stop sign. When this happened the boys were always polite, contrite and pled for mercy. As in school, they received the mercy they asked for. None ever received a ticket or was taken into the precinct by the local police.

The situation in Big Town, where the boys engaged in most of their delinquency, was only slightly different. The police there did not know the boys at all, although occasionally the boys were stopped by a patrolman. Once they were caught taking a lantern from a construction site. Another time they were stopped for running a stop sign, and on several occasions they were stopped for speeding. Their behavior was as before: contrite, polite and penitent. The urban police, like the local police, accepted their demeanor as sincere. More important, the urban police were convinced that these were good boys just out for a lark.

The Roughnecks

Hanibal townspeople never perceived the Saints' high level of delinquency. The Saints were good boys who just went in for an occasional prank. After all, they were well dressed, well mannered and had nice cars. The Roughnecks were a different story. Although the two gangs of boys were the same age, and both groups engaged in an equal amount of wild-oat sowing, everyone agreed that the not-so-well-dressed, not-so-well-mannered, not-so-rich boys were heading for trouble. Townspeople would say, "You can see the gang members at the drugstore, night after night, leaning against the storefront (sometimes drunk) or slouching around inside buying cokes, reading magazines, and probably stealing old Mr. Wall blind. When they are outside and girls walk by, even respectable girls, these boys make suggestive remarks. Sometimes their remarks are downright lewd."

From the community's viewpoint, the real indication that these kids were in for trouble was that they were constantly involved with the police. Some of them had been picked up for stealing, mostly small stuff, of course, "but still it's stealing small stuff that leads to big time crimes." "Too bad," people said. "Too bad that these boys couldn't behave like the other kids in town; stay out of trouble, be polite to adults, and look to their future."

The community's impression of the degree to which this group of six boys (ranging in age from 16 to 19) engaged in delinquency was somewhat distorted. In some ways the gang was more delinquent than the community thought; in other ways they were less.

The fighting activities of the group were fairly readily and accurately perceived by almost everyone. At least once a month, the boys would get into some sort of fight, although most fights were scraps between members of the group or involved only one member of the group and some peripheral hanger-on. Only three times in the period of observation did the group fight together: once against a gang from across town, once against two blacks and once against a group of boys from another school. For the first two fights the group went out "looking for trouble"—and they found it both times. The third fight followed a football game and began spontaneously with an argument on the football field between one of the Roughnecks and a member of the opposition's football team.

Jack had a particular propensity for fighting and was involved in most of the brawls. He was a prime mover of the escalation of arguments into fights.

More serious than fighting, had the community been aware of it, was theft. Although almost everyone was aware that the boys occasionally stole things, they did not realize the extent of the activity. Petty stealing was a frequent event for the Roughnecks. Sometimes they stole as a group and coordinated their efforts; other times they stole in pairs. Rarely did they steal alone.

The thefts ranged from very small things like paperback books, comics and ballpoint pens to expensive items like watches. The nature of the thefts varied from time to time. The gang would go through a period of systematically shoplifting items from automobiles or school lockers. Types of thievery varied with the whim of the gang. Some forms of thievery were more profitable than others, but all thefts were for profit, not just thrills.

Roughnecks siphoned gasoline from cars as often as they had access to an automobile, which was not very often. Unlike the Saints, who owned their own cars, the Roughnecks would have to borrow their parents' cars, an event which occurred only eight or nine times a year. The boys claimed to have stolen cars for joy rides from time to time.

Ron committed the most serious of the group's offenses. With an unidentified associate the boy attempted to burglarize a gasoline station. Although this station had been robbed twice previously in the same month, Ron denied any involvement in either of the other thefts. When Ron and his accomplice approached the station, the owner was hiding in the bushes beside the station. He fired both barrels of a double-barreled shotgun at the boys. Ron was severely injured; the other boy ran away and was never caught. Though he remained in critical condition for several months, Ron finally recovered and served six months of the following year in reform school. Upon release from reform school, Ron was put back a grade in school, and began running around with a different gang of boys. The Roughnecks considered the new gang less delinquent than themselves, and during the following year Ron had no more trouble with the police.

The Roughnecks, then, engaged mainly in three types of delinquency: theft, drinking and fighting. Although community members perceived that this gang of kids was delinquent, they mistakenly believed that their illegal activities were primarily drinking, fighting and being a nuisance to passersby. Drinking was limited among the gang members, although it did occur, and theft was much more prevalent than anyone realized.

Drinking would doubtless have been more prevalent had the boys had ready access to liquor. Since they rarely had automobiles at their disposal, they could not travel very far, and the bars in town would not serve them. Most of the boys had little money, and this, too, inhibited their purchase of alcohol. Their major source of liquor was a local drunk who would buy them a fifth if they would give him enough extra to buy himself a pint of whiskey or a bottle of wine.

The community's perception of drinking as prevalent stemmed from the fact that it was the most obvious delinquency the boys engaged in. When one of the boys had been drinking, even a casual observer seeing him on the corner would suspect that he was high.

There was a high level of mutual distrust and dislike between the Roughnecks and the police. The boys felt very strongly that the police were unfair and corrupt. Some evidence existed that the boys were correct in their perception.

The main source of the boys' dislike for the police undoubtedly stemmed from the fact that the police would sporadically harass the group. From the standpoint of the boys, these acts of occasional enforcement of the law were whimsical and uncalled for. It made no sense to them, for example, that the police would come to the corner occasionally and threaten them with arrest for loitering when the night before the boys had been out siphoning gasoline from cars and the police had been nowhere in sight. To the boys, the police were stupid on the one hand, for not being where they should have been and catching the boys in a serious offense, and unfair on the other hand, for trumping up "loitering" charges against them.

From the viewpoint of the police, the situation was quite different. They knew, with all the confidence necessary to be a policeman, that these boys were engaged in criminal activities. They knew this partly from occasionally catching them, mostly from circumstantial evidence ("the boys were around when those tires were slashed"), and partly because the police shared the view of the community in general that this was a bad bunch of boys. The best the police could hope to do was to be sensitive to the fact that these boys were engaged in illegal acts and arrest them whenever there was some evidence that they had been involved. Whether or not the boys had in fact committed a particular act in a particular way was not especially important. The police had a broader view: their job was to stamp out these kids' crimes; the tactics were not as important as the end result.

Over the period that the group was under observation, each member was arrested at least once. Several of the boys were arrested a number of times and spent at least one night in jail. While most were never taken to court, two of the boys were sentenced to six months' incarceration in boys' schools.

The Roughnecks in School

The Roughnecks' behavior in school was not particularly disruptive. During school hours they did not all hang around together, but tended instead to spend most of their time with one or two other members of the gang who were their special buddies. Although every member of the gang attempted to avoid school as much as possible, they were not particularly successful and most of them attended school with surprising regularity. They considered school a burden—something to be gotten through with a minimum of conflict. If they were "bugged" by a particular teacher, it could lead to trouble. One of the boys, Al, once threatened to beat up a teacher and, according to the other boys, the teacher hid under a desk to escape him.

Teachers saw the boys the way the general community did, as heading for trouble, as being uninterested in making something of themselves. Some were also seen as being incapable of meeting the academic standards of the school. Most of the teachers expressed concern for this group of boys and were willing to pass them despite poor performance, in the belief that failing them would only aggravate the problem.

The group of boys had a grade point average just slightly above "C." No one in the group failed either grade, and no one had better than a "C" average. They were very consistent in their achievement or, at least, the teachers were consistent in their perception of the boys' achievement.

Two of the boys were good football players. Herb was acknowledged to be the best player in the school and Jack was almost as good. Both boys were criticized for their failure to abide by training rules, for refusing to come to practice as often as they should, and for not playing their best during practice. What they lacked in sportsmanship they made up for in skill, apparently, and played every game no matter how poorly they had performed in practice or how many practice sessions they had missed.

Two Questions

Why did the community, the school and the police react to the Saints as though they were good, upstanding, nondelinquent youths with bright futures but to the Roughnecks as though they were tough, young criminals who were headed for trouble? Why did the Roughnecks and the Saints in fact have quite different careers after high school—careers which, by and large, lived up to the expectations of the community?

The most obvious explanation for the differences in the community's and law enforcement agencies' reactions to the two gangs is that one group of boys was "more delinquent" than the other. Which group was more delinquent? The answer to this question will determine in part how we explain the differential responses to these groups by the members of the community and, particularly, by law enforcement and school officials.

In sheer number of illegal acts, the Saints were the more delinquent. They were truant from school for at least part of the day almost every day of the week. In addition, their drinking and vandalism occurred with surprising regularity. The Roughnecks, in contrast, engaged sporadically in delinquent episodes. While these episodes were frequent, they certainly did not occur on a daily or even a weekly basis.

The difference in frequency of offenses was probably caused by the Roughnecks' inability to obtain liquor and to manipulate legitimate excuses from school. Since the Roughnecks had less money than the Saints, and teachers carefully supervised their school activities, the Roughnecks' hearts may have been as black as the Saints', but their misdeeds were not nearly as frequent.

There are really no clear-cut criteria by which to measure qualitative differences in antisocial behavior. The most important dimension of the difference is generally referred to as the "seriousness" of the offenses.

If seriousness encompasses the relative economic costs of delinquent acts, then some assessment can be made. The Roughnecks probably stole an average of about $5.00 worth of goods a week. Some weeks the figure was considerably higher, but these times must be balanced against long periods when almost nothing was stolen.

The Saints were more continuously engaged in delinquency but their acts were not for the most part costly to property. Only their vandalism and occasional theft of gasoline would so qualify. Perhaps once or twice a month they would siphon a tankful of gas. The other costly items were street signs, construction lanterns and the like. All of these acts combined probably did not quite average $5.00 a week, partly because much of the stolen equipment was abandoned and presumably could be recovered. The difference in cost of stolen property between the two groups was trivial, but the Roughnecks probably had a slightly more expensive set of activities than did the Saints.

Another meaning of seriousness is the potential threat of physical harm to members of the community and to the boys themselves. The Roughnecks were more prone to physical violence: they not only welcomed an opportunity to fight, they went seeking it. In addition, they fought among themselves frequently. Although the fighting never included deadly weapons, it was still a menace, however minor, to the physical safety of those involved.

The Saints never fought. They avoided physical conflict both inside and outside the group. At the same time, though, the Saints frequently endangered their own and other people's lives. They did so almost every time they drove a car, especially if they had been drinking. Sober, their driving was risky; under the influence of alcohol it was horrendous. In addition, the Saints endangered the lives of others with their pranks. Street excavations left unmarked were a very serious hazard.

Evaluating the relative seriousness of the two gangs' activities is difficult. The community reacted as though the behavior of the Roughnecks was a problem, and they reacted as though the behavior of the Saints was not. But the members of the community were ignorant of the array of delinquent acts that characterized the Saints' behavior. Although concerned citizens were unaware of much of the Roughnecks' behavior as well, they were much better informed about the Roughnecks' involvement in delinquency than they were about the Saints'.

Visibility

Differential treatment of the two gangs resulted in part because one gang was infinitely more visible than the other. This differential visibility was a direct function of the economic standing of the families. The Saints had access to automobiles and were able to remove themselves from the sight of the community. In as routine a decision as to where to go to have a milkshake after school, the Saints stayed away from the mainstream of community life. Lacking transportation, the Roughnecks could not make it to the edge of town. The center of town was the only practical place for them to meet, since their homes were scattered throughout the town and any noncentral meeting place put an undue hardship on some members. Through necessity the Roughnecks congregated in a crowded area where everyone in the community passed frequently, including teachers and law enforcement officers. They could easily see the Roughnecks hanging around the drugstore.

The Roughnecks, of course, made themselves even more visible by making remarks to passersby and by occasionally getting into fights on the corner. Meanwhile, just as regularly, the Saints were either at the cafe on one edge of town or in the pool hall at the other edge of town. Without any particular realization that they were making themselves inconspicuous, the Saints were able to hide their time-wasting. Not only were they removed from the mainstream of traffic, but they were almost always inside a building.

On their escapades the Saints were also relatively invisible, since they left Hanibal and travelled to Big Town. Here, too, they were mobile, roaming the city, rarely going to the same area twice.

Demeanor

To the notion of visibility must be added the difference in the responses of group members to outside intervention with their activities. If one of the Saints was confronted with an accusing policeman, even if he felt he was truly innocent of a wrongdoing, his demeanor was apologetic and penitent. A Roughneck's attitude was almost the polar opposite. When confronted with a threatening adult authority, even one who tried to be pleasant, the Roughneck's hostility and disdain were clearly observable. Sometimes he might attempt to put up a veneer of respect, but it was thin and was not accepted as sincere by the authority.

School was no different from the community at large. The Saints could manipulate the system by feigning compliance with the school norms. The availability of cars at school meant that once free from the immediate sight of the teacher, the boys could disappear rapidly. And this escape was well enough planned that no administrator or teacher was nearby when the boys left. A Roughneck who wished to escape for a few hours was in a bind. If it were possible to get free from class, downtown was still a mile away, and even if he arrived there, he was still very visible. Truancy for the Roughnecks meant almost certain detection, while the Saints enjoyed almost complete immunity from sanctions.

Bias

Community members were not aware of the transgressions of the Saints. Even if the Saints had been less discreet, their favorite delinquencies would have been perceived as less serious than those of the Roughnecks.

In the eyes of the police and school officials, a boy who drinks in an alley and stands intoxicated on the street corner is committing a more serious offense than is a boy who drinks to inebriation in a nightclub or a tavern and drives around afterwards in a car. Similarly, a boy who steals a wallet from a store will be viewed as having committed a more serious offense than a boy who steals a lantern from a construction site.

Perceptual bias also operates with respect to the demeanor of the boys in the two groups when they are confronted by adults. It is not simply that adults dislike the posture affected by boys of the Roughneck ilk; more important is the conviction that the posture adopted by the Roughnecks is an indication of their devotion and commitment to deviance as a way of life. The posture becomes a cue, just as the type of the offense is a cue, to the degree to which the known transgressions are indicators of the youths' potential for other problems.

Visibility, demeanor and bias are surface variables which explain the day-to-day operations of the police. Why do these surface variables operate as they do? Why did the police choose to disregard the Saints' delinquencies while breathing down the backs of the Roughnecks?

The answer lies in the class structure of American society and the control of legal institutions by those at the top of the class structure. Obviously, no representative of the upper class drew up the operational chart for the police which led them to look in the ghettoes and on street corners— which led them to see the demeanor of lower-class youth as troublesome and that of upper-middle-class youth as tolerable. Rather, the procedures simply developed from experience— experience with irate and influential upper-middle-class parents insisting that their son's vandalism was simply a prank and his drunkenness only a momentary "sowing of wild oats"— experience with cooperative or indifferent, powerless, lower-class parents who acquiesced to the law's definition of their son's behavior.

Adult Careers of the Saints and the Roughnecks

The community's confidence in the potential of the Saints and the Roughnecks apparently was justified. If anything, the community members underestimated the degree to which these youngsters would turn out "good" or "bad."

Seven of the eight members of the Saints went on to college immediately after high school. Five of the boys graduated from college in four years.

The sixth one finished college after two years in the army, and the seventh spent four years in the Air Force before returning to college and receiving a B.A. Of these seven college graduates, three went on for advanced degrees. One finished law school and is now active in state politics, one finished medical school and is practicing near Hanibal, and one boy is now working for a Ph.D. The other four college graduates entered submanagerial, managerial or executive training positions with larger firms.

The only Saint who did not complete college was Jerry. Jerry had failed to graduate from high school with the other Saints. During his second senior year, after the other Saints had gone on to college, Jerry began to hang around with what several teachers described as a "rough crowd"— the gang that was heir apparent to the Roughnecks. At the end of his second senior year, when he did graduate from high school, Jerry took a job as a used-car salesman, got married and quickly had a child. Although he made several abortive attempts to go to college by attending night school, when I last saw him (ten years after high school) Jerry was unemployed and had been living on unemployment for almost a year. His wife worked as a waitress.

Some of the Roughnecks have lived up to community expectations. A number of them were headed for trouble. A few were not.

Jack and Herb were the athletes among the Roughnecks, and their athletic prowess paid off handsomely. Both boys received unsolicited athletic scholarships to college. After Herb received his scholarship (near the end of his senior year), he apparently did an about-face. His demeanor became very similar to that of the Saints. Although he remained a member in good standing of the Roughnecks, he stopped participating in most activities and did not hang on the corner as often.

Jack did not change. If anything, he became more prone to fighting. He even made excuses for accepting the scholarship. He told the other gang members that the school had guaranteed him a "C" average if he would come to play football—an idea that seems far-fetched, even in this day of highly competitive recruiting.

During the summer after graduation from high school, Jack attempted suicide by jumping from a tall building. The jump would certainly have killed most people trying it, but Jack survived. He entered college in the fall and played four years of football. He and Herb graduated in four years, and both are teaching and coaching in high schools. They are married and have stable families. If anything, Jack appears to have a more prestigious position in the community than does Herb, though both are well respected and secure in their positions.

Two of the boys never finished high school. Tommy left at the end of his junior year and went to another state. That summer he was arrested and placed on probation on a manslaughter charge. Three years later he was arrested for murder; he pleaded guilty to second-degree murder and is serving a 30-year sentence in the state penitentiary.

Al, the other boy who did not finish high school, also left the state in his senior year. He is serving a life sentence in a state penitentiary for first-degree murder.

Wes is a small-time gambler. He finished high school and "bummed around." After several years he made contact with a bookmaker who employed him as a runner. Later he acquired his own area and has been working it ever since. His position among the bookmakers is almost identical to the position he had in the gang; he is always around but no one is really aware of him. He makes no trouble and he does not get into any. Steady, reliable, capable of keeping his mouth closed, he plays the game by the rules, even though the game is an illegal one.

That leaves only Ron. Some of his former friends reported that they had heard he was "driving a truck up north," but no one could provide any concrete information.

Reinforcement

The community responded to the Roughnecks as boys in trouble, and the boys agreed with that perception. Their pattern of deviancy was reinforced, and breaking away from it became increasingly unlikely. Once the boys acquired an image of themselves as deviants, they selected new friends who affirmed that self-image. As that self-conception became more firmly entrenched, they also became willing to try new and more extreme deviances. With their growing alienation came freer expression of disrespect and hostility for representatives of the legitimate society. This disrespect increased the community's negativism, perpetuating the entire process of commitment to deviance. Lack of a commitment to deviance works the same way. In either case, the process will perpetuate itself unless some event (like a scholarship to college or a sudden failure) external to the established relationship intervenes. For two of the Roughnecks (Herb and Jack), receiving college athletic scholarships created new relations and culminated in a break with the established pattern of deviance. In the case of one of the Saints (Jerry), his parents' divorce and his failing to graduate from high school changed some of his other relations. Being held back in school for a year and losing his place among the Saints had sufficient impact on Jerry to alter his self-image and to virtually assure that he would not go on to college as his peers did. Although the experiments of life can rarely be reversed, it seems likely in view of the behavior of the other boys who did not enjoy this special treatment by the school that Jerry, too, would have "become something" had he graduated as anticipated. For Herb and Jack outside intervention worked to their advantage; for Jerry it was his undoing.

Selective perception and labeling—finding, processing and punishing some kinds of criminality and not others—means that visible, poor, nonmobile, outspoken, undiplomatic "tough" kids will be noticed, whether their actions are seriously delinquent or not. Other kids, who have established a reputation for being bright (even though underachieving), disciplined and involved in respectable activities, who are mobile and monied, will be invisible when they deviate from sanctioned activities. They'll sow their wild oats—perhaps even wider and thicker than their lower-class cohorts—but they won't be noticed. When it's time to leave adolescence most will follow the expected path, settling into the ways of the middle class, remembering fondly the delinquent but unnoticed fling of their youth. The Roughnecks and others like them may turn around, too. It is more likely that their noticeable deviance will have been so reinforced by police and community that their lives will be effectively channelled into careers consistent with their adolescent background.

THINKING ABOUT THE READING

Have you ever known someone who had a "bad reputation"? How did this reputation affect the way people perceived that person? How did it affect the way people interpreted that person's actions? Compare your own "deviant" activities in high school with those of the "Saints" and the "Roughnecks." How were you able to overcome the potential negative effects of labeling? If you were labeled as a bad kid, how were you able to shed the label? Chambliss describes "deviant" activities that were relatively minor. How would the labeling processes he identifies differ if these groups were involved in serious, violent forms of deviance?

A Crime by Any Other Name . . .

Jeffrey Reiman

. . . Think of a crime, any crime. Picture the first "crime" that comes into your mind. What do you see? The odds are you are not imagining a mining company executive sitting at his desk, calculating the costs of proper safety precautions and deciding not to invest in them. Probably what you do see with your mind's eye is one person physically attacking another or robbing something from another via the threat of physical attack. Look more closely. What does the attacker look like? It's a safe bet he (and it is a *he,* of course) is not wearing a suit and tie. In fact, my hunch is that you—like me, like almost anyone else in America—picture a young, tough, lower-class male when the thought of crime first pops into your head. You (we) picture someone like the Typical Criminal described above. The crime itself is one in which the Typical Criminal sets out to attack or rob some specific person.

This last point is important. It indicates that we have a mental image not only of the Typical Criminal but also of the Typical Crime. If the Typical Criminal is a young, lower-class male, the Typical Crime is *one-on-one harm*—where harm means either physical injury or loss of something valuable or both. If you have any doubts that this is the Typical Crime, look at any random sample of police or private eye shows on television. How often do you see the cops on "NYPD Blue" investigate consumer fraud or failure to remove occupational hazards? And when Jessica Fletcher (on "Murder, She Wrote") tracks down well-heeled criminals, it is almost always for garden-variety violent crimes like murder. A study of TV crime shows by The Media Institute in Washington, D.C., indicates that, while the fictional criminals portrayed on television are on

the average both older and wealthier than the real criminals who figure in the FBI *Uniform Crime Reports,* "TV crimes are almost 12 times as likely to be violent as crimes committed in the real world."[1] A review of several decades of research confirms that violent crimes are overrepresented on TV news and fictional crime shows, and that "young people, black people, and people of low socioeconomic status are underrepresented as offenders or victims in television programs"—exactly opposite from the real world in which nonviolent property crimes far outnumber violent crimes, and young, poor and black folks predominate as offenders and victims.[2] As a result, TV crime shows broadcast the double-edged message that the one-on-one crimes of the poor are the typical crimes of all and thus not uniquely caused by the pressures of poverty; *and* that the criminal justice system pursues rich and poor alike—thus, when the criminal justice system happens mainly to pounce on the poor in real life, it is not out of any class bias.[3]

In addition to the steady diet of fictionalized TV violence and crime, there has been an increase in the graphic display of crime on many TV news programs. Crimes reported on TV news are also far more frequently violent than real crimes are.[4] An article in *The Washingtonian* says that the word around two prominent local TV news programs is, "If it bleeds, it leads."[5] What's more, a new breed of nonfictional "tabloid" TV show has appeared in which viewers are shown films of actual violent crimes—blood, screams, and all—or reenactments of actual violent crimes, sometimes using the actual victims playing themselves! Among these are "COPS," "Real Stories of the Highway Patrol," "America's

Most Wanted," and "Unsolved Mysteries." Here, too, the focus is on crimes of one-on-one violence, rather than, say, corporate pollution. The *Wall Street Journal,* reporting on the phenomenon of tabloid TV, informs us that "Television has gone tabloid. The seamy underside of life is being bared in a new rash of true-crime series and contrived-confrontation talk shows."[6] Is there any surprise that a survey by *McCall's* indicates that its readers have grown more afraid of crime in the mid-1980s—even though victimization studies show a stable level of crime for most of this period?[7]

It is important to identify this model of the Typical Crime because it functions like a set of blinders. It keeps us from calling a mine disaster a mass murder even if ten men are killed, even if someone is responsible for the unsafe conditions in which they worked and died. One study of newspaper reporting of a food-processing plant fire, in which 25 workers were killed and criminal charges were ultimately brought, concludes that "the newspapers showed little consciousness that corporate violence might be seen as a crime."[8] I contend that this is due to our fixation on the model of the Typical Crime. This particular piece of mental furniture so blocks our view that it keeps us from using the criminal justice system to protect ourselves from the greatest threats to our persons and possessions.

What keeps a mine disaster from being a mass murder in our eyes is that it is not a one-on-one harm. What is important in one-on-one harm is not the numbers but the *desire of someone (or ones) to harm someone (or ones) else.* An attack by a gang on one or more persons or an attack by one individual on several fits the model of one-on-one harm; that is, for each person harmed there is at least one individual who wanted to harm that person. Once he selects his victim, the rapist, the mugger, the murderer all want this person they have selected to suffer. A mine executive, on the other hand, does not want his employees to be harmed. He would truly prefer that there be no accident, no injured or dead miners. What he does want is something legitimate. It is what he has been hired to get: maxi-

mum profits at minimum costs. If he cuts corners to save a buck, he is just doing his job. If ten men die because he cut corners on safety, we may think him crude or callous but not a murderer. He is, at most, responsible for an *indirect harm,* not a one-on-one harm. For this, he may even be criminally indictable for violating safety regulations—but not for murder. The ten men are dead as an unwanted consequence of his (perhaps overzealous or undercautious) pursuit of a legitimate goal. So, unlike the Typical Criminal, he has not committed the Typical Crime—or so we generally believe. As a result, ten men are dead who might be alive now if cutting corners of the kind that leads to loss of life, whether suffering is specifically aimed at or not, were treated as murder.

This is my point. Because we accept the belief—encouraged by our politicians' statements about crime and by the media's portrayal of crime—that the model for crime is one person specifically trying to harm another, we accept a legal system that leaves us unprotected against much greater dangers to our lives and well-being than those threatened by the Typical Criminal. Before developing this point further, let us anticipate and deal with some likely objections. Defenders of the present legal order are likely to respond to my argument at this point with irritation. Because this will surely turn to outrage in a few pages, let's talk to them now while the possibility of rational communication still exists.

The Defenders of the Present Legal Order (I'll call them "the Defenders" for short) are neither foolish nor evil people. They are not racists, nor are they oblivious to the need for reform in the criminal justice system to make it more even-handed, and for reform in the larger society to make equal opportunity a reality for all Americans. In general, their view is that—given our limited resources, particularly the resource of human altruism—the political and legal institutions we have are the best that can be. What is necessary is to make them work better and to weed out those who are intent on making them work shoddily. Their response to my argument at this point is that the criminal justice system *should* occupy itself primarily with one-on-one harm. Harms of the sort exemplified in the "mine tragedy" are really *not* murders and are better dealt with through stricter government enforcement of safety regulations. The Defenders admit that this enforcement has been rather lax and recommend that it be improved. Basically, though, they think this division of labor is right because it fits our ordinary moral sensibilities.

The Defenders maintain that, according to our common moral notions, someone who tries to do another harm and does is really more evil than someone who jeopardizes others while pursuing legitimate goals but doesn't aim to harm anyone. The one who jeopardizes others in this way at least doesn't try to hurt them. He or she doesn't have the goal of hurting someone in the way that a mugger or a rapist does. Moreover, being directly and purposely harmed by another person, the Defenders believe, is terrifying in a way that being harmed indirectly and impersonally, say, by a safety hazard, is not—even if the resultant injury is the same in both cases. And we should be tolerant of the one responsible for lax safety measures because he or she is pursuing a legitimate goal, that is, his or her dangerous action occurs as part of a productive activity, something that ultimately adds to social wealth and thus benefits everyone—whereas doers of direct harm benefit no one but themselves. Thus, the latter are rightfully in the province of the criminal justice system with its drastic weapons, and the former appropriately dealt with by the milder forms of regulation.

Further, the Defenders insist, the crimes identified as such by the criminal justice system are imposed on their victims totally against their will, whereas the victims of occupational hazards chose to accept their risky jobs and thus have in some degree consented to subject themselves to the dangers. Where dangers are consented to, the appropriate response is not blame but requiring improved safety, and this is most efficiently done by regulation rather than with the guilt-seeking methods of criminal justice.

In sum, the Defenders make four objections: 1. That someone who purposely tries to harm

another is really more evil than someone who harms another without aiming to, even if the degree of harm is the same. 2. That being harmed directly by another person is more terrifying than being harmed indirectly and impersonally, as by a safety hazard, even if the degree of harm is the same. 3. That someone who harms another in the course of an illegitimate and purely self-interested action is more evil than someone who harms another as a consequence of a legitimate and socially productive endeavor. 4. That the harms of typical crimes are imposed on their victims against their wills, while harms like those due to occupational hazards are consented to by workers when they agree to a job. This too is thought to make the harms of typical crimes evil in a way that occupational harms are not.

All four of these objections are said to reflect our common moral beliefs, which are a fair standard for a legal system to match. Together they are said to show that the typical criminal does something worse than the one responsible for an occupational hazard, and thus deserves the special treatment provided by the criminal justice system. Some or all of these objections may have already occurred to the reader. Thus, it is important to respond to the Defenders. For the sake of clarity I shall number the paragraphs in which I start to take up each objection in turn.

1. The Defenders' first objection confuses intention with specific aim or purpose, and it is intention that brings us properly within the reach of the criminal law. It is true that a mugger aims to harm his victim in the way that a corporate executive who maintains an unsafe workplace does not. But the corporate executive acts intentionally nonetheless, and that's what makes his actions appropriately subject to criminal law. What we intend is not just what we try to make happen but what we know is likely to happen as the normal causal product of our chosen actions. As criminal law theorist Hyman Gross points out: "What really matters here is whether conduct of a particular degree of dangerousness was done intentionally."[9] Whether we want or aim for that conduct to harm someone is a different

matter, which is relevant to the actor's *degree* of culpability (not to whether he or she is culpable at all). Gross describes the degrees of culpability for intentional action by means of an example in which a sailor dies when his ship is fumigated while he is asleep in the hold. Fumigation is a dangerous activity; it involves spraying the ship with poison that is normally fatal to humans. If the fumigation was done in order to kill the sailor, we can say that his death is caused *purposely*. But suppose that the fumigation was done knowing that a sailor was in the hold but not in order to kill him. Then, according to Gross, we say that his death was brought about *knowingly*. If the fumigation was done without knowledge that someone was in the hold but without making sure that no one was, then the sailor's death is brought about *recklessly*. Finally, if the fumigation was done without knowledge that the sailor was there and some, but inadequate, precautions were taken to make sure no one was there, then the sailor's death is brought about *negligently*.

How does this apply to the executive who imposes dangerous conditions on his workers, conditions that, as in the mine explosion, do finally lead to death? The first thing to note is that the difference between purposely, knowingly, recklessly, or negligently causing death is a difference within the range of intentional (and thus to some extent culpable) action. What is done recklessly or negligently is still done intentionally. Second, culpability decreases as we go from purposely to knowingly to recklessly to negligently killing because, according to Gross, the outcome is increasingly due to chance and not to the actor; that is, the one who kills on purpose leaves less room to chance that the killing will occur than the one who kills knowingly (the one who kills on purpose will take precautions against the failure of his killing, while the one who kills knowingly won't), and likewise the one who kills recklessly leaves wholly to chance whether there is a victim at all. And the one who kills negligently reduces this chance, but insufficiently.

Now, we may say that the kernel of truth in the Defenders' objection is that the common street mugger harms on purpose, while the executive harms only knowingly or recklessly or negligently. This does not justify refusing to treat the executive killer as a criminal, however, because we have criminal laws against reckless or even negligent harming—thus the kid-glove treatment meted out to those responsible for occupational hazards and the like is no simple reflection of our ordinary moral sensibilities, as the Defenders claim. Moreover, don't be confused into thinking that, because all workplaces have some safety measures, all workplace deaths are at most due to negligence. To the extent that precautions are not taken against particular dangers (like leaking methane), deaths due to those dangers are—by Gross's standard—caused recklessly or even knowingly (because the executive knows that potential victims are in harm's way from the danger he fails to reduce). And Nancy Frank concludes from a review of state homicide statutes that "a large number of states recognize unintended deaths caused by extreme recklessness as murder."[10]

But there is more to be said. Remember that Gross attributes the difference in degrees of culpability to the greater role left to chance as we descend from purposely to recklessly to negligently harming. In this light it is important to note that the executive (say, the mine owner) imposes danger on a larger number of individuals than the typical criminal typically does. So while the typical criminal purposely harms a particular individual, the executive knowingly subjects a large number of workers to a risk of harm. But as the risk gets greater and the number of workers gets greater, it becomes increasingly likely that one or more workers will get harmed. This means that the gap between the executive and the typical criminal shrinks. By not harming workers purposely, the executive leaves more to chance; but by subjecting large numbers to risk, he leaves it less and less to chance that someone will be harmed, and thus he rolls back his advantage over the typical criminal. If you keep your workers in mines or factories with high levels of toxic gases or chemicals, you start to approach 100 percent likelihood that at least one of them will be harmed as a result. And that means that the culpability of the executive approaches that of the typical criminal.

A different way to make the Defenders' argument is to say that the executive has failed to protect his workers, while the typical criminal has positively acted to harm his victim. In general, we think it is worse to harm someone than to fail to prevent their being harmed (perhaps you should feed starving people on the other side of town or of the world, but few people will think you are a murderer if you don't and the starving die). But at least in some cases we are responsible for the harm that results from our failure to act (for example, parents are responsible for failing to provide for their children). Some philosophers go further and hold that we are responsible for all the foreseeable effects of what we do, including the foreseeable effects of failing to act certain ways.[11] While this view supports the position for which I am arguing here, I think it goes too far. It entails that we are murderers every time we are doing anything other than saving lives, which surely goes way beyond our ordinary moral beliefs. My view is that in most cases, we are responsible only for the foreseeable effects likely to be caused by our action—and not responsible for those caused by our inaction. We are, however, responsible for the effects of our inaction in at least one special type of case: where we have a special obligation to aid people. This covers the parent who causes his child's death by failing to feed him, the doctor who causes her patient's death by failing to care for her, and the coal mine owner who causes his employees' death by failing to take legally mandated safety precautions. It may also cover the society that fails to rectify harm-producing injustices in its midst. This is another way in which the moral difference between the safety-cutting executive and the typical criminal shrinks away.

Further on this first objection, I think the Defenders overestimate the importance of specifically trying to do evil in our moral estimate of people. The mugger who aims to hurt someone is no doubt an ugly character. But so too is the well-heeled executive who calmly and callously chooses to put others at risk. Compare the mine executive who cuts corners with the typical murderer. Most murders, we know, are committed in the heat of some passion like rage or jealousy. Two lovers or neighbors or relatives find themselves in a heated argument. One (often it is a matter of chance *which* one) picks up a weapon and strikes the other a fatal blow. Such a person is clearly a murderer and rightly subject to punishment by the criminal justice system. Is this person more evil than the executive who, knowing the risks, calmly chooses not to pay for safety equipment?

The one who kills in a heated argument kills from passion. What she does she probably would not do in a cooler moment. She is likely to feel "she was not herself." The one she killed was someone she knew, a specific person who at the time seemed to her to be the embodiment of all that frustrates her, someone whose very existence makes life unbearable. I do not mean to suggest that this is true of all killers, although there is reason to believe it is true of many. Nor do I mean to suggest that such a state of mind justifies murder. What it does do, however, is suggest that the killer's action, arising out of anger at a particular individual, does not show general disdain for the lives of her fellows. Here is where she is different from our mine executive. Our mine executive wanted to harm no one in particular, but he *knew his acts were likely to harm someone*—and once someone is harmed, the victim is someone in particular. Nor can our executive claim that "he was not himself." His act is done not out of passion but out of cool reckoning. Precisely here his evil shows. In his willingness to jeopardize the lives of unspecified others who pose him no real or imaginary threat in order to make a few dollars, he shows his general disdain for all his fellow human beings. Can it really be said that he is less evil than one who kills from passion? The Model Penal Code includes within the definition of murder any death caused by "extreme indifference to human life."[12] Is our executive not a murderer by this definition?

It's worth noting that in answering the Defenders here, I have portrayed harms from occupational hazards in their best light. They are not, however, all just matters of well-intentioned but excessive risk taking. Consider, for example, the Manville (formerly Johns Manville) asbestos case. It is predicted that 240,000 Americans working now or who previously worked with asbestos will die from asbestos-related cancer in the next 30 years. But documents made public during congressional hearings in 1979 show "that Manville and other companies within the asbestos industry covered up and failed to warn millions of Americans of the dangers associated with the fireproof, indestructible insulating fiber."[13] An article in the *American Journal of Public Health* attributes thousands of deaths to the cover-up.[14] Later . . . I document similar intentional cover-ups, such as the falsification of reports on coal dust levels in mines, which leads to crippling and often fatal black lung disease. Surely someone who knowingly subjects others to risks and tries to hide those risks from them is culpable in a high degree.

2. I think the Defenders are right in believing that direct personal assault is terrifying in a way that indirect impersonal harm is not. This difference is no stranger to the criminal justice system. Prosecutors, judges, and juries constantly have to consider how terrifying an attack is in determining what to charge and what to convict offenders for. This is why we allow gradations in charges of homicide or assault and allow particularly grave sentences for particularly grave attacks. In short, the difference the Defenders are pointing to here might justify treating a one-on-one murder as graver than murder due to lax safety measures, but it doesn't justify treating one as a grave crime and the other as a mere regulatory (or very minor criminal) matter. After all, although it is worse to be injured with terror than without, it is still the injury that constitutes the worst part of violent crime. Given the choice, seriously injured victims of crime would surely rather have been terrorized and not injured than injured and not terrorized. If that is so, then the worst part of violent crime is still shared by the indirect harms that the Defenders would relegate to regulation.

3. There is also something to the Defenders' claim that indirect harms, such as ones that result from lax safety measures, are part of legitimate productive activities, whereas one-on-one crimes are not. No doubt we must tolerate the risks that are necessary ingredients of productive activity (unless those risks are so great as to outweigh the gains of the productive activity). But this doesn't imply we shouldn't identify the risks, or levels of danger, that are unnecessary and excessive, and use the law to protect innocent people from them. And if those risks are great enough, the fact that they may further a productive or otherwise legitimate activity is no reason against making them crimes—if that's what's necessary to protect workers. A person can commit a crime to further an otherwise legitimate endeavor and it is still a crime. If, say, I threaten to assault my workers if they don't work faster, this doesn't make my act any less criminal. And, in general, if I do something that by itself ought to be a crime, the fact that I do it as a means to a legitimate aim doesn't change the fact that it ought to be a crime. If acts that intentionally endanger others ought to be crimes, then the fact that the acts are means to legitimate aims doesn't change the fact that they ought to be crimes.

4. . . . . The Defenders overestimate generally the degree to which workers freely consent to the conditions of their jobs. Although no one is forced at gunpoint to accept a particular job, virtually everyone is forced by the requirements of necessity to take some job. At best, workers can choose among the dangers present at various work sites, but they cannot choose to face no danger at all. Moreover, workers can choose jobs only where there are openings, which means they cannot simply pick their place of employment at will. For nonwhites and women, the choices are even more narrowed by discriminatory hiring, long-standing occupational segregation (funneling women into secretarial, nursing, or teaching jobs and blacks into janitorial and other menial occupations), not to mention subtle and not so subtle practices that keep nonwhites and women from advancing within their occupations. Consequently, for all intents and purposes, most workers *must* face the dangers of the jobs that are available to them. What's more, remember that

while here we have been focusing on harms due to occupational hazards, much of the indirect harm that I shall document in what follows is done not to workers but to consumers (of food with dangerous chemicals) and citizens (breathing dangerous concentrations of pollutants).

Finally, recall that the basis of all the Defenders' objections is that the idea that one-on-one harms are more evil than indirect harms is part of our common moral beliefs, and that this makes it appropriate to treat the former with the criminal justice system and the latter with milder regulatory measures. Here I think the Defenders err by overlooking the role of legal institutions in shaping our ordinary moral beliefs. Many who defend the criminal justice system do so precisely because of its function in educating the public about the difference between right and wrong. The great historian of English law, Sir James Fitzjames Stephens, held that a

> great part of the general detestation of crime which happily prevails amongst the decent part of the community in all civilized countries arises from the fact that the commission of offences is associated in all such communities with the solemn and deliberate infliction of punishment wherever crime is proved.[15]

One cannot simply appeal to ordinary moral beliefs to defend the criminal law because the criminal law has already had a hand in shaping ordinary moral beliefs. At least one observer has argued that making narcotics use a crime in the beginning of this century *caused* a change in the public's ordinary moral notions about drug addiction, which prior to that time had been viewed as a medical problem.[16] It is probably safe to say that in our own time, civil rights legislation has sharpened the public's moral condemnation of racial discrimination. Hence, we might speculate that if the criminal justice system began to prosecute—and if the media began to portray—those who inflict *indirect harm* as serious criminals, our ordinary moral notions would change on this point as well.

I think this disposes of the Defenders for the time being. We are left with the conclusion that

there is no moral basis for treating *one-on-one harm* as criminal and *indirect harm* as merely a regulatory affair. What matters, then, is whether the purpose of the criminal justice system will be served by including, in the category of serious crime, actions that are predictably likely to produce serious harm, yet that are done in pursuit of otherwise legitimate goals and without the aim of harming anyone. . . .

In the remainder of this [section], I identify some acts that are *crimes by any other name*—acts that cause harm and suffering comparable to that caused by acts called crimes. My purpose is to confirm the first hypothesis: that the definitions of crime in the criminal law do not reflect the only or the most dangerous behaviors in our society. To do this, we will need some measure of the harm and suffering caused by crimes with which we can compare the harm and suffering caused by noncrimes. Our measure need not be too refined because my point can be made if I can show that there are some acts that we do not treat as crimes but that cause harm *roughly comparable* to that caused by acts that we do treat as crimes. For that, it is not necessary to compare the harm caused by noncriminal acts with the harm caused by *all* crimes. I need only show that the harm produced by some type of noncriminal act is comparable to the harm produced by *any* serious crime. Because the harms caused by noncriminal acts fall into the categories of death, bodily injury (including the disabling effects of disease), and property loss, I will compare the harms done by noncriminal acts with the injuries caused by the crimes of murder, aggravated assault, and theft.

According to the FBI's *Uniform Crime Reports*, in 1995, there were 21,597 murders and nonnegligent manslaughters, and 1,099,179 aggravated assaults. "Murder and nonnegligent manslaughter" includes all "willful (nonnegligent) killing of one human being by another." "Aggravated assault" is defined as an "attack by one person on another for the purpose of inflicting severe or aggravated bodily injury."[17] Thus, as a measure of the physical harm done by crime in 1995, we can say that reported crimes lead to roughly 21,000 deaths and 1,000,000 instances of serious bodily injury short of death a year. As a measure of monetary loss due to property crime, we can use $15.1 billion—the total estimated dollar losses due to property crime in 1995 according to the *UCR*.[18] Whatever the shortcomings of these reported crime statistics, they are the statistics upon which public policy has traditionally been based. Thus, I will consider any actions that lead to loss of life, physical harm, and property loss comparable to the figures in the *UCR* as actions that pose grave dangers to the community comparable to the threats posed by crimes. They are surely precisely the kind of harmful actions from which a criminal justice system whose purpose is to protect our persons and property ought to protect us. *They are crimes by other names.*

Work May Be Dangerous to Your Health

Since the publication of *The President's Report on Occupational Safety and Health*[19] in 1972, numerous studies have documented the astounding incidence of disease, injury, and death due to hazards in the workplace *and* the fact that much or most of this carnage is the consequence of the refusal of management to pay for safety measures and of government to enforce safety standards—and sometimes of willful defiance of existing law.[20]

In that 1972 report, the government estimated the number of job-related illnesses at 390,000 per year and the number of annual deaths from industrial disease at 100,000. For 1990, the Bureau of Labor Statistics (BLS) of the U.S. Department of Labor estimated 2,900 work-related deaths.[21] Before we celebrate what appears to be a dramatic drop in work-related mortality, note that the latter figure applies only to private-sector work environments with 11 or more employees. Moreover, BLS itself "believes that the annual survey significantly understates the number of work-related fatalities."[22]

For 1994, the Bureau of Labor Statistics (BLS) reported 515,000 job-related illnesses in the private sector.[23] And there is wide agreement that occupational diseases are seriously underreported. . . . Part of the difficulty is that there may be a substantial delay between contracting a fatal disease on the job and the appearance of symptoms, and from these to death. Moreover, the Occupational Safety and Health Administration (OSHA) relies on employer reporting for its figures, and there are many incentives for underreporting. Writing in the journal *Occupational Hazards*, Robert Reid states that

> OSHA concedes that many factors—including insurance rates and supervisor evaluations based on safety performance—are incentives to underreport. And the agency acknowledges that recordkeeping violations have increased more than 27 percent since 1984, with most of the violations recorded for not maintaining the injuries and illnesses log examined by compliance officers and used for BLS' annual survey.[24]

. . .

For these reasons, plus the fact that BLS's figures on work-related deaths are only for private workplaces with 11 or more employees, we must supplement the BLS figures with other estimates. In 1982, then U.S. Secretary of Health and Human Services Richard Schweiker stated that "current estimates for overall workplace-associated cancer mortality vary within a range of five to fifteen percent."[25] With annual cancer deaths currently running at about 500,000, that translates into about 25,000 to 75,000 job-related cancer deaths per year. More recently, Edward Sondik, of the National Cancer Institute, states that the best estimate of cancer deaths attributable to occupational exposure is 4 percent of the total, with the range of acceptable estimates running between 2 and 8 percent. That translates into a best estimate of 20,000 job-related cancer deaths a year, within a range of acceptable estimates between 10,000 and 40,000.[26]

Death from cancer is only part of the picture of death-dealing occupational disease. In testimony before the Senate Committee on Labor and Human Resources, Dr. Philip Landrigan, director of the Division of Environmental and

Occupational Medicine at the Mount Sinai School of Medicine in New York City, stated that

> Recent data indicate that occupationally related exposures are responsible each year in New York State for 5,000 to 7,000 deaths and for 35,000 new cases of illness (not including work-related injuries). These deaths due to occupational disease include 3,700 deaths from cancer.... Crude national estimates of the burden of occupational disease in the United States may be developed by multiplying the New York State data by a factor of 10. New York State contains slightly less than 10 percent of the nation's workforce, and it includes a broad mix of employment in the manufacturing, service and agricultural sectors. Thus, it may be calculated that occupational disease is responsible each year in the United States for 50,000 to 70,000 deaths, and for approximately 350,000 new cases of illness.[27]

It is some confirmation of Dr. Landrigan's estimates that they imply work-related cancer deaths of approximately 37,000 a year—a figure that is toward the low end of the range in Secretary Schweiker's statement on this issue, and toward the top end of the range of acceptable estimates according to Sondik. Landrigan's estimates of deaths from occupational disease are also corroborated by a study reported by the National Safe Workplace Institute, which estimates that the number of occupational disease deaths is between 47,377 and 95,479. Mark Cullen, director of the occupational medicine program at the Yale University School of Medicine, praised this study as "a very balanced, very comprehensive overview of occupational health." The study's figures are low compared with a 1985 report of the Office of Technology Assessment (OTA) that estimated 100,000 Americans die annually from work-related illness.[28] Even if we discount OSHA's 1972 estimate of 100,000 deaths a year due to occupational disease or OTA's 1985 estimate of the same number, we would surely be erring in the other direction to accept the BLS figure of 2,900. We can hardly be overestimating the actual toll if we take the conservative route

and set it at 25,000 deaths a year resulting from occupational disease.

The 515,000 work-related illnesses reported by BLS for 1994 are of varying severity. Because I want to compare these occupational harms with those resulting from aggravated assault, I shall stay on the conservative side here too, as with deaths from occupational diseases, and say that there are annually in the United States approximately 250,000 job-related serious illnesses. Taken together with 25,000 deaths from occupational diseases, how does this compare with the threat posed by crime?

Before jumping to any conclusions, note that the risk of occupational disease and death falls only on members of the labor force, whereas the risk of crime falls on the whole population, from infants to the elderly. Because the labor force is about half the total population (131,056,000 in 1994, out of a total population of 260,651,000), to get a true picture of the *relative* threat posed by occupational diseases compared with that posed by crimes, we should *halve* the crime statistics when comparing them with the figures for industrial disease and death. Using the crime figures for 1995 . . . we note that the *comparable* figures would be

	Occupational Disease	Crime (halved)
Death	25,000	10,500
Other physical harm	250,000	500,000

If it is argued that this paints an inaccurate picture because so many crimes go unreported, my answer is this: First of all, homicides are by far the most completely reported of crimes. For obvious reasons, the general underreporting of crimes is not equal among crimes. It is easier to avoid reporting a rape or a mugging than a corpse. Second, although not the best, aggravated assaults are among the better-reported crimes. Preliminary estimates from the Justice Department's *National Crime Victimization Survey* indicate that 54 percent of aggravated assaults were reported to the police in 1995, compared with 27 percent of thefts.[29] On the other hand, we should expect more—not less—underreporting of industrial than criminal victims because diseases and deaths are likely to cost firms money in the form of workdays lost and insurance premiums raised, occupational diseases are frequently first seen by company physicians who have every reason to diagnose complaints as either malingering or not job-related, and many occupationally caused diseases do not show symptoms or lead to death until after the employee has left the job. . . . In sum, both occupational and criminal harms are underreported, though there is reason to believe that the underreporting is worse with occupational than criminal harms. Finally, I have been extremely conservative in estimating occupational deaths and other harms. However one may quibble with figures presented here, I think it is fair to say that, if anything, they understate the extent of occupational harm compared with criminal harm.

Note further that the estimates in the last chart are *only* for occupational *diseases* and deaths from those diseases. They do not include death and disability from work-related injuries. Here, too, the statistics are gruesome. The National Safety Council (NSC) reported that, in 1993, work-related accidents resulted in 9,100 workers killed on the job, and 3.2 million disabling injuries.[30] This brings the number of occupation-related deaths to 34,100 a year and other physical harms to 3,450,000. If, on the basis of these additional figures, we recalculated our chart comparing occupational harms from both disease and accident with criminal harms, it would look like this:

	Occupational Hazard	Crime (halved)
Death	34,100	10,500
Other physical harm	3,450,000	500,000

Can there be any doubt that workers are more likely to stay alive and healthy in the face of the danger from the underworld than in the work-world? If any doubt lingers, consider this: Lest we falter in the struggle against crime, the FBI includes in its annual *Uniform Crime Reports* a table of "crime clocks," which graphically illustrates the extent of the criminal menace. For 1995, the crime clock shows a murder occurring every 24 minutes. If a similar clock were constructed for occupational deaths—using the conservative estimate of 34,100 cited above and remembering that this clock ticks only for that half of the population that is in the labor force—this clock would show an occupational death about every 15 minutes! In other words, in about the time it takes for three murders on the crime clock, four workers have died *just from trying to make a living.*

To say that some of these workers died from accidents due to their own carelessness is about as helpful as saying that some of those who died at the hands of murderers asked for it. It overlooks the fact that where workers are careless, it is not because they love to live dangerously. They have production quotas to meet, quotas that they themselves do not set. If quotas were set with an eye to keeping work at a safe pace rather than to keeping the production-to-wages ratio as high as possible, it might be more reasonable to expect workers to take the time to be careful. Beyond this, we should bear in mind that the vast majority of occupational deaths result from disease, not accident, and disease is generally a function of conditions outside a worker's control. Examples of such conditions are the level of coal dust in the air, . . . textile dust, . . . asbestos fibers, . . . or coal tars. . . . The Bureau of Labor Statistics reported that, in 1994, there were 332,000 cases of repetitive strain diseases, such as carpal tunnel syndrome.[31] Repetitive strain disease "is, by all accounts, the fastest-growing health hazard in the U.S. workplace, reportedly afflicting about 1,000 keyboard operators, assembly-line workers, meat processors, grocery check-out clerks, secretaries and other employees everyday. . . . OSHA officials argue that . . . carpal tunnel problems lead the list in average time lost from work (at a median of 30 days per case), well above amputations (24 days) and fractures (20).[32]

To blame the workers for occupational disabilities and deaths is to ignore the history of governmental attempts to compel industrial firms to meet safety standards that would keep dangers (such as chemicals or fibers or dust particles in the air) that are outside the worker's control down to a safe level. This has been a continual struggle, with firms using everything from their own "independent" research institutes to more direct and often questionable forms of political pressure to influence government in the direction of loose standards and lax enforcement. So far, industry has been winning because OSHA has been given neither the personnel nor the mandate to fulfill its purpose. It is so understaffed that, in 1973, when 1,500 federal sky marshals guarded the nation's airplanes from hijackers, only 500 OSHA inspectors toured the nation's workplaces. By 1980, OSHA employed 1,581 compliance safety and health officers, but this still enabled inspection of only roughly 2 percent of the 2.5 million establishments covered by OSHA. The *New York Times* reports that in 1987 the number of OSHA inspectors was down to 1,044. As might be expected, the agency performs fewer inspections than it did a dozen years earlier.[33] . . . According to a report issued by the AFL-CIO in 1992, "The median penalty paid by an employer during the years 1972–1990 following an incident resulting in death or serious injury of a worker was just $480."[34] The same report claims that the federal government spends $1.1 billion a year to protect fish and wildlife and only $300 million a year to protect workers from health and safety hazards on the job.

An editorial in the January 1983 issue of the *American Journal of Public Health* titled "Can Reagan Be Indicted for Betraying Public Health?" answers the question in its title affirmatively by listing the Reagan administration's attempts to cut back government support for public health programs. On the issue of occupational safety and health, the editorial states:

> The Occupational Safety and Health Administration (OSHA) has delayed the cotton and lead [safe exposure level] standards. It proposes to weaken the generic carcinogen policy, the labeling standard, the access to medical and exposure records standard. Mine fatalities are rising again, but the Mine Safety and Health Administration and OSHA enforcement have been cut back. Research on occupational safety and health has been slashed more than any other research program in the Department of Health and Human Services. The National Institute for Occupational Safety and Health funding in real dollars is lower in 1983 than at any time in the 12-year history of the Institute. Reporting and data requirements have been devastated.[35]

The editorial ends by asking rhetorically, "How can anyone believe that the Reagan Administration wishes to prevent disease or promote health or preserve public health in America?"

And so it goes on.

. . .

Health Care May Be Dangerous to Your Health

More than 25 years ago, when the annual number of willful homicides in the nation was about 10,000, the President's Commission on Law Enforcement and Administration of justice reported that

> A recent study of emergency medical care found the quality, numbers, and distribution of ambulances and other emergency services severely deficient, and estimated that as many as *20,000 Americans die unnecessarily each year* as a result of improper emergency care. The means necessary for correcting this situation are very clear and would probably yield greater immediate return in reducing death than would expenditures for reducing the incidence of crimes of violence.[36]

On July 15, 1975, Dr. Sidney Wolfe of Ralph Nader's Public Interest Health Research Group testified before the House Commerce Oversight and Investigations Subcommittee that there "were 3.2 million cases of unnecessary surgery performed each year in the United States." These unneeded operations, Wolfe added, "cost close to $5 billion a year and kill as many as 16,000 Americans."[37] Wolfe's estimates of unnecessary surgery were based on studies comparing the operations performed and surgery recommended by doctors who are paid for the operations they do with those performed and recommended by salaried doctors who receive no extra income from surgery.

The figure accepted by Dr. George A. Silver, professor of public health at the Yale University School of Medicine, is 15,000 deaths a year "attributable to unnecessary surgery."[38] Silver places the annual cost of excess surgery at $4.8 billion.[39] In an article on an experimental program by Blue Cross and Blue Shield aimed at curbing unnecessary surgery, *Newsweek* reports that

> a Congressional committee earlier this year [1976] estimated that more than 2 million of the elective operations performed in 1974 were not only unnecessary—but also killed about 12,000 patients and cost nearly $4 billion.[40]

Because the number of surgical operations performed in the United States rose from 16.7 million in 1975 to 22.7 million in 1993,[41] there is reason to believe that at least somewhere between (the congressional committee's estimate of) 12,000 and (Dr. Wolfe's estimate of) 16,000 people a year still die from unnecessary surgery. In 1995, the FBI reported that 2,538 murders were committed with a "cutting or stabbing instrument."[42] Obviously, the FBI does not include the scalpel as a cutting or stabbing instrument. If they did, they would have had to report that between 14,538 and 18,538 persons were killed by "cutting or stabbing" in 1995—depending on whether you take Congress's figure or Wolfe's. No matter how you slice it, the scalpel may be more dangerous than the switchblade.

And this is only a fraction of the problem: Data from the Harvard Medical Practice Study (based on over 30,000 records from New York State Hospitals in 1984 and extrapolated to the American population as a whole) indicate that more than 1.3 million Americans are injured by medical treatment, and "that each year 150,000 people die from, rather than in spite of, their medical treatment."[43] One of the authors of the study, Dr. Lucian Leape, a surgeon and lecturer at the Harvard School of Public Health, suggests that one-quarter of these deaths are due to negligence, and two-thirds are preventable.

While they are at it, the FBI should probably add the hypodermic needle and the prescription to their list of potential murder weapons. Silver points out that these are also death-dealing instruments.

> Of the 6 billion doses of antibiotic medicines administered each year by injection or prescription, it is estimated that 22 percent are unnecessary. Of the doses given, 10,000 result in fatal or near-fatal reactions. Somewhere between 2,000 and 10,000 deaths probably would not have occurred if the drugs, meant for the patient's benefit, had not been given.[44]

These estimates are supported by the Harvard Medical Practice Study. Its authors write that, of the 1.3 million medical injuries, 19 percent (247,000) were related to medications, and 14 percent of these (34,580) resulted in permanent injury or death.[45]

The danger continues. The Public Citizen Health Research Group reports in its *Health Letter* of October 1988 that

> two major U.S. drug companies—Lilly and SmithKline—have pleaded guilty to criminal charges for having withheld information from the Food and Drug Administration (FDA) about deaths and life-threatening adverse drug reactions.

The response of the Justice Department has been predictably merciful:

> SmithKline, the actions of whose executives resulted in at least . . . 36 deaths, pleaded guilty to 14 criminal misdemeanor counts and was fined $34,000. Lilly and its executives, whose criminal negligence was responsible for deaths

to at least 49 Americans . . . , were slapped on the wrist with a total of $45,000 in fines.[46]

In fact, if someone had the temerity to publish a *Uniform Crime Reports* that really portrayed the way Americans are murdered, the FBI's statistics on the *type of weapon* used in murder would have to be changed for 1995 from those shown in Table 1A to something like those shown in Table 1B.

The figures shown in Table 1B would give American citizens a much more honest picture of what threatens them—although remember how conservative the estimates of noncriminal harm are. Nonetheless, we are not likely to see such a chart broadcast by the criminal justice system, perhaps because it would also give American citizens a more honest picture of *who* threatens them.

We should not leave this topic without noting that, aside from the other losses it imposes, un-

necessary surgery was estimated to have cost between $4 billion and $5 billion in 1974. The price of medical care roughly quadrupled between 1974 and 1994. Thus, assuming that the same number of unneeded operations were performed in 1994, the cost of unnecessary surgery would be between $16 and $20 billion. To this we should add the unnecessary 22 percent of the 6 billion administered doses of medication. Even at the extremely conservative estimate of $3 a dose, this adds about $4 billion. In short, assuming that earlier trends have continued, there is reason to believe that unnecessary surgery and medication cost the public between $20 and $24 billion annually—far outstripping the $15.1 billion taken by thieves that concern the FBI.[47] This gives us yet another way in which we are robbed of more money by practices that are not treated as criminal than by practices that are. . . .

TABLE 1A   *How Americans Are Murdered*

Total	Firearms	Knife or Other Cutting Instrument	Other Weapon: Club, Arson, Poison, Strangulation, etc.	Personal Weapon: Hands, Fists, etc.
20,043[a]	13,673	2,538	2,650	1,182

[a]Note that this figure diverges somewhat from the number of murders and nonnegligent manslaughters used elsewhere in the FBI *Uniform Crime Reports,* 1995, since the FBI has data on the weapons used in only 20,043 of the reported murders.

SOURCE: FBI *Uniform Crime Reports*, 1995: "Murder Victims, Types of Weapons Used, 1995."

TABLE 1B   *How Americans Are (Really) Murdered*

Total	Occupation Hazard & Disease	Knife or Other Cutting Instrument Including Scalpel	Firearms	Other Weapon: Club, Poison, Hypodermic, Prescription Drug, etc.	Personal Weapon: Hands, Fists, etc.
68,143	34,100	14,538[a]	13,673	4,650[a]	1,182

[a]These figures represent the relevant figures in Table 1A plus the most conservative figures for the relevant categories discussed in the text.

Summary

Once again, our investigations lead to the same result. The criminal justice system does not protect us against the gravest threats to life, limb, or possessions. Its definitions of crime are not simply a reflection of the objective dangers that threaten us. The workplace [and] the medical profession . . . lead to far more human suffering, far more death and disability, and take far more dollars from our pockets than the murders, aggravated assaults, and thefts reported annually by the FBI. What is more, this human suffering is preventable. A government really intent on protecting our well-being could enforce work safety regulation [or] police the medical profession . . . but it does not. Instead we hear a lot of cant about law and order and a lot of rant about crime in the streets. It is as if our leaders were not only refusing to protect us from the major threats to our well-being but trying to cover up this refusal by diverting our attention to crime—as if this were the only real threat.

As we have seen, the criminal justice system is a carnival mirror that presents a distorted image of what threatens us. The distortions do not end with the definitions of crime. . . . New distortions enter at every level of the system, so that in the end, when we look in our prisons to see who really threatens us, all we see are poor people. By that time, virtually all the well-to-do people who endanger us have been discreetly weeded out of the system. . . . All the mechanisms by which the criminal justice system comes down more frequently and more harshly on the poor criminal than on the well-off criminal take place *after* most of the dangerous acts of the well-to-do have been excluded from the definition of crime itself. The bias against the poor within the criminal justice system is all the more striking when we recognize that the door to that system is shaped in a way that excludes in advance the most dangerous acts of the well-to-do. . . .

NOTES

1. *Washington Post*, January 11, 1983, p. C10.
2. Voigt, Lydia, et al., *Criminology and Justice* (New York: McGraw-Hill, 1994), pp. 11–15; the quotation is at p. 15.

3. This answers Graeme Newman, who observes that most criminals on TV are white, and wonders what the "ruling class" or conservatives "have to gain by denying the criminality of Blacks." Graeme R. Newman, "Popular Culture and Criminal Justice: A Preliminary Analysis," *Journal of Criminal Justice* 18 (1990), pp. 261–274.

4. Newman, "Popular Culture and Criminal justice: A Preliminary Analysis," pp. 263–264.

5. Barbara Matusow, "If It Bleeds, It Leads," *Washingtonian*, January 1988, p. 102.

6. "Titillating Channels: TV Is Going Tabloid As Shows Seek Sleaze and Find Profits, Too," *Wall Street Journal*, May 18, 1988, p. 1.

7. "Crime in America: The Shocking Truth," *McCall's*, March 1987, p. 144.

8. John P. Wright, Francis T. Cullen, Michael B. Blankenship, "The Social Construction of Corporate Violence: Media Coverage of the Imperial Food Products Fire," *Crime & Delinquency* 41, no. 1 (January 1995), p. 32. . . .

9. Hyman Gross, *A Theory of Criminal Justice* (New York: Oxford University Press, 1979), p. 78. See generally Chapter 3, "Culpability, Intention, Motive," which I have drawn upon in making the argument of this and the following two paragraphs.

10. Nancy Frank, "Unintended Murder and Corporate Risk-Taking: Defining the Concept of Justifiability," *Journal of Criminal Justice* 16 (1988), p. 18.

11. For example, see John Harris, "The Marxist Conception of Violence," *Philosophy & Public Affairs* 3, no. 2 (Winter 1974), pp. 192–220; Jonathan Glover, *Causing Death and Saving Lives* (Hammondsworth, England: Penguin, 1977), pp. 92–112; and James Rachels, *The End of Life* (Oxford: Oxford University Press, 1986), pp. 106–150.

12. *Model Penal Code*, Final Draft (Philadelphia: American Law Institute, 1962).

13. Russell Mokhiber, *Corporate Crime and Violence: Big Business Power and the Abuse of Public Trust* (San Francisco: Sierra Club, 1988), pp. 278, 285.

14. David E. Lilienfeld, "The Silence: The Asbestos Industry and Early Occupational Cancer Research—A Case Study," *American Journal of Public Health* 81, no. 6 (June 1991), p. 791. This article shows how early the asbestos industry knew of the link between asbestos and cancer and how hard they tried to suppress this

information. See also Paul Brodeur, *Outrageous Misconduct: The Asbestos Industry on Trial* (New York: Pantheon, 1985).

15. Sir James Fitzjames Stephen, from his *History of the Criminal Law of England* 2 (1883), excerpted in *Crime, Law and Society*, Abraham S. Goldstein and Joseph Goldstein, eds. (New York: Free Press, 1971), p. 21.

16. Troy Duster, *The Legislation of Morality: Law, Drugs and Moral Judgment* (New York: Free Press, 1970), pp. 3–76.

17. *UCR-1995*, pp. 13, 31.

18. *UCR-1995*, p. 36.

19. *The President's Report on Occupational Safety and Health* (Washington, D.C.: U.S. Government Printing Office, 1972).

20. "James Messerschmidt, in a comprehensive review of research studies on job-related accidents, determined that somewhere between 35 and 57 percent of those accidents occurred because of direct safety violations by the employer. Laura Shill Schraeger and James Short, Jr. found 30 percent of industrial accidents resulted from safety violations and another 20 percent resulted from unsafe working conditions." Kappeler et al., *Mythology of Crime and Criminal Justice*, p. 104. See James Messerschmidt, *Capitalism, Patriarchy, and Crime: Toward a Socialist Feminist Criminology* (New Jersey: Rowman and Littlefield, 1986); and Laura Shill Schraeger and James Short, "Toward a Sociology of Organizational Crime," *Social Problems* 25 (April 1978), pp. 407–419. See also Joseph A. Page and Mary-Win O'Brien, *Bitter Wages: Ralph Nader's Study Group Report on Disease and Injury on the Job* (New York: Grossman, 1973); Rachel Scott, *Muscle and Blood* (New York: Dutton, 1974); Jeanne M. Stellman and Susan M. Daum, *Work Is Dangerous to Your Health* (New York: Vintage, 1973); Fran Lynn, "The Dust in Willie's Lungs," *Nation* 222, no. 7 (February 21, 1976), pp. 209–212; and Joel Swartz, "Silent Killers at Work," *Crime and Social Justice* 3 (Summer 1975), pp. 15–20.

21. *President's Report on Occupational Safety and Health*, p. 111; National Safety Council, *Accident Facts* 1992, p. 39, 50.

22. National Safety Council, *Accident Facts* 1992, p. 39.

23. Curt Suplee, "House to Consider 'Ergo Rider' Restraints on OSHA," *Washington Post*, July 11, 1996, p. A4.

24. Robert Reid, "How Accurate Are Safety and Health Statistics?" *Occupational Hazards*, March 1987, p. 49.

25. Letter from Schweiker to B. J. Pigg, Executive Director of the Asbestos Information Association, dated April 29, 1982.

26. Edward Sondik, "Progress in Cancer Prevention and Control," in Russell Maulitz, ed., *Unnatural Causes: Three Leading Killer Diseases in America* (New Brunswick: Rutgers University Press, 1989), p. 117.

27. Philip Landrigan, Testimony before the Senate Committee on Labor and Human Resources, April 18, 1988, p. 2. For cancer deaths, see *StatAbst-1988*, p. 77, Table no. 117, and p. 80, Table no. 120.

28. "Safety Group Cites Fatalities Linked to Work," *Wall Street Journal*, August 31, 1990, p. B8; and Sally Squires, "Study Traces More Deaths to Working than Driving," *Washington Post*, August 31, 1990, p. A7.

29. BJS, *National Crime Victimization Survey*, preliminary estimates (BJS Internet home page, September 17, 1996), p. 3.

30. *StatAbst-1995*, Table 688, p. 440.

31. Curt Suplee, "House to Consider 'Ergo Rider' Restraints on OSHA," *Washington Post*, July 11, 1996, p. A4.

32. Ibid.

33. "Is OSHA Falling Down on the Job?" *New York Times*, August 2, 1987, pp. A1, A6.

34. Frank Swoboda, "More for Wildlife Than for Workers," *Washington Post*, April 28, 1992, p. A13.

35. Anthony Robbins, "Can Reagan Be Indicted for Betraying Public Health?" *American Journal of Public Health* 73, no. 1 (January 1983), p. 13.

36. *Challenge*, p. 52 (emphasis added). See also p. 3 for then-prevailing homicide rates.

37. *Washington Post*, July 16, 1975, p. A3.

38. George A. Silver, "The Medical Insurance Disease," *Nation*, 222, no. 12 (March 27, 1976), p. 369.

39. Ibid., p. 371.

40. *Newsweek*, March 29, 1976, p. 67. Lest anyone think this is a new problem, compare this passage written in a popular magazine over 40 years ago:

In an editorial on medical abuse, the *Journal of the Medical Association of Georgia* referred to "surgeons who paradoxically are often cast in the role of the supreme hero by the patient and family and at the same time may be doing the greatest amount of harm to the individual."

Unnecessary operations on women, stemming from the combination of a trusting patient and a split fee, have been so deplored by honest doctors that the phrase "rape of the pelvis" has been used to describe them. The American College of Surgeons, impassioned foe of fee-splitting, has denounced unnecessary hysterectomies, uterine suspensions, Caesarian sections. [Howard Whitman, "Why Some Doctors Should Be in Jail," *Colliers,* October 30, 1953, p. 24.]

41. *StatAbst-1988*, p. 97, Table no. 153; *StatAbst-1995*, p. 130, Table no. 194; and American Hospital Association, *Hospital Statistics 1992–93*, p. xlv.

42. *UCR-1995*, p. 18.

43. Paul Weiler, Howard Hiatt, Joseph Newhouse, William Johnson, Troyen Brennan, and Lucian Leape, *A Measure of Malpractice: Medical Injury, Malpractice Litigation and Patient Compensation* (Cambridge, MA: Harvard University Press, 1993), p. 137. The data given here come from the Harvard Medical Practice Study. See also Christine Russell, "Human Error: Avoidable Mistakes Kill 100,000 Patients a Year," *Washington Post Health*, February 18, 1992, p. 7.

44. Silver, "The Medical Insurance Disease," p. 369. Silver's estimates are extremely conservative. Some studies suggest that between 30,000 and 160,000 individuals die as a result of drugs prescribed by their doctors. See Boyce Rensberger, "Thousands a Year Killed by Faulty Prescriptions," *New York Times*, January 28, 1976, p. A1, A17. If we assume with Silver that at least 20 percent are unnecessary, this puts the annual death toll from unnecessary prescriptions at between 6,000 and 32,000 persons. For an in-depth look at the recklessness with which prescription drugs are put on the market and the laxness with which the Food and Drug Administration exercises its mandate to protect the public, see the series of eight articles by Morton Mintz, "The Medicine Business," *Washington Post*, June 27–30, July 1–4, 1976.

45. Weiler et al., *A Measure of Malpractice: Medical Injury, Malpractice Litigation and Patient Compensation*, p. 54.

46. "More Crime in the Drug and Device Industry," *Health Letter*, October 1988, p. 12.

47. Rate of increase of medical costs is calculated from *StatAbst-1995*, p. 117, Table no. 167. Note that the assumption that the *number* of unnecessary operations and prescriptions has remained the same between 1974 and 1991, and between 1991 and 1994, is a conservative assumption in that it effectively assumes that the rate of these practices relative to the population has declined because population has increased in the period.

THINKING ABOUT THE READING

Why aren't the dangerous activities Reiman describes defined as serious crimes by our criminal justice system? Should they be? In other words, do you think a business executive who fails to pay for safety precautions, indirectly causing the deaths of several workers, should be considered a criminal in the same way as a mugger who kills a victim in the course of a robbery? Why, or why not? How should we as a society deal with dangerous practices that aren't considered crimes?

Building Social Relationships:
Groups and Families

In this culture, close, personal relationships are the standard by which we judge the quality and happiness of our everyday lives. Yet in a complex, individualistic society like ours, they are becoming more difficult to establish and sustain. Although we like to think that the things we do in our relationships are completely private experiences, they are continually influenced by large-scale political interests and economic pressures. Like every other aspect of our lives, these relationships can be understood only within the broader social context. Laws, customs, and social institutions often regulate the way we form these relationships, how we act inside them, and how we dispose of them when they are no longer working. At a more fundamental level, societies determine which relationships can be considered "legitimate" and therefore entitled to cultural and institutional recognition. Those relationships that lack such societal validation are often scorned and stigmatized.

In "Exiles from Kinship," Kath Weston describes the dilemmas faced by people in homosexual unions who want to be considered legitimate families. In most societies, biology (in the form of blood ties or reproduction) is the key determinant of family status. Weston, however, thinks that things are changing in American society and that "chosen families"—those tied together simply by the bonds of affection—are gaining more legitimacy. Indeed, the growing number of cities with "domestic partnership" ordinances attests to this fact. Nevertheless, there is still a profound reluctance on the part of the public to grant homosexuals complete family status.

One undeniable fact of family life in the late 20th and early 21st centuries is that both parents in a family are likely to work outside the home. Hence, most families today must figure out ways to balance home life with the demands of work. Most of us assume that "home" is the more pleasant, soothing place to be. It's where we can relax and receive emotional sustenance. Work, on the other hand, has traditionally been characterized as a harried, dehumanizing, and insecure place. It's where we go, out of economic necessity, to earn money that serves as a means to an end. If given the choice, most people would rather be at home than at work, right?

Not necessarily. Arlie Hochschild finds in her article, "The Time Bind," that the traditional images of work and home are changing. Many parents say they want to spend more time with their families and less time at work, but relatively few are taking advantage of opportunities to reduce their work time. The workers she interviewed seem to prefer being at work. Hochschild argues that new management techniques have made the workplace a more personal and appreciative place to be. At the same time, pressing time demands on working parents have made the home a frenzied, busy place where efficiency and scheduling are overriding concerns. Such a shift will have important consequences for people's family expectations and, according to Hochschild, children's lives in the future.

Exiles from Kinship

Kath Weston

*Indeed, it is not so much identical conclusions that prove minds
to be related as the contradictions that are common to them.*
—Albert Camus

Lesbian and gay San Francisco during the 1980s offered a fascinating opportunity to learn something about how ideologies arise and change as people lock in conflict, work toward reconciliation, reorganize relationships, establish or break ties, and agree to disagree. In an apartment on Valencia Street, a young lesbian reassured her gay friend that his parents would get over their initially negative reaction if he told them he was gay. On Polk Street, a 16-year-old searched for a place to spend the night because he had already come out to his parents and now he had nowhere to go. While two lovers were busy organizing an anniversary party that would bring blood relations together with their gay families, a woman on the other side of the city reported to work as usual because she feared losing her job if her employer should discover that she was mourning the passing of her partner, who had died the night before. For every lesbian considering parenthood, several friends worried about the changes children would introduce into peer relationships. For every eight or nine people who spoke with excitement about building families of friends, one or two rejected gay families as an oppressive accommodation to a heterosexual society.

Although not always codified or clear, the discourse on gay families that emerged during the 1980s challenged many cultural representations and common practices that have effectively denied lesbians and gay men access to kinship. In earlier decades gay people had also fought custody battles, brought partners home to meet their parents, filed suit against discriminatory insurance policies, and struggled to maintain ties with adoptive or blood relations. What set this new discourse apart was its emphasis on the kinship character of the ties gay people had forged to close friends and lovers, its demand that those ties receive social and legal recognition, and its separation of parenting and family formation from heterosexual relations. For the first time, gay men and lesbians systematically laid claim to families of their own. . . .

Is "Straight" to "Gay" as "Family" Is to "No Family"?

For years, and in an amazing variety of contexts, claiming a lesbian or gay identity has been portrayed as a rejection of "the family" and a departure from kinship. In media portrayals of AIDS, Simon Watney (1987:103) observes that "we are invited to imagine some absolute divide between the two domains of 'gay life' and 'the family,' as if gay men grew up, were educated, worked and lived our lives in total isolation from the rest of society." Two presuppositions lend a dubious credence to such imagery: the belief that gay men and lesbians do not have children or establish lasting relationships, and the belief that they invariably alienate adoptive and blood kin once their sexual identities become known. By presenting "the family" as a unitary object, these depictions also imply that everyone participates in identical sorts of kinship relations and subscribes to one universally agreed-upon definition of family.

Representations that exclude lesbians and gay men from "the family" invoke what Blanche Wiesen Cook (1977:48) has called "the assumption that gay people do not love and do not work," the reduction of lesbians and gay men to sexual identity, and sexual identity to sex alone. In the United States, sex apart from heterosexual marriage tends to introduce a wild card into social relations, signifying unbridled lust and the limits of individualism. If heterosexual intercourse can bring people into enduring association via the creation of kinship ties, lesbian and gay sexuality in these depictions isolates individuals from one another rather than weaving them into a social fabric. To assert that straight people "naturally" have access to family, while gay people are destined to move toward a future of solitude and loneliness, is not only to tie kinship closely to procreation, but also to treat gay men and lesbians as members of a nonprocreative species set apart from the rest of humanity (cf. Foucault 1978).

It is but a short step from positioning lesbians and gay men somewhere beyond "the family"—unencumbered by relations of kinship, responsibility, or affection—to portraying them as a menace to family and society. A person or group must first be outside another in order to invade, endanger, and threaten. My own impression from fieldwork corroborates Frances FitzGerald's (1986) observation that many heterosexuals believe not only that gay people have gained considerable political power, but also that the absolute number of lesbians and gay men (rather than their visibility) has increased in recent years. Inflammatory rhetoric that plays on fears about the "spread" of gay identity and of AIDS finds a disturbing parallel in the imagery used by fascists to describe syphilis at mid-century, when "the healthy" confronted "the degenerate" while the fate of civilization hung in the balance (Hocquenghem 1978).

A long sociological tradition in the United States of studying "the family" under siege or in various states of dissolution lent credibility to charges that this institution required protection from "the homosexual threat." Proposition 6 (the Briggs initiative), which appeared on the ballot in California in 1978, was defeated only after a massive organizing campaign that mobilized lesbians and gay men in record numbers. The text of the initiative, which would have barred gay and lesbian teachers (along with heterosexual teachers who advocated homosexuality) from the public schools, was phrased as a defense of "the family" (in Hollibaugh 1979:55):

> One of the most fundamental interests of the State is the establishment and preservation of the family unit. Consistent with this interest is the State's duty to protect its impressionable youth from influences which are antithetical to this vital interest.

Other anti-gay legislative initiative campaigns adopted the slogans "save the family" and "save the children" as their rallying cries. In 1983 the *Moral Majority Report* referred obliquely to AIDS with the headline, "Homosexual Diseases Threaten American Families" (Godwin 1983). When the *Boston Herald* opposed a gay rights bill introduced into the Massachusetts legislature, it was with an eye to "the preservation of family values" (Allen 1987).

Discourse that opposes gay identity to family membership is not confined to the political arena. A gay doctor was advised during his residency to discourage other gay people from becoming his patients, lest his waiting room become filled with homosexuals. "It'll scare away the families," warned his supervisor (Lazere 1986). Discussions of dual-career families and the implications of a family wage system usually render invisible the financial obligations of gay people who support dependents or who pool material resources with lovers and others they define as kin. Just as women have been accused of taking jobs away from "men with families to support," some lesbians and gay men in the Bay Area recalled coworkers who had condemned them for competing against "people with families" for scarce employment. Or consider the choice of words by a guard at that "all-American" institution, Disneyland, commenting on a legal suit brought by two gay men who had been prohibited from dancing with one another at a dance floor on the grounds: "This is a family park. There is no room for alternative lifestyles here" (Mendenhall 1985).

Scholarly treatments are hardly exempt from this tendency to locate gay men and lesbians beyond the bounds of kinship. Even when researchers are sympathetic to gay concerns, they may equate kinship with genealogically calculated relations. Manuel Castells' and Karen Murphy's (1982) study of the "spatial organization of San Francisco's gay community," for instance, frames its analysis using "gay territory" and "family land" as mutually exclusive categories.

From New Right polemics to the rhetoric of high school hallways, "recruitment" joins "reproduction" in allusions to homosexuality. Alleging that gay men and lesbians must seduce young people in order to perpetuate (or expand) the gay population because they cannot have children of their own, heterosexist critics have conjured up visions of an end to society, the inevitable fate of a society that fails to "reproduce." Of course, the contradictory inferences that sexual identity is "caught" rather than claimed, and that parents pass their sexual identities on to their children, are unsubstantiated. The power of this chain of associations lies in a play on words that blurs the multiple senses of the term "reproduction."

Reproduction's status as a mixed metaphor may detract from its analytic utility, but its very ambiguities make it ideally suited to argument and innuendo. By shifting without signal between reproduction's meaning of physical procreation and its sense as the perpetuation of society as a whole, the characterization of lesbians and gay men as nonreproductive beings links their supposed attacks on "the family" to attacks on society in the broadest sense. Speaking of parents who had refused to accept her lesbian identity, a Jewish woman explained, "They feel like I'm finishing off Hitler's job." The plausibility of

the contention that gay people pose a threat to "the family" (and, through the family, to ethnicity) depends upon a view of family grounded in heterosexual relations, combined with the conviction that gay men and lesbians are incapable of procreation, parenting, and establishing kinship ties.

Some lesbians and gay men in the Bay Area had embraced the popular equation of their sexual identities with the renunciation of access to kinship, particularly when first coming out. "My image of gay life was very lonely, very weird, no family," Rafael Ortiz recollected. "I assumed that my family was gone now—that's it." After Bob Korkowski began to call himself gay, he wrote a series of poems in which an orphan was the central character. Bob said the poetry expressed his fear of "having to give up my family because I was queer." When I spoke with Rona Bren after she had been home with the flu, she told me that whenever she was sick, she relived old fears. That day she had remembered her mother's grim prediction: "You'll be a lesbian and you'll be alone the rest of your life. Even a dog shouldn't be alone."

Looking backward and forward across the life cycle, people who equated their adoption of a lesbian or gay identity with a renunciation of family did so in the double-sided sense of fearing rejection by the families in which they had grown up, and not expecting to marry or have children as adults. Although few in numbers, there were still those who had considered "going straight" or getting married specifically in order to "have a family."

Bernie Margolis had been sexually involved with men since he was in his teens, but for years had been married to a woman with whom he had several children. At age 67 he regretted having grown to adulthood before the current discussion of gay families, with its focus on redefining kinship and constructing new sorts of parenting arrangements.

> I didn't want to give up the possibility of becoming a family person. Of having kids of my own to carry on whatever I built up. . . . My

mother was always talking about she's looking forward to the day when she would bring her children under the canopy to get married. It never occurred to her that I wouldn't be married. It probably never occurred to me either.

The very categories "good family person" and "good family man" had seemed to Bernie intrinsically opposed to a gay identity. In his fifties at the time I interviewed him, Stephen Richter attributed never having become a father to "not having the relationship with the woman." Because he had envisioned parenting and procreation only in the context of a heterosexual relationship, regarding the two as completely bound up with one another, Stephen had never considered children an option.

Older gay men and lesbians were not the only ones whose adult lives had been shaped by ideologies that banish gay people from the domain of kinship. Explaining why he felt uncomfortable participating in "family occasions," a young man who had no particular interest in raising a child commented, "When families get together, what do they talk about? Who's getting married, who's having children. And who's not, okay? Well, look who's not." Very few of the lesbians and gay men I met believed that claiming a gay identity automatically requires leaving kinship behind. In some cases people described this equation as an outmoded view that contrasted sharply with revised notions of what constitutes a family.

Well-meaning defenders of lesbian and gay identity sometimes assert that gays are not inherently "anti-family," in ways that perpetuate the association of heterosexual identity with exclusive access to kinship. Charles Silverstein (1977), for instance, contends that lesbians and gay men may place more importance on maintaining family ties than heterosexuals do because gay people do not marry and raise children. Here the affirmation that gays and lesbians are capable of fostering enduring kinship ties ends up reinforcing the implication that they cannot establish "families of their own," presumably because the author regards kinship as unshakably rooted in

heterosexual alliance and procreation. In contrast, discourse on gay families cuts across the politically loaded couplet of "pro-family" and "anti-family" that places gay men and lesbians in an inherently antagonistic relation to kinship solely on the basis of their nonprocreative sexualities. "Homosexuality is not what is breaking up the Black family," declared Barbara Smith (1987), a black lesbian writer, activist, and speaker at the 1987 Gay and Lesbian March on Washington. "Homophobia is. My Black gay brothers and my Black lesbian sisters are members of Black families, both the ones we were born into and the ones we create."

At the height of gay liberation, activists had attempted to develop alternatives to "the family," whereas by the 1980s many lesbians and gay men were struggling to legitimate gay families as a form of kinship. When Armistead Maupin spoke at a gathering on Castro Street to welcome home two gay men who had been held hostage in the Middle East, partners who had stood with arms around one another upon their release, he congratulated them not only for their safe return, but also as representatives of a new kind of family. Gay or chosen families might incorporate friends, lovers, or children, in any combination. Organized through ideologies of love, choice, and creation, gay families have been defined through a contrast with what many gay men and lesbians in the Bay Area called "straight," "biological," or "blood" family. If families we choose were the families lesbians and gay men created for themselves, straight family represented the families in which most had grown to adulthood.

What does it mean to say that these two categories of family have been defined through contrast? One thing it emphatically does not mean is that heterosexuals share a single coherent form of family (although some of the lesbians and gay men doing the defining believed this to be the case). I am not arguing here for the existence of some central, unified kinship system vis-à-vis which gay people have distinguished their own practice and understanding of family. In the United States, race, class, gender, ethnicity, regional origin, and context all inform differences in household organization, as well as differences in notions of family and what it means to call someone kin. . . .

Deck the Halls

Holidays, family reunions, and other celebrations culturally categorized as family occasions represent everyday arenas in which people in the Bay Area elaborated discourse on kinship. To attend was to catch a glimpse of history in the making that brought ideological oppositions to life. During the season when Hanukkah, Christmas, New Year's, and Winter Solstice converge, opportunities abounded to observe the way double-sided contrasts like the one between straight and gay families take shape. Meanings and transformations appeared far less abstract as people applied and reinterpreted them in the course of concrete activities and discussion. Their emotional power suddenly became obvious and inescapable, clearly central to ideological relations that have been approached far too cognitively in the past.

In San Francisco, gay community organizations set up special telephone hotlines during the holidays to serve as resources for lesbians and gay men battling feelings of loneliness or depression. At this time of year similar feelings were common in the population at large, given the tiring, labor-intensive character of holiday preparations and the pressure of cultural prescriptions to gather with relatives in a state of undisturbed happiness and harmony. Yet many gay people considered the "holiday blues" a more acute problem for themselves than for heterosexuals because disclosure of a lesbian or gay identity so often disrupted relations with straight relatives. The large number of gay immigrants to the Bay Area ensured that decisions about where to spend the holidays would make spatial declarations about family ties and family loyalties. . . .

For those whose sexual identity was known to biological or adoptive relatives, conflicts over gaining acknowledgment and legitimacy for relationships with lovers and others they considered gay family was never so evident as on holidays.

When Chris Davidson planned to return to her childhood home in the Bay Area for the holidays, she worried about being caught in the "same old pull" between spending time with her parents and time with her close lesbian friends. That year she had written her parents a letter in advance asking that they confront their "possessiveness" and recognize the importance of these other relationships in her life. Another woman regarded her parents' decision to allow her lover in their house to celebrate New Year's Day together with "the family" as a sign of growing acceptance. Some people had decided to celebrate holidays with their chosen families, occasionally inviting relatives by blood or adoption to join the festivities. One man voiced pride in "creating our environment, our *intimate* environment. I have an extended [gay] family. I have a lot of friends who we have shared Christmas and Thanksgiving with. Birthdays. Just as you would any other extended family." . . .

When a celebration brought chosen relatives into contact with biological or adoptive kin, family occasions sometimes became a bridge to greater integration of straight and gay families. Those who felt rejected for their sexual identities, however, could experience holidays as events that forced them to ally with one or the other of these opposed categories. The feeling was widespread that, in Diane Kunin's words, "[gay] people have to make some really excruciating choices that other people are not faced with." Because contexts such as holidays evoked the more inclusive level of the opposition *between* two types of family, they seldom elicited the positive sense of choice and creativity associated with gay families. Instead, individuals too often found themselves faced with the unwelcome dilemma of making an either/or decision when they would have preferred to choose both.

Kinship and Procreation

In the United States the notion of biology as an indelible, precultural substratum is so ingrained that people often find it difficult to take an anthropological step backward in order to examine biology as symbol rather than substance. For many in this society, biology is a defining feature of kinship: they believe that blood ties make certain people kin, regardless of whether those individuals display the love and enduring solidarity expected to characterize familial relations. Physical procreation, in turn, produces biological links. Collectively, biogenetic attributes are supposed to demarcate kinship as a cultural domain, offering a yardstick for determining who counts as a "real" relative. Like their heterosexual counterparts, lesbians and gay men tended to naturalize biology in this manner.

Not all cultures grant biology this significance for describing and evaluating relationships. To read biology as symbol is to approach it as a cultural construct and linguistic category, rather than a self-evident matter of "natural fact." At issue here is the cultural valuation given to ties traced through procreation, and the meaning that biological connection confers upon a relationship in a given cultural context. In this sense biology is no less a symbol than choice or creation. Neither is inherently more "real" or valid than the other, culturally speaking.

In the United States, Schneider (1968) argues, "sexual intercourse" is the symbol that brings together relations of marriage and blood, supplying the distinctive features in terms of which kinship relations are defined and differentiated. A relationship mediated by procreation binds a mother to a daughter, a brother to a sister, and so on, in the categories of genitor or genetrix, offspring, or members of a sibling set. Immediately apparent to a gay man or lesbian is that what passes here for sex per se is actually the *heterosexual* union of two differently gendered persons. While all sexual activity among heterosexuals certainly does not lead to the birth of children, the isolation of heterosexual intercourse as a core symbol orients kinship studies toward a dominantly procreative reading of sexualities. For a society like the United States, Sylvia Yanagisako's and Jane Collier's (1987) call to analyze gender and kinship as mutually implicated constructs must be extended to embrace sexual identity.

The very notion of gay families asserts that people who claim nonprocreative sexual identities and pursue nonprocreative relationships can lay claim to family ties of their own without necessary recourse to marriage, childbearing, or childrearing. By defining these chosen families in opposition to the biological ties believed to constitute a straight family, lesbians and gay men began to renegotiate the meaning and practice of kinship from within the very societies that had nurtured the concept. Theirs has not been a proposal to number gay families among variations in "American kinship," but a more comprehensive attack on the privilege accorded to a biogenetically grounded mode of determining what relationships will *count* as kinship.

It is important to note that some gay men and lesbians in the Bay Area agreed with the view that blood ties represent the only authentic, legitimate form of kinship. Often those who disputed the validity of chosen families were people whose notions of kinship were bound up with their own sense of racial or ethnic identity. "You've got one family, one biological family," insisted Paul Jaramillo, a Mexican-American man who did not consider his lover or friends to be kin.

> They're very good friends and I love them, but I would not call them family. Family to me is blood. . . . I feel that Western Caucasian culture, that it's much more broken down, and that they can deal with their good friends and neighbors as family. But it's not that way, at least in my background.

Because most individuals who expressed this view were well aware of the juxtaposition of blood family with families we choose, they tended to address gay kinship ideologies directly. As Lourdes Alcantara explained,

> I know a lot of lesbians think that you choose your own family. I don't think so. Because, as a Latin woman, the bonds that I got with my family are irreplaceable. They can't be replaced. They cannot. So my family is my family, my friends are my friends. My friends can be *more*

important than my family, but that doesn't mean they are my family. . . . 'Cause no matter what, they are just friends—they don't have your blood. They don't have your same connection. They didn't go through what you did. For example, I starved with my family a lot of times. They know what it is like. If I talk to my friends, they will understand me, but they will never feel the same.

What Lourdes so movingly described was a sense of enduring solidarity arising from shared experience and symbolized by blood connection. Others followed a similar line of reasoning (minus the biological signifier) when they contended that a shared history testifies to enduring solidarity, which can provide the basis for creating familial relationships of a chosen, or nonbiological, sort.

In an essay on disclosing a lesbian or gay identity to relatives, Betty Berzon (1979:89) maintains that "from early on, being gay is associated with going against the family." Many people in the Bay Area viewed families as the principal mediator of race and ethnicity, drawing on folk theories of cultural transmission in which parents hand down "traditions" and identity (as well as genes) to their children. If having a family was part of what it meant to be Chicana or Cherokee or Japanese-American, then claiming a lesbian or gay identity could easily be interpreted as losing or betraying that cultural heritage, so long as individuals conceived kinship in biogenetic terms (cf. Clunis and Green 1988:105; Tremble et al. 1989). . . .

Condemnations of homosexuality might picture race or ethnicity and gay identity as antagonists in response to a history of racist attributions of "weak" family ties to certain groups (e.g., blacks), or in response to anything that appeared to menace the legacy of "strong" kinship bonds sometimes attributed to other categories of people (e.g., Latinos, Jews). In either case, depicting lesbian or gay identity as a threat to ethnic or racial identity depended upon the cultural positioning of gay people outside familial relations. The degree to which individuals construct racial

identity *through* their notions of family remains a relatively unexplored aspect of why some heterosexuals of color reject gay or lesbian identity as a sign of assimilation, a "white thing."

Not all lesbians and gays of color or whites with a developed ethnic identity took issue with the concept of chosen families. Many African-Americans, for instance, felt that black communities had never held to a strictly biogenetic interpretation of kinship. "Blacks have never said to a child, 'Unless you have a mother, father, sister, brother, you don't have a family'" (Height 1989:137). Discourse and ideology are far from being uniformly determined by identities, experiences, or historical developments. Divergent perceptions of the relation between family ties and race or ethnicity are indicative of a situation of ideological flux, in which procreative and nonprocreative interpretations vie with one another for the privilege of defining kinship. As the United States entered the final decade of the twentieth century, lesbians and gay men from a broad spectrum of racial and ethnic identities had come to embrace the legitimacy of gay families.

From Biology to Choice

Upon first learning the categories that framed gay kinship ideologies, heterosexuals sometimes mentioned adoption as a kind of limiting case that appeared to occupy the borderland between biology and choice. In the United States, adopted children are chosen, in a sense, although biological offspring can be planned or selected as well, given the widespread availability of birth control. Yet adoption in this society "is only understandable as a way of creating the social fiction that an actual link of kinship exists. Without biological kinship as a model, adoption would be meaningless" (Schneider 1984:55). Adoption does not render the attribution of biological descent culturally irrelevant (witness the many adopted children who, later in life, decide to search for their "real" parents). But adoptive relations—unlike gay families—pose no fundamental challenge to either procreative interpretations of kinship or the culturally standardized image of a family assembled around a core of parent(s) plus children.

Mapping biological family and families we choose onto contrasting sexual identities (straight and gay, respectively) places these two types of family in a relation of opposition, but *within* that relation, determinism implicitly differentiates biology from choice and blood from creation. Informed by contrasting notions of free will and the fixedness often attributed to biology in this culture, the opposition between straight and gay families echoes old dichotomies such as nature versus nurture and real versus ideal. In families we choose, the agency conveyed by "we" emphasizes each person's part in constructing gay families, just as the absence of agency in the term "biological family" reinforces the sense of blood as an immutable fact over which individuals exert little control. Likewise, the collective subject of families we choose invokes a collective identity—who are "we" if not gay men and lesbians? In order to identify the "we" associated with the speaker's "I," a listener must first recognize the correspondence between the opposition of blood to choice and the relation of straight to gay.

Significantly, families we choose have not built directly upon beliefs that gay or lesbian identity can be chosen. Among lesbians and gay men themselves, opinions differ as to whether individuals select or inherit their sexual identities. In the aftermath of the gay movement, the trend has been to move away from the obsession of earlier decades with the etiological question of what "causes" homosexuality. After noting that no one subjects heterosexuality to similar scrutiny, many people dropped the question. Some lesbian-feminists presented lesbianism as a political choice that made a statement about sharing their best with other women and refusing to participate in patriarchal relations. In everyday conversations, however, the majority of both men and women portrayed their sexual identities as either inborn or a predisposition developed very early in life. Whether or not to act on feelings already present then became the only matter left to individual discretion. "The choice for me

wasn't being with men or being a lesbian," Richie Kaplan explained. "The choice was being asexual or being with women."

In contrast, parents who disapproved of homosexuality could convey a critical attitude by treating gay identity as something elective, especially since people in the United States customarily hold individuals responsible for any negative consequences attendant upon a "free choice." One man described with dismay his father's reaction upon learning of his sexual identity: "I said, 'I'm gay.' And he said, 'Oh. Well, I guess you made your choice.'" According to another, "My father kept saying, 'Well, you're gonna have to live by your choices that you make. It's your responsibility.' What's there to be responsible [about]? I was who I *am*." When Andy Wentworth disclosed his gay identity to his sister,

> She asked me, how could I choose to do this and to ignore the health risks . . . implying that this was a conscious, "Oh, I'd like to go to the movies today" type of choice. And I told her, I said, "Nobody in their right mind would go through this hell of being gay just to satisfy a whim." And I explained to her what it was like growing up. Knowing this other side of yourself that you can't tell anybody about, and if anybody in your family knows they will be upset and mortified.

Another man insisted he would never forget the period after coming out when he realized that he felt good about himself, and that he was not on his way to becoming "the kind of person that they're portraying gay people to be." What kind of person is that, I asked. "Well, you know, wicked, evil people who *decide* that they're going to be evil."

Rather than claiming an elective gay identity as its antecedent, the category "families we choose" incorporates the meaningful *difference* that is the product of choice and biology as two relationally defined terms. If many gay men and lesbians interpreted blood ties as a type of social connectedness organized through procreation, they tended to associate choice and creativity with a total absence of guidelines for ordering relationships within gay families. Although heterosexuals in the Bay Area also had the sense of creating something when they established families of their own, that creativity was often firmly linked to childbearing and childrearing, the "pro-" in procreation. In the absence of a procreative referent, individual discretion regulated who would be counted as kin. For those who had constructed them, gay families could evoke utopian visions of self-determination in the absence of social constraint. Of course, the contextualization of choice and creativity within the symbolic relation that opposes them to blood and biology itself lends a high degree of structure to the notion of gay families. The elaboration of gay kinship ideologies in contrast to the biogenetic symbolism of straight family illustrates the type of structured relation Roman Jakobson (1962) has called "the unexpected arising from expectedness, both of them unthinkable without the opposite."

Certainly lesbians and gay men, with their range of backgrounds and experiences, did not always mean the same thing or advance identical cultural critiques when they spoke of blood and chosen families. Ideological contrasts utilized and recognized by all need not have the same significance for all. Neither can an examination of ideology alone explain why choice should have been highlighted as an organizing principle of gay families. Only history, material conditions, and context can account for the specific content of gay kinship ideologies, their emergence at a particular point in time, and the variety of ways people have implemented those ideologies in their daily lives. In themselves, gay families comprise only a segment of the historical transformation sequence that mapped the contrast between straight and gay first onto "family/no family," and then onto "biological family/families we choose." Gone are the days when embracing a lesbian or gay identity seemed to require a renunciation of kinship. The symbolic groundwork for gay families, laid during a period when coming out to relatives witnessed a kind of institutionalization, has made it possible to claim a sexual identity that is not linked to procreation,

face the possibility of rejection by blood or adoptive relations, yet still conceive of establishing a family of one's own.

REFERENCES

Allen, Ronnie. 1987. "Times Have Changed at the Herald." *Gay Community News* (June 28–July 4).

Berzon, Betty. 1979. "Telling the Family You're Gay." In Betty Berzon and Robert Leighton, eds., *Positively Gay*, pp. 88–100. Los Angeles: Mediamix Associates.

Castells, Manuel and Karen Murphy. 1982. "Cultural Identity and Urban Structure: The Spatial Organization of San Francisco's Gay Community." In Norman I. Fainstein and Susan S. Fainstein, eds., *Urban Policy Under Capitalism*, pp. 237–259. Beverly Hills, Calif.: Sage.

Clunis, D. Merilee and G. Dorsey Green. 1988. *Lesbian Couples.* Seattle: Seal Press.

Cook, Blanche Wiesen. 1977. "Female Support Networks and Political Activism: Lillian Wald, Crystal Eastman, Emma Goldman." *Chrysalis* 3:44–61.

FitzGerald, Frances. 1986. *Cities on a Hill: A Journey Through Contemporary American Cultures.* New York: Simon & Schuster.

Foucault, Michel. 1978. *The History of Sexuality.* Vol 1. New York: Vintage.

Godwin, Ronald S. 1983. "AIDS: A Moral and Political Time Bomb." *Moral Majority Report* (July).

Height, Dorothy. 1989. "Self-Help—A Black Tradition." *The Nation* (July 24–31):136–138.

Hocquenghem, Guy. 1978. *Homosexual Desire.* London: Alison & Busby.

Hollibaugh, Amber. 1979. "Sexuality and the State: The Defeat of the Briggs Initiative and Beyond." *Socialist Review* 9(3):55–72.

Jakobson, Roman. 1962. *Selected Writings.* The Hague: Mouton.

Lazere, Arthur. 1986. "On the Job." *Coming Up!* (June).

Mendenhall, George. 1985. "Mickey Mouse Lawsuit Remains Despite Disney Dancing Decree." *Bay Area Reporter* (Aug. 22).

Schneider, David M. 1968. *American Kinship: A Cultural Account.* Englewood Cliffs, N.J.: Prentice-Hall.

_____. 1984. *A Critique of the Study of Kinship.* Ann Arbor: University of Michigan Press.

Silverstein, Charles. 1977. *A Family Matter: A Parents' Guide to Homosexuality.* New York: McGraw-Hill.

Smith, B. 1987. "From the Stage." *Gay Community News* (Nov. 8–14).

Tremble, Bob, Margaret Schneider, and Carol Appathurai. 1989. "Growing Up Gay or Lesbian in a Multicultural Context." In Gilbert Herdt, ed., *Gay and Lesbian Youth*, pp. 253–264. New York: Haworth Press.

Watney, Simon. 1987. *Policing Desire: Pornography, AIDS, and the Media.* Minneapolis: University of Minnesota Press.

Yanagisako, Sylvia Junko and Jane Fishburne Collier. 1987. "Toward a Unified Analysis of Gender and Kinship." In Jane Fishburne Collier and Sylvia Junko Yanagisako, eds., *Gender and Kinship: Essays Toward a Unified Analysis*, pp. 14–50. Stanford: Stanford University Press.

THINKING ABOUT THE READING

Why do you suppose there is so much reluctance in this society to acknowledge the family status of gay couples? Why are gay relationships considered by many to be a threat to the institution of family? The larger sociological issue here is: Should individuals have the freedom to define their living arrangements as a family? Should we be able to call anything we want a "family"? What is society's interest in controlling who can and can't be considered a family? Can you envision a society based on "families of choice" rather than on procreation or blood? How would such a society differ from the one you currently live in? How would other social institutions—economics, politics, religion, education, and so on—be affected?

The Time Bind

When Work Becomes Home and Home Becomes Work

Arlie Russell Hochschild

. . . I had come to Spotted Deer [Day Care Center] to explore a question I'd been left with after finishing my last book, *The Second Shift: Working Parents and the Revolution at Home.* In that work I had examined the tensions that arise at home in two-job marriages when working women also do the lion's share of the childcare and housework. Such marriages were far less strained, I found, when men committed themselves to sharing what I came to call "the second shift," the care of children and home. But even with the work shared out, there seemed to be less and less time for the second shift, not to mention relaxed family life. Something was amiss, and whatever it was, I sensed that I would not find out simply by looking at home life by itself.

Everything I already knew or would soon learn pointed to the workplace as the arena that needed to be explored. As a start, I was well aware that, while in 1950 12.6 percent of married mothers with children under age seventeen worked for pay, by 1994, 69 percent did so; and 58.8 percent of wives with children age one or younger were in the workforce. Many of these wives also had a hand in caring for elderly relatives. In addition, the hours both men and women put in at work had increased—either for college-educated workers or, depending on which scholars you read, for all workers. In her book *The Overworked American,* the economist Juliet Schor has claimed that over the last two decades the average worker has added an extra 164 hours—a month of work—to his or her work year. Workers now take fewer unpaid leaves, and even fewer paid ones. In the 1980s alone, vacations shortened by 14 percent. According to the economist Victor Fuchs, between 1960 and 1986 parental time available to children per week fell ten hours in white households and twelve hours in black households. It was also evident, however you cut the figures, that life was coming to center more on work. More women were on board the work train, and the train was moving faster. It wasn't just that ever larger numbers of mothers of young children were taking paying jobs, but that fewer of those jobs were part time; and fewer of those mothers were taking time off even in the summer, as they might once have done, to care for school-aged children on vacation. Women moving into the workforce—whether or not they were mothers—were less inclined than ever to move out of it. It was apparent, in fact, that working mothers were increasingly fitting the profile of working fathers. But those fathers, far from cutting back to help out at home, studies told us, were now working even longer hours. In fact, their hours were as long as those of childless men.

All this could be read in the numbers—as well as in the tensions in many of the households I had visited. I was left with a nagging question: given longer workdays—and more of them—how could parents balance jobs with family life? Or, to put the matter another way, was life at work winning out over life at home? If so, was there not some way to organize work to avoid penalizing employees, male and female, for having lives outside of work and to ease the burden on their children?

I was thinking about these questions when a surprising event occurred. I was asked to give a talk at Amerco, a company about which I knew little except that it had been identified as one of the ten most "family-friendly" companies in America by the Families and Work Institute, by

Working Mother magazine, and by the authors of *Companies That Care*. At a dinner given after my talk, a company spokesman seated next to me asked if I had ever thought of studying family-friendly policies in the workplace itself. To tell the truth, I could not believe my luck. If there was ever a chance for families to balance home and work, I thought to myself, it would be at a place like this. Amerco's management clearly hoped my findings would help them answer a few questions of their own. In the late 1980s, the company had been distressed to discover a startling fact: they were losing professional women far faster than they were losing professional men. Each time such a worker was lost, it cost the company a great deal of money to recruit and train a replacement. The company had tried to eliminate this waste of money and talent by addressing one probable reason women were leaving: the absence of what was called "work-family balance." Amerco now offered a range of remedial programs including options for part-time work, job sharing, and flextime. Did these policies really help Amerco? Given current trends, it seemed crucial to top management to know the answer. Six months later I found myself lodged at a cozy bed-and-breakfast on a tree-lined street in Spotted Deer, ready to begin finding out. . . .

I interviewed top and middle managers, clerks and factory workers—a hundred and thirty people in all. Most were part of two-job couples, some were single parents, and a few were single without children. Sometimes we met in their offices or in a plant breakroom, sometimes in their homes, often in both places. Early mornings and evenings, weekends and holidays, I sat on the lawn by the edge of a series of parking lots that circled company headquarters, watching people walk to and from their vans, cars, or pick-up trucks to see when they came to work and when they left.

I talked with psychologists in and outside the company, childcare workers hired by Amerco, homemakers married to Amerco employees, and company consultants. Along with the Spotted Deer Childcare Center, I visited local YWCA after-school programs as well as a Parent Re-

source Center funded by the company. I attended company sessions of the Women's Quality Improvement Team and the Work Family Progress Committee, a Valuing Diversity workshop, and two High Performance Team meetings. A team in Amerco's Sales Division allowed me to sit in on its meetings. To their surprise—and mine—I also became the fifth wheel on a golfing expedition designed to build team spirit. During several night shifts at an Amerco factory, tired workers patiently talked with me over coffee in the breakroom. One even took me to a local bar to meet her friends and relatives.

The company gave me access to a series of its internal "climate surveys" of employee attitudes, and I combed through research reports on other companies, national opinion polls, and a burgeoning literature on work and family life. I also attended work-family conferences held in New York, San Francisco, Los Angeles, and Boston by The Conference Board, a respected organization that gathers and disseminates information of interest to the benefit of the business management community.

[In addition,] six families—four two-parent families and two single-mother families—allowed me to follow them on typical workdays from dawn until dusk and beyond. . . .

An Angel of an Idea

Almost from the beginning of my stay in Spotted Deer, I could tell that the family-friendly reforms introduced with so much fanfare in 1985 were finding a curious reception. Three things seemed true. First, Amerco's workers declared on survey after survey that they were strained to the limit. Second, the company offered them policies that would allow them to cut back. Third, almost no one cut back. . . . Programs that allowed parents to work undistracted by family concerns were endlessly in demand, while policies offering shorter hours that allowed workers more free or family time languished.

To try to make sense of this paradox I began, first of all, to scrutinize the text of the policy and the results of employee surveys. Amerco defines a part-time job as one that requires thirty-five hours or less, with full or prorated benefits.[1] A job share is a full-time position shared by two people with benefits and salary prorated. As with all attempts to change work schedules, I learned, the worker has to get the permission of a supervisor, a division head, or both. In addition, workers under union contract—a full half of Amerco's workforce including factory hands and maintenance crews—were not eligible for policies offering shorter or more flexible hours.

But I discovered that among eligible employees with children thirteen and under, only 3 percent worked part time. In fact, in 1990, only 53 out of Amerco's 21,070 employees in the United States, less than one-quarter of 1 percent of its workforce, were part-timers, and less than 1 percent of Amerco's employees shared a job.

Amerco also offered its employees a program called "flexplace," which allowed workers to do their work from home or some other place. One percent of employees used it. Likewise, under certain circumstances, an employee could take a temporary leave from full-time work. The standard paid parental leave for a new mother was six weeks (to be divided with the father as the couple wished). If permission was granted, a parent could then return to work part time with full benefits, to be arranged at his or her supervisor's discretion. Most new mothers took the paid weeks off, and sometimes several months more of unpaid leave, but then returned to their full-time schedules. Almost no Amerco fathers took advantage of parental leave, and no Amerco father has ever responded to the arrival of a new baby in the family by taking up a part-time work schedule.

By contrast, "flextime," a policy allowing workers to come and go early or late, or to be in other ways flexible about when they do their work, was quite popular. By 1993, a quarter of all workers—and a third of working parents—used it. In other words, of Amerco's family-friendly policies only flextime, which rearranged but did not cut back on hours of work, had any significant impact on the workplace. According to one survey, 99 percent of Amerco employees worked full time, and

full-time employees averaged forty-seven hours a week. As I looked more closely at the figures I discovered some surprising things. Workers with young children actually put in more hours at work as those without children. Although a third of all parents had flexible schedules, 56 percent of employees with children regularly worked on weekends. Seventy-two percent of parents regularly worked overtime; unionized hourly workers were paid for this time (though much of their overtime was required), while salaried workers weren't. In fact, during the years I was studying Amerco, parents and nonparents alike began to work *longer* hours. By 1993, virtually everyone I spoke with told me they were working longer hours than they had only a few years earlier, and most agreed that Amerco was "a pretty workaholic place."

Amerco is not alone. A 1990 study of 188 Fortune 500 manufacturing firms found that while 88 percent of them informally offered part-time work, only 3 to 5 percent of their employees made use of it. Six percent of the companies surveyed formally offered job sharing, but only 1 percent or less of their employees took advantage of that. Forty-five percent of these companies officially offered flextime, but only 10 percent of their employees used it. Three percent of the companies offered flexplace—work at home—and less than 3 percent of their employees took advantage of it.[2]*

As Amerco's experience would suggest, American working parents seem to be putting in longer and longer hours. Of workers with children aged twelve and under, only 4 percent of men, and 13 percent of women, worked less than forty hours a week.[3] According to a study by Arthur Emlen of Portland State University,

---

*The 1993 Family and Medical Leave Act requires all companies employing fifty or more workers to offer three months of unpaid time off for medical or family emergencies. Although it is not yet clear what effect this law will have, research suggests few workers are likely to take advantage of it. Studies of earlier state family and medical leave laws show that less than 5 percent of employees actually use the leave.

whether or not a worker has a child makes re-markably little difference to his or her atten-dance record at work. Excluding vacation and holidays, the average employee misses nine days of work a year. The average parent of a child who is left home alone on weekdays misses fourteen and a half days a year: only five and a half days more. Fathers with young children only miss half a day more a year than fathers without children.[4]

The idea of more time for family life seems to have died, gone to heaven, and become an angel of an idea. But why? Why don't working parents, and others too, take the opportunity available to them to reduce their hours at work?

The most widely accepted explanation is that working parents simply can't *afford* to work shorter hours. With the median income of U.S. households in 1996 at $32,264, it is true that many workers could not pay their rent and food bills on three-quarters or half of their salaries. But notwithstanding the financial and time pres-sures most parents face, why do the majority not even take all of the paid vacation days due to them? Even more puzzling, why are the best-paid employees—upper-level managers and profes-sionals—among the least interested in part-time work or job sharing? In one Amerco survey, only one-third of top-level female employees (who belong to what is called the "A-payroll") thought part time was of "great value." The percentage of women favoring part time rose as pay levels went down: 45 percent of "B-payroll" (lower-level managers and professionals) and "adminis-trative" women (who provide clerical support) thought part time was of "great value." Thus, those who earned more money were less inter-ested in part-time work than those who earned less. Few men at any level expressed interest in part-time work.

Again, if income alone determined how often or how long mothers stayed home after the birth of their babies, we would expect poorer mothers to go back to work more quickly, and richer mothers to spend more time at home. But that's not what we find. Nationwide, well-to-do new mothers are not significantly more likely to stay home with a new baby than low-income new mothers. A quarter of poor new mothers in one study returned to work after three months, but so did a third of well-to-do new mothers. Twenty-three percent of new mothers with household in-comes of $15,000 or under took long leaves (fifty-three weeks or more), and so did 22 percent of new mothers with household incomes of $50,000 or more.[5]

In a 1995 national study, 48 percent of Ameri-can working women and 61 percent of men claimed they would still want to work even if they had enough money to live as "comfortably as you would like."[6] When asked what was "very important" to their decision to take their current job, only 35 percent of respondents in one na-tional study said "salary/wage," whereas 55 per-cent mentioned "gaining new skills" as very im-portant, and 60 percent mentioned "effect on personal/family life."[7] Money matters, of course, but other things do too.

According to a second commonly believed ex-planation, workers extend their hours, not be-cause they need the money, but because they are afraid of being laid off. They're working scared. By fostering a climate of fear, the argument goes, many companies take away with one hand the helpful policies they lightly offer with the other.

Downsizing is a serious problem in American companies in the 1990s but there's scant evi-dence that employees at Amerco were working scared. During the late 1980s and early 1990s, there was very little talk of layoffs. When I asked employees whether they worked long hours be-cause they were afraid of getting on a layoff list, virtually everyone said no. (Although there were, in fact, small-scale layoffs in certain divisions of the company, the process was handled delicately through "internal rehiring" and "encouraged" early retirement.) And when I compared hours of work in the few downsized Amerco divisions with those in non-downsized divisions, they were basically the same. Supervisors in the two kinds of divisions received just about the same number of requests for shorter hours. . . .

One possible explanation is that workers in-terested in and eligible for flexible or shorter hours don't know they can get them. After all, even at a place like Amerco, such policies are fairly new. Yet on closer inspection, this proved not to be the case. According to a 1990 survey, most Amerco workers were aware of company policies on flextime and leaves. Women were better informed than men, and higher-level workers more so than lower-level workers. The vast majority of people I talked with knew that the company offered "good" policies and were proud to be working for such a generous company. Employees who weren't clear about the details knew they could always ask someone who was. As one secretary remarked, "I don't know exactly how long the parental leave is, but I know how to find out." So why didn't they? . . .

Family Values and Reversed Worlds

If working parents are "deciding" to work full time and longer, what experiences at home and work might be influencing them to do so? When I first began [my] research, . . . I assumed that home was "home" and work was "work"—that each was a stationary rock beneath the moving feet of working parents. I assumed as well that each stood in distinct opposition to the other. In a family, love and commitment loom large as ends in themselves and are not means to any further end. As an Amerco parent put it, "I work to live; I don't live to work." However difficult family life may be at times, we usually feel family ties offer an irreplaceable connection to generations past and future. Family is our personal embrace with history.

Jobs, on the other hand, earn money that, to most of us, serves as the means to other ends. To be sure, jobs can also allow us to develop skills or friendships, and to be part of a larger work community. But we seldom envision the workplace as somewhere workers would freely choose to spend their time. If in the American imagination the family has a touch of the sacred, the realm of work seems profane.

In addition, I assumed, as many of us do, that compared to the workplace, home is a more pleasant place to be. This is after all one reason why employers pay workers to work and don't pay them to stay home. The very word "work" suggests to most of us something unpleasant, involuntary, even coerced.

If the purpose and nature of family and work differ so drastically in our minds, it seemed reasonable to assume that people's emotional experiences of the two spheres would differ profoundly, too. In *Haven in a Heartless World*, the social historian Christopher Lasch drew a picture of family as a "haven" where workers sought refuge from the cruel world of work.[8] Painting in broad strokes, we might imagine a picture like this: At the end of a long day, a weary worker opens his front door and calls out, "Hi, Honey! I'm home!" He takes off his uniform, puts on a bathrobe, opens a beer, picks up the paper, and exhales. Whatever its strains, home is where he's relaxed, most himself. At home, he feels that people know him, understand him, appreciate him for who he really is. At home, he is safe.

At work, our worker is "on call," ready to report at a moment's notice, working flat out to get back to the customer right away. He feels "like a number." If he doesn't watch out, he can take the fall for somebody else's mistakes. This, then, is Lasch's "heartless world." . . .

It was just such images of home and work that were challenged in one of my first interviews at Amerco. Linda Avery, a friendly thirty-eight-year-old mother of two daughters, is a shift supervisor at the Demco Plant, ten miles down the valley from Amerco headquarters. Her husband, Bill, is a technician in the same plant. Linda and Bill share the care of her sixteen-year-old daughter from a previous marriage and their two-year-old by working opposite shifts, as a full fifth of American working parents do. "Bill works the 7 A.M. to 3 P.M. shift while I watch the baby," Linda explained. "Then I work the 3 P.M. to 11 P.M. shift and he watches the baby. My older daughter works at Walgreens after school."

When we first met in the factory's breakroom over a couple of Cokes, Linda was in blue jeans and a pink jersey, her hair pulled back in a long blond ponytail. She wore no makeup, and her manner was purposeful and direct. She was working overtime, and so I began by asking whether Amerco required the overtime, or whether she volunteered for it. "Oh, I put in for it," she replied with a low chuckle. But, I wondered aloud, wouldn't she and her husband like to have more time at home together, finances and company policy permitting. Linda took off her safety glasses, rubbed her whole face, folded her arms, resting her elbows on the table, and approached the question by describing her life at home:

> I walk in the door and the minute I turn the key in the lock my older daughter is there. Granted, she needs somebody to talk to about her day. . . . The baby is still up. She should have been in bed two hours ago and that upsets me. The dishes are piled in the sink. My daughter comes right up to the door and complains about anything her stepfather said or did, and she wants to talk about her job. My husband is in the other room hollering to my daughter, "Tracy, I don't *ever* get any time to talk to your mother, because you're always monopolizing her time before I even get a chance!" They all come at me at once.

To Linda, her home was not a place to relax. It was another workplace. Her description of the urgency of demands and the unarbitrated quarrels that awaited her homecoming contrasted with her account of arriving at her job as a shift supervisor:

> I usually come to work early just to get away from the house. I get there at 2:30 P.M., and people are there waiting. We sit. We talk. We joke. I let them know what's going on, who has to be where, what changes I've made for the shift that day. We sit there and chit-chat for five or ten minutes. There's laughing, joking, fun. My coworkers aren't putting me down for any reason. Everything is done with humor and fun from beginning to end, though it can get stressful when a machine malfunctions.

For Linda, home had become work and work had become home. Somehow, the two worlds had been reversed. Indeed, Linda felt she could only get relief from the "work" of being at home by going to the "home" of work. As she explained,

> My husband's a great help watching our baby. But as far as doing housework or even taking the baby when I'm at home, no. He figures he works five days a week; *he's* not going to come

home and clean. But he doesn't stop to think that I work *seven* days a week. Why should I have to come home and do the housework without help from anybody else? My husband and I have been through this over and over again. Even if he would just pick up from the kitchen table and stack the dishes for me, that would make a big difference. He does nothing. On his weekends off, I have to provide a sitter for the baby so he can go fishing. When I have a day off, I have the baby all day long without a break. He'll help out if I'm not here, but the minute I am, all the work at home is mine.

With a light laugh, she continued, "So I take a lot of overtime. The more I get out of the house, the better I am. It's a terrible thing to say, but that's the way I feel." Linda said this not in the manner of a new discovery, a reluctant confession, or collusion between two working mothers—"Don't you just want to get away sometimes?"—but in a matter-of-fact way. This was the way life was.

Bill, who was fifty-six when I first met him, had three grown children from a contentious first marriage. He told me he felt he had already "put in his time" to raise them and now was at a stage of life in which he wanted to enjoy himself Yet when he came home afternoons he had to "babysit for Linda."

In a previous era, men regularly escaped the house for the bar, the fishing hole, the golf course, the pool hall, or, often enough, the sweet joy of work. Today, as one of the women who make up 45 percent of the American workforce, Linda Avery, overloaded and feeling unfairly treated at home, was escaping to work, too. Nowadays, men and women both may leave unwashed dishes, unresolved quarrels, crying tots, testy teenagers, and unresponsive mates behind to arrive at work early and call out, "Hi, fellas, I'm here!"

Linda would have loved a warm welcome from her family when she returned from work, a reward for her day of labors at the plant. At a minimum, she would have liked to relax, at least for a little while. But that was hard to do because Bill, on *his* second shift at home, would nap and watch television instead of engaging the children. The more Bill slacked off on his shift at home, the more Linda felt robbed of rest when she was there. The more anxious the children were, or the messier the house was when she walked in the door, the more Linda felt she was simply returning to the task of making up for being gone.

For his part, Bill recalled that Linda had wanted a new baby more than he had. So now that they were the parents of a small child, Bill reasoned, looking after the baby should also be more Linda's responsibility. Caring for a two-year-old after working a regular job was hard enough. Incredibly, Linda wanted him to do more. That was her problem though, not his. He had "earned his stripes" with his first set of children. . . .

Both Linda and Bill felt the need for time off, to relax, to have fun, to feel free, but they had not agreed that it was Bill who needed a break more than Linda. Bill simply . . . took his free time. This irritated Linda because she felt he *took* it at her expense. Largely in response to her resentment, Linda grabbed what she also called "free time"—at work.

Neither Linda nor Bill Avery wanted more time at home, not as things were arranged. Whatever images they may have carried in their heads about what family and work should be like, the Averys did not feel their actual home was a haven or that work was a heartless world.

Where did Linda feel most relaxed? She laughed more, joked more, listened to more interesting stories while on break at the factory than at home. Working the 3 P.M. to 11 P.M. shift, her hours off didn't coincide with those of her mother or older sister who worked in town, nor with those of her close friends and neighbors. But even if they had, she would have felt that the true center of her social world was her plant, not her neighborhood. The social life that once might have surrounded her at home she now found at work. The sense of being part of a lively, larger, ongoing community—that, too, was at work. In an emergency, Linda told me, she would sacrifice everything for her family. But in the meantime, the everyday "emergencies" she most wanted to attend to, that challenged rather than exhausted her, were those she encountered at the factory. Frankly, life there was more fun.

How do Linda and Bill Avery fit into the broader picture of American family and work life? Psychologist Reed Larson and his colleagues studied the daily emotional experiences of mothers and fathers in fifty-five two-parent Chicago families with children in the fifth to eighth grades. Some of the mothers cared for children at home, some worked part time, others full time, while all the fathers in the study worked full time. Each participant wore a pager for a week, and whenever they were beeped by the research team, each wrote down how he or she felt: "happy, unhappy, cheerful-irritable, friendly-angry." The researchers found that men and women reported a similar range of emotional states across the week. But fathers reported more "positive emotional states" at home; mothers, more positive emotional states at work. This held true for every social class. Fathers like Bill Avery relaxed more at home; while mothers like Linda Avery did more housework there. Larson suggests that "because women are constantly on call to the needs of other family members, they are less able to relax at home in the way men do."[9] Wives were typically in better moods than their husbands at home only when they were eating or engaging in "family transport." They were in worse moods when they were doing "child-related activities" or "socializing" there.[10] Men and women each felt most at ease when involved in tasks they felt less obliged to do, Larson reports. For women, this meant first shift work; for men, second.

A recent study of working mothers made another significant discovery. Problems at home tend to upset women more deeply than problems at work. The study found that women were most deeply affected by family stress—and were more likely to be made depressed or physically ill by it—even when stress at the workplace was greater. For women, current research on stress does not support the common view of home as a sanctuary and work as a "jungle." However hectic their lives, women who do paid work, researchers have consistently found, feel less depressed, think better of themselves, and are more satisfied with life than women who don't do paid work.[11] One study reported that, paradoxically, women who work feel more valued at home than women who stay home.[12]

In sum, then, women who work outside the home have better physical and mental health than those who do not, and not simply because healthier women go to work. Paid work, the psychologist Grace Baruch argues, "offers such benefits as challenge, control, structure, positive feedback, self-esteem . . . and social ties."[13] Reed Larson's study found, for example, that women were no more likely than men to see coworkers as friendly, but when women made friendly contact it was far more likely to lift their spirits.[14]

As a woman quoted by Baruch put it, "A job is to a woman as a wife is to a man."[15]

For Linda Avery self-satisfaction, well-being, high spirits, and work were inextricably linked. It was mainly at work, she commented, that she felt really good about herself As a supervisor, she saw her job as helping people, and those she helped appreciated her. . . .

Often relations at work seemed more manageable. The "children" Linda Avery helped at work were older and better able to articulate their problems than her own children. The plant where she worked was clean and pleasant. She knew everyone on the line she supervised. Indeed, all the workers knew each other, and some were even related by blood, marriage, or, odd as it may sound, by divorce. One coworker complained bitterly that a friend of her husband's ex-wife was keeping track of how much overtime she worked in order to help this ex-wife make a case for increasing the amount of his child support. Workers sometimes carried such hostilities generated at home into the workplace. Yet despite the common assumption that relations at work are emotionally limited, meaningful friendships often blossom. When Linda Avery joined coworkers for a mug of beer at a nearby bar after work to gossip about the "spy" who was tracking the deadbeat dad's new wife's overtime, she was among real friends. Research shows that work friends can be as important as family members in helping both men and women cope with the blows of life. The gerontologist Andrew Sharlach studied how middle-aged people in Los Angeles dealt with the death of a parent. He

found that 73 percent of the women in the sample, and 64 percent of the men, responded that work was a "helpful resource" in coping with a mother's death.[16]

Amerco regularly reinforced the family-like ties of coworkers by holding recognition ceremonies honoring particular workers or entire self-managed production teams. The company would decorate a section of the factory and serve food and drink. The production teams, too, had regular get-togethers. The halls of Amerco were hung with plaques praising workers for recent accomplishments. Such recognition luncheons, department gatherings, and, particularly in the ranks of clerical and factory workers, exchange of birthday gifts were fairly common workday events.

At its white-collar offices, Amerco was even more involved in shaping the emotional culture of the workplace and fostering an environment of trust and cooperation in order to bring out everyone's best. At the middle and top levels of the company, employees were invited to periodic "career development seminars" on personal relations at work. The centerpiece of Amerco's personal-relations culture was a "vision" speech that the CEO had given called "Valuing the Individual," a message repeated in speeches, memorialized in company brochures, and discussed with great seriousness throughout the upper reaches of the company. In essence, the message was a parental reminder to respect others. Similarly, in a new-age recasting of an old business slogan ("The customer is always right"), Amerco proposed that its workers "Value the internal customer." This meant: Be as polite and considerate to your coworkers as you would be to Amerco customers. "Value the internal customer" extended to coworkers the slogan "Delight the customer." Don't just work with your coworkers, delight them.

"Employee empowerment," "valuing diversity," and "work-family balance"—these catchphrases, too, spoke to a moral aspect of work life. Though ultimately tied to financial gain, such exhortations—and the policies that followed from them—made workers feel the company was concerned with people, not just money.

In many ways, the workplace appeared to be a site of benign social engineering where workers came to feel appreciated, honored, and liked. On the other hand, how many recognition ceremonies for competent performance were going on at home? Who was valuing the internal customer there?

After thirty years with Amerco, Bill Avery felt, if anything, overqualified for his job, and he had a recognition plaque from the company to prove it. But when his toddler got into his fishing gear and he blew up at her and she started yelling, he felt impotent in the face of her rageful screams— and nobody was there to back him up. When his teenage stepdaughter reminded him that she saw him, not as an honorable patriarch, but as an infantile competitor for her mother's attention, he felt humiliated. At such moments, he says, he had to resist the impulse to reach for the whiskey he had given up five years earlier.

Other fathers with whom I talked were less open and self-critical about such feelings, but in one way or another many said that they felt more confident they could "get the job done" at work than at home. As one human resource specialist at Amerco reflected,

> We used to joke about the old "Mother of the Year Award." That doesn't exist anymore. Now, we don't know a meaningful way to reward a parent. At work, we get paid and promoted for doing well. At home, when you're doing the right thing, chances are your kids are giving you hell for it.

If a family gives its members anything, we assume it is surely a sense of belonging to an ongoing community. In its engineered corporate cultures, capitalism has rediscovered communal ties and is using them to build its new version of capitalism. Many Amerco employees spoke warmly, happily, and seriously of "belonging to the Amerco family," and everywhere there were visible symbols of this belonging. While some married people have dispensed with their wedding rings, people proudly wore their "Total Quality" pins or "High Performance Team" tee-shirts, symbols of their loyalty to the company and of its loyalty to them. In my interviews, I heard little about festive reunions of extended families, while throughout the year, employees flocked to the many company-sponsored ritual gatherings. . . .

We may be seeing here a trend in modern life destined to affect us all. To be sure, few people feel totally secure either at work or at home. In the last fifteen years, massive waves of downsizing have reduced the security workers feel even in the most apparently stable workplaces. At the same time, a rising divorce rate has reduced the security they feel at home. Although both Linda and Bill felt their marriage was strong, over the course of their lives, each had changed relationships more often than they had changed jobs. Bill had worked steadily for Amerco for thirty years, but he had been married twice; and in the years between marriages, he had lived with two women and dated several more. Nationwide, half the people who marry eventually divorce, most within the first seven years of marriage. Three-quarters of divorced men and two-thirds of divorced women remarry, but remarried couples are more likely than those in first marriages to divorce. Couples who only live together are even more likely to break up than couples who marry. Increasing numbers of people are getting their "pink slips" at home. Work may become their rock. . . .

The social world that draws a person's allegiance also imparts a pattern to time. The more attached we are to the world of work, the more its deadlines, its cycles, its pauses and interruptions shape our lives and the more family time is forced to accommodate to the pressures of work. In recent years at Amerco it has been possible to detect a change in the ways its workers view the proper use of their time: Family time, for them, has taken on an "industrial" tone.

As the social worlds of work and home reverse, working parents' experience of time in each sphere changes as well. Just how, and how much, depends on the nature of a person's job, company, and life at home. But at least for people . . . at Amerco, it's clear that family time is succumbing to a cult of efficiency previously associated with the workplace. Meanwhile, work time, with its ever longer hours, becomes newly hospitable to sociability—periods of talking with friends on e-mail, patching up quarrels, gossiping. . . .

The Third Shift

. . .

. . . Why *weren't* Amerco working parents putting up a bigger fight for family time, given the fact that most said they needed more? Many of them may have been responding to a powerful process that is devaluing what was once the essence of family life. The more women and men do what they do in exchange for money and the more their work in the public realm is valued or honored, the more, almost by definition, private life is devalued and its boundaries shrink. For women as well as men, work in the marketplace is less often a simple economic fact than a complex cultural value. If in the early part of the century it was considered unfortunate that a woman had to work, it is now thought surprising when she doesn't.

People generally have the urge to spend more time on what they value most and on what they are most valued for. . . . The valued realm of work is registering its gains in part by incorporating the best aspects of home. The devalued realm, the home, is meanwhile taking on what were once considered the most alienating attributes of work. However one explains the failure of Amerco to create a good program of work-family balance, though, the fact is that in a cultural contest between work and home, working parents are voting with their feet, and the workplace is winning.

In this respect, we may ask, are working parents at Amerco an anomaly or are they typical of working parents nationwide? In search of an answer, I contacted a company called Bright Horizons, which runs 125 company-based childcare centers associated with corporations, hospitals, real estate developers, and federal agencies in nineteen states.[17] Bright Horizons allowed me to add a series of new questions to a questionnaire the company was sending out to seven thousand parents whose children were attending Bright Horizons Children's Centers. A third of the par-

ents who received questionnaires filled them out. The resulting 1,446 responses came from mainly middle- or upper-middle-class parents in their early thirties.[18] Since many of them worked for Fortune 500 companies—including IBM, American Express, Sears, Roebuck, Eastman Kodak, Xerox, Bausch and Lomb, and Dunkin' Donuts—this study offers us a highly suggestive picture of what is happening among managers and professional working parents at Amerco's counterparts nationwide.

These parents reported time pressures similar to those Amerco parents complained about. As at Amerco, the longest hours at work were logged by the most highly educated professionals and managers, among whom six out of ten regularly averaged over forty hours a week. A third of the parents in this sample had their children in childcare forty hours a week or more.[19] As at Amerco, the higher the income of their parents, the longer the children's shifts in childcare.

When asked, "Do you ever consider yourself a workaholic?" a third of fathers and a fifth of mothers answered yes. One out of three said their *partner* was workaholic. In response to the question "Do you experience a problem of 'time famine'?" 89 percent responded yes. Half reported that they typically brought work home from the office.[20] Of those who complained of a time famine, half agreed with the statement "I feel guilty that I don't spend enough time with my child." Forty-three percent agreed that they "very often" felt "too much of the time I'm tired when I'm with my child." When asked, "Overall, how well do you feel you can balance the demands of your work and family?" only 9 percent said "very well."

If many of these Bright Horizons working parents were experiencing a time bind of the sort I heard about from Amerco employees, were they living with it because they felt work was more rewarding than family life? To find out, I asked, "Does it sometimes feel to you like home is a 'workplace'?" Eighty-five percent said yes (57 percent "very often"; 28 percent "fairly often"). Women were far more likely to agree than men. I asked this question the other way around as well: "Is it sometimes true that work feels like home should feel?" Twenty-five percent answered "very often" or "quite often," and 33 percent answered "occasionally." Only 37 percent answered "very rarely."

One reason some workers may feel more "at home" at work is that they feel more appreciated and more competent there. Certainly, this was true for many Amerco workers I interviewed, and little wonder, for Amerco put great effort into making its workers feel appreciated. In a large-scale nationwide study, sociologists Diane Burden and Bradley Googins found that 59 percent of employees rated their family performances "good or unusually good," while 86 percent gave that rating to their performances on the job—that is, workers appreciated *themselves* more at work than at home.[21] In the Bright Horizons national survey, only 29 percent felt appreciated "mainly at home," and 52 percent "equally" at home and work. Surprisingly, women were not more likely than men to say they felt more appreciated at home.

Often, working parents feel more at home at work because they come to expect that emotional support will be more readily available there. As at Amerco, work can be where their closest friends are, a pattern the Bright Horizons survey reflected. When asked, "Where do you have the most friends?" 47 percent answered "at work"; 16 percent, "in the neighborhood"; and 6 percent, "at my church or temple." Women were far more likely than men to have the most friends at work.[22]

Some workers at Amerco felt more at home at work because work was where they felt most relaxed. To the question "Where do you feel the most relaxed?" only a slight majority in the Bright Horizons survey, 51 percent, said "home." To the question "Do you feel as if your life circumstances or relationships are more secure at work or at home?" a similarly slim majority answered "home." I also asked, "How many times have you changed jobs since you started working?" The average was between one and two times. Though I didn't ask how many times a person had changed primary loved ones, the national picture suggests that by the early thirties, one or two such changes is not unusual. Work

may not "always be there" for the employee, but then home may not either....

For this sample, then, we find some evidence that a cultural reversal of workplace and home is present at least as a theme. Unsurprisingly, more people in the survey agreed that home felt like work than that work felt like home. Still, only to half of them was home a main source of relaxation or security. For many, work seemed to function as a backup system to a destabilizing family. For women, in particular, to take a job is often today to take out an emotional insurance policy on the uncertainties of home life....

The Hydro-Compressed Sterilized Mouth Wiper

Working parents often face difficult problems at home without much outside support or help in resolving them. In itself time is, of course, no cure-all. But having time together is an important precondition for building family relations. What, then, is happening to family time?

Working parents exhibit an understandable desire to build sanctuaries of family time, free from pressure, in which they can devote themselves to only one activity or one relationship. So, for instance, the time between 8 and 8:45 P.M. may be cordoned off as "quality time" for parents and child, and that between 9:15 and 10 P.M. as quality time for a couple (once the children are in bed). Such time boundaries must then be guarded against other time demands—calls from the office, from a neighbor to arrange tomorrow's car pool, from a child's friend about homework. Yet these brief respites of "relaxed time" themselves come to look more and more like little segments of job time, with parents punching in and out as if on a time clock....

Paradoxically, what may seem to harried working parents like a solution to their time bind—efficiency and time segmentation—can later feel like a problem in itself. To be efficient with whatever time they do have at home, many working parents try to go faster if for no other reason than to clear off some space in which to go slowly. They do two or three things at once. They plan ahead. They delegate. They separate home events into categories and try to outsource some of them. In their efficiency, they may inadvertently trample on the emotion-laden symbols associated with particular times of day or particular days of the week. They pack one activity closer to the next and disregard the "framing" around each of them, those moments of looking forward to or looking back on an experience, which heighten its emotional impact. They ignore the contribution that a leisurely pace can make to fulfillment, so that a rapid dinner, followed by a speedy bath and bedtime story for a child—if part of "quality time"—is counted as "worth the same" as a slower version of the same events. As time becomes something to "save" at home as much as or even more than at work, domestic life becomes quite literally a second shift; a cult of efficiency, once centered in the workplace, is allowed to set up shop and make itself comfortable at home. Efficiency has become both a means to an end—more home time—and a way of life, an end in itself. . . .

. . . *Working Mother* magazine, for example, carries ads that invite the working mother to cook "two-minute rice," a "five-minute chicken casserole," a "seven-minute Chinese feast." One ad features a portable phone to show that the working mother can make business calls while baking cookies with her daughter.

Another typical ad promotes cinnamon oatmeal cereal for breakfast by showing a smiling mother ready for the office in her square-shouldered suit, hugging her happy son. A caption reads, "In the morning, we are in such a rush, and my son eats so slowly. But with cinnamon oatmeal cereal, I don't even have to coax him to hurry up!" . . .

A Third Shift: Time Work

As the first shift (at the workplace) takes more time, the second shift (at home) becomes more hurried and rationalized. The longer the workday at the office or plant, the more we feel pressed at home to hurry, to delegate, to delay, to forgo, to segment, to hyperorganize the precious remains of family time. Both their time deficit and what seem like solutions to it (hurrying, segmenting, and organizing) force parents . . . to engage in a third shift—noticing, understanding, and coping with the emotional consequences of the compressed second shift.

Children respond to the domestic work-bred cult of efficiency in their own ways. Many, as they get older, learn to protest it. Parents at Amerco and elsewhere then have to deal with their children, as they act out their feelings about the sheer scarcity of family time. For example, Dennis Long, an engineer at Amerco, told me about what happened with his son from a previous marriage when he faced a project deadline at work. Whenever Dennis got home later than usual, four-year-old Joshua greeted him with a tantrum. As Dennis ruefully explained,

> Josh gets really upset when I'm not home. He's got it in his head that the first and third weeks of every month, he's with me, not with his mom. He hasn't seen me for a while, and I'm supposed to be there. When a project deadline like this one comes up and I come home late, he gets to the end of his rope. He gives me hell. I understand it. He's frustrated. He doesn't know what he can rely on.

This father did his "third shift" by patiently sitting down on the floor to "receive" Josh's tantrum, hearing him out, soothing him, and giving him some time. For a period of six months, Joshua became upset at almost any unexpected delay or rapid shift in the pace at which events were, as he saw it, supposed to happen. Figuring out what such delays or shifts in pace meant to Joshua became another part of Dennis Long's third shift.

Such episodes raise various questions: If Josh's dad keeps putting off their dates to play together, does it mean he doesn't care about Josh? Does Josh translate the language of time the same way his father does? What if time symbolizes quite different things to the two of them? Whose understanding counts the most? Sorting out such emotional tangles is also part of the third shift.

Ironically, many Amerco parents were challenged to do third-shift work by their children's reactions to "quality time." As one mother explained,

Quality time is seven-thirty to eight-thirty at night, and then it's time for bed. I'm ready at seven-thirty, but Melinda has other ideas. As soon as quality time comes she wants to have her bath or watch TV; *no way* is she going to play with Mommy. Later, when I'm ready to drop, *then* she's ready for quality time.

. . .

In such situations, pressed parents often don't have time to sort through their children's responses. They have no space to wonder what their gift of time means. Or whether a parent's visit to daycare might seem to a child like a painfully prolonged departure. Is a gift of time what a parent wants to give, or what a child wants to receive? Such questions are often left unresolved.

Time-deficit "paybacks" lead to another kind of difficult emotional work. For example, like many salespeople at Amerco, Phyllis Ramey spent about a fifth of her work time traveling. She always kept in touch by phone with her husband and their two children—Ben, three, and Pete, five—and at each sales stop, she bought the boys gifts. Ben enjoyed them but thought little about them; Pete, on the other hand, fixated anxiously on "what mommy's bringing me"—a Tonka truck, a Batman cape, a bubble-making set. . . . Phyllis believed that Pete "really needed more time" with her, and she sensed that she was buying him things out of guilt. Indeed, she talked and joked about guilt-shopping with co-workers. But in Pete's presence she had a hard time separating his anxiety about gifts from his relationship with her.

Amerco parents like Phyllis are not alone, of course. Spending on toys has soared from $6.7 billion in 1980 to $17.5 billion in 1995. According to psychologist Marilyn Bradford, preschoolers looking forward to Christmas ask for an average of 3.4 toys but receive on average 11.6.[23] As employers buy growing amounts of time from employees, parents half-consciously "buy" this time from their children. But children rarely enter into these "trades" voluntarily, and parents are tempted to avoid the "time work" it takes to cope with their children's frustration. . . .

Most Amerco working parents held on to some fantasy of a more leisurely and gratifying family life. Their wishes seemed so modest—to have time to throw a ball with their children, or to read to them, or simply to witness the small dramas of their development, not to speak of having a little fun and romance themselves. Yet often even those modest wishes seemed strangely out of reach. So many of these parents had come to live in a small town and work for a family-friendly company precisely because they thought it would be a good place to raise children. They had wanted some kind of balance. . . .

Still, family-friendly Amerco put steady pressure on its employees to lead a more work-centered life, and while some working parents resisted, most did not. As a result, they were giving their children, their marriages, their communities, and themselves far less time than they imagined giving. They were, in a sense, leading one life and imagining another. . . .

But how are working parents at Amerco—or any of us—to face the time bind? And once we face it, what are we to do about it—not just in our imaginations but in real life? One course of action is to deal with the time bind as a purely personal problem, and to develop personal strategies for coping with it in one's own life. At Amerco the most common response by far was to try to limit the pull of home by needs reduction, outsourcing, and dreams of a potential time-rich self, but these strategies merely avoided, and even exacerbated, the time bind. . . .

A more daunting yet ultimately more promising approach to unknotting the time bind requires collective—rather than individual—action: workers must directly challenge the organization, and the organizers, of the American workplace. For this to occur, Amerco employees and their counterparts across the country would have to become new kinds of political activists who would—to borrow a slogan from the environmental movement—"think globally and act locally." Together, they might create a time movement. For the truth of the matter is that many working parents lack time because the workplace has a prior claim on it. It solves very little to either adapt to that claim or retreat from the workplace. The moment has come to address that claim, to adjust the old workplace to the new workforce....

...A movement to reform work time should not limit itself to encouraging companies to offer policies allowing shorter or more flexible hours. ...Such policies may serve as little more than fig leaves concealing long-hour work cultures. A time movement would also need to challenge the premises of that work culture. It would ask, Are workers judged mainly on the excellence of their performance, or mainly on the amount of time they are present in the workplace? Is there a "culture of trust" that allows workers to pinch-hit for one another as needs arise? Is there job security? The answers to these questions are crucial, for there can be little appeal to shorter hours when employees fear that the long hours they now work may disappear entirely....

A time movement cannot stop at the company level, however. In the long run, no work–family balance will ever fully take hold if the social conditions that might make it possible—men who are willing to share parenting and housework, communities that value work in the home as highly as work on the job, and policymakers and elected officials who are prepared to demand family-friendly reforms—remain out of reach. And it is by helping foster these broader conditions that a social movement could have its greatest effect.

Any push for more flexible work time must confront a complex reality: many working families are both prisoners and architects of the time bind in which they find themselves. A time movement would have to explore the question of why working parents have yet to protest collectively the cramped quarters of the temporal "housing" in which they live. It would have to force a public reckoning about the private ways out of the time bind—emotional asceticism, the love affair with capitalism, the repeatedly postponed plans of the potential self—that only seem to worsen the situation.

Then, too, a time movement must not shy away from opening a national dialogue on the most difficult and frightening aspect of our time bind: the need for "emotional investment" in family life in an era of familial divestiture and deregulation. How much time and energy ought we to devote to the home? How much time and energy do we dare subtract from work? Current arguments about what should and should not count as "a family" do little to help the families that already exist. What is needed instead is a public debate about how we can properly value relationships with loved ones and ties to communities that defy commodification.

NOTES

1. These part-time jobs are not to be confused with jobs without benefits or job security, jobs in the so-called contingency labor force. The growth of "bad" part-time jobs may, indeed, be chilling the quest for "good" ones. See Vicki Smith, "Flexibility in Work and Employment: Impact on Women," *Research in the Sociology of Organizations* 11 (1993): 195–216.

2. ... See also Galinsky et al., *The Corporate Reference Guide* (1991), pp. 85–87. Nationwide, a far higher proportion of firms claim to offer flexible schedules than report workers using them. In one study of flexible staffing and scheduling, of the twenty-nine firms offering the family-friendly benefit flexplace, for example, eighteen of the companies had five or fewer employees working from home (Kathleen Christensen, *Flexible Staffing and Scheduling in U.S. Corporations* [New York: The Conference Board, 1989], p. 18).

What people *do* with the time freed up by flexible schedules is another story. One study of the use of flex benefits by workers in two federal agencies found no increase in working parents' time spent with children—although they did find an increase in women's time doing housework (Halcyone Bohen and Anamaria Viveros-Long, *Balancing Jobs and Family Life: Do Flexible Schedules Help?* [Philadelphia: Temple University Press, 1981]).

A 1992 study conducted by Johnson & Johnson Company found that only 6 percent of employees used their "family-care leave" (unpaid leave for up to a year), and 18 percent used the "family-care absence" (time off with pay for short-term emergency care) (Families and Work Institute, "An Evaluation of Johnson and Johnson's Work-Family Initiative," April

1993, p. 20). Despite the fact that in 1983, 37 percent of American companies made parental leave available to new fathers, one study of 384 companies found that only nine reported even one father taking a formal leave (Dana Friedman, *Linking Work–Family Issues to the Bottom Line* [New York: The Conference Board, 1991], p. 50).

3. Galinsky et al., *The Corporate Reference Guide* (1991), p. 123.

4. Arthur Emlen, "Employee Profiles: 1987 Dependent Care Survey, Selected Companies" (Portland: Oregon Regional Research Institute for Human Services, Portland State University, 1987), reported in Friedman, *Linking Work–Family Issues to the Bottom Line* (1991), p. 13.

5. Hofferth et al., *National Child Care Survey 1990* (1991), p. 374. See also Bond and Galinksy, *Beyond the Parental Leave Debate* (1991), p. 74.

6. Families and Work Institute, *Women: The New Providers*, Whirlpool Foundation Study, Part 1, survey conducted by Louis Harris and Associates, Inc., May 1995, p. 12.

7. See Galinsky et al., *The Changing Workforce* (1993), p. 17.

8. Christopher Lasch, *Haven in a Heartless World* (New York: Basic Books, 1977). To Lasch what matters about the family is its privacy, its capacity to protect the individual from the "cruel world of politics and work"; this privacy has been invaded, he argues, by the cruel world it was set up to guard against.

9. Reed Larson, Maryse Richards, and Maureen Perry-Jenkins, "Divergent Worlds: The Daily Emotional Experience of Mothers and Fathers in the Domestic and Public Spheres," *Journal of Personality and Social Psychology* 67 (1994):1035.

10. Larson et al., "Divergent Worlds" (1994), pp. 1039, 1040.

11. Grace Baruch, Lois Biener, and Rosalind Barnett, "Women and Gender in Research on Work and Family Stress," *American Psychologist* 42 (1987):130–136; Glenna Spitze, "Women's Employment and Family Relations: A Review," *Journal of Marriage and the Family* 50 (1988):595–618. Even when researchers take into account the fact that the depressed or less mentally fit would be less likely to find or keep a job in the first place, working women come out slightly ahead in mental health (see Rena Repetti, Karen Matthews, and Ingrid Waldron, "Employment and Women's Health: Effects of Paid Employment on Women's Mental and Physical Health," *American Psychologist* 44 [1989]:1394–1401).

12. Families and Work Institute, *Women: The New Providers* (1995), p. 10.

13. Baruch et al., "Women and Gender in Research" (1987), p. 132.

14. Larson et al., "Divergent Worlds" (1994), p. 1041. See also Shelley MacDermid, Margaret Williams, Stephen Marks, and Gabriela Heilbrun, "Is Small Beautiful? Influence of Workplace Size on Work-Family Tension," *Family Relations* 43 (1994):159–167.

15. For supporting research about the importance of work to women, see Baruch et al., "Women and Gender in Research" (1987), esp. p. 132. Also see Diane Burden and Bradley Googins, "Boston University Balancing Job and Homelife Study: Managing Work and Family Stress in Corporations" (Boston: Boston University School of Social Work, 1987). Researchers also find that simply being a mother doesn't raise satisfaction with life (E. Spreitzer, E. Snyder, and D. Larson, "Multiple Roles and Psychological Well-Being," *Sociological Focus* 12 [1979]: 141–148; and Ethel Roskies and Sylvie Carrier, "Marriage and Children for Professional Women: Asset or Liability?" paper presented at the APA convention "Stress in the 90s," Washington, D.C., 1992).

See also L. Verbrugge, "Role Burdens and Physical Health of Women and Men," in Faye Crosby, ed., *Spouse, Parent, Worker: On Gender and Multiple Roles* (New Haven, CT: Yale University Press, 1987). However, many factors come into play when we talk about working mothers' emotional well-being and mental health. For example, Kessler and McCrae found that a job improved mental health for women only if their husbands shared the load at home (R. Kessler and J. McCrae, "The Effect of Wives' Employment on the Mental Health of Men and Women," *American Sociological Review* 47 [1982]:216–227).

16. Andrew Scharlach and Esme Fuller-Thomson, "Coping Strategies Following the Death of an Elderly Parent," *Journal of Gerontological Social Work* 21 (1994): 90. In response to a mother's death, work was a more "helpful resource" than spouse or religion for women. For men, work was more helpful than family, friends, and religion.

17. Founded in 1986, Bright Horizons was named the nation's leading work-site childcare organization in 1991 by the Child Care Information Exchange. The

company offers a range of services: drop-in care, weekend programs, and programs for infants, toddlers, preschoolers, and school-age children. Bright Horizons pays its teachers 10 percent more than whatever the going rate may be at nearby childcare centers and has a rate of teacher turnover that averages only half of the industry-wide 40 to 50 percent a year.

18. Thirty-five percent of parents responded (9 percent were male and 90 percent female; 92 percent were married and 7 percent single). Percentages may not add up to 100 for some questions either because some respondents didn't answer that question or because the percentages that are reported were rounded to the nearest whole number.

19. Twenty percent of parents reported that their children were in childcare 41–45 hours a week; 13 percent, 46–50 hours; 2 percent, 51–60 hours. In the lowest income group in the study ($45,000 or less), 25 percent of parents had children in childcare 41 hours a week or longer. In the highest income group ($140,000 or higher), 39 percent did.

20. Parents were asked how many hours they spent doing work they brought home from the office "on a typical weekday." Eighteen percent didn't answer. Of those remaining, half said they did bring work home. The largest proportion—19 percent—brought home "between six and ten hours of work [per week]." They estimated even longer hours for their partners.

21. Burden and Googins, "Boston University Balancing Job and Homelife Study" (1987), p. 30.

22. Yet friends may not be a working parent's main source of social support. When asked which were the "three most important sources of support in your life," nine out of ten men and women mentioned their spouses or partners. Second came their mothers, and third "other relatives." So people turned for support to kin first. Among *friendships*, however, those at work proved more significant than those around home. As sources of emotional support, 10 percent of the respondents also mentioned "books and magazines," the same percentage as mentioned "church or temple"; only 5 percent mentioned neighbors. Thirteen percent turned for support first to friends at work—as many as turned to their own fathers.

23. Gary Cross, "If Not the Gift of Time, At Least Toys," *New York Times*, 3 December 1995.

THINKING ABOUT THE READING

What does Hochschild mean when she says that "work has become home and home has become work"? Why does she think home life has become so stressful and harried in recent years? Think of the enduring effects of the shift that Hochschild describes. How will these changes influence people's expectations about their family lives? What impact will they have on marriage? On the bearing and rearing of children? If people aren't taking advantage of available family leave policies as Hochschild claims, how might the workplace change in the coming years? Hochschild implies that, in the past, people's work and family lives were very different than they are today. Was the workplace of the past as awful and dehumanizing as she implies? Was home life as warm and glorious?

III

Social Structure, Institutions, and Everyday Life

CHAPTER 9

Building the Structure of Society: Organizations and Social Institutions

One of the great sociological paradoxes of our existence is that in a society that so fiercely extols the virtues of rugged individualism and personal accomplishment, we spend most of our lives responding to the influence of larger organizations and social institutions. From the nurturing environments of our churches and schools to the cold depersonalizations of massive bureaucracies, organizations and institutions are a fundamental part of our everyday lives.

Organizations are both a source of predictability and a source of problems in everyday life. Sometimes individual interests coincide with organizational needs; other times they conflict. Consider the workplace. For most Americans, their place of employment is the most important organization in their lives. For better or worse, our jobs are what define us. In recent years, the service sector of the labor force—those jobs that involve workers interacting with customers—has increasingly dominated the U.S. economy. For the most part, these jobs are low-paying and highly routinized, requiring little problem-solving skills on the part of workers. In her article, "Fast Food, Fast Talk," sociologist Robin Leidner shows how two large companies— McDonald's Restaurants and Combined Insurance Company—try to routinize the workplace by tightly regulating their workers' words, thoughts, actions, moods, appearance, ideas, and so on. The result is that workers are often forced into artificial identities while on the job, undermining their sense of individuality and authenticity.

Organizations are more than structures, rules, policies, goals, job descriptions, and standard operating procedures. Each organization, and each division within an organization, develops its own norms, values, and language. Furthermore, no matter how strict and unyielding a particular organization may appear to be, individuals within them are usually able to exert some control over their lives. Rarely is an organization what it appears to be on the surface.

In larger organizations, distinct cultures develop where similar meanings and perspectives are cultivated. As in society as a whole, however, distinct subcultures can develop. In "The Smile Factory," John Van Maanen examines the organizational culture of one of American society's most enduring icons: Disney theme parks. Disneyland and Disneyworld have a highly codified and strict set of conduct standards. Variations from tightly defined employee norms are not tolerated. You'd expect in such a place that employees would be a rather homogeneous group. However, Van Maanen discovers that beneath the surface of this self-proclaimed "Happiest Place on Earth" lies a mosaic of distinct groups that have created their own status system and that work hard to maintain the status boundaries between one another.

Fast Food, Fast Talk

Service Work and the Routinization of Everyday Life

Robin Leidner

Working on People

The logic of work routinization is simple, elegant, and compelling. Adam Smith's famous discussion of pin manufacture laid the groundwork: instead of paying high-priced, skilled workers to do a job from start to finish, employers could split the job into its constituent parts and assign each task to minimally qualified workers, thus greatly reducing costs and increasing output (Smith 1776). Frederick Taylor's system of scientific management, aimed at removing decision making from all jobs except managers' and engineers', pushed the division of labor still further. Routinizing work processes along these lines offers several benefits to managers. First, designing jobs so that each worker repeatedly performs a limited number of tasks according to instructions provided by management increases efficiency, through both greater speed and lower costs. Second, it results in products of uniform quality. And its final and most enticing promise is that of giving management increased control over the enterprise.

These systems for dividing and routinizing work were conceived for manual labor and were first widely implemented in manufacturing; therefore most sociological work on routinization has been based on studies of this sector (e.g., Blauner 1964; Burawoy 1979; Sabel 1982). As the clerical work force grew in importance, the principles of routinization were applied to what had been considered "brain work," transforming some clerical functions into rote manual tasks and reducing the scope, variety, and opportunity for decision making in many jobs (see Braverman 1974; Garson 1975; Glenn

and Feldberg 1979a; Mills 1951). In recent years the service sector has come increasingly to dominate the U.S. economy (Mills 1986; Noyelle 1987; Smith 1984), and the routinization of jobs that require workers to interact directly with customers or clients—what I call "interactive service work"—has been expanding as well, challenging employers to find ways to rationalize workers' self-presentation and feelings as well as their behavior. As routinization spills over the boundaries of organizations to include customers as well as employees, employers' strategies for controlling work affect not only workers but the culture at large.

Although many of the rationales, techniques, and outcomes associated with routinizing other kinds of work are applicable to interactive service work, the presence of customers or clients complicates the routinization process considerably. When people are the raw materials of the work process, it is difficult to guarantee the predictability of conditions necessary for routinization. Organizations attempting routinization must try to standardize the behavior of nonemployees to some extent in order to make such routinization possible (see Mills 1986). It is part of the labor process of many interactive service workers to induce customers and clients to behave in ways that will not interfere with the smooth operation of work routines.

In addition to the issues of deskilling, autonomy, and power already associated with work routinization, the routinization of interactive service work raises questions about personal identity and authenticity. In this sort of work there are no clear distinctions among the product being sold, the work process, and the worker. Employers of interactive service workers may therefore claim authority over many more aspects of workers' lives than other kinds of employers do, seeking to regulate workers' appearance, moods, demeanors, and attitudes. But even when management makes relatively little effort to reshape the workers, interactive service workers and their customers or clients must negotiate interactions in which elements of manipulation, ritual, and genuine social exchange are subtly mixed.

Routinized interactive service work thus involves working on people in two senses. The workers work on the people who are their raw materials, including themselves, and the organizations work on their employees. These processes can be problematic, both practically and morally. This [article] explores these practical difficulties and moral and psychological stresses through case studies of two organizations that have taken the routinization of interactive service work to extremes, McDonald's and Combined Insurance. . . .

The Research

I did not choose to study McDonald's and Combined Insurance because I thought they were typical interactive service organizations. Rather, both companies took routinization to an extreme, and I was interested in examining how far working on people could be pushed. I believed that extreme cases would best illuminate the kinds of tensions and problems that routinizing human interactions creates, and that a study of long-established and successful companies would provide clues to the attractions of routinization and the means by which managers can overcome the difficulties of standardizing workers and service-recipients.

Although these two companies both pushed routinization almost to its logical limits, their public-contact employees did very different kinds of work and had different kinds of relations with service-recipients. The companies therefore adopted dissimilar approaches to routinization, with distinctive ramifications for

workers and service-recipients. McDonald's took a classic approach to routinization, making virtually all decisions about how work would be conducted in advance and imposing them on workers. Since Combined's sales agents worked on their own and faced a broader range of responses than McDonald's workers did, their company had to allow them some decision-making scope. It did create routines that were as detailed as possible, but it pushed the limits of routinization in another direction, extending it to many aspects of workers' selves both on and off the job. It aimed to make a permanent, overall change in the ways its agents thought about themselves and went about their lives.

At each company, I collected information through interviewing and participant-observation. I examined routinization at two levels. First, I learned as much as I could about the company's goals and strategies for routinization by attending corporate training programs and interviewing executives. Next, I explored how the routines worked out in practice by doing or observing the work and by interviewing interactive service workers.

At both McDonald's and Combined Insurance I received official permission to do my research. The managers I interviewed, the trainees I accompanied through classes, and the workers I interviewed, observed, and worked with were all aware that I was conducting a study and that my project had been approved by higher levels of management. The customers I served and observed were the only participants who did not know that I was collecting data. . . .

The Routine [at McDonald's]
McDonald's had routinized the work of its crews so thoroughly that decision making had practically been eliminated from the jobs. As one window worker told me, "They've tried to break it down so that it's almost idiot-proof." Most of the workers agreed that there was little call for them to use their own judgment on the job, since there were rules about everything. If an unusual problem arose, the workers were supposed to turn it over to a manager.

Many of the noninteractive parts of the window workers' job had been made idiot-proof through automation. The soda machines, for example, automatically dispensed the proper amount of beverage for regular, medium, and large cups. Computerized cash registers performed a variety of functions handled elsewhere by human waitresses, waiters, and cashiers, making some kinds of skill and knowledge unnecessary. As a customer gave an order, the window worker simply pressed the cash register button labeled with the name of the selected product. There was no need to write the orders down, because the buttons lit up to indicate which products had been selected. Nor was there any need to remember prices, because the prices were programmed into the machines. Like most new cash registers, these added the tax automatically and told workers how much change customers were owed, so the window crew did not need to know how to do those calculations. The cash registers also helped regulate some of the crew's interactive work by reminding them to try to increase the size of each sale. For example, when a customer ordered a Big Mac, large fries, and a regular Coke, the cash register buttons for cookies, hot apple pies, ice cream cones, and ice cream sundaes would light up, prompting the worker to suggest dessert. It took some skill to operate the relatively complicated cash register, as my difficulties during my first work shift made clear, but this organizationally specific skill could soon be acquired on the job.

In addition to doing much of the workers' thinking for them, the computerized cash registers made it possible for managers to monitor the crew members' work and the store's inventory very closely. For example, if the number of Quarter Pounder with Cheese boxes gone did not match the number of Quarter Pounders with Cheese sold or accounted for as waste, managers might suspect that workers were giving away or taking food. Managers could easily tell which workers had brought in the most money during a given interval and who was doing the best job of persuading customers to buy a particular item. The computerized system could also com-

plicate what would otherwise have been simple customer requests, however. For example, when a man who had not realized the benefit of ordering his son's food as a Happy Meal came back to the counter to ask whether his little boy could have one of the plastic beach pails the Happy Meals were served in, I had to ask a manager what to do, since fulfilling the request would produce a discrepancy between the inventory and the receipts. Sometimes the extreme systematization can induce rather than prevent idiocy, as when a window worker says she cannot serve a cup of coffee that is half decaffeinated and half regular because she would not know how to ring up the sale.

The interactive part of window work is routinized through . . . rules aimed at standardizing attitudes and demeanors as well as words and actions. The window workers were taught that they represented McDonald's to the public and that their attitudes were therefore an important component of service quality. Crew people could be reprimanded for not smiling, and often were. The window workers were supposed to be cheerful and polite at all times, but they were also told to be themselves while on the job. McDonald's does not want its workers to seem like robots, so part of the emotion work asked of the window crew is that they act naturally. "Being yourself" in this situation meant behaving in a way that did not seem stilted. Although workers had some latitude to go beyond the script, the short, highly schematic routine obviously did not allow much room for genuine self-expression.

Workers were not the only ones constrained by McDonald's routines, of course. The cooperation of service-recipients was crucial to the smooth functioning of the operation. In many kinds of interactive service work, . . . constructing the compliance of service-recipients is an important part of the service worker's job. The routines such workers use may be designed to maximize the control each worker has over customers. McDonald's window workers' routines were not intended to give them much leverage over customers' behavior, however. The window workers interacted only with people who had already decided to do business with McDonald's and who therefore did not need to be persuaded to take part in the service interaction. Furthermore, almost all customers were familiar enough with McDonald's routines to know how they were expected to behave. For instance, I never saw a customer who did not know that she or he was supposed to come up to the counter rather than sit down and wait to be served. This customer training was accomplished through advertising, spatial design, customer experience, and the example of other customers, making it unnecessary for the window crew to put much effort into getting customers to fit into their work routines.

McDonald's ubiquitous advertising trains consumers at the same time that it tries to attract them to McDonald's. Television commercials demonstrate how the service system is supposed to work and familiarize customers with new products. Additional cues about expected customer behavior are provided by the design of the restaurants. For example, the entrances usually lead to the service counter, not to the dining area, making it unlikely that customers will fail to realize that they should get in line, and the placement of waste cans makes clear that customers are expected to throw out their own trash. Most important, the majority of customers have had years of experience with McDonald's, as well as with other fast-food restaurants that have similar arrangements. The company estimates that the average customer visits a McDonald's twenty times a year (Koepp 1987a: 58), and it is not uncommon for a customer to come in several times per week. For many customers, then, ordering at McDonald's is as routine an interaction as it is for the window worker. Indeed, because employee turnover is so high, steady customers may be more familiar with the work routines than the workers serving them are. Customers who are new to McDonald's can take their cue from more experienced customers.

Not surprisingly, then, most customers at the McDonald's I studied knew what was expected of them and tried to play their part well. They sorted themselves into lines and gazed up at the menu boards while waiting to be served. They usually gave their orders in the conventional sequence: burgers or other entrees, french fries or other side orders, drinks, and desserts. Hurried customers with savvy might order an item "only if it's in the bin," that is, ready to be served. Many customers prepared carefully so that they could give their orders promptly when they got to the counter. This preparation sometimes became apparent when a worker interrupted to ask, "What kind of dressing?" or "Cream and sugar?", flustering customers who could not deliver their orders as planned.

McDonald's routines, like those of other interactive service businesses, depend on the predictability of customers, but these businesses must not grind to a halt if customers are not completely cooperative. Some types of deviations from standard customer behavior are so common that they become routine themselves, and these can be handled through subroutines (Stinchcombe 1990b: 39). McDonald's routines work most efficiently when all customers accept their products exactly as they are usually prepared; indeed, the whole business is based on this premise. Since, however, some people give special instructions for customized products, such as "no onions," the routine allows for these exceptions. At the franchise I studied, workers could key the special requests into their cash registers, which automatically printed out "grill slips" with the instructions for the grill workers to follow. Under this system, the customer making the special order had to wait for it to be prepared, but the smooth flow of service for other customers was not interrupted. Another type of routine difficulty was customer dissatisfaction with food quality. Whenever a customer had a complaint about the food—cold fries, dried-out burger—window workers were authorized to supply a new product immediately without consulting a supervisor.

These two kinds of difficulties—special orders and complaints about food—were the only irregularities window workers were authorized to handle. The subroutines increased the flexibility of the service system, but they did not increase the workers' discretion, since procedures were in place for dealing with both situations. All other kinds of demands fell outside the window crew's purview. If they were faced with a dispute about money, an extraordinary request, or a furious customer, workers were instructed to call a manager; the crew had no authority to handle such problems.

Given the almost complete regimentation of tasks and preemption of decision making, does McDonald's need the flexibility and thoughtfulness of human workers? As the declining supply of teenagers and legislated increases in the minimum wage drive up labor costs, it is not surprising that McDonald's is experimenting with electronic replacements. So far, the only robot in use handles behind-the-scenes work rather than customer interactions. ARCH (Automated Restaurant Crew Helper) works in a Minnesota McDonald's where it does all the frying and lets workers know when to prepare sandwich buns, when supplies are running low, and when fries are no longer fresh enough to sell. Other McDonald's stores (along with Arby's and Burger King units) are experimenting with a touchscreen computer system that lets customers order their meals themselves, further curtailing the role of the window worker. Although it requires increased customer socialization and cooperation, early reports are that the system cuts service time by thirty seconds and increases sales per window worker 10–20 percent (Chaudhry 1989: F61)....

The Routine [at Combined Life Insurance]

The basic routine of Combined's life insurance agents was a good deal longer, more flexible, and more complex than that of the workers at McDonald's. Several features of the agents' job account for these differences. Unlike the window workers, the life insurance agents met with potential customers one-to-one on the customers' own turf. The agents worked without supervision, but also without any of the environmental supports that can be built into a central workplace to guide or control customers. Because the agents did not deal with people who had sought out their services, they encountered much resistance as they tried to carry out their routines.

McDonald's workers interacted with "guests" who had chosen to patronize McDonald's, but the agents called on "prospects" who had to be turned into customers. The transformation of prospects into customers was in fact the agents' basic task. Most prospects, however, did their best to prevent this outcome by cutting the interaction short. The agents, of course, were strongly motivated to overcome the opposition they faced, since their income depended entirely on their success in doing so. Their routine was designed to help them succeed.

The interactive routine, if completed, had six distinct stages. Progress from one stage to the next could not be taken for granted; each step was a challenge for the agents. The routine was meant to make it as difficult as possible for the prospect to refuse to listen to the agent, to interrupt him, to sustain objections to the policies, or to decline to buy. The first stage of the routine was to find a prospect at home or at work, introduce oneself, and get inside. "Warming up the prospect" was the next stage, three to five minutes of informal chat during which the agent tried to establish rapport and to pick up information that could help him tailor the sales presentation to the prospect's circumstances and attitudes. During this period, the agent also tried to "get into a selling situation," that is, to find an advantageous setting for the sales presentation and position himself and the prospect to maximize his chances for success. In the third stage, after "verifying some information" on the prospect's lead card, the agent delivered the formal sales presentation, a memorized monologue supported by charts and other illustrations in a presentation book. Fourth, the agent tried to close the sale. At this stage the agent usually had to deliver one or more rebuttals to objections raised by the customer and generally had to make several attempts to close. Next, if the prospect did agree to buy a policy, the agent filled out the application, carefully reviewed the policy's provisions with the prospect to "solidify the sale," "sowed the seeds" for future renewals and amendments of the policy, and took payment. Whether or not the agent succeeded in making a sale, the last stage of the routine was to ask the prospect for referrals to other potential customers and to leave on cordial terms.

The routine was necessarily quite flexible, but the company tried as far as possible to prescribe how agents would adjust the sales pitch and their self-presentations to adapt to various circumstances. In fact, the most striking thing about Combined Insurance's training for its life insurance agents was the amazing degree of standardization for which the company was striving. The agents were told, in almost hilarious detail, what to say and do. . . .

Scripting

Large parts of the agents' routines were supposed to be memorized and recited precisely as written. In training class, the new agents memorized a complete presentation for each of the two policies then available, rebuttals of the most common objections to each of the sales talks, and shorter scripts for renewing and amending policies. The trainees were expected to learn these speeches word for word. The trainer, Mark, conceded that in the field the agents could make small adjustments to the scripts based on what they found to work best, but he encouraged them to try to be word-perfect while in school.

The stress on exact memorization underscored how far management went in trying to make skill and decision making unnecessary. The trainees were assured that the routines had been proven effective over many years and that anyone with the right personal characteristics who used the routines could succeed in selling insurance. The message, as one executive told me, was "If you follow this [sales presentation] precisely as it is, you'll win. If you start deviating, you'll get into trouble." Mark illustrated the power of the scripts (and of good mental attitudes) with stories of successful foreign-born agents:

> Mark tells us about a Czech guy who didn't know any English except for the sales talk. He learned the script phonetically and didn't even know what the words meant. . . . He sold twenty applications on his first day and is now a top

executive. Combined also has an Iranian agent who is doing well. Mark says that when prospects say no, she claims not to be able to understand them.

The company gave several reasons for this strict scripting. The most important one was that the routines worked. If the agents used the presentations exactly as written, they were told, they would have fewer interruptions, they would be sure to cover all the necessary information, and they would sell policies. Having the presentations perfectly memorized would also give the agents the self-confidence necessary for success, since they would not have to fear being at a loss for words, offending anyone, or getting their facts wrong. Yet another benefit was that if the agents were so familiar with the scripts that they could rattle them off without having to think about them, their minds would be free to consider what strategies would help to make a particular sale (training manual).

The fear that agents might get the facts wrong was an important incentive for the company to script the sales presentations. The insurance business is subject to government regulation, and misrepresentation is a serious concern throughout the industry. The use of standard sales presentations made it less likely that agents would inadvertently misrepresent the policies.

For the most part, the trainees accepted these justifications of the scripting and did not resist the standardization. Some of them did have reservations about it, though. For example, one trainee's reaction to the first day of training was, "It's OK if I can get past the phoniness"; he explained that he thought it would be hard to seem natural and casual if he was reciting a script. Mark undercut such feelings of discomfort by occasionally acknowledging that there was a comic element to the scripting. For instance, the script called for agents to ask, "Isn't that true?" and nod, as they made statements that anyone would have to agree with. This technique was supposed to put prospects in a "yes frame of mind." Mark sometimes used the technique jocularly in class, as in, "I bet you're ready for a break now, isn't that true?", thus giving trainees a chance to laugh at the scripting without calling its usefulness into question.

Some members of the class did resist specific elements of the script that they thought could not be delivered in a way that sounded natural. For instance, several people asserted during a class break that they would never use the introductory phrase they had just been taught for use in amending policies ("Pardon me a moment, if you will"), because they thought it sounded ridiculously stilted. There was more general resistance to the Standard Joke that was supposed to be included in every life insurance presentation:

> This policy is so good that the president of our company says ... "Once you have it, you will live forever!!!" How's that? [original punctuation, including ellipses]

Upon hearing a salesman in a videotaped demonstration give a particularly wooden delivery of the joke, one trainee said firmly, "I'm not using that in the field. Forget it!" Mark willingly conceded that the joke was not funny, but he insisted that it worked well as a means of dispelling tension, especially when the agent laughed at it heartily himself. Mark recognized that this was hard to do:

> We don't care why you laugh, as long as you laugh. You can laugh at yourself for telling it. You can laugh at the customer for laughing at it.

This acknowledgment that some resistance to the standardization was understandable helped assuage the trainees' discontent.

Agents were supposed to use the scripts for sales presentations, rebuttals, renewals, and amendments according to fixed decision rules: if the prospect is more than sixty-five years old, give the presentation for the senior citizens' policy; if the prospect says she already has insurance, deliver Rebuttal Number One. In addition to these standard scripts, the agents learned a variety of less rigid subroutines they could choose from, using their own judgment about the specific context. For example, quite a bit of time was spent, in class and on homework assignments,

on creating and learning "interruption-stoppers," quick phrases that allowed the agent to return to the sales presentation after a prospect interrupted him. Although one trainer told the class to practice them until "you become a computer and spit these things out," this part of the routine allowed agents some discretion. It was clear that any of a variety of responses might be used to deal with the same interruption successfully, and the agents were encouraged to experiment to find the ones that worked best for them. Similarly, Mark gave us a long list of suggestions on "How to Get the Money" when prospects who wanted to buy said that they did not have the cash. These scripts were presented as helpful suggestions, not as inflexible routines. They expanded the agents' ability to accomplish their work while allowing them some discretion.

Another way the trainers standardized agents' speech was by teaching them general rules about what sorts of things should and should not be said during sales calls, so that the agents could improvise on the job without alienating prospects. Among the rules the agents were taught were: never ask prospects why they have said no to a policy, since that would force them to solidify their reasons for saying no and make it harder for them to change their mind; literally "never say 'die'" when speaking to a prospect (given the nature of the product, this rule required a creative use of euphemism); respond to all questions from prospects by saying, "I'm glad you asked"; preface questions prospects might be reluctant to answer with a casual "By the way," or conclude them airily with "Do you remember offhand?"

These sorts of tips made the trainees feel better able to conduct their sales calls successfully without making them feel constrained by inflexible rules. . . .

Standardizing Attitudes and Ways of Thinking

Combined's overall approach to standardizing its workers' characters and personalities was through Positive Mental Attitude training. That training was intended to ensure that the agents had the enthusiasm, optimism, and determination necessary for success in sales.

In addition to the general PMA orientation, Combined's training for its insurance agents included specific attitudinal guidelines and psychic strategies for dealing with the work. Some of these guidelines were intended, like PMA, to prevent the agents from becoming discouraged. For example, Mark advised the trainees never to tell themselves that they had been assigned a "bum town." Should they be assigned to work in a town with very high unemployment, they should not think, "Forget it, no one has any money, I'll never sell anything." Instead, they should keep in mind that many people will have lost the insurance benefits they had at work and that Combined's small policies would be attractive to them. Mark also taught the agents to protect their positive attitudes by quickly ending interactions with very negative prospects: "Spend the time with people who show interest, and get away from those who are giving you a hard time." He told the agents, "Reject them before they reject you. You can't sell everybody, and it's much better to leave graciously."

Similarly, Combined Insurance tried to control interactions among its employees in the field, so that they would not reinforce or transmit disappointment, cynicism, or other negative attitudes. At a morning sales meeting I attended, for example, the sales manager interrupted an agent who had started to criticize his own previous week's performance, reminding him that they were supposed to be sharing good news. The sales team I observed spent plenty of time grousing, but company policy encouraged agents to share goals and successes, not gripes.

Much of the standardization of workers' attitudes and ways of thinking that Combined Insurance undertook was intended to persuade agents that their own interests coincided both with those of the prospects and with those of the company. If the company and the individual agents were to succeed, for example, the agents would have to be willing to put considerable pressure on prospects to buy. Combined Insur-

ance trained its agents to think that they were acting in the prospects' interests even when the prospects clearly asserted that they did not wish to participate in the interaction. On the first day of class Mark emphasized that "people buy what they want; they have to be *sold* what they need." The agents were taught that everyone needs life insurance and that Combined's policies were extremely good ones. If people showed reluctance to discuss buying life insurance—an understandable reaction, since such a discussion would make them think about their own death—it was the agents' duty to make them see the importance of protecting their loved ones from financial disaster. If people tried to brush off the agents by saying that they already had life insurance, it was important to find out whether their present policies were now inadequate because of inflation or changed financial responsibilities. Throughout the training the agents were frequently reminded that their services were needed and that a certain amount of persistence was not only morally justifiable but morally required.

The company tried to overcome the reluctance new agents might feel to put pressure on prospects, but it was equally concerned about the possibility that, in order to maximize their own profits, agents would put too much pressure on prospects or would even try to cheat them. Mark argued that it was in the agents' own interests to behave ethically and to refrain from high-pressure sales techniques. Although the agents were taught to create a sense of urgency about buying insurance, they were also taught that being too pushy would only increase prospects' resistance. A low-key approach was more likely to increase prospects' trust, Mark told us. He mentioned one successful agent who went so far as to yawn while waiting for the prospect to make a decision, to show that he was not overly concerned with making money on the sale. Ideally, the agents would not push prospects into buying but would lead them along so that they came to see why they should buy. That way, Mark said,

> the customer will feel good about the sale, and it will stick [he or she won't cancel the policy or fail to renew it]. If you put service and the

customers' needs number one, your needs will be taken care of.

The agents were taught that the proper attitude was one of sincere interest in meeting prospects' needs. An overly insistent or demanding approach would make prospects wary and resentful, and prospects might cancel policies they had been bullied into buying.

Combined's training emphasized business ethics. The agents were urged to "do the right thing because it is right" ("Statement on Representatives' Conduct") and also because it was in their own interest to behave ethically. Mark argued:

> If you're doing anything remotely unethical, it affects your sincerity, your confidence, and your commitment, and the customer can pick up on this.

Among the sales practices that were expressly forbidden were "abusive or overly aggressive sales tactics"; misrepresenting policy coverage, benefits, or premiums; encouraging prospects to cancel an existing policy in favor of a new one; and selling policies to people who were obviously too poor to afford them ("Statement on Representatives' Conduct").

Combined Insurance tried to make the agents identify their interests with those of the company as well as with those of their prospects. For example, because Combined's life-insurance policies did not require medical examinations but became effective immediately upon issue, the company had to rely on its agents to follow its underwriting guidelines strictly, declining to sell policies to people whose health, as described by themselves, was not good enough to qualify them for coverage. "Always visualize that the claim is being paid out of your checking account," Mark urged the agents. He pointed out that Combined Insurance could preissue policies and keep its prices low (both important selling points) only if the agents followed the underwriting rules precisely. Therefore, he argued, it was not in the agents' long-term interests to maximize their commissions by increasing the company's risk. . . .

Meanings of Routinized Work

. . . For workers, the routinization of interactive service work makes individuality, authenticity, and identity everyday concerns. For example, I noticed that one of Combined's agents, Kevin, had a little note stuck to the dashboard of his car that said, "BE KEVIN." As he explained it, this was not a statement of a metaphysical imperative, but a practical reminder. When how one presents oneself is minutely prescribed, being oneself is problematic, so Kevin had to work at it. Furthermore, he did not want to be himself so that he would *feel* better, but so that he would *do* better. He had found he was more likely to sell policies when more of himself came through, so he consciously worked on being genuine.

In all areas of social life, people have to struggle with the relation between what they do and say and what sorts of people they want to be. Erving Goffman, who regarded organizations as "place[s] for generating assumptions about identity" (1961c: 186), analyzed the problems faced by people who do not want to accept the assumptions that are generated by their participation in an organization. The mental patients he observed found ways to discount the implications participation had for their self-definitions. Similarly, for both the worker and the person being served, highly routinized service interactions can create tensions between the ways they want to think about themselves and what the situation implies about them.

Consumers of services, by and large, have already accepted the overriding assumption built into service routines, that people are generally interchangeable, at least for the limited purposes of the organization. Consumers do not approach encounters with representatives of large bureaucratic organizations with the expectation that they will be treated as whole individuals or that they will be allowed to define what matters will be considered relevant. . . .

Service organizations that have to compete for customers realize that although most customers accept anonymity, the implications of interchangeability are not flattering or pleasing to them. Such organizations try to construct routines in which workers uniformly inject into the interactions some of the attributes of authentic humanity, such as friendliness, consideration, and personal attention (see Hochschild 1983). The idea is to make standardization more palatable by reliably producing good feelings without greatly interfering with efficiency, which remains the dominant goal.

The implications of participation in routinized interactions are different for workers. Although the effects vary according to the nature of the job, all sorts of interactive service workers face tensions resulting from the discrepancy between how they normally deal with people and how they are required by the routines to deal with them. Inevitably, then, employers who routinize interactions create problems of identity and authenticity for their workers. One such problem is the necessity of disguising some feelings and simulating others.

Whether workers experience the discrepancy between their authentic feelings and the feelings they need to express as part of the job as a problem is, to some extent, culturally variable. According to Trilling (1972), personal authenticity is a relatively new cultural ideal. Hochschild (1983) argues that contemporary Americans are unusually concerned with authenticity, and she analyzes the socioeconomic determinants of this preoccupation. Since "phoniness" is considered a serious failing in the United States, jobs that require the manipulation of one's own and others' feelings may raise painful questions of identity for workers in this culture. . . .

. . . Constructions of gender are also at issue in the design and implementation of interactive service routines. In many cases, these routines draw on widely accepted understandings of how men and women think and behave. Workers' and service-recipients' enactment of the routines can bolster the taken-for-granted status of these beliefs. The case studies of McDonald's and Combined Insurance suggest, however, that cultural definitions of masculine and feminine work are quite elastic, allowing workers to interpret their jobs as expressive of their gendered nature regardless of content. Nevertheless, even when women's and men's jobs draw on skills or traits usually associated with the other gender, the gender segregation of jobs helps sustain the notion that women and men have essentially different characters.

Problems of Identity

McDonald's window workers and Combined's agents had to find ways to reconcile their sense of themselves with the identity their job conferred upon them. Some of their difficulties arose because neither job was held in high esteem by the public. This low public regard affected both customers' treatment of workers and the workers' responses to their roles:

> . . . Dennis, a host, speaks very disparagingly about working at McDonald's. He says, "This isn't really a job." I ask what he means, and he says, "It's about as low as you can get. Everyone knows it."

Although the Combined Insurance salesmen did not regard their work as low-status, they were well aware that insurance agents are widely regarded as bores or pests, to be avoided if possible. Moreover, they frequently had to deal with rude and dismissive behavior from prospects. Some of the hostility insurance agents face is based on mistrust of their motives (Oakes 1990; Zelizer 1979). The intelligence of McDonald's workers was doubted, but it was the integrity of Combined's agents that was suspect.

Further challenges to identity were raised by the companies' extensive attempts to control their workers' self-presentation, including the workers' looks, demeanor, and personal style. For example, many McDonald's workers regarded the polyester tunic outfits they had to wear as ugly and degrading, and they were greatly cheered when those uniforms were replaced by ones that more closely resembled ordinary street clothes. The lack of control the window workers had over self-presentation was brought home most clearly during a special promotion of "Shanghai McNuggets," when they were forced to wear big Chinese peasant hats made of styrofoam. Most of the workers felt that the hats made them ridiculous:

Katie says that McDonald's ought to pay another ten cents an hour for making them wear the hats: "No one should have to wear those. It's TORTURE."

The selfhood of the workers was challenged most severely by routines that imposed particular types of interaction with other people. The problems of identity set up by McDonald's differed from those created by Combined Insurance.

The central duty of McDonald's window workers was to serve, and their major psychic task was to control or suppress the self. Their job required them to be nice to one person after another in a way that was necessarily quite unindividualized, and to keep their temper no matter how they were treated.... The workers were supposed to be efficient, courteous, and friendly in short bursts and within a very narrow range. They were told to be themselves, but their routines gave them little scope to express their personality.

Combined Insurance placed very different sorts of demands on its workers. While McDonald's merely instructed workers to smile and behave pleasantly to customers, Combined Insurance tried to affect its employees' psyches quite fundamentally through Positive Mental Attitude training. The company strove to inculcate optimism, determination, enthusiasm, and confidence and to destroy habits of negative thinking. The message for agents was somewhat paradoxical: you should do everything exactly the way we tell you to, but success depends on your own strength of character.

The main task for Combined's agents was not to serve but to sell, to take prospects and turn them into customers. Since the salesmen normally faced substantial resistance, their routines were designed to make it easier for them to impose their wills on prospects. Furthermore, the agents worked on their own rather than in a central workplace, and their interactions with customers could be much longer and cover a broader range than the McDonald's workers' did, so the agents were called on to use much more of their selves than were the window workers. They had to motivate themselves and keep up their

enthusiasm, and they had to adjust their behavior to respond to the problems presented by each prospect. Although their basic routine was unvaried, they needed to be chameleonlike to a certain extent and adapt to circumstances. As Tom put it, "You have to learn to read people, to figure out what they want in a salesperson and BE that person." Like the workers at McDonald's, the agents were required to control themselves, but their focus was always on controlling the prospect and the interaction.

These two jobs, then, posed distinct problems of identity for the workers. At McDonald's, workers needed to suppress the self and to serve others. The implications for the self that the window workers might have wished to resist were self-abnegation and depersonalization. Workers in nonroutinized service jobs also face the problem of having to enact self-abnegation, but the sense of depersonalization is especially acute for workers who must speak sentences they have not constructed to people who take no notice of them as people. For Combined's agents, the job was not so much to suppress the self as to transform it, and not so much to serve others as to control them. In these circumstances the basic danger for workers was self-alienation: having to be, while at work, someone they did not want to be. To do their job well, the agents were required to be insincere and manipulative. That problem might well be shared by other salespeople, even those working on their own. Combined's agents, however, faced the additional problem of holding on to their sense of themselves as autonomous and authentic people while reciting a script. Kevin's efforts to be himself inside the bounds of his script reflected this difficulty. Scripting could also challenge the agents' sense of manliness.

These problems arose in concrete ways during the work process. The companies, aware of the problems, tried to provide workers with psychic strategies that minimized some of the difficulties, and workers looked for ways to reconcile their sense of themselves with the identity they enacted on the job. Because the service interactions often bore little resemblance to genuine interpersonal exchanges, they raised questions about workers' real selves.

One question both workers and customers had to confront in every interaction was whether it was a real conversation. At McDonald's, the lines window workers used were extremely schematic: "Welcome to McDonald's"; "Will that be a *large* Coke?"; "For here or to go?" These standard lines, repeated over and over again, were extremely familiar to workers and customers, and both parties, as a rule, maintained a lesser degree of engagement in the interactions than they would in ordinary conversations. The mechanical nature of the exchange was highlighted, to my embarrassment, in one exchange I had with a customer:

> CUSTOMER: A hamburger and a large Coke.
>
> RL (while punching the order into the cash register): Something to drink?
>
> CUSTOMER: I said, a Coke.
>
> RL: Oh, I meant to say, "For here or to go?"

I had, in fact, heard and understood the order. Not giving my full attention to the conversation, I had absent-mindedly said the wrong line when it was my turn to speak, just as if I had pushed the wrong button on a tape recorder.

Not only did the form of the interactions tend to highlight the distance between these exchanges and ordinary conversations, but the content of the scripts also violated conversational norms, as when the workers were required to try suggestive selling to customers who had said, "That's it." This difficulty was especially acute during a promotion of Bacon Double Cheeseburgers, when the window workers were directed to suggest that product to every customer. Since it was summertime, when many customers stopped in just for a cold drink or an ice cream cone, the managers soon recognized that it was ridiculous for workers to respond to such orders by asking, "Would you like to try our Bacon Double Cheeseburger?" The solution they provided was for workers to ask this question *before* the customer gave the order. Customers, unfortunately, were likely to respond to a hurriedly delivered "Hi-welcome-to-McDonald's-would-you-like-to-try-our-Bacon-Double-Cheeseburger?" with a baffled "What?" Nevertheless, this practice was enforced, the goal of actual communication having been abandoned.

Under these circumstances, some customers did not even attempt to treat their interactions with workers as real conversations. They would fail to answer direct questions, for example, or even to look at the workers. . . .

Such customers apparently were not looking for personalized human contact. They wanted to expend a minimum of emotional effort in the service interactions, and they did not pretend that the encounters were anything but anonymous and routine. McDonald's attempts to standardize good cheer and enthusiasm were wasted on people who simply wanted to get their food as quickly as possible, with no emotional involvement whatever. Indeed, some of these customers seemed to regard the forms of routinized friendliness as intrusive, impertinent, or a waste of time.

Some workers also conducted the interactions by rote, withholding full involvement (see Goffman 1961b). I was surprised, for instance, at how a worker I knew treated me as a customer:

> I stand on line to buy a meal. Marisa recognizes me but waits on me without any variation in her routine or manner that would indicate that she's serving someone she knows—"Will that be all?" . . . "Have a nice day."

Even though some workers tried to divorce their selves from the service interactions, the divergence of the routine from the practices of ordinary conversation presented problems for workers' sense of self. Being treated as non-people by some customers could be hurtful in itself:

> Pat complains about suggestive selling: "I say, 'Would you like to try the raspberry shake?' They ignore you." She laughs. "They just go ahead on and give you their order. You'll be, like, 'Well—guess they didn't want it.' It makes you feel so embarrassed, 'cause . . . they just ignore you."

Furthermore, in enacting the routine workers were made to behave as though they did not know any better than to violate taken-for-granted interaction practices—to behave, in short, like badly socialized idiots. They felt some pressure to devise strategies to undercut this impression. For example, I found myself actively striving *not* to sound natural:

> As I'm taking an order, one of the crew trainers (I don't even have a moment to turn around to see who it is) says in my ear, "You have to push the Bacon Double Cheeseburgers." . . . I do start some of my orders by saying, "Would you like to try our Bacon Double Cheeseburger today?" I sometimes camp it up a bit—sort of saying the line in quotes, with a big smile and a "have-I-got-an-offer-for-you" tone of voice. Some guests smile or laugh in response, especially if they just want an ice cream cone. Most say "No" or "No, thank you," and go on to give their orders. One guy says, "You read my mind!" I reply, "We do our best." I don't say the line to everyone, though, by a long shot. I'm especially reluctant to do so when there are lines of people who can hear what I've said to the previous customer.

The intention of my humorous delivery was to convey that, although it was part of my job to deliver the line, I realized it was slightly ridiculous.

For the Combined Insurance agents, the question of whether they were involved in real conversations arose in drawing the boundary between genuine, relatively noninstrumental conversation and the sales pitch. During the "warming up the prospect" portion of the sales calls, the agents engaged in friendly, apparently idle chat that seemed to be at least as "real" as much social interaction. At a certain point, however, they needed to shift into the sales presentation. This transition was especially clear-cut in the presentation for the Senior Citizens' Policy. On these calls, the agents wanted to find out relatively early in the visit whether the prospect was healthy enough to qualify for the policy, so they would not waste a lot of time talking with someone who could not become a customer.

They might ask casually, "How have you been feeling lately?" and listen sympathetically to the prospects' descriptions of their health. At some point, though, the agents would have to ask, "More specifically, during the last five years, have you had any advice or treatment for stroke? heart attack or heart condition? cancer or any malignant growth?" It would then be clear that the previous conversation had not been idle talk at all, but part of the sales process. The transition had to be handled somewhat delicately, lest the prospect be offended by the now-apparent insincerity of the agent.

Beyond this issue of how real their conversations were, the work roles of interactive service workers presented broader questions for the jobholders. What is their relation to other people? How do they treat them? At McDonald's, the workers' task was to serve others. The design of the window workers' routines, including the requirement of constant cheerfulness, was intended to convey deference to customers. Since the workers were at the command of anyone who chose to come into the restaurant, they had to serve, politely, even those they considered to be their social inferiors, such as small children or homeless people, and even those who treated them disrespectfully. The servile behavior demanded of window workers could certainly be considered demeaning.

Combined's agents were expected to relate to other people by controlling them. The numerous compliance techniques built into their routines helped the agents to maintain control of interactions and prevent prospects from gaining the upper hand. A determined prospect could manage to get rid of an agent despite his use of clever interruption-stoppers, of course, but the agent's practiced tactics for turning prospects' responses to his own purposes and his refusal to accept the intended message of interruptions made it more difficult for prospects to control events. To carry out their routines the agents had to be pushy and manipulative, qualities some agents might not care to embrace. The lack of autonomy inherent in following a detailed script could further challenge agents' images of themselves.

The routines of interactive service workers, in short, are structured to make them *be* certain kinds of people. Some of the qualities built into their routines are ones that workers might well judge positively—cheerfulness or aggressiveness, helpfulness or control. Similarly, routines may match workers' ideas of appropriate manliness or womanliness. Other aspects of the routines, such as those demanding subordination, passivity, or insincerity, may be harder for workers to incorporate into their self-images. Interactive service workers have to determine whether they want to be the kinds of people their routines demand, and whether it is possible for them, while at work, to be the kinds of people they do want to be. When their job makes them behave in ways that do not coincide with their preferred identity, they must determine whether it will still be possible for them to hold on to the belief that they really are the kinds of people they want to be, and not the kinds they are constrained to be at work.

Organizations want to make it easy for their workers to accept the identity embodied in their routines, or at least to minimize workers' resistance to doing their jobs. Employers therefore provide psychic strategies to help workers reconcile their work with their self-image. They supply ways of thinking about the work and of interpreting events that are palatable to workers. For instance, since both Combined Insurance and McDonald's workers sometimes had to deal with insulting or even abusive behavior, the companies provided practical ways for the workers to deal with the assault on the self such incidents represented without responding in kind. They defined acceptance of abuse, not as demeaning oneself, but as proving oneself to be better than the customer exhibiting a lack of self-control. Mark, the Combined Insurance trainer, told the agents they should be glad that some people gave them a hard time: "If people bought insurance without help, there would be no need for representatives to sell it." Similarly, the Combined Insurance agents were taught to think of their work, not as manipulating people, but as keeping control, achieving their goals, and being winners.

Despite employers' efforts to provide face-saving psychic strategies, workers may still not be entirely happy with the identity implied by their routines. In that case, how did workers think about themselves and what they were doing? How could they maintain their dignity while enacting a script? The high turnover rates at McDonald's and Combined Insurance suggest that the modal response to these particular jobs was to leave. Those who stayed used diverse strategies to cope with the strains of their work, but the structure of each job closed off some possibilities and made others more likely.

At McDonald's, workers took a variety of approaches to reconciling the way they had to act with the self they wanted to be. Some workers tried to be good actors, delivering the standard lines with enthusiasm and a degree of sincerity. The struggle for verisimilitude could be rather difficult to sustain, though, given how unlifelike some aspects of the routines were and how frenetic the pace could get. I sometimes had a hard time sounding natural on the job. . . .

A related strategy for coping with the routine was to use the script as a starting point and inject one's own personality into the interactions. Thus, some window workers joked or chatted with customers and tried to make the exchanges enjoyable for both parties. This stance implied an assertion of equality with customers and a refusal to suppress the self completely. The problem, from the workers' point of view, was that the more workers were themselves on the job and the greater their efforts to make the interactions pleasant, the more painful or infuriating it was when customers were unresponsive or mean. . . .

Both of these strategies involved a large degree of acceptance of the terms of the interactions set by management. The workers tried to match the cheery, efficient, eager-to-please image that McDonald's advertises. Other workers tried to establish greater distance from that role (see Goffman 1961b). One strategy, familiar to most fast-food customers, was to refuse to take on the upbeat, enthusiastic persona that management tried to impose. Thus, some workers delivered their lines and carried out their tasks as assigned, but they did so with a minimum of emotional commitment. Their unsmiling faces conveyed the message, "I have to do this, but I don't have to like it." ...

Even workers who were usually willing to be cheerful and smiling might make subtle adjustments in their manner to protect their sense of dignity. The window workers were in the position of servant to all customers, but when the customers were perceived to have a lower social standing than the workers or were unappreciative of the crew's efforts, workers could try to distance themselves from the extra indignity that role implied:

> The homeless woman I've served before comes into the store. She's barefoot, and despite the heat she's wearing a down jacket. She asks Edward for a key to the downstairs washroom. He answers her, but I notice that he's less nice to her than he is to "respectable" customers.

. . . As limiting as McDonald's routine was, within its constraints the workers did find ways to express their sense of themselves and to protect their dignity.

Another strategy by which workers avoided enacting deference was to concentrate on an aspect of the routine that did allow them to feel that they were in charge and that they were good at their work. At McDonald's, this most often meant focusing on speed of service. Some workers barked questions at customers in a no-nonsense manner, making it clear to customers that by hesitating over their order or neglecting to give sufficiently detailed information they were holding things up. In this way the workers tried to impose their priorities on the service interactions. Since speed of service was a primary value at McDonald's, the managers at the franchise where I worked held up some of these extremely efficient but minimally civil workers as positive examples.

An especially interesting worker strategy was one that combined complete detachment with perfect enactment of the role. For example, Edward told me that when he came to work he assumed a McDonald's persona quite separate from his own. This practice enabled him to execute his duties with a show of good cheer and with consistent courtesy, but without thinking much and without engaging his personality. . . . When I asked Edward how he dealt with difficult customers, he answered, "I become a smiling little toady. . . . 'Whatever you say, sir. You're right and I'm an asshole.'" His detachment enabled him to enact subservience in these situations without feeling that his act was an acknowledgment of true inferiority. Edward did not perceive either the false cheeriness or the false self-abnegation as touching his real self.

This strategy of distancing, however good a shield against injuries to the self, also acted as a shield against some of the pleasures the job could provide. In contrast to the great majority of workers I interviewed, who said they frequently found it pleasant to deal with customers, Edward said, "It's almost too clinical for that. . . . Is it pleasant, is it unpleasant, I don't think about that."

How willing a worker was to accept the persona McDonald's prescribed was related not only to whether the worker was normally outgoing and personable but also to how much that worker was in fact defined by the job. Edward, who willingly became "a smiling little toady," was a part-time college student majoring in psychology. His acceptance of the McDonald's role was relatively untroubled because he did not see working at McDonald's as defining the limits of his talents and prospects. Furthermore, Edward was the only white male window worker in my sample. Shows of deference might well have a different meaning for him than they would for nonwhite and female workers, especially those for whom this job was the best available.

For the Combined Insurance agents it was a great deal more difficult to hold the self in reserve, because their job demanded that they throw themselves into their role to a much greater extent than the McDonald's workers did. If they were unwilling to be pushy or manipulative or if they recited their lines mechanically and without conviction, they could not sell insurance. Because their job required them to use a lot of themselves, they needed to find ways to reconcile their self-concept with the qualities their routines required them to embody. The agents I met therefore consciously worked on their selves in a way that was not necessary for most McDonald's workers. The agents saw it as a process of transformation to a better self, a more skillful and successful self. Most of them used the terminology of Combined's Positive Mental Attitude ideology in conversations and recognized that it was up to them to keep their spirits and their motivation high.

The transformation of their selves into the kinds of personalities that could succeed in Combined's system presented two related problems for the agents' self-identities. First, agents might wish to avoid thinking of themselves as manipulative and insincere. Second, they might find it hard to hold on to a sense of autonomy and of manliness while enacting their routines. Agents responded to the issue of manipulativeness in two ways. Some fully embraced this aspect of their roles. They took pleasure in outmaneuvering prospects and believed that Combined's routines enabled them to be smarter, smoother, more effective people than they were before. Other agents, who valued sincerity and ethical behavior more highly, discounted the manipulativeness of the role by interpreting their work as providing an important service. Despite the manipulativeness built into their sales routines, Tom and Kevin both believed that they could do their job without compromising their ethics. As Tom told me:

> I'm big on ethics. I don't push if people don't need it, if they have enough insurance. I'm not pushy at all—I won't waste my time or theirs.

Kevin expressed a similar attitude, adding that good intentions promote his own interests:

> It's not worth it to me to lie. I'm *big* on ethics. . . . When you push real hard, and there's greed in your eyes, and you're really struggling for the money, the sales won't be there. If you're more laid-back, it starts to happen. [Kevin criticizes himself for his attitude during a call that morning:] I had money on my mind.

Even these agents took pleasure in their ability to manipulate prospects, though. For example,

Kevin, noticing that a prospect's car had a garter hanging from the rear-view mirror and a license-plate frame reading "No Fat Chicks," gleefully said, "OK, a stud. I'll melt him."

The second problem, that of reconciling autonomy and manliness with the agent role, had two elements. The recitation of a script and the enactment of carefully prescribed movements always imply a lack of self-determination that can be demeaning in itself. In addition, several requirements of the Combined Insurance routine could be seen as further undercutting the workers' sense of dignity and of manliness. . . .

Overview

Routinizing interactive service work inevitably sets up tensions concerning the identity and individuality of workers, and, to a lesser extent, of customers as well. The sorts of identity issues created for workers vary, however, with the type of work and the type of relations with customers that are organized by the company. The possible ways of handling these tensions or of reconciling conflict between workers' preferred self-images and the identities imposed on them by their routines are likewise structured by the organization of the work. How possible is it to hold one's self in reserve while on the job? How compromising is it to a worker's feelings of dignity and individuality to embrace the routine? How far is it possible to interpret the role in ways that are compatible with a self-identity the worker is willing to accept?

The identities of workers in all sorts of jobs are shaped by the work they do, but the routinization of interactive service work tends to give employers more explicit and, in some areas, more extensive rights to define workers' looks, demeanor, attitudes, and outlooks. Braverman (1974), in his account of the history of work routinization, emphasized that deskilling jobs was the most important goal and outcome of employers' efforts to rationalize work. The jobs I have described have been deskilled to some extent. McDonald's window workers need fewer skills than do waiters or waitresses in conventional restaurants, and Combined's agents need fewer skills than do insurance agents who sell a wide variety of products without formal scripting, although the agents' training did give them skills that let them control their work more effectively. Nevertheless, a focus on skills does not capture some of the most significant features of the routinization of interactive service work. The qualities that allow workers to succeed in these jobs, and that employers try to control, are personal attributes, character traits, interactional styles, and the like. Some aspects of these dimensions can be regarded as skills, but only in an ambiguous and complicated sense. For instance, if workers are required to control their emotions on the job, would one call their loss of decision-making authority over their own behavior deskilling? Or would one say that the job requires the skill of self-control? The ability to get along well with people can easily be regarded as a skill, but what about the ability to tolerate abuse?

The concept of deskilling, appropriate as it is for understanding the standardization of tasks and the reduction of job complexity, does not illuminate the distinctive aspects of the routinization of interactive service work. Employers of these types of workers may find that to routinize work they must undertake the transformation of their employees' identities, ways of thinking, and sources of motivation, much as, for instance, religious orders and armies transform their recruits. Until now, research on work routinization has tended to downplay the relevance of social psychological theory, except in denouncing the attempts of managers of the human relations school to manipulate their workers. To understand the full impact of routinization in interactive service work, more serious attention to issues of identity, authenticity, and individuality is required. Investigations of workers' subjectivity must take into account not only employers' efforts to shape workers' consciousness but also workers' determined agency in providing justifications and interpretations of their experiences.

REFERENCES

Blauner, Robert. 1964. *Alienation and Freedom*. Chicago: University of Chicago Press.

Braverman, Harry. 1974. *Labor and Monopoly Capital: The Degradation of Work in the Twentieth Century*. New York: Monthly Review Press.

Burawoy, Michael. 1979. *Manufacturing Consent: Changes in the Labor Process Under Capitalism*. Chicago: University of Chicago Press.

Chaudhry, Rajan. 1989. "Burger Giants Singed by Battle." *Nation's Restaurant News* (August 7): F36.

Garson, Barbara. 1975. *All the Livelong Day: The Meaning and Demeaning of Routine Work*. New York: Doubleday.

Glenn, Evelyn Nakano, and Roslyn L. Feldberg. 1979a. "Proletarianizing Clerical Work: Technology and Control." Pp. 51–72 in Andrew Zimbalist, ed., *Case Studies on the Labor Process*. New York: Monthly Review Press.

Goffman, Erving. 1961b. "Role Distance." Pp. 83–152 in *Encounters: Two Studies in the Sociology of Interaction*. Indianapolis, Ind.: Bobbs-Merrill.

———. 1961c. "The Underlife of a Public Institution: A Study of Ways of Making Out in a Mental Hospital." Pp. 125–170 in *Asylums: Essays on the Social Situation of Mental Patients and Other Inmates*. Garden City, NY: Anchor Books.

Hochschild, Arlie Russell. 1983. *The Managed Heart: Commercialization of Human Feeling*. Berkeley: University of California Press.

Koepp, Stephen. 1987a. "Big Mac Strikes Back." *Time* (April 13): 58–60.

Lamont, Michele. 1992. *Money, Morals, and Manners: The Culture of the French and American Upper Middle Class*. Chicago: University of Chicago Press.

Mills, C. Wright. 1951. *White Collar: The American Middle Class*. New York: Oxford University Press.

Mills, Peter K. 1986. *Managing Service Industries: Organizational Practices in a Postindustrial Economy*. Cambridge, MA: Ballinger.

Noyelle, Thierry J. 1987. *Beyond Industrial Dualism: Market and Job Segmentation in the New Economy*. Boulder, CO: Westview Press.

Oakes, Guy. 1990. *The Soul of the Salesman: The Moral Ethos of Personal Sales*. Atlantic Highlands, NJ: Humanities Press International.

Sabel, Charles F. 1982. *Work and Politics: The Division of Labor in Industry*. Cambridge: Cambridge University Press.

Smith, Adam. 1982 [1776]. *The Wealth of Nations*. New York: Penguin.

Smith, Joan. 1984. "The Paradox of Women's Poverty: Wage-earning Women and Economic Transformation." *Signs* 10: 291–310.

Stinchcombe, Arthur L. 1990a. "Work Institutions and the Sociology of Everyday Life." Pp. 99–116 in Kai Erikson and Steven Peter Vallas, eds., *The Nature of Work: Sociological Perspectives.* New Haven, CT: Yale University Press.

———. 1990b. *Information and Organizations.* Berkeley: University of California Press.

Trilling, Lionel. 1972. *Sincerity and Authenticity.* Cambridge, MA: Harvard University Press.

Zelizer, Viviana A. Rotman. 1979. *Morals and Markets: The Development of Life Insurance in the United States.* New York: Columbia University Press.

THINKING ABOUT THE READING

How do the routinized experiences of McDonald's workers and Combined Insurance agents workers differ? What do these different experiences tell us about the different organizational needs of these two companies? In which company are individuals most likely to experience a threat to their own identity? Discuss the necessity of routinization from the perspective of organizations. Could these companies function if workers' behaviors and attitudes weren't so tightly controlled? Explain. If you've ever worked for a company that practiced the sort of routinization of activity described in this article, describe how it affected your sense of self and your feelings of individuality.

The Smile Factory

Work at Disneyland

John Van Maanen

Part of Walt Disney Enterprises includes the theme park Disneyland. In its pioneering form in Anaheim, California, this amusement center has been a consistent money maker since the gates were first opened in 1955. Apart from its sociological charm, it has, of late, become something of an exemplar for culture vultures and has been held up for public acclaim in several best-selling publications as one of America's top companies. . . . To outsiders, the cheerful demeanor of its employees, the seemingly inexhaustible repeat business it generates from its customers, the immaculate condition of park grounds, and, more generally, the intricate physical and social order of the business itself appear wondrous.

Disneyland as the self-proclaimed "Happiest Place on Earth" certainly occupies an enviable position in the amusement and entertainment worlds as well as the commercial world in general. Its product, it seems, is emotion—"laughter and well-being." Insiders are not bashful about promoting the product. Bill Ross, a Disneyland

executive, summarizes the corporate position nicely by noting that "although we focus our attention on profit and loss, day-in and day-out we cannot lose sight of the fact that this is a feeling business and we make our profits from that."

The "feeling business" does not operate, however, by management decree alone. Whatever services Disneyland executives believe they are providing to the 60 to 70 thousand visitors per day that flow through the park during its peak summer season, employees at the bottom of the organization are the ones who most provide them. The work-a-day practices that employees adopt to amplify or dampen customer spirits are therefore a core concern of this feeling business. The happiness trade is an interactional one. It rests partly on the symbolic resources put into place by history and park design but it also rests on an animated workforce that is more or less eager to greet the guests, pack the trams, push the buttons, deliver the food, dump the garbage, clean the streets, and, in general, marshal the will to meet and perhaps exceed customer expectations. False moves, rude words, careless disregard, detected insincerity, or a sleepy and bored presence can all undermine the enterprise and ruin a sale. The smile factory has its rules.

It's a Small World

. . . This rendition is of course abbreviated and selective. I focus primarily on such matters as the stock appearance (vanilla), status order (rigid), and social life (full), and swiftly learned codes of conduct (formal and informal) that are associated with Disneyland ride operators. These

Author's Note: This paper has been cobbled together using three-penny nails of other writings. Parts come from a paper presented to the American Anthropological Association Annual Meetings in Washington D.C. on November 16, 1989 called "Whistle While You Work." Other parts come from J. Van Maanen and G. Kunda, 1989. "Real feelings: Emotional expressions and organization culture." In B. Staw & L. L. Cummings (Eds.), *Research in Organization Behavior* (Vol. 11, pp. 43–103). Greenwich, CT: JAI Press. In coming to this version, I've had a good deal of help from my friends Steve Barley, Nicloe Biggart, Michael Owen Jones, Rosanna Hertz, Gideon Kunda, Joanne Martin, Maria Lydia Spinelli, Bob Sutton, and Bob Thomas.

employees comprise the largest category of hourly workers on the payroll. During the summer months, they number close to four thousand and run the 60-odd rides and attractions in the park.

They are also a well-screened bunch. There is—among insiders and outsiders alike—a rather fixed view about the social attributes carried by the standard-make Disneyland ride operator. Single, white males and females in their early twenties, without facial blemish, of above average height and below average weight, with straight teeth, conservative grooming standards, and a chin-up, shoulder-back posture radiating the sort of good health suggestive of a recent history in sports are typical of these social identifiers. There are representative minorities on the payroll but because ethnic displays are sternly discouraged by management, minority employees are rather close copies of the standard model Disneylander, albeit in different colors.

This Disneyland look is often a source of some amusement to employees who delight in pointing out that even the patron saint, Walt himself, could not be hired today without shaving off his trademark pencil-thin mustache. But, to get a job in Disneyland and keep it means conforming to a rather exacting set of appearance rules. These rules are put forth in a handbook on the Disney image in which readers learn, for example, that facial hair or long hair is banned for men as are aviator glasses and earrings and that women must not tease their hair, wear fancy jewelry, or apply more than a modest dab of makeup. Both men and women are to look neat and prim, keep their uniforms fresh, polish their shoes, and maintain an upbeat countenance and light dignity to complement their appearance—no low spirits or cornball raffishness at Disneyland.

The legendary "people skills" of park employees, so often mentioned in Disneyland publicity and training materials, do not amount to very much according to ride operators. Most tasks require little interaction with customers and are physically designed to practically insure that is the case. The contact that does occur typically is fleeting and swift, a matter usually of only a few seconds. In the rare event sustained interaction with customers might be required, employees are taught to deflect potential exchanges to area supervisors or security. A Training Manual offers the proper procedure: "On misunderstandings, guests should be told to call City Hall. . . . In everything from damaged cameras to physical injuries, don't discuss anything with guests . . . there will always be one of us nearby." Employees learn quickly that security is hidden but everywhere. On Main Street security cops are Keystone Kops; in Frontierland, they are Town Marshalls; on Tom Sawyer's Island, they are Cavalry Officers, and so on.

Occasionally, what employees call "line talk" or "crowd control" is required of them to explain delays, answer direct questions, or provide directions that go beyond the endless stream of recorded messages coming from virtually every nook and cranny of the park. Because such tasks are so simple, consisting of little more than keeping the crowd informed and moving, it is perhaps obvious why management considers the sharp appearance and wide smile of employees so vital to park operations. There is little more they could ask of ride operators whose main interactive tasks with visitors consist of being, in their own terms, "information booths," "line signs," "pretty props," "shepherds," and "talking statues."

A few employees do go out of their way to initiate contact with Disneyland customers but, as a rule, most do not and consider those who do to be a bit odd. In general, one need do little more than exercise common courtesy while looking reasonably alert and pleasant. Interactive skills that are advanced by the job have less to do with making customers feel warm and welcome than they do with keeping each other amused and happy. This is, of course, a more complex matter.

Employees bring to the job personal badges of status that are of more than passing interest to peers. In rough order, these include: good looks, college affiliation, career aspirations, past achievements, age (directly related to status up to about age 23 or 24 and inversely related thereafter), and assorted other idiosyncratic matters. Nested closely alongside these imported status badges are organizational ones that are also of concern and value to employees.

Where one works in the park carries much social weight. Postings are consequential because the ride and area a person is assigned provide rewards and benefits beyond those of wages. In-the-park stature for ride operators turns partly on whether or not unique skills are required. Disneyland neatly complements labor market theorizing on this dimension because employees with the most differentiated skills find themselves at the top of the internal status ladder, thus making their loyalties to the organization more predictable.

Ride operators, as a large but distinctly middle-class group of hourly employees on the floor of the organization, compete for status not only with each other but also with other employee groupings whose members are hired for the season from the same applicant pool. A loose approximation of the rank ordering among these groups can be constructed as follows:

1. The upper-class prestigious Disneyland Ambassadors and Tour Guides (bilingual young women in charge of ushering—some say rushing—little bands of tourists through the park);
2. Ride operators performing coveted "skilled work" such as live narrations or tricky transportation tasks like those who symbolically control customer access to the park and drive the costly entry vehicles such as the antique trains, horse-drawn carriages, and Monorail);
3. All other ride operators;
4. The proletarian Sweepers (keepers of the concrete grounds);
5. The sub-prole or peasant status Food and Concession workers (whose park sobriquets reflect their lowly social worth—"pancake ladies," "peanut pushers," "coke blokes," "suds divers," and the seemingly irreplaceable "soda jerks").

Pay differentials are slight among these employee groups. The collective status adheres, as it does internally for ride operators, to assignment or functional distinctions. As the rank order suggests, most employee status goes to those who work jobs that require higher degrees of special skill, relative freedom from constant and direct supervision, and provide the opportunity to organize and direct customer desires and behavior rather than to merely respond to them as spontaneously expressed.

The basis for sorting individuals into these various broad bands of job categories is often unknown to employees—a sort of deep, dark secret of the casting directors in personnel. When prospective employees are interviewed, they interview for "a job at Disneyland," not a specific one. Personnel decides what particular job they will eventually occupy. Personal contacts are considered by employees as crucial in this job-assignment process as they are in the hiring decision. Some employees, especially those who wind up in the lower ranking jobs, are quite disappointed with their assignments as is the case when, for example, a would-be Adventureland guide is posted to a New Orleans Square restaurant as a pot scrubber. Although many of the outside acquaintances of our pot scrubber may know only that he works at Disneyland, rest assured, insiders will know immediately where he works and judge him accordingly.

Uniforms are crucial in this regard for they provide instant communication about the social merits or demerits of the wearer within the little world of Disneyland workers. Uniforms also correspond to a wider status ranking that casts a significant shadow on employees of all types. Male ride operators on the Autopia wear, for example, untailored jump-suits similar to pit mechanics and consequently generate about as much respect from peers as the grease-stained outfits worn by pump jockeys generate from real motorists in gas stations. The ill-fitting and homogeneous "whites" worn by Sweepers signify lowly institutional work tinged, perhaps, with a reminder of hospital orderlies rather than street cleanup crews. On the other hand, for males, the crisp, officer-like Monorail operator stands alongside the swashbuckling Pirate of the Caribbean, the casual cowpoke of Big Thunder Mountain, or the smartly vested Riverboat pilot as carriers of valued symbols in and outside the park. Employees lust for these higher status positions and the rights to small advantages such uniforms provide. A lively internal labor market exists wherein there is much scheming for the more prestigious assignments.

For women, a similar market exists although the perceived "sexiness" of uniforms, rather than social rank, seems to play a larger role. To wit, the rather heated antagonisms that developed years ago when the ride "It's a Small World" first opened and began outfitting the ride operators with what were felt to be the shortest skirts and most revealing blouses in the park. Tour Guides, who traditionally headed the fashion vanguard at Disneyland in their above-the-knee kilts, knee socks, tailored vests, black English hats, and smart riding crops were apparently appalled at being upstaged by their social inferiors and lobbied actively (and, judging by the results, successfully) to lower the skirts, raise the necklines, and generally remake their Small World rivals.

Important, also, to ride operators are the break schedules followed on the various rides. The more the better. Work teams develop inventive ways to increase the number of "time-outs" they take during the work day. Most rides are organized on a rotational basis (e.g., the operator moving from a break, to queue monitor, to turnstile overseer, to unit loader, to traffic controller, to driver, and, again, to a break). The number of break men or women on a rotation (or ride) varies by the number of employees on duty and by the number of units on line. Supervisors, foremen, and operators also vary as to what they regard as appropriate break standards (and, more importantly, as to the value of the many situational factors that can enter the calculation of break rituals—crowd size, condition of ride, accidents, breakdowns, heat, operator absences, special occasions, and so forth). Self-monitoring teams with sleepy supervisors and lax (or savvy) foremen can sometimes manage a shift comprised of 15 minutes on and 45 minutes off each hour. They are envied by others, and rides that

have such a potential are eyed hungrily by others who feel trapped by their more rigid (and observed) circumstances.

Movement across jobs is not encouraged by park management, but some does occur (mostly within an area and job category). Employees claim that a sort of "once a sweeper, always a sweeper" rule obtains but all know of at least a few exceptions to prove the rule. The exceptions offer some (not much) hope for those working at the social margins of the park and perhaps keep them on the job longer than might otherwise be expected. Dishwashers can dream of becoming Pirates, and with persistence and a little help from their friends, such dreams just might come true next season (or the next).

These examples are precious, perhaps, but they are also important. There is an intricate pecking order among very similar categories of employees. Attributes of reward and status tend to cluster, and there is intense concern about the cluster to which one belongs (or would like to belong). To a degree, form follows function in Disneyland because the jobs requiring the most abilities and offering the most interest also offer the most status and social reward. Interaction patterns reflect and sustain this order. Few Ambassadors or Tour Guides, for instance, will stoop to speak at length with Sweepers who speak mostly among themselves or to Food workers. Ride operators, between the poles, line up in ways referred to above with only ride proximity (i.e., sharing a break area) representing a potentially significant intervening variable in the interaction calculation. . . .

Paid employment at Disneyland begins with the much renowned University of Disneyland whose faculty runs a day-long orientation program (Traditions I) as part of a 40-hour apprenticeship program, most of which takes place on the rides. In the classroom, however, newly hired ride operators are given a very thorough introduction to matters of managerial concern and are tested on their absorption of famous Disneyland fact, lore, and procedure. Employee demeanor is governed, for example, by three rules:

First, we practice the friendly smile.

Second, we use only friendly and courteous phrases.

Third, we are not stuffy—the only Misters in Disneyland are Mr. Toad and Mr. Smee.

Employees learn too that the Disneyland culture is officially defined. The employee handbook put it in this format:

Dis-ney Cor-po-rate Cul-ture (diz'ne kor'pr'it kul'cher) *n* 1. Of or pertaining to the Disney organization, as a: the philosophy underlying all business decisions; b: the commitment of top leadership and management to that philosophy; c: the actions taken by individual cast members that reinforce the image.

Language is also a central feature of university life, and new employees are schooled in its proper use. Customers at Disneyland are, for instance, never referred to as such, they are "guests." There are no rides at Disneyland, only "attractions." Disneyland itself is a "Park," not an amusement center, and it is divided into "backstage," "on-stage," and "staging" regions. Law enforcement personnel hired by the park are not policemen, but "security hosts." Employees do not wear uniforms but check out fresh "costumes" each working day from "wardrobe." And, of course, there are no accidents at Disneyland, only "incidents.". . .

The university curriculum also anticipates probable questions ride operators may someday face from customers, and they are taught the approved public response. A sample:

Question (posed by trainer): What do you tell a guest who requests a rain check?
Answer (in three parts): We don't offer rain checks at Disneyland because (1) the main attractions are all indoors; (2) we would go broke if we offered passes; and (3) sunny days would be too crowded if we gave passes.

Shrewd trainees readily note that such an answer blissfully disregards the fact that waiting areas of Disneyland are mostly outdoors and that there are no subways in the park to carry guests from land to land. Nor do they miss the economic assumption concerning the apparent frequency of Southern California rains. They discuss such matters together, of course, but rarely raise them in the training classroom. In most respects, these are recruits who easily take the role of good student.

Classes are organized and designed by professional Disneyland trainers who also instruct a well-screened group of representative hourly employees straight from park operations on the approved newcomer training methods and materials. New-hires seldom see professional trainers in class but are brought on board by enthusiastic peers who concentrate on those aspects of park procedure thought highly general matters to be learned by all employees. Particular skill training (and "reality shock") is reserved for the second wave of socialization occurring on the rides themselves as operators are taught, for example, how and when to send a mock bobsled caroming down the track or, more delicately, the proper ways to stuff an obese adult customer into the midst of children riding the Monkey car on the Casey Jones Circus Train or, most problematically, what exactly to tell an irate customer standing in the rain who, in no uncertain terms, wants his or her money back and wants it back now.

During orientation, considerable concern is placed on particular values the Disney organization considers central to its operations. These values range from the "customer is king" verities to the more or less unique kind, of which "everyone is a child at heart when at Disneyland" is a decent example. This latter piety is one few employees fail to recognize as also attaching to everyone's mind as well after a few months of work experience. Elaborate checklists of appearance standards are learned and gone over in the classroom and great efforts are spent trying to bring employee emotional responses in line with such standards. Employees are told repeatedly that if they are happy and cheerful at work, so, too, will the guests at play. Inspirational films, hearty pep talks, family imagery, and exemplars of corporate performance are all representative of the strong symbolic stuff of these training rites. . . .

Yet, like employees everywhere, there is a limit to which such overt company propaganda can be effective. Students and trainers both seem to agree on where the line is drawn, for there is much satirical banter, mischievous winking, and playful exaggeration in the classroom. As young seasonal employees note, it is difficult to take seriously an organization that provides its retirees "Golden Ears" instead of gold watches after 20 or more years of service. All newcomers are aware that the label "Disneyland" has both an unserious and artificial connotation and that a full embrace of the Disneyland role would be as deviant as its full rejection. It does seem, however, because of the corporate imagery, the recruiting and selection devices, the goodwill trainees hold toward the organization at entry, the peer-based employment context, and the smooth fit with real student calendars, the job is considered by most ride operators to be a good one. The University of Disneyland, it appears, graduates students with a modest amount of pride and a considerable amount of fact and faith firmly ingrained as important things to know (if not always accept).

Matters become more interesting as new hires move into the various realms of Disneyland enterprise. There are real customers "out there" and employees soon learn that these good folks do not always measure up to the typically well mannered and grateful guest of the training classroom. Moreover, ride operators may find it difficult to utter the prescribed "Welcome Voyager" (or its equivalent) when it is to be given to the 20-thousandth human being passing through the Space Mountain turnstile on a crowded day in July. Other difficulties present themselves as well, but operators learn that there are others onstage to assist or thwart them.

Employees learn quickly that supervisors and, to a lesser degree, foremen are not only on the premises to help them, but also to catch them when they slip over or brazenly violate set procedures or park policies. Because most rides are tightly designed to eliminate human judgment and minimize operational disasters, much of the supervisory monitoring is directed at activities ride operators consider trivial: taking too long a break; not wearing parts of one's official uniform such as a hat, standard-issue belt, or correct shoes; rushing the ride (although more frequent violations seem to be detected for the provision of longer-than-usual rides for lucky customers); fraternizing with guests beyond the call of duty; talking back to quarrelsome or sometimes merely querisome customers; and so forth. All are matters covered quite explicitly in the codebooks ride operators are to be familiar with, and violations of such codes are often subject to instant and harsh discipline. The firing of what to supervisors are "malcontents," "trouble-makers," "bumblers," "attitude problems," or simply "jerks" is a frequent occasion at Disneyland, and among part-timers, who are most subject to degradation and being fired, the threat is omnipresent. There are few workers who have not witnessed firsthand the rapid disappearance of a co-worker for offenses they would regard as "Mickey Mouse." Moreover, there are few employees who themselves have not violated a good number of operational and demeanor standards and anticipate, with just cause, the violation of more in the future.

In part, because of the punitive and what are widely held to be capricious supervisory practices in the park, foremen and ride operators are usually drawn close and shield one another from suspicious area supervisors. Throughout the year, each land is assigned a number of area supervisors who, dressed alike in short-sleeved white shirts and ties with walkie-talkies hitched to their belts, wander about their territories on the lookout for deviations from park procedures (and other signs of disorder). Occasionally, higher level supervisors pose in "plainclothes" and ghost-ride the various attractions just to be sure everything is up to snuff. Some area supervisors are well-known among park employees for the variety of surreptitious techniques they employ when going about their monitoring duties. Blind observation posts are legendary, almost sacred, sites within the park ("This is where Old Man

Weston hangs out. He can see Dumbo, Story-book, the Carousel, and the Tea Cups from here"). Supervisors in Tomorrowland are, for example, famous for their penchant of hiding in the bushes above the submarine caves, timing the arrivals and departures of the supposedly fully loaded boats making the 8½ minute cruise under the polar icecaps. That they might also catch a submarine captain furtively enjoying a cigarette (or worse) while inside the conning tower (his upper body out of view of the crowd on the vessel) might just make a supervisor's day—and unmake the employee's. In short, supervisors, if not foremen, are regarded by ride operators as sneaks and tricksters out to get them and representative of the dark side of park life. Their presence is, of course, an orchestrated one and does more than merely watch over the ride operators. It also draws operators together as cohesive little units who must look out for one another while they work (and shirk). . . .

Employees are also subject to what might be regarded as remote controls. These stem not from supervisors or peers but from thousands of paying guests who parade daily through the park. The public, for the most part, wants Disneyland employees to play only the roles for which they are hired and costumed. If, for instance, Judy of the Jets is feeling tired, grouchy, or bored, few customers want to know about it. Disneyland employees are expected to be sunny and helpful; and the job, with its limited opportunities for sustained interaction, is designed to support such a stance. Thus, if a ride operator's behavior drifts noticeably away from the norm, customers are sure to point it out—"Why aren't you smiling?" "What's wrong with you?" "Having a bad day?" "Did Goofy step on your foot?" Ride operators learn swiftly from the constant hints, glances, glares, and tactful (and tactless) cues sent by their audience what their role in the park is to be, and as long as they keep to it, there will be no objections from those passing by.

I can remember being out on the river looking at the people on the Mark Twain looking down

on the people in the Keel Boats who are looking up at them. I'd come by on my raft and the y'd all turn and stare at me. If I gave them a little wave and a grin, they'd all wave back and smile; all ten thousand of them. I always wondered what would happen if I gave them the finger? (Ex-ride operator, 1988)

Ride operators also learn how different categories of customers respond to them and the parts they are playing on-stage. For example, infants and small children are generally timid, if not frightened, in their presence. School-age children are somewhat curious, aware that the operator is at work playing a role but sometimes in awe of the role itself. Nonetheless, these children can be quite critical of any flaw in the operator's performance. Teenagers, especially males in groups, present problems because they sometimes go to great lengths to embarrass, challenge, ridicule, or outwit an operator. Adults are generally appreciative and approving of an operator's conduct provided it meets their rather minimal standards, but they sometimes overreact to the part an operator is playing (positively) if accompanied by small children. . . .

The point here is that ride operators learn what the public (or, at least, their idealized version of the public) expects of their role and find it easier to conform to such expectations than not. Moreover, they discover that when they are bright and lively others respond to them in like ways. This . . . balancing of the emotional exchange is such that ride operators come to expect good treatment. They assume, with good cause, that most people will react to their little waves and smiles with some affection and perhaps joy. When they do not, it can ruin a ride operator's day.

With this interaction formula in mind, it is perhaps less difficult to see why ride operators detest and scorn the ill-mannered or unruly guest. At times, these grumpy, careless, or otherwise unresponsive characters insult the very role the operators play and have come to appreciate—"You can't treat the Captain of the USS Nautilus like that!" Such out-of-line visitors offer breaks from routine, some amusement, consternation, or the occasional job challenge that occurs when remedies are deemed necessary to restore employee and role dignity.

By and large, however, the people-processing tasks of ride operators pass good naturedly and smoothly, with operators hardly noticing much more than the bodies passing in front of view (special bodies, however, merit special attention as when crew members on the subs gather to assist a young lady in a revealing outfit on board and then linger over the hatch to admire the view as she descends the steep steps to take her seat on the boat). Yet, sometimes, more than a body becomes visible, as happens when customers overstep their roles and challenge employee authority, insult an operator, or otherwise disrupt the routines of the job. In the process, guests become "dufusses," "ducks," and "assholes" (just three of many derisive terms used by ride operators to label those customers they believe to have gone beyond the pale). Normally, these characters are brought to the attention of park security officers, ride foremen, or area supervisors who, in turn, decide how they are to be disciplined (usually expulsion from the park).

Occasionally, however, the alleged slight is too personal or simply too extraordinary for a ride operator to let it pass unnoticed or merely inform others and allow them to decide what, if anything, is to be done. Restoration of one's respect is called for, and routine practices have been developed for these circumstances. For example, common remedies include: the "seatbelt squeeze," a small token of appreciation given to a deviant customer consisting of the rapid cinching-up of a required seatbelt such that the passenger is doubled-over at the point of departure and left gasping for the duration of the trip; the "break-toss," an acrobatic gesture of the Autopia trade whereby operators jump on the outside of a norm violator's car, stealthily unhitching the safety belt, then slamming on the brakes, bringing the car to an almost instant stop while the driver flies on the hood of the car (or beyond); the "seatbelt slap," an equally distinguished (if primitive) gesture by which an offending customer receives a sharp, quick snap of a hard plastic belt across the face (or other parts of the body) when entering or exiting a seat-belted ride; the "break-up-the-party" gambit, a queuing device put to use in officious fashion whereby bothersome pairs are separated at the last minute into different units, thus forcing on them the pain of strange companions for the duration of a ride through the Haunted Mansion or a ramble on Mr. Toad's Wild Ride; the "hatch-cover ploy," a much beloved practice of Submarine pilots who, in collusion with mates on the loading dock, are able to drench offensive guests with water as their units pass under a waterfall; and, lastly, the rather ignoble variants of the "Sorry-I-didn't-see-your-hand" tactic, a savage move designed to crunch a particularly irksome customer's hand (foot, finger, arm, leg, etc.) by bringing a piece of Disneyland property to bear on the appendage, such as the door of a Thunder Mountain railroad car or the starboard side of a Jungle Cruise boat. This latter remedy is, most often, a "near miss" designed to startle the little criminals of Disneyland.

All of these unofficial procedures (and many more) are learned on the job. Although they are used sparingly, they are used. Occasions of use provide a continual stream of sweet revenge talk to enliven and enrich colleague conversation at break time or after work. Too much, of course, can be made of these subversive practices and the rhetoric that surrounds their use. Ride operators are quite aware that there are limits beyond which they dare not pass. If they are caught, they know that restoration of corporate pride will be swift and clean.

In general, Disneyland employees are remarkable for their forbearance and polite good manners even under trying conditions. They are taught, and some come to believe, for a while at least, that they are really "on-stage" at work. And, as noted, surveillance by supervisory personnel certainly fades in light of the unceasing glances an employee receives from the paying guests who tromp daily through the park in the summer. Disneyland employees know well that they are part of the product being sold and learn to check their more discriminating manners in favor of the generalized countenance of a cheerful lad or lassie whose enthusiasm and dedication is obvious to all.

At times, the emotional resources of employees appear awesome. When the going gets tough and the park is jammed, the nerves of all employees are frayed and sorely tested by the crowd, din, sweltering sun, and eyeburning smog. Customers wait in what employees call "bullpens" (and park officials call "reception areas") for up to several hours for a 3½ minute ride that operators are sometimes hell-bent on cutting to 2½ minutes. Surely a monument to the human ability to suppress feelings has been created when both users and providers alike can maintain their composure and seeming regard for one another when in such a fix.

It is in this domain where corporate culture and the order it helps to sustain must be given its due. Perhaps the depth of a culture is visible only when its members are under the gun. The orderliness—a good part of the Disney formula for financial success—is an accomplishment based not only on physical design and elaborate procedures, but also on the low-level, part-time employees who, in the final analysis, must be willing, even eager, to keep the show afloat. The ease with which employees glide into their kindly and smiling roles is, in large measure, a feat of social engineering. Disneyland does not pay well; its supervision is arbitrary and skin-close; its working conditions are chaotic; its jobs require minimal amounts of intelligence or judgment; and asks a kind of sacrifice and loyalty of its employees that is almost fanatical. Yet, it attracts a particularly able workforce whose personal backgrounds suggest abilities far exceeding those required of a Disneyland traffic cop, people stuffer, queue or line manager, and button pusher. As I have suggested, not all of Disneyland is covered by the culture put forth by management. There are numerous pockets of resistance and various degrees of autonomy maintained by employees. Nonetheless, adherence and support for the organization are remarkable. And, like swallows returning to

Capistrano, many part-timers look forward to their migration back to the park for several seasons.

The Disney Way

Four features alluded to in this unofficial guide to Disneyland seem to account for a good deal of the social order that obtains within the park. First, socialization, although costly, is of a most selective, collective, intensive, serial, sequential, and closed sort. These tactics are notable for their penetration into the private spheres of individual thought and feeling. . . . Incoming identities are not so much dismantled as they are set aside as employees are schooled in the use of new identities of the situational sort. Many of these are symbolically powerful and, for some, laden with social approval. It is hardly surprising that some of the more problematic positions in terms of turnover during the summer occur in the food and concession domains where employees apparently find little to identify with on the job. Cowpokes on Big Thunder Mountain, Jet Pilots, Storybook Princesses, Tour Guides, Space Cadets, Jungle Boat Skippers, or Southern Belles of New Orleans Square have less difficulty on this score. Disneyland, by design, bestows identity through a process carefully set up to strip away the job relevance of other sources of identity and learned response and replace them with others of organizational relevance. It works.

Second, this is a work culture whose designers have left little room for individual experimentation. Supervisors, as apparent in their focused wandering and attentive looks, keep very close tabs on what is going on at any moment in all the lands. Every bush, rock, and tree in Disneyland is numbered and checked continually as to the part it is playing in the park. So too are employees. Discretion of a personal sort is quite limited while employees are "on-stage." Even "back-stage" and certain "off-stage" domains have their corporate monitors. Employees are indeed aware that their "off-stage" life beyond the picnics, parties, and softball games is subject to some scrutiny, for police checks are made on potential and current employees. Nor do all employees discount the rumors that park officials make periodic inquiries on their own as to a person's habits concerning sex and drugs. Moreover, the sheer number of rules and regulations is striking, thus making the grounds for dismissal a matter of multiple choice for supervisors who discover a target for the use of such grounds. The feeling of being watched is, unsurprisingly, a rather prevalent complaint among Disneyland people, and it is one that employees must live with if they are to remain at Disneyland.

Third, emotional management occurs in the park in a number of quite distinct ways. From the instructors at the university who beseech recruits to "wish every guest a pleasant good day," to the foremen who plead with their charges to, "say thank you when you herd them through the gate," to the impish customer who seductively licks her lips and asks, "what does Tom Sawyer want for Christmas?" appearance, demeanor, and etiquette have special meanings at Disneyland. Because these are prized personal attributes over which we normally feel in control, making them commodities can be unnerving. Much self-monitoring is involved, of course, but even here self-management has an organizational side. Consider ride operators who may complain of being "too tired to smile" but, at the same time, feel a little guilty for uttering such a confession. Ride operators who have worked an early morning shift on the Matterhorn (or other popular rides) tell of a queasy feeling they get when the park is opened for business and they suddenly feel the ground begin to shake under their feet and hear the low thunder of the hordes of customers coming at them, oblivious of civil restraint and the small children who might be among them. Consider, too, the discomforting pressures of being "on-stage" all day and the cumulative annoyance of having adults ask permission to leave a line to go to the bathroom, whether the water in the lagoon is real, where the well-marked entrances might be, where Walt

Disney's cryogenic tomb is to be found, or—the real clincher—whether or not one is "really real."

The mere fact that so much operator discourse concerns the handling of bothersome guests suggests that these little emotional disturbances have costs. There are, for instance, times in all employee careers when they put themselves on "automatic pilot," "go robot," "can't feel a thing," "lapse into a dream," "go into a trance," or otherwise "check out" while still on duty. Despite a crafty supervisor's (or curious visitor's) attempt to measure the glimmer in an employee's eye, this sort of willed emotional numbness is common to many of the "on-stage" Disneyland personnel. Much of this numbness is, of course, beyond the knowledge of supervisors and guests because most employees have little trouble appearing as if they are present even when they are not. It is, in a sense, a passive form of resistance that suggests there still is a sacred preserve of individuality left among employees in the park.

Finally, taking these three points together, it seems that even when people are trained, paid, and told to be nice, it is hard for them to do so all of the time. But, when efforts to be nice have succeeded to the degree that is true of Disneyland, it appears as a rather towering (if not always admirable) achievement. It works at the collective level by virtue of elaborate direction. Employees—at all ranks—are stage-managed by higher ranking employees who, having come through themselves, hire, train, and closely supervise those who have replaced them below. Expression rules are laid out in corporate manuals. Employee time-outs intensify work experience. Social exchanges are forced into narrow bands of interacting groups. Training and retraining programs are continual. Hiding places are few. Although little sore spots and irritations remain for each individual, it is difficult to imagine work roles being more defined (and accepted) than those at Disneyland. Here, it seems, is a work culture worthy of the name.

THINKING ABOUT THE READING

What is the significance of the title, "The Smile Factory"? What, exactly, is the factory-made product that Disney sells in its theme parks? How does the Disney organizational culture shape the lives of employees? Disney is frequently criticized for its strict—some would say oppressive—employee rules and regulations. But would it be possible to run a "smile factory" with a more relaxed code of conduct where employees could regularly make their own decisions and act as they pleased? Explain. Disney theme parks abroad (in Japan and France, for instance) have not been nearly as successful as Disneyland and Disneyworld. Why has it been so difficult to export the "feeling business" to other countries? Consider also how Van Maanen describes the ways in which employees define the social rank of different positions within Disneyland. Describe an organizational situation you've been in where such a ranking of members occurred. What were the criteria upon which such rankings were made?

CHAPTER 10

The Architecture of Stratification: Power, Class, and Privilege

Inequality is woven into the fabric of all societies through a structured system of *social stratification*. Social stratification is a ranking of entire groups of people that perpetuates unequal rewards and life chances in society. The structural-functionalist explanation of stratification is that the stability of society depends on all social positions being filled—that is, there are people around to do all the jobs that need to be done. Higher rewards, such as prestige and large salaries, are afforded to the most important positions, thereby ensuring that the most qualified individuals will occupy the highest positions. In contrast, conflict theory argues that stratification reflects an unequal distribution of power in society and is a primary source of conflict and tension.

Social class is the primary means of stratification in American society. Contemporary sociologists are likely to define one's class standing as a combination of income, wealth, occupational prestige, and educational attainment. It is tempting to see class differences as simply the result of an economic stratification system that exists at a level above the individual. Although inequality is created and maintained by larger social institutions, however, it is often felt most forcefully and is reinforced most effectively in the chain of interactions that take place in our day-to-day lives.

Sociologists are particularly concerned with how power and authority are distributed within our economic and political institutions. The pluralist perspective, which emphasizes the role of competing interest groups, and the ruling-class perspective, which emphasizes the role of a small group of wealthy individuals, are two competing explanations of institutional power.

William Domhoff, in "The Bohemian Grove," argues that there is a tiny but cohesive ruling class in American society that makes decisions of national and international significance in its own narrowly defined interests. Often these decisions are made not in corporate boardrooms, the halls of Congress, or the White House, but in the comfortable, relaxing, and secluded confines of private, exclusive social clubs. Not only are business and political relationships among wealthy, powerful individuals formed here, but marriages between members of wealthy, powerful families are often arranged as well, thereby sustaining and strengthening the boundary between the ruling class and the other classes.

It is important to remember that inequality and stratification extend beyond national borders. Third-world laborers have become a crucial part of the global economic marketplace and an important foreign resource for multinational corporations. Low-skilled jobs are frequently exported to developing countries that have cheaper labor costs. On the surface, it would appear that such an arrangement benefits all involved: The multinational corporations benefit from higher profits, the developing countries benefit from higher rates of employment, the workers themselves benefit from earning a wage that would have otherwise been unavailable to them, and consumers in wealthy countries benefit from less expensive products.

But most of us are unaware of and unconcerned with the harsh conditions under which our most coveted products are made. William Greider, in "These Dark Satanic Mills," discusses the exploitative potential of relying on third-world factories. He uses a particular tragedy, the 1993 industrial fire at the Kader Industrial Toy Company in Thailand, to illustrate how global economics create and sustain international inequality. Greider shows us the complex paradox of the global marketplace: While foreign manufacturing facilities free factory workers from certain poverty, they also ensnare the workers in new and sometimes lethal forms of domination.

The Bohemian Grove

G. William Domhoff

Picture yourself comfortably seated in a beautiful open-air dining hall in the midst of twenty-seven hundred acres of giant California redwoods. It is early evening and the clear July air is still pleasantly warm. Dusk has descended, you have finished a sumptuous dinner, and you are sitting quietly with your drink and your cigar, listening to nostalgic welcoming speeches and enjoying the gentle light and the eerie shadows that are cast by the two-stemmed gaslights flickering softly at each of the several hundred outdoor banquet tables.

You are part of an assemblage that has been meeting in this redwood grove sixty-five miles north of San Francisco for over a hundred years. It is not just any assemblage, for you are a captain of industry, a well-known television star, a banker, a famous artist, or maybe a member of the President's Cabinet. You are one of fifteen hundred men gathered together from all over the country for the annual encampment of the rich and the famous at the Bohemian Grove.

[Recent "Bohemians" include former presidents Ronald Reagan, George Bush, Gerald Ford and Richard Nixon; former Attorney General William French Smith; former cabinet members George Shultz, Richard Cheney and James Baker III; journalist William F. Buckley; and various wealthy investment bankers, university presidents, entertainers, high level government officials and Fortune 500 CEO's. In June of 1993 White House counselor David Gergen resigned his membership in the club at the behest of the President.]

The Cremation of Care is the most spectacular event of the midsummer retreat that members and guests of San Francisco's Bohemian Club have taken every year since 1878. However, there are several other entertainments in store. Before the Bohemians return to the everyday world, they will be treated to plays, variety shows, song fests, shooting contests, art exhibits, swimming, boating, and nature rides. . . .

A cast for a typical Grove play easily runs to seventy-five or one hundred people. Add in the orchestra, the stagehands, the carpenters who make the sets, and other supporting personnel, and over three hundred people are involved in creating the High Jinks each year. Preparations begin a year in advance, with rehearsals occurring two or three times a week in the month before the encampment, and nightly in the week before the play.

Costs are on the order of $20,000 to $30,000 per High Jinks, a large amount of money for a one-night production which does not have to pay a penny for salaries (the highest cost in any commercial production). "And the costs are talked about, too," reports my second informant. "'Hey, did you hear the High Jinks will cost $25,000 this year?' one of them will say to another. The expense of the play is one way they can relate to its worth." . . .

Entertainment is not the only activity at the Bohemian Grove. For a little change of pace, there is intellectual stimulation and political enlightenment every day at 12:30 P.M. Since 1932 the meadow from which people view the Cremation of Care also has been the setting for informal talks and briefings by people as varied as Dwight David Eisenhower (before he was President), Herman Wouk (author of *The Caine Mu-*

tiny), Bobby Kennedy (while he was Attorney General), and Neil Armstrong (after he returned from the moon).

Cabinet officers, politicians, generals, and governmental advisers are the rule rather than the exception for Lakeside Talks, especially on weekends. Equally prominent figures from the worlds of art, literature, and science are more likely to make their appearance during the week-days of the encampment, when Grove atten-dance may drop to four or five hundred (many of the members only come up for one week or for the weekends because they cannot stay away from their corporations and law firms for the full two weeks).

Members vary as to how interesting and in-formative they find the Lakeside Talks. Some find them useful, others do not, probably de-pending on their degree of familiarity with the topic being discussed. It is fairly certain that no inside or secret information is divulged, but a good feel for how a particular problem will be handled is likely to be communicated. Whatever the value of the talks, most members think there is something very nice about hearing official government policy, orthodox big-business ideol-ogy, and new scientific information from a fellow Bohemian or one of his guests in an informal at-mosphere where no reporters are allowed to be present.

One person who seems to find Lakeside Talks a useful forum is President Richard M. Nixon, a Bohemian Club member since 1953. A speech he gave at the Grove in 1967 was the basis for a pub-lic speech he gave a few months later. Richard J. Whalen, one of Nixon's speech writers in the late sixties, tells the story as follows:

> He would speak at the Hoover Institution, before a conference on the fiftieth anniversary of the Bolshevik revolution. "I don't want it to be the typical anti-Communist harangue—you know, there's Nixon again. Try to *lift* it. I want to take a *sophisticated* hard line. I'd like to be very fair and objective about their achieve-ments—in fifty years they've come from a cellar conspiracy to control of half the world. But I

also want to underline the horrible costs of their methods and system." He handed me a copy of his speech the previous summer at Bohemian Grove, telling me to take it as a model for outlining the changes in the Com-munist world and the changing U.S. Policy toward the Soviet Union.[1]

The ease with which the Bohemian Grove is able to attract famous speakers for no remunera-tion other than the amenities of the encampment attests to the high esteem in which the club is held in the higher circles. Down through the years the Lakeside podium has hosted such luminaries as Lee DuBridge (science), David Sarnoff (business), Wernher von Braun (space technology), Senator Robert Taft, Lucius Clay (military and business), Earl Warren (Supreme Court), former California Republican Governor Goodwin J. Knight, and former California Democratic Governor Pat Brown. For many years former President Herbert C. Hoover, who joined the club in 1913, was a regular feature of the Lakeside Talks, with the final Saturday afternoon being reserved for his anach-ronistic counsel.

Politicians apparently find the Lakeside Talks especially attractive. "Giving a Lakeside" provides them with a means for personal exposure with-out officially violating the injunction "Weaving spiders, come not here." After all, Bohemians ra-tionalize, a Lakeside Talk is merely an informal chat by a friend of the family.

Some members, at least, know better. They re-alize that the Grove is an ideal off-the-record at-mosphere for sizing up politicians. "Well, of course when a politician comes here, we all get to see him, and his stock in trade is his personality and his ideas," a prominent Bohemian told a *New York Times* reporter who was trying to cover Nelson Rockefeller's 1963 visit to the Grove for a Lakeside Talk. The journalist went on to note that the midsummer encampments "have long been a major showcase where leaders of business, industry, education, the arts, and politics can come to examine each other." . . .

For 1971, [then] President Nixon was to be the featured Lakeside speaker. However, when newspaper reporters learned that the President planned to disappear into a redwood grove for an off-the-record speech to some of the most powerful men in America, they objected loudly and vowed to make every effort to cover the event. The flap caused the club considerable embarrassment, and after much hemming and hawing back and forth, the club leaders asked the President to cancel his scheduled appearance. A White House press secretary then announced that the President had decided not to appear at the Grove rather than risk the tradition that speeches there are strictly off the public record.[2]

However, the President was not left without a final word to his fellow Bohemians. In a telegram to the president of the club, which now hangs at the entrance to the reading room in the San Francisco clubhouse, he expressed his regrets at not being able to attend. He asked the club president to continue to lead people into the woods, adding that he in turn would redouble his efforts to lead people out of the woods. He also noted that, while anyone could aspire to be President of the United States, only a few could aspire to be president of the Bohemian Club.

Not all the entertainment at the Bohemian Grove takes place under the auspices of the committee in charge of special events. The Bohemians and their guests are divided into camps which evolved slowly over the years as the number of people on the retreat grew into the hundreds and then the thousands. These camps have become a significant center of enjoyment during the encampment.

At first the camps were merely a place in the woods where a half-dozen to a dozen friends would pitch their tents. Soon they added little amenities like their own special stove or a small permanent structure. Then there developed little camp "traditions" and endearing camp names like Cliff Dwellers, Moonshiners, Silverado Squatters, Woof, Zaca, Toyland, Sundodgers, and Land of Happiness. The next steps were special emblems, a handsome little lodge or specially constructed tepees, a permanent bar, and maybe a grand piano.[3] Today there are 129 camps of varying sizes, structures, and statuses. Most have

between 10 and 30 members, but there are one or two with about 125 members and several with less than 10. A majority of the camps are strewn along what is called the River Road, but some are huddled in other areas within five or ten minutes of the center of the Grove.

The entertainment at the camps is mostly informal and impromptu. Someone will decide to bring together all the jazz musicians in the Grove for a special session. Or maybe all the artists or writers will be invited to a luncheon or a dinner at a camp. Many camps have their own amateur piano players and informal musical and singing groups which perform for the rest of the members.

But the joys of the camps are not primarily in watching or listening to performances. Other pleasures are created within them. Some camps become known for their gastronomical specialties, such as a particular drink or a particular meal. The Jungle Camp features mint juleps, Halcyon has a three-foot-high martini maker constructed out of chemical glassware. At the Owl's Nest [former President Reagan's club] it's the gin-fizz breakfast—about a hundred people are invited over one morning during the encampment for eggs Benedict, gin fizzes, and all the trimmings.

Poison Oak is famous for its Bulls' Balls Lunch. Each year a cattle baron from central California brings a large supply of testicles from his newly castrated herds for the delectation of Poison Oakers and their guests. No one goes away hungry. Bulls' balls are said to be quite a treat. Meanwhile, one small camp has a somewhat different specialty, which is not necessarily known to members of every camp. It houses a passé pornographic collection which is more amusing than erotic. Connoisseurs do not consider it a great show, but it is an easy way to kill a lazy afternoon. . . .

The men of Bohemia are drawn in large measure from the corporate leadership of the United States. They include in their numbers directors from major corporations in every sector of the American economy. An indication of this fact is that one in every five resident members and one in every three nonresident members is found in Poor's *Register of Corporations, Executives, and Directors,* a huge volume which lists the leadership of tens of thousands of companies from every major business field except investment banking, real estate, and advertising.

Even better evidence for the economic prominence of the men under consideration is that at least one officer or director from 40 of the 50 largest industrial corporations in America was present, as a member or a guest, on the lists at our disposal. Only Ford Motor Company and Western Electric were missing among the top 25! Similarly, we found that officers and directors from 20 of the top 25 commercial banks (including all of the 15 largest) were on our lists. Men from 12 of the first 25 life-insurance companies were in attendance (8 of these 12 were from the top 10). Other business sectors were represented somewhat less: 10 of 25 in transportation, 8 of 25 in utilities, 7 of 25 in conglomerates, and only 5 of 25 in retailing. More generally, of the top-level businesses ranked by *Fortune* for 1969 (the top 500 industrials, the top 50 commercial banks, the top 50 life-insurance companies, the top 50 transportation companies, the top 50 utilities, the top 50 retailers, and the top 47 conglomerates), *29 percent of these 797 corporations were "represented" by at least 1 officer or director....*

Do Bohemians Rule America?

The foregoing material on [Bohemian Grove], which I have presented in as breezy a manner as possible, is relevant to highly emotional questions concerning the distribution of power in modern America. In this final [section] I will switch styles somewhat and discuss these charged questions in a sober, simple, and straightforward way.

It is my hypothesis that there is a ruling social class in the United States. This class is made up of the owners and managers of large corporations, which means the members have many economic and political interests in common, and many conflicts with ordinary working people. Comprising at most 1 percent of the total popu-

lation, members of this class own 25 to 30 percent of all privately held wealth in America, own 60 to 70 percent of the privately held corporate wealth, receive 20 to 25 percent of the yearly income, direct the large corporations and foundations, and dominate the federal government in Washington.

Most social scientists disagree with this view. Some dismiss it out of hand, others become quite vehement in disputing it. The overwhelming majority of them believe that the United States has a "pluralistic" power structure, in which a wide variety of "veto groups" (e.g., businessmen, farmers, unions, consumers) and "voluntary associations" (e.g., National Association of Manufacturers, Americans for Democratic Action, Common Cause) form shifting coalitions to influence decisions on different issues. These groups and associations are said to have differing amounts of interest and influence on various questions. Contrary to my view, pluralists assert that no one group, not even the owners and managers of large corporations, has the cohesiveness and ability to determine the outcome of a wide variety of social, economic, and political issues....

This means that wealthy families from all over the country, and particularly from major cities like New York, San Francisco, Chicago, and Houston, are part of interlocking social circles which perceive each other as equals, belong to the same clubs, interact frequently, and freely intermarry.

Whether we call it a "social class" or a "status group," many pluralistic social scientists would deny that such a social group exists. They assert that there is no social "cohesiveness" among the various rich in different parts of the country. For them, social registers, blue books, and club membership lists are merely collections of names which imply nothing about group interaction.

There is a wealth of journalistic evidence which suggests the existence of a national upper class. It ranges from Cleveland Amory's *The Proper Bostonians and Who Killed Society?* to Lucy Kavaler's *The Private World of High Society* and Stephen Birmingham's *The Right People.* But what is the systematic evidence which I can present for my thesis? There is first of all the evidence that has been developed from the study of attendance at private schools. It has been shown that a few dozen prep schools bring together children of the upper class from all over the country. From this evidence it can be argued that young members of the upper class develop lifetime friendship ties with like-status age-mates in every section of the country.[4]

There is second the systematic evidence which comes from studying high-status summer resorts. Two such studies show that these resorts bring together upper-class families from several different large cities.[5] Third, there is the evidence of business interconnections. Several different studies have demonstrated that interlocking directorships bring wealthy men from all over the country into face-to-face relationships at the board meetings of banks, insurance companies, and other corporations.[6]

And finally, there is the evidence developed from studying exclusive social clubs. Such studies have been made in the past, but the present investigation of the Bohemian Club is a more comprehensive effort. *In short, I believe the present [study] to be significant evidence for the existence of a cohesive American upper class.*

The Bohemian Grove, as well as other watering holes and social clubs, is relevant to the problem of class cohesiveness in two ways. First, the very fact that rich men from all over the country gather in such close circumstances as the Bohemian Grove is evidence for the existence of a socially cohesive upper class. It demonstrates that many of these men do know each other, that they have face-to-face communications, and that they are a social network. In this sense, we are looking at the Bohemian Grove and other social retreats as a *result* of social processes that lead to class cohesion. But such institutions also can be viewed as facilitators of social ties. Once formed, these groups become another avenue by which the cohesiveness of the upper class is maintained.

In claiming that clubs and retreats like the Bohemians are evidence for my thesis of a national upper class, I am assuming that cohesion develops

within the settings they provide. Perhaps some readers will find that assumption questionable. So let us pause to ask: Are there reasons to believe that the Bohemian Grove and its imitators lead to greater cohesion within the upper class?

For one thing, we have the testimony of members themselves. There are several accounts by leading members of these groups, past and present, which attest to the intimacy that develops among members. John J. Mitchell, El Presidente of Los Rancheros Visitadores [a club similar to Bohemian Grove] from 1930 to 1955, wrote as follows on the twenty-fifth anniversary of the group:

> All the pledges and secret oaths in the universe cannot tie men, our kind of men, together like the mutual appreciation of a beautiful horse, the moon behind a cloud, a song around the campfire, or a ride down the Santa Ynez Valley. These are experiences common on our ride, but unknown to most of our daily lives. Our organization, to all appearances, is the most informal imaginable. Yet there are men here who see one another once a year, yet feel a bond closer than between those they have known all their lives.[7]

A second reason for stressing the importance of retreats and clubs like the Bohemian Grove is a body of research within social psychology which deals with group cohesion. "Group dynamics" suggests the following about cohesiveness: (1) *Physical proximity is likely to lead to group solidarity.* Thus, the mere fact that these men gather together in such intimate physical settings implies that cohesiveness develops. (The same point can be made, of course, about exclusive neighborhoods, private schools, and expensive summer resorts.) (2) *The more people interact, the more they will like each other.* This is hardly a profound discovery, but we can note that the Bohemian Grove and other watering holes maximize personal interactions. (3) *Groups seen as high in status are more cohesive.* The Bohemian Club fits the category of a high-status group, further, its stringent membership requirements, long waiting lists, and high dues also serve to heighten its valuation in the eyes of its members. Members are likely to think of themselves as "special" people, which would heighten their attractiveness to each other, and increase the likelihood of interaction and cohesiveness. (4) *The best atmosphere for increasing group cohesiveness is one that is relaxed and cooperative.* Again the Bohemian Grove [is an] ideal example of this kind of climate. From a group-dynamics point of view, then, we could argue that one of the reasons for upper-class cohesiveness is the fact that the class is organized into a wide variety of small groups which encourage face-to-face interaction and ensure status and security for members.[8]

In summary, if we take these several common settings together—schools, resorts, corporation directorships, and social clubs—and assume on the basis of members' testimony and the evidence of small-group research that interaction in such settings leads to group cohesiveness, then I think we are justified in saying that wealthy families from all over the United States are linked together in a variety of ways into a national upper class.

Even if the evidence and arguments for the existence of a socially cohesive national upper class are accepted, there is still the question of whether or not this class has the means by which its members can reach policy consensus on issues of importance to them.

A five-year study based upon information obtained from confidential informants, interviews, and questionnaires has shown that social clubs such as the Bohemian Club are an important consensus-forming aspect of the upper class and big-business environment. According to sociologist Reed Powell, "the clubs are a repository of the values held by the upper-level prestige groups in the community and are a means by which these values are transferred to the business environment." Moreover, the clubs are places where problems are discussed:

> On the other hand, the clubs are places in which the beliefs, problems, and values of the industrial organization are discussed and related to

other elements in the larger community. Clubs, therefore, are not only effective vehicles of informal communication, but also valuable centers where views are presented, ideas are modified, and new ideas emerge. Those in the interview sample were appreciative of this asset; in addition, they considered the club as a valuable place to combine social and business contacts.[9]

The revealing interview work of Floyd Hunter, an outstanding pioneer researcher on the American power structure, also provides evidence for the importance of social clubs as informal centers of policy making. Particularly striking for our purposes is a conversation he had with one of the several hundred top leaders that he identified in the 1950s. The person in question was a conservative industrialist who was ranked as a top-level leader by his peers:

> Hall [a pseudonym] spoke very favorably of the Bohemian Grove group that met in California every year. He said that although over the entrance to the Bohemian Club there was a quotation, "Weaving spiders come not here," there was a good deal of informal policy made in this association. He said that he got to know Herbert Hoover in this connection and that he started work with Hoover in the food administration of World War I.[10]

Despite the evidence presented by Powell and Hunter that clubs are a setting for the development of policy consensus, I do not believe that such settings are the only, or even the primary, locus for developing policy on class-related issues. For policy questions, other organizations are far more important, organizations like the Council on Foreign Relations, the Committee for Economic Development, the Business Council, and the National Municipal League. These organizations, along with many others, are the "consensus-seeking" and "policy-planning" organizations of the upper class. Directed by the same men who manage the major corporations, and financed by corporation and foundation monies, these groups sponsor meetings and discussions wherein wealthy men from all over the country gather to iron out differences and formulate policies on pressing problems.

No one discussion group is *the* leadership council within the upper class. While some of the groups tend to specialize in certain issue areas, they overlap and interact to a great extent. Consensus slowly emerges from the interplay of people and ideas within and among the groups.[11] This diversity of groups is made very clear in the following comments by Frazar B. Wilde, chairman emeritus of Connecticut General Life Insurance Company and a member of the Council on Foreign Relations and the Committee for Economic Development. Mr Wilde was responding to a question about the Bilderbergers, a big-business meeting group which includes Western European leaders as well as American corporation and foundation directors:

> Business has had over the years many different seminars and discussion meetings. They run all the way from large public gatherings like NAM [National Association of Manufacturers] to special sessions such as those held frequently at Arden House. Bilderberg is in many respects one of the most important, if not the most important, but this is not to deny that other strictly off-the-record meetings and discussion groups such as those held by the Council on Foreign Relations are not in the front rank.[12]

Generally speaking, then, it is in these organizations that leaders within the upper class discuss the means by which to deal with problems of major concern. Here, in off-the-record settings, these leaders try to reach consensus on general issues that have been talked about more casually in corporate boardrooms and social clubs. These organizations, aided by funds from corporations and foundations, also serve several other functions:

1. They are a training ground for new leadership within the class. It is in these organizations, and through the publications of these organizations, that younger lawyers, bankers, and businessmen become acquainted with general issues in the areas of foreign, domestic, and municipal policy.

2. They are the place where leaders within the upper class hear the ideas and findings of their hired experts.

3. They are the setting wherein upper-class leaders "look over" young experts for possible service as corporation or governmental advisers.

4. They provide the framework for expert studies on important issues. Thus, the Council on Foreign Relations undertook a $1 million study of the "China question" in the first half of the 1960s. The Committee for Economic Development created a major study of money and credit about the same time. Most of the money for these studies was provided by the Ford, Rockefeller, and Carnegie foundations.[13]

5. Through such avenues as books, journals, policy statements, discussion groups, press releases, and speakers, the policy-planning organizations greatly influence the "climate of opinion" within which major issues are considered. For example, *Foreign Affairs,* the journal of the Council on Foreign Relations, is considered the most influential journal in its field, and the periodic policy statements of the Committee for Economic Development are carefully attended to by major newspapers and local opinion leaders.

It is my belief, then, that the policy-planning groups are essential in developing policy positions which are satisfactory to the upper class as a whole. As such, I think they are a good part of the answer to any social scientist who denies that members of the upper class have institutions by which they deal with economic and political challenges.

However, the policy-planning groups could not function if there were not some common interests within the upper class in the first place. The most obvious, and most important, of these common interests have to do with the shared desire of the members to maintain the present monopolized and subsidized business system which so generously overrewards them and makes their jet setting, fox hunting, art collecting, and other extravagances possible. But it is not only shared economic and political concerns which make consensus possible. The Bohemian Grove and other upper-class social institutions also contribute to this process: *Group-dynamics research suggests that members of socially cohesive groups are more open to the opinions of other members, and more likely to change their views to those of fellow members.*[14] Social cohesion is a factor in policy consensus because it creates a desire on the part of group members to reconcile differences with other members of the group. It is not enough to say that members of the upper class are bankers, businessmen, and lawyers with a common interest in profit maximization and tax avoidance who meet together at the Council on Foreign Relations, the Committee of Economic Development, and other policy-planning organizations. We must add that they are Bohemians.

NOTES

1. Richard J. Whalen, *Catch the Falling Flag: A Republican's Challenge to His Party* (Boston: Houghton Mifflin, 1972), p. 25. Earlier in this book, on page 4, Whalen reports that his own speech in 1969 at the Bohemian Grove, which concerned the U.S.-Soviet nuclear balance, was distributed by President Nixon to cabinet members and other administration officials with a presidential memorandum commending it as an "excellent analysis." I am grateful to sociologist Richard Hamilton of McGill University for bringing this material to my attention.

2. James M. Naughton, "Nixon Drops Plan for Coast Speech" (*New York Times,* July 31, 1971), p. 11.

3. There is a special moisture-proof building at the Grove to hold the dozens of expensive Steinway pianos belonging to the club and various camps.

4. Baltzell, *Philadelphia Gentlemen,* chapter 12. Domhoff, *The Higher Circles,* p. 78.

5. Baltzell, *Philadelphia Gentlemen,* pp. 248–51. Domhoff, *The Higher Circles,* pp. 79–82. For recent anecdotal evidence on this point, see Stephen Birmingham, *The Right People* (Boston: Little, Brown, 1968), Part 3.

6. *Interlocks in Corporate Management* (Washington: U.S. Government Printing Office, 1965) summarizes much of this information and presents new evidence as well. See also Peter Dooley, "The Interlocking Directorate" (*American Economic Review,* December, 1969).

7. Neill C. Wilson, *Los Rancheros Visitadores,* p. 2.

8. Dorwin Cartwright and Alvin Zander, *Group Dynamics* (New York: Harper & Row, 1960), pp. 74–82; Albert J. Lott and Bernice E. Lott, "Group Cohesiveness as Interpersonal Attraction" (*Psychological Bulletin,* 64, 1965), pp. 259–309; Michael Argyle, *Social Interaction* (Chicago: Aldine Publishing Company, 1969), pp. 220–23. I am grateful to sociologist John Sonquist of the University of California, Santa Barbara, for making me aware of how important the small-groups literature might be for studies of the upper class. Findings on influence processes, communication patterns, and the development of informal leadership also might be applicable to problems in the area of upper-class research.

9. Reed M. Powell, *Race, Religion, and the Promotion of the American Executive* (College of Administrative Science Monograph No AA-3, Ohio State University, 1969), p. 50.

10. Floyd Hunter, *Top Leadership, U.S.A.* (Chapel Hill: University of North Carolina Press, 1959), p. 109. Hunter also reported (p. 199) that the most favored clubs of his top leaders were the Metropolitan, Links, Century, University (New York), Bohemian, and Pacific Union. He notes (p. 223 n.) that he found clubs to be less important in policy formation on the national level than they are in communities.

11. For a detailed case study of how the process works, see David Eakins, "Business Planners and America's Postwar Expansion," in David Horowitz, editor, *Corporations and the Cold War* (New York: Monthly Review Press, 1969). For other examples and references, see Domhoff, *The Higher Circles,* chapters 5 and 6.

12. Carl Gilbert, personal communication, June 30, 1972. Mr. Gilbert has done extensive research on the Bilderberg group, and I am grateful to him for sharing his detailed information with me. For an excellent discussion of this group, whose role has been greatly distorted and exaggerated by ultra-conservatives, see Eugene Pasymowski and Carl Gilbert, "Bilderberg, Rockefeller, and the CIA" (*Temple Free Press,* November

16, 1968). The article is most conveniently located in a recently revised form in the *Congressional Record,* September 15, 1971, under the title "Bilderberg: The Cold War Internationale."

13. The recent work of arch-pluralist Nelson Polsby is bringing him dangerously close to this formulation. Through studies of the initiation of a number of new policies, Polsby and his students have tentatively concluded that "innovators are typically professors or interest group experts." Where Polsby goes wrong is in failing to note that the professors are working on Ford Foundation grants and/or Council on Foreign Relations fellowships. If he would put his work in a sociological framework, people would not gain the false impression that professors are independent experts sitting in their ivory towers thinking up innovations for the greater good of humanity. See Nelson Polsby, "Policy Initiation in the American Political System," in Irving Louis Horowitz, editor, *The Use and Abuse of Social Science* (New Brunswick, N.J.: TransAction Books, 1971), p. 303.

14. Cartwright and Zander, *Group Dynamics,* p. 89; Lott and Lott, "Group Cohesiveness as Interpersonal Attraction," pp. 291–96.

THINKING ABOUT THE READING

What do you think of Domhoff's argument about a cohesive upper class? Can recreational clubs provide the sort of "social cohesiveness" necessary for a self-contained ruling class to exist? How do you think places like Bohemian Grove contribute to class stratification in American society? How does the existence of such clubs change your thinking about the way important political and economic decisions are made in this country?

These Dark Satanic Mills

William Greider

. . . If the question were put now to everyone, everywhere—do you wish to become a citizen of the world?—it is safe to assume that most people in most places would answer, no, they wish to remain who they are. With very few exceptions, people think of themselves as belonging to a place, a citizen of France or Malaysia, of Boston or Tokyo or Warsaw, loyally bound to native culture, sovereign nation. The Chinese who aspire to get gloriously rich, as Deng instructed, do not intend to become Japanese or Americans. Americans may like to think of themselves as the world's leader, but not as citizens of "one world."

The deepest social meaning of the global industrial revolution is that people no longer have free choice in this matter of identity. Ready or not, they are already of the world. As producers or consumers, as workers or merchants or investors, they are now bound to distant others through the complex strands of commerce and finance reorganizing the globe as a unified marketplace. The prosperity of South Carolina or Scotland is deeply linked to Stuttgart's or Kuala Lumpur's. The true social values of Californians or Swedes will be determined by what is tolerated in the factories of Thailand or Bangladesh. The energies and brutalities of China will influence community anxieties in Seattle or Toulouse or Nagoya.

. . . Unless one intends to withdraw from modern industrial life, there is no place to hide from the others. Major portions of the earth, to be sure, remain on the periphery of the system, impoverished bystanders still waiting to be included in the action. But the patterns of global interconnectedness are already the dominant reality. Commerce has leapt beyond social consciousness and, in doing so, opened up challenging new vistas for the human potential. Most people, it seems fair to say, are not yet prepared to face the implications. . . .

The process of industrialization has never been pretty in its primitive stages. Americans or Europeans who draw back in horror at the present brutalities in Asia or Latin America should understand that they are glimpsing repetitions of what happened in their own national histories, practices that were forbidden as inhumane in their own countries only after long political struggle. To make that historical point complicates the moral responses, but does not extinguish the social question.

The other realm, of course, is the wealthy nation where the established social structure is under assault, both from market forces depressing wages and employment and from the political initiatives to dismantle the welfare state. The governments' obligations to social equity were erected during the upheavals of the last century to ameliorate the harsher edges of unfettered capitalism; now they are in question again. The economic pressures to shrink or withdraw public benefits are relentless, yet no one has explained how wealthy industrial nations will maintain the social peace by deepening their inequalities.

A standard response to all these social concerns is the reassuring argument that market forces will eventually correct them—if no one interferes. The new wealth of industrialization, it is said, will lead naturally to middle-class democracy in the poorer countries and the barbarisms will eventually be eradicated. In the older societies, it is assumed that technology will create new realms of work that in time replace the lost employment, restore living wages and spread the prosperity widely again. People need only be patient with the future and not interrupt the revolution.

The global system has more or less been proceeding on these assumptions for at least a generation and one may observe that the unfolding reality has so far gravely disappointed these expectations. Nor does the free-market argument conform with the actual history of how democratic development or social equity was advanced over the last two centuries, neither of which emerged anywhere without titanic political struggles. A more pointed contradiction is the hypocrisy of those who make these arguments. If multinational enterprises truly expect greater human freedom and social equity to emerge from the marketplace, then why do they expend so much political energy to prevent these conditions from developing?

In any case, the theoretical arguments about the future do not satisfy the moral question that exists concretely at present. If one benefits tangibly from the exploitation of others who are weak, is one morally implicated in their predicament? Or are basic rights of human existence confined to those civilized societies wealthy enough to afford them? Everyone's values are defined by what they will tolerate when it is done to others. Everyone's sense of virtue is degraded by the present reality....

Two centuries ago, when the English industrial revolution dawned with its fantastic invention and productive energies, the prophetic poet William Blake drew back in moral revulsion. Amid the explosion of new wealth, human destruction was spread over England—peasant families displaced from their lands, paupers and poorhouses crowded into London slums, children sent to labor at the belching ironworks or textile looms. Blake delivered a thunderous rebuke to the pious Christians of the English aristocracy with these immortal lines:

And was Jerusalem builded here
Among these dark Satanic mills?

Blake's "dark Satanic mills" have returned now and are flourishing again, accompanied by the same question.[1]

On May 10, 1993, the worst industrial fire in the history of capitalism occurred at a toy factory on the outskirts of Bangkok and was reported on page 25 of the *Washington Post*. The *Financial Times* of London, which styles itself as the daily newspaper of the global economy, ran a brief item on page 6. The *Wall Street Journal* followed a day late with an account on page 11. The *New York Times* also put the story inside, but printed a dramatic photo on its front page: rows of small shrouded bodies on bamboo pallets—dozens of them—lined along the damp pavement, while dazed rescue workers stood awkwardly among the corpses. In the background, one could see the collapsed, smoldering structure of a mammoth factory where the Kader Industrial Toy Company of Thailand had employed three thousand workers manufacturing stuffed toys and plastic dolls, playthings destined for American children.[2]

The official count was 188 dead, 469 injured, but the actual toll was undoubtedly higher since the four-story buildings had collapsed swiftly in the intense heat and many bodies were incinerated. Some of the missing were never found; others fled home to their villages. All but fourteen of the dead were women, most of them young, some as young as thirteen years old. Hundreds of the workers had been trapped on upper floors of the burning building, forced to jump from third- or fourth-floor windows, since the main exit doors were kept locked by the managers, and the narrow stairways became clotted with trampled bodies or collapsed.

When I visited Bangkok about nine months later, physical evidence of the disaster was gone—the site scraped clean by bulldozers—and Kader was already resuming production at a new toy factory, built far from the city in a rural province of northeastern Thailand. When I talked with Thai labor leaders and civic activists, people who had rallied to the cause of the fire victims, some of them were under the impression that a worldwide boycott of Kader products was under way, organized by conscience-stricken Americans and Europeans. I had to inform them that the civilized world had barely noticed their tragedy.

As news accounts pointed out, the Kader fire surpassed what was previously the worst industrial fire in history—the Triangle Shirtwaist Company fire of 1911—when 146 young immigrant women died in similar circumstances at a garment factory on the Lower East Side of Manhattan. The Triangle Shirtwaist fire became a pivotal event in American politics, a public scandal that provoked citizen reform movements and energized the labor organizing that built the International Ladies Garment Workers Union and other unions. The fire in Thailand did not produce meaningful political responses or even shame among consumers. The indifference of the leading newspapers merely reflected the tastes of their readers, who might be moved by human suffering in their own communities but were inured to news of recurring calamities in distant places. A fire in Bangkok was like a typhoon in Bangladesh, an earthquake in Turkey.

The Kader fire might have been more meaningful for Americans if they could have seen the thousands of soot-stained dolls that spilled from the wreckage, macabre litter scattered among the dead. Bugs Bunny, Bart Simpson and the Muppets. Big Bird and other *Sesame Street* dolls. Playskool "Water Pets." Santa Claus. What the initial news accounts did not mention was that Kader's Thai factory produced most of its toys for American companies—Toys "R" Us, Fisher-Price, Hasbro, Tyco, Arco, Kenner, Gund and J. C. Penney—as well as stuffed dolls, slippers and souvenirs for Europe.[3]

Globalized civilization has uncovered an odd parochialism in the American character: Americans worried obsessively over the everyday safety of their children, and the U.S. government's regulators diligently policed the design of toys to avoid injury to young innocents. Yet neither citizens nor government took any interest in the brutal and dangerous conditions imposed on the people who manufactured those same toys, many of whom were mere adolescent children themselves. Indeed, the government position, both in Washington and Bangkok, assumed that there was no social obligation connecting consumers with workers, at least none that governments could enforce without disrupting free trade or invading the sovereignty of other nations.

The toy industry, not surprisingly, felt the same. Hasbro Industries, maker of Playskool, subsequently told the *Boston Globe* that it would no longer do business with Kader, but, in general, the U.S. companies shrugged off responsibility. Kader, a major toy manufacturer based in Hong Kong, "is extremely reputable, not sleaze bags," David Miller, president of the Toy Manufacturers of America, assured *USA Today*. "The responsibility for those factories," Miller told ABC News, "is in the hands of those who are there and managing the factory."[4]

The grisly details of what occurred revealed the casual irresponsibility of both companies and governments. The Kader factory compound consisted of four interconnected, four-story industrial barns on a three-acre lot on Buddhamondhol VI Road in the Sampran district west of Bangkok. It was one among Thailand's thriving new industrial zones for garments, textiles, electronics and toys. More than 50,000 people, most of them migrants from the Thai countryside, worked in the district at 7,500 large and small firms. Thailand's economic boom was based on places such as this, and Bangkok was almost choking on its own fantastic growth, dizzily erecting luxury hotels and office towers.

The fire started late on a Monday afternoon on the ground floor in the first building and spread rapidly upward, jumping to two adjoining buildings, all three of which swiftly collapsed. Investigators noted afterwards that the structures had been cheaply built, without concrete reinforcement, so steel girders and stairways crumpled easily in the heat. Thai law required that in such a large factory, fire-escape stairways must be sixteen to thirty-three feet wide, but Kader's were a mere four and a half feet. Main doors were locked and many windows barred to prevent pilfering by the employees. Flammable raw materials—fabric, stuffing, animal fibers—were stacked everywhere, on walkways and next to electrical boxes. Neither safety drills nor fire alarms and sprinkler systems had been provided.

Let some of the survivors describe what happened.

A young woman named Lampan Taptim: "There was the sound of yelling about a fire. I tried to leave the section but my supervisor told me to get back to work. My sister who worked on the fourth floor with me pulled me away and insisted we try to get out. We tried to go down the stairs and got to the second floor; we found that the stairs had already caved in. There was a lot of yelling and confusion. . . . In desperation, I went back up to the windows and went back and forth, looking down below. The smoke was thick and I picked the best place to jump in a pile of boxes. My sister jumped, too. She died."

A young woman named Cheng: "There is no way out [people were shouting], the security guard has locked the main door out! It was horrifying. I thought I would die. I took off my gold ring and kept it in my pocket and put on my name tag so that my body could be identifiable. I had to decide to die in the fire or from jumping down from a three stories' height." As the walls collapsed around her, Cheng clung to a pipe and fell downward with it, landing on a pile of dead bodies, injured but alive.

An older woman named La-iad Nada-nguen: "Four or five pregnant women jumped before me. They died before my eyes." Her own daughter jumped from the top floor and broke both hips.

Chauweewan Mekpan, who was five months pregnant: "I thought that if I jumped, at least my parents would see my remains, but if I stayed, nothing would be left of me." Though her back was severely injured, she and her unborn child miraculously survived.

An older textile worker named Vilaiwa Satieti, who sewed shirts and pants at a neighboring factory, described to me the carnage she encountered: "I got off work about five and passed by Kader and saw many dead bodies lying around, uncovered. Some of them I knew. I tried to help the workers who had jumped from the factory. They had broken legs and broken arms and broken heads. We tried to keep them alive until they got to the hospital, that's all you could do. Oh, they were teenagers, fifteen to twenty years, no more than that, and so many of them, so many."

This was not the first serious fire at Kader's factory, but the third or fourth. "I heard some-body yelling 'fire, fire,' " Tumthong Podhirun testified, ". . . but I did not take it seriously because it has happened before. Soon I smelled smoke and very quickly it billowed inside the place. I headed for the back door but it was locked. . . . Finally, I had no choice but to join the others and jumped out of the window. I saw many of my friends lying dead on the ground beside me."[5]

In the aftermath of the tragedy, some Bangkok activists circulated an old snapshot of two smiling peasant girls standing arm in arm beside a thicket of palm trees. One of them, Praphai Prayonghorm, died in the 1993 fire at Kader. Her friend, Kammoin Konmanee, had died in the 1989 fire. Some of the Kader workers insisted afterwards that their factory had been haunted by ghosts, that it was built on the site of an old graveyard, disturbing the dead. The folklore expressed raw poetic truth: the fire in Bangkok eerily resembled the now-forgotten details of the Triangle Shirtwaist disaster eighty years before. Perhaps the "ghosts" that some workers felt present were young women from New York who had died in 1911.

Similar tragedies, large and small, were now commonplace across developing Asia and elsewhere. Two months after Kader, another fire at a Bangkok shirt factory killed ten women. Three months after Kader, a six-story hotel collapsed and killed 133 people, injuring 351. The embarrassed minister of industry ordered special inspections of 244 large factories in the Bangkok region and found that 60 percent of them had basic violations similar to Kader's. Thai industry was growing explosively—12 to 15 percent a year—but workplace injuries and illnesses were growing even faster, from 37,000 victims in 1987 to more than 150,000 by 1992 and an estimated 200,000 by 1994.

In China, six months after Kader, eighty-four women died and dozens of others were severely burned at another toy factory fire in the burgeoning industrial zone at Shenzhen. At Dongguan, a Hong Kong–owned raincoat factory burned in 1991, killing more than eighty people (Kader Industries also had a factory at Dongguan where two fires have been reported since 1990). In late 1993, some sixty women died at the Taiwanese-owned Gaofu textile plant in Fuzhou Province, many of them smothered in their dormitory beds by toxic fumes from burning textiles. In 1994, a shoe factory fire killed ten persons at Jiangmen; a textile factory fire killed thirty-eight and injured 160 at the Qianshan industrial zone.[6]

"Why must these tragedies repeat themselves again and again?" the *People's Daily* in Beijing asked. The official *Economic Daily* complained: "The way some of these foreign investors ignore international practice, ignore our own national rules, act completely lawlessly and immorally and lust after wealth is enough to make one's hair stand on end."[7]

America was itself no longer insulated from such brutalities. When a chicken-processing factory at Hamlet, North Carolina, caught fire in 1991, the exit doors there were also locked and twenty-five people died. A garment factory discovered by labor investigators in El Monte, California, held seventy-two Thai immigrants in virtual peonage, working eighteen hours a day in "sub-human conditions." One could not lament the deaths, harsh working conditions, child labor and subminimum wages in Thailand or across Asia and Central America without also recognizing that similar conditions have reappeared in the United States for roughly the same reasons.

Sweatshops, mainly in the garment industry, scandalized Los Angeles, New York and Dallas. The grim, foul assembly lines of the poultry-processing industry were spread across the rural South; the *Wall Street Journal's* Tony Horwitz won a Pulitzer Prize for his harrowing description of this low-wage work. "In general," the U.S. Government Accounting Office reported in 1994, "the description of today's sweatshops differs little from that at the turn of the century."[8]

That was the real mystery: Why did global commerce, with all of its supposed modernity and wondrous technologies, restore the old barbarisms that had long ago been forbidden by law? If the information age has enabled multinational corporations to manage production and marketing spread across continents, why were

their managers unable—or unwilling—to organize such mundane matters as fire prevention?

The short answer, of course, was profits, but the deeper answer was about power: Firms behaved this way because they could, because nobody would stop them. When law and social values retreated before the power of markets, then capitalism's natural drive to maximize returns had no internal governor to check its social behavior. When one enterprise took the low road to gain advantage, others would follow.

The toy fire in Bangkok provided a dramatic illustration for the much broader, less visible forms of human exploitation that were flourishing in the global system, including the widespread use of children in manufacturing, even forced labor camps in China or Burma. These matters were not a buried secret. Indeed, American television has aggressively exposed the "dark Satanic mills" with dramatic reports. ABCs *20/20* broadcast correspondent Lynn Sherr's devastating account of the Kader fire; CNN ran disturbing footage. Mike Wallace of CBS's *60 Minutes* exposed the prison labor exploited in China. NBC's *Dateline* did a piece on Wal-Mart's grim production in Bangladesh. CBS's *Street Stories* toured the shoe factories of Indonesia.

The baffling quality about modern communications was that its images could take us to people in remote corners of the world vividly and instantly, but these images have not as yet created genuine community with them. In terms of human consciousness, the "global village" was still only a picture on the TV screen.

Public opinion, moreover, absorbed contradictory messages about the global reality that were difficult to sort out. The opening stages of industrialization presented, as always, a great paradox: the process was profoundly liberating for millions, freeing them from material scarcity and limited life choices, while it also ensnared other millions in brutal new forms of domination. Both aspects were true, but there was no scale on which these opposing consequences could be easily balanced, since the good and ill effects were not usually apportioned among the same people. Some human beings were set free, while other lives were turned into cheap and expendable commodities.

Workers at Kader, for instance, earned about 100 baht a day for sewing and assembling dolls, the official minimum wage of $4, but the constant stream of new entrants meant that many at the factory actually worked for much less—only $2 or $3 a day—during a required "probationary" period of three to six months that was often extended much longer by the managers. Only one hundred of the three thousand workers at Kader were legally designated employees; the rest were "contract workers" without permanent rights and benefits, the same employment system now popularized in the United States.

"Lint, fabric, dust and animal hair filled the air on the production floor," the International Confederation of Free Trade Unions based in Brussels observed in its investigative report. "Noise, heat, congestion and fumes from various sources were reported by many. Dust control was nonexistent; protective equipment inadequate. Inhaling the dust created respiratory problems and contact with it caused skin diseases." A factory clinic dispensed antihistamines or other drugs and referred the more serious symptoms to outside hospitals. Workers paid for the medication themselves and were reimbursed, up to $6, only if they had contributed 10 baht a month to the company's health fund.

A common response to such facts, even from many sensitive people, was: yes, that was terrible, but wouldn't those workers be even worse off if civil standards were imposed on their employers since they might lose their jobs as a result? This was the same economic rationale offered by American manufacturers a century before to explain why American children must work in the coal mines and textile mills. U.S. industry had survived somehow (and, in fact, flourished) when child labor and the other malpractices were eventually prohibited by social reforms. Furthermore, it was not coincidence that industry always assigned the harshest conditions and lowest pay to the weakest members of a society—women, children, uprooted migrants. Whether the factory was in Thailand or the United States or Mexico's

maquiladora zone, people who were already quite powerless were less likely to resist, less able to demand decency from their employers.

Nor did these enterprises necessarily consist of small, struggling firms that could not afford to treat their workers better. Small sweatshops, it was true, were numerous in Thailand, and I saw some myself in a working-class neighborhood of Bangkok. Behind iron grillwork, children who looked to be ten to twelve years old squatted on the cement floors of the open-air shops, assembling suitcases, sewing raincoats, packing T-shirts. Across the street, a swarm of adolescents in blue smocks ate dinner at long tables outside a two-story building, then trooped back upstairs to the sewing machines.

Kader Holding Company, Ltd., however, was neither small nor struggling. It was a powerhouse of the global toy industry—headquartered in Hong Kong, incorporated in Bermuda, owned by a wealthy Hong Kong Chinese family named Ting that got its start after World War II making plastic goods and flashlights under procurement contracts from the U.S. military. Now Kader controlled a global maze of factories and interlocking subsidiaries in eight countries, from China and Thailand to Britain and the United States, where it owned Bachmann toys.[9]

After the fire Thai union members, intellectuals and middle-class activists from social rights organizations (the groups known in developing countries as nongovernmental organizations, or NGOs) formed the Committee to Support Kader Workers and began demanding justice from the employer. They sent a delegation to Hong Kong to confront Kader officials and investigate the complex corporate linkages of the enterprise. What they discovered was that Kader's partner in the Bangkok toy factory was actually a fabulously wealthy Thai family, the Chearavanonts, ethnic Chinese merchants who own the Charoen Pokphand Group, Thailand's own leading multinational corporation.

The CP Group owns farms, feed mills, real estate, air-conditioning and motorcycle factories, food-franchise chains—two hundred companies worldwide, several of them listed on the New

York Stock Exchange. The patriarch and chairman, Dhanin Chearavanont, was said by *Fortune* magazine to be the seventy-fifth richest man in the world, with personal assets of $2.6 billion (or 65 billion baht, as the *Bangkok Post* put it). Like the other emerging "Chinese multinationals," the Pokphand Group operates through the informal networks of kinfolk and ethnic contacts spread around the world by the Chinese diaspora, while it also participates in the more rigorous accounting systems of Western economies.

In the mother country, China, the conglomerate nurtured political-business alliances and has become the largest outside investor in new factories and joint ventures. In the United States, it maintained superb political connections. The Chearavanonts co-sponsored a much-heralded visit to Bangkok by ex-president George Bush, who delivered a speech before Thai business leaders in early 1994, eight months after the Kader fire. The price tag for Bush's appearance, according to the Bangkok press, was $400,000 (equivalent to one month's payroll for all three thousand workers at Kader). The day after Bush's appearance, the Chearavanonts hosted a banquet for a leading entrepreneur from China—Deng Xiaoping's daughter.[10]

The Pokphand Group at first denied any connection to the Kader fire, but reformers and local reporters dug out the facts of the family's involvement. Dhanin Chearavanont himself owned 11 percent of Honbo Investment Company and with relatives and corporate directors held majority control. Honbo, in turn, owned half of KCP Toys (KCP stood for Kader Charoen Pokphand), which, in turn, owned 80 percent of Kader Industrial (Thailand) Company. Armed with these facts, three hundred workers from the destroyed factory marched on the Pokphand Group's corporate tower on Silom Road, where they staged a gentle sit-down demonstration in the lobby, demanding just compensation for the victims.[11]

In the context of Thai society and politics, the workers' demonstration against Pokphand was itself extraordinary, like peasants confronting the nobility. Under continuing pressures from the support group, the company agreed to pay much larger compensation for victims and their families—$12,000 for each death, a trivial amount in American terms but more than double the Thai standard. "When we worked on Kader," said Professor Voravidh Charoenloet, an economist at Chulalongkorn University, "the government and local entrepreneurs and factory owners didn't want us to challenge these people; even the police tried to obstruct us from making an issue. We were accused of trying to destroy the country's reputation."

The settlement, in fact, required the Thai activists to halt their agitation and fall silent. "Once the extra compensation was paid," Voravidh explained, "we were forced to stop. One of the demands by the government was that everything should stop. Our organization had to accept it. We wanted to link with the international organizations and have a great boycott, but we had to cease."

The global boycott, he assumed, was going forward anyway because he knew that international labor groups like the ICFTU and the AFL-CIO had investigated the Kader fire and issued stinging denunciations. I told him that aside from organized labor, the rest of the world remained indifferent. There was no boycott of Kader toys in America. The professor slumped in his chair and was silent, a twisted expression on his face.

"I feel very bad," Voravidh said at last. "Maybe we should not have accepted it. But when we came away, we felt that was what we could accomplish. The people wanted more. There must be something more."

In the larger context, this tragedy was not explained by the arrogant power of one wealthy family or the elusive complexities of interlocking corporations. The Kader fire was ordained and organized by the free market itself. The toy industry—much like textiles and garments, shoes, electronics assembly and other low-wage sectors—existed (and thrived) by exploiting a crude ladder of desperate competition among the poorest nations. Its factories regularly hopped to new locations where wages were even lower, where the governments would be even more tolerant of abusive practices. The contract work assigned to foreign firms, including thousands of small sweatshops, fitted neatly into the systems of far-flung production of major brand names and distanced the capital owners from personal responsibility. The "virtual corporation" celebrated by some business futurists already existed in these sectors and, indeed, was now being emulated in some ways by advanced manufacturing—cars, aircraft, computers.

Over the last generation, toy manufacturers and others have moved around the Asian rim in search of the bottom-rung conditions: from Hong Kong, Korea and Taiwan to Thailand and Indonesia, from there to China, Vietnam and Bangladesh, perhaps on next to Burma, Nepal or Cambodia. Since the world had a nearly inexhaustible supply of poor people and supplicant governments, the market would keep driving in search of lower rungs; no one could say where the bottom was located. Industrial conditions were not getting better, as conventional theory assured the innocent consumers, but in many sectors were getting much worse. In America, the U.S. diplomatic opening to Vietnam was celebrated as progressive politics. In Southeast Asia, it merely opened another trapdoor beneath wages and working conditions.

A country like Thailand was caught in the middle: if it conscientiously tried to improve, it would pay a huge price. When Thai unions lobbied to win improvements in minimum-wage standards, textile plants began leaving for Vietnam and elsewhere or even importing cheaper "guest workers" from Burma. When China opened its fast-growing industrial zones in Shenzhen, Dongguan and other locations, the new competition had direct consequences on the factory floors of Bangkok.

Kader, according to the ICFTU, opened two new factories in Shekou and Dongguan where young people were working fourteen-hour days, seven days a week, to fill the U.S. Christmas orders for Mickey Mouse and other American dolls. Why should a company worry about sprinkler systems or fire escapes for a dusty factory in Bangkok when it could hire brand-new workers in China for only $20 a month, one fifth of the labor cost in Thailand?

The ICFTU report described the market forces: "The lower cost of production of toys in China changes the investment climate for countries like Thailand. Thailand competes with China to attract investment capital for local toy production. With this development, Thailand has become sadly lax in enforcing its own legislation. It turns a blind eye to health violations, thus allowing factory owners to ignore safety standards. Since China entered the picture, accidents in Thailand have nearly tripled."

The Thai minister of industry, Sanan Kachornprasart, described the market reality more succinctly: "If we punish them, who will want to invest here?" Thai authorities subsequently filed charges against three Kader factory managers, but none against the company itself nor, of course, the Chearavanont family.[12]

In the aftermath, a deputy managing director of Kader Industrial, Pichet Laokasem, entered a Buddhist monastery "to make merit for the fire victims," *The Nation* of Bangkok reported. Pichet told reporters he would serve as a monk until he felt better emotionally. "Most of the families affected by the fire lost only a loved one," he explained. "I lost nearly two hundred of my workers all at once."

The fire in Bangkok reflected the amorality of the marketplace when it has been freed of social obligations. But the tragedy also mocked the moral claims of three great religions, whose adherents were all implicated. Thais built splendid golden temples exalting Buddha, who taught them to put spiritual being before material wealth. Chinese claimed to have acquired superior social values, reverence for family and community, derived from the teachings of Confucius. Americans bought the toys from Asia to celebrate the birth of Jesus Christ. Their shared complicity was another of the strange convergences made possible by global commerce. . . .

In the modern industrial world, only the ignorant can pretend to self-righteousness since only the primitive are truly innocent. No advanced society has reached that lofty stage without enduring barbaric consequences and despoliation along the way; no one who enjoys the uses of electricity or the internal combustion engine may claim to oppose industrialization for others without indulging in imperious hypocrisy.

Americans, one may recall, built their early national infrastructure and organized large-scale agriculture with slave labor. The developing American nation swept native populations from their ancient lands and drained the swampy prairies to grow grain. It burned forests to make farmland, decimated wildlife, dammed the wild rivers and displaced people who were in the way. It assigned the dirtiest, most dangerous work to immigrants and children. It eventually granted political rights to all, but grudgingly and only after great conflicts, including a terrible civil war.

The actual history of nations is useful to remember when trying to form judgments about the new world. Asian leaders regularly remind Americans and Europeans of exactly how the richest nation-states became wealthy and observe further that, despite their great wealth, those countries have not perfected social relations among rich and poor, weak and powerful. The maldistribution of incomes is worsening in America, too, not yet as extreme as Thailand's, but worse than many less fortunate nations.

Hypocrisies run the other way, too, however. The fashionable pose among some leaders in developing Asia is to lecture the West on its decadent ways and hold up "Asian values" as morally superior, as well as more productive. If their cultural claims sound plausible at a distance, they seem less noble, even duplicitous up close. The Asian societies' supposed reverence for family, for instance, is expressed in the "dark Satanic mills" where the women and children are sent to work. "Family" and "social order" are often mere euphemisms for hierarchy and domination. A system that depends upon rigid control from above or the rank exploitation of weaker groups is not about values, but about power. Nothing distinctive about that. Human societies have struggled to overcome those conditions for centuries.

My point is that any prospect of developing a common global social consciousness will inevi-

tably force people to reexamine themselves first and come to terms with the contradictions and hypocrisies in their own national histories. Americans, in particular, are not especially equipped for that exercise. A distinguished historian, Lawrence Goodwyn of Duke University, once said to me in frustration: You cannot teach American history to American students. You can teach the iconic version, he said, that portrays America as beautiful and unblemished or you can teach a radical version that demonizes the country. But American culture does not equip young people to deal with the "irreconcilable conflicts" embedded in their own history, the past that does not yield to patriotic moralisms. "Race is the most obvious example of what I mean," he said.

Coming to terms with one's own history ought not only to induce a degree of humility toward others and their struggles, but also to clarify what one really believes about human society. No one can undo the past, but that does not relieve people of the burden of making judgments about the living present or facing up to its moral implications. If the global system has truly created a unified marketplace, then every worker, every consumer, every society is already connected to the other. The responsibility exists and invoking history is not an excuse to hide from the new social questions.

Just as Americans cannot claim a higher morality while benefiting from inhumane exploitation, neither can developing countries pretend to become modern "one world" producers and expect exemption from the world's social values. Neither can the global enterprises. The future asks: Can capitalism itself be altered and reformed? Or is the world doomed to keep renewing these inhumanities in the name of economic progress?

The proposition that human dignity is indivisible does not suppose that everyone will become equal or alike or perfectly content in his or her circumstances. It does insist that certain well-understood social principles exist internationally which are enforceable and ought to be the price of admission in the global system. The idea is very simple: every person—man, woman and child—regardless of where he or she exists in time and place or on the chain of economic development, is entitled to respect as an individual being.

For many in the world, life itself is all that they possess; an economic program that deprives them of life's precious possibilities is not only unjust, but also utterly unnecessary. Peasants may not become kings, but they are entitled to be treated with decent regard for their sentient and moral beings, not as cheap commodities. Newly industrialized nations cannot change social patterns overnight, any more than the advanced economies did before them, but they can demonstrate that they are changing.

This proposition is invasive, no question, and will disturb the economic and political arrangements within many societies. But every nation has a sovereign choice in this matter, the sort of choice made in the marketplace every day. If Thailand or China resents the intrusion of global social standards, it does not have to sell its toys to America. And Americans do not have to buy them. If Singapore rejects the idea of basic rights for women, then women in America or Europe may reject Singapore—and multinational firms that profit from the subordination of women. If people do not assert these values in global trade, then their own convictions will be steadily coarsened.

In Bangkok, when I asked Professor Voravidh to step back from Thailand's problems and suggest a broader remedy, he thought for a long time and then said: "We need cooperation among nations because the multinational corporations can shift from one country to another. If they don't like Thailand, they move to Vietnam or China. Right now, we are all competing and the world is getting worse. We need a GATT on labor conditions and on the minimum wage, we need a standard on the minimum conditions for work and a higher standard for children."

The most direct approach, as Voravidh suggested, is an international agreement to incorporate such standards in the terms of trade, with penalties and incentives, even temporary embar-

goes, that will impose social obligations on the global system, the firms and countries. Most of the leading governments, including the United States, have long claimed to support this idea—a so-called social clause for GATT—but the practical reality is that they do not. Aside from rhetoric, when their negotiators are at the table, they always yield readily to objections from the multinational corporations and developing nations. Both the firms and the governing elites of poor countries have a strong incentive to block the proposition since both profit from a free-running system that exploits the weak. A countering force has to come from concerned citizens. Governments refuse to act, but voters and consumers are not impotent, and, in the meantime, they can begin the political campaign by purposefully targeting the producers—boycotting especially the well-known brand names that depend upon lovable images for their sales. Americans will not stop buying toys at Christmas, but they might single out one or two American toy companies for Yuletide boycotts, based on their scandalous relations with Kader and other manufacturers. Boycotts are difficult to organize and sustain, but every one of the consumer-goods companies is exquisitely vulnerable.

In India, the South Asian Coalition on Child Servitude, led by Kailash Satyarthi, has created a promising model for how to connect the social obligations of consumers and workers. Indian carpet makers are notorious for using small children at their looms—bonded children like Thailand's bonded prostitutes—and have always claimed economic necessity. India is a poor nation and the work gives wage income to extremely poor families, they insist. But these children will never escape poverty if they are deprived of schooling, the compulsory education promised by law.

The reformers created a "no child labor" label that certifies the rugs were made under honorable conditions and they persuaded major importers in Germany to insist upon the label. The exporters in India, in turn, have to allow regular citizen inspections of their workplaces to win the label for their rugs. Since this consumer-led certification system began, the carpet industry's use of children has fallen dramatically. A Textile Ministry official in New Delhi said: "The government is now contemplating the total eradication of child labor in the next few years."[13]

Toys, shoes, electronics, garments—many consumer sectors are vulnerable to similar approaches, though obviously the scope of manufacturing is too diverse and complex for consumers to police it. Governments have to act collectively. If a worldwide agreement is impossible to achieve, then groups of governments can form their own preferential trading systems, introducing social standards that reverse the incentives for developing countries and for capital choosing new locations for production.

The crucial point illustrated by Thailand's predicament is that global social standards will help the poorer countries escape their economic trap. Until a floor is built beneath the market's social behavior, there is no way that a small developing country like Thailand can hope to overcome the downward pull of competition from other, poorer nations. It must debase its citizens to hold on to what it has achieved. The path to improvement is blocked by the economics of an irresponsible marketplace.

Setting standards will undoubtedly slow down the easy movement of capital—and close down the most scandalous operations—but that is not a harmful consequence for people in struggling nations that aspire to industrial prosperity or for a global economy burdened with surpluses and inadequate consumption. When global capital makes a commitment to a developing economy, it ought not to acquire the power to blackmail that nation in perpetuity. Supported by global rules, those nations can begin to improve conditions and stabilize their own social development. At least they would have a chance to avoid the great class conflicts that others have experienced.

In the meantime, the very least that citizens can demand of their own government is that it no longer use public money to finance the brutal upheavals or environmental despoliation that have flowed from large-scale projects of the World Bank and other lending agencies. The so-cial distress in the cities begins in the countryside, and the wealthy nations have often financed it in the name of aiding development. The World Bank repeatedly proclaims its new commitment to strategies that address the development ideas of indigenous peoples and halt the destruction of natural systems. But social critics and the people I encountered in Thailand and elsewhere have not seen much evidence of real change.

The terms of trade are usually thought of as commercial agreements, but they are also an implicit statement of moral values. In its present terms, the global system values property over human life. When a nation like China steals the property of capital, pirating copyrights, films or technology, other governments will take action to stop it and be willing to impose sanctions and penalty tariffs on the offending nation's trade. When human lives are stolen in the "dark Satanic mills," nothing happens to the offenders since, according to the free market's sense of conscience, there is no crime.

NOTES

1. William Blake's immortal lines are from "Milton," one of his "prophetic books" written between 1804 and 1808. *The Portable Blake,* Alfred Kazin, editor (New York: Penguin Books, 1976).

2. *Washington Post, Financial Times* and *New York Times,* May 12, 1993, and *Wall Street Journal,* May 13, 1993.

3. The U.S. contract clients for Kader's Bangkok factory were cited by the International Confederation of Free Trade Unions headquartered in Brussels in its investigatory report, "From the Ashes: A Toy Factory Fire in Thailand," December 1994. In the aftermath, the ICFTU and some nongovernmental organizations attempted to mount an "international toy campaign" and a few sporadic demonstrations occurred in Hong Kong and London, but there never was a general boycott of the industry or any of its individual companies. The labor federation met with associations of British and American toy manufacturers and urged them to adopt a "code of conduct" that might discourage the abuses. The proposed codes were inadequate, the ICFTU acknowledged, but it was optimistic about their general adoption by the international industry.

4. Mitchell Zuckoff of the *Boston Globe* produced a powerful series of stories on labor conditions in developing Asia and reported Hasbro's reaction to the Kader fire, July 10, 1994. David Miller was quoted in *USA Today*, May 13, 1993, and on ABC News *20/20*, July 30, 1993.

5. The first-person descriptions of the Kader fire are but a small sampling from survivors' horrifying accounts, collected by investigators and reporters at the scene. My account of the disaster is especially indebted to the investigative report by the International Confederation of Free Trade Unions; Bangkok's English-language newspapers, the *Post* and *The Nation;* the Asia Monitor Resource Center of Hong Kong; and Lynn Sherr's devastating report on ABCs *20/20*, July 30, 1993. Lampan Taptim and Tumthong Podhirun, "From the Ashes," ICFTU, December 1994; Cheng: *Asian Labour Update*, Asia Monitor Resource Center, Hong Kong, July 1993; La-iad Nads-nguen: *The Nation*, Bangkok, May 12, 1993; and Chaweewan Mekpan: *20/20*.

6. Details on Thailand's worker injuries and the litany of fires in China are from the ICFTU report and other labor bulletins, as well as interviews in Bangkok.

7. The *People's Daily* and *Economic Daily* were quoted by Andrew Quinn of Reuters in *The Daily Citizen* of Washington, DC, January 18, 1994.

8. Tony Horwitz described chicken-processing employment as the second fastest growing manufacturing job in America: *Wall Street Journal*, December 1, 1994. U.S. sweatshops were reviewed in "Garment Industry: Efforts to Address the Prevalence and Conditions of Sweatshops," U.S. Government Accounting Office, November 1994.

9. Corporate details on Kader are from the ICFTU and the Asia Monitor Resource Center's *Asian Labour Update*, July 1993.

10. Dhanin Chearavanont's wealth: *Bangkok Post*, June 15, 1993; Pokphand Group ventures in China and elsewhere: *Far Eastern Economic Review*, October 21, 1993; George Bush's appearance in Bangkok: *Bangkok Post*, January 22, 1994. The dinner for Deng's daughter, Deng Nan, was reported in *The Nation*, Bangkok, January 28, 1994.

11. The complex structure of ownership was used to deflect corporate responsibility. Kader's Kenneth Ting protested after the fire that his family's firm owned only a 40 percent stake in the Thai factory, but people blamed them "because we have our name on it. That's the whole problem." The lesson, he said, was to "never lend your name or logo to any company if you don't have managing control in the company." That lesson, of course, contradicted the basic structure of how the global toy industry was organized: *Bangkok Post*, May 17, 1993. The chain of ownership was reported in several places, including *The Nation* of Bangkok, May 28, 1993. Details of the Kader workers' sit-in: *Bangkok Post*, July 13, 1993.

12. Sanan was quoted in the *Bangkok Post*, May 29, 1993.

13. The New Delhi–based campaign against child labor in the carpet industry is admittedly limited to a narrow market and expensive product, but its essential value is demonstrating how retailers and their customers can be connected to a distant factory floor. See, for instance, Hugh Williamson, "Stamp of Approval," *Far Eastern Economic Review*, February 2, 1995, and N. Vasuk Rao in the *Journal of Commerce*, March 1, 1995.

THINKING ABOUT THE READING

Greider argues that the tragedy of the Kader industrial fire cannot be explained simply by focusing on greedy families and multinational corporations. Instead, he blames global economics and the organization of the international toy industry. He writes, "The Kader fire was ordained and organized by the free market itself." What do you suppose he means by this? Given the enormous economic pressures that this and other multinational industries operate under, are such tragedies inevitable? Why have attempts to improve the working conditions in Third World factories been so ineffective?

CHAPTER 11

The Architecture of Disadvantage: Poverty and Wealth

It is impossible to fully examine the American stratification system without addressing the plight of those at the bottom. Despite the much publicized economic recovery of the late 1990s, poverty continues to be a large and, in many cases, deadly social problem. The face of American poverty has changed somewhat over the past several decades. The economic status of single mothers and their children has deteriorated while that of people over age 65 has improved somewhat.

What hasn't changed is the ever widening gap between the rich and the poor. Poverty persists because in a free-market and competitive society it serves economic and social functions. In addition, poverty receives institutional "support" in the form of segmented labor markets and inadequate educational systems. The ideology of competitive individualism—that to succeed in life all one has to do is work hard and win in competition with others—creates a belief that poor people are to blame for their own suffering. So although the problem of poverty remains serious, worse, public attitudes toward poverty and poor people are frequently indifferent or even hostile. Furthermore, important social institutions can perpetuate the problem.

In "Savage Inequalities in Americas Schools," Jonathan Kozol provides a troubling portrait of inequality in the American educational system by comparing the school experiences of children in two very different cities. Although the children of destitute East St. Louis, Illinois, and affluent Rye, New York, are citizens of the same country, they live in two very different worlds. Kozol draws compelling contrasts between the broken-down classrooms, outdated textbooks, and faulty plumbing in East St. Louis and the sparkling new auditoriums and up-to-date computers in Rye. These vastly different educational experiences make it difficult to sustain the myth that all children, no matter where they live, are competing in a fair race for society's resources.

We hear a lot of talk these days about the need to reduce "welfare dependency" in this country. In 1996, President Clinton signed into law an unprecedented welfare reform bill designed to reduce poor people's reliance on government aid and to "end welfare as we know it." The new welfare system includes, among other things, a mandatory work requirement after 2 years of receiving assistance (or enrollment in vocational training or community service) and a 5-year lifetime limit to benefits for any family. Kathryn Edin and Laura Lein, in "Making Ends Meet," describe the precarious economic experiences of poor single mothers as they face hardships and devise strategies to survive. Although they collected their data *before* federal welfare reforms went into effect, Edin and Lein show persuasively that most poor single mothers want to work and want to be off welfare. But these mothers are hard-pressed to find a job that pays a wage which can support them and their children. They are frequently forced to choose between the need to be with their children and the need to earn money, a choice often made with the knowledge that getting off welfare has some potentially serious costs.

Savage Inequalities in America's Schools

Life on the Mississippi: East St. Louis, Illinois

Jonathan Kozol

"East of anywhere," writes a reporter for the *St. Louis Post-Dispatch*, "often evokes the other side of the tracks. But, for a first-time visitor suddenly deposited on its eerily empty streets, East St. Louis might suggest another world." The city, which is 98 percent black, has no obstetric services, no regular trash collection, and few jobs. Nearly a third of its families live on less than $7,500 a year; 75 percent of its population lives on welfare of some form. The U.S. Department of Housing and Urban Development describes it as "the most distressed small city in America."

Only three of the 13 buildings on Missouri Avenue, one of the city's major thoroughfares, are occupied. A 13-story office building, tallest in the city, has been boarded up. Outside, on the sidewalk, a pile of garbage fills a ten-foot crater.

The city, which by night and day is clouded by the fumes that pour from vents and smoke-stacks at the Pfizer and Monsanto chemical plants, has one of the highest rates of child asthma in America.

It is, according to a teacher at the University of Southern Illinois, "a repository for a nonwhite population that is now regarded as expendable." The *Post-Dispatch* describes it as "America's Soweto."

Fiscal shortages have forced the layoff of 1,170 of the city's 1,400 employees in the past 12 years. The city, which is often unable to buy heating fuel or toilet paper for the city hall, recently announced that it might have to cashier all but 10 percent of the remaining work force of 230. In 1989 the mayor announced that he might need to sell the city hall and all six fire stations to raise needed cash. Last year the plan had to be scrapped after the city lost its city hall in a court judgment to a creditor. East St. Louis is mortgaged into the next century but has the highest property-tax rate in the state.

Since October 1987, when the city's garbage pickups ceased, the backyards of residents have been employed as dump sites. In the spring of 1988 a policeman tells a visitor that 40 plastic bags of trash are waiting for removal from the back-yard of his mother's house. Public health officials are concerned the garbage will attract a plague of flies and rodents in the summer. The policeman speaks of "rats as big as puppies" in his mother's yard. They are known to the residents, he says, as "bull rats." Many people have no cars or funds to cart the trash and simply burn it in their yards. The odor of smoke from burning garbage, says the *Post-Dispatch*, "has become one of the scents of spring" in East St. Louis.

Railroad tracks still used to transport hazardous chemicals run through the city. "Always present," says the *Post-Dispatch*, "is the threat of chemical spills. . . . The wail of sirens warning residents to evacuate after a spill is common." The most recent spill, the paper says, "was at the Monsanto Company plant. . . . Nearly 300 gallons of phosphorous trichloride spilled when a railroad tank was overfilled. About 450 residents were taken to St. Mary's Hospital. . . . The frequency of the emergencies has caused Monsanto to have a 'standing account' at St. Mary's." . . .

The dangers of exposure to raw sewage, which backs up repeatedly into the homes of residents in East St. Louis, were first noticed, in the spring of 1989, at a public housing project, Villa Griffin. Raw sewage, says the *Post-Dispatch*, overflowed into a playground just behind the housing project, which is home to 187 children, "forming an oozing lake of . . . tainted water." Two schoolgirls, we are told, "experienced hair loss since raw sewage flowed into their homes."

While local physicians are not certain whether loss of hair is caused by the raw sewage, they have issued warnings that exposure to raw sewage can provoke a cholera or hepatitis outbreak. A St. Louis health official voices her dismay that children live with waste in their backyards. "The development of working sewage systems made cities livable a hundred years ago," she notes. "Sewage systems separate us from the Third World."

The sewage, which is flowing from collapsed pipes and dysfunctional pumping stations, has also flooded basements all over the city. The city's vacuum truck, which uses water and suction to unclog the city's sewers, cannot be used because it needs $5,000 in repairs. Even when it works, it sometimes can't be used because there isn't money to hire drivers. A single engineer now does the work that 14 others did before they were laid off. By April the pool of overflow behind the Villa Griffin project has expanded into a lagoon of sewage. Two million gallons of raw sewage lie outside the children's homes. . . .

The Daughters of Charity, whose works of mercy are well known in the Third World, operate a mission at the Villa Griffin homes. On an afternoon in early spring of 1990, Sister Julia Huiskamp meets me on King Boulevard and drives me to the Griffin homes.

As we ride past blocks and blocks of skeletal structures, some of which are still inhabited, she slows the car repeatedly at railroad crossings. A seemingly endless railroad train rolls past us to the right. On the left: a blackened lot where garbage has been burning. Next to the burning garbage is a row of 12 white cabins, charred by fire. Next: a lot that holds a heap of auto tires and a mountain of tin cans. More burnt houses. More trash fires. The train moves almost imperceptibly across the flatness of the land.

Fifty years old, and wearing a blue suit, white blouse, and blue head-cover, Sister Julia points to the nicest house in sight. The sign on the front reads MOTEL. "It's a whorehouse," Sister Julia says.

When she slows the car beside a group of teen-age boys, one of them steps out toward the car, then backs away as she is recognized.

The 99 units of the Villa Griffin homes—two-story structures, brick on the first floor, yellow wood above—form one border of a recessed park and playground that were filled with fecal matter last year when the sewage mains exploded. The sewage is gone now and the grass is very green and looks inviting. When nine-year-old Serena and her seven-year-old brother take me for a walk, however, I discover that our shoes sink into what is still a sewage marsh. An inch-deep residue of fouled water still remains.

Serena's brother is a handsome, joyous little boy, but troublingly thin. Three other children join us as we walk along the marsh: Smokey, who is nine years old but cannot yet tell time; Mickey, who is seven; and a tiny child with a ponytail and big brown eyes who talks a constant stream of words that I can't always understand.

"Hush, Little Sister," says Serena. I ask for her name, but "Little Sister" is the only name the children seem to know.

"There go my cousins," Smokey says, pointing to two teen-age girls above us on the hill.

The day is warm, although we're only in the second week of March; several dogs and cats are playing by the edges of the marsh. "It's a lot of squirrels here," says Smokey. "There go one!"

"This here squirrel is a friend of mine," says Little Sister.

None of the children can tell me the approximate time that school begins. One says five o'clock. One says six. Another says that school begins at noon.

When I ask what song they sing after the flag pledge, one says "Jingle Bells."

Smokey cannot decide if he is in the second or third grade.

Seven-year-old Mickey sucks his thumb during the walk.

The children regale me with a chilling story as we stand beside the marsh. Smokey says his sister was raped and murdered and then dumped behind his school. Other children add more details: Smokey's sister was 11 years old. She was beaten with a brick until she died. The murder was committed by a man who knew her mother.

The narrative begins when, without warning, Smokey says, "My sister has got killed."

"She was my best friend," Serena says.

"They had beat her in the head and raped her," Smokey says.

"She was hollering out loud," says Little Sister.

I ask them when it happened. Smokey says, "Last year." Serena then corrects him and she says, "Last week."

"It scared me because I had to cry," says Little Sister.

"The police arrested one man but they didn't catch the other," Smokey says.

Serena says, "He was some kin to her."

But Smokey objects, "He weren't no kin to me. He was my momma's friend."

"Her face was busted," Little Sister says.

Serena describes this sequence of events: "They told her go behind the school. They'll give her a quarter if she do. Then they knock her down and told her not to tell what they had did."

I ask, "Why did they kill her?"

"They was scared that she would tell," Serena says.

"One is in jail," says Smokey. "They can't find the other."

"Instead of raping little bitty children, they should find themselves a wife," says Little Sister.

"I hope," Serena says, "her spirit will come back and get that man."

"And *kill* that man," says Little Sister.

"Give her another chance to live," Serena says.

"My teacher came to the funeral," says Smokey.

"When a little child dies, my momma say a star go straight to Heaven," says Serena.

"My grandma was murdered," Mickey says out of the blue. "Somebody shot two bullets in her head."

I ask him, "Is she really dead?"

"She dead all right," says Mickey. "She was layin' there, just dead."

"I love my friends," Serena says. "I don't care if they no kin to me. I care for them. I hope his mother have another baby. Name her for my friend that's dead."

"I have a cat with three legs," Smokey says.

"Snakes hate rabbits," Mickey says, again for no apparent reason.

"Cats hate fishes," Little Sister says.

"It's a lot of hate," says Smokey.

Later, at the mission, Sister Julia tells me this: "The Jefferson School, which they attend, is a decrepit hulk. Next to it is a modern school, erected two years ago, which was to have replaced the one that they attend. But the construction was not done correctly. The roof is too heavy for the walls, and the entire structure has begun to sink. It can't be occupied. Smokey's sister was raped and murdered and dumped between the old school and the new one."

As the children drift back to their homes for supper, Sister Julia stands outside with me and talks about the health concerns that trouble people in the neighborhood. In the setting sun, the voices of the children fill the evening air. Nourished by the sewage marsh, a field of wild daffodils is blooming. Standing here, you wouldn't think that anything was wrong. The street is calm. The poison in the soil can't be seen. The sewage is invisible and only makes the grass a little greener. Bikes thrown down by children lie outside their kitchen doors. It could be an ordinary twilight in a small suburban town.

Night comes on and Sister Julia goes inside to telephone a cab. In another hour, the St. Louis taxis will not come into the neighborhood. . . .

East St. Louis—which the local press refers to as "an inner city without an outer city"—has some of the sickest children in America. Of 66 cities in Illinois, East St. Louis ranks first in fetal death, first in premature birth, and third in infant death. Among the negative factors listed by the city's health director are the sewage running in the streets, air that has been fouled by the local plants, the high lead levels noted in the soil, poverty, lack of education, crime, dilapidated housing, insufficient health care, unemployment. Hospital care is deficient too. There is no place to have a baby in East St. Louis. The maternity ward at the city's Catholic hospital, a 100-year-old structure, was shut down some years ago. The only other hospital in town was forced by lack of funds to close in 1990. The closest obstetrics service open to the women here is seven miles away. The infant death rate is still rising.

As in New York City's poorest neighborhoods, dental problems also plague the children here. Although dental problems don't command the instant fears associated with low birth weight, fetal death or cholera, they do have the consequence of wearing down the stamina of children and defeating their ambitions. Bleeding gums, impacted teeth and rotting teeth are routine matters for the children I have interviewed in the South Bronx. Children get used to feeling constant pain. They go to sleep with it. They go to school with it. Sometimes their teachers are alarmed and try to get them to a clinic. But it's all so slow and heavily encumbered with red tape and waiting lists and missing, lost or canceled welfare cards, that dental care is often delayed. Children live for months with pain that grown-ups would find unendurable. The gradual attrition of accepted pain erodes their energy and aspiration. I have seen children in New York with teeth that look like brownish, broken sticks. I have also seen teenagers who were missing half their teeth. But, to me, most shocking is to see a child with an abscess that has been inflamed for weeks and that he has simply lived with and accepts as part of the routine of life. Many teachers in the urban schools have seen this. It is almost commonplace.

Compounding these problems is the poor nutrition of the children here—average daily food expenditure in East St. Louis is $2.40 for one child—and the underimmunization of young children. Of every 100 children recently surveyed in East St. Louis, 55 were incompletely immunized for polio, diphtheria, measles and whooping cough. In this context, health officials look with all the more uneasiness at those lagoons of sewage outside public housing.

On top of all else is the very high risk of death by homicide in East St. Louis. In a recent year in which three cities in the state of roughly the same size as East St. Louis had an average of four homicides apiece, there were 54 homicides in

East St. Louis. But it is the heat of summer that officials here particularly dread. The heat that breeds the insects bearing polio or hepatitis in raw sewage also heightens asthma and frustration and reduces patience. "The heat," says a man in public housing, "can bring out the beast...."

The fear of violence is very real in East St. Louis. The CEO of one of the large companies out on the edge of town has developed an "evacuation plan" for his employees. State troopers are routinely sent to East St. Louis to put down disturbances that the police cannot control. If the misery of this community explodes someday in a real riot (it has happened in the past), residents believe that state and federal law-enforcement agencies will have no hesitation in applying massive force to keep the violence contained....

The problems of the streets in urban areas, as teachers often note, frequently spill over into public schools. In the public schools of East St. Louis this is literally the case.

"Martin Luther King Junior High School," notes the *Post-Dispatch* in a story published in the early spring of 1989, "was evacuated Friday afternoon after sewage flowed into the kitchen.... The kitchen was closed and students were sent home." On Monday, the paper continues, "East St. Louis Senior High School was awash in sewage for the second time this year." The school had to be shut because of "fumes and backed-up toilets." Sewage flowed into the basement, through the floor, then up into the kitchen and the students' bathrooms. The backup, we read, "occurred in the food preparation areas."

School is resumed the following morning at the high school, but a few days later the overflow recurs. This time the entire system is affected, since the meals distributed to every student in the city are prepared in the two schools that have been flooded. School is called off for all 16,500 students in the district. The sewage backup, caused by the failure of two pumping stations, forces officials at the high school to shut down the furnaces.

At Martin Luther King, the parking lot and gym are also flooded. "It's a disaster," says a legislator. "The streets are underwater; gaseous fumes are being emitted from the pipes under the schools," she says, "making people ill."

In the same week, the schools announce the layoff of 280 teachers, 166 cooks and cafeteria workers, 25 teacher aides, 16 custodians and 18 painters, electricians, engineers and plumbers. The president of the teachers' union says the cuts, which will bring the size of kindergarten and primary classes up to 30 students, and the size of fourth to twelfth grade classes up to 35, will have "an unimaginable impact" on the students. "If you have a high school teacher with five classes each day and between 150 and 175 students . . . , it's going to have a devastating effect." The school system, it is also noted, has been using more than 70 "permanent substitute teachers," who are paid only $10,000 yearly, as a way of saving money.

Governor Thompson, however, tells the press that he will not pour money into East St. Louis to solve long-term problems. East St. Louis residents, he says, must help themselves. "There is money in the community," the governor insists. "It's just not being spent for what it should be spent for."

The governor, while acknowledging that East St. Louis faces economic problems, nonetheless refers dismissively to those who live in East St. Louis. "What in the community," he asks, "is being done right?" He takes the opportunity of a visit to the area to announce a fiscal grant for sewer improvement to a relatively wealthy town nearby.

In East St. Louis, meanwhile, teachers are running out of chalk and paper, and their paychecks are arriving two weeks late. The city warns its teachers to expect a cut of half their pay until the fiscal crisis has been eased.

The threatened teacher layoffs are mandated by the Illinois Board of Education, which, because of the city's fiscal crisis, has been given supervisory control of the school budget. Two weeks later the state superintendent partially relents. In a tone very different from that of the governor, he notes that East St. Louis does not

have the means to solve its education problems on its own. "There is no natural way," he says, that "East St. Louis can bring itself out of this situation." Several cuts will be required in any case—one quarter of the system's teachers, 75 teacher aides, and several dozen others will be given notice—but, the state board notes, sports and music programs will not be affected.

East St. Louis, says the chairman of the state board, "is simply the worst possible place I can imagine to have a child brought up. . . . The community is in desperate circumstances." Sports and music, he observes, are, for many children here, "the only avenues of success." Sadly enough, no matter how it ratifies the stereotype, this is the truth; and there is a poignant aspect to the fact that, even with class size soaring and one quarter of the system's teachers being given their dismissal, the state board of education demonstrates its genuine but skewed compassion by attempting to leave sports and music untouched by the overall austerity.

Even sports facilities, however, are degrading by comparison with those found and expected at most high schools in America. The football field at East St. Louis High is missing almost everything—including goalposts. There are a couple of metal pipes—no crossbar, just the pipes. Bob Shannon, the football coach, who has to use his personal funds to purchase footballs and has had to cut and rake the football field himself, has dreams of having goalposts someday. He'd also like to let his students have new uniforms. The ones they wear are nine years old and held together somehow by a patchwork of repairs. Keeping them clean is a problem, too. The school cannot afford a washing machine. The uniforms are carted to a corner laundromat with fifteen dollars' worth of quarters. . . .

In the wing of the school that holds vocational classes, a damp, unpleasant odor fills the halls. The school has a machine shop, which cannot be used for lack of staff, and a woodworking shop. The only shop that's occupied this morning is the auto-body class. A man with long blond hair and wearing a white sweat suit swings a paddle to get children in their chairs. "What we need the most is new equipment," he reports. "I have equipment for alignment, for example, but we don't have money to install it. We also need a better form of egress. We bring the cars in through two other classes." Computerized equipment used in most repair shops, he reports, is far beyond the high school's budget. It looks like a very old gas station in an isolated rural town.

The science labs at East St. Louis High are 30 to 50 years outdated. John McMillan, a soft-spoken man, teaches physics at the school. He shows me his lab. The six lab stations in the room have empty holes where pipes were once attached. "It would be great if we had water," says McMillan. . . .

Leaving the chemistry labs, I pass a double-sized classroom in which roughly 60 kids are sitting fairly still but doing nothing. "This is supervised study hall," a teacher tells me in the corridor. But when we step inside, he finds there is no teacher. "The teacher must be out today," he says.

Irl Solomon's history classes, which I visit next, have been described by journalists who cover East St. Louis as the highlight of the school. Solomon, a man of 54 whose reddish hair is turning white, has taught in urban schools for almost 30 years. A graduate of Brandeis University in 1961, he entered law school but was drawn away by a concern with civil rights. "After one semester, I decided that the law was not for me. I said, 'Go and find the toughest place there is to teach. See if you like it.' I'm still here. . . ."

Teachers like Mr. Solomon, working in low-income districts such as East St. Louis, often tell me that they feel cut off from educational developments in modern public schools. "Well, it's amazing," Solomon says. "I have done without so much so long that, if I were assigned to a suburban school, I'm not sure I'd recognize what they are doing. We are utterly cut off."

"Very little education in the school would be considered academic in the suburbs. Maybe 10 to 15 percent of students are in truly academic programs. Of the 55 percent who graduate, 20 percent may go to four-year colleges: something like 10 percent of any entering class. Another 10 to 20 percent may get some other kind of higher education. An equal number join the military. . . .

"Sometimes I get worried that I'm starting to burn out. Still, I hate to miss a day. The department frequently can't find a substitute to come here, and my kids don't like me to be absent."

Solomon's advanced class, which soon comes into the room, includes some lively students with strong views.

"I don't go to physics class, because my lab has no equipment," says one student. "The typewriters in my typing class don't work. The women's toilets. . . ." She makes a sour face. "I'll be honest," she says. "I just don't use the toilets. If I do, I come back into class and I feel dirty."

"I wanted to study Latin," says another student. "But we don't have Latin in this school."

"We lost our only Latin teacher," Solomon says.

A girl in a white jersey with the message DO THE RIGHT THING on the front raises her hand. "You visit other schools," she says. "Do you think the children in this school are getting what we'd get in a nice section of St. Louis?"

I note that we are in a different state and city.

"Are we citizens of East St. Louis or America?" she asks. . . .

Clark Junior High School is regarded as the top school in the city. I visit, in part, at the request of school officials, who would like me to see education in the city at its very best. Even here, however, there is a disturbing sense that one has entered a backwater of America.

"We spend the entire eighth grade year preparing for the state exams," a teacher tells me in a top-ranked English class. The teacher seems devoted to the children, but three students sitting near me sleep through the entire period. The teacher rouses one of them, a girl in the seat next to me, but the student promptly lays her head back on her crossed arms and is soon asleep again. Four of the 14 ceiling lights are broken. The corridor outside the room is filled with voices. Outside the window, where I see no schoolyard, is an empty lot.

In a mathematics class of 30 children packed into a space that might be adequate for 15 kids, there is one white student. The first white student I have seen in East St. Louis, she is polishing her nails with bright red polish. A tiny black girl next to her is writing with a one-inch pencil stub.

In a seventh grade social studies class, the only book that bears some relevance to black concerns—its title is *The American Negro*—bears a publication date of 1967. The teacher invites me to ask the class some questions. Uncertain where to start, I ask the students what they've learned about the civil rights campaigns of recent decades.

A 14-year-old girl with short black curly hair says this: "Every year in February we are told to read the same old speech of Martin Luther King. We read it every year. 'I have a dream. . . .' It does begin to seem—what is the word?" She hesitates and then she finds the word: "perfunctory."

I ask her what she means.

"We have a school in East St. Louis named for Dr. King," she says. "The school is full of sewer water and the doors are locked with chains. Every student in that school is black. It's like a terrible joke on history."

It startles me to hear her words, but I am startled even more to think how seldom any press reporter has observed the irony of naming segregated schools for Martin Luther King. Children reach the heart of these hypocrisies much quicker than the grown-ups and the experts do.

Public Education in New York

The train ride from Grand Central Station to suburban Rye, New York, takes 35 to 40 minutes. The high school is a short ride from the station. Built of handsome gray stone and set in a landscaped campus, it resembles a New England prep school. On a day in early June of 1990, I enter the school and am directed by a student to the office.

The principal, a relaxed, unhurried man who, unlike many urban principals, seems gratified to have me visit in his school, takes me in to see the auditorium, which, he says, was recently restored with private charitable funds ($400,000) raised by parents. The crenellated ceiling, which is white and spotless, and the polished dark-wood paneling contrast with the collapsing structure

of the auditorium at Morris High. The principal strikes his fist against the balcony: "They made this place extremely solid." Through a window, one can see the spreading branches of a beech tree in the central courtyard of the school.

In a student lounge, a dozen seniors are relaxing on a carpeted floor that is constructed with a number of tiers so that, as the principal explains, "they can stretch out and be comfortable while reading."

The library is wood-paneled, like the auditorium. Students, all of whom are white, are seated at private carrels, of which there are approximately 40. Some are doing homework; others are looking through the *New York Times*. Every student that I see during my visit to the school is white or Asian, though I later learn there are a number of Hispanic students and that 1 or 2 percent of students in the school are black.

According to the principal, the school has 96 computers for 546 children. The typical student, he says, studies a foreign language for four or five years, beginning in the junior high school, and a second foreign language (Latin is available) for two years. Of 140 seniors, 92 are now enrolled in AP classes. Maximum teacher salary will soon reach $70,000. Per-pupil funding is above $12,000 at the time I visit.

The students I meet include eleventh and twelfth graders. The teacher tells me that the class is reading Robert Coles, Studs Terkel, Alice Walker. He tells me I will find them more than willing to engage me in debate, and this turns out to be correct. Primed for my visit, it appears, they arrow in directly on the dual questions of equality and race.

Three general positions soon emerge and seem to be accepted widely. The first is that the fiscal inequalities "do matter very much" in shaping what a school can offer ("That is obvious," one student says) and that any loss of funds in Rye, as a potential consequence of future equalizing, would be damaging to many things the town regards as quite essential.

The second position is that racial integration—for example, by the busing of black children from the city or a nonwhite suburb to this school—would meet with strong resistance, and the reason would not simply be the fear that certain standards might decline. The reason, several students say straightforwardly, is "racial" or, as others say it, "out-and-out racism" on the part of adults.

The third position voiced by many students, but not all, is that equity is basically a goal to be desired and should be pursued for moral reasons, but "will probably make no major difference" since poor children "still would lack the motivation" and "would probably fail in any case because of other problems."

At this point, I ask if they can truly say "it wouldn't make a difference" since it's never been attempted. Several students then seem to rethink their views and say that "it might work, but it would have to start with preschool and the elementary grades" and "it might be 20 years before we'd see a difference."

At this stage in the discussion, several students speak with some real feeling of the present inequalities, which, they say, are "obviously unfair," and one student goes a little further and proposes that "we need to change a lot more than the schools." Another says she'd favor racial integration "by whatever means—including busing —even if my parents disapprove." But a contradictory opinion also is expressed with a good deal of fervor and is stated by one student in a rather biting voice: "I don't see why we should do it. How could it be of benefit to us?"

Throughout the discussion, whatever the views the children voice, there is a degree of unreality about the whole exchange. The children are lucid and their language is well chosen and their arguments well made, but there is a sense that they are dealing with an issue that does not feel very vivid, and that nothing that we say about it to each other really matters since it's "just a theoretical discussion." To a certain degree, the skillfulness and cleverness that they display seem to derive precisely from this sense of unreality. Questions of unfairness feel more like a geometric problem than a matter of humanity or conscience. A few of the students do break through the note of unreality but, when they do, they cease to be so agile in their use of words and

speak more awkwardly. Ethical challenges seem to threaten their effectiveness. There is the sense that they were skating over ice and that the issues we addressed were safely frozen underneath. When they stop to look beneath the ice they start to stumble. The verbal competence they have acquired here may have been gained by building walls around some regions of the heart.

"I don't think that busing students from their ghetto to a different school would do much good," one student says. "You can take them out of the environment, but you can't take the environment out of *them*. If someone grows up in the South Bronx, he's not going to be prone to learn." His name is Max and he has short black hair and speaks with confidence. "Busing didn't work when it was tried," he says. I ask him how he knows this and he says he saw a television movie about Boston.

"I agree that it's unfair the way it is," another student says. "We have AP courses and they don't. Our classes are much smaller." But, she says, "putting them in schools like ours is not the answer. Why not put some AP classes into *their* school? Fix the roof and paint the halls so it will not be so depressing."

The students know the term "separate but equal," but seem unaware of its historical associations. "Keep them where they are but make it equal," says a girl in the front row.

A student named Jennifer, whose manner of speech is somewhat less refined and polished than that of the others, tells me that her parents came here from New York. "My family is originally from the Bronx. Schools are hell there. That's one reason that we moved. I don't think it's our responsibility to pay our taxes to provide for *them*. I mean, my parents used to live there and they wanted to get out. There's no point in coming to a place like this, where schools are good, and then your taxes go back to the place where you began."

I bait her a bit: "Do you mean that, now that you are not in hell, you have no feeling for the people that you left behind?"

"It has to be the people in the area who want an education. If your parents just don't care, it won't do any good to spend a lot of money. Someone else can't want a good life for you. You have got to want it for yourself." Then she adds, however, "I agree that everyone should have a chance at taking the same courses. . . ."

I ask her if she'd think it fair to pay more taxes so that this was possible.

"I don't see how that benefits me," she says.

It occurs to me how hard it would have been for anyone to make that kind of statement, even in the wealthiest suburban school, in 1968. Her classmates would have been unsettled by the voicing of such undisguised self-interest. Here in Rye, in 1990, she can say this with impunity. She's an interesting girl and I reluctantly admire her for being so straightforward.

Max raises a different point. "I'm not convinced," he says, "that AP courses would be valued in the Bronx. Not everyone is going to go to college."

Jennifer picks up on this and carries it a little further. "The point," she says, "is that you cannot give an equal chance to every single person. If you did it, you'd be changing the whole economic system. Let's be honest. If you equalize the money, someone's got to be shortchanged. I don't doubt that children in the Bronx are getting a bad deal. But do we want *everyone* to get a mediocre education?"

"The other point," says Max, "is that you need to match the money that you spend to whether children in the school can profit from it. We get twice as much as kids in the South Bronx, but our school is *more* than twice as good and that's because of who is here. Money isn't the whole story. . . ."

"In New York," says Jennifer, "rich people put their kids in private school. If we equalize between New York and Rye, you would see the same thing happen here. People would pull out their kids. Some people do it now. So it would happen a lot more."

An eleventh grader shakes her head at this. "Poor children need more money. It's as simple as that," she says. "Money comes from taxes. If we have it, we should pay it."

It is at this point that a boy named David picks up on a statement made before. "Someone said just now that this is not our obligation, our responsibility. I don't think that that's the question. I don't think you'd do it, pay more taxes or whatever, out of obligation. You would do it just because . . . it is unfair the way it is." He falters on these words and looks a bit embarrassed. Unlike many of the other students who have spoken, he is somewhat hesitant and seems to choke up on his words. "Well, it's easy for me to be sitting here and say I'd spend my parents' money. I'm not working. I don't earn the money. I don't need to be conservative until I do. I can be as openminded and unrealistic as I want to be. You can be a liberal until you have a mortgage."

I ask him what he'd likely say if he were ten years older. "Hopefully," he says, "my values would remain the same. But I know that having money does affect you. This, at least, is what they tell me."

Spurred perhaps by David's words, another student says, "The biggest tax that people pay is to the federal government. Why not take some money from the budget that we spend on armaments and use it for the children in these urban schools?"

A well-dressed student with a healthy tan, however, says that using federal taxes for the poor "would be like giving charity," and "charitable things have never worked. . . . Charity will not instill the poor with self-respect."

Max returns to something that he said before: "The environment is everything. It's going to take something more than money." He goes on to speak of inefficiency and of alleged corruption in the New York City schools. "Some years ago the chancellor was caught in borrowing $100,000 from the schools. I am told that he did not intend to pay it back. These things happen too much in New York. Why should we pour money in, when they are wasting what they have?"

I ask him, "Have we *any* obligations to poor people?"

"I don't think the burden is on us," says Jennifer again. "Taxing the rich to help the poor— we'd be getting nothing out of it. I don't understand how it would make a better educational experience for me."

"A child's in school only six hours in a day," says Max. "You've got to deal with what is happening at home. If his father's in the streets, his mother's using crack . . . how is money going to make a difference?"

David dismisses this and tells me, "Here's what we should do. Put more money into preschool, kindergarten, elementary years. Pay college kids to tutor inner-city children. Get rid of the property tax, which is too uneven, and use income taxes to support these schools. Pay teachers more to work in places like the Bronx. It has to come from taxes. Pay them extra to go into the worst schools. You could forgive their college loans to make it worth their while."

"Give the children Head Start classes," says another student. "If they need more buildings, give them extra money so they wouldn't need to be so crowded."

"It has got to come from taxes," David says again.

"I'm against busing," Max repeats, although this subject hasn't been brought up by anybody else in a long while.

"When people talk this way," says David, "they are saying, actually—" He stops and starts again: "They're saying that black kids will never learn. Even if you spend more in New York. Even if you bring them here to Rye. So what it means is— you are writing people off. You're just dismissing them. . . ."

"I'd like it if we had black students in this school," the girl beside him says.

"It seems rather odd," says David when the hour is up, "that we were sitting in an AP class discussing whether poor kids in the Bronx deserve to get an AP class. We are in a powerful position."

THINKING ABOUT THE READING

What do you suppose would happen if a student from a place like East St. Louis were to attend a school in a place like Rye? Or vice versa? At one point in the reading, one of the students from Rye says, "You can take them out of the environment, but you can't take the environment out of them." Do you agree or disagree with that assessment of the problem of unequal education? Do you think this is a common attitude in American society? Does it enhance or impede progress regarding inequality in this country?

Making Ends Meet

How Single Mothers Survive Welfare and Low-Wage Work

Kathryn Edin and Laura Lein

On December 18, 1994, the cover of the *New York Times Magazine* featured an African American single mother of four. In the photograph, Mary Ann Moore stands in an apron and sanitary cap in front of an industrial-sized stove, ready to start her ten-hour work day as a cook in a Chicago soup kitchen. When *New York Times* journalist Jason DeParle interviewed Moore in the fall of that year, she had been working at this job for almost twelve months.

As the article revealed, thirty-three-year-old Moore had held at least two dozen service-sector jobs since leaving high school. Between these jobs she had relied on Aid to Families with Dependent Children (AFDC). At the time DeParle interviewed her, Moore was paid $8 an hour and could work up to sixty hours a week. It was the highest-paying position she had ever held. To land the job, she had to complete training at a Chicago city college and obtain a food and sanitation license. To keep the job, she had to wake her family at 3:30 each morning; dress, feed, and transport them eleven miles from her subsidized South Chicago apartment to her mother's apartment in the Cabrini Green housing project (her mother got the older children to school and the younger children to their day care center); and then travel six more miles to the North Side to begin her work day at 6:00 A.M.

Although this job netted Moore about $1,600 in a typical month (she worked an average of fifty-six hours a week), leaving welfare for work had substantially increased her expenses. The Chicago Housing Authority raised her rent from roughly $100 to $300 a month; she had to purchase a used car that cost her $300 a month; she had to pay for liability insurance and gasoline

($100 a month); and she had to spend $100 a month on day care for her two-year-old twins. This left Moore with roughly $800 a month with which to feed and clothe her family of five, buy diapers for the twins and school supplies for her two school-aged boys, pay her phone bill and household expenses, and meet out-of-pocket medical expenses. In addition, she paid $67 a month toward a student loan for the training she had needed to land her job.

Of the thousands of welfare-related stories appearing in major newspapers in recent years, DeParle's rendering of Mary Ann Moore's situation was one of only a handful that took a serious look at the working lives of former welfare recipients. DeParle used Moore's story to test the assumptions of those who wanted to replace welfare with work. After spending several weeks living with Moore's family, observing her daily routine, asking countless questions, and tallying up her monthly budget, DeParle concluded that, even for mothers who can get a relatively good job like Moore's, trading welfare for work is far more problematic than most reformers presume. Moore was—and would almost certainly remain—one sick child away from destitution.

Economic Well-Being of Mother-Only Families

National data suggest that despite her tight budget, Moore was more fortunate than most former welfare recipients. Not only did she earn more money per hour than most women with similar skills and education, she was able to work more hours than most, and she had not been laid off. She was fortunate enough to live in a subsidized apartment and had a day care subsidy for her preschool children. Finally, Moore's mother was willing and able to take on many of the parenting tasks while Moore was at work.

Moore's income placed her just above the official poverty line, but about half of all single mothers and their children fall below this threshold. Fifty-five percent of all African American children living in a mother-only family were officially poor in 1990, as were 41 percent of white children. Twenty-two percent of all children lived in mother-only families in that year, up from 11 percent in 1970. Among whites, the proportion of children living with two parents fell from nine in ten to roughly seven in ten. For African Americans, the proportion dropped from about six in ten to just under four of every ten children (Levy 1995, 40). Some of this decline was due to growing nonmarital births (three of Moore's children were born while she was unmarried) and some to divorce or separation.

Like Moore, most unskilled and semiskilled mothers who try to support their children by working are hard-pressed to find a job that pays a living wage.... In the 1970s, few unskilled and semiskilled women who worked full time earned enough to support a family.... During the 1980s and 1990s, these mothers' prospects for a living wage job did not improve (Bianchi 1995, 127–133).

Neither did their chances of getting financial help from their children's fathers, though federal and state lawmakers have made repeated efforts to improve these chances. In 1988, the Family Support Act required states to increase the percentage of welfare-reliant children who had legally identifiable fathers, mandated improvements in collection rates, forced fathers' employers to begin withholding child support from their wages, required states to adopt uniform standards for setting child support awards, and obligated child support officials to update these awards at least every three years. In addition, some states implemented computerized systems for locating delinquent parents and have required the putative fathers of nonmarital children to take genetic paternity tests. Other states intercept tax returns and lottery winnings, garnish bank accounts, suspend driver's licenses, and put nonpaying fathers in jail. Unfortunately, these measures have not improved the financial situations of most low-income single mothers (Edin 1994; Edin 1995; Sorensen and Turner 1996).

Given their limited ability to glean income from either work or their children's fathers, it is not surprising that, at any given point over the last few decades, half of all mothers raising children alone have relied on welfare to help pay their bills. However, the value of a welfare check declined dramatically (more than 40 percent) between the mid-1970s and the mid-1990s as inflation eroded the purchasing power of benefits. As welfare devolves to the states, this erosion will almost certainly continue because federal block grants to states are not likely to increase as living costs rise. As states begin to implement the new federal work requirements and time limits, fewer mothers will be eligible for the program at all.

Nearly three decades of stagnant wages, ineffective child support enforcement, and dwindling welfare benefits have made single mothers and their children America's poorest demographic group. Because 60 percent of all children born during the 1980s will spend part of their childhood in a mother-only family, and because current trends suggest that an even higher proportion of children born during the current decade will be raised by single mothers, we believe the economic well-being of mother-only families should be of concern to every American (Martin and Bumpass 1989; Sweet and Bumpass 1987)....

The Dual Demands on Single Mothers

It is virtually impossible to understand the economic behavior of the mothers we interviewed without considering the overall context within which this behavior occurred—that of single motherhood. Our mothers' accounts show that all over America, unskilled and semiskilled single mothers face desperate economic and personal situations that they can seldom resolve satisfactorily. Most want to be good providers *and* good mothers. For these parents, good mothering means, at minimum, keeping their children out of danger—off the streets, off drugs, out of gangs, not pregnant, and in school. Most of us would endorse these goals, but few realize just how difficult they are to achieve for mothers who must support their children on low-wage employment.

These widely shared social definitions of good mothering affected how our respondents spent their money. Good mothers, they believed, should treat their children on occasion. Consequently, some mothers would occasionally forgo necessities to pay for a basic cable television subscription, a movie rental, a trip to a fast food restaurant, new clothes for the first day of school, or name-brand sneakers. Although these items are not essential for a child's material well-being, a cable television subscription is a relatively inexpensive way for mothers to keep their children off the streets and away from undesirable peers. Likewise, buying a pair of expensive sneakers is insurance against the possibility that children will be tempted to steal them or sell drugs to get them.

The importance of being a good mother also limited women's access to the more financially lucrative survival strategies available to them. Although a few mothers sold sex, drugs, or stolen goods when other strategies failed, almost all believed that good mothering and routine criminal activity were incompatible. Thus, few mothers engaged in well-paid side-work like prostitution. Instead, they opted for cleaning houses, maintaining apartment buildings, mowing lawns, babysitting, collecting bottles and aluminum cans, or other poorly paid work.

Finally, concerns about good mothering profoundly affected the way that mothers thought about the advantages of welfare and low-wage work. The regular jobs open to unskilled and semiskilled women were precisely those jobs that are least compatible with mothering. The jobs our mothers held seldom provided health benefits, so mothers who chose them often had to forgo medical care for themselves or their children. Many of these jobs offered unpredictable or limited hours, required workers to take shifts at odd or irregular times, provided few if any paid vacation or sick days, and did not allow mothers to take or make personal calls to check on children left home alone. In sum, the nature of their jobs often made it difficult for mothers to fulfill their parenting roles satisfactorily.

Because virtually all the women we interviewed were at least as concerned with parenting as with providing, many chose not to work for a time. As low-income single mothers' option to withdraw from the labor market and rely on welfare is increasingly restricted, it is hard to gauge what impact this may have on their ability to parent their children effectively. We believe that this will largely depend on the type of jobs and the kinds of long-term support services states will be able to provide unskilled and semiskilled single mothers who work. . . .

The Decision to Stay on Welfare

Social scientists often analyze individual decision making processes in terms of incentives and disincentives, or what social scientists call "rational choice" models (Bane and Ellwood 1994). These models assume that women . . . choose between welfare and work by calculating the costs and benefits of each option, and then determining which has the biggest payoff. When economists apply these models, they typically focus on the *economic* costs and benefits associated with welfare as opposed to work and assume that individuals consider the long-run as well as the short-run economic consequences of their choices. Sociologists usually concentrate on the short run and take into account a somewhat broader array of costs and benefits. . . .

Our data lend a good deal of support to the idea that mothers choose between welfare and work by weighing the costs and benefits of each. Most of the welfare-reliant mothers we interviewed had an accurate view of the benefits they would lose by going to work—although they did not always know the exact dollar amount—and they made reasonable assessments of how much they would need to earn to offset the added costs of work. Mothers' views of the incentives and disincentives of each, however, were quite different from those assumed by many social scientists. . . .

For poor single mothers, the welfare/work choice was not merely a problem of maximizing income or consumption. Rather, each woman's choice was set against a backdrop of survival and serious potential material hardship. The mothers with whom we spoke were less interested in maximizing consumption than in minimizing the risk of economic disaster. . . .

We interviewed 214 welfare-reliant women, most of whom said that their decision regarding whether to leave welfare was predicated on their past labor-market experiences. These experiences shaped their estimates of their current job prospects. Contrary to popular rhetoric, mothers did not choose welfare because of a *lack* of work experience or because they were ignorant of their job options. Most of the welfare-reliant mothers we interviewed had held a job in the formal sector of the labor market in the past: 83 percent had some work experience and 65 percent had worked within the last five years. National data, though not directly comparable, suggest an even higher rate of labor-market participation; 60 percent of all welfare recipients surveyed by the Panel Study of Income Dynamics (PSID) had worked during the previous two years (U.S. House of Representatives 1993, 718). On average, our welfare recipients had accumulated 5.6 years of work experience before their current spell on welfare.

Elsewhere, we have demonstrated that their experience in the low-wage labor market taught these mothers several lessons about their likely job prospects (Edin and Lein forthcoming). First, returning to the kinds of jobs they had held in the past would not make them better off—either financially or emotionally—than they were on welfare. Indeed, this was precisely why most mothers were receiving welfare rather than working. Second, most mothers believed that taking a low-wage job might well make them *worse* off, because the job might vanish and they might be without any income for a time, since it took months for the welfare department to redetermine welfare eligibility and cut the first check. Consequently, working might put them and their children at risk of serious hardship. Third, no matter how long they stayed at a job and no matter how diligently they worked, jobs in what some called "the five-dollar-an-hour ghetto" seldom led to better jobs over time. Fourth, since job clubs and other components of the federal JOBS [Job Opportunities and Basic Skills] program were designed to place mothers in the types of jobs they held in the past, they saw little reason to participate in these programs: JOBS training programs added little to mothers' earning power. Finally, mothers took noneconomic as well as economic factors into account when deciding between welfare and work. Although most mothers felt that accepting welfare carried a social stigma, they also feared that work—and the time they would have to spend away from home—could jeopardize the safety and well-being of their children.

Given these realities, it was surprising to us that most mothers still had plans to leave welfare for work. Some planned to delay leaving welfare until their children were older and the cost of working was lower. Others . . . planned to use their time on welfare to improve their skills so they could get a better job when they reentered the labor force. In the long run, the goal of most mothers was to earn enough to eliminate the need for any government welfare program and to minimize their dependence on family, friends, boyfriends, side-jobs, and agencies.

. . . Half the mothers in the welfare-reliant group were engaged in some form of work (formal or informal) to make ends meet. Most had also worked at a job in the formal sector at some time in the past, and the vast majority planned to do so in the future. Indeed, they all knew that they would have to work in due course, since their children would eventually reach adulthood, making the family ineligible for welfare. Only a tiny portion had no concrete plans to work in the formal sector.

When welfare-reliant mothers thought about welfare and work, the vast majority calculated not only how their prospective wages would compare with their cash welfare and food stamp benefits but how much they would lose in housing subsidies and other means-tested benefits. They also calculated how much more they would have to spend on child care, medical care, transportation, and suitable work clothing if they were to take a job. This mother's comment was typical:

> One day, I sat down and figured out the balance of everything that I got on welfare [including fuel assistance and Medicaid] and everything that I [earn] and have to spend working. And you know what? You're definitely better off on welfare! I mean absolutely every woman wants to work. I always want to work, but it's hard.

Because the costs and benefits associated with leaving welfare for work were constantly on their minds, many of the women we interviewed could do these calculations off the top of their heads, and some were able to show us the backs of envelopes and scraps of notebook paper on which they had scribbled such calculations in the last few weeks. Although respondents' estimates were seldom exact, most mothers were able to describe their prospective loss in benefits and potential increase in expenses. They were also able to calculate how holding a regular job would affect their ability to supplement their income in various ways. . . . In addition, mothers considered a variety of noneconomic "costs" of working: whether full-time work would leave them enough time to be competent parents and whether they could manage to keep their children safe from the potentially lethal effects of their neighborhoods. Mothers' concerns about their children's welfare were often as important as purely economic gains or losses in their decisions.

"A Total Trap"

One Boston woman had only recently gone on welfare after seven years of working as a police dispatcher. Her top wage at this job was $7 an hour—a relatively high wage compared with the other women in our sample. She made ends meet on this wage only because she had a housing subsidy and a live-in boyfriend who paid a lot of the expenses. Despite the fact that she worked full time, she could not afford to move out of the projects. After her boyfriend left her

and stopped contributing to her budget, she could not pay her bills. Thus, after seven years, she returned to welfare and went back to school:

> There's nothing in a low salary job because . . . your rent be so high . . . you know, people don't believe that people who work and live in the projects be paying $400–$500 for rent. But that's true because you can't really afford—for three bedroom, you can't really afford to go out and be paying $1,000 for a private apartment. You go out and get a job and then they take your rent subsidy away from you. You pay that much rent and it's hard just trying to maintain the low standard of living you had on welfare. You're in the same position, so it don't matter if you're working or not.

For women living in subsidized housing, working meant a double tax on earnings because housing subsidies are determined on the basis of cash income. For welfare-reliant mothers, only the cash welfare payment (and not food stamp benefits or the value of Medicaid) is used in determining rent. This means that even if a mother took a job that paid the equivalent of her combined cash welfare, food stamp, and Medicaid benefits, she would have had to pay more rent. . . .

Mothers also had to calculate the effect that work would have on their abilities to garner the additional income that allowed them to survive on welfare. Those mothers who relied exclusively on their social networks for extra help each month felt they could more easily afford the time spent working at a job in the formal sector; mothers who relied on side-jobs or agency handouts were far less sanguine about their ability to keep up these strategies while working a full-time job. One mother captured this sentiment particularly well:

> I'm going to have to lose a lot in terms of what I earn from under-the-table housecleaning to gain anything from a job. I'm a workaholic. I'm so unhappy with welfare. But I can't leave welfare for work. I'm ready to move back home with my mother, tell welfare to screw—excuse my French—and try to get child support so I

could live off of work. Even if I get a part-time job, though, they take so much from you. I'm very creative, I'm very smart, and I know that I could get my way out of this. But, now, I just feel like I'm all boxed in.

Apart from believing that working was a financial wash, women also felt they would gain little self-respect from the minimum-wage jobs they could get with their current skills. Nearly all of our welfare-reliant respondents said they would feel better about themselves if they could make it without welfare, but this boost to their self-esteem seemed to depend on a working life that offered somewhat higher wages and better prospects for advancement than most of the jobs they thought they could get with their current skills and job experience.

Risking the Future

The cost-benefit calculations that mothers made about leaving welfare for work were colored by the economic and social contexts of these women's lives. As we mentioned earlier, the mothers we interviewed had to weigh the utility of work against the real possibility that a subsequent layoff or reduction in hours could lead to serious material hardship. The jobs these mothers could get were among the least reliable in the U.S. economy. Typically, they demanded work at irregular hours, did not guarantee how many hours a worker would be able to work in a given week, and were subject to frequent layoffs. Nowhere was this more true than in the fast food industry. . . . Fast food chains typically impose unpredictable schedules on workers, sending them home when business is slow. As a result, women could not predict how many hours they would be able to work. . . .

Even worse, if the job failed, it usually took several months to get their benefits going again, leaving these mothers with no source of legal income in the interim. A Chicago respondent expressed the frustration with the lag in benefits this way:

[Because of the way the system is set up] it's just really hard to get off of [welfare]. When you go

get a job, you lose everything, just about. For every nickel you make, they take a dime from you. [I have been] on and off welfare. Like when I [tried] working at a nursing home, I was making $4.50 an hour [and] they felt like I ma[de] too much money. Then they cut me off. And I just couldn't make ends meet with $4.50 an hour, because I was paying for day care too. So I [had] to quit my job to get back on it. It took me forever to get back on, and meanwhile I had to starve and beg from friends.

Another woman commented,

One thing they should change is not to wait three months for things to catch up with you. They're like three months behind so like, say if I worked in April [I wouldn't get any benefits] in June, [even though I had no work] income in June. That's where a lot of people can't make it. That's what threw me off. Because like in April I made so much money with my job, and I was expecting my check to go down, but by the time it caught up with me I no longer had a job.

. . . To aggravate matters, a large proportion of those respondents who stayed at one job in order to work their way up were eventually laid off. Gottschalk and Danziger (1989) found that women working in low-wage jobs were three times more prone to job layoffs than other workers (see also Blank 1995). One might expect that unemployment insurance would provide a safety net for such workers, but this is seldom the case. The percentage of job losers who collected unemployment declined throughout the 1980s. At the end of the decade, less than one in three jobless workers reported receiving unemployment benefits (about 34 percent were eligible), and those in the low-wage sector were the least likely to have coverage (Burtless 1994, 69; U.S. House of Representatives 1987, 330). This is presumably because an increasing proportion of Americans are working at jobs that are not covered by these benefits. Roberta Spalter-Roth, Heidi Hartmann, and Beverly Burr (1994) found that only 11 percent of welfare recipients with substantial work hours were eligible for unemployment insurance.

Dead-End Jobs

The vast majority of those who had worked also found that hard work rarely led to anything better. Their past jobs had seldom produced the type of "human capital" (training, experience, or education) that they could parley into better jobs. Nor did they produce the "social capital" (professional contacts and links with other jobs or employers) that might improve their career prospects, since they worked with other women in equally low-level jobs. In short, these women were unable to build careers; if they chose to work, they were much more likely to move from one dead-end job to another. Thus, women learned that the kinds of jobs available to them were not avenues to success or even to bare-bones self-sufficiency; they were dead ends.

One respondent from the low-wage worker group, an African American woman in her late thirties with a high school diploma, had spent twenty years working for a large regional grocery chain. She worked the first fifteen years as a cashier, earning the minimum wage. In 1986, management promoted her to the service counter and raised her hourly wage from $3.35 to $4.00 an hour. In 1991, after five years in her new position, she had worked her way up to $5 an hour, the highest wage she had ever received. She had virtually never been late or taken a sick day, and her boss told her she was one of his most competent employees, yet her hourly salary over the past twenty years had risen by a total of $1.65.

Nonetheless, this mother was able to make ends meet for three reasons. First, her children were all in their teens and needed no day care; their truancy rate, however, was so high that she felt they would not finish high school. Second, she had a Section 8 housing subsidy, which allowed her to live in a private apartment within walking distance of her job. Third, she had lived with a succession of steadily employed boyfriends (three men over the past twenty years) who paid a lot of her bills. Her twenty-year-old daughter was raising her two-year-old twins on welfare and was a part of our welfare-reliant sample. Although her daughter also lived in a Section 8 apartment close to the central business district, she had two children who would have required day care if she went to work, and she did not have a boyfriend who could pay her bills. Because of this, she turned down a job where her mother worked.

Most of the welfare-reliant mothers we interviewed felt they could get a job if they were willing to do minimum-wage work. Even in Boston and San Antonio, where the labor market was slack, most mothers thought they could get work. At a minimum, however, they wanted a job that would leave them slightly better off than they had been on welfare. The mothers' most common dream was to earn enough to move out of project housing and into a better neighborhood. Other mothers wanted to buy better clothing for their children so their peers would not ridicule them. Yet, few mothers had had work experiences that led them to expect such rewards from work; they knew first-hand that a minimum-wage job would get them nowhere.

Most mothers told us they had originally entered the labor market with high hopes. They believed that if they could manage to stay at one job long enough or, alternatively, use each job as a stepping stone to a better one, they could make ends meet through work. After a few years in the low-wage job sector, they saw that instead of achieving their goals they were getting further and further behind in their bills. Not surprisingly, mothers concluded that the future they were building through low-wage work was a house of cards.

Iris, a Chicago welfare-reliant mother with twelve years of low-wage work experience, had spent her last seven working years as head housekeeper at a large hotel. Although this job gave her benefits and a two-week paid vacation, after seven years she had gone from $4.90 to only $5.15 an hour. Two years prior to our interviews, she had left this job for welfare with the hope that she could use the time off to search full-time for a better job. After months of persistent searching, she concluded that better jobs were simply not available for someone with her skills and experience.

One displaced housewife, Bonnie Jones, applied for AFDC when her husband deserted her and her savings ran dry. Because she had substantial secretarial experience, she found a job quickly. Her persistently low earnings, however, meant that she was back on welfare after two years.

> I went on Public Aid when my ex left [1987]. He just up and poof, that was it. My daughter was four. And I was like "Oh God." I hadn't worked in five years. I lived on my savings until it ran out and then I went on welfare. After a few months on AFDC I went on an interview and I was hired at a computer supply store . . . for $5.50. I took it because I was living free with my mother and I figured it was a foot in the door. I already had office experience, but I had a five-year gap in my work history because of my child. I figured I would get in as a switchboard operator and push my way up as high as I could. [But] there's no ladder. It's unbelievable. I just quit there in September. They drilled me to the ground. My top wage there was $6.90 in two years when I quit.

National data echo these mothers' experiences. First, a large body of research has shown that low-wage work does not pay a living or family wage. Charles Michalopoulos and Irwin Garfinkel (1989) estimate that workers with demographic profiles resembling those of typical welfare-reliant mothers could expect to earn only $5.15 an hour (in 1991 dollars) if they left welfare for work. Diana Pearce's (1991) analysis of PSID data also shows that for 70 percent of welfare-reliant mothers in the 1980s, spells of low-wage employment left them no better off than they had been before. The kinds of jobs that are available to these women more often end up being "chutes" not ladders.

Second, there is growing evidence that low-wage jobs provide little or no access to better future jobs. . . .

Unless the typical unskilled or semiskilled single mother finds an unusually well-paying job or has medical benefits, a child care subsidy, and very low housing and transportation costs, she cannot work her way from dependency to self-sufficiency. Despite this reality, many single

mothers remained committed to the work ethic and tried to leave welfare again and again. Many had such varied job histories that their employment records sounded like the newspaper's "help wanted" advertisements. Most mothers had moved from one job to another, always looking for some slight advantage—more hours, a better shift, a lower copayment on a health plan, more convenient transportation, less strenuous manual labor, or less monotonous work—without substantially improving their earnings over the long term.

Nonetheless, some researchers have criticized women workers in the low-wage sector both for not moving enough and for moving too much. Lawrence Mead (1992), for example, argues that,

> The notion of the dead-end job misrepresents the nature of mobility in the economy. Most jobs are dead-end in the sense that any given employer usually offers employees only limited chances for promotion. Most workers move up, not by rising within the organization, but by leaving it and getting a better job elsewhere. Mobility comes not in a given job but from a work history that convinces each employer that the job seeker will be a reliable employee. Advancement is something workers must largely seek out for themselves, not something given to them by employers. (p. 96)

At the same time, Mead (1992) remonstrates that "These workers exhibit what Hall termed 'pathological instability' in holding jobs" (p. 96).

Past Experience with Job Training

Ironically, the types of jobs our welfare-reliant mothers had held in the past were precisely those that the mothers' JOBS caseworkers recommended that they work toward in their training programs, which is perhaps why mothers placed so little faith in them. Typically, these programs had several components. In the work-readiness or Job Club component, recipients learned to write a resume and practice their interviewing skills. The Job Search component required recipients to show proof that they had applied for a substantial number of jobs each month. A third component, the Community Work Experience Program (CWEP), required recipients to work half time for a nonprofit agency in exchange for their benefits. Finally, recipients judged to be in need of remedial training could exempt themselves from the other components of workfare while they were enrolled full time in school or in on-the-job training.

Participation in the component programs varied by state. In Illinois, two-thirds of JOBS participants were enrolled in educational or job skills programs in 1993, with smaller numbers in the Job Club and Job Search components. Massachusetts also enrolled about two-thirds of JOBS participants in educational programs, but placed nearly one-quarter in Job Search. In South Carolina, placement in educational programs was somewhat less common (about one-third of JOBS participants were enrolled); the state opted instead for Job Club (30 percent) and Job Search (25 percent). In Texas, 64 percent were enrolled in Job Club, 43 percent in educational programs, and 6 percent in Job Search (some mothers are enrolled in multiple programs). None of the states we studied used either on-the-job training or the CWEP components to any great extent (U.S. House of Representatives 1993).

Among our mothers, the least popular components were Job Club and Job Search. Women who had been through them believed the jobs that the caseworkers recommended were not a realistic alternative to welfare. They knew from their own experience and that of their friends that these jobs were "stupid" jobs—little better than the ones they could have acquired on their own. One Chicago-area mother who attended several Job Club meetings commented,

> It was disgusting. Here were these women getting jobs at a fast food restaurant for minimum wage, and people were clapping and cheering. And then they would find out that they couldn't make it on that amount, so they would just come right back on welfare a month or so later. And that was the best they seemed to do. They didn't offer any real good jobs to anyone.

. . .

Evaluations at the national level show rather convincingly that these mothers' assessments of low-cost, short-term job training are accurate: the wage rates of trainees increased very little or not at all (Blank 1994; Friedlander and Gueron 1992). The seeming futility of welfare-sponsored job training programs was another factor causing some women to choose welfare over work while they sought out better quality educational programs on their own.

Noneconomic Costs of Work

The chance to get ahead through work is what welfare-reliant women wanted and believed they deserved, particularly when they considered the added strain that work would bring to their lives. The single mothers we interviewed were therefore skeptical about working a job for years on end if they were just going to scrape by month after month. Indeed, they reported to us that the endless strain left them worn down and depressed. Nor were they willing to go continually to friends or relatives for substantial handouts. Thus, most mothers, while they wanted to trade welfare for work, were unwilling to do so unless that job held a reasonable promise of helping them to become self-sufficient.

One mother with more than ten years of work experience told us,

> There were many days where I got my paycheck and I just looked at it and cried. It was not enough to pay my rent, and I had to work almost the full month to pay the rent. It never was enough that I could go buy groceries. And I had the two kids and they had to watch one another and I didn't want welfare. And it is just one up and down after another.
>
> Suppose you have to go up to the school. You've got to be a full-time mother, then you've got to be a breadwinner, then you've got to be a nursemaid and you've just got to always be there. It's like you're being stretched so many different ways. Maybe your child is having behavioral or learning problems at the same time in school.

I know from my experience, I've had to deal with it. I would get depressed and I would withdraw. Somehow, you can even feel like you're not even a part of society because you're standing there looking at the American Dream and you feel like it's passing you over. Just the basics. To pay rent, to buy the food and to make sure your kids have decent clothing so they can go to school and look like they belong to somebody. You don't always have that when you're working.

The majority of American families still have two parents to share childrearing responsibilities and most can afford some form of child care for their children, but many poor families have only one parent and can hardly afford any child care. Faced with a job that does not pay the bills, some have argued that the poor should surmount their difficulties by working more hours (Mead 1992). For parents who have sole responsibility for their children, this solution may work in the short term but not in the long run. Every hour spent in the workplace is an hour children must spend without their parent (and often without any other adult supervision). Lack of supervision is clearly bad for younger children, but it can also have serious repercussions for older children. A mother's absence usually means that the influence of the peer group expands. Eventually, many single parents lose control. While they work, their adolescent children may stop doing their homework, stop attending school, drift into sexual activity, or get in trouble with the law.

Our respondents convinced us that they had one overriding concern in their lives—to provide for their children. That is why they turned to welfare in the first place, why they "worked" the system, why they cycled between welfare and low-wage reported work, and why they left the low-wage labor market for welfare and school.

Welfare-Reliant Mothers as Long-Term Strategists

In the face of the welfare/work dilemma, one might assume welfare-reliant mothers would simply resign themselves to welfare or look for a husband with a good job. Although a small number of the women we interviewed had clearly settled for one of these alternatives, most had not. Not only did most mothers plan to get out of their current situations, but these plans reflected their belief that they might never be able (or, in some cases, willing) to rely on a man to solve their economic problems. Although few were averse to the possibility of marriage, they were not counting on it. Rather, these women saw the responsibility of providing for their families as their own.

Although some women were either too sick, too deeply involved in the underground economy, or experiencing too much personal turmoil to believe that their circumstances would change, the vast majority of mothers we interviewed had spent a good deal of time thinking about how to make their lives better in the future. These mothers were making plans to leave welfare for work as soon as their skills or their health care and child care arrangements allowed them to make ends meet on their earnings.

. . . Only 14 percent of the welfare-reliant mothers we interviewed (twenty-nine mothers) had no clear plans to leave welfare for work. Of them, more than one-third (ten mothers) were receiving disability payments for themselves or a child because of a permanent disability. Although a child's disability might not preclude a mother's working, disabled children typically missed a lot of school and had to be taken to a lot of medical specialists. These mothers received welfare because their disability payments did not cover their nondisabled family members. That left nineteen mothers who had no plans to leave welfare for a job. About half of these (ten mothers) believed they were better off combining welfare with unreported work in the informal or underground economy. That way they could keep their housing subsidies and medical benefits. Of the nine mothers remaining, five planned to marry to get off welfare, and four claimed their current situations were simply too unstable to allow them to think about the future.

This means that the vast majority of our sample—86 percent (or 185 mothers)—was planning to leave welfare for work. This is not surprising: survey researchers have repeatedly found highly favorable attitudes toward work among the welfare poor (Goodwin 1972; Tienda and Stier 1991). Yet only 13 percent of all those in the sample who wanted to work (twenty-seven mothers) believed they could afford to leave welfare at the time we interviewed them. Seventy-three percent of the total (158 mothers) said that, while they both wanted and planned to leave welfare for work, they could not afford to take the kind of job they thought they could get at the time.

Want to Work Now

The twenty-seven mothers who wanted to work immediately had more education and work experience than other mothers in the sample. The work-ready group was significantly more likely to have earned a high school diploma or General Equivalency Diploma (GED) (89 percent versus 68 percent of all the welfare recipients), and more than one-third had participated in post–high school training (37 percent versus 12 percent). Furthermore, nearly all had worked during the previous five years, versus three-fifths of all recipients. The work-ready group also had significantly more years of work experience (6.6 years versus 4.4 years) than the other mothers in the sample. Finally, only one-third of these mothers had preschool children compared with 93 percent of the others, and all work-ready mothers with young children told us they had a friend or relative who could watch their child while they worked.

These work-ready welfare-reliant mothers were not willing to take a minimum-wage job. Without exception, mothers in this group were holding out for jobs that paid above the minimum wage, had the potential for advancement, and offered benefits. Mothers in this group cited hourly reservation wages in the $8 to $10 range, which translated into $16,000 to $20,000 a year. But most were willing to take less initially if they could work their way up to these levels in a relatively short period of time (less than two years). Unfortunately, the U.S. economy does not produce nearly enough of these jobs to go around, particularly for unskilled and semiskilled women (Reskin 1993).

National data show that white mothers have a greater chance of commanding wages in this range than nonwhites. In 1989, white women who worked full time and year round earned an average of $19,880. Their African American counterparts earned only $17,680 a year. White full-time female workers whose earnings fell in the bottom quintile earned $13,920 a year, while their African American counterparts earned an average of $12,250 (U.S. House of Representatives 1993, 592). To make matters even worse, many women who wanted to work full time could not get the hours. This is not likely to change very soon, since part-time, temporary, or subcontracted employees are now the fastest-growing category of workers in the United States (Heclo 1994, 420–421).

Want to Work, but Not Now

Seventy-three percent of our welfare-reliant mothers said they wanted to work but could not afford to do so now because of the gap between what they needed to pay their monthly bills and expenses and their present earning potential. Mothers told us that although some work-related costs were constant (transportation, clothing, medical care, and loss of some of their housing subsidy), some varied according to their current situations (the cost of day care and health care) and could be reduced when their situations changed.

Twenty-four of the mothers who did not think they could afford to work at present were experiencing a temporary disability (such as an injury sustained in an accident or a high-risk pregnancy) or were caring for a temporarily disabled family member (a child with a serious illness or a parent who was critically ill and needed constant care). These women remained on welfare partly because their disability (or that of their family member) prevented them from working and partly because they needed to maintain their family's Medicaid eligibility to cover the cost of treatment. Most had worked in the past and planned to return to work once the health crisis had abated.

Another obstacle to work was a lack of child care. A total of 121 mothers said they could not afford to work at least in part because they had no access to low-cost child care. All these women had children under the age of six, and half had children under the age of three. One Boston mother commented,

> The babysitting up here is expensive . . . it almost doesn't pay to work. So, that's why I'm not working right now. I want to work, because I hate not working. I hate sitting home. They offered me a job at a fast food restaurant, but . . . if you figure out the babysitting expense and stuff like that . . . that was more than I was making.

Under the federal rules the welfare system subsidized the costs of day care for a year. But mothers doubted that their incomes would increase fast enough to assume the full costs once the subsidies lapsed. Mothers felt it would be a waste of time to take a job only to quit a year later and return to welfare, especially because of the time it would take to get their benefits going again.

Although child care concerns posed a significant barrier to work, only 16 of the 121 mothers in this group felt that a day care subsidy alone would make work affordable. The other mothers believed a significant gap would remain between what they could earn and what they would need to pay their bills. For these 105 women, the answer was twofold: wait until their children no longer needed day care and, in the interim, pursue further education. The following quotation is typical of what mothers in this group told us,

> If I got a job where I made $200 every week, day care would cost me $180! They won't help you with day care when you get a job. But you know, it's still better to work because then it's my money. I can't wait to get away from welfare. I'm going to start a job training program. I want to go to business school. I have a cousin who went to business school and makes $10 an hour. Good, huh? Three years from now, I hope to be working and to have finished school. I love school.

An additional thirteen mothers did not have day care problems, but still believed their educa-tional deficiencies prevented them from leaving welfare.

Altogether, 118 mothers believed they needed to improve their skills before they could afford to leave welfare for work. One San Antonio welfare-reliant mother with twelve years of work experi-ence left her low-wage factory job in 1985 and began to combine welfare with part-time school-ing. At the time of our 1991 interviews, she was a few months away from completing a four-year degree in elementary education. She told us that she viewed the strategy of combining welfare with schooling as the best way of "looking out for the future." . . .

Most other mothers also believed that com-bining welfare with quality training was the best way to achieve self-sufficiency. Almost half (42 percent) who told us they could not afford to leave welfare without further training were al-ready enrolled in an educational program. We should note, however, that only 12.5 percent of the total U.S. caseload in 1991 was enrolled in school or training, whereas 23 percent of our sample told us they were in school (U.S. House of Representatives 1993, 699). We doubt our sample is as unrepresentative as this contrast im-plies, because many of our mothers told us they were hiding their schooling for fear that their caseworkers would disapprove and force them to trade their current educational pursuits for an immediate job search or short-term training.

Mothers told us that the first question they asked regarding a training program was how much they could earn when they completed it. The vast majority wanted to enroll in programs that led to "meal-ticket jobs" rather than four-year college programs in the liberal arts that had no immediate application to a specific career. The most common four-year educational goals were nursing and teaching—jobs that have tradition-ally offered moderate wages and flexible schedules to women. Mothers who did not feel they could spend that much time in school typically wanted to pursue high-quality training in vocational and technical colleges. Although the women with whom we spoke were not enthusiastic about JOBS training, they showed tremendous excitement about pursuing two-year degrees in pharmaceutical, dental, and medical technology and in accounting, business, and cosmetology....

The women with whom we spoke also believed that it was nearly impossible to combine childrearing, full-time work, and full-time schooling; they felt it was possible to combine welfare with schooling and still take care of their children. Just as important, women on welfare had full access to Pell grants and other tuition remission, whereas they would have received less assistance if they were working and their countable incomes were higher.

What Must a Single Mother Earn to Leave Welfare?

We asked each welfare-reliant mother what she felt she would need to earn in order to leave welfare for work. Roughly 70 percent of mothers cited what economists call a "reservation wage" between $8 to $10 an hour. Mothers with only one child gave slightly lower estimates—averaging roughly $7.50 an hour—while mothers with more than three children and mothers whose children would need full-time child care tended to give slightly higher estimates.

The loss of health benefits so often associated with leaving welfare for work pushed reservation wages toward the upper end of this $8 to $10 range. We asked one work-ready Boston-area mother, "What is a decent wage? What could you support your family with?" She told us, "at least $8 an hour and with benefits." We then asked, "What would you do if you were offered a job for $8 an hour with no benefits and without possibility for advancement?" She answered, "I wouldn't take it. I would go into training or back to school, but I wouldn't take it."

This respondent's children had experienced serious health problems in the past, making it necessary for her to retain her medical benefits. Mothers whose families had no history of medical problems were more willing to risk their health benefits, but even these mothers believed that a job without benefits would have to pay more. Mothers' estimates of how much more

varied, depending mostly on a family's health history and current health status.

How much did these mothers need to earn to maintain the same standard of living that welfare afforded? ... The average welfare-reliant mother in 1991 needed $876 a month to pay her expenses; those who paid market rent needed over $1,000 a month. It seems reasonable to argue that if welfare-reliant mothers needed to spend an average of $876 a month to meet their expenses, working mothers would need to spend even more, because working adds extra costs to the monthly budget. Working mothers usually spend substantially more on medical care because they lose Medicaid, because few low-wage employers offer health care benefits, and because those employers that do usually require co-payments and have deductibles. Most working mothers also pay more for transportation because of commuting costs and travel to and from their day care provider. In addition, working mothers probably need to spend more for child care than welfare-reliant mothers. Finally, some working mothers need to purchase more and better clothing than they had on welfare.

In previous work, Edin and Jencks (1992) used the 1984–1985 Consumer Expenditure Survey to provide rough estimates of how much more working single mothers spent on these items than their welfare-reliant counterparts. They found that single mothers who worked spent $2,800 more each year on these four items—medical care, transportation, child care, and clothing—than their welfare-reliant counterparts. If we inflate these numbers to 1991 levels, the figure is roughly $3,500. We also looked at a group of 165 working mothers ... who earned about what our welfare-reliant mothers reported having earned in the past. These mothers spent about $37 a month more for health care, $67 a month more for transportation, $58 a month more for child care, and $27 a month more for clothing than welfare-reliant mothers did. Taken together, these additional expenses total $189 a month, or $2,268 a year.

By adding the extra costs of working to the average amount privately-housed welfare recipients spent each month ($1,077 + $189), we calculate what the average mother would need to take home each month from a job if she were to maintain the standard of living she had on welfare—roughly $1,300 in take-home pay. On an annual basis, she would have to gross roughly $16,000, or between $8 and $9 an hour depending on how many hours she could be expected to work. Yet, Michalopoulos and Garfinkel (1989) have shown that a full-time, year-round worker with characteristics similar to the average welfare-reliant single mother in the 1980s could expect to earn only $5.15 an hour. Kathleen Mullan Harris (1996) has made comparable estimates using PSID data for all women who left welfare for work during the 1980s. On average, during this ten-year period, she found that women who left welfare for work were paid $6.11 an hour in 1991 dollars. The difference between Michalopoulos and Garfinkel's predictions and Harris's results reflects the fact that women who actually leave welfare for work have greater earning power than those who remain on welfare (or leave the rolls for other reasons).

If a single mother worked forty hours a week for fifty weeks of the year at $5.15 an hour, she would earn $858 a month, or about $10,000 a year after subtracting taxes and adding the EITC [earned income tax credit]. If she worked thirty-five hours a week for fifty weeks—the average number of hours our low-wage sample reported working—she would earn only $751 a month, or about $9,000 after taxes and the EITC. These figures mean that the average mother who left welfare for full-time work would experience, at minimum, a 33 percent gap between what she could expect to earn and what she would need to maintain her standard of living.

The break-even point—using our own data and national-level expenditure data—thus ranges from $8 to $9 an hour. Recall that our mothers' reservation wages ranged from about $8 to $10 an hour. Because most mothers in our sample knew they could not expect to earn this much given their current skills, it seems reasonable that they chose to delay work until their potential work-related costs decreased or until they had enhanced their education and training to a point where they could earn more.

The "Welfare Trap"

The Omnibus Budget Reconciliation Act of 1981, the Family Support Act of 1988, and the welfare reform law of 1996 all tried to push the welfare poor into low-wage employment. All evolved from two related assumptions:

1. Most welfare-reliant mothers have little or no work experience;
2. Employment at a low-wage job will provide access to better jobs in the future.

In other words, the welfare problem has been defined as an issue of labor force participation—once a mother gets a job, any job, policymakers assume she can move up. For this reason, welfare reform has focused on pushing unskilled and semiskilled mothers "out of the nest" as soon as possible. The astoundingly high rates of welfare recidivism show, however, that while such tactics may marginally reduce costs, fledgling working mothers more often crash than fly. Using longitudinal data from the PSID, Harris (1993, table 4) estimates that nearly one-quarter of all mothers who exit welfare for work return within one year, 35 percent within two years, and 54 percent within six years. Subsequent exits from welfare are also rapid: within twelve months of their return, half leave welfare again. Some of them then return to welfare yet again (Harris 1993, table 2).

The Institute for Women's Policy Research (IWPR) has studied the work behavior of welfare-reliant mothers using data from the Survey of Income and Program Participation (SIPP). IWPR found that seven of ten mothers reported some participation in the formal sector of the U.S. labor market during the two-year period of its study. However, their jobs were unstable (averaging only forty-six weeks), seldom provided health coverage (workers were covered in only one-third of the months they worked), paid poorly (an average of $4.29 an hour in 1990 dollars), and were concentrated in the lowest rungs of the occupational ladder (39 percent worked as maids, cashiers, nurse's aides, child care workers, or waitresses) (Spalter-Roth et al. 1995).

. . . Many single mothers spend much of their adult lives cycling between welfare and work. The essence of this "welfare trap" is not that public aid warps women's personalities or makes them pathologically dependent, although that may occasionally happen. Rather, it is that low-wage jobs usually make single mothers even worse off than they were on welfare.

Because our data represent a snapshot rather than a longitudinal portrait of how welfare-reliant mothers were living in the early 1990s, we cannot fully describe how single mothers moved between the federal welfare system and work over time. Our data do allow us, however, to present monthly budgets (ones that balance) for poor persons—something that no national survey of low-income families has managed to accomplish. These budgets provide a clear picture of the cost that welfare-reliant mothers must take into account when making the decision between welfare and work. Our open-ended interviews with mothers also offered insights into how many women viewed the trade-off between welfare and work, and how they thought these trade-offs might affect their children.

What is interesting, then, is the continuing attraction of work for these women. Like mothers everywhere, these women dreamed of moving to a better neighborhood, making it a month without running out of food, regularly giving their children and loved ones birthday and Christmas gifts, taking their children down South to meet their kinfolk, buying their children good enough clothing that they would not be ridiculed at school, and maybe having a little nest egg for emergencies. Faced with the reality that welfare would never get them any of these things, and with the deadening knowledge that welfare receipt was daily eating away at their own and their children's self-respect, mothers planned ways in which they could make work more profitable for themselves and less of a threat to their children's well-being.

REFERENCES

Bane, Mary Jo, and David T. Ellwood. 1994. *Welfare Realities: From Rhetoric to Reform.* Cambridge, MA: Harvard University Press.

Bianchi, Suzanne. 1995. "Changing Economic Roles of Women and Men." In *State of the Union,* edited by Reynolds Farley. New York: Russell Sage Foundation.

Blank, Rebecca M. 1994. "The Employment Strategy: Public Policies to Increase Work and Earnings." In *Confronting Poverty,* edited by Sheldon H. Danziger, Gary D. Sandefur, and Daniel H. Weinberg. Cambridge, MA: Harvard University Press; New York: Russell Sage Foundation.

———. 1995. "Outlook for the U.S. Labor Market and Prospects for Low-Wage Entry Jobs." in *The Work Alternative,* edited by Demetra Smith Nightingale and Robert H. Haveman. Washington, DC: The Urban Institute Press; Cambridge, MA: Harvard University Press.

Burtless, Gary. 1994. "Public Spending on the Poor: Historical Trends and Economic Limits." In *Confronting Poverty,* edited by Sheldon H. Danziger, Gary D. Sandefur, and Daniel H. Weinberg. Cambridge, MA: Harvard University Press; New York: Russell Sage Foundation.

Edin, Kathryn. 1994. "The Myths of Dependency and Self-Sufficiency." Working Paper. New Brunswick, NJ: Center for Urban Policy Research, Rutgers University.

———. 1995. "Single Mothers and Child Support: The Possibilities and Limits of Child Support Policy." *Children and Youth Services Review* 17: 203–230.

Edin, Kathryn, and Christopher Jencks. 1992. "Welfare." In *Rethinking Social Policy,* edited by Christopher Jencks. Cambridge, MA: Harvard University Press.

Edin, Kathryn, and Laura Lein. Forthcoming. "Work, Welfare, and Single Mothers' Economic Survival Strategies." *American Sociological Review.*

Friedlander, Daniel, and Judith M. Gueron. 1992. "Are High-Cost Services More Effective Than Low-Cost Services?" In *Evaluating Welfare and Training Programs,* edited by Charles F. Manski and Irwin Garfinkel. Cambridge, MA: Harvard University Press.

Goodwin, Leonard. 1972. *Do the Poor Want to Work? A Social-Psychological Study of Work Orientation.* Washington, DC: The Brookings Institution.

Gottschalk, Peter, and Sheldon Danziger. 1989. "Unemployment Insurance and the Safety Net for the Unemployed." Working Paper.

Harris, Kathleen Mullan. 1993. "Work and Welfare Among Single Mothers in Poverty." *American Journal of Sociology* 99: 317–352.

———. 1996. "Life After Welfare: Women, Work and Repeat Dependency." *American Sociological Review* 61: 207–246.

Heclo, Hugh. 1994. "Poverty Politics." In *Confronting Poverty,* edited by Sheldon H. Danziger, Gary D. Sandefur, and Daniel H. Weinberg. Cambridge, MA: Harvard University Press; New York: Russell Sage Foundation.

Levy, Frank. 1995. "Incomes and Income Inequality." In *State of the Union,* edited by Reynolds Farley. New York: Russell Sage Foundation.

Martin, Theresa Castro, and Larry L. Bumpass. 1989. "Report on Trends in Marital Disruption." *Demography* 26: 37–51.

Mead, Lawrence M. 1992. *The New Politics of Poverty: The Nonworking Poor in America.* New York: Basic Books.

Michalopoulos, Charles, and Irwin Garfinkel. 1989. "Reducing Welfare Dependence and Poverty of Single Mothers by Means of Earnings and Child Support: Wishful Thinking and Realistic Possibilities." Discussion Paper 882–89. Madison: Institute for Research on Poverty, University of Wisconsin.

Pearce, Diana. 1991. "Chutes and Ladders." Paper presented at the American Sociological Association Annual Meeting. Cincinnati, Ohio (August).

Reskin, Barbara. 1993. "Sex Segregation in the Workplace." *Annual Review of Sociology* 19: 241–270.

Sorensen, Elaine, and Mark Turner. 1996. "Barriers in Child Support Policy: A Literature Review." Paper LB-SB-96-04. Philadelphia: National Center on Fathers and Families, University of Pennsylvania.

Spalter-Roth, Roberta, Beverly Burr, Heidi Hartmann, and Louise Shaw. 1995. "Welfare That Works: The Working Lives of AFDC Recipients." Report to the Ford Foundation. Washington, DC: Institute for Women's Policy Research.

Spalter-Roth, Roberta, Heidi Hartmann, and Beverly Burr. 1994. *Income Insecurity: The Failure of Unemployment Insurance to Reach Working AFDC Mothers.* Washington, DC: Institute for Women's Policy Research.

Sweet, James A., and Larry L. Bumpass. 1987. *American Families and Households.* New York: Russell Sage Foundation.

Tienda, Marta, and Haya Stier. 1991. "Joblessness and Shiftlessness: Labor Force Activity in Chicago's Inner City." In *The Urban Underclass,* edited by Christopher Jencks and Paul E. Peterson. Washington, DC: Brookings Institution.

U.S. House of Representatives, Committee on Ways and Means. 1987. Overview of Entitlement Programs (Green Book). Washington, DC: U.S. Government Printing Office.

———. 1993. Overview of Entitlement Programs (Green Book). Washington, DC: U.S. Government Printing Office.

THINKING ABOUT THE READING

According to Edin and Lein, what prevents welfare-reliant mothers from taking paid jobs? Many social observers criticize middle-class mothers for putting their children in day care or leaving them with a private caregiver so they can go to work. Yet mothers on welfare are criticized for *not* doing so. How can you account for these very different responses? Why do you suppose there is such a strong tendency in American society to demonize welfare recipients? If the problem welfare recipients face is that low-wage jobs available to them don't pay enough to support a family, would you advocate increasing wages to ensure these jobs paid them enough to get off welfare permanently? What kinds of problems would such a solution create? What benefits? How has this article changed your perception of welfare recipients?

CHAPTER 12

The Architecture of Inequality: Race and Ethnicity

The history of race in American society is an ambivalent one. Our famous sayings about equality conflict with the experiences of most racial and ethnic minorities: oppression, violence, and exploitation. Opportunities for life, liberty, and the pursuit of happiness have always been distributed along racial and ethnic lines. American society is built on the assumption that different immigrant groups will ultimately assimilate, changing their way of life to conform to that of the dominant culture. But the increasing diversity of the population has shaped people's ideas about what it means to be an American and has influenced our relationships with one another and with our social institutions.

Racial inequality is both a personal and structural phenomenon. On the one hand, it is lodged in individual prejudice and discrimination. On the other hand, it resides in our language, collective beliefs, and important social institutions. This latter manifestation of racism is more difficult to detect than personal racism, hence it is more difficult to stop. Because such racism exists at a level above personal attitudes, it will not disappear simply by reducing people's prejudices.

Consider, for instance, life in the "inner city." In "The Code of the Streets," Elijah Anderson shows us that for many African Americans growing up in poor, depressed neighborhoods, violence and despair are consistent parts of everyday life. The highly publicized economic boom of the late 1990s barely touched these areas. Institutional racism is still rampant. Access to jobs that pay a living wage—and therefore a traditional means of gaining respect—is almost nonexistent. The result is that many poor inner-city African American youth develop a profound sense of alienation from mainstream society and its institutions. Anderson shows us that in such an environment a "code of the streets" emerges with a set of informal rules governing all aspects of public interaction, including violence. This code is so powerful that it even holds the most well intentioned, "decent" families in its grip.

Higher education is usually seen as a ticket out of the inner city. In the United States, universities are typically viewed as tolerant, open-minded places where people can share ideas in an atmosphere of mutual respect. The formal exclusion of certain ethnic or religious groups is a thing of the past. Indeed, some social commentators argue that racism in American universities has all but disappeared. However, Joe Feagin, Hernán Vera, and Nikitah Imani, in their article, "The Agony of Education," show that students of color who attend predominantly White universities often find that their presence is unwelcome, that their academic skills are doubted, and that they don't enjoy access to the same intellectual opportunities and institutional support that White students enjoy. Based on focus-group interviews with both students and their parents, the authors capture the painful racist realities African American students face in their pursuit of a college education. They find that racial insensitivity and inequality are well entrenched in the presumably tolerant halls of higher education.

Cultural attitudes toward race can sometimes be internalized to the point of individuals trying to surgically alter their appearance to conform to Anglo standards. In her article, " 'Opening' Faces," Eugenia Kaw describes how some Asian American women have come to judge their own bodies through the eyes of White America. Although many of these women claim that by undergoing cosmetic surgery they are simply exercising their right to become more desirable and don't see any racism in their decisions, their attitudes reflect a deeper belief in the social inferiority of Asian features.

The Code of the Streets

Elijah Anderson

Of all the problems besetting the poor inner-city black community, none is more pressing than that of interpersonal violence and aggression. It wreaks havoc daily with the lives of community residents and increasingly spills over into downtown and residential middle-class areas. Muggings, burglaries, carjackings, and drug-related shootings, all of which may leave their victims or innocent bystanders dead, are now common enough to concern all urban and many suburban residents. The inclination to violence springs from the circumstances of life among the ghetto poor—the lack of jobs that pay a living wage, the stigma of race, the fallout from rampant drug use and drug trafficking, and the resulting alienation and lack of hope for the future.

Simply living in such an environment places young people at special risk of falling victim to aggressive behavior. Although there are often forces in the community which can counteract the negative influences, by far the most powerful being a strong, loving, "decent" (as inner-city residents put it) family committed to middle-class values, the despair is pervasive enough to have spawned an oppositional culture, that of "the streets," whose norms are often consciously opposed to those of mainstream society. These two orientations—decent and street—socially organize the community, and their coexistence has important consequences of residents, particularly children growing up in the inner city. Above all, this environment means that even youngsters whose home lives reflect mainstream values—and the majority of homes in the community do—must be able to handle themselves in a street-oriented environment.

This is because the street culture has evolved what may be called a code of the streets, which amounts to a set of informal rules governing interpersonal public behavior, including violence. The rules prescribe both a proper comportment and a proper way to respond if challenged. They regulate the use of violence and so allow those who are inclined to aggression to precipitate violent encounters in an approved way. The rules have been established and are enforced mainly by the street-oriented, but on the streets the distinction between street and decent is often irrelevant; everybody knows that if the rules are violated, there are penalties. Knowledge of the code is thus largely defensive; it is literally necessary for operating in public. Therefore, even though families with a decency orientation are usually opposed to the values of the code, they often reluctantly encourage their children's familiarity with it to enable them to negotiate the inner-city environment.

At the heart of the code is the issue of respect—loosely defined as being treated "right," or granted the deference one deserves. However, in the troublesome public environment of the inner city, as people increasingly feel buffeted by forces beyond their control, what one deserves in the way of respect becomes more and more problematic and uncertain. This in turn further opens the issue of respect to sometimes intense interpersonal negotiation. In the street culture, especially among young people, respect is viewed as almost and external entity that is hard-won but easily lost, and so must constantly be guarded. The rules of the code in fact provide a framework for negotiating respect. The person whose very appearance—including his clothing, demeanor, and way of moving—deters transgressions feels that he possesses, and may be considered by others to possess, a measure of respect. With the right amount of respect, for instance, he can avoid "being bothered" in public. If he is bothered, not only may he be in physical danger but he has been disgraced or "dissed" (disrespected). Many of the forms that dissing can take might seem petty to middle-class people (maintaining eye contact for too long, for example), but to those invested in the street code, these actions become serious indications of the other person's intentions. Consequently, such people become very sensitive to advances and slights, which could well serve as warnings of imminent physical confrontation.

This hard reality can be traced to the profound sense of alienation from mainstream society and its institutions felt by many poor inner-city black people, particularly the young. The code of the streets is actually a cultural adaptation to a profound lack of faith in the police and the judicial system. The police are most often seen as representing the dominant white society and not caring to protect inner-city residents. When called, they may not respond, which is one reason many residents feel they must be prepared to take extraordinary measures to defend themselves and their loved ones against those who are inclined to aggression. Lack of police accountability has in fact been incorporated into the status system: the person who is believed capable of "taking care of himself" is accorded a certain deference, which translates into a sense of physical and psychological control. Thus the street code emerges where the influence of the police ends and personal responsibility for one's safety is felt to begin. Exacerbated by the proliferation of drugs and easy access to guns, this volatile situation results in the ability of the street-oriented minority (or those who effectively "go for bad") to dominate the public spaces.

Decent and Street Families

Although almost everyone in poor inner-city neighborhoods is struggling financially and

therefore feels a certain distance from the rest of America, the decent and the street family in a real sense represent two poles of value orientation, two contrasting conceptual categories. The labels "decent" and "street," which the residents themselves use, amount to evaluative judgments that confer status on local residents. The labeling is often the result of a social contest among individuals and families of the neighborhood. Individuals of the two orientations often coexist in the same extended family. Decent residents judge themselves to be so while judging others to be of the street, and street individuals often present themselves as decent, drawing distinctions between themselves and other people. In addition, there is quite a bit of circumstantial behavior—that is, one person may at different times exhibit both decent and street orientations, depending on the circumstances. Although these designations result from so much social jockeying, there do exist concrete features that define each conceptual category.

Generally, so-called decent families tend to accept mainstream values more fully and attempt to instill them in their children. Whether married couples with children or single-parent (usually female) households, they are generally "working poor" and so tend to be better off financially than their street-oriented neighbors. They value hard work and self-reliance and are willing to sacrifice for their children. Because they have a certain amount of faith in mainstream society, they harbor hopes for a better future for their children, if not for themselves. Many of them go to church and take a strong interest in their children's schooling. Rather than dwelling on the real hardships and inequities facing them, many such decent people, particularly the increasing number of grandmothers raising grandchildren, see their difficult situation as a test from God and derive great support from their faith and from the church community.

Extremely aware of the problematic and often dangerous environment in which they reside, decent parents tend to be strict in their child-rearing practices, encouraging children to respect authority and walk a straight moral line. They have an almost obsessive concern about trouble of any kind and remind their children to be on the lookout for people and situations that might lead to it. At the same time, they are themselves polite and considerate of others, and teach their children to be the same way. At home, at work, and in church, they strive hard to maintain a positive mental attitude and a spirit of cooperation.

So-called street parents, in contrast, often show a lack of consideration for other people and have a rather superficial sense of family and community. Though they may love their children, many of them are unable to cope with the physical and emotional demands of parenthood, and find it difficult to reconcile their needs with those of their children. These families, who are more fully invested in the code of the streets than the decent people are, may aggressively socialize their children into it in a normative way. They believe in the code and judge themselves and others according to its values.

In fact the overwhelming majority of families in the inner-city community try to approximate the decent-family model, but there are many others who clearly represent the worst fears of the decent family. Not only are their financial resources extremely limited, but what little they have may easily be misused. The lives of the street-oriented are often marked by disorganization. In the most desperate circumstances people frequently have a limited understanding of priorities and consequences, and so frustrations mount over bills, food, and, at times, drink, cigarettes, and drugs. Some tend toward self-destructive behavior; many street-oriented women are crack-addicted ("on the pipe"), alcoholic, or involved in complicated relationships with men who abuse them. In addition, the seeming intractability of their situation, caused in large part by the luck of well-paying jobs and the persistence of racial discrimination, has engendered deep-seated bitterness and anger in many of the most desperate and poorest blacks, especially young people. The need both to exercise a measure of control and to lash out at somebody is often reflected in the adults' relations with their children. At the least, the frustrations of persistent poverty shorten the fuse in

such people—contributing to a lack of patience with anyone, child or adult, who irritates them.

In these circumstances a woman—or a man, although men are less consistently present in children's lives—can be quite aggressive with children, yelling at and striking them for the least little infraction of the rules she has set down. Often little if any serious explanation follows the verbal and physical punishment. This response teaches children a particular lesson. They learn that to solve any kind of interpersonal problem one must quickly resort to hitting or other violent behavior. Actual peace and quiet, and also the appearance of calm, respectful children conveyed to her neighbors and friends, are often what the young mother most desires, but at times she will be very aggressive in trying to get them. Thus she may be quick to beat her children, especially if they defy her law, not because she hates them but because this is the way she knows to control them. In fact, many street-oriented women love their children dearly. Many mothers in the community subscribe to the notion that there is a "devil in the boy" that must be beaten out of him or that socially "fast girls need to be whupped." Thus much of what borders on child abuse in the view of social authorities is acceptable parental punishment in the view of these mothers.

Many street-oriented women are sporadic mothers whose children learn to fend for themselves when necessary, foraging for food and money any way they can get it. The children are sometimes employed by drug dealers of become addicted themselves. These children of the street, growing up with little supervision, are said to "come up hard." They often learn to fight at an early age, sometimes using short-tempered adults around them as role models. The street-oriented home may be fraught with anger, verbal disputes, physical aggression, and even mayhem. The children observe these goings-on, learning the lesson that might makes right. They quickly learn to hit those who cross them, and the dog-eat-dog mentality prevails. In order to survive, to protect oneself, it is necessary to marshal inner resources and be ready to deal with adversity in a hands-on way. In these circumstances physical prowess takes on great significance.

In some of the most desperate cases, a street-oriented mother may simply leave her young children alone and unattended while she goes out. The most irresponsible women can be found at local bars and crack houses, getting high and socializing with other adults. Sometimes a troubled woman will leave very young children alone for days at a time. Reports of crack addicts abandoning their children have become common in drug-infested inner-city communities. Neighbors or relatives discover the abandoned children, often hungry and distraught over the absence of their mother. After repeated absences, a friend or relative, particularly a grandmother, will often step in to care for the young children, sometimes petitioning the authorities to send her, as guardian of the children, the mother's welfare check, if the mother gets one. By this time, however, the children may well have learned the first lesson of the streets: survival itself, let alone respect, cannot be taken for granted; you have to fight for your place in the world.

Campaigning for Respect

These realities of inner-city life are largely absorbed on the streets. At an early age, often even before they start school, children from street-oriented homes gravitate to the streets, where they "hang"—socialize with their peers. Children from these generally permissive homes have a great deal of latitude and are allowed to "rip and run" up and down the street. They often come home from school, put their books down, and go right back out the door. On school nights eight- and nine-year-olds remain out until nine or ten o'clock (and teenagers typically come in whenever they want to). On the streets they play in groups that often become the source of their primary social bonds. Children from decent homes tend to be more carefully supervised and are thus likely to have curfews and to be taught how to stay out of trouble.

When decent and street kids come together, a kind of social shuffle occurs in which children have a chance to go either way. Tension builds as

a child comes to realize that he must choose an orientation. The kind of home he comes from influences but does not determine the way he will ultimately turn out—although it is unlikely that a child from a thoroughly street-oriented family will easily absorb decent values on the streets. Youths who emerge from street-oriented families but develop a decency orientation almost always learn those values in another setting—in school, in a youth group, in church. Often it is the result of their involvement with a caring "old head" (adult role model).

In the street, through their play, children pour their individual life experiences into a common knowledge pool, affirming, confirming, and elaborating on what they have observed in the home and matching their skills against those of others. And they learn to fight. Even small children test one another, pushing and shoving, and are ready to hit other children over circumstances not to their liking. In turn, they are readily hit by other children, and the child who is toughest prevails. Thus the violent resolution of disputes, the hitting and cursing, gains social reinforcement. The child in effect is initiated into a system that is really a way of campaigning for respect.

In addition, younger children witness the disputes of older children, which are often resolved through cursing and abusive talk, if not aggression or outright violence. They see that one child succumbs to the greater physical and mental abilities of the other. They are also alert and attentive witnesses to the verbal and physical fights of adults, after which they compare notes and share their interpretations of the event. In almost every case the victor is the person who physically won the altercation, and this person often enjoys the esteem and respect of onlookers. These experiences reinforce the lessons the children have learned at home: might makes right, and toughness is a virtue, while humility is not. In effect they learn the social meaning of fighting. When it is left virtually unchallenged, this understanding becomes an ever more important part of the child's working conception of the world. Over time the code of the streets becomes refined.

Those street-oriented adults with whom children come in contact—including mothers, fathers, brothers, sisters, boyfriends, cousins, neighbors, and friends—help them along in forming this understanding by verbalizing the messages they are getting through experience: "Watch your back." "Protect yourself." "Don't punk out." "If somebody messes with you, you got to pay them back." "If someone disses you, you got to straighten them out." Many parents actually impose sanctions if a child is not sufficiently aggressive. For example, if a child loses a fight and comes home upset, the parent might respond, "Don't you come in here crying that somebody beat you up; you better get back out there and whup his ass. I didn't raise no punks! Get back out there and whup his ass. If you don't whup his ass, I'll whup your ass when you come home." Thus the child obtains reinforcement for being tough and showing nerve.

While fighting, some children cry as though they are doing something they are ambivalent about. The fight may be against their wishes, yet they may feel constrained to fight or face the consequences—not just from peers but also from caretakers or parents, who may administer another beating if they back down. Some adults recall receiving such lessons from their own parents and justify repeating them to their children as a way to toughen them up. Looking capable of taking care of oneself as a form of self-defense is a dominant theme among both street-oriented and decent adults who worry about the safety of their children. There is thus at times a convergence in their child-rearing practices, although the rationales behind them may differ.

Self-Image Based on "Juice"

By the time they are teenagers, most youths have either internalized the code of the streets or at least learned the need to comport themselves in accordance with its rules, which chiefly have to do with interpersonal communication. The code revolves around the presentation of self. Its basic requirement is the display of a certain predisposition to violence. Accordingly, one's bearing must send the unmistakable if sometimes subtle message to "the next person" in public that one is capable of violence and mayhem when the situation requires it, that one can take care of oneself. The nature of this communication is largely determined by the demands of the circumstances but can include facial expressions, gait, and verbal expressions—all of which are geared mainly to deterring aggression. Physical appearance, including clothes, jewelry, and grooming, also plays an important part in how a person is viewed; to be respected, it is important to have the right look.

Even so, there are no guarantees against challenges, because there are always people around looking for a fight to increase their share of respect—or "juice," as it is sometimes called on the street. Moreover, if a person is assaulted, it is important, not only in the eyes of his opponent but also in the eyes of his "running buddies," for him to avenge himself. Otherwise he risks being "tried" (challenged) or "moved on" by any number of others. To maintain his honor he must show he is not someone to be "messed with" or "dissed." In general, the person must "keep himself straight" by managing his position of respect among others; this involves in part his self-image, which is shaped by what he thinks others are thinking of him in relation to his peers.

Objects play an important and complicated role in establishing self-image. Jackets, sneakers, gold jewelry, reflect not just a person's taste, which tends to be tightly regulated among adolescents of all social classes, but also a willingness to possess things that may require defending. A boy wearing a fashionable, expensive jacket, for example, is vulnerable to attack by another who covets the jacket and either cannot afford to buy one or wants the added satisfaction of depriving someone else of his. However, if they boy forgoes the desirable jacket and wears one that isn't "hip," he runs the risk of being teased and possibly even assaulted as an unworthy person. To be allowed to hang with certain prestigious crowds, a boy must wear a different set of expensive clothes—sneakers and athletic suit—every day. Not to be able to do so might make him appear socially deficient. The youth comes to covet such items—especially when he sees easy prey wearing them.

In acquiring valued things, therefore, a person shores up his identity—but since it is an identity based on having things, it is highly precarious. This very precariousness gives a heightened sense of urgency to staying even with peers, with whom the person is actually competing. Young men and women who are able to command respect through their presentation of self—by allowing their possessions and their body language to speak for them—may not have to campaign for regard but may, rather, gain it by the force of their manner. Those who are unable to command respect in this way must actively campaign for it—and are thus particularly alive to slights.

One way of campaigning for status is by taking the possessions of others. In this context, seemingly ordinary objects can become trophies imbued with symbolic value that far exceeds their monetary worth. Possession of the trophy can symbolize the ability to violate somebody—to "get in his face," to take something of value from him, to "dis" him, and thus to enhance one's own worth by stealing someone else's. The trophy does not have to be something material. It can be another person's sense of honor, snatched away with a derogatory remark. It can be the outcome of a fight. It can be the imposition of a certain standard, such as a girl's getting herself recognized as the most beautiful. Material things, however, fit easily into the pattern. Sneakers, a pistol, even somebody else's girlfriend, can become a trophy. When a person can take something from another and then flaunt it, he gains a certain regard by being the owner, or the controller, of that thing. But this display of ownership can then provoke other people to challenge him. This game of who controls what is thus constantly being played out on inner-city streets, and the trophy—extrinsic or intrinsic, tangible or intangible—identifies the current winner.

An important aspect of this often violent give-and-take is its zero-sum quality. That is, the extent to which one person can raise himself up depends on his ability to put another person down. This underscores the alienation that permeates the inner-city ghetto community. There is a generalized sense that very little respect is to be had, and therefore everyone competes to get what affirmation he can of the little that is available. The craving for respect that results gives people thin skins. Shows of deference by others can be highly soothing, contributing to a sense of security, comfort, self-confidence, and self-respect. Transgressions by others which go unanswered diminish these feelings and are believed to encourage further transgressions. Hence one must be ever vigilant against the transgressions of others or even *appearing* as if transgressions will be tolerated. Among young people, whose sense of self-esteem is particularly vulnerable, there is an especially heightened concern with being disrespected. Many inner-city young men in particular crave respect to such a degree that they will risk their lives to attain and maintain it.

The issue of respect is thus closely tied to whether a person has an inclination to be violent, even as a victim. In the wider society people may not feel required to retaliate physically after an attack, even though they are aware that they have been degraded or taken advantage of. They may feel a great need to defend themselves *during* an attack, or to behave in such a way as to deter aggression (middle-class people certainly can and do become victims of street-oriented youths), but they are much more likely than street-oriented people to feel that they can walk away from a possible altercation with their self-esteem intact. Some people may even have the strength of character to flee, without any thought that their self-respect or esteem will be diminished.

In impoverished inner-city black communities, however, particularly among young males and perhaps increasingly among females, such flight would be extremely difficult. To run away would likely leave one's self-esteem in tatters. Hence people often feel constrained not only to stand up and at least attempt to resist during an assault but also to "pay back"—to seek revenge— after a successful assault on their person. This may include going to get a weapon or even getting relatives involved. Their very identity and self-respect, their honor, is often intricately tied up with the way they perform on the streets during and after such encounters. This outlook reflects the circumscribed opportunities of the inner-city poor. Generally people outside the ghetto have other ways of gaining status and regard, and thus do not feel so dependent on such physical displays.

By Trial of Manhood

On the street, among males these concerns about things and identity have come to be expressed in the concept of "manhood." Manhood in the inner city means taking the prerogatives of men with respect to strangers, other men, and women—being distinguished as a man. It implies physicality and a certain ruthlessness. Regard and respect are associated with this concept in large part because of its practical application: if others have little or no regard for a person's manhood, his very life and those of this loved ones could be in jeopardy. But there is a chicken-and-egg aspect to this situation: one's physical safety is more likely to be jeopardized in public *because* manhood is associated with respect. In other words, an existential link has been created between the idea of manhood and one's self-esteem, so that it has become hard to say which is primary. For many inner-city youths, manhood and respect are flip sides of the same coin; physical and psychological well-being are inseparable, and both require a sense of control, of being in charge.

The operating assumption is that a man, especially a real man, knows what other men know—the code of the streets. And if one is not a real man, one is somehow diminished as a person, and there are certain valued things one simply does not deserve. There is thus believed to be a certain justice to the code, since it is considered that everyone has the opportunity to know it. Implicit in this is that everybody is held responsible for being familiar with the code. If the victim of a mugging, for example, does not know the code and so responds "wrong," the perpetrator may feel justified even in killing him and may

feel no remorse. He may think, "Too bad, but it's his fault. He should have known better."

So when a person ventures outside, he must adopt the code—a kind of shield, really—to prevent others from "messing with" him. In these circumstances it is easy for people to think they are being tried or tested by others even when this is not the case. For it is sensed that something extremely valuable is at stake in every interaction, and people are encouraged to rise to the occasion, particularly with strangers. For people who are unfamiliar with the code—generally people who live outside the inner city—the concern with respect in the most ordinary interactions can be frightening and incomprehensible. But for those who are invested in the code, the clear object of their demeanor is to discourage strangers from even thinking about testing their manhood. And the sense of power that attends the ability to deter others can be alluring even to those who know the code without being heavily invested in it—the decent inner-city youths. Thus a boy who has been leading a basically decent life can, in trying circumstances, suddenly resort to deadly force.

Central to the issue of manhood is the widespread belief that one of the most effective ways of gaining respect is to manifest "nerve." Nerve is shown when one takes another person's possessions (the more valuable the better), "messes with" someone's woman, throws the first punch, "gets in someone's face," or pulls a trigger. Its proper display helps on the spot to check others who would violate one's person and also helps to build a reputation that works to prevent future challenges. But since such a show of nerve is a forceful expression of disrespect toward the person on the receiving end, the victim may be greatly offended and seek to retaliate with equal or greater force. A display of nerve, therefore, can easily provoke a life-threatening response, and the background knowledge of that possibility has often been incorporated into the concept of nerve.

True nerve exposes a lack of fear of dying. Many feel that it is acceptable to risk dying over the principle of respect. In fact, among the hard-core street-oriented, the clear risk of violent death may be preferable to being "dissed" by another. The youths who have internalized this attitude and convincingly display it in their public bearing are among the most threatening people of all, for it is commonly assumed that they fear no man. As the people of the community say, "They are the baddest dudes on the street." They often lead an existential life that may acquire meaning only when they are faced with the possibility of imminent death. Not to be afraid to die is by implication to have few compunctions about taking another's life. Not to be afraid to die is the quid pro quo of being able to take somebody else's life—for the right reasons, if the situation demands it. When others believe this is one's position, it gives one a real sense of power on the streets. Such credibility is what many inner-city youths strive to achieve, whether they are decent or street-oriented, both because of its practical defensive value and because of the positive way it makes them feel about themselves. The difference between the decent and the street-oriented youth is often that the decent youth makes a conscious decision to appear tough and manly; in another setting—with teachers, say, or at his part-time job—he can be polite and deferential. The street-oriented youth, on the other hand, has made the concept of manhood a part of his very identity; he has difficulty manipulating it—it often controls him.

Girls and Boys

Increasingly, teenage girls are mimicking the boys and trying to have their own version of "manhood." Their goal is the same—to get respect, to be recognized as capable of setting or maintaining a certain standard. They try to achieve this end in the ways that have been established by the boys, including posturing, abusive language, and the use of violence to resolve disputes, but the issues for the girls are different. Although conflicts over turf and status exist among the girls, the majority of disputes seem rooted in assessments of beauty (which girl in a group is "the cutest"), competition over boyfriends, and attempts to regulate other people's

knowledge of and opinions about a girl's behavior or that of someone close to her, especially her mother.

A major cause of conflicts among girls is "he say, she say." This practice begins in the early school years and continues through high school. It occurs when "people," particularly girls, talk about others, thus putting their "business in the streets." Usually one girl will say something negative about another in the group, most often behind the person's back. The remark will then get back to the person talked about. She may retaliate or her friends may feel required to "take up for" her. In essence this is a form of group gossiping in which individuals are negatively assessed and evaluated. As with much gossip, the things said may or may not be true, but the point is that such imputations can cast aspersions on a person's good name. The accused is required to defend herself against the slander, which can result in arguments and fights, often over little of real substance. Here again is the problem of low self-esteem, which encourages youngsters to be highly sensitive to slights and to be vulnerable to feeling easily "dissed." To avenge the dissing, a fight is usually necessary.

Because boys are believed to control violence, girls tend to defer to them in situations of conflict. Often if a girl is attacked or feels slighted, she will get a brother, uncle, or cousin to do her fighting for her. Increasingly, however, girls are doing their own fighting and are even asking their male relatives to teach them how to fight. Some girls form groups that attack other girls or take things from them. A hard-core segment of inner-city girls inclined toward violence seems to be developing. As one thirteen-year-old girl in a detention center for youths who have committed violent acts told me, "To get people to leave you alone, you gotta fight. Talking don't always get you out of stuff." One major difference between girls and boys: girls rarely use guns. Their fights are therefore not life-or-death struggles. Girls are not often willing to put their lives on the line for "manhood." The ultimate form of respect on the male-dominated inner-city street is thus reserved for men.

"Going for Bad"

In the most fearsome youths such a cavalier attitude toward death grows out of a very limited view of life. Many are uncertain about how long they are going to live and believe they could die violently at any time. They accept this fate; they live on the edge. Their manner conveys the message that nothing intimidates them; whatever turn the encounter takes, they maintain their attack—rather like a pit bull, whose spirit many such boys admire. The demonstration of such tenacity "shows heart" and earns their respect.

This fearlessness has implications for law enforcement. Many street-oriented boys are much more concerned about the threat of "justice" at the hands of a peer than at the hands of the police. Moreover, many feel not only that they have little to lose by going to prison but that they have something to gain. The toughening-up one experiences in prison can actually enhance one's reputation on the streets. Hence the system loses influence over the hard core who are without jobs, with little perceptible stake in the system. If mainstream society has done nothing *for* them, they counter by making sure it can do nothing *to* them.

At the same time, however, a competing view maintains that true nerve consists in backing down, walking away from a fight, and going on with one's business. One fights only in self-defense. This view emerges from the decent philosophy that life is precious, and it is an important part of the socialization process common in decent homes. It discourages violence as the primary means of resolving disputes and encourages youngsters to accept nonviolence and talk as confrontational strategies. But "if the deal goes down," self-defense is greatly encouraged. When there is enough positive support for this orientation, either in the home or among one's peers, then nonviolence has a chance to prevail. But it prevails at the cost of relinquishing a claim to being bad and tough, and therefore sets a young person up as at the very least alienated from street-oriented peers and quite possibly a target of derision or even violence.

Although the nonviolent orientation rarely overcomes the impulse to strike back in an encounter, it does introduce a certain confusion and so can prompt a measure of soul-searching, or even profound ambivalence. Did the person back down with his respect intact or did he back down only to be judged a "punk"—a person lacking manhood? Should he or she have acted? Should he or she have hit the other person in the mouth? These questions beset many young men and women during public confrontations. What is the "right" thing to do? In the quest for honor, respect, and local status—which few young people are uninterested in—common sense most often prevails, which leads many to opt for the tough approach, enacting their own particular versions of the display of nerve. The presentation of oneself as rough and tough is very often quite acceptable until one is tested. And then that presentation may help the person pass the test, because it will cause fewer questions to be asked about what he did and why. It is hard for a person to explain why he lost the fight or why he backed down. Hence many will strive to appear to "go for bad," while hoping they will never be tested. But when they are tested, the outcome of the situation may quickly be out of their hands, as they become wrapped up in the circumstances of the moment.

An Oppositional Culture

The attitudes of the wider society are deeply implicated in the code of the streets. Most people in inner-city communities are not totally invested in the code, but the significant minority of hard-core street youths who are have to maintain the code in order to establish reputations, because they have—or feel they have—few other ways to assert themselves. For these young people the standards of the street code are the only game in town. The extent to which some children—particularly those who through upbringing have become most alienated and those lacking in strong and conventional social support—experience, feel, and internalize racist rejection and contempt from mainstream society may strongly encourage them to express contempt for the more conventional society in turn. In dealing with this contempt and rejection, some youngsters will consciously invest themselves and their considerable mental resources in what amounts to an oppositional culture to preserve themselves and their self-respect. Once they do, any respect they might be able to garner in the wider system pales in comparison with the respect available in the local system; thus they often lose interest in even attempting to negotiate the mainstream system.

At the same time, many less alienated young black have assumed a street-oriented demeanor as a way of expressing their blackness while really embracing a much more moderate way of life; they, too, want a nonviolent setting in which to live and raise a family. These decent people are trying hard to be part of the mainstream culture, but the racism, real and perceived, that they encounter helps to legitimate the oppositional culture. And so on occasion they adopt street behavior. In fact, depending on the demands of the situation, many people in the community slip back and forth between decent and street behavior.

A vicious cycle has thus been formed. The hopelessness and alienation many young inner-city black men and women feel, largely as a result of endemic joblessness and persistent racism, fuels the violence they engage in. This violence serves to confirm the negative feelings many whites and some middle-class blacks harbor toward the ghetto poor, further legitimating the oppositional culture and the code of the streets in the eyes of many poor young blacks. Unless this cycle is broken, attitudes on both sides will become increasingly entrenched, and the violence, which claims victims, black and white, poor and affluent, will only escalate.

THINKING ABOUT THE READING

What is Anderson referring to when he speaks of a "code of the streets"? What role do poverty and racism play in the development of such a code? He makes a distinction between "street families" and "decent families." How useful is such a disctinction? How do these different types of families adapt to the code of the streets? Anderson implies that *all* young people in the inner city, no matter how mainstream their values, must know, and at times live, by the code of the streets. Do you agree? If it's true that young people feel that in order to gain respect they must show a willingness to be agressive when publicly confronted, how can the vicious cycle of violence in the inner city ever by broken?

The Agony of Education

Black Students at White Colleges and Universities

Joe R. Feagin, Hernán Vera, and Nikitah Imani

The Modern University: Under Attack from "Barbarians"?

In the United States public and private universities have long been viewed as particularly open and tolerant places. Universities are seen as intellectual settings that house and disseminate the best knowledge society has to offer. Essential to the ideal of the university is that it be a place where diverse students and teachers seek knowledge without hindrance and intolerance. The university is usually viewed as guiding serious inquiry, verifying discoveries, and exposing errors through, to quote John Henry Newman, "the collision of mind with mind, and knowledge with knowledge."[1] In this vision, as Newman put it, a university is "a seat of wisdom, a light of the world . . . and Alma Mater of the rising generation."[2] Critical to this ideal is the view that excellence should be the only criterion for the admission of students and teachers to its ranks, as well as the criterion for the quest for knowledge.

In recent years this ideal of the liberal university has been featured in mainstream critiques of racial events and multicultural trends on our university campuses. The values of excellence and tolerance are frequently viewed as under attack from misguided administrators, radical professors, multiculturalists, and students and professors of color. According to widely publicized analysts like Allan Bloom, Dinesh D'Souza, Arthur Schlesinger, and Richard Bernstein, traditionally white colleges and universities have experienced a "revolution" that sets aside concern for excellence in favor of the allegedly corrupting goals of certain racial groups, particularly African Americans. Indeed, the problem with the modern university, many critics suggest, is that it has become *too* tolerant of the views and interests of African Americans and other people of color.[3] . . .

For these analysts of higher education, . . . the predominantly white colleges and universities are under siege. At the heart of this threat are black students, who from this perspective are seen as challenging the hoary ideals of excellence and tolerance. Bloom has argued that there is "a large black presence in major universities, frequently equivalent to the black proportion in the general population" and that this black presence has become "indigestible" because of black student desires for self-segregation and political power. Bloom blames black students for being unwilling to melt into the melting pot, "as have *all* other groups."[4] Black students, with their allegedly exaggerated assessments of universities as racist and their pressure for political change, are viewed as a threat to the ideal of the university. Shelby Steele contends that most black students have "an unconscious need to exaggerate the level of racism on campus—to make it a matter of the system, not just a handful of students."[5] . . .

At the heart of this analysis of U.S. educational institutions is the view that racial barriers and impediments are not important problems at predominantly white colleges and universities. These authors, like many media analysts, political commentators, and politicians, deny the reality of discrimination and other aspects of racism not only in education but also in society at large. As a result, the problems faced by students of color in education are often said to be located in the students themselves, their families, or their communities. For example, the educational analyst, George Keller, has attributed the lack of black advancement in education to causes primarily within the black community. Faulting community leadership, he argues that "petulant and accusatory black spokespersons will need to climb off their soapboxes and walk through the unpleasant brambles of their young people's new preferences and look at their young honesty. . . . Critics will need to stop the fashionable practice of lambasting the colleges as if they were the central problem."[6]

Many conventional analysts have joined the chorus suggesting that racism is no longer a serious problem that needs government action, except perhaps in the confused minds of many African Americans. For example, Martin Seligman, a prominent psychologist, has echoed the common white accusation that black Americans are generally wrong-headed in focusing on racism in U.S. institutions. Black explanations of their problems that often accent white racism or the "system" are, he argues, "superficially appealing," but they are not nearly as good as personalized explanations like "bad housing," "drugs," or "poor education." . . . Like many conventional white analysts of U.S. society today, Seligman goes on to suggest that this blaming-racism view should also be avoided by government policymakers: It is time to question the view that "racism is to blame for all the barriers between African Americans and success in our society."[7]

A Strikingly Different View of Campus Racism

In a national interview study that included a number of African American college students, one black honor student at a public university reviewed her pre-college trip to a leading Ivy League school:

> I applied to a lot of different schools besides here, and I got accepted to a major Ivy League university. And I went up there, checked it out. . . . I deserved to be there, simply because

of my merit. And I felt bad; I felt out of place. One reason I didn't go to there, besides the money (I couldn't afford it), one reason I didn't go was because it reeked of whiteness. And that is no joke. And I am not exaggerating. I was only there for two days, and after one day I wanted to leave. And I mean, really, it just reeked, everywhere I went, reeked of old white men, just lily whiteness, oozing from the corners! [laughs] I wanted to leave. And I knew that socially I would just be miserable. And I talked to other black students; I talked to all of them because there aren't a lot. And so I said, "do you like it here?" And they were like, "no, we're miserable."[8]

If white students and faculty members are as receptive to black students as is claimed by the conventional commentators on education cited above, why is it that this black student feels "bad" and "out of place"? Why is it that the other black students at this Ivy League school feel "miserable"?

Or take the case of Michigan's Olivet College. During the spring of 1992 trouble began brewing when some white students openly objected to black male students dating white females. Then there was a major incident. A white female student reported that she was sitting in the dorm with a white male friend when four students, three of whom were black, came to her door to discuss various matters. One black student had come to ask about a paper the female student was typing for him. After some discussion, the black students departed. Later, the female student telephoned friends to report receiving a threatening phone call, which she felt had come from the black students. As a result, a dozen or so white fraternity men came to the dorm, where they confronted two of the black students. The white students directed racial epithets at the black students, who responded in kind; more students gathered, and an interracial fight ensued.[9]

Over the next few days black students became worried that they might be attacked on the campus. White students and anonymous callers directed more threats at the black students, and someone distributed Ku Klux Klan literature on the campus.[10] Many white and black students who were friends ceased speaking to each other.[11] Significantly, two thirds of the black students left the campus within a few days of the initial incident. Soon after the interracial fight, moreover, black students organized a "black caucus," which would come to play an important role in pressing the Olivet administration to take action to promote racial justice on campus.[12]

One black student present at the fight noted reported hearing comments like "We're sick of these niggers. We're going to get them."[13] Later the black student commented: "Many students you thought were your friends, roommates, teammates, guys who'd give you answers during tests were . . . calling you all types of names—coon, spearchucker, nigger. . . . [Were] everyone's true colors shown that night? And were the first three years a facade, a fake, and finally everybody showed how they really felt?"[14]

One black student leader commented: "Right now we're in the midst of a civil war on this campus, and you can't turn your back on it. You have to face it. . . . I feel as though I have to make a stand here."[15] One of the black students who remained on campus following the incidents commented on feeling unwanted and isolated: "People I never would have expected have called me names. None of us feel we can trust white people anymore."[16] A student who returned home told a reporter that they "recruit us here, but they offer nothing to keep us here. I think the blacks you see here are the last you will see here in a long while. I wouldn't advise them to come here. They can see there is racial violence, and they are not going to want to come here."[17]

Could these black students be talking about the same type of college setting that the critics of higher education are discussing? Was this college, which was founded by a white abolitionist in the 1800s, a place where the multiculturism philosophy was so pervasive that whites were no longer dominant in determining the campus climate or curriculum?

At a number of colleges and universities, African American students and other students of color have recently organized to protest various types of racism on campus. For example, early in 1995 at Iowa's Grinnell College more than sixty students of color, most of them African American, organized a protest over racist incidents on campus, including the use of racial slurs by disc jockeys on the campus radio and by white spectators at a basketball game. The students reportedly wore tape over their mouths on campus, with the message, according to a student leader, of "Through our silence, you will hear our rage."[18]

Is this a college where racial barriers are no longer of any significance, as many of the critics of higher education allege? Is this a place where black students and faculty members dominate the campus climate?

Racial Intolerance on College Campuses

Recent studies of students at predominantly white institutions of higher education have found that black students have higher attrition rates and lower rates of going to graduate school. On the average, they do not perform as well academically or adjust as well psychosocially as white students.[19] In the mainstream literature there is a debate as to why black students do not do as well as whites. As we have seen, many contemporary critics of higher education blame the black students, their families, or community leaders for the students' college troubles.

This view of higher education is myopic because it fails to examine the persisting role of white racism in creating serious barriers and dilemmas for black students and other students of color, the point emphasized by the students quoted above. One analyst of higher education, Walter R. Allen, has underscored the finding that U.S. schools and colleges have been settings for black "contest and struggle, as African Americans fought for full citizenship and participation in the society. Historically, educational institutions and educators have been among the most active and effective instruments for the oppression of black people."[20]

... On predominantly white college campuses racial barriers and impediments are still commonplace. This racism is situated in particular places and at particular times as it is practiced by numerous white students, faculty, staff members, police officers, and administrators. Today as in the past, racial discrimination involves erecting physical, legal, and social barriers to make certain places, situations, and positions inaccessible to, or difficult for members of racial outgroups. In the process of developing strategies to cope with racial barriers, black and other targets of discrimination are injured physically, psychologically, and socially and forced to waste much energy and time.

For the white-on-black racism ... racial discrimination can be viewed as the *socially organized set of practices that deny African Americans the dignity, opportunities, spaces, time, positions, and rewards this nation offers to white Americans.* What we call *racism* encompasses subtle and overt discriminatory practices, their institutional contexts, and the attitudes and ideologies that shape or rationalize them. Discriminatory practices— for example, the legal exclusion of black students from many colleges until the 1950s or the informal discrimination directed against these students at majority-white colleges today—are generated by a range of white motivations, including prejudice, fear and hope of personal gain....

Today ... racial discrimination is well entrenched in higher education in the United States. This institutionalized discrimination both reflects and molds the attitudes and ideologies many whites hold in regard to racial matters. Racially restrictive practices in U.S. educational institutions have occurred over a large geographical area and for centuries. Clearly, isolated bigotry is not sufficient to explain the past or present racial picture in education. The coordinated repetition of discriminatory practices suggests that their roots are not just in individual psyches; individual perpetrators are compelled, in part, by social forces and perspectives that they feel to be irresistible. Many harmful racial actions taken by whites are supported by their families, social networks, and organizational contexts. For a long period, bla-

tantly antiblack discrimination at most colleges and universities was prescribed by law or local customs. In many areas no African American students were allowed; in most others they were discouraged from attending or restricted once on campus.

Although outright exclusion is now illegal, much discrimination persists in a variety of forms, ranging from blatant actions to subtle but still destructive practices, and is carried out by a range of white perpetrators. Discrimination targeting black students on contemporary college campuses is still carried out by a large number of whites guided by the informal norms of white-dominated social networks and organizations. The examples of discrimination on campus today include racist joking, the recurring use of racist epithets, racist skits and floats by white fraternities, the neglect or rejection of black students' goals and interests, the mistreatment of black students by white professors, and racial harassment by white police officers.[21] Most damaging is the taking for granted by most white administrators, faculty, staff, and students that the campus is a "white" place in which blacks are admitted, at best, as guests....

White Professors and Educational Change

Many critics of higher education have recently portrayed the faculty members in contemporary colleges and universities as flocking to the cause of multiculturalism. In large numbers, according to this theory, many professors are significantly altering their courses to reflect closely the new language and materials associated with what critics call "political correctness." However, these ideologues ignore the substantial evidence that contradicts their arguments. Research studies since the 1970s indicate that only a modest number of white faculty members have made any significant concessions to the presence of African American students on their campuses or in their classrooms. One study, for example, found that when white faculty members were asked the degree to which black issues or pressures had changed their role as faculty members, most replied "very little." Moreover, a majority of the faculty members said that faculty support for black-oriented programs was more likely to be passive than active.[22]

. . . Everyday life on college campuses is structured in terms of historical and collective memories, as well as in terms of racialized places and interaction. We have shown how different forms of racialized space, time, and recognition shape the everyday life experiences of African American students and parents. In this [article] we examine accounts of black students' experiences with their instructors, who bear the responsibility of nurturing and teaching students, the university's purpose. Recall the ideal of the modern university: A singularly open and tolerant place for the transmission of learning. The instructors pass on the collective wisdom and understandings of the past to the new learners in the present. They play the central role in the university as the "Alma Mater of the rising generation."[23] Basic to this ideal is the provision of a place where students and teachers can come together to seek knowledge without serious prejudices, barriers, and impediments.

Today, however, the reality of the predominantly white university often does not reflect this distinctive ideal. Thus, on the exit questionnaire the black students at State University were asked, "How often have you been mistreated by white professors at this campus because of your race?" Half replied that it had happened once or twice, while six percent said several times. Thirty-nine percent said never, and the rest replied that they were not sure.

Surveys on student-faculty interaction at other major university campuses have found a similar situation, although the proportions of students facing problems vary. For instance, a 1990s survey of "ethnic minority" (mostly black, Latino, and Asian) students at the University of Nevada (Las Vegas) found only thirty-seven percent of those with an opinion said that they had almost never felt discriminated against on campus by instructors.[24] A survey of black students at a historically white Southern university, half of whom were first-year or second-year students, found that one-fifth of the students had already encountered racial discrimination at the hands of faculty members—and that another ten percent were uncertain whether they had faced discrimination.[25] Moreover, a 1995 report on the experiences of black graduate students at Michigan State University found that more than seventy percent had witnessed or experienced acts of racial condescension from faculty members, while twenty-eight percent reported witnessing or experiencing incidents of racial hostility involving faculty members.[26] . . .

White Professors and Course Content: "I Got Full Support from My White Humanities Professor"

The experiences of black students with faculty at mostly white campuses are regularly confusing and contradictory. Sometimes, white instructors are supportive and encouraging. They seem committed to fair treatment and a respect for different life experiences and perspectives. In other cases, however, white instructors, like other whites on campus, engage in hostile practices or adopt a viewpoint that is aggressively Euro-American. The fact that many discriminatory acts are unpredictable in timing or character makes their effects even more disruptive and painful to their targets.

In one focus group a student commented on positive support from a faculty member in a humanities department:

> In my humanities class, my first humanities class, one of our projects was you had to write a letter to an influential figurehead on campus, and I wrote a letter to our university's president, basically bitching him out about the minority retention rate. And I got full support from my white humanities professor.

As we noted previously, the black student dropout rate is really a "push-out" rate that affects too many black students. Here the professor appears to be doing nothing out of the ordinary, and yet, this student considers the incident worth mentioning. The student is manifesting an apprehension about expressing his feelings about a racial problem on campus. The lives of black students in white-dominated places are frequently limited by a reluctance to express openly their feelings about racial matters.

Discussing recurring incidents, one student noted the contrast between the attitude of some white students and that of a white professor who specializes in African American studies:

> . . . As soon as we started talking about books by black people, everybody was like this [she sits closed-lipped, with arms crossed]. They sat there, and they looked [strangely] at me . . . because they think that I'm really stupid, like they usually do. And as it is, they like claim to be so open, and how they're understanding and everything. All [open], but then when it comes to racial issues or even like gender and stuff or politics, they'll be, like they're afraid to say what they believe, or either they have no opinion. They're like really ignorant. My teacher is like— he's white—but he, I guess he's a scholar of black studies, which really surprised them. So it's kind of that you don't just have just the black teachers pushing you to read black materials and learn about black books and stuff.

The experience here is not unique. When racial issues come up in this classroom, some white students are tight-lipped, and a black student becomes the center of attention. . . . One critical aspect of modern racism is the white *misrecognition* of African Americans, the failure of whites to see a black person as fully human, as like a white person. As this black student interprets these incidents, some of her white peers misrecognize her as "really stupid." Her position in the classroom is socially constructed and defined negatively by some whites because of her skin color and, apparently, her viewpoint. This injurious white view is highlighted, paradoxically, by the teacher's assigning African American materials to read and discuss. As we see it, the inclusion of texts by black authors in the curriculum should be commonplace, not noteworthy as

here, because it broadens the knowledge of black and white students about the contributions of Africans and African Americans to world history and to U.S. society. . . .

. . . The last . . . statement on [a] positive experience with [a] white instructor took place in a university context in which black intellectual concerns and political interests, according to the student, are only occasionally given serious attention. As female scholars and male scholars of color slowly make their way into academia, the interests, ideas, and literature previously ignored by the white-male professoriat are finally being incorporated into a few course syllabi, discussions, and lectures. This intellectual broadening is very important for the health and survival of African American students in these white-normed places, but it is still the exception rather than the rule in courses on contemporary college campuses.

Stereotyping by White Instructors: "Their Preference Was Not to Have Blacks"

Several students in the group interviews discussed racial stereotyping by some faculty members. For example, one male athlete described the view of his professor about an absence from class:

> I didn't go to class for like maybe a week or two because we have a tournament and everything. And I talked to the [white] teacher on the telephone. . . . The teacher thought I was right and she gave me a break. [The teacher apparently failed him on a test.] And, then, when I confronted [her], and she was like, "You just didn't go to class because you didn't want to," when she found out who I was. [What's your sport?] Soccer. And when I told her I was an athlete, she automatically thought—"Well, the track team wasn't away this weekend." Then, like afterwards, I had to go to my coach and everything . . . so I could take the test over.

The problem arose when the teacher did not trust the student's veracity in regard to the athletic commitments he had claimed. The student's humiliation is compounded by having to obtain a formal excuse from his coach, who is thus informed the student is not trusted. This is a painful situation to be put in, especially when one is a member of a group whites have long stereotyped as undependable and untrustworthy. . . .

. . . The old stereotype of black incompetence seems to lie just beneath the surface of certain professorial assumptions about African American students. . . .

One male student reported another type of stereotyping of non-European students by a white professor:

> I don't want to take a lot of time with this professor. One time she was taking attendance, and there were these two Asian kids. One was like Japanese and the other was like Vietnamese, right. So she . . . said the one kid's name wrong. And she was like, "Oh well it doesn't matter because like you guys all look alike." She said that . . . I mean she said that! [No one said anything to her?] Well, most of the people were white people, so they were just like, whatever? But we . . . the black people just connected right there. One of these kids dropped the course. I don't know if that's why, but I'd have dropped it if she said that to me.

Here we see a kind of crude insensitivity that some white professors still show toward students of color. This comment was disrespectful not only to its Asian targets but also to the black students who also felt victimized by such a barbed remark. This type of faculty insensitivity is reproduced on college campuses because it can . . . usually be expressed with impunity. To challenge a professor in such circumstances requires more status or power than students, black or nonblack, ordinarily have.

As with other types of human interaction, that between students and their instructors cannot be expected to be free from difficulties and misunderstandings. However, the racial definition of the problems documented in this chapter makes them distinctive. One way these problems are different from many run-of-the-mill classroom problems is that their impact frequently extends beyond the students to their circle of friends and into their families. Serious incidents accumulate and become part of the collective memory. We see this in the accounts of some parents who spoke of classroom problems at State University. For example, in a lengthy discussion one mother noted that she encouraged her daughter to go to SU:

> She's a graduate. I did encourage her. And she transferred into State University. She'd gone to another school and after a year decided to try them and had an essentially positive experience. . . . I'm not saying that it was a typical experience or it was the standard. But it wasn't as negative as we anticipated. . . . I expected racial incidents, and they happened. I expected discrimination in the classroom, and she had it. [Like what?] Instructors who actually let it be known that their preference was not to have blacks in their classroom or that blacks didn't have the thinking ability to be in those particular classes. And they let them know. And they have no reservations about making a comment about African Americans. Like giving them, [and example of] "An African American woman who is below thirty, and to look for her to be whorish." That's not an unusual comment, and with African Americans sitting in the class.

In addition to the stereotyped image of young black men as criminal, a common white image is of young black women as whores or welfare "queens." This gendered racism undergirds the misrecognition of black women as not fully human and has a very negative effect on young black female students. . . .

As these accounts suggest, the agonizing struggle to deal with racial barriers is a recurring and stressful aspect of black students' lives. Psychological studies of black students on predominantly white campuses have found relatively high levels of stress, some of it generated by faculty and other staff members. For instance, one research project interviewed 284 black students at the University of North Carolina (Charlotte) in an attempt to inventory stress factors for students in such areas as personal identity, interpersonal relationships, and career plans. Among the environmental stressors found were insensitive white faculty, low academic expectations, unfair grading, and poor academic advising. The study concluded that assessments of stress levels needed to be culture-specific in order to determine accurately the distinctive needs of students of color.[27] . . .

Professorial Inquiries: "They Put the Whole Black Race on Your Shoulders"

The historical absence of black students in traditionally white universities, as well as their continuing underrepresentation there, contribute to whites' lack of knowledge or awareness of the histories, lives, and racial burdens of African Americans. We have noted how black students often become objects of attention when racial issues arise in class. White professors and students can construct social situations where black students are placed in awkward or painful positions. Social situations of this kind deserve a closer look because of the damaging effects they can have.

In the focus groups several students talked of being forced to be the spokesperson "for the race" in and out of the classroom. One student commented:

> Another thing I wanted to say is like in the classroom when it's like a situation when you're like the only black person in your classroom, and they put the whole black race on your shoulders. [How often does that happen? That you are the only one in your class?] [Several voices] A lot!

A characteristic experience of black students in predominantly white universities is feeling the burden placed on them by whites to act as defenders and explainers of their group. This problem seems to be commonplace in colleges and universities across the United States. For example, a 1990s report on the racial climate at a major University of California campus noted that black students talked starkly about problems of academic adjustment there "in terms of their high visibility in classes."[28]

In one focus group a male student noted that sometimes in the classroom white professors

> can be talking about a whole other subject . . . [and] they use the word "minority" in a sentence. And their eyes just look right to you.

The impact of such professorial gestures can be enhanced by their unthinking spontaneity. Even the expectation of unwanted attention can create pressure and discomfort, as another student explained:

> Especially like this social science department. We're just sitting there in the class. And the teacher . . . you can always tell when they want to get a little discussion, a little smile, [a] look at their notes. "So what about the racial situation and detention we had down at [names a local place]?" And you're sitting there like, "OK this is going to be on me, this is big trouble." You're like the only black person sitting there, and it just happens to be an issue dealing with your race. You feel a lot of pressure, a lot of pressure.

Being the unwanted center of attention is stressful and serves to remind black students of the racial position that they are often assigned in predominantly white classroom settings. The pressure reported by the black students does not come from one isolated act, but from a recurrence of similar situations over several years at SU. The repetition of such acts creates a racialized social structure on campus, which the black students have little power to define or significantly alter. In some cases the questioning by whites can take on a probing and personal character, as in the following account:

> One of my teachers . . . was talking to me about black issues. She was trying to drain me of information or something. . . . I would go there [to her office] and she would start talking about my family. And she was like, "Well what do you think about their racial atmosphere?" and "When I was growing up as a white woman. . . ." She really pissed me off because she thought I was going to sit there and discuss it with her, so

she could better understand how black people were. She was using me as a book or something saying, "Let me try and understand this." That's the thing. . . . I guess [whites] think all black people are dumb from the get-go. And [if] you've got a little bit of sense they're like, "Oh, wow. Maybe I can like probe you." And then when you don't want to talk about it she's like, "I don't understand." I mean if you want to know something you go out and find out yourself, like I had to find out. Then they get mad at you and say, "Oh you're bitter," and all that stuff. . . . And it seems like white people feel the need to get in your business and stuff.

The student leaves little doubt about the discomfort and pain this professor caused her. She is caught in a dilemma: If she responds, she has to control her anger at being placed in such a position. Yet if she remains silent, she may chastise herself for failing to confront established stereotypes. The student is reacting against being treated as a research object. Some white instructors may probe a student out of well-intentioned ignorance or out of insensitivity, but others may be expressing a deeper racial motivation. Whatever the motivation, many white instructors may become irritated when rebuffed. Both the probing and the displeasure at being rebuffed underscore the reality of racially determined power relations on campus. Moreover, this professorial inquisition signals as much about implicit white conceptions of whiteness, such as the presumed right to get familiar with or to probe African Americans, as it does about white images of African Americans.[29]

On college campuses today students of color seem to face more problems which racially insensitive faculty members, who are unreflective about their racial stereotypes or proclivities, than with openly bigoted professors. In another research study conducted by the senior author a talented student at another predominantly white university described how a white professor made a comment on religion that assumed the student was a Baptist. She was Episcopalian and resented the professor's implication that most African Americans were Baptist. She added:

Probably the thing that angers me the most about white people is their insensitivity and their total inability to see you as an individual. You're always seen as a black person. And as a black woman, you're seen as a black person before you're seen as a woman. It's just a constant struggle. You're always trying to assert your personality, or your style, your individuality. If you want recognition, you practically have to go overboard to get people to see that you are unique with your own style and your own goals, and your own way of thinking about things.[30]

. . .

As we have noted, the mistreatment of students of color on a college campus is often more than an individual matter. Racial incidents can have an impact on friends and family members. In the parent focus groups, some spoke about relatives and acquaintances who had felt singled out in the classroom, as in the case of this mother:

. . . I can think of a friend of mine saying from her experience being in a classroom. . . . You're almost intimidated to put your hand up and contribute to the conversation because you are outnumbered so greatly in a classroom. One experience she had was when she actually got the courage to raise her hand. . . . And she put her hand up and the teacher stopped and looked at her and said, "Your name is?" And she didn't know her name, and she finally came up with her name. And she—when the teacher called her name, all the students, [were] looking you know like the E. F. Hutton [advertisement], "This person speaks," like, "Oh this thing can talk." And the intimidation was so great to her, and that was a struggle for her. . . .

Here we observe again the intimidation that a black student perceives in a sea of white faces on a majority-white college campus and the social isolation this produces. Not surprisingly, black students experience being targeted in this manner as social marginalization.

These narratives relate the pain and tribulations of black students at predominantly white institutions. The black students and parents sometimes do not attribute any negative intention to the white professors and students who caused the pain or discomfort. Some of the white teachers were apparently unaware of the hurt or damage that they inflicted. The fact that white teachers, sometimes in well-meaning or spontaneous ways, are able to inflict such pain on African American students signals a more serious problem than if the white actions represented only hostility and ill will. The institutionalization of racism means that certain hurtful ways of acting have become more or less routinized, as taken-for-granted actions linked to traditional ways of doing a professor's job. Unless the black students' side of the story is heard, and heard clearly, there is little hope for eradicating the racial divide that persists in higher education.

Differential Treatment from White Professors: "Things That Build Up Rage"

In any society the subtle and overt distinctions that are made in everyday interactions define the character of the social positions one occupies in interaction with others. Being singled out for differential treatment by a professor can cause much pain, no matter what the motivation may be, and this distress effectively marks the actual position one occupies on campus. For example, one young woman noted what seems at first glance to be a solely positive experience:

> I've had a lot of teachers say, I mean if there's only like two or three blacks in my class, [that they want to help]. And I've even had one teacher who held the blacks after class and was like, "I really want my black students to do well." You know I was surprised she said it, you know, she's not a good teacher.

This student notes differential treatment that seems to favor black students; at least, some white teachers seem sincere in trying to help the black students do well in their classes. However, this extra attention has a special treatment aspect and may communicate to the black students, and to white students who become aware of it, that in

the view of some faculty members black students are expected to do less well than whites, thereby stigmatizing the black students. Indeed, surveys on several college campuses have found that many black students report that white professors expect them to be less successful in academic pursuits than white students. A survey of black graduate students at Michigan State University, for instance, found that more than half knew faculty members who had differential expectations for white students and students of color.[31] . . .

The parallel here with some research on women students is interesting. For example, Roberta Hall and Bernice Sandler have reported on the "chilly classroom climate" for female students. They found that male teachers often use sexist humor, language, and disparaging remarks about women's abilities and do not draw women into classroom discussions as often as they do men.[32] Classroom obstacles for women or students of color can be blatant or subtle, even subtle enough to be imperceptible to outside observers. Some contemporary patterns of discrimination on college campuses are so hidden, novel, or subtle that students may struggle for the words with which to describe it. One University of California (Berkeley) report noted that black students there sometimes do not have "a textured and nuanced language to fit the newer and more subtly perceived forms of discomforting racism" and thus often self-censor instances of racism "before they can give language to it."[33] In one group discussion there a black professor asked a group of black students what they meant by racism. One student said in frustration: "You know, you know . . . they just act like you don't belong here."[34] . . .

. . . Social groups are rooted in the "we feeling" of their members, an emotion conveyed through expressions of solidarity, social integration, and cooperation. A pivotal finding of our research is that the marginalized social position from which black students often interact with their white peers and with white faculty members is defined in everyday interactions and encounters. Every day the African American students go through a series of interpersonal exchanges on campus, interactions from which they learn how they are viewed and how they must act and react.

These students do not react solely on the basis of one negative exchange but use their intellect and individual and collective memories to make sense of what is going on around them. The following statement illustrates how one black student came to make sense of a singular incident, integrating it into a stock of knowledge that would help him understand future incidents:

> Another incident that I was involved in was trying to . . . subscribe a class. And the professor was white, and she gave me the impression fully—I mean quote, unquote "indirectly"— that I was not quite wanted in there. I was number one for the entire week waiting to get into the class. And I was attending classes, participating and what have you, and there were about two or three other white guys that was numbers two, three, and four on the wait list. And I asked her if she would oversubscribe me, since the waiting list came in and I did not get the class. And she started hitting me about how she is all busy, she's got so much other stuff to do, that taking on additional student would become a problem, and that grading an extra paper would just be too much As if I'm really asking her to bend backwards, et cetera. And what I was told a couple weeks later when I did not get the class is that another guy got in. . . .
> . . . That just let me know what time it was. And it just goes to show that when you think things are not going on, things are definitely going on. And it's a shame because we all need this kind of stuff in terms of trying to provide positive momentum to try and get the job done. These are things that build up rage. And then certain people have a problem controlling inner rage, and they do things perhaps that they may regret.

This student describes the painful effects of a situation of anomie, a situation where one cannot trust the existing rules to be applied in one's case. It is likely that his prior experiences on campus, and those of his friends, lead him to believe that discriminatory "things are definitely going on." After using the first person singular throughout most of the account, he concludes in an impersonal voice that describes the effects such incidents generate. This shift in language is a device to put some distance between him and his feelings. He apparently shifts to a description of a general black situation, but the rage he attributes to "certain people" is no doubt his own.

This account points toward the significant impact that racial barriers can have on the health and well-being of those targeted. Research studies have found rage over recurring racism to be common among African Americans. This rage, when repressed, can create serious health problems, such as hypertension, and can explode at inopportune times. According to a 1993 Princeton University report, students of color there frequently react to recurring discrimination "by storing up their responses. This often leads to a kind of accumulated rage that evokes strong reactions in instances which would not seem to warrant such a response." In turn, the report notes, such an overreaction reinforces whites in their notions that African Americans and other people of color are thin-skinned and volatile.[35]

This accumulated rage over racism is central to recent discussions of black and white Americans. Recently, the arch-conservative analyst Dinesh D'Souza has argued that racism is disappearing from U.S. society and that middle-class African Americans have a rage that indicates a "questionable grip on reality" and a frustration over "pursuing unearned privileges." In his view the rage is unjustified and unrelated to continuing racial barriers these middle-class African Americans face in this society.[36] In contrast, in a very perceptive analysis of black rage, the scholar bell hooks has shown that it is useful for a white-dominated society "to make all black rage appear pathological rather than identify the structure wherein that rage surfaces." In her view, black rage is very much grounded in persisting racist barriers in U.S. society. While this rage can lead to pathological actions, it can also lead to constructive actions that empower African Americans. What she has in mind is the way in which rage can become "a passion for freedom and justice that illuminates, heals, and makes redemptive struggle possible."[37] Regularly, in our student and parent commentaries we see this passion for freedom and racial justice, a passion that has significant educational relevance for all students and staff members on contemporary college campuses.

The situation of anomie, of unclear norms, described in the last account may be more widespread than one might think on college campuses. A major factor determining satisfactory progress toward a college degree is fair grading and evaluation by the professoriat. Whether one is a white student or a student of color, one has the right to expect grades to be based on the same standards. Certainly, the image of the university as an especially open and tolerant place might lead students to expect that grading will be done impartially and without restraint on freedom of expression. However, these conventional academic guarantees are often not enjoyed by black students. Research surveys at State University and on other campuses indicate that from a fifth to half of African American students report they have received unfair grades because of their skin color. A recent study of the experiences of black graduate students at Michigan State University found that a third knew faculty members who graded students of color lower than whites, and thirty percent knew faculty members who gave less help to their students of color than to white students.[38] . . .

. . . Fair grading criteria and honest explanations are important for all students, but especially for African American students who are veterans of campus and social unfairness. Interestingly, most black students seem willing to give white teachers the benefit of the doubt wherever possible. Differential grading practices constitute racial maltreatment in that they see to affix to black students the label of weak achievement or failure. As a result, academic transcripts will not measure accurately the black achievements.

Another male student was able to discern the likely reason for certain grades he received:

I wrote a paper in a humanities course about how Africa was a civilization long before other civilizations. . . . I don't know what it is about the teachers but they really come down on you for attempting to write papers, something, you know, that has to do with [black] topics. If it's controversial, it's not good. If you're not writing about peace and love or whatever, or something that's just neutral, it's not good. . . . I mean you can see it . . . if you write some papers, you're writing, you get B's, B+'s, A's. And then all of a sudden you write this paper on Africa, and you get a C–. You're like "What! How did this happen?" Or you know when they try to invalidate your material. . . . All of a sudden, "You can't do this in your paper." . . . If I wrote about how great Abraham Lincoln was, I probably would have gotten an A. But I'm writing about Africa; I'm getting a C–. It doesn't, you know, it just doesn't click.

All students who write on creative topics run the risk of displeasing teachers who are not informed on such topics or who have a different perspective. However, at a predominantly white institution, it is too often the views and knowledge of African American students in regard to certain historical, political, or racial matters that are deemed inappropriate or odd by certain white instructors. Many black students like to do research on and write about topics such as the history of Africa, a continent that evokes strong positive emotions in many blacks and negative stereotypes in the minds of many whites. Most critical here is the intellectual censorship of topics of importance to black students, a censorship that again makes them feel like aliens in white territory.

Contesting grades can bring into play other white racial concerns and stereotypes, as in this example from a male student:

I'm in [names a course] right now, and I'm doing pretty good in it, but I have another friend who's black who's not doing that well. And the teacher, he's kind of an ass because like, my friend, he went up to him and was asking a question, "Why did you put all these circles on my paper and grade it this way?" And then the teacher says something like,"Well, come back. I think you're not in the right mood to discuss this." He was like the way I am now. Not like yelling or nothing, but just asking him a question. He says, "I don't think you're in a mood to discuss it. Come back after you've calmed down a little bit." [Moderator: Do you think it was racially motivated?] I think so.

Again, the position of black students in the campus social structure is made clear. The teacher's dismissal of the student's question is based on the way the professor read a black student's demeanor. This white teacher devalued the black student's question, and the injury was compounded when the teacher suggested the questions were rooted in anger or agitation. As college teachers ourselves, we are aware that students are sometimes not objective about the grades they receive and often want to discuss them. Yet, here this common situation was apparently not read as ordinary by the white teacher. Instead it seems the student was stereotyped as a threatening young black man....

Grades are part of the performance record that becomes central to an individual's academic history, one that follows a student well beyond the university. *Recurring* accounts of grading problems at predominantly white universities raise questions about the integrity of the academic system. The last few accounts demonstrate how professors' grading practices can become a problem for black students when they are rooted in inconsistent standards for class performance.

... Social neglect or isolation on a majority-white college campus is more difficult for some students than for others.... On such campuses the average white student has more chances to "make it" than the average black student, who, because of campus and societal racism, may need extra support and encouragement from faculty members.

... One mother commented on her son's problems with support at State University:

I don't think that they have the same support system ... at the State University, that they would at a historically [black] college. I don't think that the teachers or the professors are as interested or [that] they ... give them the certain help that they need. That's how I see it.... And that's why I did not want my youngest son to go there.... His brother went to a historically black college; and I tried to get him there.... So then he said, "Well, I'll go to the university, Mom, because I know I'll do well there." So that's where he's at. I don't know whether he likes it or what, but he's just there. I don't feel good about it, but you know, that's it.

... Aware of the agony black students frequently go through at predominantly white colleges, this mother tried to get her son to go to a historically black college. Our interviews suggest how black colleges and universities, although declining in number in recent decades, are frequently viewed as places of strong individual and educational support and as refuges from the vagaries of white racism. In our groups, as well as in other research studies we have cited, many black parents and students indicate that at predominantly white universities black students often do not get the same kind or amount of attention that white students receive or that black students receive at historically black colleges. The parents' and students' conclusions are not unsubstantiated, but are based on a familial and communal stock of knowledge about the racial slant of certain educational institutions. Such knowledge is usually grounded in the experiences of numerous black individuals over some period of time....

The Case of Black Faculty Members: "The Teachers Weren't That Black"

... The prevailing whiteness of the SU campus quickly becomes clear to new students in the scarcity of black instructors, who make up a very small percentage of the campus faculty. The relative shortage of black faculty comes as a blow to many students, as this young man explained:

And when I got here like, the students weren't black. The teachers weren't that black. And it was like I go through this science department, and there are no black teachers or no black TA's even. I mean there's none; and at first it really screwed me up. I'm walking around, and . . . it just didn't seem normal. It seemed like I commute into this place, and I'm like in the twilight zone where there's no one I could possibly relate to in the whole department. . . . But it just made me feel like I had no hope to go through.

The "twilight zone" metaphor suggests the unreality black students often sense at predominantly white universities, as well as the personal wounds a white-centered campus can inflict. Having "no hope" to get through is a serious burden to bear on top of the usual difficulties associated with leaving home for college and becoming a university student.

Several focus group participants pointed out the utility of black instructors for informal counseling and support rooted in the collective black experience. . . . The presence of African American faculty is one antidote for the condition of hopelessness many black students describe. These faculty members are perceived as having suffered some of the same tensions and pain faced by the students, experiences that even the most sympathetic white instructors cannot be expected to have.

One SU student was surprised and excited in finding a black professor teaching her course:

> I have an adjunct professor this semester who's black. . . . And it freaked me out, because I didn't expect it. I walked into class, and you look, and it's like "whoa." You know? I'm like excited, and other people are like, "Why is she so excited?"

. . .

In the group interviews a few parents also spoke about the importance of black faculty members. After explaining that her experience with white professors had left her with the feeling that SU was a "cold" place, one mother commented on issues linked to the absence of black professors:

> . . . I don't see that many blacks on campus. At least when I was there, I didn't see that many blacks there. And of all of the four professors that I had in my department, none of them were black. I did not see any black people, really, except a few people that were in my classes. But I did not see any black professors, so I didn't know if they had any or not. But visibly, it is a very white-looking campus.

We have seen that "white-looking" is a key dimension of the space at SU. Certain recurring messages for black students and parents signal that SU is a place where they are unusual and unwelcome. In the group interviews most participants seemed to be saying that the recruitment of black graduate students and faculty members is a critical part of the corrective action that would be necessary to make this predominantly white environment much more hospitable.

The Difficult Position of Black Faculty and Staff: "You Are an Associate Professor, and You Work for the Dean"

For all the importance that black students and parents attributed to the presence of black faculty, they were not naive about the role that they could play. Some in the parent groups dealt critically with remedial measures being taken by the university, including the hiring of black staff members. These token efforts were viewed as inadequate to solving the range of individual and systemic racial problems. One father noted that

> I was there months ago. . . . The change is that you have big black people in places that are supposed to be to help you, in equal opportunity offices and so forth. [But they are] really there just there in name only. Well, you know the typical environment—you are [an] associate professor and you work for the dean. You're

not going to do anything to cut your throat in getting your promotion and so forth. It's less than tokenism. The people are sincere and so forth, you pull them aside and talk to them, and they'll tell you what it is. But how do you break through that?

In such cases, the apparent tokenism is not even tokenism in practice. The black parents are sensitive to the problems of black faculty members put into relatively powerless positions where they cannot speak out aggressively on racial issues. Pressures on faculty of color to fit into the white campus atmosphere are great. For example, a 1993 survey of forty-two mostly black, Latino, and Asian faculty members at the University of Nevada (Las Vegas) found that forty-three percent of those replying to a question about assimilation said they had to abandon some or all of the important parts of their cultures to be successful in their university departments. Two-thirds of those replying to a related question reported that they sometimes or all the time felt pressure to ascribe to white colleagues' values. Moreover, thirty-five percent of those replying to a question about decision making in their university unit said that they were excluded from the decisions some or all of the time.[39]

Putting a significant number of black faculty into positions of power is very important for black parents and students. One mother noted how she felt about the recent hiring of a few black professors at State University:

Negative. . . . In their key positions, then, I know two people came from a black university to State University. And they're in top positions, so maybe they can work with each other to do the things that they want. [To] try and act like they're helping you. . . . Then I know about five that [left] the State University because they felt things weren't going right with them as far as benefits and how they were being treated. And they left. . . . The change from what I see is not better.

Earlier in the group discussion the same parent had commented about

All this kind of stuff you read it in the papers about the university. And a few years ago I remember . . . they had just hired a black administrator, somebody in a high position, and they kept talking about this thing as if he were the only black person in the world.

A father commented on the same appointment:

There have been some changes that we've seen that have been cosmetic anyhow. [Moderator: Like what? What do you mean by cosmetic?] You have a black administrator over there few years ago, you've had a black administrator? . . . The [black] enrollment is up, but I can't say that the graduation is up.

The parents recognize the changes in recent years at SU and approve of having more black faculty members and administrators. But, as we have noted previously, they and the students are wary of a tokenism that means little real change. Indeed, the "minoritization" of certain university programs or positions is usually a cosmetic process in which a few black professors or other staff members are placed as legitimizing tokens that make the institution look good in regard to racial diversification. Black faculty members and administrators provide, as some of them actually say, a kind of "fire insurance" for the white administrators of these universities. Yet their token positions usually offer them little power to effect significant changes in the campus operations or racial climate.

The situation on predominantly white campuses can be very rough for black faculty and staff members. One survey of several hundred black faculty members at mostly white colleges found that a substantial proportion thought that racism was the important barrier to black employment in their educational institutions.[40] Another report on the quality of life for black faculty at predominantly white colleges found that, where the number of black faculty members is small, "the burdens of institutional and individual racism weigh heavily. The psychological safety associated with numbers is not available to persons who work in these isolated situations."[41]

The difficult position of black staff members was made clear in a recent interview we conducted with a female African American educator who has taught at two mostly white colleges in the 1990s. Reflecting on her own recent college experiences, which also took place at a mostly white college, she commented on remarks made by white faculty, staff, and students:

> The difficulties came, however, in ignorant racial remarks, and the comparison of my success with the media's hyperbole of my people's failures. I was seen as a "credit to my race" for my many accomplishments and academic success. I was often asked to speak for my entire race, and covertly asked why other inner city black youth didn't pull it together like I had.

Continuing her interview, this educator related how she encountered overt racism in the form of a mock slave auction set up by a group of white students to raise money for religious purposes:

> This was one of the most painful racial experiences that I ever encountered. A group on campus decided to do a fundraiser which would allow professors to bid on students in a centralized location (the cafeteria) to do grunt work for them. In return the students would use the money raised to do ministry. As staff and faculty began to jestingly poke and pick at students on the auction block, onlookers began to cheer and shout demeaning epithets that I interpreted as being characteristic of white masters toward black slaves. The few black students that were present in the cafeteria looked on as I did in horror and disbelief. After all, this was an academic and religious institution. After stuffing down my lunch and trying to downplay my initial outrage, I questioned other students to get their perceptions of this recent event, in hopes that collectively we could confront the college president and participating staff with this grotesque display of the many improprieties suffered by persons of color and the poor. To my dismay no one had much to say about it: "What was the big deal, the money was

being used for a good cause!" Perhaps my voice of justice was silenced because I was a newcomer, or maybe because I was so young, but whatever the case my concern never went much further than my immediate colleagues.

Next in her account she explains that after graduation, she went on to get a graduate degree elsewhere. Later, a white administrator at her undergraduate college called her with a job offer, which she took. As the only black staff member, she soon ran into the same type of racism:

> After being warmly accepted by the students of color, I became an advocate and outlet for many of their frustrations. Upon my second term at the institution, a close colleague of mine vivaciously announced, at a staff meeting, that her students were planning a slave auction as a fundraiser for outreach! As other staff members openly gave their approval, I braced myself for the confrontation that I knew had to take place. History would not repeat itself, at least not without some kicking and fighting by this black woman. As the flyer for the event displayed an African bound in chains on an auction block, I knew that my freshman feelings of outrage were not an exaggeration, nor was my rekindled hurt and anger unjustified.

After speaking with her supervisor about what she saw as "the atrocity of such an event," and having gotten some support from him, she approached the well-educated white colleague who was setting up the fundraiser with the students:

> Confidently, I approached my colleague sponsoring the event, and conveyed the dehumanizing elements of such an event, not expecting any resistance, nor what came next. She stared blankly into my face as if to say "What's your problem?" As I tried to constructively share my personal encounter as a freshman and the detrimental effects of such an event on everyone in the community, she retorted with, "Slavery has been over for hundreds of years, no one thinks of it in terms of black and white any more, so why make a big deal of it?" Had she heard anything I said? And

why didn't the man on the flyer have straight hair instead of an Afro? After talking to her a few more minutes, in vain, she finally agreed not to hold this profitable event "if it bothered me!" If it bothered me?! I could have hurt someone at that point, so I turned and walked away. I was at least pleased that the event would not take place, even if the people didn't understand why it shouldn't. I was successful, with the help of my supervisor, at getting any future slave auctions banned on campus. . . . Although some backlash came from students who had to think of a more creative way of raising money, and staff who thought I was playing the victim role, I felt a small victory had been won.

This educator's experiences echo those of the students and parents in the SU focus groups. In this example some whites, both students and professors, thought nothing of holding a mock African-slave auction. For them, it appears to have been just another fundraiser. Yet, slave auctions are among the *most* demeaning and cruel events in the family and community memories of African Americans. While in the mind of some whites, slave auctions are not important and happened "hundreds of years" ago (an exaggeration, since slavery existed just 130 years before the statement was made), in the black educator's mind they are oppressive and still vivid memories and a cause for outrage. This personal narrative illustrates how the same historical events can evoke very different feelings and memories, and have quite different meanings, for black and white Americans. For most whites involved, a mock slave auction is an opportunity to have fun and raise funds, ironically in this case, for religious ministries. For the black students and staff, however, it is the cause of more frustration, anguish, and painful memories.

Like many whites in similar situations, the white colleague here appears not to have understood the black staff member's position, and she dismisses her concerns with the comment that "no one thinks of it in terms of black and white any more." This white assertion places the black staff member outside the circle of people who think correctly about U.S. history. In effect, the white protagonist tells the black woman that her "place" in campus space is marginal. A white person fails to recognize the feelings and understandings of an African American. The white staff member agreed to cancel the slave auction, but only because it bothered her black colleague. By this act she granted her black associate as an act of personal favor something to which the latter had a legitimate expectation—and something the white protagonist herself should have ruled out as a matter of historical knowledge and moral conscience.

Conclusion

In this [article] we have focused on what is perhaps the most central social and intellectual exchange in higher education—that between professors and students. The voices of black students at predominantly white institutions are worth attending to because they have come from an important group of the consumers of higher learning who are, at the same time, part of its distinctive product.[42] In this age of large college enrollments and of computerized, bureaucratic processing of students, higher education still rests at base on the regular interaction between teachers and students.

Students, black and nonblack, occupy distinctive positions in the social structure of a predominantly white campus, and these positions are defined and redefined within a complex web of interracial relationships. Social scientists have long described many human realities as being socially constructed. What is taken as socially "real" is at heart a collection of shared understandings, but these understandings have a past and a future. Social meanings generally transcend particular individuals at one point in historical time. Because of these individual and collective understandings, the world around an individual becomes socially structured and personally predictable. Individuals and groups accumulate memories and stocks of knowledge that help them in the process of making sense out of the world around them. When human beings become part of a new physical and social environment, such as a college campus, they must interpret the signs and symbols, as well as others' behavior toward them, in order to know "their place." As we have seen, the voices of the black students and parents describe not only their interactions with whites, but also the social structure of the university campus as it is lived and processed by these key actors. In the student and parent reports we often observe the social positions defined for black students in what is still fundamentally white educational territory.

The SU students' experiences with white faculty members suggest that racial insensitivity and inequality are well-institutionalized in what may at first seem to be an unlikely place—the presumably tolerant halls of higher education. Yet, the long history of racial restriction and exclusion at traditionally white colleges and universities provides ample reason for expecting racial insensitivity and inequality to be present today at such places. Over the course of U.S. history, one generation of white male professors has, for the most part, been succeeded by another generation of white male professors. Today, most college professors continue to be white men of European background, and the majority seem more or less comfortable with their racial privileges. Few, indeed, wish to actively intervene to root out racist barriers in academia. In addition, the intellectual discourse at traditionally white colleges and universities is for the most part parochial and restricted by subtle or overt Eurocentric interests and biases.

On predominantly white campuses across the nation, African American students who come to see that some, or many, of their white professors are insensitive, prejudiced, or discriminating are less likely to go to them for advice. They know that they will not get the recognition and respect they deserve. They are not likely to adopt these instructors as role models. As a result, many black students dissociate themselves from the important reference group of white scholars and have no real option but to create a support structure of fellow black students and, if they are available and willing, black faculty members. Not surprisingly, a campus situation of pervasive racial hurdles and

impediments can affect the academic performance and success of many black students. As we have seen, SU is not unique; the difficult struggle for academic survival and success has been reported by students of color at many predominantly white colleges and universities. Indeed, students of color who were recently interviewed at Princeton explained that persistent racial bias on campus affected their "rapport with members of the instructional staffs—both faculty and assistants-in-instruction—so that their studies are not as satisfying as they would like."[43] Under such circumstances the black attrition rate often increases, and the severe cost of campus racism again becomes conspicuous.

NOTES

1. As quoted in Jo Ann Gerdeman Thompson, *The Modern Idea of the University* (New York: Peter Lang, 1984), 266–267.

2. John Henry Newman, "The Idea of a University," in *The Idea of a University,* ed. M. J. Svalic (San Francisco: Rinehart Press, 1960 [1852]), 15–16.

3. See Allan Bloom, *The Closing of the American Mind* (New York: Simon & Schuster, 1987), 91; Dinesh D'Souza, *Illiberal Education: The Politics of Race and Sex on Campus* (New York: Vintage, 1991), 13–15, 229–244; Richard Bernstein, *Dictatorship of Virtue: Multiculturalism and the Battle for America's Future* (New York: Alfred A. Knopf, 1994); Arthur Schlesinger, Jr., *The Disuniting of America: Reflections on a Multicultural Society* (New York: Norton, 1991).

4. Bloom, *The Closing of the American Mind,* 93. His italics.

5. Steele, "The Recoloring of Campus Life," 51.

6. George Keller, "Black Students in Higher Education: Why So Few?" *Planning for Higher Education* 17 (1988–1989): 50–56.

7. Martin E. P. Seligman, "When Black Americans Play the Blame Game, They're Bound to Lose," *Chicago Tribune* (February 10, 1993): Zone N, 19.

8. Joe R. Feagin and Melvin P. Sikes, *Living with Racism: The Black Middle Class Experience* (Boston: Beacon Press, 1994), 94.

9. Lynne Duke, "Ugly Racial Melee Shakes Students, Officials at Small Michigan College," *Washington Post* (April 26, 1992): A3, Jerry Thomas, "Brawl

May Empty College of All Blacks," *Chicago Tribune* (April 26, 1992): C23. This section draws on Joe R. Feagin and Hernán Vera, *White Racism: The Basics* (New York: Routledge, 1995), chapter 2.

10. Don Gonyea, "Olivet College Copes with Racial Tension," All Things Considered, National Public Radio, April 29, 1992.

11. Isabel Wilkerson, "Racial Tension Erupts, Tearing a College Apart," *New York Times* (April 13, 1992): A14.

12. "Olivet Disciplinary Panel to Begin Investigation of Racial Brawl," United Press International (April 15, 1992): BC cycle. n.p.; Charles Grose, "Racial Relations as a Catalyst for Institutional Change," unpublished research paper, Mankato State University, 1995.

13. Gonyea, "Olivet College Copes with Racial Tension."

14. Gonyea, "Olivet College Copes with Racial Tension."

15. Duke, "Ugly Racial Melee Shakes Students." A3.

16. Wilkerson, "Racial Tension Erupts, Tearing a College Apart," A14.

17. Thomas, "Brawl May Empty College of All Blacks," C23.

18. Reported from the *Des Moines Register* (January 3, 1995) in "Racism in Education," *The Race Relations Reporter* (May 15, 1995): 3.

19. Jacqueline Fleming, *Blacks in College: A Comparative Study of Students' Success in Black and in White Institutions* (San Francisco: Jossey-Bass, 1984), 47–63; Walter R. Allen, Edgar G. Epps, and Nesha Z. Haniff (Eds.), *College in Black and White* (Albany: SUNY Press, 1991); Walter R. Allen, "The Color of Success," *Harvard Educational Review* 62 (Spring 1992): 27.

20. Walter R. Allen, "Introduction," in *College in Black and White*, eds. Walter R. Allen, Edgar G. Epps, and Nesha Z. Haniff (Albany: SUNY Press, 1991), 12.

21. A number of recent reports have cited the growing racial unrest on college campuses. See Gail E. Thomas, "Race Relations and Campus Climate for Minority Students at Majority and Minority Institutions: Implications for Higher Education Desegregation," report prepared for the Southern Education Foundation, Texas A&M University, 1995.

22. Cited in Denice Ward Hood, "Academic and Noncognitive Factors Affecting the Retention of Black Men at a Predominantly White University," *Journal of Negro Education* 61 (1992): 518.

23. John Henry Newman, "The Idea of a University," in *The Idea of a University*, ed. M. J. Svalic (San Francisco: Rinehart Press, 1960 [1852]), 15–16.

24. Center for Applied Research, "Survey of Ethnic Minority Students," University of Nevada at Reno, August 1993, 52.

25. Joe R. Feagin, *Final Report: Survey of Minority Undergraduate Students,* unpublished, 1993.

26. Urban Affairs Programs, *The Graduate School Climate at MSU: Perceptions of Three Diverse Racial/Ethnic Groups* (East Lansing: Office of the Provost, 1995), Table 20.

27. Gloria J. Edmunds, "Needs Assessment Strategy for Black Students: An Examination of Stressors and Program Implications," *Journal of Non-White Concerns in Personnel and Guidance* 12 (1984): 48–56.

28. Institute for the Study of Social Change, *The Diversity Project: Final Report* (Berkeley: University of California, 1991), 29.

29. For a discussion of the importance of white conceptions of the white self, see Joe R. Feagin and Hernán Vera, *White Racism: The Basics* (New York: Routledge, 1995). 135–162.

30. Joe R. Feagin, "Barriers to Black Students in Higher Education: Learning from Qualitative Research," published position paper, Center for Research on Minority Education, University of Oklahoma, 1989.

31. Urban Affairs Programs, *The Graduate School Climate at MSU,* Tables 20 and 22.

32. Roberta M. Hall and Bernice R. Sandler, *The Classroom Climate: A Chilly One for Women?* (Washington, DC: Association of American Colleges, 1982); see also Joe R. Feagin and Nijole Benokraitis, *Modern Sexism: Blatant, Subtle and Covert Discrimination,* 2nd ed. (Englewood Cliffs, N.J.: Prentice Hall, 1995).

33. Institute for the Study of Social Change, *The Diversity Project,* 17.

34. Institute for the Study of Social Change, *The Diversity Project,* 17, note.

35. Ruth J. Simmons, "Report on Campus Race Relations," Princeton University, March 1, 1993, p. 11.

36. Dinesh D'Souza, *The End of Racism: Principles for a Multiracial Society* (New York: Free Press, 1995), 491–493.

37. bell hooks, *Killing Rage: Enduring Racism* (New York: Henry Holt and Co., 1995), 20, 29.

38. Urban Affairs Programs, *The Graduate School Climate at MSU,* Tables 20 and 22.

39. Affirmative Action Office, "Faculty Survey," University of Nevada at Las Vegas, September, 1993, 3.

40. Kenneth W. Jackson, "Black Faculty in Academia," in *The Racial Crisis in American Higher Education*, eds. Philip G. Altbach and Kofi Lomotey (Albany: SUNY Press, 1991), 143.

41. Washington and Harvey, *Affirmative Rhetoric, Negative Action*, 26.

42. See Pierre Bourdieu and Jean-Claude Passeron, *Les Héritiers: Les Étudiants et La Culture* (Paris: Les Edition de Minuit, 1964), 25.

43. Ruth J. Simmons, "Report on Campus Race Relations," Princeton University, March 1, 1993, 2.

THINKING ABOUT THE READING

Why do you think that so many students of color at predominantly white universities feel "out of place"? How can you explain the tendency of many professors described in this article—even those who are supportive and encouraging—to subtly and not-so-subtly discriminate against the African American students in their classes? Would you characterize this treatment as "institutional" or "personal" racism? Explain. How do the experiences of students at State University compare to those of students of color at your school? How do your instructors address issues of racial and ethnic diversity in the classroom? What steps might a university take to ensure that all students have access to the same educational and social opportunities on campus?

"Opening" Faces

The Politics of Cosmetic Surgery and Asian American Women

Eugenia Kaw

Ellen, a Chinese American in her forties, informed me she had had her upper eyelids surgically cut and sewed by a plastic surgeon twenty years ago in order to get rid of "the sleepy look," which her naturally "puffy" eyes gave her. She pointed out that the sutures, when they healed, became a crease above the eye which gave the eyes a more "open appearance." She was quick to tell me that her decision to undergo "double-eyelid" surgery was not so much because she was vain or had low self-esteem, but rather because the "undesirability" of her looks before the surgery was an undeniable fact.

During my second interview with Ellen, she showed me photos of herself from before and after her surgery in order to prove her point. When Stacy, her twelve-year-old daughter, arrived home from school, Ellen told me she wanted Stacy to undergo similar surgery in the near future because Stacy has only single eyelids and would look prettier and be more successful in life if she had a fold above each eye. Ellen brought the young girl to where I was sitting and said, "You see, if you look at her you will know what I mean when I say that I had to have surgery done on my eyelids. Look at her eyes. She looks just like me before the surgery." Stacy seemed very shy to show me her face. But I told the girl truthfully that she looked fine and beautiful the way she was. Immediately she grinned at her mother in a mocking, defiant manner, as if I had given her courage, and put her arm up in the manner that bodybuilders do when they display their bulging biceps.

As empowered as Stacy seemed to feel at the moment, I could not help but wonder how many times Ellen had shown her "before" and "after" photos to her young daughter with the remark that "Mommy looks better after the surgery." I also wondered how many times Stacy had been asked by Ellen to consider surgically "opening" her eyes like "Mommy did." And I wondered about the images we see on television and in magazines and their often negative, stereotypical portrayal of "squinty-eyed" Asians (when Asians are featured at all). I could not help but wonder how normal it is to feel that an eye without a crease is undesirable and how much of that feeling is imposed. And I shuddered to think how soon it might be before twelve-year-old Stacy's defenses gave away and she allowed her eyes to be cut.

The permanent alteration of bodies through surgery for aesthetic purposes is not a new phenomenon in the United States. As early as World War I, when reconstructive surgery was performed on disfigured soldiers, plastic surgery methods began to be refined for purely cosmetic purposes (that is, not so much for repairing and restoring but for transforming natural features a person is unhappy with). Within the last decade, however, an increasing number of people have opted for a wide array of cosmetic surgery procedures, from tummy tucks, facelifts, and liposuction to enlargement of chests and calves. By 1988, two million Americans had undergone cosmetic surgery (Wolf 1991:218), and a 69 percent increase had occurred in the number of cosmetic surgery procedures between 1981 and 1990, according to the ASPRS, or American Society of Plastic and Reconstructive Surgeons (n.d.).

Included in these numbers are an increasing number of cosmetic surgeries undergone by people like Stacy who are persons of color (American Academy of Cosmetic Surgery press release, 1991). In fact, Asian Americans are more likely than any other ethnic group (white or nonwhite) to pursue cosmetic surgery. ASPRS reports that over thirty-nine thousand of the aesthetic procedures performed by its members in 1990 (or more than 6 percent of all procedures performed that year) were performed on Asian Americans, who make up 3 percent of the U.S. population (Chen 1993:15). Because Asian Americans seek cosmetic surgery from doctors in Asia and from doctors who specialize in fields other than surgery (e.g., ear, nose, and throat specialists and opthamologists), the total number of Asian American patients is undoubtedly higher (Chen 1993:16).

The specific procedures requested by different ethnic groups in the United States are missing from the national data, but newspaper reports and medical texts indicate that Caucasians and nonwhites, on the average, seek significantly different types of operations (Chen 1993; Harahap 1982; Kaw 1993; LeFlore 1982; McCurdy 1980; Nakao 1993; Rosenthal 1991). While Caucasians primarily seek to augment breasts and to remove wrinkles and fat through such procedures as facelifts, liposuction, and collagen injection, African Americans more often opt for lip and nasal reduction operations; Asian Americans more often choose to insert an implant on their nasal dorsum for a more prominent nose or undergo double-eyelid surgery whereby parts of their upper eyelids are excised to create a fold above each eye, which makes the eye appear wider.

Though the American media, the medical establishment, and the general public have debated whether such cosmetic changes by nonwhite persons reflect a racist milieu in which racial minorities must deny their racial identity and attempt to look more Caucasian, a resounding no appears to be the overwhelming opinion of people in the United States. Many plastic surgeons have voiced the opinion that racial minorities are becoming more assertive about their right to choose and that they are choosing not to look Caucasian. Doctors say that nonwhite persons' desire for thinner lips, wider eyes, and pointier noses is no more than a wish to enhance their features in order to attain "balance" with all their other features (Kaw 1993; Merrell 1994; Rosenthal 1991).

Much of the media and public opinion also suggests that there is no political significance inherent in the cosmetic changes made by people of color which alter certain conventionally known, phenotypic markers of racial identity. On a recent Phil Donahue show where the racially derogatory nature of blue contact lenses for African American women was contested, both white and nonwhite audience members were almost unanimous that African American women's use of these lenses merely reflected their freedom to choose in the same way that Bo Derek chose to wear corn rows and white people decided to get tans (Bordo 1990). Focusing more specifically on cosmetic surgery, a *People Weekly* magazine article entitled "On the Cutting Edge" (January 27, 1992, p. 3) treats Michael Jackson (whose nose has become narrower and perkier and whose skin has become lighter through the years) as simply one among many Hollywood stars whose extravagant and competitive lifestyle has motivated and allowed them to pursue cosmetic self-enhancement. Clearly, Michael Jackson's physical transformation within the last decade has been more drastic than Barbara Hershey's temporary plumping of her lips to look younger in *Beaches* or Joan Rivers's facelift, yet his reasons for undergoing surgery are not differentiated from those of Caucasian celebrities; the possibility that he may want to cross racial divides through surgery is not an issue in the article.

When critics speculate on the possibility that a person of color is attempting to look white, they often focus their attack on the person and his or her apparent lack of ethnic pride and self-esteem. For instance, a *Newsweek* article, referring to Michael Jackson's recent television interview with Oprah Winfrey, questioned Jackson's emphatic claim that he is proud to be a black American: "Jackson's dermatologist confirmed that the star has vitiligo, a condition that blocks the skin's ability to produce pigment . . . [however,] most vitiligo sufferers darken their light patches with makeup to even the tone. Jackson's makeup solution takes the other tack: less ebony, more ivory" (Fleming and Talbot 1993:57). Such criticisms, sadly, center around Michael Jackson the person instead of delving into his possible feelings of oppression or examining society as a potential source of his motivation to alter his natural features so radically.

. . . Based on structured, open-ended interviews with Asian American women like Ellen who have or are thinking about undergoing cosmetic surgery for wider eyes and more heightened noses, I attempt to convey more emphatically the lived social experiences of people of color who seek what appears to be conventionally recognized Caucasian features. Rather than mock their decision to alter their features or treat it lightly as an expression of their freedom to choose an idiosyncratic look, I examine everyday cultural images and social relationships which influence Asian American women to seek cosmetic surgery in the first place. Instead of focusing, as some doctors do (Kaw 1993), on the size and width of the eyelid folds the women request as indicators of the women's desire to look Caucasian, I examine the cultural, social, and historical sources that allow the women in my study to view their eyes in a negative fashion—as "small" and "slanted" eyes reflecting a "dull," "passive" personality, a "closed" mind, and a "lack of spirit" in the person. I explore the reasons these women reject the natural shape of their eyes so radically that they willingly expose themselves to a surgery that is at least an hour long, costs one thousand to three thousand dollars, entails administering local anesthesia and sedation, and carries the following risks: "bleeding and hematoma," "hemorrhage," formation of a "gaping wound," "discoloration," scarring, and "asymmetric lid folds" (Sayoc 1974:162–166).

In our feminist analyses of femininity and beauty we may sometimes find it difficult to account for cosmetic surgery without undermining the thoughts and decisions of women who opt

for it (Davis 1991). However, I attempt to show that the decision of the women in my study to undergo cosmetic surgery is often carefully thought out. Such a decision is usually made only after a long period of weighing the psychological pain of feeling inadequate prior to surgery against the possible social advantages a new set of features may bring. Several of the women were aware of complex power structures that construct their bodies as inferior and in need of change, even while they simultaneously reproduced these structures by deciding to undergo surgery (Davis 1991:33).

I argue that as women and as racial minorities, the psychological burden of having to measure up to ideals of beauty in American society falls especially heavy on these Asian-American women. As women, they are constantly bombarded with the notion that beauty should be their primary goal (Lakoff and Scherr 1984, Wolf 1991). As racial minorities, they are made to feel inadequate by an Anglo American–dominated cultural milieu that has historically both excluded them and distorted images of them in such a way that they themselves have come to associate those features stereotypically identified with their race (i.e., small, slanty eyes, and a flat nose) with negative personality and mental characteristics.

In a consumption-oriented society such as the United States, it is often tempting to believe that human beings have an infinite variety of needs which technology can endlessly fulfill, and that these needs, emerging spontaneously in time and space, lack any coherent patterns, cultural meanings, or political significance (Bordo 1991; Goldstein 1993; O'Neill 1985:98). However, one cannot regard needs as spontaneous, infinite, harmless, and amorphous without first considering what certain groups feel they lack and without first critically examining the lens with which the larger society has historically viewed this lack. Frances C. MacGregor, who between 1946 and 1959 researched the social and cultural motivations of such white ethnic minorities as Jewish and Italian Americans to seek rhinoplasty, wrote, "The statements of the patients . . . have a certain face validity and explicitness that reflect both the values of our society and the degree to which these are perceived as creating problems for the deviant individual" (MacGregor 1967:129).

Social scientific analyses of ethnic relations should include a study of the body. As evident in my research, racial minorities may internalize a body image produced by the dominant culture's racial ideology and, because of it, began to loathe, mutilate, and revise parts of their bodies. Bodily adornment and mutilation (the cutting up and altering of essential parts of the body; see Kaw 1993) are symbolic mediums most directly and concretely concerned with the construction of the individual as social actor or cultural subject (Turner 1980). Yet social scientists have only recently focused on the body as a central component of social self-identity (Blacking 1977; Brain 1979; Daly 1978; Lock and Scheper-Hughes 1990; ONeill 1985; Turner 1980; Sheets-Johnstone 1992). Moreover, social scientists, and sociocultural anthropologists in particular, have not yet explored the ways in which the body is central to the everyday experience of racial identity.

Method and Description of Subjects

In this article, I present the findings of an ethnographic research project completed in the San Francisco Bay Area. I draw on data from structured interviews with doctors and patients, basic medical statistics, and relevant newspaper and magazine articles. The sampling of informants for this research was not random in the strictly statistical sense since informants were difficult to find. Both medical practitioners and patients treat cases of cosmetic surgery as highly confidential, as I later discuss in more detail. To find a larger, more random sampling of Asian American informants, I posted fliers and placed advertisements in various local newspapers. Ultimately, I was able to conduct structured, open-ended interviews with eleven Asian American women, four of whom were referred to me by the doctors in my study and six by mutual acquaintances; I found one through an advertisement. Nine had

had cosmetic surgery of the eye or the nose; one recently considered a double-eyelid operation; one is considering undergoing double-eyelid operation in the next few years. The women in my study live in the San Francisco Bay Area, except for two who reside in the Los Angeles area. Five were operated on by doctors who I also interviewed for my study, while four had their operations in Asia—two in Seoul, Korea, one in Beijing, China, and one in Taipei, Taiwan. Of the eleven women in my study, only two (who received their operations in China and in Taiwan) had not lived in the United States prior to their operations. The ages of the Asian American women in my study range from eighteen to seventy-one; one woman was only fifteen at the time of her operation. Their class backgrounds are similar in that they were all engaged in middle-class, white-collar occupations: there were three university students, one art student, one legal assistant, one clerk, one nutritionist, one teacher, one law student, and two doctors' assistants.

Although I have not interviewed Asian American men who have or are thinking of undergoing cosmetic surgery, I realize that they too undergo double-eyelid and nose bridge operations. Their motivations are, to a large extent, similar to those of the women in my study (Iwata 1991). Often their decision to undergo surgery also follows a long and painful process of feeling marginal in society (Iwata 1991). I did not purposely exclude Asian American male patients from my study; rather, none responded to my requests for interviews.

To understand how plastic surgeons view the cosmetic procedures performed on Asian Americans, five structured, open-ended interviews were conducted with five plastic surgeons, all of whom practice in the Bay Area. I also examined several medical books and plastic surgery journals which date from the 1950s to 1990. And I referenced several news releases and informational packets distributed by such national organizations as the American Society of Plastic and Reconstructive Surgeons, an organization which represents 97 percent of all physicians certified by the American Board of Plastic Surgery.

To examine popular notions of cosmetic surgery, in particular how the phenomenon of Asian American women receiving double-eyelid and nose bridge operations is viewed by the public and the media, I have referenced relevant newspaper and magazine articles.

I obtained national data on cosmetic surgery from various societies for cosmetic surgeons, including the American Society of Plastic and Reconstructive Surgeons. Data on the specific types of surgery sought by different ethnic groups in the United States, including Asian Americans, were missing from the national statistics. At least one public relations coordinator told me that such data are unimportant to plastic surgeons. To compensate for this lack of data, I asked the doctors in my study to provide me with figures from their respective clinics. Most told me they had little data on their cosmetic patients readily available.

Colonization of Asian American Women's Souls: Internalization of Gender and Racial Stereotypes

Upon first talking with my Asian American women informants, one might conclude that the women were merely seeking to enhance their features for aesthetic reasons and that there is no cultural meaning or political significance in their decision to surgically enlarge their eyes and heighten their noses. As Elena, a twenty-one-year-old Chinese American who underwent double-eyelid surgery three years ago from a doctor in my study, stated: "I underwent my surgery for personal reasons. It's not different from wanting to put makeup on . . . I don't intend to look Anglo-Saxon. I told my doctor, 'I would like my eyes done with definite creases on my eyes, but I don't want a drastic change.' "Almost all the other women similarly stated that their unhappiness with their eyes and nose was individually motivated and that they really did not desire Caucasian features. In fact, one Korean American woman, Nina, age thirty-four, stated she was not satisfied with the results of her surgery from

three years ago because her doctor made her eyes "too round" like that of Caucasians. One might deduce from such statements that the women's decision to undergo cosmetic surgery of the eye and nose is harmless and may be even empowering to them, for their surgery provides them with a more permanent solution than makeup for "personal" dissatisfactions they have about their features.

However, an examination of their descriptions of the natural shape of their eyes and nose suggests that their "personal" feelings about their features reflect the larger society's negative valuation and stereotyping of Asian features in general. They all said that "small, slanty" eyes and a "flat" nose suggest, in the Asian person, a personality that is "dull," "unenergetic," "passive," and "unsociable" and a mind that is narrow and "closed." For instance, Elena said, "When I look at other Asians who have no folds and their eyes are slanted and closed, I think of how they would look better more awake." Nellee, a twenty-one-year-old Chinese American, said that she seriously considered surgery for double eyelids in high school so that she could "avoid the stereotype of the 'oriental bookworm' " who is "dull and doesn't know how to have fun." Carol, a thirty-seven-year-old Chinese American who received double eyelids seven years ago, said: "The eyes are the window of your soul . . . [yet] lots of oriental people have the outer corners of their eyes a little down, making them look tired. [The double eyelids] don't make a big difference in the size of our eyes but they give your eyes more spirit." Pam, a Chinese American, age forty-four, who received double-eyelid surgery from another doctor in my study, stated, "Yes. Of course. Bigger eyes look prettier. . . . Lots of Asians' eyes are so small they become little lines when the person laughs, making the person look sleepy." Likewise, Annie, an eighteen-year-old Korean American woman who had an implant placed on her nasal dorsum to build up her nose bridge at age fifteen, said: "I guess I always wanted that sharp look—a look like you are smart. If you have a roundish kind of nose it's like you don't know what's going on. If you have that sharp look, you know, with black eyebrows, a pointy nose, you look more alert. I always thought that was cool." The women were influenced by the larger society's negative valuation of stereotyped Asian features in such a way that they evaluated themselves and Asian women in general with a critical eye. Their judgments were based on a set of standards, stemming from the eighteenth- and nineteenth-century European aesthetic ideal of the proportions in Greek sculpture, which are presumed by a large amount of Americans to be within the grasp of every woman (Goldstein 1993:150, 160).

Unlike many white women who may also seek cosmetic surgery to reduce or make easier the daily task of applying makeup, the Asian American women in my study hoped more specifically to ease the task of creating with makeup the illusion of features they do not have as women who are Asian. Nellee, who has not yet undergone double-eyelid surgery, said that at present she has to apply makeup everyday "to give my eyes an illusion of a crease. When I don't wear makeup I feel my eyes are small." Likewise, Elena said that before her double-eyelid surgery she checked almost every morning in the mirror when she woke up to see if a fold had formed above her right eye to match the more prominent fold above her left eye: "[on certain mornings] it was like any other day when you wake up and don't feel so hot, you know. My eye had no definite folds, because when Asians sleep their folds change in and out—it's not definite." Also, Jo, a twenty-eight-year-old Japanese American who already has natural folds above each eye but wishes to enlarge them through double-eyelid surgery, explained:

> I guess I just want to make a bigger eyelid [fold] so that they look bigger and not slanted. I think in Asian eyes it's the inside corner of the fold [she was drawing on my notebook] that goes down too much. . . . Right now I am still self-conscious about leaving the house without any makeup on, because I feel just really ugly without it. I try to curl my eyelashes and put on mascara. I think it makes my eyes look more

open. But surgery can permanently change the shape of my eyes. I don't think that a bigger eyelid fold will actually change the slant but I think it will give the perception of having less of it, less of an Asian eye.

For the women in my study, their oppression is a double encounter: one under patriarchal definitions of femininity (i.e., that a woman should care about the superficial details of her look), and the other under Caucasian standards of beauty. The constant self-monitoring of their anatomy and their continuous focus on detail exemplify the extent to which they feel they must measure up to society's ideals.

In the United States, where a capitalist work ethic values "freshness," "a quick wit," and assertiveness, many Asian American women are already disadvantaged at birth by virtue of their inherited physical features which society associates with dullness and passivity. In this way, their desire to look more spirited and energetic through the surgical creation of folds above each eye is of a different quality from the motivation of many Anglo Americans seeking facelifts and liposuction for a fresher, more youthful appearance. Signs of aging are not the main reason Asian American cosmetic patients ultimately seek surgery of the eyes and the nose; often they are younger (usually between eighteen and thirty years of age) than the average Caucasian patient (Kaw 1993). Several of the Asian American women in my study who were over thirty years of age at the time of their eyelid operation sought surgery to get rid of extra folds of skin that had developed over their eyes due to age; however, even these women decided to receive double eyelids in the process. When Caucasian patients undergo eyelid surgery, on the other hand, the procedure is almost never to create a double eyelid (for they already possess one); in most cases, it is to remove sagging skin that results from aging. Clearly, Asian American women's negative image of their eyes and nose is not so much a result of their falling short of the youthful, energetic beauty ideal that influences every American as it is a direct product of society's racial stereotyping.

The women in my study described their own features with metaphors of dullness and passivity in keeping with many Western stereotypes of Asians. Stereotypes, by definition, are expedient caricatures of the "other," which serve to set them apart from the "we"; they serve to exclude instead of include, to judge instead of accept (Gilman 1985:15). Asians are rarely portrayed in the American print and electronic media. For instance, Asians (who constitute 3 percent of the U.S. population) account for less than 1 percent of the faces represented in magazine ads, according to a 1991 study titled "Invisible People" conducted by New York City's Department of Consumer Affairs (cited in Chen 1993:26). When portrayed, they are seen in one of two forms, which are not representative of Asians in general: as Eurasian-looking fashion models and movie stars (e.g., Nancy Kwan who played Suzy Wong) who already have double eyelids and pointy noses; and as stereotypically Asian characters such as Charlie Chan, depicted with personalities that are dull, passive, and nonsociable (Dower 1986; Kim 1986; Ramsdell 1983; Tajima 1989). The first group often serves as an ideal toward which Asian American women strive, even when they say they do not want to look Caucasian. The second serves as an image from which they try to escape.

Asian stereotypes, like all kinds of stereotypes, are multiple and have changed throughout the years; nevertheless they have maintained some distinct characteristics. Asians have been portrayed as exotic and erotic (as epitomized by Suzie Wong, or the Japanese temptress in the film *The Berlin Affair*), and especially during the U.S. war in the Pacific during World War II, they were seen as dangerous spies and mad geniuses who were treacherous and stealthy (Dower 1986; Huhr and Kim 1989). However, what remains consistent in the American popular image of Asians is their childishness, narrow-mindedness, and lack of leadership skills. Moreover, these qualities have long been associated with the relatively roundish form of Asian faces, and in particular with the "puffy" smallness of their eyes. Prior to the Japanese attack on Pearl Harbor, for instance, the Japanese were considered incapable of planning successful dive bombing attacks due to their "myopic," "squinty" eyes. During the war in the Pacific, their soldiers were caricatured as having thick horn-rimmed glasses through which they must squint to see their targets (Dower 1986). Today, the myopic squinty-eyed image of the narrow-minded Asian persists in the most recent stereotype of Asians as "model minorities" (as eptimoized in the Asian exchange student character in the film *Sixteen Candles*). The term *model minority* was first coined in the 1960s when a more open-door U.S. immigration policy began allowing an unprecedented number of Asian immigrants into the United States, many of whom were the most elite and educated of their own countries (Takaki 1989). Despite its seemingly complimentary nature, *model minority* refers to a person who is hardworking and technically skilled but desperately lacking in creativity, worldliness, and the ability to assimilate into mainstream culture (Huhr and Kim 1989; Takaki 1989). Representations in the media, no matter how subtle, of various social situations can distort and reinforce one's impressions of one's own nature (Goffman 1979).

Witnessing society's association of Asian features with negative personality traits and mental characteristics, many Asian Americans become attracted to the image of Caucasian, or at least Eurasian, features. Several of the women in my study stated that they are influenced by images of fashion models with Western facial types. As Nellee explained: "I used to read a lot of fashion magazines which showed occidental persons how to put makeup on. So I used to think a crease made one's eyes prettier. It exposes your eyelashes more. Right now they all go under the hood of my eyes." Likewise, Jo said she thought half of her discontent regarding her eyes is a self-esteem problem, but she blames the other half on society: "When you look at all the stuff that they portray on TV and in the movies and in Miss America Pageants, the epitome of who is beautiful is that all-American look. It can even include African Americans now but not Asians." According to Jo, she is influenced not only by representations of Asians as passive, dull, and narrow-minded, but also by a lack of representation of Asians in general because society considers them un-American, unassimilable, foreign, and to be excluded.

Similar images of Asians also exist in East and Southeast Asia, and since many Asian Americans are immigrants from Asia, they are likely influenced by these images as well. Multinational corporations in Southeast Asia, for example, consider the female work force biologically suited for the most monotonous industrial labor because they claim the "Oriental girl" is "diligent" and has "nimble fingers" and a "slow-wit" (Ong 1987:151). In addition, American magazines and films have become increasingly available in many parts of Asia since World War II, and Asian popular magazines and electronic media depict models with Western facial types, especially when advertizing Western products. In fact, many of my Asian American women informants possessed copies of such magazines, available in various Asian stores and in Chinatown. Some informants, like Jane, a twenty-year-old Korean American who underwent double-eyelid surgery at age sixteen and nasal bridge surgery at age eighteen, thumbed through Korean fashion magazines which she stored in her living room to show me photos of the Western and Korean models who she thought looked Caucasian, Eurasian, or had had double-eyelid and nasal bridge surgeries. She said these women had eyes that were too wide and noses that were too tall and straight to be on Asians. Though she was born and raised in the United States, she visits her relatives in Korea often. She explained that the influences the media had on her life in Korea and in the United States were, in some sense, similar: "When you turn on the TV [in Korea] you see people like Madonna and you see MTV and American movies and magazines. In any fashion magazine you don't really see a Korean-type woman; you see Cindy Crawford. My mother was telling me that when she was a kid, the ideal beauty was someone with a totally round, flat face. Kind of small and five feet tall. I guess things began to change in the 1950s when

Koreans started to have a lot of contact with the West." The environment within which Asian women develop a perspective on the value and meaning of their facial features is most likely not identical in Asia and the United States, where Asian women are a minority, but in Asia one can still be influenced by Western perceptions of Asians.

Some of the women in my study maintained that although racial inequality may exist in many forms, their decision to widen their eyes had little to do with racial inequality; they were attempting to look like other Asians with double eyelids, not like Caucasians. Nina, for example, described a beautiful woman as such: "Her face should not have very slender eyes like Chinese, Korean, or Japanese but not as round as Europeans. Maybe Filipino, Thai, or other Southeast Asian faces are ideal. Basically I like an Asian's looks. . . . I think Asian eyes [not really slender ones] are sexy and have character." The rest of her description, however, makes it more difficult for one to believe that the Asian eyes she is describing actually belong on an Asian body: "The skin should not be too dark . . . and the frame should be a bit bigger than that of Asians." Southeast Asians, too, seek cosmetic surgery for double eyelids and nose bridges. One doctor showed me "before" and "after" photos of many Thai, Indonesian, and Vietnamese American women, who, he said, came to him for wider, more definite creases so that their eyes, which already have a double-eyelid, would look deeper-set.

In the present global economy, where the movement of people and cultural products is increasingly rapid and frequent and the knowledge of faraway places and trends is expanding, it is possible to imagine that cultural exchange happens in a multiplicity of directions, that often people construct images and practices that appear unconnected to any particular locality or culture (Appadurai 1990). One might perceive Asian American women in my study as constructing aesthetic images of themselves based on neither a Caucasian ideal nor a stereotypical Asian face. The difficulty with such constructions, however, is that they do not help Asian

Americans to escape at least one stereotypical notion of Asians in the United States—that they are "foreign" and "exotic." Even when Asians are considered sexy, and attractive in the larger American society, they are usually seen as exotically sexy and attractive (Yang and Ragaz 1993:21). Since their beauty is almost always equated with the exotic and foreign, they are seen as members of an undifferentiated mass of people. Even though the women in my study are attempting to be seen as individuals, they are seen, in some sense, as less distinguishable from each other than white women are. As Lumi, a Japanese former model recently told *A. Magazine: The Asian American Quarterly,* "I've had bookers tell me I'm beautiful, but that they can't use me because I'm 'type.' All the agencies have their one Asian girl, and any more would be redundant" (Chen 1993:21).

The constraints many Asian Americans feel with regard to the shape of their eyes and nose are clearly of a different quality from almost every American's discontent with weight or signs of aging; it is also different from the dissatisfaction many women, white and nonwhite alike, feel about the smallness or largeness of their breasts. Because the features (eyes and nose) Asian Americans are most concerned about are conventional markers of their racial identity, a rejection of these markers entails, in some sense, a devaluation of not only oneself but also other Asian Americans. It requires having to imitate, if not admire, the characteristics of another group more culturally dominant than one's own (i.e., Anglo Americans) in order that one can at least try to distinguish oneself from one's own group. Jane, for instance, explains that looking like a Caucasian is almost essential for socioeconomic success: "Especially if you go into business, or whatever, you kind of have to have a Western facial type and you have to have like their features and stature—you know, be tall and stuff. So you can see that [the surgery] is an investment in your future."

Unlike those who may want to look younger or thinner in order to find a better job or a happier social life, the women in my study must take into consideration not only their own socioeconomic future, but also more immediately that of their offspring, who by virtue of heredity, inevitably share their features. Ellen, for instance, said that "looks are not everything. I want my daughter, Stacy, to know that what's inside is important too. Sometimes you can look beautiful because your nice personality and wisdom inside radiate outward, such as in the way you talk and behave." Still, she has been encouraging twelve-year-old Stacy to have double-eyelid surgery because she thinks "having less sleepy looking eyes would make a better impression on people and help her in the future with getting jobs." Ellen had undergone cosmetic surgery at the age of twenty on the advice of her mother and older sister and feels she has benefited. Indeed, all three women in the study under thirty who have actually undergone cosmetic surgery did so on the advice of their mother and in their mother's presence at the clinic. Elena, in fact, received her double-eyelid surgery as a high school graduation present from her mother, who was concerned for her socioeconomic future. The mothers, in turn, are influenced not so much by a personal flaw of their own which drives them to mold and perfect their daughters as by a society that values the superficial characteristics of one race over another.

A few of the women's dating and courtship patterns were also affected by their negative feelings toward stereotypically Asian features. Jo, for example, who is married to a Caucasian man, said she has rarely dated Asian men and is not usually attracted to them, partly because they look too much like her: "I really am sorry to say that I am not attracted to Asian men. And it's not to say that I don't find them attractive on the whole. But I did date a Japanese guy once and I felt like I was holding my brother's hand [she laughs nervously]."

A Mutilation of the Body

Although none of the women in my study denied the fact of racial inequality, almost all insisted that the surgical alteration of their eyes and nose was a celebration of their bodies, reflecting their right as women and as minorities to do what they wished with their bodies. Many, such as Jane, also said the surgery was a rite of passage or a routine ceremony, since family members and peers underwent the surgery upon reaching eighteen. Although it is at least possible to perceive cosmetic surgery of the eyes and nose for many Asian Americans as a celebration of the individual and social bodies, as in a rite of passage, this is clearly not so. My research has shown that double-eyelid and nasal bridge procedures performed on Asian Americans do not hold, for either the participants or the larger society, cultural meanings that are benign and spontaneous. Rather, these surgeries are a product of society's racial ideologies, and for many of the women in my study, the surgeries are a calculated means for socioeconomic success. In fact, most describe the surgery as something to "get out of the way" before carrying on with the rest of their lives.

Unlike participants in a rite of passage, these Asian American women share little *communitas* (an important element of rites of passage) with each other or with the larger society. Arnold Van Gennup defined rites of passage as "rites which accompany every change of place, state, social position, and age" (quoted in Turner 1969:94). These rites create an almost egalitarian type of solidarity (communitas) between participants and between the participants and a larger social group. A body modification procedure which is an example of such a rite is the series of public head-scarification rituals for pubescent boys among the Kabre of Togo, West Africa (Brain 1979:178). The final scars they acquire make them full adult members of their group. Their scarification differs considerably from the cosmetic surgery procedures of Asian American women in my study in at least two of its aspects: (1) an egalitarian bond is formed between the participants (between and among those who are doing the scarring and those who are receiving it); and (2) both the event and the resulting feature (i.e., scars) signify the boy's incorporation into a larger social group (i.e., adult men), and therefore, both are unrelentingly made public.

The Asian American women who undergo double-eyelid and nasal bridge surgeries do not usually create bonds with each other or with their plastic surgeons. Their surgery, unlike the scarification rite of the Kabre, is a private event that usually occurs in the presence of the patient, the doctor, and the doctor's assistants only. Moreover, there is little personal connection between doctor and patient. Though a few of the Asian American women in my study were content with their surgery and with their doctors, most describe their experience on the operating table as one of fear and loneliness, and some described their doctors as impersonal, businesslike, and even tending toward profit-making. Annie, for instance, described the fear she felt being alone with the doctor and his assistants in the operating room, when her mother suddenly left the room because she could not bear to watch:

> They told me to put my thumbs under my hips so I didn't interfere with my hands. I received two anesthesia shots on my nose—this was the only part of the operation that hurt, but it hurt! I closed my eyes. I didn't want to look. I didn't want to see like the knives or anything. I could feel like the snapping of scissors and I was aware when they were putting that thing up my nose. My mom didn't really care. They told her to look at my nose. They were wondering if I wanted it sharper and stuff. She said, "Oh no. I don't want to look" and just ran away. She was sitting outside. I was really pissed.

Elena described her experience of surgery in a similar manner: "I had no time to be nervous. They drugged me with valium, I think. I was awake but drugged, conscious but numb. I remember being on the table. They [doctor and nurses] continued to keep up a conversation. I would wince sometimes because I could feel little pinches. He [the doctor] would say, 'Okay. Pumpkin, Sweetheart, it will be over soon.' . . . I didn't like it, being called Pumpkin and being touched by a stranger. . . . I wanted to say Shut up! to all three people." Clearly, the event of surgery did not provide an opportunity or the atmosphere for the women in my study to forge meaningful relationships with their doctors.

Asian American women who undergo cosmetic surgery also have a very limited chance of bonding with each other by sharing experiences of the surgery, because unlike participants in a Kabre puberty rite, these women do not usually publicize either their operation or their new features. All informed me that apart from me and their doctors, few people knew about their surgery since at the most they had told three close friends and/or family members about it. As Annie stated, "I don't mind if people found out [that I had a nose operation], but I won't go around telling them." Jane explained: "It's nothing to be ashamed of, not at all, but it's not something you brag about either. . . . To this day my boyfriend doesn't notice I had anything done. That makes me feel pretty good. It's just that you want to look good, but you don't want them [other people] to know how much effort goes into it." In fact, all the women in my study said they wanted a "better" look, but one that was not so drastically different from the original that it looked "unnatural." Even those who underwent revision surgeries to improve on their first operation said they were more at ease and felt more effective in social situations (with boyfriends, classmates, and employers) after their primary operation, mainly because they looked subtly "better," not because they looked too noticeably different from the way they used to look. Thus, it is not public awareness of these women's cosmetic surgery or the resulting features which win them social acceptance. Rather, the successful personal concealment of the operation and of any glaring traces of the operation (e.g., scars or an "unnatural" look) is paramount for acceptance. Clearly, the alteration of their features is not a rite of passage celebrating the incorporation of individual bodies into a larger social body; rather, it is a personal quest by marginal people seeking acceptance in a society where the dominant culture's ideals loom large and are constraining. The extent to which the Asian American women have internalized society's negative valuation of their natural features is best exemplified by the fact that these women feel more self-confident in social interactions as a result of this slight alteration of their eyelids—that is, with one minor alteration in their whole anatomy—which others may not even notice.

Medicine and the "Disembodiment" of the Asian American Female Consumer

Some sectors of the medical profession fail to recognize that Asian American women's decision to undergo cosmetic surgery of the eyelid and the nose is not so much triggered by a simple materialistic urge to feel better with one more status item that money can buy as much as it is an attempt to heal a specific doubt about oneself which society has unnecessarily brought on. For instance, one doctor in my study stated the following about double-eyelid surgery on Asian American women: "It's like when you wear certain shoes, certain clothes, or put certain makeup on, well—why do you wear those? Why this brand of clothes and not another? . . . You can label these things different ways, but I think that it [the double-eyelid surgery of Asian Americans] is just a desire to look better. You know, it's like driving a brand-new car down the street or having something bought from Nordstrom." By viewing cosmetic surgery and items bought from a department store as equally arbitrary, plastic surgeons, like economists, sometimes assume that the consumer (in this case, the cosmetic surgery client) is disembodied (O'Neill 1985:103). They view her as an abstract, nonhuman subject whose choice of items is not mediated by any historical circumstances, symbolic meaning, or political significance.

With "advances" in science and technology and the proliferation of media images, the number of different selves one can become appears arbitrary and infinite to many Americans, including the women in my study. Thus, many of them argue, as do some plastic surgeons (see Kaw 1993), that the variation in the width of the crease requested by Asian Americans (from six to ten millimeters) is indicative of a whole range of personal and idiosyncratic styles in double-eyelid operations. The idea is that the women are not conforming to any standard, that they are molding their own standards of beauty. However, they ignore that a primary goal in all double-eyelid operations, regardless of how high or how far across the eyelid the crease is cut, is to have a more open appearance of the eye, and the trend in all cases is to create a fold where there was none. These operations are an instance of the paradoxical "production of variety within standardization" in American consumer culture (Goldstein 1993:152). Thus, there is a double bind in undergoing a double-eyelid operation. On the one hand, the women are rebelling against the notion that one must be content with the physical features one is born with, that one cannot be creative in molding one's own idea of what is beautiful. On the other hand, they are conforming to Caucasian standards of beauty.

The women in the study seem to have an almost unconditional faith that science and technology will help them feel satisfied with their sense of self. And the plastic surgery industry, with its scientific advances and seemingly objective stance, makes double-eyelid surgery appear routine, necessary, and for the most part, harmless (Kaw 1993). The women in my study had read advertisements of cosmetic surgery clinics, many of them catering to their specific "needs." In my interviews with Nellee, who had once thought about having double-eyelid surgery, and Jo, who is thinking about it for the near future, I did not have to tell them that the operation entailed creating a crease on the upper eyelid through incision and sutures. They told me. Jo, for instance, said, "I know the technology and it's quite easy, so I am not really afraid of it messing up."

Conclusion: Problem of Resistance in a Culture Based on Endless Self-Fashioning

My research has shown that Asian American women's decision to undergo cosmetic surgery for wider eyes and more prominent noses is very much influenced by society's racial stereotyping of Asian features. Many of the women in my study are aware of the racial stereotypes from which they suffer. However, all have internalized these negative images of themselves and of other Asians, and they judge the Asian body, including their own, with the critical eye of the oppressor.

Moreover, almost all share the attitude of certain sectors of the media and medicine in regard to whether undergoing a surgical operation is, in the end, harmful or helpful to themselves and other Asian Americans; they say it is yet another exercise of their freedom of choice.

The American value of individualism has influenced many of the women to believe that the specific width and shape they choose for their eyelid folds and nose bridges indicate that they are molding their own standards of beauty. Many said they wanted a "natural" look that would be uniquely "in balance" with the rest of their features. However, even those such as Jane, who openly expressed the idea that she is conforming to a Western standard of beauty, emphasized that she is not oppressed but rather empowered by her surgical transformation: "Everything is conforming as I see it. It's just a matter of recognizing it. . . . Other people—well, they are also conforming to something else. Nothing anybody has ever done is original. And it's very unlikely that people would go out and be dressed in any way if they hadn't seen it somewhere. So I don't think it's valid to put a value judgment on [the type of surgery I did]. I'm definitely for self-improvement. So if you don't like a certain part of your body, there's no reason not to change it."

The constraints Asian American women in my study feel every day with regard to their natural features are a direct result of unequal race relationships in the United States. These women's apparent lack of concern for their racial oppression is symptomatic of a certain postmodern culture arising in the United States which has the effect of hiding structural inequalities from public view (Bordo 1990). In its attempt to celebrate differences and to shun overgeneralizations and totalizing discourses that apparently efface diversity among people in modern life, this postmodern culture actually obscures differences; that is, by viewing differences as all equally arbitrary, it effaces from public consciousness historically determined differences in power between groups of people. Thus, blue contact lenses for African American women, and double eyelids and nose bridges for Asian women are both seen as forms of empowerment and indistinguishable in form and function from perms for white women, corn rows on Bo Derek, and tans on Caucasians. All cosmetic changes are seen in the same way—as having no cultural meaning and no political significance. In this process, what is trivialized and obscured is the difficult, and often frustrated struggle with which subordinate groups must assert their difference as something to be proud of in the face of dominant ideologies (Bordo 1990:666).

With the proliferation of scientific and technological industries, the many selves one can become appear infinite and random. Like the many transformations of the persona of Madonna throughout her career or the metamorphosis of Michael Jackson's face during his "Black and White" video, the alteration of bodies through plastic surgery has become for the American public simply another means of self-expression and self-determination. As Ellen said, "You can be born Chinese. But if you want to look like a more desirable one, and if surgery is available like it is now, then why not do it?" She said that instead of having to undergo the arduous task of placing thin strips of transparent plastic tape over the eyelids to create a temporary crease (a procedure which, she said, many Asians unhappy with single eyelids used to do), Asians now have the option to permanently transform the shape of their eyes.

Thus, instead of becoming a battleground for social and cultural resistance, the body has become a playground (Bordo 1990:667). Like Michael Jackson's lyrics in the song "Man in the Mirror" ("If you want to make the world a better place, then take a look at yourself and make a change"; Jackson 1987), it is ambiguous whether political change and social improvement are best orchestrated through changing society or through an "act of creative interpretation" (Bordo 1990) of the superficial details of one's appearance. The problem and dilemma of resistance in U.S. society are best epitomized in this excerpt of my interview with Jo, the twenty-eight-year-old law student who is thinking of having double-eyelid surgery:

JO: In my undergraduate college, every Pearl Harbor Day I got these phone calls and people would say, "Happy Pearl Harbor Day," and they made noises like bombs and I'd find little toy soldiers at my dorm door. Back then, I kind of took it as a joke. But now, I think it was more malicious. . . . [So] I think the surgery is a lot more superficial. Affecting how society feels about a certain race is a lot more beneficial. And it goes a lot deeper and lasts a lot longer.

INTERVIEWER: Looking into the future, do you think you will do both?

JO: Yeah [nervous laughter]. I do. I do.

Jo recognizes that undergoing double-eyelid surgery, that is, confirming the undesirability of Asian eyes, is in contradiction to the work she would like to do as a teacher and legal practitioner. However, she said she cannot easily destroy the negative feelings she already possesses about the natural shape of her eyes.

Implications: Asian Americans and the American Dream

The psychological burden of having constantly to measure up has been often overlooked in the image of Asian Americans as model minorities, as people who have achieved the American dream. The model minority myth assumes not only that all Asian Americans are financially well-to-do, but also that those Asian Americans who are from relatively well-to-do, non-working-class backgrounds (like many of the women in my study) are free from the everyday constraints of painful racial stereotypes (see Takaki 1989; Hurh and Kim 1989). As my research has shown, the cutting up of Asian Americans' faces through plastic surgery is a concrete example of how, in modern life, Asian Americans, like other people of color, can be influenced by the dominant culture to loathe themselves in such a manner as to begin mutilating and revising parts of their body.

Currently, the eyes and nose are those parts of the anatomy which Asian Americans most typically cut and alter since procedures for these are relatively simple with the available technology.

However, a few of the women in my study said that if they could, they would also want to increase their stature, and in particular, to lengthen their legs; a few also suggested that when safer implants were found, they wanted to augment their breasts; still others wanted more prominent brow bridges and jawlines. On the one hand, it appears that through technology women can potentially carve an endless array of new body types, breaking the bounds of racial categories. On the other hand, these desired body types are constructed in the context of the dominant culture's beauty ideals. The search for the ideal body may have a tremendous impact, in terms of racial discrimination, on patterns of artificial genetic selection, such as occurs at sperm banks, egg donation centers, and in the everyday ritual of courtship.

REFERENCES

American Society of Plastic and Reconstructive Surgeons (ASPRS). N.d. "Estimated Number of Cosmetic Surgery Procedures Performed by ASPRS Members in 1990." Pamphlet.

Appadurai, Arjun. 1990. "Disjuncture and Difference in the Global Cultural Economy." *Public Culture* 2(2): 1–24.

Blacking, John. 1977. *The Anthropology of the Body.* London: Academic Press.

Bordo, Susan. 1990. "Material Girl: The Effacements of Postmodern Culture." *Michigan Quarterly Review* 29:635–676.

Brain, Robert. 1979. *The Decorated Body.* New York: Harper and Row.

Chen, Joanne. 1993. "Before and After: For Asian Americans, the Issues Underlying Cosmetic Surgery Are Not Just Skin Deep." *A. Magazine: The Asian American Quarterly* 2(1): 15–18, 26–27.

Daly, Mary. 1978. *Gyn/ecology: The Metaethics of Radical Feminism.* Boston: Beacon Press.

Davis, Kathy. 1991. "Remaking the She-Devil: A Critical Look at Feminist Approaches to Beauty." *Hypatia* 6(2): 21–43.

Dower, John. 1986. *War without Mercy: Race and Power in the Pacific War.* New York: Pantheon.

Ellison, Katherine. 1990. "Mexico Puts on a Foreign Face." *San Jose Mercury News,* December 16, p. 14a.

Fleming, Charles, and Mary Talbot. 1993. "The Two Faces of Michael Jackson." *Newsweek,* February 22, p. 57.

Gilman, Sander L. 1985. *Difference and Pathology: Stereotypes of Sexuality, Race and Madness.* Ithaca, NY: Cornell University Press.

Goffman, Erving. 1979. *Gender Advertisement.* Cambridge: Harvard University Press.

Goldstein, Judith. 1993. "The Female Aesthetic Community." *Poetics Today* 14(1): 143–163.

Harahap, Marwali. 1982. "Oriental Cosmetic Blepharoplasty." In *Cosmetic Surgery for Non-white Patients,* ed. Harold Pierce, pp. 79–97. New York: Grune & Stratton.

Hurh, Won Moo, and Kwang Chung Kim. 1989. "The 'Success' Image of Asian Americans: Validity, and Its Practical and Theoretical Implications." *Ethnic and Racial Studies* 12(4):512–537.

Iwata, Edward. 1991. "Race without Face." *San Francisco Image Magazine,* May, pp. 51–55.

Jackson, Michael. 1987. "Man in the Mirror." On *Bad.* Epic Records, New York.

Kaw. Eugenia. 1993. "Medicalization of Racial Features: Asian American Women and Cosmetic Surgery." *Medical Anthropology Quarterly* 7(1):74–89.

Kim, Elaine. 1986. "Asian-Americans and American Popular Culture." In *Dictionary of Asian-American History,* ed. Hyung-Chan Kim. New York: Greenwood Press.

Kristof, Nicholas. 1991. "More Chinese Look 'West.' " *San Francisco Examiner and Chronicle,* July 7.

Lakoff, Robin T., and Raquel L. Scherr. 1984. *Face Value: The Politics of Beauty.* Boston: Routledge & Kegan Paul.

LeFlore, Ivens C. 1982. "Face Lift, Chin Augmentation and Cosmetic Rhinoplasty in Blacks." In *Cosmetic Surgery in Non-White Patients,* ed. Harold Pierce. New York: Grune & Stratton.

Lock, Margaret, and Nancy Scheper-Hughes. 1990. "A Critical-Interpretive Approach in Medical Anthropology: Rituals and Routines of Discipline and Dissent." In *Medical Anthropology: Contemporary Theory and Method,* ed., Thomas Johnson and Carolyn Sargent, pp. 47–72. New York: Praeger.

McCurdy, John A. 1990. *Cosmetic Surgery of the Asian Face.* New York: Thieme Medical Publishers.

MacGregor, Frances C. 1967. "Social and Cultural Components in the Motivations of Persons Seeking Plastic Surgery of the Nose." *Journal of Health and Social Behavior* 8(2):125–135.

Merrell, Kathy H. 1994. "Saving Faces." *Allure,* January, pp. 66–68.

Millard, Ralph, Jr. 1964. "The Original Eyelid and Its Revision." *American Journal of Opthamology* 57:546–649.

Molnar, Stephen. 1983. *Human Variation: Races, Types, and Ethnic Groups.* Englewood Cliffs, NJ: Prentice Hall.

Nakao, Annie. 1993. "Faces of Beauty: Light Is Still Right." *San Francisco Examiner and Chronicle,* April 11, p. D4.

O'Neill, John. 1985. *Five Bodies.* Ithaca, NY: Cornell University Press.

Ong, Aihwa. 1987. *Spirits of Resistance and Capitalist Discipline: Factory Women in Malaysia.* Albany: State University of New York Press.

Ramsdell, Daniel. 1983. "Asia Askew: U.S. Best-sellers on Asia. 1931–1980." *Bulletin of Concerned Asian Scholars* 15(4):2–25.

Rosenthal, Elisabeth. 1991. "Ethnic Ideals: Rethinking Plastic Surgery." *New York Times,* September 25, p. B7.

Sayoc, B. T. 1954. "Plastic Construction of the Superior Palpebral Fold." *American Journal of Opthamology* 38:556–559.

———. 1974. "Surgery of the Oriental Eyelid." *Clinics in Plastic Surgery* 1(1): 157–171.

Sheets-Johnstone, Maxine, ed. 1992. *Giving the Body Its Due.* Albany: State University of New York Press.

Tajima, Renee E. 1989. "Lotus Blossoms Don't Bleed: Images of Asian Women." In *Making Waves: An Anthology of Writings by and about Asian American Women,* ed. Diane Yeh-Mei Wong, pp. 308–317. Boston: Beacon Press.

Takaki. Ronald. 1989. *Strangers from a Different Shore.* Boston: Little, Brown.

Turner, Terence. 1980. "The Social Skin." In *Not Work Alone,* ed. J. Cherfas and R. Lewin, pp. 112–114. London: Temple Smith.

Turner, Victor. 1969. *The Ritual Process: Structure and Anti-Structure.* Chicago: Aldine.

Wolf, Naomi. 1991. *The Beauty Myth: How Images of Beauty Are Used Against Women.* New York: Morrow.

Yang, Jeff, and Angelo Ragaz. 1993. "The Beauty Machine." *A. Magazine: The Asian American Quarterly* 2(1):20–21.

THINKING ABOUT THE READING

What is meant by the term "the politics of cosmetic surgery?" How can the private act of undergoing plastic surgery be linked to broader political, or for that matter, economic or cultural issues? Is there anything wrong with Asian American women trying to look more Caucasian? When considering an alteration to their physical appearance, should people feel obligated to maintain their "ethnically unique" features? In other words, at what point does loyalty to one's ethnic group identity override their personal desire to enhance their attractiveness? Is there any difference between altering one's body to fit prevailing White standards and, say, changing one's name or one's wardrobe to accomplish the same goal?

CHAPTER 13

The Architecture of Inequality: Gender

Along with racial and class inequality, sexual inequality—and the struggle against it—has been a fundamental part of the historical development of our national identity. Along the way it has influenced the lives and dreams of individual people, shaped popular culture, and created or maintained social institutions. Gender is a major criterion for the distribution of important economic, political, and educational resources in most societies. Sexual inequality is perpetuated by a dominant cultural ideology that devalues women on the basis of presumed biological differences between men and women. This ideology overlooks the equally important role of social forces in determining male and female behavior.

Expressions of personal sexism are most apparent during the course of everyday interactions—in the form of communication patterns and gestures. While sometimes dismissed as playful and harmless, they can be particularly dangerous when expressed in the form of sexual harassment and sexual violence. The inequality created by such actions is particularly apparent when women are forced to reconstruct their lives to decrease the likelihood of being victimized.

In her article, "Nothing Bad Happens to Good Girls," Esther Madriz analyzes women's perceptions of their risk of being victimized by crime and the effect these perceptions have on their behavior. Madriz argues that women in our society operate under strict rules of conduct that limit their lives and activities. Women are constantly forced to forego enjoyable activities—for instance, taking a walk at night or going to a park by themselves—because of an ideology of crime, which suggests that if they do these things "something bad" is likely to happen to them. If these rules are not followed, women often get the blame for their own victimization.

Institutional sexism exists in the law, in the family (in terms of such things as the domestic division of labor), and in economics. Not only are social institutions sexist, in that women are systematically segregated, exploited, and excluded, they are also gendered. Institutions themselves are structured along gender lines so that traits associated with success are usually stereotypically male characteristics: tough-mindedness, rationality, assertiveness, competitiveness, and so forth.

Women have made significant advances politically, economically, educationally, and socially over the past decades. The traditional obstacles to advancement continue to fall. Women have entered the labor force in unprecedented numbers. Yet despite their growing presence in the labor force and their entry into historically male occupations, rarely do women work alongside men or perform the same tasks and functions.

Jobs within an occupation still tend to be divided into "men's work" and "women's work." Such sex segregation has serious consequences for women in the form of blocked advancement and lower salaries. But looking at sex segregation on the job as something that happens only to women gives us an incomplete picture of the situation. It is just as important to examine what keeps men out of "female" jobs as it is to examine what keeps women out of "male" jobs. The proportion of women in male jobs has increased over the past several decades, but the proportion of men in female jobs has remained virtually unchanged. In "Still a Man's World," Christine Williams looks at the experiences of male nurses, social workers, elementary school teachers, and librarians. She finds that although these men do feel somewhat stigmatized by their nontraditional career choices, they still enjoy significant gender advantages.

Nothing Bad Happens to Good Girls

Fear of Crime in Women's Lives

Esther Madriz

For Your Own Sake

One of the most significant mechanisms in the control of women's lives is the fear of crime. Its influence is masked by the common belief that fear of crime imposes limitations upon women's lives "for their own sake." . . .

Fear of crime is embedded in the prevailing "ideologies" or conceptions of crime that members of society share. These ideologies not only seek to explain the nature of crime, its causes, the way to control it, and how to avoid being victimized (Hall et al. 1978); they also contain a reservoir of images of criminals, victims, and the relations between them.

Two major conceptions, or ideologies, shape our images of crime and criminals in today's America. The more "conservative" view sees crime as the result of the deterioration of important social values—respectability, discipline, the work ethic, morality—all of which are represented and transmitted to us by a major social institution, the family. The way to control crime, according to the conservative view, is to restore these values through a more traditional family structure, and to control those who deviate with tougher laws, more police, and more prisons. The concept of family values has been at the forefront of Democratic and Republican agendas alike, with both parties competing to depict themselves as the ultimate moral crusaders (Becker 1964). According to the conservative view, criminals are undisciplined, they lack fundamental moral values, and many are unemployed, promiscuous, poor, and, of course, minorities. Conservatives believe that individuals and not social forces are to blame for the de-

struction of fundamental family values, yet they never address some of the systemic and historic roots of this erosion, for example, the split of extended and even nuclear families who are forced to relocate constantly in search of new jobs.

The "liberal" view of crime, on the other hand, blames forces outside the control of the individual such as failures in the socialization process, lack of education and opportunity, psychological problems, or all the above. According to the liberal view, criminals may be disturbed or psychotic individuals who go astray through no fault of their own or poor, undersocialized people who need to be brought back into the mainstream of society by re-education, job training, and the creation of role models to teach them how to be "good."

Of course, the liberal and conservative positions described here are only rough representations of the most common views of crime and criminals. We should not deny that a myriad of views depart from or in some way combine these two major conceptions. Nevertheless, they are particularly pertinent for the theme of this [article] because they are among the most commonly held views, and thus they offer us a general perspective on the public images of crime and criminals in the United States. . . .

I maintain that female fear is exacerbated by images and representations of crime contained in the prevailing ideology of crime (Hall et al. 1978). This ideology is shaped by dominant assumptions about what is criminal, who is more likely to commit a crime and who is more likely to become a victim, what the connections are between criminals and victims, where and when a crime is more likely to occur, and what the best ways are to control or prevent crime. These ideas reflect "attitudes so deeply embedded in tradition as to appear natural" (Reiman 1995, 6). By appealing to fundamental beliefs, these issues tend to rally Americans around politicians who vow to fight against crime and for "American values." In fact, these images are translated into a social ideology that cuts across class, race, and gender, creating a convincing, almost nationalized vision of crime and criminals. These images are held as valid by most members of our society regardless of their position in the various social hierarchies and regardless of their diverse and sometimes contradictory life experiences. They are incorporated into an uncodified, emotional, and enormously powerful ideological construct that is shared, at least to a certain extent, by almost everyone in our society (Hall et al. 1978). As Gramsci stated, the power of the eltites is based not only on the use of force, but above all on the ability to control the intellectual and moral direction of a society and to provide models of "exemplary behavior" for its citizens (Pellicani 1981).

Liberal and conservative views overlap in one fundamental respect: both see the family as the place where crime control must occur, while the social structure in which the family exists remains immune from criticism. Family values thus become the solution to many maladies, especially crime, and the transmission of these values rests heavily on the shoulders of women. The belief that women's primary responsibility is the care and protection of their children still prevails in most of American society. Women are convinced that it is their fault if something happens to their children, or if their children take the "wrong path." This is not, by any means, only fantasy or delusion. Several recent court rulings unmistakably confirm the social reality of these attitudes. A Washington judge recently denied a Senate aide custody of her children because he deemed the mother more devoted to her career than to the care of her offspring. A Michigan college student also lost custody of her daughter because she put her in a child care center to attend a good university (Chira 1994).

Feminist legal scholars claim that working mothers are penalized because some judges consider career women "unmaternal" (Chira 1994). Women understand this and have internalized the feelings and beliefs of their society. . . .

Women who have to leave their children in child care centers feel "as if we were doing something wrong." Many mothers feel scared by reports that child care centers are flawed (Quindlen 1994). A recent book by Penelope Leach, the British, so-called child care guru has given women more reasons to worry and to feel guilty if they have to work. Leach claims that "unless society allows children more time with their parents in the early years, when IQ, temperament, values and a child's chances for success are largely determined . . . babies harmed by part-time parenting will cost society more than it can afford later: Violence, crime, drug addiction, all the main problems of Western postindustrial societies" (Kinkead 1994). . . .

The reality is that most women work because they have to. Most families cannot afford to live with only one salary. Moreover, the United States has the highest rate of divorce of any country in the world: for every two marriages in one year, there is one divorce. In other words, 50 percent of the marriages today end in divorce (U.S. Bureau of Census 1990). Furthermore, increasing numbers of homes are headed by single women, especially by women of color (Sidel 1992). But even in two-parent families, women are still the primary caregivers of the children and the primary guardians of family values.

Many images associated with women as guardians of family values have traditionally been used as a means of social control. For example, Barbara Ehrenreich and Deirdre English (1978) explain how twentieth-century psychology has helped to develop the figure of the "bad mother" by portraying maternal deprivation as one of the major causes of children's psychological and behavioral problems. Quoting from John Bowlby's book, *Maternal Care and Mental Health,* Ehrenreich and English explain how family failure has been attributed to factors ranging from "death of a parent" to "full employment of the mother." Thus a major fear is placed in a mother's mind: if she fails, her children may become drug addicts or even criminals. Women are the ones that have to be home to be sure that their children become "responsible citizens," don't get involved in drugs, and don't get into trouble. The message is: be a good mother; stay home or your family will fail, and it will be your fault. Thus the fear of crime reinforces gender roles within the family, with women seen as the primary caretakers and guardians of the children and their safety.

Women's fear about the possible victimization of their children or about their possible involvement in deviant or criminal behaviors has political consequences. It induces social conformity by corralling women within the parameters of rigid gender expectations, perpetuating gendered relations not only at home but also in different domains of social life: work and public space. Women, more often than men, have to limit their activities so they can be "good mothers" and protect their children by driving or walking them to school, picking them up, helping with their homework. All these activities place limits upon the educational level women can achieve, the type of work they can get, and the nature of their work schedules. In addition, as we have said, women bear an enormous share of the responsibility in the control of crime. Because women need to take care of themselves, they don't go to the "wrong places" (like the Central Park jogger), do the "wrong things" (like Carol Ann Artutis, the woman whose body was discovered in a trailer in New York City), wear the "wrong clothes," or interact in the "wrong way" with the "wrong people." But they also have to protect their children so they do not become "bad." Thus women, in most instances, do not need the police, the courts, the prisons to be controlled, because their control is informal and internalized, but no less insidious and constraining.

Fear of crime is indeed an extremely dominant force in the control of women's lives. Images of crime, criminals, victims, and the relationships among them help to organize public consent around issues such as what places are safe for women to be in and at what times, what behaviors are appropriate for women and what for men, and what roles are proper for males and what for females. . . .

From birth, invisible walls are built around women, limiting their lives and activities. The strict rules of conduct imposed upon women under the flag of "keeping them safe" make the need for formal control agencies less significant. Consequently, the study of the social constraints on women must take into account the fear of crime. Such a study should be conducted outside the context of traditional criminological theories of crime and punishment. Rather it should examine the material, everyday conditions of women's lives, using forms of language and communication that facilitate the sharing and understanding of women's diverse experiences, according to their age, race, socioeconomic class, and sexual orientation.

Current ideologies of crime are filled with representations of women as victims of crimes and men as offenders; with images of who is a criminal, who is a victim, and where, when, and why a crime is likely to occur. Women are constantly forced to forgo activities that are enjoyable to them, such as taking a walk during a summer night, going to a public park by themselves, or . . . even going to a movie or to a restaurant. The fear that "something bad can happen to them" teaches women at a very early age what "their place" is; who is expected to be strong and who weak; who should be protected and who should protect; what type of clothes women should wear and what type of activities they should or should not engage in. If these clear, gendered rules of behavior are not strictly followed, women get the blame for their own victimization, because good women are supposed to "know better."

Coping with Fear

. . .

Women's responses to fear of crime are varied: some lock themselves within the invisible or, oftentimes, tangible walls of their apartments, houses, or nursing homes, constraining their lives considerably. Others develop protection rituals that allow them to continue with their lives without consuming too much of their time or energy worrying about crime. Still others respond by "not letting fear control my life" or by carrying forms of protection such as Mace or pepper spray, or even a weapon such as a knife, scissors, or a gun. . . .

Women respond to their fears of victimization in a variety of ways. Some of their responses may seem acquiescent, submissive, and even passive to us: locking themselves inside their homes, avoiding certain streets and activities, refraining from civic or religious activities. Others may seem more assertive and forceful, showing the women's determination to continue with their lives and not allow their fears to dictate their behavior. Some coping strategies may seem to reinforce the gender patterns of protected/protector or weak/strong, while others may challenge such patterns. Some strategies reveal a great deal of resourcefulness—as well as significant dissatisfaction with the social situation that constrains women's lives. Most women have to spend a great amount of energy, time, and economic resources to shield themselves from criminal victimization and to minimize their fears: take a cab; buy Mace; purchase alarms, locks, Clubs, or other devices; spend money in parking garages; and walk on streets that take them out of their way. Although men also have to take some precautions, studies show that women employ more avoidance strategies (Stanko 1990, 14).

Michel de Certeau mentions how "the act of walking is to the urban system what speech is to language" (1984, 97). Walking through a city has several functions, says de Certeau: (1) the appropriation of certain streets or places by individuals, similar to the appropriation of language by the speaker; (2) the spatial acting-out of the place by individual actors, as speech becomes an acting-out of language; (3) the creation of relations among different actors in that particular space and among that unique place and other areas of the city, just as speech establishes relations between the speaker and the interlocutor (de Certeau 1984, 97–98). The process of choosing

certain streets and not others reinforces the assumptions that certain places should be avoided and others should be sought out as "inviting." In urban centers, "inviting" places are normally those with beautiful or charming stores—which sell clothes and commodities that most of us cannot afford—and those with middle- or upper-class homes and neat lawns. As individuals walk through these places and not others, they are, through their presence, making the place safer from crime and reinforcing class hierarchies in the urban space. By avoiding of certain places, they are buttressing the belief that poor neighborhoods are dangerous and should be circumvented.

Many of the participants in this research gave clear indications of the personal maps they create as they walk through the city, especially in New York City and the surrounding boroughs. "I never walk down [name of the street]," or "I don't go to [name of a certain neighborhood]" were common expressions. And the places commonly avoided were lower-class, predominantly Black and Latino, areas.

In discussing their different strategies, some women at first said that they did not do too much to protect themselves, because "I am not really afraid," while in the next sentence, they shared the different manners in which they respond to the fear in their lives. In focus groups, some participants pointed out to other members of the group the conflicting nature of these assertions. But what becomes evident in such contradictory statements is the emotional nature of the fear of crime. By emotional I do not mean, as other authors have suggested, that fear of crime is irrational or unrealistic. On the contrary, the fear of crime is a response to threats and criminal incidents that many women and their relatives encounter daily at home, in the workplace, or on the streets. It is emotional, however, because the fear of crime encompasses a multitude of symbols, representations, and codes that go beyond the reality of crime and are embodied in the image of the faceless stranger and in the horror stories of abductions and decapitated female bodies.

Although a few women, especially elderly women, admit to limiting their lives to the extreme of becoming prisoners in their own homes, the majority deal with their fears in a less confining manner. Most women have developed their own protection rituals and regularly use more than one coping strategy to deal with their fears. Some women depicted these rituals as, "You know, I do the normal things that we all do." On many occasions, lower-class and minority women expressed frustration at being forced by their circumstances to engage in activities that put them at risk, in spite of the perils to which such activities expose them. Some must work night shifts and have no other option but to take public transportation during late hours of the evening. If they were given the choice, many of them would gladly work day shifts or use a private vehicle. Other participants expressed frustration at having to attend evening classes. However, they must support themselves and their children and pay for their own education, so they have to work full-time. Some participants asserted that, "If I could, I would like to move from this neighborhood to a better area, but I can't afford it." Therefore, it became very clear throughout the study that many of the rituals and the avoidance strategies used by the participants are mediated by socioeconomic constraints.

Women's coping strategies are also mediated by physical constraints. The elderly and women with disabilities or health conditions mentioned avoiding crowded places, public transportation, and night activities more often than those who were physically fit. Terry, a forty-three-year-old African American woman who is blind, reported such an experience:

> I need someone to take me out. Although I can go out by myself, the fear that someone might try to mug me or rob me scares me to death. You hear so many stories about blind people being pushed into the tracks or being pushed down the stairs . . . for nothing. . . . I don't take no chances.

Several of the most common reactions to the fear of crime include self-isolation, target hard-

ening, altering personal appearance, looking for guardians, ignoring fears, guarding one's children, carrying protection, and fighting back. Women commonly said that they use or have used more than one of these strategies. Some of them expressed anger and frustration for "having to live my life this way." Only a couple of participants in the study expressed the belief that the limitations that fear of victimization imposes upon their lives violate their rights to the use of public space or to equal treatment in society. . . .

A Strategy of Self-Isolation

Studies show that women and the elderly are particularly likely to restrict their activities for fear of criminal victimization (Clemente and Kleiman 1977; Gordon and Riger 1991; Riger and Gordon 1991; Riger et al. 1978; Skogan 1987). In this research, although the use of isolation strategies such as staying inside the home and avoiding certain places were documented by most women regardless of their age, race, and socioeconomic background, some strategies were favored by certain groups of women. For example, elderly women avoided going out of their homes more often than younger women. Among elderly Latina women, especially, avoiding the streets almost entirely was a frequent strategy. During a focus group with these women, three of them, Beatriz, Lola, and Maga, discussed their strategies with a certain degree of sadness in their voices:

> Yes, I am older and not as quick as I used to be. This fear, I know, has stopped me from enjoying my retirement. Last year I was mugged. . . . Now I stay in more often, almost all the time. *Me siento aislada y muy sola* [I feel isolated and very lonely]. . . . Thank God I have the soap operas to keep me company and my *novenas* [prayers].

> I used to go to church, but now I don't even go to mass because I am afraid of walking the streets of this neighborhood. Even during Christmas. . . . I used to go to the midnight mass . . . I loved it. But in our church, they had to change the midnight mass on Christmas eve

to 8:00 P.M. because people were afraid to go out that late. . . . You know, life is not the same.

Since I was robbed after cashing my social security check, I do not go out by myself anymore. I go out only if I have to, which is twice a month, at the most.

The increased life expectancy of people in this country has lengthened their retirement years. Therefore, the quality of life of those millions of Americans now in retirement is a matter of great importance for social research. The fear of crime, such as that expressed by these three Latina women, clearly affects the quality of life of elderly persons, contributing to their sense of isolation and loneliness. The fact that women live longer than men makes it imperative to comprehend the way in which fear of crime restricts the behavior of elderly women. Fátima, another elderly Latina woman, also shared with me that she only goes to those places where she has to go and not to places she wishes to go: she never takes a walk or goes out of her house unless she has "something to buy or something specific to do. I used to go to the movies," she said, but "I don't go anymore because I am afraid of being mugged. You know, I am old and if someone mugs me, I could be hurt," she concluded. "Would you like to go out more often?" I asked Fátima. "Of course," she emphatically declared. "But I can't. I am just terrified of being mugged." . . .

Among elderly white women who live in the suburbs, the situation is less restrictive than for other elderly women because they have private automobiles and can drive to certain "safe" places where they feel less vulnerable. Nevertheless, one of them commented, "I only go out during the day." Two of them, Rose and Norma, engaged in the following conversation:

If I want to go for a walk, I only go to the malls. That is the only place where I walk. There is a lot of security there. . . . And I do not take anything with me. Only my car keys. That's all I take.

I used to be an outdoor person. . . . I love nature, and I used to go for walks in the woods.

But there is no way I would do something like that now. . . . Besides, my children would think that I am crazy. Why worry them?

. . .

Other women avoid going out in the evening or avoid engaging in night activities. For example, some react to their fears by restricting their leisure activities. A group of Latina teenagers said that they no longer go dancing, because they are afraid. Some teenagers said that they have restricted their participation in sports and after-school activities out of fear of crime. "I love to play basketball," one of them said. "But I can't because the practice is during the evening and I don't have a ride home."

Studies show that women's control of leisure is not merely a matter of personal enjoyment and gratification, it is "an integral part of social relations" (Green et al. 1991, 78). Leisure is necessary not only for physical, mental, and spiritual well-being but also for the formation of social networks, which are fundamental to the social and professional advancement of individuals. Social contacts initiated during leisure activities—sports, dinners, parties, and other forms of recreation—become important sources of information on educational and career opportunities. For those with limited social networks, these contacts are restricted. Thus women's lower rate of participation in leisure activities has a profound influence on their lives. Such activities are to some degree constrained by men's control of the economic resources within the family, as studies have shown (Green et al. 1991, 78). Few researchers have focused on the control that fear of crime imposes on leisure and the impact of this control on the quality of life and opportunities for development of millions of women. Some studies indicate that women's participation in activities outside of the home are lower than men's (Green et al. 1991, 77). Indeed, as some of the interviewees in this study reveal, one factor contributing to women's lower rates of participation in leisure activities is their own or their families' fear of criminal victimization.

Other forms of self-isolation include walking fast and "shutting everyone out." "I just walk and do not look at anyone's eyes. If someone tries to talk to me, I just ignore him." This attitude, considered commonplace among people in large cities such as New York, was used by many women as a means of protection. Even though this reaction is comprehensible given the sexual harassment that many women face on the streets, it also has some detrimental consequences. For example, it contributes to decreased social solidarity among people by severely constraining personal interaction. Several women reported that they refuse to help someone in need of assistance because of their fear of victimization. "If someone asks me for directions, I just walk away. You take a big chance if you try to help," an elderly white woman reported. Edith, an elderly Latina woman, used this interesting phrase: *el que se mete a redentor sale crucificado* (whoever pretends to be the Redeemer, dies crucified). Edith's words mean that the person who tries to do good by helping others easily ends up being hurt. This type of attitude certainly contributes to individual cynicism, lack of cooperation, and decreased social solidarity.

Several of the women interviewed, especially those who live in New York City, mentioned that they "walk with an attitude," so people do not "mess with me." One twenty-seven-year-old African American woman said:

> Often strangers, and even my friends wonder why I constantly possess a tough attitude. I feel that if I act "tough," like a man is supposed to act, I feel the harm will not come to me.

. . .

Hardening the Target

"Hardening the target" means "crime-proofing" one's property, or at least making it more difficult for an offender to steal it (Clarke 1983). It involves securing homes, businesses, and vehicles and also guarding personal items such as wallets, purses, and jewelry. According to a National Crime Victimization Survey (NCVS), people take various measures to feel safer at home: installing alarms, window bars, and warning signs;

keeping dogs; engraving valuables with an identification number; and participating in neighborhood watch programs (Whitaker 1986). Most of the participants in this research said that they lock the doors and windows at home—"even during the summer," one of them said. Others buy special locks and alarm systems, lights, and timers; and install bars on their windows and doors in an attempt to build their cocoons of safety. Women use other measures to give the impression that someone is at home "protecting" them. During, the discussion with a group of suburban white teenagers, the following exchange took place:

> When I am alone I put up my radio and pretend that there are many people at home.
>
> Or the TV.
>
> I talk to myself.
>
> The other day I was at home alone and someone called on the phone asking for my mother. I said . . . she is in the bathroom. No way I am going to tell them that I am alone [everyone laughed].

. . .

Those women who have private cars use Clubs, alarm systems, and radios that can be removed from the car. Several of the participants who drive said that they always check the back seat to be sure that nobody is there. "Since I saw that movie . . . in which a woman is kidnapped and the man is hiding in the back of the car . . . I always check," Gina, a middle-class thirty-five-year-old white woman mentioned. "I am especially careful in the parking garages; anyone can walk there and hide inside of your car."

Among the most common target-hardening techniques reported by the participants in this research are hiding or not wearing their jewelry, holding their purses in a way that makes them more difficult to steal, hiding their money in their shoes or in their underwear, and not carrying cash or any property of value. For example, Angela, a twenty-three-year-old African American woman, said that she used to wear gold, but after being robbed she now wears only silver or fake jewelry. Some women said that they look for purses that are difficult to reach into, such as those that have a flap and a zipper. Frances, a middle-class white woman in her seventies, shared with the group:

> Crime is always in my mind when I shop for a purse. I try to buy the ones with long straps, so I can carry them across my chest. I also see if they are easy to open by someone trying to rob you . . . like in a crowded place. That makes me feel that at least I have some control. . . . I like especially the ones that have a flap, because they are harder to be opened by someone trying to pull your wallet out of your purse.

Other women reported that during winter they keep their purses under their coats, so they become less visible. "I bought an extra-large coat," one of the participants said, "so my pocketbook fits under it." Other women do not carry handbags, but use only belts where they can keep their money, credit cards, and identification. Some students said that although they use their book bags, they keep their money in their pockets. . . .

Clearly, target-hardening strategies are mediated by class, race, and gender. Since it is more common for women to carry purses and handbags and to wear jewelry, they are more likely to be victims of crimes such as purse or chain snatching. Therefore, it becomes a woman's individual responsibility to take care of herself. The underlying assumption is that if she exposes her jewelry or if her purse gets stolen, it is her fault for not being careful enough. . . .

Strategies of Disguise

Fear of crime also influences the way women dress because of the fear of being robbed, sexually molested, or harassed in the streets. Fashion designers, eager to sell their expensive dresses, are capitalizing on women's fear by introducing "comfort clothes and body armor for an increasingly dangerous world." According to an April 8, 1995, *New York Times* article, body protection was Donna Karan's theme in one of her latest shows. "Men's suits, quilted jackets, coat dressing

that stays on all day long, layers of fabric covering the body, padding along dresses and jackets." The idea in most American shows, according to the article, was "the need of a woman to feel safe in her clothes, physically and emotionally." The designs favor a "uniform, the suit as seen for years by the Japanese, by Wall Street, and now by women who are wary of unwelcome attention" (Spindler 1995, 31). Since most women obviously cannot afford Donna Karan's dresses, they are designing their own armor to protect themselves against possible acts of aggression.

A large number of the women interviewed shared with me the many ways in which they alter their looks. In general, adult middle-class white, Black, and Latina women, as well as white teenagers were more likely to report changing their appearance than were African American or Latina teenage women. Josephine, a twenty-three-year-old middle-class white woman, recounted:

> I work in a store that sells nice and expensive clothes. So, I have to dress nicely. But, before I leave work, I change my clothes. I hide my jewelry inside of my handbag, wear my raggy jeans and my sneakers, put my long hair up, wear a cap, so I don't call attention. . . . I don't dare to take the subway, a bus . . . or even a cab dressed in my nice clothes.

. . .

In order to protect themselves against crime, then, women often feel that they must defend or hide their bodies and even masculinize themselves. Under a system of patriarchy, the body of a woman becomes the object of males' desires and fantasies. This view is periodically reinforced by the media in films, advertisements, TV programs, magazines, and even the daily news. The persistently reinforced myth is that men cannot resist their urges when they see a desirable woman. The counterpart to this myth, for many women, is that the female body is something that a man can have access to if he wishes. It becomes a commodity, something shameful or dangerous to reveal—therefore, it needs to be disguised. As a result, it is a woman's responsibility to take care of herself by dressing conservatively and by concealing her feminine features. "I wear clothes that don't show my body," was a common phrase used by many women, especially by white women and some of the middle-class Latinas. Many of them explained in detail the types of costumes they have to wear to camouflage their bodies, such as extra-large jackets, baggy pants, and oversized coats.

Carol Brooks Gardner (1995, 25) points out that "for women in public, crime prevention does not mean to refrain from pulling a bank heist or turning a mean penny as a pickpocket: For women, crime prevention is essentially, evading the role of a target for men criminals by muting personal attractiveness." As some feminist researchers have concluded, women's bodies are constantly defined as the property of men and therefore as vulnerable to unwanted male attacks (Radford 1991; Radford and Russell 1992). Thus many women find that one way to protect themselves against becoming a victim is to bury their bodies under an armor of oversized or masculinized pieces of clothing. Thus the motto becomes: "Good girls don't show their bodies, they dress decently."

Those who do not follow the dress code are demonized. In fact, during a discussion with a group of Latina teenagers, two of the participants, Marietta and Camille, conferred about the way they think a woman should dress:

> I dress the way I want. That's nobody's problem. I even wear my gold. I love big earrings and gold chains.

> We should be able to dress the way we want. . . . That is nobody's business. . . . If they think we look too sexy, that's their fucking problem, not mine.

> Why is it that men can dress the way they want and women cannot? . . . I dress for myself, not for anyone else.

However, one of the participants, Mercedes, shared with the group how her own victimization made her change her mind:

> You don't know what you are saying. . . . I used to think like you . . . I wear whatever I want and nobody messes with me. . . . That's the way I

used to think . . . until I was robbed at gunpoint. . . . This guy put a gun to my head. . . . I thought that he was going to shoot me dead right there, . . . you know? I said shit . . . don't kill me . . . and he took all my gold. . . . Now I don't take no chances. I don't wear no gold.

. . .

Looking for Guardians

According to risk victimization theory, "All else equal, offenders prefer targets that are less well-guarded to those that are more well-guarded. Therefore, the greater the guardianship the less the risk of criminal victimization" (Cohen et al. 1981). One way that women prefer to deal with their fear of crime is by looking for guardians or protectors. In fact, many of the women interviewed said that they feel safe only in the company of others. For instance, some of the white and Latina teenagers reported that they do not go out unless they are in a group. Jody, a white teenager, said:

> We always go out like . . . ten or twenty of us . . . you know, to the malls, or to skate. If I don't have someone, I stay home. It is too scary . . . and boring to go out without my friends.

Eugenia, a Latina teenager who lives in the suburbs of New Jersey, said that she and her friends don't go to the clubs unless there are twenty or thirty in the group. In her own words,

> I don't dare to go by myself. Even when we go to parties we go in groups of like twenty or thirty or we meet at the party. I go to parties only if all my friends go. . . . I am afraid of people that I don't know. . . . And those who drive bring us home. If not I call mom. . . . Mom can you pick me up? [pretending to be talking over the telephone].

Although a handful of participants stated that it did not matter if the company was that of a man or a woman, the majority of them said that being with a man made them feel safer. After a discussion with the rest of the group, Eugenia concluded:

I rather have some boys in the group.... With boys you feel as if they are there to protect you. Like if they will prevent something from happening.

The most common protective figures mentioned by the participants were those considered "safe" men, such as husbands, fathers, boyfriends, and brothers (Stanko 1993, 132). For example, Maytena, a nineteen-year-old Latina student, said:

The main thing that helps me feel protected is my boyfriend. He is a 6'2" Black male and has a muscular body, you know. I feel that because he is Black nobody messes with him and when I am with him nobody messes with me.

. . .

Some women feel that they need to be accompanied, even when they go to the bathroom. Two fifteen-year-old white high-school students, Adriana and Gloria, commented:

I am afraid of going to the bathroom in the school by myself. I always ask a friend to come with me and wait for me while I go to the bathroom.

Me too. Several girls have been molested when they are in the bathroom.... Some boys get into the bathroom and look at them while they are using the toilet.... I heard that one girl was raped in the bathroom of my school.

. . .

When women do not have live bodyguards available, some improvise. One of my students, a twenty-two-year-old white female, Natasha, told me that one of her friends, who commutes more than one hour between home and school, got an inflatable latex man that sits beside her in the car. "People believe that she is with a man and they leave her alone," she concluded. "She used to have a lot of problems. Her inflatable friend has stopped them," she concluded, laughing.

Others look for spiritual protection. Several of the women mentioned the fact that they pray to feel protected. A Latina woman in her forties shared with the group that she always carries her Bible. "So, I do not have to make eye contact with anyone's eyes ... I always read my Bible, or pray, especially in the subway," she explained....

Although most women reported feeling safer when accompanied by a male, there were some exceptions. Some of the Black and Latina teenagers and women who had been abused by their partners reported feeling safer being by themselves or in company of a female friend or relative than when accompanied by a man. The difference between these and other women is that they know that their safety is not in the hands of a male because they have experienced or witnessed violence by those men that were supposed to be "safe."

Ignoring or Denying Fears

Of all the women participants in this research, teenagers were more likely to report that they ignore fears and continue with their lives. In one of the discussion groups with working-class Latina teenagers, I asked them, "What do you do with your fears? How do you react toward them?" The following conversation took place among four of them, Rosa, Daniela, Kathy, and Mercedes:

I bottle them up. Because I can do nothing about it.

The only thing I can do is to run.

I never think about them.

We should recognize that this fear is part of life ... well I deal with it. Because if you are paranoid about it you will get nowhere with it. Deal with the fact that you are living in the ghetto, and this is not a nice place to be.... America made this ghetto for us in Manhattan ... for us to grow up here and to fuck us up. Every city has its ghetto for poor people like us.... And they bring the drugs.... Then they say ... oh, there is crime in that neighborhood.... They know it.... I deal with my fears by understanding that they want to keep us here.... I will leave as soon as I can and take my family with me.... And then just go on with my life.

Mercedes's narrative is especially striking for it reveals her belief that it is not her fault that she lives in the ghetto. She understands that she is there for a reason: because she is a poor Puerto Rican woman. She believes that "they know" that there are drugs and crime there but "they want to keep us here." "Who are they?" I asked her. "People who have power. You know; you are a professor: the government, rich people," she concluded, staring at me. . . .

Several adult women, regardless of their race, explained that they just ignore sexual harassers. Eve, a middle-class woman in her late thirties, said: "If you just ignore them . . . that is your best defense. . . . I just look somewhere else and keep walking." Only a handful of women mentioned that they disagree with this strategy, because they believe it is their responsibility to teach men how to behave toward women. These participants tended to adopt a political perspective on the roles of women and men in society. "They have to learn to respect women," an African American woman in her early forties emphatically concluded. Finally, a few women mentioned that they try to embarrass their harassers by thanking them. One working-class white woman in her early twenties said that when she responds to a harasser with a smile and a thank-you, "they get shocked because they do not expect you to act nice toward them. They want to scare you and you show them that they can't do it." . . .

Carrying Protection

Several women in the study reported carrying a weapon or a sharp instrument to protect themselves and to feel safer. The devices mentioned range from beepers to Mace or pepper spray and from scissors to guns. Carmela, twenty-one, a working-class Latina student, . . . reported that her boyfriend gave her a beeper as a birthday present to make her, himself, and her mother feel safer. Another student, Paulette, a white woman also in her early twenties, said that her father bought her Mace when "I told him that I was going to school in New York City." In both of these

cases, as well as in others mentioned during the study, some women explained that men were the ones that bought the Mace, the pepper spray, or the beeper for them. Since men may not be there constantly to protect "their women," they are the ones that provide their daughters, wives, sisters, and girlfriends with something else to protect them, reinforcing the notion of men = protector/ women = protected. In many ways, the perception of safety provided by the device becomes an extension of the father, brother, husband, or boyfriend's protection.

Some women explained that they use sharp instruments such as scissors, keys, and even rings. Carmen is a sixteen-year-old Latina high-school student who lives on the Upper West Side of Manhattan and seems very shy. She transforms herself as she begins to talk, especially when she shows me the two big sharp-pointed rings that she wears on her right hand.

> There are not enough security guards in the high school. . . . I was almost raped by a teacher who had raped another student and had been in jail. If he approaches me again, I can hit him on the face right here . . . [pointing her fingers toward her forehead, between the eyes] in the eyes and blind him. He almost got me once. But I am ready for the next time that he or another dog wants to go for it.

Several participants said that they keep blunt instruments at home in easily accessible places. One Latina student said that she keeps a machete in her room. Similarly, Katheleen, an African American teenager who reported being abused by her mate, said that she keeps a baseball bat in her room "just in case that the asshole comes back." . . .

Gun ownership was also reported among a few of the white women. . . . A couple of them, however, said that their husbands are the ones that own the guns, "but they keep [them] at home," one of them concluded. Other middle-class white women also explained that they carry something sharp with them "like a small pocket knife" or "a scissors." Another woman said that she carries a whistle, "to call attention."

According to an article published in *Harper's Bazaar,* the gun industry and the National Rifle Association began to target potential women buyers when handgun production dropped from 2.6 million in 1982 to 1.4 million in 1986. Two appeals were used in the sales campaign: feminism and motherhood. Some images even depicted a woman with a gun tucking her children into bed! Colt Manufacturing Company published an ad in the July 1992 *Ladies' Home Journal,* instructing women to guard their children and themselves: "Self-protection is more than your right . . . it is your responsibility" (Horowitz 1994).

Fighting Back

Some parents are examining the crime statistics before choosing the college that their daughters will attend. "Before I came to this college," said Lillian, a middle-class woman who attends college in a small town in upstate New York, "my parents and I asked for the college's crime reports." Diane, another white college student, said "I wanted to go to another college, but it was in a bad section of the city, and my parents thought that it was too dangerous for me."

Several colleges and universities are now offering self-defense classes (McLarin 1994). Indeed, a handful of participants said that they had taken or were planning to take such classes. "I may not be able to protect myself if someone has a gun," Gwendolyn, a white student, said. "But I am sure it would make me feel stronger." Students who were involved in self-defense training mentioned that most of the instructors are males. "It is amazing," Gwendolyn said. "The self-defense class is for women but is given by males." Other students, such as Caro, a Latina teenager, take similar measures to protect themselves. "I am getting stronger by working out. I go to the gym everyday and do weights. It makes me feel stronger and safer." . . .

Working-class Black and Latina teenagers frequently expressed their belief that nobody is there to defend them. Thus they must learn to fight back. Most of them have lived their lives in a con-

tinuum of violence—sexual, physical, and psychological—at home and in the streets (Kelly 1991). They are clear about the fact that, for them, there are no "safe" men. Very early in their lives, they realize that they are responsible for their own protection and that there are no protectors. The only allies that they have, on occasion, are their girlfriends. Many of them believe—from experience—that they cannot count on the police. Indeed, if they turn to the police for their protection, they expect to encounter suspicion, mistrust, and further abuse. . . .

What Can Women Do?

One of the last questions asked of the participants was: "What do you recommend to other women to deal with their fear of crime?" The responses ranged from traditional measures that clearly enhance existing gender divisions to measures that challenge the status quo. Without a doubt, the most frequent responses reinforced traditional women's roles, confirming the major argument of this book: fear of crime helps reinforce gender hierarchies in U.S. society and organize consent about an appropriate code of behavior for women. The recommendations of María, a Dominican woman in her early forties, exemplify some of the most common answers:

> Do not dress provocative, do not go out by yourself, do not go out during the night, but above all pray a lot and ask God for protection.
>
> . . .

Although most of the advice was consistent with traditional roles, a few responses reflected a more politicized attitude toward fear of crime and its impact upon women's lives. Particularly relevant for this study was the response of Connie, a fourteen-year-old lower-middle-class white teenager, whose mother, Marilyn, is a student in a Women's Studies Program at a college in New York City. In a very clear and eloquent manner, Connie shared with me her views:

> I am a woman and I can do something, instead of [raising the pitch of her voice] well, I need my husband to walk me down the street! Even if

they need a can of Mace. I think women around the city and around the world should do something. . . . Have a protest. Say, look media, you have to project a better image of us because we are not wimps and we are not people who stay home and take care of children all the time. Not because that is a bad thing to do, but we are women who go out and make something of our lives. I think women should have a protest or boycott certain things. . . . Especially if they present a negative image of us. And girls should be educated more, such as math classes for girls so they think better of themselves. If they think better of themselves, they are more likely to protect themselves.

. . .

In brief, the measures that the participants recommended can be arranged along a continuum. At one extreme are strategies that reinforce traditional sex-role orientations: they accept the view that women are safer at home than on the streets, that women's predominant role is to protect children, and that there are "safe" men that can protect them. Most of the responses fall into this traditional category. At the other extreme are strategies that imply a more "proactive" attitude toward fear of crime and challenge conventional etiquettes regarding women's behavior. Such strategies range from becoming involved in physical fights to entirely rejecting the idea that there are proper behaviors for women.

REFERENCES

Becker, Howard. 1964. *The Other Side: Perspectives on Deviance.* New York: Free Press.

Bureau of Justice Statistics. 1994b. *Source Book of Criminal Justice Statistics, 1993.* Washington, DC: U.S. Department of Justice.

Chira, Susan. 1994. "Solomon's Rules for the 90's." *New York Times,* 25 September, sec. 4, 1, 3.

Clarke, Ronald. 1983. "Situational Crime Prevention: Its Theoretical Basis and Practical Scope." In Michael Tonry and Norval Morris, eds., *Annual Review of Criminal Justice Research,* 225–256. Chicago: University of Chicago Press.

Clemente, Frank, and Michael B. Kleiman. 1977. "Fear of Crime in the United States: A Multivariate Analysis." *Social Forces* 56: 518–531.

Cohen, Lawrence E., James R. Kluegel, and Kenneth C. Land. 1981. "Social Inequality and Predatory Criminal Victimization: An Exposition and Test of a Formal Theory." *American Sociological Review* 48: 505–524.

de Certeau, Michel. 1984. *The Practice of Everyday Life.* Berkeley: University of California Press.

Ehrenreich, Barbara, and Deidre English. 1978. *For Her Own Good: 150 Years of the Experts' Advice to Women.* New York: Doubleday.

Gardner, Carol Brooks. 1995. *Passing By: Gender and Public Harassment.* Berkeley: University of California Press.

Gordon, Margaret T., and Stephanie Riger. 1991. *The Female Fear: The Social Cost of Rape.* Chicago: University of Illinois Press.

Green, Eileen, Sandra Hebron, and Diana Woodward. 1991. "Women, Leisure, and Social Control." In Jalna Hanmer and Mary Maynard, eds., *Women, Violence, and Social Control,* 75–92. Atlantic Highlands, NJ: Humanities Press International.

Hall, Stuart, Chas Critcher, Tony Jefferson, John Clarke, and Brian Roberts. 1978. *Policing the Crisis: Mugging, the State and Law and Order.* New York: Holmes and Meier.

Horowitz, Joy. 1994. "Arms and the Woman." *Harper's Bazaar,* February, 166–169.

Kelly, Liz. 1991. "The Continuum of Sexual Violence." In Jalna Hanmer and Mary Maynard, eds., *Women, Violence, and Social Control,* 46–60. Atlantic Highlands, NJ: Humanity Press International.

Kinkead, Gwen. 1994. "Spock, Brazelton, and Now . . . Penelope Leach." *New York Times Magazine,* 10 April, 32–35.

McLarin, Kimberly J. 1994. "Fear Prompts Self-Defense as Crime Comes to College." *New York Times,* 2 September, A-1, B-11.

Pellicani, Luciano. 1981. *Gramsci: An Alternative Communism?* Stanford, CA: Hoover Institution Press.

Quindlen, Anna. 1994. "Playing Perfect Pattycake. The Mythical Mother." *New York Times,* 13 April, A-21.

Radford, Jill. 1991. "Policing Male Violence, Policing Women." In Jalna Hanmer and Mary Maynard, eds., *Women, Violence, and Social Control,* 30–45. Atlantic Highlands, NJ: Humanities Press International.

Radford, Jill, and Diana E. H. Russell, eds. 1992. *Femicide: The Politics of Woman Killing.* New York: Twayne.

Reiman, Jeffrey. 1995. *The Rich Get Richer and the Poor Get Prison.* Boston, MA: Allyn & Bacon.

Riger, Stephanie, and Margaret T. Gordon. 1991. "The Fear of Rape. A Study in Social Control." *Journal of Social Issues* 37: 71–92.

Riger, Stephanie, Margaret T. Gordon, and R. LeBailly. 1978. "Women's Fear of Crime: From Blaming to Restricting the Victim." *Victimology* 3:274–283.

Sidel, Ruth. 1992. *Women and Children Last. The Plight of Poor Women in Affluent America.* New York: Penguin.

Skogan, Wesley. 1987. "The Impact of Victimization on Fear," *Crime and Delinquency* 33: 135–154.

Spindler, Amy M. 1995. "Luxurious Armor by Karan, Klein, Mizrahi." *New York Times,* 8 April, 31.

Stanko, Elizabeth. 1993. "Ordinary Fear: Women, Violence, and Personal Safety." In Pauline Bart and Eileen Geil Moran, eds., *Violence Against Women, the Bloody Footprints,* 155–164. Newbury Park, CA: Sage.

———. 1990. *Everyday Violence: How Women and Men Experience Sexual and Physical Danger.* London: Pandora.

U. S. Bureau of Census. 1990. *Statistical Abstract of the United States.* Washington, DC: U.S. Government Printing Office.

Whitaker, Catherine. 1986. *Crime Prevention Measures.* Washington, DC: Bureau of Justice Statistics.

THINKING ABOUT THE READING

Discuss the significance of the title, "Nothing Bad Happens to Good Girls." Describe the strategies women use to cope with their fear of crime. What does Madriz mean when she says that female fear is made worse by prevailing ideologies of crime, which represent women as victims and men as offenders? How can social concern with the safety of women actually harm them? Discuss the effect that race and class have on women's fear of crime and their crime-prevention strategies.

Still a Man's World

Men Who Do "Women's Work"

Christine L. Williams

Gendered Jobs and Gendered Workers

A 1959 article in *Library Journal* entitled "The Male Librarian—An Anomaly?" begins this way:

> My friends keep trying to get me out of the library. . . . Library work is fine, they agree, but they smile and shake their heads benevolently and charitably, as if it were unnecessary to add that it is one of the dullest, most poorly paid, unrewarding, off-beat activities any man could be consigned to. If you have a heart condition, if you're physically handicapped in other ways, well, such a job is a blessing. And for women there's no question library work is fine; there are some wonderful women in libraries and we all ought to be thankful to them. But let's face it, no healthy man of normal intelligence should go into it.[1]

Male librarians still face this treatment today, as do other men who work in predominantly female occupations. In 1990, my local newspaper featured a story entitled "Men Still Avoiding Women's Work" that described my research on men in nursing, librarianship, teaching, and social work. Soon afterwards, a humor columnist for the same paper wrote a spoof on the story that he titled, "Most Men Avoid Women's Work Because It Is Usually So Boring."[2] The columnist poked fun at hairdressing, librarianship, nursing, and babysitting—in his view, all "lousy" jobs requiring low intelligence and a high tolerance for boredom. Evidently people still wonder why any "healthy man of normal

intelligence" would willingly work in a "woman's occupation."

In fact, not very many men do work in these fields, although their numbers are growing. In 1990, over 500,000 men were employed in these four occupations, constituting approximately 6 percent of all registered nurses, 15 percent of all elementary school teachers, 17 percent of all librarians, and 32 percent of all social workers. These percentages have fluctuated in recent years: As Table 1 indicates, librarianship and social work have undergone slight declines in the proportions of men since 1975; teaching has remained somewhat stable; while nursing has experienced noticeable gains. The number of men in nursing actually doubled between 1980 and 1990; however, their overall proportional representation remains very low.

Very little is known about these men who "cross over" into these nontraditional occupations. While numerous books have been written about women entering male-dominated occupations, few have asked why men are underrepresented in traditionally female jobs.[3] The underlying assumption in most research on gender and work is that, given a free choice, both men and women would work in predominantly male occupations, as they are generally better paying and more prestigious than predominantly female occupations. The few men who willingly "cross over" must be, as the 1959 article suggests, "anomalies."

Popular culture reinforces the belief that these men are "anomalies." Men are rarely portrayed working in these occupations, and when they

TABLE 1 *Men in the "Women's Professions":*
Number (in thousands) and Distribution of Men
Employed in the Occupations, Selected Years

Profession	1975	1980	1990
Registered Nurses			
Number of men	28	46	92
% men	3.0	3.5	5.5
Elementary Teachers[a]			
Number of men	194	225	223
% men	14.6	16.3	14.8
Librarians			
Number of men	34	27	32
% men	18.9	14.8	16.7
Social Workers			
Number of men	116	134	179
% men	39.2	35.0	21.8

Sources: U.S. Department of Labor, Bureau of Labor Statistics, *Employment and Earnings* 38 no. 1 (January 1991), table 22 (employed civilians by detailed occupation), p. 185; vol. 28, no. 1 (January 1981), table 23 (employed persons by detailed occupation), p. 180; vol. 22, no. 7 (January 1976), table 2 (employed persons by detailed occupation), p. 11.

[a]Excludes kindergarten teachers.

are, they are represented in extremely stereotypical ways. For example, in the 1990 movie *Kindergarten Cop,* muscle-man Arnold Schwarzenegger played a detective forced to work undercover as a kindergarten teacher; the otherwise competent Schwarzenegger was completely overwhelmed by the five-year-old children in his class. . . .

[I] challenge these stereotypes about men who do "women's work" through case studies of men in four predominantly female occupations: nursing, elementary school teaching, librarianship, and social work. I show that men maintain their masculinity in these occupations, despite the popular stereotypes. Moreover, male power and privilege is preserved and reproduced in these occupations through a complex interplay between gendered expectations embedded in organizations, and the gendered interests workers bring with them to their jobs. Each of these occupations

is "still a man's world" even though mostly women work in them.

I selected these four professions as case studies of men who do "women's work" for a variety of reasons. First, because they are so strongly associated with women and femininity in our popular culture, these professions highlight and perhaps even exaggerate the barriers and advantages men face when entering predominantly female environments. Second, they each require extended periods of educational training and apprenticeship, requiring individuals in these occupations to be at least somewhat committed to their work (unlike those employed in, say, clerical or domestic work). Therefore I thought they would be reflective about their decisions to join these "nontraditional" occupations, making them "acute observers" and, hence, ideal informants about the sort of social and psychological processes I am interested in describing.[4] Third, these occupations vary a great deal in the proportion of men working in them. Although my aim was not to engage in between-group comparisons, I believed that the proportions of men in a work setting would strongly influence the degree to which they felt accepted and satisfied with their jobs.[5]

I traveled across the United States conducting in-depth interviews with seventy-six men and twenty-three women who work in nursing, teaching, librarianship, and social work. Like the people employed in these professions generally, those in my sample were predominantly white (90 percent). Their ages ranged from twenty to sixty-six, and the average age was thirty-eight. I interviewed women as well as men to gauge their feelings and reactions to men's entry into "their" professions. Respondents were intentionally selected to represent a wide range of specialties and levels of education and experience. I interviewed students in professional schools, "front line" practitioners, administrators, and retirees, asking them about their motivations to enter these professions, their on-the-job experiences, and their opinions about men's status and prospects in these fields. . . .

Riding the Glass Escalator

Men earn more money than women in every oc-cupation—even in predominantly female jobs (with the possible exceptions of fashion model-ing and prostitution).[6] Table 2 shows that men outearn women in teaching, librarianship, and social work; their salaries in nursing are virtually identical. The ratios between women's and men's earnings in these occupations are higher than those found in the "male" professions, where women earn 74 to 90 percent of men's salaries. That there is a wage gap at all in predominantly female professions, however, attests to asymme-tries in the workplace experiences of male and female tokens. These salary figures indicate that the men who do "women's work" fare as well as, and often better than, the women who work in these fields. . . .

Hiring Decisions

Contrary to the experience of many women in the male-dominated professions, many of the men and women I spoke to indicated that there is a *preference* for hiring men in these four occu-pations. A Texas librarian at a junior high school said that his school district "would hire a male over a female":

[CW: Why do you think that is?]

Because there are so few, and the . . . ones that they do have, the library directors seem to really . . . think they're doing great jobs. I don't know, maybe they just feel they're being progressive or something, [but] I have had a real sense that they really appreciate having a male, particularly at the junior high. . . . As I said, when seven of us lost our jobs from the high schools and were redistributed, there were only four positions at junior high, and I got one of them. Three of the librarians, some who had been here longer than I had with the school district, were put down in elementary school as librarians. And I definitely think that being male made a difference in my being moved to the junior high rather than an elementary school.

Many of the men perceived their token status as males in predominantly female occupations as an *advantage* in hiring and promotions. When I asked an Arizona teacher whether his specialty (elementary special education) was an unusual area for men compared to other areas within education, he said,

Much more so. I am extremely marketable in special education. That's not why I got into the field. But I am extremely marketable because I am a man.

TABLE 2   *Median Weekly Earnings of Full-Time Professional Workers, by Sex, and Ratio of Female:Male Earnings, 1990*

Occupation	Both	Men	Women	Ratio
Registered Nurses	608	616	608	.99
Elementary Teachers	519	575	513	.89
Librarians	489	—*	479	—
Social Workers	445	483	427	.88
Engineers	814	822	736	.90
Physicians	892	978	802	.82
College Teachers	747	808	620	.77
Lawyers	1,045	1,178	875	.74

Source: U.S. Department of Labor, Bureau of Labor Statistics, *Employment and Earnings* 38, no. 1 (January 1991), table 56, p. 223.

*The Labor Department does not report income averages for base sample sizes consisting of fewer than 50,000 individuals.

... Sometimes the preference for men in these occupations is institutionalized. One man landed his first job in teaching before he earned the appropriate credential "because I was a wrestler and they wanted a wrestling coach." A female math teacher similarly told of her inability to find a full-time teaching position because the schools she applied to reserved the math jobs for people (presumably men) who could double as coaches....

... Some men described being "tracked" into practice areas within their professions which were considered more legitimate for men. For example, one Texas man described how he was pushed into administration and planning in social work, even though "I'm not interested in writing policy; I'm much more interested in research and clinical stuff." A nurse who is interested in pursuing graduate study in family and child health in Boston said he was dissuaded from entering the program specialty in favor of a concentration in "adult nursing." And a kindergarten teacher described his difficulty finding a job in his specialty after graduation: "I was recruited immediately to start getting into a track to become an administrator. And it was men who recruited me. It was men that ran the system at that time, especially in Los Angeles."

This tracking may bar men from the most female-identified specialties within these professions. But men are effectively being "kicked upstairs" in the process. Those specialties considered more legitimate practice areas for men also tend to be the most prestigious, and better-paying specialties as well. For example, men in nursing are overrepresented in critical care and psychiatric specialties, which tend to be higher paying than the others.[7] The highest paying and most prestigious library types are the academic libraries (where men are 35 percent of librarians) and the special libraries which are typically associated with businesses or other private organizations (where men constitute 20 percent of librarians).[8]

A distinguished kindergarten teacher, who had been voted citywide "Teacher of the Year," described the informal pressures he faced to advance in his field. He told me that even though

people were pleased to see him in the classroom, "there's been some encouragement to think about administration, and there's been some encouragement to think about teaching at the university level or something like that, or supervisory-type position."

The effect of this "tracking" is the opposite of that experienced by women in male-dominated occupations. Researchers have reported that many women encounter "glass ceilings" in their efforts to scale organizational and professional hierarchies. That is, they reach invisible barriers to promotion in their careers, caused mainly by the sexist attitudes of men in the highest positions.[9] In contrast to this "glass ceiling," many of the men I interviewed seem to encounter a "glass escalator." Often, despite their intentions, they face invisible pressures to move up in their professions. Like being on a moving escalator, they have to work to stay in place....

Supervisors and Colleagues:
The Working Environment

... Respondents in this study were asked about their relationships with supervisors and female colleagues to ascertain whether men also experienced "poisoned" work environments when entering nontraditional occupations.

A major difference in the experience of men and women in nontraditional occupations is that men are far more likely to be supervised by a member of their own sex. In each of the four professions I studied, men are overrepresented in administrative and managerial capacities, or, as in the case of nursing, the organizational hierarchy is governed by men. For example, 15 percent of all elementary school teachers are men, but men make up over 80 percent of all elementary school principals and 96 percent of all public school superintendents and assistant superintendents.[10] Likewise, over 40 percent of all male social workers hold administrative or managerial positions, compared to 30 percent of all female social workers.[11] And 50 percent of male librarians hold administrative positions, compared to 30 percent of female librarians, and the majority of deans and directors of major university and public libraries are men.[12] Thus, unlike women who enter "male fields," the men in these professions often work under the direct supervision of other men.

Many of the men interviewed reported that they had good rapport with their male supervisors. It was not uncommon in education, for example, for the male principal to informally socialize with the male staff, as a Texas special education teacher describes:

> Occasionally I've had a principal who would regard me as "the other man on the campus" and "it's us against them," you know? I mean, nothing really that extreme, except that some male principals feel like there's nobody there to talk to except the other man. So I've been in that position.

These personal ties can have important consequences for men's careers. For example, one California nurse, whose performance was judged marginal by his nursing superiors, was transferred to the emergency room staff (a prestigious promotion) due to his personal friendship with the physician in charge. And a Massachusetts teacher acknowledged that his principal's personal interest in him landed him his current job:

> [CW: You had mentioned that your principal had sort of spotted you at your previous job and had wanted to bring you here [to this school]. Do you think that has anything to do with the fact that you're a man, aside from your skills as a teacher?]
>
> Yes, I would say in that particular case, that was part of it. . . . We have certain things in common, certain interests that really lined up.
>
> [CW: Vis-à-vis teaching?]
>
> Well, more extraneous things—running specifically, and music. And we just seemed to get along real well right off the bat. It is just kind of a guy thing; we just liked each other. . . .

Interviewees did not report many instances of male supervisors discriminating against them, or refusing to accept them because they were male. Indeed, these men were much more likely to report that their male bosses discriminated against the *females* in their professions. . . .

Of course, not all the men who work in these occupations are supervised by men. Many of the men interviewed who had female bosses also reported high levels of acceptance—although the level of intimacy they achieved with women did not seem as great as with other men. But in some cases, men reported feeling shut-out from decision making when the higher administration was constituted entirely by women. I asked this Arizona librarian whether men in the library profession were discriminated against hiring because of their sex:

> Professionally speaking, people go to considerable lengths to keep that kind of thing out of their [hiring] deliberations. Personally, is another matter. It's pretty common around here to talk about the "old girl network." This is one of the few libraries that I've had any intimate knowledge of which is actually controlled by women. . . . Most of the department heads and upper level administrators are women. And there's an "old girl network" that works just like the "old boy network," except that the important conferences take place in the women's room rather than on the golf course. But the political mechanism is the same, the exclusion of the other sex from decision making is the same. The reasons are the same. It's somewhat discouraging. . . .

Although I did not interview many supervisors, I did include twenty-three women in my sample to ascertain their perspectives about the presence of men in their professions. All of the women I interviewed claimed to be supportive of their male colleagues, but some conveyed ambivalence. For example, a social work professor said she would like to see more men enter the social work profession, particularly in the clinical specialty (where they are underrepresented). She said she would favor affirmative action hiring guidelines for men in the profession, and yet, she resented the fact that her department hired "another white male" during a recent search. I confronted her about this apparent ambivalence:

[CW: I find it very interesting that, on the one hand, you sort of perceive this preference and perhaps even sexism with regard to how men are evaluated and how they achieve higher positions within the profession, yet, on the other hand, you would be encouraging of more men to enter the field. Is that contradictory to you, or . . . ?]

Yeah, it's contradictory. . . .

Men's reception by their female colleagues is thus somewhat mixed. It appears that women are generally eager to see men enter "their" occupations, and the women I interviewed claimed they were supportive of their male peers. Indeed, several men agreed with this social worker that their female colleagues had facilitated their careers in various ways (including college mentorship). At the same time, however, women often resent the apparent ease with which men seem to advance within these professions, sensing that men at the higher levels receive preferential treatment, and thus close off advancement opportunities for women.

But this ambivalence does not seem to translate into the "poisoned" work environment described by many women who work in male-dominated occupations. Among the male interviewees, there were no accounts of sexual harassment (indeed, one man claimed this was a disappointment to him!) However, women do treat their male colleagues differently on occasion. It is not uncommon in nursing, for example, for men to be called upon to help catheterize male patients, or to lift especially heavy patients. Some librarians also said that women asked them to lift and move heavy boxes of books because they were men. . . .

Another stereotype confronting men, in nursing and social work in particular, is the expectation that they are better able than women to handle aggressive individuals and diffuse violent situations. An Arizona social worker who was the first male caseworker in a rural district, described this preference for men:

They welcomed a man, particularly in child welfare. Sometimes you have to go into some tough parts of towns and cities, and they felt it was nice to have a man around to accompany them or be present when they were dealing with a difficult client. Or just doing things that males can do. I always felt very welcomed.

But this special treatment bothered some respondents: Getting assigned all the violent patients or discipline problems can make for difficult and unpleasant working conditions. Nurses, for example, described how they were called upon to subdue violent patients. A traveling psychiatric nurse I interviewed in Texas told how his female colleagues gave him "plenty of opportunities" to use his wrestling skills. . . .

But many men claimed that this differential treatment did not distress them. In fact, several said they liked being appreciated for the special traits and abilities (such as strength) they could contribute to their professions.

Furthermore, women's special treatment of men sometimes enhanced—rather than detracted from—the men's work environments. One Texas librarian said he felt "more comfortable working with women than men" because "I think it has something to do with control. Maybe it's that women will let me take control more than men will." Several men reported that their female colleagues often cast them into leadership roles. . . .

The interviews suggest that the working environment encountered by "nontraditional" male workers is quite unlike that faced by women who work in traditionally male fields. Because it is not uncommon for men in predominantly female professions to be supervised by other men, they tend to have closer rapport and more intimate social relationships with people in management. These ties can facilitate men's careers by smoothing the way for future promotions. Relationships with female supervisors were also described for the most part in positive terms, although in some cases, men perceived an "old girls'" network in place that excluded them from decision making. But in sharp contrast to the reports of women in nontraditional occupations, men in these fields did not complain of feeling discriminated against because they were men. If anything, they felt that being male was an asset that enhanced their career prospects.

Those men interviewed for this study also described congenial workplaces, and a very high level of acceptance from their female colleagues. The sentiment was echoed by women I spoke to who said that they were pleased to see more men enter "their" professions. Some women, however, did express resentment over the "fast-tracking" that their male colleagues seem to experience. But this ambivalence did not translate into a hostile work environment for men: Women generally included men in their informal social events and, in some ways, even facilitated men's careers. By casting men into leadership roles, presuming they were more knowledgeable and qualified, or relying on them to perform certain critical tasks, women unwittingly contributed to the "glass escalator effect" facing men who do "women's work."

Relationships with Clients

Workers in these service-oriented occupations come into frequent contact with the public during the course of their work day. Nurses treat patients; social workers usually have client case loads; librarians serve patrons; and teachers are in constant contact with children, and often with parents as well. Many of those interviewed claimed that the clients they served had different expectations of men and women in these occupations, and often treated them differently.

People react with surprise and often disbelief when they encounter a man in nursing, elementary school teaching, and, to a lesser extent, librarianship. (Usually people have no clear expectations about the sex of social workers.) The stereotypes men face are often negative. For example, according to this Massachusetts nurse, it is frequently assumed that male nurses are gay:

> Fortunately, I carry one thing with me that protects me from [the stereotype that male nurses are gay], and the one thing I carry with me is a wedding ring, and it makes a big

difference. The perfect example was conversations before I was married. . . . [People would ask], "Oh, do you have a girlfriend?" Or you'd hear patients asking questions along that idea, and they were simply implying, "Why is this guy in nursing? Is it because he's gay and he's a pervert?" And I'm not associating the two by any means, but this is the thought process.

. . . It is not uncommon for both gay and straight men in these occupations to encounter people who believe that they are "gay 'til proven otherwise," as one nurse put it. In fact, there are many gay men employed in these occupations. But gender stereotypes are at least as responsible for this general belief as any "empirical" assessment of men's sexual lifestyles. To the degree that men in these professions are perceived as not "measuring up" to the supposedly more challenging occupational roles and standards demanded of "real" men, they are immediately suspected of being effeminate—"like women"—and thus, homosexual.

An equally prevalent sexual stereotype about men in these occupations is that they are potentially dangerous and abusive. Several men described special rules they followed to guard against the widespread presumption of sexual abuse. For example, nurses were sometimes required to have a female "chaperone" present when performing certain procedures or working with specific populations. This psychiatric nurse described a former workplace:

> I worked on a floor for the criminally insane. Pretty threatening work. So you have to have a certain number of females on the floor just to balance out. Because there were female patients on the floor too. And you didn't want to be accused of rape or any sex crimes.

Teachers and librarians described the steps they took to protect themselves from suspicions of sexual impropriety. A kindergarten teacher said:

> I know that I'm careful about how I respond to students. I'm careful in a number of ways—in my physical interaction with students. It's

mainly to reassure parents. . . . For example, a little girl was very affectionate, very anxious to give me a hug. She'll just throw herself at me. I need to tell her very carefully: "Sonia, you need to tell me when you want to hug me." That way I can come down, crouch down. Because you don't want a child giving you a hug on your hip. You just don't want to do that. So I'm very careful about body position.

. . . Although negative stereotypes about men who do "women's work" can push men out of specific jobs, their effects can actually benefit men. Instead of being a source of negative discrimination, these prejudices can add to the "glass escalator effect" by pressuring men to move *out* of the most feminine-identified areas and *up* to those regarded as more legitimate for men.

The public's reactions to men working in these occupations, however, are by no means always negative. Several men and women reported that people often assume that men in these occupations are more competent than women, or that they bring special skills and expertise to their professional practice. For example, a female academic librarian told me that patrons usually address their questions to the male reference librarian when there is a choice between asking a male or a female. A male clinical social worker in private practice claimed that both men and women generally preferred male psychotherapists. And several male nurses told me that people often assume that they are physicians and direct their medical inquiries to them instead of to the female nurses.[13]

The presumption that men are more competent than women is another difference in the experience of token men and women. Women who work in nontraditional occupations are often suspected of being incompetent, unable to survive the pressures of "men's work." As a consequence, these women often report feeling compelled to prove themselves and, as the saying goes, "work twice as hard as men to be considered half as good." To the degree that men are assumed to be competent and in control, they may have to be twice as incompetent to be considered half as bad.

One man claimed that "if you're a mediocre male teacher, you're considered a better teacher than if you're a female and a mediocre teacher. I think there's that prejudice there." . . .

There are different standards and assumptions about men's competence that follow them into nontraditional occupations. In contrast, women in both traditional and nontraditional occupations must contend with the presumption that they are neither competent nor qualified. . . .

The reasons that clients give for preferring or rejecting men reflect the complexity of our society's stereotypes about masculinity and femininity. Masculinity is often associated with competence and mastery, in contrast to femininity, which is often associated with instrumental incompetence. Because of these stereotypes, men are perceived as being stricter disciplinarians and stronger than women, and thus better able to handle violent or potentially violent situations. . . .

Conclusion

Both men and women who work in nontraditional occupations encounter discrimination, but the forms and the consequences of this discrimination are very different for the two groups. Unlike "nontraditional" women workers, most of the discrimination and prejudice facing men in the "female" professions comes from clients. For the most part, the men and women I interviewed believed that men are given fair—if not preferential—treatment in hiring and promotion decisions, are accepted by their supervisors and colleagues, and are well-integrated into the workplace subculture. Indeed, there seem to be subtle mechanisms in place that enhance men's positions in these professions—a phenomenon I refer to as a "glass escalator effect."

Men encounter their most "mixed" reception in their dealings with clients, who often react negatively to male nurses, teachers, and to a lesser extent, librarians. Many people assume that the men are sexually suspect if they are employed in these "feminine" occupations either because they do or they do not conform to stereotypical masculine characteristics.

Dealing with the stress of these negative stereotypes can be overwhelming, and it probably pushes some men out of these occupations.[14] The challenge facing the men who stay in these fields is to accentuate their positive contribution to what our society defines as essentially "women's work."...

NOTES

1. Allan Angoff, "The Male Librarian—An Anomaly?" *Library Journal*, February 15, 1959, p. 553.

2. *Austin-American Statesman*, January 16, 1990; response by John Kelso, January 18, 1990.

3. Some of the most important studies of women in male-dominated occupations are: Rosabeth Moss Kanter, *Men and Women of the Corporation* (New York: Basic Books, 1977); Susan Martin, *Breaking and Entering: Policewomen on Patrol* (Berkeley: University of California Press, 1980); Cynthia Fuchs Epstein, *Women in Law* (New York: Basic Books, 1981); Kay Deaux and Joseph Ullman, *Women of Steel* (New York: Praeger, 1983); Judith Hicks Stiehm, *Arms and the Enlisted Woman* (Philadelphia: Temple University Press, 1989); Jerry Jacobs, *Revolving Doors: Sex Segregation and Women's Careers* (Stanford: Stanford University Press, 1989); Barbara Reskin and Patricia Roos, *Job Queues, Gender Queues: Explaining Women's Inroads into Male Occupations* (Philadelphia: Temple University Press, 1990).

Among the few books that do examine men's status in predominantly female occupations are Carol Tropp Schreiber, *Changing Places: Men and Women in Transitional Occupations* (Cambridge: MIT Press, 1979); Christine L. Williams, *Gender Differences at Work: Women and Men in Nontraditional Occupations* (Berkeley: University of California Press, 1989); and Christine L. Williams, ed., *Doing "Women's Work": Men in Nontraditional Occupations* (Newbury Park, CA: Sage Publications, 1993).

4. In an influential essay on methodological principles, Herbert Blumer counseled sociologists to "sedulously seek participants in the sphere of life who are acute observers and who are well informed. One such person is worth a hundred others who are merely unobservant participants." See "The Methodological Position of Symbolic Interactionism," in *Symbolic Interactionism: Perspective and Method* (Berkeley: University of California Press, 1969), p. 41.

5. The overall proportions in the population do not necessarily represent the experiences of individuals in my sample. Some nurses, for example, worked in groups that were composed almost entirely of men, while some social workers had the experience of being the only man in their group. The overall statistics provide a general guide, but relying on them exclusively can distort the actual experiences of individuals in the workplace. The statistics available for research on occupational sex segregation are not specific enough to measure internal divisions among workers. Research that uses firm-level data finds a far greater degree of segregation than research that uses national data. See William T. Bielby and James N. Baron, "A Woman's Place Is with Other Women: Sex Segregation within Organizations," in *Sex Segregation in the Workplace: Trends, Explanations, Remedies,* ed. Barbara Reskin (Washington, D.C.: National Academy Press, 1984), pp. 27–55.

6. Catharine MacKinnon, *Feminism Unmodified* (Cambridge: Harvard University Press, 1987), pp. 24–25.

7. Howard S. Rowland, *The Nurse's Almanac,* 2d ed. (Rockville, MD: Aspen Systems Corp., 1984), p. 153; Johw W. Wright, *The American Almanac of Jobs and Salaries,* 2d ed. (New York: Avon, 1984), p. 639.

8. King Research, Inc., *Library Human Resources: A Study of Supply and Demand* (Chicago: American Library Association, 1983), p. 41.

9. See, for example, Sue J. M. Freeman, *Managing Lives: Corporate Women and Social Change* (Amherst: University of Massachusetts Press, 1990).

10. Patricia A. Schmuck, "Women School Employees in the United States," in *Women Educators: Employees of Schools in Western Countries* (Albany: State University of New York Press, 1987), p. 85; James W. Grimm and Robert N. Stern, "Sex Roles and Internal Labor Market Structures: The Female Semi-Professions," *Social Problems* 21(1974): 690–705.

11. David A. Hardcastle and Arthur J. Katz, *Employment and Unemployment in Social Work: A Study of NASW Members* (Washington, D.C.: NASW, 1979), p. 41; Reginold O. York, H. Carl Henley and Dorothy N. Gamble, "Sexual Discrimination in Social Work: Is

It Salary or Advancement?" *Social Work* 32 (1987): 336–340; Grimm and Stern, "Sex Roles and Internal Labor Market Structures."

12. Leigh Estabrook, "Women's Work in the Library/Information Sector," in *My Troubles Are Going to Have Trouble with Me,* ed. Karen Brodkin Sacks and Dorothy Remy (New Brunswick, NJ: Rutgers University Press, 1984), p. 165.

13. Liliane Floge and D. M. Merrill found a similar phenomenon in their study of male nurses. See "To-kenism Reconsidered: Male Nurses and Female Physicians in a Hospital Setting," Social Forces 64 (1986): 931–932.

14. Jim Allan makes this argument in "Male Elementary Teachers: Experiences and Perspectives," in *Doing "Women's Work": Men in Nontraditional Occupations,* ed. Christine L. Williams (Newbury Park, CA: Sage Publications, 1993), pp. 113–127.

THINKING ABOUT THE READING

Compare the discrimination men experience in traditionally female occupations to that experienced by women in traditionally male occupations. What is the "glass escalator effect"? In what ways can the glass escalator actually be harmful to men? What do you suppose might happen to the structure of the American labor force if men did in fact begin to enter predominantly female occupations in the same proportion as women entering predominantly male occupations?

CHAPTER 14

The Dynamics of Population: Demographic and Global Trends

In the past several chapters we have examined the various interrelated sources of social stratification. Race, class, and gender continue to determine access to cultural, economic, and political opportunities. Yet another source of inequality that we don't think much about but has enormous local, national, and global significance is the changing size and shape of the human population. Globally, population imbalances between richer and poorer societies underlie most if not all of the other important forces for change that are taking place today. Poor, developing countries are expanding rapidly, while the populations in wealthy, developed countries have either stabilized or, in some cases, declined. When the population of a country grows rapidly, the age structure is increasingly dominated by young people. In slow-growth countries with low birthrates and high life expectancy, the population is much older.

Often overlooked in our quest to identify the structural factors that shape our everyday experiences are the effects of our *birth cohort*. Birth cohorts are more than just a collection of individuals born within a few years of each other; they are distinctive generations tied together by historical events, national and global population trends, and large-scale societal changes. We hear a lot of criticism about the youthful generation of Americans in their teens and twenties. The news media depict them as a directionless wasteland of academic underachievement, political apathy, disease-ridden sex, and reckless self-absorption. Older generations often see them as "hard-to-like kids who deserve not a break but a kick. . . ." Making predictions about the future of a large group of people is always risky business, but in their article, "The 21st Century Breathing Down Our Necks," Neil Howe and Bill Strauss offer some provocative thoughts about what is going to become of America's "13th Generation" (people born between 1961 and 1981) over the next 40 years. In doing so, they provide a vivid illustration of the importance of birth cohorts on our everyday experiences.

As social and demographic conditions in poor, developing countries grow worse, pressures to migrate increase, creating a variety of cultural, political, and economic fears in countries experiencing high levels of immigration. Immigration—both legal and illegal—has become one of the most contentious political issues in the United States today. While politicians debate proposed immigration restrictions, people from all corners of the globe continue to come to this country looking for a better life. In his article, "Across the Wire," Luis Urrea provides us with a first-hand account of life on the border between the United States and Mexico. Urrea puts a human face on immigration as a social issue. Not only do we get a sense of the dangers of illegal immigration, but we also see that the culture that emerges on the border differs from that of either country it dissects.

Once immigrants arrive in a new country, they often face disapproving, often hostile reactions from others. In the article, "The Melting Pot," Anne Fadiman examines the experiences of Hmong refugees in the United States. Some 150,000 Hmong people have fled Laos since that country fell to communist forces in 1975. Most have settled in the United States. Virtually every element of Hmong culture and tradition lies in stark contrast to the everyday assumptions of American life. They have been described in the American media as simplistic, primitive, and throwbacks to the Stone Age. Hmong immigrants have had a particularly difficult time adapting to American society because they are a proud, independent people who are quick to reject the customs of other cultures. This article vividly portrays the everyday conflicts immigrants face as they straddle two vastly different cultures.

The 21st Century Breathing Down Our Necks

Neil Howe and Bill Strauss

. . . To figure out where any generation is heading, you have to know two things: its current location and its future direction.

Location is the easy part. You can find out where a generation is today by identifying its collective personality, its cultural center of gravity, and its attitudes, habits, and skills. To answer any number of trivial questions about the future, current location may be all you need to know. Take music, for example. Even in old age, a generation retains a special fondness for the songs it first hears in its mid-teens to early 20s. Thus, we could have predicted many years ago that today's senior citizens would still be listening to Glenn Miller and Benny Goodman. And we can safely predict that, sometime around 2040, America's 70-year-olds will feel a special nostalgia for (believe it or not) the staccato rhythm of a vintage urban rapper.

Yet even if a generation can't alter many of the specific traits it acquires young, it is equally true that such traits get applied to new purposes and are shaped by new attitudes over the course of its life cycle. Along the way, a generation typically finds that its personality in old age is very different from its personality in youth. . . .

To make more important predictions, therefore, you need some understanding of a generation's sense of *direction*—what Ortega y Gasset called its "preestablished vital trajectory" and Karl Mannheim its "essential destiny." It's not easy to identify this direction. It's like unwrapping some hidden sociogenetic code. You have to read motives and questions and dreams that are hidden inside a generation like an oak within an acorn and that don't become fully apparent until they are expressed in history.

But one thing is certain: If you don't know the direction, you'll be clueless about the future, because no generation ever starts and ends its collective journey in the same location. Consider a generation (like the G.I.s [today's senior citizens]) that comes of age saving, working, and building big things. Who would guess that this same group of people, entering retirement, would create the biggest consumption and leisure lobby in world history? Or consider a generation (like the Silent [the 40 million Americans now in their 50s]) that spends the first half of its life doing everything by the rules—and ever since midlife yearns to break all the taboos. Or consider a generation (like the Baby Boomers) that celebrates the libido at age 18—and then three decades later begins to engage in what marketers call "non-ism," the ascetic art of celebrating whatever it is you're *not* enjoying.

To understand how generations acquire a sense of direction, you have to ask how they interpret their world early in life. Coming of age, what is their agenda? What's their greatest challenge—the biggest problem they want to solve or the obstacle they need to overcome? For G.I.s in the early 1930s, the challenge was national poverty and pessimism—which helps explain the affluent, upbeat image of today's senior citizen. For the Silent in the early '50s, it was "yes sir" determination and conformism—hence the ambivalent, open-minded image of today's midlifer. For the Boomers in the early '70s, soulless abundance and complacency—hence the (still evolving) values-fixated image of today's 40-year-old.

This brings us to the future of the 13th Generation [Americans born between 1961 and 1981]. What is it about America's current social mood that is likely to leave the most lasting impression on Americans now coming of age? We don't know for sure, but we can make some fair guesses: chaotic individualism; social fragmentation; cultural openness; institutions grown over-complex and irrelevant; a consumption-based economy that devours its own future; a political system that debates everything but chooses nothing. Were you to extrapolate the future strictly on the basis of how 13ers are now coping with this world, you could indeed draw a very dismal scenario. Imagine a place in which civilization has crumbled into dust, leaving only a bunch of aging Road Warriors and Blade Runners. But this scenario is likely to be as wildly inaccurate as the totalitarian 1984 projections made for the compliant young Silent Generation in the wake of Hitler and Stalin. It's wrong because it looks at where a generation is without paying attention to what's happening *inside* that generation—where it's going, what it's on the way to becoming.

So what *is* the 13er direction? Here's where history helps. . . . If 13ers follow the trajectory of prior generations . . . we can make a good number of informed predictions about how their collective personality will evolve as they grow older; which attitudes and habits will stay constant, and which will reverse; what lifelong lessons they will carry with them from the circa-'80s and '90s world in which they are coming of age; how they will behave toward other generations, and how other generations will behave toward them; what kind of leadership they will someday provide; and how history will someday remember them.

The most important lesson of history is this: Once previous 13er-like generations reached midlife, they underwent a profound personality transformation. Their risk-taking gave way to caution, their wildness and alienation turned into exhaustion and conservatism, and their nomadic individualism matured into a preference for strong community life. The same unruly rebels and adventurers who alarmed older colonists during the 1760s later became the crusty old Patrick Henrys and George Washingtons who warned younger statesmen against gambling with the future. The same gold-chasing '49ers and Civil War

brigands whom Oliver Wendell Holmes, Jr., called "a generation touched with fire" later became the stodgy "Old Guard" Victorians of the Gilded Era. The same gin-fizz "Flaming Youth" who electrified America during the 1920s later became the Norman Rockwells and Dwight Eisenhowers who calmed America during the 1950s.

With history as a guide, we offer 13 predictions for the 13th Generation:

1. *Over the next fifteen years, the festering quarrel between 13ers and Boomers will grow into America's next great "generation gap."* As their stamp on American culture increasingly looks, tastes, smells, and sounds anti-Boom, everything 13ers do that Boomers already consider frenetic, shallow, or shocking will grow even more so, confirming public opinion that this truly is a "wasted" generation. Like the Lost Generation of the 1920s, 13ers will have their greatest cultural impact on the marketplace (entertainment, products, styles, advertising), yet over time their what-you-see-is-what-you-get brassiness will spill over into religion and politics. Thirteeners will vent their social alienation by stressing bucks and deals where their next-elders once talked about ideas and values. In response, midlife Boomers will try to insulate their families from a mainstream culture gone rotten and will project heavy-handed value judgments into public life. Interpreting these judgments as pitiless and Scroogelike, 13ers will blast away at Boomer hypocrisy and pomposity—and get blasted back for their own cynicism and wildness. Only during the first decade of the next century, when Atari-wave 13ers reach midlife, will this age war subside.

2. *Thirteeners will never outgrow their "bad" image.* The children allowed to grow up unskilled, unschooled, and unwanted in the 1970s and '80s will carry those pathologies with them. They will be just as unemployable and socially undesirable at age forty as they are today at age twenty. Remedial adult education will lose funding, young-adult welfare will be cut further, and expanded health-care benefits will help young parents only to the extent that it targets their kids.

Many of today's youth gangsters will ripen into their adult facsimile, waging Capone-like wars with police. Already the most incarcerated generation in American history, 13ers will in time be (thanks to Boomer legislators, judges, and juries) the most executed generation as well. Efforts to prevent antisocial behavior and to encourage cooperation and teamwork will be focused exclusively on the young. By the year 2020—roughly [twenty] years from now—Americans in their fifties will be generally regarded as worse-behaved (and worse-educated) than Americans in their twenties—exactly the opposite of today.

3. *The 13th will become one of the most important immigrant generations in U.S. history.* Ultimately, its membership will include the highest percentage of naturalized U.S. citizens of any generation born in the twentieth century. The politics of ethnic group rivalry and the cultural impact of racial diversity will play a far more serious role in the lives of 13ers than they ever did in the lives of the Boom and Silent. As immigrants and nonwhites flaunt their unique identities, many white 13ers will see themselves as endangered, sparking social movements that others will regard as know-nothing nativism. Over time, the perception that large numbers of 13er immigrants threaten to fragment society beyond repair will persuade Americans of all ages to clamp down on immigration—ensuring that the foreign-born share of the next generation will be smaller. Meanwhile, foreign-born high-achievers will catapult new ethnic groups, especially Asians and Hispanics, into national prominence much as [earlier] generations did for the Italians, Eastern Europeans . . . Irish, and Germans.

4. *Early in life, the most successful 13ers will be risk takers who exploit opportunities overlooked by established businesses.* The leading 13er frontier will be overseas, where this generation can most fully apply its entrepreneurial instincts and take advantage of its linguistic, computer, and marketing skills. At home, 13ers will revitalize the unskilled service sector, turn small manufacturers into exporters, mount gray-market challenges to credentialed monopolies (law, medicine, fi-

nance), and set up profitable alternatives to rule-encrusted state enterprises (mail, schools, waste disposal, security). As contract work employees, many will dart from job to job, while others mix steady wages during the day with get-rich-quick deals at night—discouraging companies from offering job training, career ladders, or pension programs. As managers, 13ers will seek market niches where quick deals matter more than long memos. Professional and union loyalties will continue to decline. The bottom line is that 13ers will leave public and private bureaucracies leaner, more personalized, and more oriented toward doing the job than staffing the process.

5. *Reaching midlife, the 13ers' economic fears will be confirmed: They will become the only generation born this century . . . to suffer a one-generation backstep in living standards.* Compared to their own parents at the same age, the 13ers' poverty rate will be higher, their rate of home ownership lower, their pension and health-care benefits skimpier. They will not match the Boomers' inflation-adjusted levels of disposable income or wealth, at the same age. Thirteeners will also experience a much wider distribution of income and wealth than today's older generations, with startling proportions either falling into destitution or shooting from rags to riches. They will change the focus of class politics—away from raising low-income families to the median toward preventing the rootless poor from sinking into a total abyss. Finding their youthful dreams broken on the shoals of marketplace reality, 13ers will internalize their disappointment. Around the year 2020, accumulated "hard knocks" will give midlife 13ers much of the same gritty determination about life that the Great Depression gave the midlife Lost [Generation]. . . .

6. *Thirteeners will restrengthen the American family.* Dedicated spouses, they will work hard to shield their marriages from the risk and stress of their work lives. Around the year 2000, these efforts will be reflected in a marked downturn in the national divorce rate. First as parents and later as community leaders, 13ers will practice and advocate a heavily protective, even smother-

ing style of nurture. They will revive the innocence of childhood by deliberately shielding their own kids from the harsher realities of life, and by prohibiting those kids from taking the same liberties they themselves once took at the same age. Having no illusions about sex themselves, they will appreciate the advantages of creating illusions (and resurrecting modesty) for their children. . . .

7. *Reaching their fifties in a mood of collective exhaustion, 13ers will settle into the midlife role of national anchor, calming the social mood and slowing the pace of social change.* As senior educators, political leaders, and media executives, 13ers will reverse the frenzied and centrifugal cultural directions of their younger years. In alliance with old Boomers, they will clean up entertainment, de-diversify the culture, reinvent core symbols of national unity, reaffirm rituals of family and neighborhood bonding, and re-erect barriers to cushion communities from unwanted social upheaval. As architects and civic officials, they will oversee the rebuilding of urban America and pioneer the next great era of (high-tech) infrastructure. Cities will define and energize them—but Boomer-run exurbs will surround them and constantly preach to them. . . . As elder role models, 13ers will make near-perfect 50-year-olds: irascible, full of mischief, with that Twainlike twinkle in the eye, but also worldly wise and experienced in the stark realities of pleasure and pain. . . .

8. *Throughout their lives, 13ers will be America's most politically conservative generation [since the turn of the century].* Until their mid-40s, the dominant brand of 13er conservatism will have a strong libertarian and free-market leave-me-alone flavor; later in life, it will lean toward cautious, pragmatic stewardship. Their attachment to the "conservative" banner will be sealed if aging Boomers rely on liberal standards to rekindle a spirit of national community and to rally younger generations to their cause—say, through some new . . . mandatory youth service. Ever the social contrarians, 13ers will be tempted to take the other side and try to keep their elders (and juniors) from going off the deep end. Regardless

of party or ideology, 13ers will be drawn to candidates who avoid hype, spell out the bottom line, do what it takes to get the job done, and shed no tears. In politics as in other spheres of social life, they will be most effective where the issues are local and personal. They will press to simplify the complex, narrow the bloated, and eliminate the unworkable. They will gain their first Senate seats and governorships before the year 2000. Their weak political profile in national affairs, however, will prevent them from winning a generational plurality in Congress until relatively late in life, perhaps not until around 2020. . . .

9. *As they reach their turn for national leadership, 13ers will produce no-nonsense winners who will excel at cunning, flexibility, and deft timing.* If 13ers turn out like every earlier generation of their type . . . they will ultimately become a stellar generation of get-it-done warriors, able to take charge of whatever raging conflicts are initiated by their elders and bring them to successful conclusions. In the tradition of George Washington, Ulysses Grant, and Dwight Eisenhower, the most memorable 13er Presidents may themselves be ex-generals. Military or not—and regardless of sex—13er leaders will be cagey, jockish, unpretentious, inelegant with words, more inclined to deal than to argue, and more admired for their personality than for their vision or learning. As they come to power around the year 2020, younger voters will view them as a welcome change from the ponderous, principles-first Boomer style. In public, they'll come across a bit shallow. But, as any 13er already knows, low expectations can be a game you can use to your advantage—in a poker game or in the White House.

10. *Before the year 2030, events will call on pockmarked 13ers to make aging Boomers get real—and, perhaps, to stop some righteous old Aquarian from doing something truly catastrophic.* Gazing down the road, some 13ers already wonder how they're going to cope with their next elders when those crusading Boomers finally go gaga. It's not an idle worry. Just think about it: Of all of today's living generations, which one is someday most likely to risk blowing up the

world just to prove a point? When that nightmare possibility appears, it may compel a grownup cadre of shouted-at Breakfast Clubbers to insist on having the last word after all—and to demand that principle defer to survival. . . .

11. *Throughout their lives, 13ers will neither ask for nor receive much assistance from government.* In their thirties, they will vote to cut young-adult welfare benefits. In their fifties, they will vote to raise income taxes. In their seventies, they will vote to cut Social Security. A generation of low collective self-esteem, 13ers will never voice much objection to their own "bad" reputation in the eyes of others (today their elders, forty years from now their juniors). Nor will 13ers ever effectively organize or vote in their own self-interest. Instead, they will take pride in the handouts they don't receive, in their lifelong talent for getting by on their own, and in their ability to divert government resources to help those younger than themselves. Policy experts who today worry about the cost of Social Security and Medicare past the year 2025 seldom reflect on the political self-image of those who will then be entering their late sixties. Will they become entitled "senior citizens"? Hardly. Like Lost Generation elders in 1964—who voted more for Barry Goldwater than any younger generation even after he promised to slash their retirement benefits—old 13ers will feel less deserving of public attention than richer and smarter young people who lack their fatalism about life.

12. *As mature leaders and voters, 13ers will favor investment over consumption, endowments over enticements, the needs of the very young over the needs of the very old.* Whether by raising taxes, by freezing the money supply, by discouraging debt, or by shifting public budgets toward education, public works, and child welfare, elder 13ers will tilt the economy back toward the future. They will use any available policy lever to raise national savings far above what private households would otherwise choose on their own— exactly the opposite of the national choice they will remember from their own youth. . . . 13ers will leave behind a smaller federal debt than they

inherited; . . . they will prefer recession to an out-of-kilter national balance sheet. . . . 13ers will be national survivalists, determined to store up capital for future contingencies and opposed to doing anything too risky, too wasteful, or too ambitious. Exiting power, they will—like the elder Washington, Twain, and Eisenhower—warn against the danger of pushing too fast in a world rigged with pitfalls.

13. *Thirteeners will make caustic, independent, yet self-effacing elders. When old, 13ers will watch America (once again) lose interest in people their own age and rediscover a fascination with the energy and promise of youth.* They will watch younger generations ignore their "old fogey" warnings and unleash new dreams of national ambition. They will watch younger people zoom past them economically. But 13er oldsters won't mind. They'll have reason to take pride in what they see happening down the age ladder. Pride in having pulled America back together and in having restored ballast to the ship of state. Pride in having rebuilt the social foundations that will by then be supporting a renaissance in public confidence and cultural optimism. Pride in having produced more than they consumed, in having made simple things work again, *in having done more for others than others ever did for them.*

Life is a sneaky fortune wheel for the 13th Generation. It spins, it turns—and just when you think you've lost, it tantalizes. Just when you think you've won, it clicks again, and you lose. But, by losing, 13ers help others gain. That could well be the story of their future.

History is not invariant, with predetermined outcomes. Any generation can bring forward good or bad leaders, or just run into good or bad luck. But each generation gets only one script. And how history turns out often depends on how well each generation plays its script.

To date, 13ers are a generation without a self-perceived mission. They know full well that they can't do or be what the G.I.s or Silent or Boomers did or were. Unite in the face of global crisis? Add nuance to a conformist society? Scream out against spirit-dead affluence? It makes no sense for them to attempt even a pale imitation of their elders—nor for those elders to condemn them for not following the paths others blazed in youth. Instead, 13ers have to find their own path, to develop their own sense of mission, to follow their own script.

Over a half-century ago, historian James Truslow Adams first defined the "American Dream" as giving every young person "the chance to grow into something bigger and finer, as bigger and finer appeared to him." This Dream is each generation's unique vision of progress, each generation's unique sense of how to improve on the legacy that has been handed down by its ancestors. The G.I.s defined their Dream through economics. The Silent defined it through social justice. Boomers defined it through inner consciousness.

So where do 13ers fit in? Have all the dreams been defined? Is anything left for them?

Yes, 13ers *do* have a mission. Theirs is the American generation that history has charged with the task of cleaning up after everybody else's mess. (Somebody had better—before it's too late.) So too is theirs the generation charged with showing others how, in this millennial era, Americans can still enjoy "life, liberty, and the pursuit of happiness" without letting the world fly to pieces, without bankrupting the nation, and without squandering scarce global resources. History is calling on the 13th Generation to provide the youthful entrepreneurship, midlife investments, and elder generosity that will enable future generations once again to define the American Dream in economic terms, if that is what they wish to do.

Do the dirty work, have a little fun, help the kids behind them. Not bad. Let others call 13ers "underachievers." They can take it. We, their elders, will never live to see how their story turns out. They will. The rest of us can only imagine how, when their job's done, they'll look history straight in the eye, give a little smile, and move on.

THINKING ABOUT THE READING

Summarize the predictions Howe and Strauss offer about the future of today's youth. Do you think they are overly optimistic or pessimistic? Given all you've heard about the 13th Generation (or, as they're more commonly called, Generation X), do you think these predictions are warranted? If you are a member of this generation, how would you characterize those older and younger than you? If you are a member of an older generation (like the Baby Boom or the Silent Generation), what is your assessment of "13ers"? How do you personally feel the effects of conflict with other generations? Is generation conflict inevitable? Explain.

Across the Wire

Life and Hard Times on the Mexican Border

Luis Alberto Urrea

When I was younger, I went to war. [The author worked as a relief worker, providing aid to refugees in the Mexican borderlands.] The Mexican border was the battlefield. There are many Mexicos; there are also many Mexican borders, any one of which could fill its own book. I, and the people with me, fought on a specific front. We sustained injuries and witnessed deaths. There were machine guns pointed at us, knives, pistols, clubs, even skyrockets. I caught a street-gang member trying to stuff a lit cherry bomb into our gas tank. On the same night, a drunk mariachi opened fire on the missionaries through the wall of his house.

We drove five beat-up vans. We were armed with water, medicine, shampoo, food, clothes, milk, and doughnuts. At the end of a day, like returning veterans from other battles, we carried secrets in our hearts that kept some of us awake at night, gave others dreams and fits of crying. Our faith sustained us—if not in God or "good," then in our work.

Others of us had no room for or interest in such drama, and came away unscathed—and unmoved. Some of us sank into the mindless joy of fundamentalism, some of us drank, some of us married impoverished Mexicans. Most of us took it personally. Poverty *is* personal: it smells and it shocks and it invades your space. You come home dirty when you get too close to the poor. Sometimes you bring back vermin: they hide in your hair, in your underpants, in your intestines. These unpleasant possibilities are a given. They are the price you occasionally have to pay.

In Tijuana and environs, we met the many ambassadors of poverty: lice, scabies, tapeworm, pinworm, ringworm, fleas, crab lice. We met diphtheria, meningitis, typhoid, polio, *turista* (diarrhea), tuberculosis, hepatitis, VD, impetigo, measles, chronic hernia, malaria, whooping cough. We met madness and "demon possession."

These were the products of dirt and disregard—bad things afflicting good people. Their world was far from our world. Still, it would take you only about twenty minutes to get there from the center of San Diego.

For me, the worst part was the lack of a specific enemy. We were fighting a nebulous, all-pervasive *It*. Call it hunger. Call it despair. Call it the Devil, the System, Capitalism, the Cycle of Poverty, the Fruits of the Mexican Malaise. It was a seemingly endless circle of disasters. Long after I'd left, the wheel kept on grinding.

At night, the Border Patrol helicopters swoop and churn in the air all along the line. You can sit in the Mexican hills and watch them herd humans on the dusty slopes across the valley. They look like science fiction crafts, their hard-focused lights raking the ground as they fly.

Borderlands locals are so jaded by the sight of nightly people-hunting that it doesn't even register in their minds. But take a stranger to the border, and she will *see* the spectacle: monstrous Dodge trucks speeding into and out of the landscape; uniformed men patrolling with flashlights, guns, and dogs; spotlights; running figures; lines of people hurried onto buses by armed guards; and the endless clatter of the helicopters with their harsh white beams. A Dutch woman once told me it seemed altogether "un-American."

But the Mexicans keep on coming—and the Guatemalans, the Salvadorans, the Panamanians, the Colombians. The seven-mile stretch of Interstate 5 nearest the Mexican border is, at times, so congested with Latin American pedestrians that it resembles a town square.

They stick to the center island. Running down the length of the island is a cement wall. If the "illegals" (currently, "undocumented workers"; formerly, "wetbacks") are walking north and a Border Patrol vehicle happens along, they simply hop over the wall and trot south. The officer will have to drive up to the 805 interchange, or Dairy Mart Road, swing over the overpasses, then drive south. Depending on where this pursuit begins, his detour could entail five to ten miles of driving. When the officer finally reaches the group, they hop over the wall and trot north. Furthermore, because freeway arrests would endanger traffic, the Border Patrol has effectively thrown up its hands in surrender.

It seems jolly on the page. But imagine poverty, violence, natural disasters, or political fear driving you away from everything you know. Imagine how bad things get to make you leave behind your family, your friends, your lovers; your home, as humble as it might be; your church, say. Let's take it further—you've said good-bye to the graveyard, the dog, the goat, the mountains where you first hunted, your grade school, your state, your favorite spot on the river where you fished and took time to think.

Then you come hundreds—or thousands—of miles across territory utterly unknown to you. (Chances are, you have never traveled farther than a hundred miles in your life.) You have walked, run, hidden in the backs of trucks, spent part of your precious money on bus fare. There is no AAA or Travelers Aid Society available to you. Various features of your journey north might include police corruption; violence in the forms of beatings, rape, murder, torture, road accidents; theft; incarceration. Additionally, you might experience loneliness, fear, exhaustion, sorrow, cold, heat, diarrhea, thirst, hunger. There is no medical attention available to you. There isn't even Kotex.

Weeks or months later, you arrive in Tijuana. Along with other immigrants, you gravitate to

the bad parts of town because there is nowhere for you to go in the glittery sections where the *gringos* flock. You stay in a run-down little hotel in the red-light district, or behind the bus terminal. Or you find your way to the garbage dumps, where you throw together a small cardboard nest and claim a few feet of dirt for yourself. The garbage-pickers working this dump might allow you to squat, or they might come and rob you or burn you out for breaking some local rule you cannot possibly know beforehand. Sometimes the dump is controlled by a syndicate, and goon squads might come to you within a day. They want money, and if you can't pay, you must leave or suffer the consequences.

In town, you face endless victimization if you aren't streetwise. The police come after you, street thugs come after you, petty criminals come after you; strangers try your door at night as you sleep. Many shady men offer to guide you across the border, and each one wants all your money now, and promises to meet you at a prearranged spot. Some of your fellow travelers end their journeys right here—relieved of their savings and left to wait on a dark corner until they realize they are going nowhere.

If you are not Mexican, and can't pass as *tijuanense*, a local, the tough guys find you out. Salvadorans and Guatemalans are routinely beaten up and robbed. Sometimes they are disfigured. Indians—Chinantecas, Mixtecas, Guasaves, Zapotecas, Mayas—are insulted and pushed around; often they are lucky—they are merely ignored. They use this to their advantage. Often they don't dream of crossing into the United States: a Mexican tribal person would never be able to blend in, and they know it. To them, the garbage dumps and street vending and begging in Tijuana are a vast improvement over their former lives. As Doña Paula, a Chinanteca friend of mine who lives at the Tijuana garbage dump, told me, "This is the garbage dump. Take all you need. There's plenty here for *everyone!*"

If you are a woman, the men come after you. You lock yourself in your room, and when you must leave it to use the pestilential public bathroom at the end of your floor, you hurry, and you check every corner. Sometimes the lights are out in the toilet room. Sometimes men listen at the door. They call you "good-looking" and "bitch" and "*mamacita*," and they make kissing sounds at you when you pass.

You're in the worst part of town, but you can comfort yourself—at least there are no death squads here. There are no torturers here, or bandit land barons riding into your house. This is the last barrier, you think, between you and the United States—*los Yunaites Estaites*.

You still face police corruption, violence, jail. You now also have a wide variety of new options available to you: drugs, prostitution, white slavery, crime. Tijuana is not easy on newcomers. It is a city that has always thrived on taking advantage of a sucker. And the innocent are the ultimate suckers in the Borderlands.

If you have saved up enough money, you go to one of the *coyotes* (people-smugglers), who guide travelers through the violent canyons immediately north of the border. Lately, these men are also called *polleros*, or "chicken-wranglers." Some of them are straight, some are land pirates. Negotiations are tense and strange: *polleros* speak a Spanish you don't quite understand—like the word *polleros*. Linguists call the new border-speak "Spanglish," but in Tijuana, Spanglish is mixed with slang and *pochismos* (the polyglot hip talk of Mexicans infected with *gringoismo;* the *cholos* in Mexico, or Chicanos on the American side).

Suddenly, the word for "yes," *sí*, can be *simón* or *siról*. "No" is *chale*. "Bike" (*bicicleta*) is *baica*. "Wife" (*esposa*) is *waifa*. "The police" (*la policía*) are *la chota*. "Women" are *rucas* or *morras*. You don't know what they're talking about.

You pay them all your money—sometimes it's your family's lifelong savings. Five hundred dollars should do it. "*Orale*," the dude tells you, which means "right on." You must wait in Colonia Libertad, the most notorious *barrio* in town, ironically named "Liberty."

The scene here is baffling. Music blares from radios. Jolly women at smoky taco stands cook food for the journeys, sell jugs of water. You can see the Border Patrol agents cruising the other side of the fence; they trade insults with the locals.

When the appointed hour comes, you join a group of *pollos* (chickens) who scuttle along behind the *coyote*. You crawl under the wires, or, if you go a mile east, you might be amazed to find that the famous American Border Fence simply stops. To enter the United States, you merely step around the end of it. And you follow your guide into the canyons. You might be startled to find groups of individuals crossing the line without *coyotes* leading them at all. You might wonder how they have mastered the canyons, and you might begin to regret the loss of your money.

If you have your daughters or mothers or wives with you—or if you are a woman—you become watchful and tense, because rape and gang rape are so common in this darkness as to be utterly unremarkable. If you have any valuables left after your various negotiations, you try to find a sly place to hide them in case you meet *pandilleros* (gang members) or *rateros* (thieves—ratmen). But, really, where can you put anything? Thousands have come before you, and the hiding places are pathetically obvious to robbers: in shoulder bags or clothing rolls, pinned inside clothes, hidden in underwear, inserted in body orifices.

If the *coyote* does not turn on you suddenly with a gun and take everything from you himself, you might still be attacked by the *rateros*. If the *rateros* don't get you, there are roving zombies that you can smell from fifty yards downwind—these are the junkies who hunt in shambling packs. If the junkies somehow miss you, there are the *pandilleros*—gang-bangers from either side of the border who are looking for some bloody fun. They adore "taking off" illegals because it's the perfect crime: there is no way they can ever be caught. They are Tijuana *cholos*, or Chicano *vatos*, or Anglo head-bangers.

Their sense of fun relies heavily on violence. Gang beatings are their preferred sport, though rape in all its forms is common, as always. Often the *coyote* will turn tail and run at the first sight of *pandilleros*. What's another load of desperate chickens to him? He's just making a living, taking care of business.

If he doesn't run, there is a good chance he will be the first to be assaulted. The most basic punishment these young toughs mete out is a good beating, but they might kill him in front of the *pollos* if they feel the immigrants need a lesson in obedience. For good measure, these boys—they are mostly *boys,* aged twelve to nineteen, bored with Super Nintendo and MTV—beat people and slash people and thrash the women they have just finished raping.

Their most memorable tactic is to hamstring the *coyote* or anyone who dares speak out against them. This entails slicing the muscles in the victim's legs and leaving him to flop around in the dirt, crippled. If you are in a group of *pollos* that happens to be visited by these furies, you are learning border etiquette.

Now, say you are lucky enough to evade all these dangers on your journey. Hazards still await you and your family. You might meet white racists, complimenting themselves with the tag "Aryans"; they "patrol" the scrub in combat gear, carrying radios, high-powered flashlights, rifles, and bats. Rattlesnakes hide in bushes—you didn't count on that complication. Scorpions, tarantulas, black widows. And, of course, there is the Border Patrol (*la migra*).

They come over the hills on motorcycles, on horses, in huge Dodge Ramcharger four-wheel drives. They yell, wear frightening goggles, have guns. Sometimes they are surprisingly decent; sometimes they are too tired or too bored to put much effort into dealing with you. They collect you in a large group of fellow *pollos,* and a guard (a Mexican Border Patrol agent!) jokes with your group in Spanish. Some cry, some sulk, most laugh. Mexicans hate to be rude. You don't know what to think—some of your fellow travelers take their arrest with aplomb. Sometimes the officers know their names. But you have been told repeatedly that the Border Patrol sometimes beats or kills people. Everyone talks about the Mexican girl molested inside its building.

The Border Patrol puts you into trucks that take you to buses that take you to compounds that load you onto other buses that transport you back to Tijuana and put you out. Your *coyote* isn't bothered in the least. Some of the regulars who were with you go across and get brought back a couple of times a night. But for you, things are different. You have been brought back with no place to sleep. You have already spent all your money. You might have been robbed, so you have only your clothes—maybe not all of them. The robbers may have taken your shoes. You might be bloodied from a beating by *pandilleros,* or an "accident" in the Immigration and Naturalization Service compound. You can't get proper medical attention. You can't eat, or afford to feed your family. Some of your compatriots have been separated from their wives or their children. Now their loved ones are in the hands of strangers, in the vast and unknown United States. The Salvadorans are put on planes and flown back to the waiting arms of the military. As you walk through the cyclone fence, back into Tijuana, the locals taunt you and laugh at your misfortune.

If you were killed, you have nothing to worry about.

Now what?

Perhaps you'll join one of the other groups that break through the Tortilla Curtain every night. The road-runners. They amass at dusk along the cement canal that separates the United States from Mexico. This wide alley is supposedly the Tijuana River, but it's usually dry, or running with sewage that Tijuana pumps toward the U.S. with great gusto.

As soon as everybody feels like it—there are no *coyotes* needed here—you join the groups passing through the gaping holes in the fence. Houses and alleys and cantinas back up against it, and in some spots, people have driven stolen cars into the poles to provide a wider passage. You rush across the canal and up the opposite slope, timing your dash between passing *migra* trucks and the overflights of helicopters. Following the others, you begin your jog toward the freeway. Here, there are mostly just Border Patrol officers to outrun—not that hard if you're in good shape. There are still some white-supremacist types bobbling around, but the cops will get them if they do anything serious. No, here the problem is the many lanes of I-5.

You stand at the edge of the road and wonder how you're going to cut across five lanes of traffic going sixty miles an hour. Then, there is the problem of the next five lanes. The freeway itself is constructed to run parallel to the border, then swing north. Its underpasses and storm-drain pipes offer another subterranean world, but you don't know about them. All you know is you have to get across at some point, and get far from the hunters who would take you back.

If you hang around the shoulder of I-5 long enough, you will find that many of your companions don't make it. So many have been killed and injured that the *gringos* have put up warning signs to motorists to watch for running people. The orange signs show a man, a woman, and a child charging across. Some *gringos* are so crazy with hate for you that they speed up, or aim for you as you run.

The vague blood of over a hundred slain runners shadows the concrete.

On either side of the border, clustered near the gates, there are dapper-looking men, dressed in nice cowboy clothes, and they speak without looking anyone in the eye. They are saying, "Los Angeles. San Bernardino. San Francisco."

They have a going concern: business is good.

Once you've gotten across the line, there will always be the question of *Where do I go now?* "Illegal aliens" have to eat, sleep, find work. Once across, you must begin another journey.

Not everyone has the energy to go on. Even faith—in Jesus, the Virgin Mary, or the Streets of Gold—breaks down sooner or later. Many of these immigrants founder at the border. There is a sad swirl of humanity in Tijuana. Outsiders eddy there who have simply run out of strength. If North America does not want them, Tijuana wants them even less. They become the outcasts of an outcast region. We could all see them if we looked hard enough: they sell chewing gum. Their children sing in traffic. In bars downtown,

the women will show us a breast for a quarter. They wash our windshields at every stoplight. But mostly, they are invisible. To see them, we have to climb up the little canyons all around the city, where the cardboard shacks and mud and smoke look like a lost triptych by Hieronymus Bosch. We have to wade into the garbage dumps and the orphanages, sit in the little churches and the hospitals, or go out into the back country, where they raise their goats and bake red bricks and try to live decent lives.

They are not welcome in Tijuana. And, for the most part, Tijuana itself is not welcome in the Motherland. Tijuana is Mexico's cast-off child. She brings in money and *gringos,* but nobody would dare claim her. As a Mexican diplomat once confided to me, "We both know Tijuana is not Mexico. The border is nowhere. It's a no-man's-land." . . .

I was born in Tijuana, to a Mexican father and an American mother. I was registered with the U.S. government as an American Citizen, Born Abroad. Raised in San Diego, I crossed the border all through my boyhood with abandon, utterly bilingual and bicultural. In 1977, my father died on the border, violently. . . .

In the Borderlands, anything can happen. And if you're in Tijuana long enough, anything *will* happen. Whole neighborhoods appear and disappear seemingly overnight. For example, when I was a boy, you got into Tijuana by driving through the Tijuana River itself. It was a muddy floodplain bustling with animals and belching old cars. A slum that spread across the riverbed was known as "Cartolandia." In border-speak, this meant "Land of Cardboard."

Suddenly, it was time for Tijuana to spruce up its image to attract more American dollars, and Cartolandia was swept away by a flash flood of tractors. The big machines swept down the length of the river, crushing shacks and toppling fences. It was like magic. One week, there were choked multitudes of sheds; the next, a clear, flat space awaiting the blank concrete of a flood channel. Town—no town.

The inhabitants of Cartolandia fled to the outskirts, where they were better suited to Tijuana's new image as Shopping Mecca. They had effectively vanished. Many of them homesteaded the Tijuana municipal garbage dump. The city's varied orphanages consumed many of their children.

Tijuana's characteristic buzz can be traced directly to a mixture of dread and expectation: there's always something coming....

THINKING ABOUT THE READING

Describe the various ways that illegal Mexican immigrants to the United States are victimized. Faced with the sorts of dangers Urrea describes, why do you think people are still willing to take the risk and enter this country illegally? Do you think that tightening the border and increasing Border Patrol surveillance will ever reduce illegal immigration? If not, how would you reduce illegal immigration? How does Urrea's depiction of crossing the border affect your beliefs and attitudes about illegal immigration?

The Melting Pot

Anne Fadiman

The Lee family—Nao Kao, Foua, Chong, Zoua, Cheng, May, Yer, and True—arrived in the United States on December 18, 1980. Their luggage consisted of a few clothes, a blue blanket, and a wooden mortar and pestle that Foua had chiseled from a block of wood in Houaysouy. They flew from Bangkok to Honolulu, and then to Portland, Oregon, where they were to spend two years before moving to Merced. Other refugees told me that their airplane flights—a mode of travel that strained the limits of the familiar Hmong concept of migration—had been fraught with anxiety and shame: they got airsick, they didn't know how to use the bathroom but were afraid to soil themselves, they thought they had to pay for their food but had no money, they tried to eat the Wash'n Dris. The Lees, though perplexed, took the novelties of the trip in stride. Nao Kao remembers the airplane as being "just like a big house."

Their first week in Portland, however, was miserably disorienting. Before being placed by a local refugee agency in a small rented house, they spent a week with relatives, sleeping on the floor. "We didn't know anything so our relatives had to show us everything," Foua said. "They knew because they had lived in America for three or four months already. Our relatives told us about electricity and said the children shouldn't touch those plugs in the wall because they could get hurt. They told us that the refrigerator is a cold box where you put meat. They showed us how to open the TV so we could see it. We had never seen a toilet before and we thought maybe the water in it was to drink or cook with. Then our relatives told us what it was, but we didn't know

whether we should sit or whether we should stand on it. Our relatives took us to the store but we didn't know that the cans and packages had food in them. We could tell what the meat was, but the chickens and cows and pigs were all cut up in little pieces and had plastic on them. Our relatives told us the stove is for cooking the food, but I was afraid to use it because it might explode. Our relatives said in America the food you don't eat you just throw away. In Laos we always fed it to the animals and it was strange to waste it like that. In this country there were a lot of strange things and even now I don't know a lot of things and my children have to help me, and it still seems like a strange country."

Seventeen years later, Foua and Nao Kao use American appliances, but they still speak only Hmong, celebrate only Hmong holidays, practice only the Hmong religion, cook only Hmong dishes, sing only Hmong songs, play only Hmong musical instruments, tell only Hmong stories, and know far more about current political events in Laos and Thailand than about those in the United States. When I first met them, during their eighth year in this country, only one American adult, Jeanine Hilt, had ever been invited to their home as a guest. It would be hard to imagine anything further from the vaunted American ideal of assimilation, in which immigrants are expected to submerge their cultural differences in order to embrace a shared national identity. *E pluribus unum:* from many, one.

During the late 1910s and early 1920s, immigrant workers at the Ford automotive plant in Dearborn, Michigan, were given free, compulsory "Americanization" classes. In addition to

English lessons, there were lectures on work habits, personal hygiene, and table manners. The first sentence they memorized was "I am a good American." During their graduation ceremony they gathered next to a gigantic wooden pot, which their teachers stirred with ten-foot ladles. The students walked through a door into the pot, wearing traditional costumes from their countries of origin and singing songs in their native languages. A few minutes later, the door in the pot opened, and the students walked out again, wearing suits and ties, waving American flags, and singing "The Star-Spangled Banner."

The European immigrants who emerged from the Ford Motor Company melting pot came to the United States because they hoped to assimilate into mainstream American society. The Hmong came to the United States for the same reason they had left China in the nineteenth century: because they were trying to *resist* assimilation. As the anthropologist Jacques Lemoine has observed, "they did not come to our countries only to save their lives, they rather came to save their selves, that is, their Hmong ethnicity." If their Hmong ethnicity had been safe in Laos, they would have preferred to remain there, just as their ancestors—for whom migration had always been a problem-solving strategy, not a footloose impulse—would have preferred to remain in China. Unlike the Ford workers who enthusiastically, or at least uncomplainingly, belted out the "The Star-Spangled Banner" (of which Foua and Nao Kao know not a single word), the Hmong are what sociologists call "involuntary migrants." It is well known that involuntary migrants, no matter what pot they are thrown into, tend not to melt.

What the Hmong wanted here was to be left alone to be Hmong: clustered in all-Hmong enclaves, protected from government interference, self-sufficient, and agrarian. Some brought hoes in their luggage. General Vang Pao has said, "For many years, right from the start, I tell the American government that we need a little bit of land where we can grow vegetables and build homes like in Laos. . . . I tell them it does not have to be

the best land, just a little land where we can live." This proposal was never seriously considered. "It was just out of the question," said a spokesman for the State Department's refugee program. "It would cost too much, it would be impractical, but most of all it would set off wild protests from [other Americans] and from other refugees who weren't getting land for themselves.". . .

Just as newly arrived immigrants in earlier eras had been called "FOBs"—Fresh Off the Boat—some social workers nicknamed the incoming Hmong, along with the other Southeast Asian refugees who entered the United States after the Vietnamese War, "JOJs": Just Off the Jet. Unlike the first waves of Vietnamese and Cambodian refugees, most of whom received several months of vocational and language training at regional "reception centers," the Hmong JOJs, who arrived after the centers had closed, were all sent directly to their new homes. (Later on, some were given "cultural orientation" training in Thailand before flying to the United States. Their classes covered such topics as how to distinguish a one-dollar bill from a ten-dollar bill and how to use a peephole.) The logistical details of their resettlement were contracted by the federal government to private nonprofit groups known as VOLAGs, or national voluntary resettlement agencies, which found local sponsors. Within their first few weeks in this country, newly arrived families were likely to deal with VOLAG officials, immigration officials, public health officials, social service officials, employment officials, and public assistance officials. The Hmong are not known for holding bureaucrats in high esteem. As one proverb puts it, "To see a tiger is to die; to see an official is to become destitute." In a study of adaptation problems among Indochinese refugees, Hmong respondents rated "Difficulty with American Agencies" as a more serious problem than either "War Memories" or "Separation from Family." Because many of the VOLAGs had religious affiliations, the JOJs also often found themselves dealing with Christian ministers, who, not surprisingly, took a dim view of shamanistic animism. A sponsoring pastor in

Minnesota told a local newspaper, "It would be wicked to just bring them over and feed and clothe them and let them go to hell. The God who made us wants them to be converted. If anyone thinks that a gospel-preaching church would bring them over and not tell them about the Lord, they're out of their mind." The proselytizing backfired. According to a study of Hmong mental health problems, refugees sponsored by this pastor's religious organization were significantly more likely, when compared to other refugees, to require psychiatric treatment.

The Hmong were accustomed to living in the mountains, and most of them had never seen snow. Almost all their resettlement sites had flat topography and freezing winters. The majority were sent to cities, including Minneapolis, Chicago, Milwaukee, Detroit, Hartford, and Providence, because that was where refugee services—health care, language classes, job training, public housing—were concentrated. To encourage assimilation, and to avoid burdening any one community with more than its "fair share" of refugees, the Immigration and Naturalization Service adopted a policy of dispersal rather than clustering. Newly arrived Hmong were assigned to fifty-three cities in twenty-five different states: stirred into the melting pot in tiny, manageable portions, or, as John Finck, who worked with Hmong at the Rhode Island Office of Refugee Resettlement, put it, "spread like a thin layer of butter throughout the country so they'd disappear." In some places, clans were broken up. In others, members of only one clan were resettled, making it impossible for young people, who were forbidden by cultural taboo from marrying within their own clan, to find local marriage partners. Group solidarity, the cornerstone of Hmong social organization for more than two thousand years, was completely ignored.

Although most Hmong were resettled in cities, some nuclear families, unaccompanied by any of their extended relations, were placed in isolated rural areas. Disconnected from traditional supports, these families exhibited unusually high levels of anxiety, depression, and paranoia. In one such case, the distraught and delusional father of the Yang family—the only Hmong family sponsored by the First Baptist Church of Fairfield, Iowa—attempted to hang himself in the basement of his wooden bungalow along with his wife and four children. His wife changed her mind at the last minute and cut the family down, but she acted too late to save their only son. An Iowa grand jury declined to indict either parent, on the grounds that the father was suffering from Post-Traumatic Stress Disorder, and the mother, cut off from all sources of information except her husband, had no way to develop an independent version of reality.

Reviewing the initial resettlement of the Hmong with a decade's hindsight, Lionel Rosenblatt, the former United States Refugee Coordinator in Thailand, conceded that it had been catastrophically mishandled. "We knew at the start their situation was different, but we just couldn't make any special provisions for them," he said. "I still feel it was no mistake to bring the Hmong here, but you look back now and say, 'How could we have done it so shoddily?'" Eugene Douglas, President Reagan's ambassador-at-large for refugee affairs, stated flatly, "It was a kind of hell they landed into. Really, it couldn't have been done much worse."

The Hmong who sought asylum in the United States were, of course, not a homogeneous lump. A small percentage, mostly the high-ranking military officers who were admitted first, were multilingual and cosmopolitan, and a larger percentage had been exposed in a desultory fashion to some aspects of American culture and technology during the war or while living in Thai refugee camps. But the experience of tens of thousands of Hmong was much like the Lees'. It is possible to get some idea of how monumental the task of adjustment was likely to be by glancing at some of the pamphlets, audiotapes, and videos that refugee agencies produced for Southeast Asian JOJs. For example, "Your New Life in the United States," a handbook published by the Language and Orientation Resource Center in Washington, D.C., included the following tips:

Learn the meaning of "WALK"–"DON'T WALK" signs when crossing the street.

To send mail, you must use stamps.

To use the phone:
1) Pick up the receiver
2) Listen for dial tone
3) Dial each number separately
4) Wait for person to answer after it rings
5) Speak.

The door of the refrigerator must be shut.

Never put your hand in the garbage disposal.

Do not stand or squat on the toilet since it may break.

Never put rocks or other hard objects in the tub or sink since this will damage them.

Always ask before picking your neighbor's flowers, fruit, or vegetables.

In colder areas you must wear shoes, socks, and appropriate outerwear. Otherwise, you may become ill.

Always use a handkerchief or a kleenex to blow your nose in public places or inside a public building.

Never urinate in the street. This creates a smell that is offensive to Americans. They also believe that it causes disease.

Spitting in public is considered impolite and unhealthy. Use a kleenex or handkerchief.

Picking your nose or your ears in public is frowned upon in the United States.

The customs they were expected to follow seemed so peculiar, the rules and regulations so numerous, the language so hard to learn, and the emphasis on literacy and the decoding of other unfamiliar symbols so strong, that many Hmong were overwhelmed. Jonas Vangay told me, "In America, we are blind because even though we have eyes, we cannot see. We are deaf because even though we have ears, we cannot hear." Some newcomers wore pajamas as street clothes; poured water on electric stoves to extinguish them; lit charcoal fires in their living rooms; stored blankets in their refrigerators; washed rice in their toilets; washed their clothes in swimming pools; washed their hair with Lestoil; cooked with motor oil and furniture polish; drank Clorox; ate cat food; planted crops in public parks; shot and ate skunks, porcupines, woodpeckers, robins, egrets, sparrows, and a bald eagle; and hunted pigeons with crossbows in the streets of Philadelphia.

If the United States seemed incomprehensible to the Hmong, the Hmong seemed equally incomprehensible to the United States. Journalists seized excitedly on a label that is still trotted out at regular intervals: "the most primitive refugee group in America." (In an angry letter to the *New York Times*, in which that phrase had appeared in a 1990 news article, a Hmong computer specialist observed, "Evidently, we were not too primitive to fight as proxies for United States troops in the war in Laos.") Typical phrases from newspaper and magazine stories in the late seventies and eighties included "low-caste hill tribe," "Stone Age," "emerging from the mists of time," "like Alice falling down a rabbit hole." Inaccuracies were in no short supply. A 1981 article in the *Christian Science Monitor* called the Hmong language "extremely simplistic"; declared that the Hmong, who have been sewing *paj ntaub* [embroidered cloth] with organic motifs for centuries, make "no connection between a picture of a tree and a real tree"; and noted that "the Hmong have no oral tradition of literature. . . . Apparently no folk tales exist." Some journalists seemed to shed all inhibition, and much of their good sense as well, when they were loosed on the Hmong. My favorite passage is a 1981 *New York Times* editorial about the large number of Hmong men who had died unexpectedly in their sleep, killed—or so it was widely believed at the time—by their own nightmares.[1] After explaining that the Hmong "attributed conscious life to natural objects," the writer asked,

What were these nightmares? Did a palm tree's fronds turn into threatening fingers? Did a forest move and march with the implacability of the tide? Did a rose stretch on its stalk and throttle the sleeper?

Or did a gasoline hose curl and crush like a python? Was one of the dreamers pinned by a perambulating postbox? Or stabbed by scissors run amok?

("Or did the editorial writer drop acid?" I wrote in the newspaper margin when I first read this.)

Timothy Dunnigan, a linguistic anthropologist who has taught a seminar at the University of Minnesota on the media presentation of Hmong and Native Americans, once remarked to me, "The kinds of metaphorical language that we use to describe the Hmong say far more about us, and our attachment to our own frame of reference, than they do about the Hmong." So much for the Perambulating Postbox Theory. Dunnigan's comment resonates with Dwight Conquergood's observation about the uneasiness Westerners feel when confronted with the Other—for who could be more Other than the Hmong? Not only did they squat on toilets and eat skunks, not only did they bang gongs and sacrifice cows, but they also displayed what struck many people as an offensively selective interest in adopting the customs of the majority culture. For example, many Hmong quickly learned how to use telephones and drive cars, because those skills fit their own agenda of communicating with other Hmong, but failed to learn English. In 1987, when Senator Alan Simpson, then the ranking minority member of the Senate Subcommittee on Immigration and Refugee Affairs, called the Hmong "the most indigestible group in society," he sounded much like the authorities in China long ago, who were grievously insulted when the Hmong refused to speak Chinese or eat with chopsticks.

It could not be denied that the Hmong were genuinely mysterious—far more so, for instance, than the Vietnamese and Cambodians who were streaming into the United States at the same time. Hardly anyone knew how to pronounce the word "Hmong." Hardly anyone—except the anthropology graduate students who suddenly realized they could write dissertations on patrilineal exoga-

mous clan structures without leaving their hometowns—knew what role the Hmong had played during the war, or even what war it had been, since our government had succeeded all too well in keeping the Quiet War quiet. Hardly anyone knew they had a rich history, a complex culture, an efficient social system, and enviable family values. They were therefore an ideal blank surface on which to project xenophobic fantasies.

The most expedient mode of projection has always been the rumor, and the Hmong attracted more than their share. This was to be expected. After all, the Hmong of China had had wings under their armpits and small tails. In prevalence and nastiness, American rumors about the Hmong are at least an even match for the Hmong rumors about America that circulated in the refugee camps of Thailand. Some samples: The Hmong run a white slave trade. The Hmong are given cars by the government. The Hmong force their children to run in front of cars in order to get big insurance settlements. The Hmong sell their daughters and buy their wives. Hmong women think speed bumps are washboards for scrubbing clothes, and they get run over by eighteen-wheelers. The Hmong eat dogs.[2] (That one comes complete with its own set of racist jokes. "What's the name of the Hmong cookbook? *101 Ways to Wok Your Dog*.") The dog-eating rumor has joined the national pantheon of deathless urban legends, right up there with alligators in the sewers and worms in the Big Macs. . . .

Not everyone who wanted to make the Hmong feel unwelcome stopped at slander. In the words of the president of a youth center in Minneapolis, his Hmong neighbors in the mid-eighties were "prime meat for predators." In Laos, Hmong houses had no locks. Sometimes they had no doors. Cultural taboos against theft and intracommunity violence were poor preparation for life in the high-crime, inner-city neighborhoods in which most Hmong were placed. Some of the violence directed against them had nothing to do with their ethnicity; they were simply easy marks. But a good deal of it was motivated by resentment, particularly in urban areas, for what was perceived as preferential welfare treatment.[3]

In Minneapolis, tires were slashed and windows smashed. A high school student getting off a bus was hit in the face and told to "go back to China." A woman was kicked in the thighs, face, and kidneys, and her purse, which contained the family's entire savings of $400, was stolen; afterwards, she forbade her children to play outdoors, and her husband, who had once commanded a fifty-man unit in the Armée Clandestine, stayed home to guard the family's belongings. In Providence, children were beaten walking home from school. In Missoula, teenagers were stoned. In Milwaukee, garden plots were vandalized and a car was set on fire. In Eureka, California, two burning crosses were placed on a family's front lawn. In a random act of violence near Springfield, Illinois, a twelve-year-old boy was shot and killed by three men who forced his family's car off Interstate 55 and demanded money. His father told a reporter, "In a war, you know who your enemies are. Here, you don't know if the person walking up to you will hurt you."

In Philadelphia, anti-Hmong muggings, robberies, beatings, stonings, and vandalism were so commonplace during the early eighties that the city's Commission on Human Relations held public hearings to investigate the violence. One source of discord seemed to be a $100,000 federal grant for Hmong employment assistance that had incensed local residents, who were mostly unemployed themselves and believed the money should have been allocated to American citizens, not resident aliens. In one of the most grievous incidents, Seng Vang, a Hmong resident of Quebec who was visiting his mother, brothers, and sisters in west Philadelphia, was beaten with steel rods and a large rock, and left on the street with two broken legs and a brain injury. Later that day, a rifle shot was fired into his mother's apartment, breaking a window near the spot where she stood washing dishes. When Vang was treated at the University of Pennsylvania hospital, he was given a blood transfusion that was probably tainted. He was gravely ill for months with a rare form of hepatitis, and, seized by justifiable paranoia, became convinced that his doctors, too, had tried to kill him.

One thing stands out in all these accounts: the Hmong didn't fight back. I pondered that fact one day as I was thumbing through the index of Charles Johnson's *Dab Neeg Hmoob: Myths, Legends and Folk Tales from the Hmong of Laos*, which contained the following entries:

Fighting
  Enemies fighting . . . 29–46, 52–58, 198, 227, 470–471
Revenge
  Murdered man reincarnated to revenge his death . . . 308–309
  Cruel 9-tongued eagle has tongues cut out . . . 330
  Ngao Njua boils king who sent away her husband . . . 362
  Family kills tiger murderer of daughter, husband & children . . . 403
  . . .
Vengeance
  Punishment of evil-doers by lightning . . . 11, 20
  Wildcat tortured & killed to avenge murder of woman . . . 436–437

To quote from the last folktale cited: "Quickly, the rooster came down, seized the cat, threw him into the mortar of the rice mill, and started in immediately pounding him with the heavy pestle: DA DUH NDUH! DA DUH NDUH! He kept pounding until all the wildcat's bones were completely broken. And that's how the wildcat died, and that's how the story ends." It was clear that the Hmong were hardly the docile, passive, mild-mannered Asians of popular stereotype. Why hadn't the Americans who tormented the Hmong ended up like that wildcat?

Charles Johnson's background notes to another tale in *Dab Neeg Hmoob* provide a partial explanation:

Our interviews indicate that the Hmong do not fight very much. When they do, it is with fists and feet. (In contrast with some neighboring peoples [in Laos] who tend to fight a lot, seem to take it lightly, and can be friends later, if two Hmong fight once, they are likely to take it very seriously, as a big issue which they do not forget, and may remain enemies forever.)

. . . The Hmong do have an ideal of patience and stoical self-control, alluded to in the idiomatic expression often used by the Hmong to admonish someone who is acting impatiently or impulsively, or by parents in teaching good behavior to their children: "Ua siab ntev" (literally, Make, do, or act with a long liver, that is, a spirit or attitude of long-suffering, patient endurance of wrongs or difficulties).

Although on the battlefield the Hmong were known more for their fierceness than for their long livers, in the United States many were too proud to lower themselves to the level of the petty criminals they encountered, or even to admit they had been victims. An anthropologist named George M. Scott, Jr., once asked a group of Hmong in San Diego, all victims of property damage or assault, why they had not defended themselves or taken revenge. Scott wrote, "several Hmong victims of such abuse, both young and old, answered that to have done so, besides inviting further, retaliatory, abuse, would have made them feel 'embarrassed' or ashamed. . . . In addition, the current president of Lao Family [a Hmong mutual assistance organization], when asked why his people did not 'fight back' when attacked here as they did in Laos, replied simply, 'because nothing here is worth defending to us.'"

There were exceptions, of course. If he was threatened with what he perceived as unbearable *poob ntsej muag* (loss of face), a Hmong sometimes decided that his shame and embarrassment would be even greater if he didn't fight back than if he did. Several Hmong in Fresno, hearing rumors that their welfare grants might be terminated because they owned cars, sent death threats ("You take away my grant and I'm going to blow your head off") to the county Social Services Department. As visual aids, they enclosed bullets and pictures of swords in their envelopes. (The grants were not terminated, and the bullets and swords were never used.) In Chicago, an elderly Hmong man and his son, in-

sulted because an American driver had honked at them loudly and persistently, hit the American over the head with a steering-wheel locking device. The injury required thirteen stitches. When the men, Ching and Bravo Xiong, were brought to trial for aggravated battery, they asked the judge to allow each party to tell his side of the story and then drink a mixture of water and the blood of a sacrificed rooster. According to Hmong tradition, anyone who drinks rooster blood after telling a lie is destined to die within a year, so if a man partakes willingly, he is recognized as a truthteller. The judge denied this request. Instead, he sentenced the younger Xiong to two weekends in jail and six hundred hours of community service. He also ordered both men to learn English and study American culture.

Such incidents were rare. Most Hmong kept an apprehensive distance from the American penal system, which was radically different from their own. There were no prisons in their villages in Laos. The Hmong sense of justice was pragmatic and personal: how would incarceration benefit the victim? Corporal punishment was also unknown. Instead, various forms of public humiliation—a powerful deterrent in a society where loss of face was considered a worse fate than death—were employed. For example, a thief who had stolen four bars of silver might be forced to repay five bars to the victim and then be hauled off to the village chief with his hands tied, while the entire community jeered. The victim ended up enriched, the criminal suffered the shame he deserved, the criminal's innocent family kept its primary provider in the household, and any would-be thieves in the village were discouraged from potential crimes by witnessing the disgraceful spectacle. The Hmong who came to this country had heard that if they hurt someone, for whatever the reason, they would be sent to an American prison, and most of them were willing to do almost anything to avoid such an unimaginable calamity. Chao Wang Vang, a Fresno resident who had been charged with misdemeanor manslaughter after a fatal traffic accident, hanged himself in the county jail before his case came to court, not knowing he had the right to a trial and believing he would be imprisoned for the rest of his life.

In any case, Hmong who were persecuted by their neighbors could exercise a time-honored alternative to violence: flight. . . . Between 1982 and 1984, three quarters of the Hmong population of Philadelphia simply left town and joined relatives in other cities. During approximately the same period, one third of all the Hmong in the United States moved from one city to another. When they decided to relocate, Hmong families often lit off without notifying their sponsors, who were invariably offended. If they couldn't fit one of their possessions, such as a television set, in a car or bus or U-Haul, they left it behind, seemingly without so much as a backward glance. Some families traveled alone, but more often they moved in groups. When there was an exodus from Portland, Oregon, a long caravan of overloaded cars motored together down Interstate 5, bound for the Central Valley of California. With this "secondary migration," as sociologists termed it, the government's attempt to stir the Hmong evenly into the melting pot was definitively sabotaged.

Although local violence was often the triggering factor, there were also other reasons for migrating. In 1982, when all refugees who had lived in the United States for more than eighteen months stopped receiving Refugee Cash Assistance—the period of eligibility had previously been three years—many Hmong who had no jobs and no prospects moved to states that provided welfare benefits to two-parent families. Their original host states were often glad to get rid of them. For a time, the Oregon Human Resources Department, strapped by a tight state budget, sent refugees letters that pointedly detailed the levels of welfare benefits available in several other states. California's were among the highest. Thousands of Hmong also moved to California because they had heard it was an agricultural state where they might be able to farm. But by far the most important reason for relocating was reunification with other members of

one's clan. Hmong clans are sometimes at odds with each other, but within a clan, whose thousands of members are regarded as siblings, one can always count on support and sympathy. A Hmong who tries to gain acceptance to a kin group other than his own is called a *puav,* or bat. He is rejected by the birds because he has fur and by the mice because he has wings. Only when a Hmong lives among his own subspecies can he stop flitting restlessly from group to group, haunted by the shame of not belonging.

The Hmong may have been following their venerable proverb, "There's always another mountain," but in the past, each new mountain had yielded a living. Unfortunately, the most popular areas of secondary resettlement all had high unemployment rates, and they got higher. For example, in the Central Valley—which had no Hmong in 1980 and more than 20,000 three years later—the economic recession of 1982 shut down dozens of factories and other businesses, driving up local unemployment and forcing the Hmong to compete with out-of-work Americans for even the most unskilled jobs. The dream of farming quickly fizzled for all but a few hundred. Hmong farmers knew a great deal about torching fields for slash-and-burn agriculture, planting mountain rice with dibble sticks, and tapping opium pods, but they had much to learn (to quote from the course plan for a not-very-successful Hmong training program) about

> crop varieties, soil preparation, machinery and equipment, timing and succession of planting, seeds and transplants, fertilizer, pest and weed management, disease control, irrigation, erosion control, record-keeping, harvesting, washing and handling, grading and size selection, packing, conditioning, market selection, product planning, pricing strategies, shipping and receiving, advertising, merchandising, verbal and non-verbal communication skills for dealing with consumers, etc.

By 1985, at least eighty percent of the Hmong in Merced, Fresno, and San Joaquin counties were on welfare.

That didn't halt the migration. Family reunification tends to have a snowball effect. The more Thaos or Xiongs there were in one place, the more mutual assistance they could provide, the more cultural traditions they could practice together, and the more stable their community would be. Americans, however, tended to view secondary migration as an indication of instability and dependence. . . .

Seeing that the Hmong were redistributing themselves as they saw fit, and that they were becoming an economic burden on the places to which they chose to move, the federal Office of Refugee Resettlement tried to slow the migratory tide. The 1983 Highland Lao Initiative, a three-million-dollar "emergency effort" to bolster employment and community stability in Hmong communities outside California, offered vocational training, English classes, and other enticements for the Hmong to stay put. Though the initiative claimed a handful of modest local successes, the California migration was essentially unstoppable. By this time, most Hmong JOJs were being sponsored by relatives in America rather than by voluntary organizations, so the government no longer had geographic control over their placements. The influx therefore came—and, in smaller increments, is still coming—from Thailand as well as from other parts of America. Therefore, in addition to trying to prevent the Hmong from moving to high-welfare states, the Office of Refugee Resettlement started trying to encourage the ones who were already there to leave. Spending an average of $7,000 per family on moving expenses, job placement, and a month or two of rent and food subsidies, the Planned Secondary Resettlement Program, which was phased out in 1994, relocated about 800 unemployed Hmong families from what it called "congested areas" to communities with "favorable employment opportunities"—i.e., unskilled jobs with wages too low to attract a full complement of local American workers.

Within the economic limitations of blue-collar labor, those 800 families have fared well. Ninety-five percent have become self-sufficient.

They work in manufacturing plants in Dallas, on electronics assembly lines in Atlanta, in furniture and textile factories in Morganton, North Carolina. More than a quarter of them have saved enough money to buy their own houses, as have three quarters of the Hmong families who live in Lancaster County, Pennsylvania, where the men farm or work in food-processing plants, and the women work for the Amish, sewing quilts that are truthfully advertised as "locally made." Elsewhere, Hmong are employed as grocers, carpenters, poultry processors, machinists, welders, auto mechanics, tool and die makers, teachers, nurses, interpreters, and community liaisons. In a survey of Minnesota employers, the respondents were asked "What do you think of the Hmong as workers?" Eighty-six percent rated them "very good." . . .

Some younger Hmong have become lawyers, doctors, dentists, engineers, computer programmers, accountants, and public administrators. Hmong National Development, an association that promotes Hmong self-sufficiency, encourages this small corps of professionals to serve as mentors and sponsors for other Hmong who might thereby be induced to follow suit. The cultural legacy of mutual assistance has been remarkably adaptive. Hundreds of Hmong students converse electronically, trading gossip and information—opinions on the relevance of traditional customs, advice on college admissions, personal ads—via the Hmong Channel on the Internet Relay Chat system. . . . There is also a Hmong Homepage on the World Wide Web (http://www.stolaf.edu/people/cdr/hmong/) and several burgeoning Hmong electronic mailing lists, including Hmongnet, Hmongforum, and Hmong Language Users Group.[4]

The M.D.s and J.D.s and digital sophisticates constitute a small, though growing, minority. Although younger, English-speaking Hmong who have been educated in the United States have better employment records than their elders, they still lag behind most other Asian-Americans. As for Hmong workers over thirty-five, the majority are immovably wedged at or near entry level. They can't get jobs that require better English, and they can't learn English on their current jobs. The federal *Hmong Resettlement Study* cited, as an example, a Hmong worker in Dallas who after three years on the job was unable to name the machine he operated. He stated that he never expected a promotion or a pay raise other than cost-of-living increases. Other Hmong have been thwarted by placing a higher value on group solidarity than on individual initiative. In San Diego, the manager of an electronics plant was so enthusiastic about one Hmong assembly worker that he tried to promote him to supervisor. The man quit, ashamed to accept a job that would place him above his Hmong coworkers.

For the many Hmong who live in high-unemployment areas, questions of advancement are often moot. They have no jobs at all. This is the reason the Hmong are routinely called this country's "least successful refugees." It is worth noting that the standard American tests of success that they have flunked are almost exclusively economic. If one applied social indices instead—such as rates of crime, child abuse, illegitimacy, and divorce—the Hmong would probably score better than most refugee groups (and also better than most Americans), but those are not the forms of success to which our culture assigns its highest priority. Instead, we have trained the spotlight on our best-loved index of failure, the welfare rolls. In California, Minnesota, and Wisconsin, where, not coincidentally, benefits tend to be relatively generous and eligibility requirements relatively loose, the percentages of Hmong on welfare are approximately forty-five, forty, and thirty-five (an improvement over five years ago, when they were approximately sixty-five, seventy, and sixty). The cycle of dependence that began with rice drops in Laos and reinforced with daily handouts at Thai refugee camps has been completed here in the United States. The conflicting structures of the Hmong culture and the American welfare system make it almost impossible for the average family to become independent. In California, for example, a man with seven children—a typical Hmong family size—would have to make $10.60 an hour, working forty hours a week, to equal his welfare stipend and food stamp allowance. But with few marketable skills and little English, he would probably be ineligible for most jobs that paid more than minimum wage, at which, even at the newly elevated rate of $5.15 an hour, he would have to work an improbable eighty-two hours a week in order to equal his welfare allotment. In addition, until the mid-nineties in most states, if he worked more than one hundred hours a month—as a part-time worker trying to acquire job skills, for example, or a farmer in the start-up phase—his family would lose their entire welfare grant, all their food stamps, and their health insurance.[5]

The 1996 welfare reform bill, which in its present form promises to deny benefits to legal immigrants, has stirred up monumental waves of anxiety among the Hmong. Faced with the possibility of having their assistance cut off, some have applied for citizenship, although many middle-aged Hmong find the English language requirement an insuperable obstacle. (The hurdles are lower for older Hmong who came to the United States shortly after the end of the war in Laos. The language rule is waived for "lawful permanent residents" age fifty or older who have been in this country for at least twenty years, and for those age fifty-five or older who have been here at least fifteen years. The Lees, who are considering applying for citizenship, would qualify for this waiver.) Some Hmong have moved, or are planning to move, to states with better job markets. Some will become dependent on their relatives. Because a few states will probably elect to use their own funds to assist legal immigrants, some will simply continue to depend on welfare in altered, reduced, and more precarious forms.

Few things gall the Hmong more than to be criticized for accepting public assistance. For one thing, they feel they deserve the money. Every Hmong has a different version of what is commonly called "The Promise": a written or verbal contract, made by CIA personnel in Laos, that if they fought for the Americans, the Americans would aid them if the Pathet Lao won the war. After risking their lives to rescue downed American pilots, seeing their villages flattened by incidental

American bombs, and being forced to flee their country because they had supported the "American War," the Hmong expected a hero's welcome here. According to many of them, the first betrayal came when the American airlifts rescued only the officers from Long Tieng, leaving nearly everyone else behind. The second betrayal came in the Thai camps, when the Hmong who wanted to come to the United States were not all automatically admitted. The third betrayal came when they arrived here and found they were ineligible for veterans' benefits. The fourth betrayal came when Americans condemned them for what the Hmong call "eating welfare." The fifth betrayal came when the Americans announced that the welfare would stop.

Aside from some older people who consider welfare a retirement benefit, most Hmong would prefer almost any other option—if other options existed. What right-thinking Hmong would choose to be yoked to one of the most bureaucratic institutions in America? (A tip from "Your New Life in the United States," on applying for cash assistance: "You should have as many of the following documents available as possible: I-94—take the original, if you can; rent bill or lease; Social Security card; any pay stubs; bank account statement or savings passbook; utility bills; medical bills or proof of medical disability; employment registration card.") What Hmong would choose to become addicted to a way of life that some clan leaders have likened to opium? And what Hmong would choose the disgrace of being *dev mus nuam yaj,* a dog waiting for scraps? Dang Moua, the Merced businessman who had kept his family alive en route to Thailand by shooting birds with a homemade crossbow, once told me, "One time when I am first in America, a Korean man tell me that if someone is lazy and doesn't work, the government still pay them. I say, you crazy! That doesn't ring my bell at all! I am not afraid of working! My parents raised me as a man! I work till the last day I leave this earth!" And indeed, Dang held three concurrent nearly full-time jobs, as a grocer, an interpreter, and a pig farmer. He was once a clerk-typist in the American Embassy in Vientiane and speaks five languages, so

his success is not one most Hmong could reasonably be expected to emulate. More typical are two middle-aged men who were interviewed in San Diego for a survey on refugee adaptation. The first said:

> I used to be a real man like any other man, but not now any longer. . . . We only live day by day, just like the baby birds who are only staying in the nest opening their mouths and waiting for the mother bird to bring the worms.

The second said:

> We are not born to earth to have somebody give us feed; we are so ashamed to depend on somebody like this. When we were in our country, we never ask anybody for help like this. . . . I've been trying very hard to learn English and at the same time looking for a job. No matter what kind of job, even the job to clean people's toilets; but still people don't even trust you or offer you such work. I'm looking at me that I'm not even worth as much as a dog's stool. Talking about this, I want to die right here so I won't see my future.

These men were both suffering from a global despair to which their economic dependence was only one of many contributing factors. In the survey for which they were interviewed, part of a longitudinal study of Hmong, Cambodians, Vietnamese, and Chinese-Vietnamese refugees, the Hmong respondents scored lowest in "happiness" and "life satisfaction." In a study of Indochinese refugees in Illinois, the Hmong exhibited the highest degree of "alienation from their environment." According to a Minnesota study, Hmong refugees who had lived in the United States for a year and a half had "very high levels of depression, anxiety, hostility, phobia, paranoid ideation, obsessive compulsiveness and feelings of inadequacy." (Over the next decade, some of these symptoms moderated, but the refugees' levels of anxiety, hostility, and paranoia showed little or no improvement.) The study that I found most disheartening was the 1987 California Southeast Asian Mental Health Needs Assessment, a statewide epidemiological survey funded by the Office of Refugee Resettlement and the National Institute of Mental Health. It was shocking to look at the bar graphs comparing the Hmong with the Vietnamese, the Chinese-Vietnamese, the Cambodians, and the Lao—all of whom, particularly the Cambodians, fared poorly compared to the general population—and see how the Hmong stacked up: Most depressed. Most psychosocially dysfunctional. Most likely to be severely in need of mental health treatment. Least educated. Least literate. Smallest percentage in labor force. Most likely to cite "fear" as a reason for immigration and least likely to cite "a better life."

The same bleak ground was covered from the Hmong point of view by Bruce Thowpaou Bliatout, a public health administrator in Portland, Oregon. Dr. Bliatout, who is Hmong, explained in an article on mental health concepts that such issues as job adjustment and family happiness are regarded by the Hmong as problems of the liver. If patience, as Charles Johnson noted in *Dab Neeg Hmoob,* is attributed to a long—that is, a robust and healthy—liver, what Americans would call mental illness is attributed to a liver that has become diseased or damaged through soul loss. According to Bliatout, who provided case histories for each one, some illnesses common among Hmong in the United States are:

Nyuab Siab
Translation: Difficult liver.
Causes: Loss of family, status, home, country, or any important item that has a high emotional value.
Symptoms: Excessive worry; crying; confusion; disjointed speech; loss of sleep and appetite; delusions.

Tu Siab
Translation: Broken liver.
Causes: Loss of family member; quarrel between family members; break of family unity.
Symptoms: Grief; worry; loneliness; guilt; feeling of loss; insecurity.

Lwj Siab
Translation: Rotten liver.

Causes: Stressful family relations; constant unfulfillment of goals.
Symptoms: Loss of memory; short temper; delusions.

Before I came to Merced, Bill Selvidge described to me the first Hmong patient he had ever seen. Bruce Thowpaou Bliatout would have diagnosed this patient as having a difficult liver; Bill thought of it, not so differently, as a broken heart. "Mr. Thao was a man in his fifties," said Bill. "He told me through an interpreter that he had a bad back, but after I listened for a while I realized that he'd really come in because of depression. It turned out he was an agoraphobe. He was afraid to leave his house because he thought if he walked more than a couple of blocks he'd get lost and never find his way home again. What a metaphor! He'd seen his entire immediate family die in Laos, he'd seen his country collapse, and he never *was* going to find his way home again. All I could do was prescribe antidepressants."

Mr. Thao turned out to be the first of a long procession of depressed Hmong patients whom Bill was to treat over the next three years. Bill cut to the nub of the matter when he described the man's profound loss of "home." For the Hmong in America—where not only the social mores but also the sound of every birdsong, the shape of every tree and flower, the smell of the air, and the very texture of the earth are unfamiliar—the ache of homesickness can be incapacitating. . . .

The home to which the older Hmong dream of returning—which they call *peb lub tebchaws,* "our fields and our lands"—is prewar Laos. Their memories of wartime Laos are almost unrelievedly traumatic: a "bereavement overload" that critically magnifies all their other stresses. Richard Mollica, a psychiatrist who helped found the IndoChinese Psychiatry Clinic in Boston, found that during the war and its aftermath, Hmong refugees had experienced an average of fifteen "major trauma events," such as witnessing killings and torture. Mollica has observed of his patients, "Their psychological reality is both full and empty. They are 'full' of the past; they are 'empty' of new ideas and life experiences."

"Full" of both past trauma and past longing, the Hmong have found it especially hard to deal with present threats to their old identities. I once went to a conference on Southeast Asian mental health at which a psychologist named Evelyn Lee, who was born in Macao, invited six members of the audience to come to the front of the auditorium for a role-playing exercise. She cast them as a grandfather, a father, a mother, an eighteen-year-old son, a sixteen-year-old daughter, and a twelve-year-old daughter. "Okay," she told them, "line up according to your status in your old country." Ranking themselves by traditional notions of age and gender, they queued up in the order I've just mentioned, with the grandfather standing proudly at the head of the line. "Now they come to America," said Dr. Lee. "Grandfather has no job. Father can only chop vegetables. Mother didn't work in the old country, but here she gets a job in a garment factory. Oldest daughter works there too. Son drops out of high school because he can't learn English. Youngest daughter learns the best English in the family and ends up at U.C. Berkeley. Now you line up again." As the family reshuffled, I realized that its power structure had turned completely upside down, with the twelve-year-old girl now occupying the head of the line and the grandfather standing forlornly at the tail.

Dr. Lee's exercise was an eloquent demonstration of what sociologists call "role loss." Of all the stresses in the Hmong community, role loss . . . may be the most corrosive to the ego. Every Hmong can tell stories about colonels who became janitors, military communications specialists who became chicken processors, flight crewmen who found no work at all. Dang Moua's cousin Moua Kee, a former judge, worked first in a box factory and then on the night shift in a machine shop. "When you have no country, no land, no house, no power, everyone is the same," he said with a shrug. Major Wang Seng Khang, a former battalion commander who served as leader for 10,000 Hmong in his refugee camp, took five years to find a job as a part-time church liaison. Even then, he depended on his wife's wages from a jewelry factory to pay the rent and on his children to translate for him. Of himself and his fellow leaders, he said, "We have become children in this country."

And in this country the real children have assumed some of the power that used to belong to their elders. The status conferred by speaking English and understanding American conventions is a phenomenon familiar to most immigrant groups, but the Hmong, whose identity has always hinged on tradition, have taken it particularly hard. "Animals are responsible to their masters, and children to their parents," advised a Hmong proverb that survived unquestioned for countless generations. In prewar Laos, where families worked in the fields all day and shared a single room at night, it was not uncommon for children and their parents to be together around the clock. Remoteness and altitude insulated their villages from the majority culture. Hmong children here spend six hours in school and often several more at large in their communities, soaking up America. "My sisters don't feel they're Hmong at all," my interpreter, May Ying Xiong, once told me. "One of them has spiked hair. The youngest one speaks mostly English. I don't see the respect I gave elders at that age." Lia's sister May said, "I know how to do *paj ntaub,* but I hate sewing. My mom says, why aren't you doing *paj ntaub*? I say, Mom, this is America."

Although Americanization may bring certain benefits—more job opportunities, more money, less cultural dislocation—Hmong parents are likely to view any earmarks of assimilation as an insult and a threat. "In our families, the kids eat hamburger and bread," said Dang Moua sadly, "whereas the parents prefer hot soup with vegetables, rice, and meat like tripes or liver or kidney that the young ones don't want. The old ones may have no driver's licenses and they ask the young ones to take them some place. Sometimes the kid say I'm too busy. That is a serious situation when the kid will not obey us. The old ones are really upset." Rebellious young Hmong sometimes go beyond refusing to chauffeur their parents, and tangle with drugs or violence. In

1994, Xou Yang, a nineteen-year-old high-school dropout from Banning, California, robbed and murdered a German tourist. His father, a veteran of the war in Laos, told a reporter, "We have lost all control. Our children do not respect us. One of the hardest things for me is when I tell my children things and they say, 'I already know that.' When my wife and I try to tell my son about Hmong culture, he tells me people here are different, and he will not listen to me."

Sukey Waller, Merced's maverick psychologist, once recalled a Hmong community meeting she had attended. "An old man of seventy or eighty stood up in the front row," she said, "and he asked one of the most poignant questions I have ever heard: 'Why, when what we did worked so well for two hundred years, is everything breaking down?'" When Sukey told me this, I understood why the man had asked the question, but I thought he was wrong. Much has broken down, but not everything. Jacques Lemoine's analysis of the postwar hegira—that the Hmong came to the West to save not only their lives but their ethnicity—has been at least partially confirmed in the United States. I can think of no other group of immigrants whose culture, in its most essential aspects, has been so little eroded by assimilation. Virtually all Hmong still marry other Hmong, marry young, obey the taboo against marrying within their own clans, pay bride-prices, and have large families. Clan and lineage structures are intact, as is the ethic of group solidarity and mutual assistance. On most weekends in Merced, it is possible to hear a death drum beating at a Hmong funeral or a *txiv neeb's* gong and rattle sounding at a healing ceremony. Babies wear strings on their wrists to protect their souls from abduction by *dabs*. People divine their fortunes by interpreting their dreams. (If you dream of opium, you will have bad luck; if you dream you are covered with excrement, you will have good luck; if you dream you have a snake on your lap, you will become pregnant.) Animal sacrifices are common, even among Christian converts, a fact I first learned when May Ying Xiong told me that she would be un-

available to interpret one weekend because her family was sacrificing a cow to safeguard her niece during an upcoming open-heart operation. When I said, "I didn't know your family was so religious," she replied, "Oh yes, we're Mormon."

Even more crucially, the essential Hmong temperament—independent, insular, antiauthoritarian, suspicious, stubborn, proud, choleric, energetic, vehement, loquacious, humorous, hospitable, generous—has so far been ineradicable. Indeed, as George M. Scott, Jr., has observed, the Hmong have responded to the hardships of life in the United States "by becoming *more* Hmong, rather than less so." Summing up his impressions of the Hmong in 1924, François Marie Savina, the French missionary, attributed their ethnic durability to six factors: religion; love of liberty; traditional customs; refusal to marry outside their race; life in cold, dry, mountainous areas; and the toughening effects of war. Even though their experience here has been suffused with despair and loss, the 180,000 Hmong who live in the United States are doing passably or better on the first four counts.[6]

I was able to see the whole cycle of adjustment to American life start all over again during one of my visits to Merced. When I arrived at the Lees' apartment, I was surprised to find it crammed with people I'd never met before. These turned out to be a cousin of Nao Kao's named Joua Chai Lee, his wife, Yeng Lor, and their nine children, who ranged in age from eight months to twenty-five years. They had arrived from Thailand two weeks earlier, carrying one piece of luggage for all eleven of them. In it were packed some clothes, a bag of rice, and, because Joua is a *txiv neeb's* assistant, a set of rattles, a drum, and a pair of divinatory water-buffalo horns. The cousins were staying with Foua and Nao Kao until they found a place of their own. The two families had not seen each other in more than a decade, and there was a festive atmosphere in the little apartment, with small children dashing around in their new American sneakers and the four barefooted adults frequently throwing back their heads and laughing.

Joua said to me, via May Ying's translation, "Even though there are a lot of us, you can spend the night here too." May Ying explained to me later that Joua didn't really expect me to lie down on the floor with twenty of his relatives. It was simply his way, even though he was in a strange country where he owned almost nothing, of extending a face-saving bit of Hmong hospitality.

I asked Joua what he thought of America. "It is really nice but it is different," he said, "It is very flat. You cannot tell one place from another. There are many things I have not seen before, like that"—a light switch—"and that"—a telephone—"and that"—an air conditioner. "Yesterday our relatives took us somewhere in a car and I saw a lady and I thought she was real but she was fake." This turned out to have been a mannequin at the Merced Mall. "I couldn't stop laughing all the way home," he said. And remembering how funny his mistake had been, he started to laugh again.

Then I asked Joua what he hoped for his family's future here. "I will work if I can," he said, "but I think I probably cannot. As old as I am, I think I will not be able to learn one word of English. If my children put a heart to it, they will be able to learn English and get really smart. But as for myself, I have no hope."

NOTES

1. Sudden Unexpected Death Syndrome, which until the early 1980s was the leading cause of death among young Hmong males in the United States, is triggered by cardiac failure, often during or after a bad dream. No one has been able to explain what produces the cardiac irregularity, although theories over the years have included potassium deficiency, thiamine deficiency, sleep apnea, depression, culture shock, and survivor guilt. Many Hmong have attributed the deaths to attacks by an incubuslike *dab* [spirit] who sits on the victim's chest and presses the breath out of him.

2. Like most false rumors, these all grew from germs of truth. The white-slavery rumor originated in press accounts of Vietnamese crimes in California, most of which were themselves probably unfounded. The car rumor originated in the Hmong custom of pooling the savings of several families to buy cars and other items too expensive for one family to afford. The insurance rumor originated in the $78,000 that a Hmong family in Wisconsin was awarded after their fourteen-year-old son was killed after being hit by a car. The daughter-selling rumor originated in the Hmong custom of brideprice, or "nurturing charge," as it is now sometimes called in the United States in order to avoid just such misinterpretations. The speed-bump rumor originated in the many nonlethal domestic faux pas the Hmong have actually committed. The dog-eating rumor, which, as I've mentioned elsewhere, is current in Merced, originated in Hmong ritual sacrifices.

3. Like all low-income refugees, newly arrived Hmong were automatically eligible for Refugee Cash Assistance. The RCA program enabled Hmong who would otherwise have been ineligible for welfare in some states—for instance, because an able-bodied male was present in the home—to receive benefits. But it did not enable Hmong families to receive more money than American families. In a given state, Refugee Cash Assistance payments were always identical to benefits from AFDC (Aid to Families with Dependent Children, the form of public assistance most people mean by the word "welfare").

4. The Hmong Channel is accessed almost exclusively by Hmong users. The Hmong Homepage and the electronic mailing lists also have an audience of Americans with an academic or professional interest in Hmong culture, as well as a number of Mormon elders who have been assigned missionary work in Hmong communities.

5. At the request of local public assistance agencies, the infamous "100-Hour Rule," which prevented so many Hmong from becoming economically self-sufficient, was waived in the majority of states, starting with California, between 1994 and 1996. "Basically, it required people not to work," explained John Cullen, who directed Merced's Human Services Agency during the last years of the rule's sway. The 100-Hour Rule was replaced by a formula of gradually decreasing benefits based on earnings.

6. About 150,000 Hmong—some of whom resettled in countries other than the United States, and some of whom are still in Thailand—fled Laos. The Hmong now living in the United States exceed that number because of their high birthrate.

THINKING ABOUT THE READING

Why has it been so difficult for Hmong refugees to adjust to the American way of life? Why are the Hmong such as popular target of anti-immigrant violence and persecution? Why is American society so unwilling to grant their wish to be "left alone?" In other words, why is there such a strong desire to assimilate them into American culture? On a more general level, why is there such distaste in this society when new immigrant groups retain their traditional way of life? How do the experiences of younger Hmong immigrants compare to those of their elders?

CHAPTER 15

Architects of Change: Reconstructing Society

Throughout this book you've seen examples of how society is socially constructed and how these social constructions, in turn, affect the lives of individuals. It's hard not to feel a little helpless when discussing the control that culture, massive bureaucratic organizations, social institutions, systems of social stratification and population trends have over our individual lives. However, social change is as much a part of society as social stability. Whether at the personal, cultural, or institutional level, change is the preeminent feature of modern societies.

Religious institutions are often intertwined with movements for widespread social change. Sometimes the religious ideology that underlies a particular movement is one that emphasizes peace and justice. The civil rights movement of the 1950s and the antiwar movement of the 1960s are two such examples. Other times, however, the supportive religious ideology of a movement can be used to deny civil rights and even incite violence. In his article, "Popular Christianity and Political Extremism in the United States," James Aho describes the relationship between Christianity and violent right-wing extremism. Every American generation, he argues, has experienced movements built on religiously inspired hatred. Today, however, these movements have been able to take advantage of sophisticated weapons and communications technology, making them especially lethal.

In the end, the nature of society, from its large institutions to its small, unspoken rules of everyday life, can be understood only by examining what people do and think. Individuals, acting collectively, can shape institutions, influence government policy, and alter the course of society. It's easy to forget that social movements consist of flesh-and-blood individuals acting together for a cause they believe in. In "The U.S. Central America Peace Movement: The Individual Activists," Christian Smith puts a human face on the Americans who organized to try to alter U.S. policy in Nicaragua and El Salvador during the 1980s. From close to 600 surveys he provides some interesting answers to the questions: What kinds of people joined the Central America peace movement, and why did they join?

Popular Christianity and Political Extremism in the United States

James Aho

December 8, 1984. In a shootout on Puget Sound, Washington, involving several hundred federal and local law enforcement officials, the leader of a terrorist group compromised of self-proclaimed Christian soldiers is killed, ending a crime spree involving multi-state robberies, armored car heists, arson attacks, three murders, and a teenage suicide. (Flynn and Gerhardt 1989)

Christmas Eve, 1985. A "Christian patriot soldier" in Seattle trying to save America by eliminating the Jewish-Communist leader of the so-called one-world conspiracy, murders an innocent family of four, including two pre-teen children. (Aho 1994: 35–49)

August 1992. In northern Idaho, three persons are killed and two others critically injured in the course of a stand-off between federal marshals, ATF officers, the FBI, and a white separatist Christian family seeking refuge from the "Time of Tribulations" prophesied in the Book of Revelations. (Aho 1994: 50–65)

Three isolated incidents, twelve dead bodies, scores of young men imprisoned, shattered families, millions of dollars in litigation fees and investigation expenses. Why? What can sociology tell us about the causes of these events that they might be averted in the future? In particular, insofar as Christianity figures so prominently in these stories, what role has this religion played in them? Has Christianity been a cause of right-wing extremism in the United States? Or has it been an excuse for extremism occasioned by other factors? Or is the association between right-wing extremism and Christianity merely anecdotal and incidental? Our object is to address these questions.

Extremism Defined

The word "extremism" is used rhetorically in everyday political discourse to disparage and undermine one's opponents. In this sense, it refers essentially to anyone who disagrees with me politically. In this chapter, however, "extremism" will refer exclusively to particular kinds of behaviors, namely, to non-democratic actions, regardless of their ideology—that is, regardless of whether we agree with the ideas behind them or not (Lipset and Raab 1970: 4–17). Thus, extremism includes: (1) efforts to deny civil rights to certain people, including their right to express unpopular views, their right to due process at law, to own property, etc.; (2) thwarting attempts by others to organize in opposition to us, to run for office, or vote; (3) not playing according to legal constitutional rules of political fairness: using personal smears like "Communist Jew-fag" and "nigger lover" in place of rational discussion; and above all, settling differences by vandalizing or destroying the property or life of one's opponents. The test is not the end as such, but the means employed to achieve it.

Cycles of American Right-Wing Extremism

In this [article] we are concerned with the most rabid right-wing extremists, those who have threatened or succeeded in injuring and killing their opponents. We are interested, furthermore, only in such activities as are connected at least indirectly to Christianity. By no means is this limitation of focus intended to suggest that American Christians are characteristically more violent than their non-Christian neighbors. Nor are we arguing that American Christians engage only in right-wing activities. We are focusing on Christianity and on rightist extremism because in America today this connection has become newsworthy and because it is sociologically problematic.

American political history has long been acquainted with Christian-oriented rightist extremism. As early as the 1790s, for example, Federalist Party activists, inspired partly by Presbyterian and Congregationalist preachers, took-up arms against a mythical anti-Christian cabal known as the Illuminati—Illuminati = bringers of light = Lucifer, the devil.

The most notable result of anti-Illuminatism was what became popularly known as the "Reign of Terror": passage of the Alien and Sedition acts (1798). These required federal registration of recent immigrants to America from Ireland and France, reputed to be the homes of Illuminatism, lengthened the time of naturalization to become a citizen from five to fourteen years, restricted "subversive" speech and newspapers—that is, outlets advocating liberal Jeffersonian or what were known then as "republican" sentiments—and permitted the deportation of "alien enemies" without trial.

The alleged designs of the Illuminati were detailed in a three hundred-page book entitled *Proofs of a Conspiracy Against All the Religions and Governments of Europe Carried on in the Secret Meetings of . . . Illuminati* (Robison 1967 [1798]). Over two hundred years later *Proofs of a Conspiracy* continues to serve as a sourcebook for right-wing extremist commentary on American social issues. Its basic themes are: (1) *manichaenism:* that the world is divided into the warring principles of absolute good and evil; (2) *populism:* that the citizenry naturally would be inclined to ally with the powers of good, but have become in-

dolent, immoral, and uninformed of the present danger to themselves; (3) *conspiracy:* that this is because the forces of evil have enacted a scheme using educators, newspapers, music, and intoxicants to weaken the people's will and intelligence; (4) *anti-modernism:* that the results of the conspiracy are the very laws and institutions celebrated by the unthinking masses as "progressive": representative government, the separation of church and State, the extension of suffrage to the propertyless, free public education, public-health measures, etc.; and (5) *apocalypticism:* that the results of what liberals call social progress are increased crime rates, insubordination to "natural" authorities (such as royal families and property-owning Anglo-Saxon males), loss of faith, and the decline of common decency—in short, the end of the world.

Approximately every thirty years America has experienced decade-long popular resurrections of these five themes. While the titles of the alleged evil-doers in each era have been adjusted to meet changing circumstances, their program is said to have remained the same. They constitute a diabolic *Plot Against Christianity* (Dilling 1952). In the 1830s, the cabal was said to be comprised of the leaders of Masonic lodges: in the 1890s, they were accused of being Papists and Jesuits; in the 1920s, they were the Hidden Hand; in the 1950s, the Insiders or Force X; and today they are known as Rockefellerian "one-world" Trilateralists or Bilderbergers.

Several parallels are observable in these periods of American right-wing resurgence. First, while occasionally they have evolved into democratically-organized political parties holding conventions that nominate slates of candidates to run for office—the American Party, the Anti-Masonic Party, the People's Party, the Prohibition Party—more often, they have become secret societies in their own right, with arcane passwords, handshakes, and vestments, plotting campaigns of counter-resistance behind closed doors. That is, they come to mirror the fantasies against which they have taken up arms. Indeed, it is this ironic fact that typically occasions the public ridicule and undoing of these groups. The most notable examples are the Know Nothings, so-called because under interrogation they were directed to deny knowledge of the organization; the Ku Klux Klan, which during the 1920s had several million members; the Order of the Star Spangled Banner, which flourished during the 1890s; the Black Legion of Michigan, circa 1930; the Minutemen of the late 1960s; and most recently, the *Bruders Schweigen,* Secret Brotherhood, or as it is more widely known, The Order.

Secondly, the thirty-year cycle noted above evidently has no connection with economic booms and busts. While the hysteria of the 1890s took place during a nation-wide depression, McCarthyism exploded on the scene during the most prosperous era in American history. On close view, American right-wing extremism is more often associated with economic good times than with bad, the 1920s, the 1830s, and the 1980s being prime examples. On the contrary, the cycle seems to have more to do with the length of a modern generation than with any other factor.

Third, and most important for our purposes, Christian preachers have played pivotal roles in all American right-wing hysterias. The presence of Dan Gayman, James Ellison, and Bertrand Comparet spear-heading movements to preserve America from decline today continues a tradition going back to Jedidiah Morse nearly two centuries ago, continuing through Samuel D. Burchard, Billy Sunday, G. L. K. Smith, and Fred Schwarz's Christian Anti-Communist Crusade.

In the nineteenth century, the honorary title "Christian patriot" was restricted to white males with Protestant credentials. By the 1930s, however, Catholic ideologues, like the anti-Semitic radio priest Father Coughlin, had come to assume leadership positions in the movement. Today, somewhat uneasily, Mormons are included in the fold. The Ku Klux Klan, once rabidly anti-Catholic and misogynist, now encourages Catholic recruits and even allows females into its regular organization, instead of requiring them to form auxiliary groups.

Christianity: A Cause of Political Extremism?

The upper Rocky Mountain region is the heartland of American right-wing extremism in our time. Montana, Idaho, Oregon, and Washington have the highest per capita rates of extremist groups of any area in the entire country (Aho 1994: 152–153). Research on the members of these groups show that they are virtually identical to the surrounding population in all respects but one (Aho 1991: 135–163)—they are not less formally educated than the surrounding population. Furthermore, as indicated by their rates of geographic mobility, marital stability, occupational choice, and conventional political participation, they are no more estranged from their local communities than those with whom they live. And finally, their social status seems no more threatened than that of their more moderate neighbors. Indeed, there exists anecdotal evidence that American right-wing extremists today are drawn from the more favored, upwardly-mobile sectors of society. They are college-educated, professional suburbanites residing in the rapidly-growing, prosperous Western states (Simpson 1983).

In other words, the standard sociological theories of right-wing extremism—theories holding, respectively, that extremists are typically under-educated, if not stupid, transient and alienated from ordinary channels of belonging, and suffer inordinately from status insecurity—find little empirical support. Additionally, the popular psychological notion that right-wing extremists are more neurotic than the general population, perhaps paranoid to the point of psychosis, can not be confirmed. None of the right-wing political murderers whose psychiatric records this author has accessed have been medically certified as insane (Aho 1991: 68–82; Aho 1994: 46–49). If this is true for right-wing murderers, it probably also holds for extremists who have not taken the lives of others.

The single way in which right-wing extremists *do* differ from their immediate neighbors is seen in their religious biographies. Those with

Christian backgrounds generally, and Presbyterians, Baptists and members of independent fundamentalist Protestant groups specifically, all are overrepresented among intermountain radical patriots (Aho 1991: 164–182). Although it concerns a somewhat different population, this finding is consistent with surveys of the religious affiliations of Americans with conservative voting and attitudinal patterns (Lipset and Raab 1970: 229–232, 359–361, 387–392, 433–437, 448–452; Shupe and Stacey 1983; Wilcox 1992).

Correlations do not prove causality. Merely because American extremists are members of certain denominations and sects does not permit the conclusion that these religious groups compel their members to extremism. In the first place, the vast majority of independent fundamentalists, Baptists, and Presbyterians are not political extremists, even if they are inclined generally to support conservative causes. Secondly, it is conceivable that violently-predisposed individuals are attracted to particular religions because of what they hear from the pulpit; and what they hear channels their *already* violent inclinations in political directions.

Today, a man named Gary Yarbrough, gaunt-faced and red-bearded, languishes in federal prison because of his participation in the *Bruders Schweigen*. Although he was recruited into terrorism from the Church of Jesus Christian—Aryan Nations—it was not the church itself that made him violent, at least not in a simplistic way. On the contrary, Yarbrough was the offspring of a notorious Pima, Arizona, family that one reporter (Ring 1985) describes as "very volatile—very anti-police, anti-social, anti-everybody." Charges against its various members have ranged from burglary and robbery to witness-intimidation.

Lloyd, Steve, and Gary Yarbrough are sons of a family of drifters. Red, the father, works as an itinerant builder and miner. Rusty, his wife, tends bar and waitresses. Child rearing, such as it was, is said to have been "severely heavy handed." Nor was much love lost between the parents. Fist fights were common and once Rusty stabbed Red so badly he was hospitalized.

Not surprisingly, "the boys did not get very good schooling." Still, mother vehemently defends her boys. One night, she jumped over a bar to attack an overly inquisitive detective concerning their whereabouts.

After a spree of drugs, vandalism, and thievery, Gary, like his brothers, eventually found himself behind bars at the Arizona State Prison. It was there that he was contacted, first by letter and later personally, by the Aryan Nations prison ministry in Idaho. He was the kind of man the church was searching for: malleable, fearless, sentimental, tough. Immediately upon release, Yarbrough moved with his wife and daughter to Idaho to be close to church headquarters. He finally found his calling: working with like-minded souls in the name of Christ to protect God's chosen people, the white race, from mongrelization.

Yarbrough purchased the requisite dark blue twill trousers, postman's shirt, Nazi pins, Sam Browne holster-belt, and 9 mm. semi-automatic pistol. The pastor of the church assigned him to head the security detail. At annual church conventions, he helped conduct rifle training. But Yarbrough was a man of action; he soon became bored with the routine of guarding the compound against aliens who never arrived. He met others in the congregation who shared his impatience. Together in a farm building, deep in the woods, over the napping figure of one of the member's infant children, they founded the *Bruders Schweigen*, swearing together an oath to war against what they called ZOG—Zionist Occupation Government (Flynn and Gerhardt 1989).

The point is not that every extremist is a violent personality searching to legitimize criminality with religion. Instead, the example illustrates the subtle ways in which religious belief, practice, and organization all play upon individual psychology to produce persons prepared to violate others in the name of principle. Let us look at each of these factors separately, understanding that in reality they intermesh in complicated, sometimes contradictory ways that can only be touched upon here.

Belief

American right-wing politics has appropriated from popular Christianity several tenets: the concept of unredeemable human depravity, the idea of America as a specially chosen people, covenant theology and the right to revolt, the belief in a national mission, millennialism, and anti-Semitism. Each of these in its own way has inspired rightist extremism.

The New Israel

The notion of America as the new Israel, for example, is the primary axiom of a fast-growing religiously-based form of radical politics known as Identity Christianity. Idaho's Aryan Nations Church is simply the most well-known Identity congregation. The adjective "identity" refers to its insistence that Anglo-Saxons are in truth the Israelites. They are "Isaac's-sons"—the Saxons—and hence the Bible is *their* historical record, not that of the Jews (Barkun 1994). The idea is that after its exile to what today is northern Iran around seven hundred B.C., the Israelites migrated over the Caucasus mountains—hence their racial type, "caucasian"—and settled in various European countries. Several of these allegedly still contain mementos of their origins: the nation of Denmark is said to be comprised of descendants from the tribe of Dan; the German-speaking Jutland, from the tribe of Judah; Catalonia, Scotland, from the tribe of Gad.

Covenant Theology

Identity Christianity is not orthodox Christianity. Nevertheless, the notion of America as an especially favored people, or as Ronald Reagan once said, quoting Puritan founders, a "city on a hill," the New Jerusalem, is widely shared by Americans. Reagan and most conservatives, of course, consider the linkage between America and Israel largely symbolic. Many right-wing extremists, however, view the relationship literally as an historical fact and for them, just as the ancient Israelites entered into a covenant with the Lord, America has done the same. According to

radical patriots America's covenant is what they call the "organic Constitution." This refers to the original articles of the Constitution plus the first ten amendments, the Bill of Rights. Other amendments, especially the 16th establishing a federal income tax, are considered to have questionable legal status because allegedly they were not passed according to constitutional strictures.

The most extreme patriots deny the constitutionality of the 13th, 14th, and 15th amendments—those outlawing slavery and guaranteeing free men civil and political rights as full American citizens. Their argument is that the organic Constitution was written by white men exclusively for themselves and their blood descendents (Preamble 1986). Non-caucasians residing in America are considered "guest peoples" with no constitutional rights. Their continued residency in this country is entirely contingent upon the pleasure of their hosts, the Anglo-Saxon citizenry. According to some, it is now time for the property of these guests to be confiscated and they themselves exiled to their places of origin (Pace 1985).

All right-wing extremists insist that if America adheres to the edicts of the organic Constitution, she, like Israel before her, shall be favored among the world's nations. Her harvests shall be bountiful, her communities secure, her children obedient to the voices of their parents, and her armies undefeated. But if she falters in her faith, behaving in ways that contravene the sacred compact, then calamities, both natural and human-made, shall follow. This is the explanation for the widespread conviction among extremists today for America's decline in the world. In short, the federal government has established agencies and laws contrary to America's divine compact: these include the Internal Revenue Service; the Federal Reserve System; the Bureau of Alcohol, Tobacco and Firearms; the Forest Service; the Bureau of Land Management; Social Security; Medicare and Medicaid; the Environmental Protection Agency; Housing and Urban Development; and the official apparatus enforcing civil rights for "so-called" minorities.

Essentially, American right-wing extremists view the entire executive branch of the United States government as little more than "jack-booted Nazi thugs," to borrow a phrase from the National Rifle Association fund-raising letter: a threat to freedom of religion, the right to carry weapons, freedom of speech, and the right to have one's property secure from illegal search and seizure.

Clumsy federal-agency assaults, first on the Weaver family in northern Idaho in 1992, then on the Branch Davidian sect in Waco, Texas, in 1993, followed by passage of the assault weapons ban in 1994, are viewed as indicators that the organic Constitution presently is imperiled. This has been the immediate impetus for the appearance throughout rural and Western America of armed militias since the summer of 1994. The terrorists who bombed a federal building in Oklahoma City in the spring of 1995, killing one hundred sixty-eight, were associated with militias headquartered in Michigan and Arizona. One month after the bombing, the national director of the United States Militia Association warned that after the current government falls, homosexuals, abortionists, rapists, "unfaithful politicians," and any criminal not rehabilitated in seven years will be executed. Tax evaders will no longer be treated as felons; instead they will lose their library privileges (Sherwood 1995).

Millennialism

Leading to both the Waco and Weaver incidents was a belief on the victims' parts that world apocalypse is imminent. The Branch Davidians split from the Seventh-Day Adventists in 1935 but share with the mother church its own millenarian convictions. The Weavers received their apocalypticism from *The Late Great Planet Earth* by fundamentalist lay preacher Hal Lindsey (1970), a book that has enjoyed a wide reading on the Christian right.

Both the Davidians and the Weavers were imbued with the idea that the thousand-year-reign of Christ would be preceded by a final battle between the forces of light and darkness. To this end both had deployed elaborate arsenals to protect themselves from the anticipated invasion of "Babylonish troops." These, they feared, would be comprised of agents from the various federal bureaucracies mentioned above, together with UN troops stationed on America's borders awaiting orders from Trilateralists. Ever alert to "signs" of the impending invasion, both fired at federal officers who had come upon their property; and both ended up precipitating their own martyrdom. Far from quelling millenarian fervor, however, the two tragedies were immediately seized upon by extremists as further evidence of the approaching End Times.

Millenarianism is not unique to Christianity, nor to Western religions; furthermore, millenarianism culminating in violence is not new—in part because one psychological effect of end-time prophesying is a devaluation of worldly things, including property, honors, and human life. At the end of the first Christian millennium (A.D. 1000) as itinerant prophets were announcing the Second Coming, their followers were taking-up arms to prepare the way, and uncounted numbers died (Cohn 1967). It should not surprise observers if, as the second millennium draws to a close and promises of Christ's imminent return increase in frequency, more and more armed cults flee to the mountains, there to prepare for the final conflagration.

Anti-Semitism

Many post-Holocaust Christian and Jewish scholars alike recognize that a pervasive anti-Judaism can be read from the pages of the New Testament, especially in focusing on the role attributed to Jews in Jesus' crucifixion. Rosemary Ruether, for example, argues that anti-Judaism constitutes the "left-hand of Christianity," its archetypal negation (Ruether 1979). Although pre-Christian Greece and Rome were also critical of Jews for alleged disloyalty, anti-Semitism reached unparalleled heights in Christian theology, sometimes relegating Jews to the status of Satan's spawn, the human embodiments of Evil itself.

During the Roman Catholic era, this association became embellished with frightening myths and images. Jews—pictured as feces-eating swine and rats—were accused of murdering Christian children on high feast days, using their blood to make unleavened bread, and poisoning wells. Added to these legends were charges during the capitalist era that Jews control international banking and by means of usury have brought simple, kind-hearted Christians into financial ruin (Hay 1981 [1950]). All of this was incorporated into popular Protestant culture through, among other vehicles, Martin Luther's diatribe, *On the Jews and Their Lies,* a pamphlet that still experiences brisk sales from patriotic bookstores. This is one possible reason for a survey finding by Charles Glock and Rodney Stark that created a minor scandal in the late 1960s. Rigidly orthodox American Christians, they found, displayed far higher levels of Jew-hatred than other Christians, regardless of their education, occupation, race, or income (Glock and Stark 1966).

In the last thirty years there has been "a sharp decline" in anti-Semitic prejudice in America, according to Glock (1993: 68). Mainline churches have played some role in this decline by facilitating Christian-Jewish dialogue, de-emphasizing offensive scriptural passages, and ending missions directed at Jews. Nevertheless, ancient anti-Jewish calumnies continue to be raised by leaders of the groups that are the focus of interest in this [article]. Far from being a product of neurotic syndromes like the so-called Authoritarian (or fascist) Personality, the Jew-hatred of many right-wing extremists today is directly traceable to what they have absorbed from these preachments, sometimes as children.

Human Depravity

There is none righteous, no not one; . . . there is none that doeth the good, no, no one. Their throat is an open sepulchre. With their tongues they have used deceit; the poison of asps in under their lips. In these words of the apostle Paul, John Calvin says God inveighs not against particular individuals, but against all mankind. "Let it be admitted, then, that men . . . are . . . corrupt . . . by a depravity of nature" (Calvin 1966: 34–36; see Romans 3:11–24).

One of the fundamentals of Calvinist theology, appropriated into popular American Christianity, is this: a transcendent and sovereign God resides in the heavens, relative to whom the earth and its human inhabitants are utterly, hopelessly fallen. True, Calvin only developed a line of thought already anticipated in Genesis and amplified repeatedly over the centuries. However, with a lawyer's penetrating logic, Calvin brought this tradition to its most stark, pessimistic articulation. It is this belief that accompanied the Pilgrims in their venture across the Atlantic, eventually rooting itself in the American psyche.

From its beginnings, a particular version of the doctrine of human depravity has figured prominently in American right-wing extremist discourse. It has served as the basis of its perennial misogyny, shared by both men and women. The female, being supposedly less rational and more passive, is said to be closer to earth's evil. Too, the theology of world devaluation is the likely inspiration for the right-wing's gossipy preoccupation with the body's appetites and the "perilous eroticism of emotion," for its prudish fulminations against music, dance, drink, and dress, and for its homophobia. Here, too, is found legitimation for the right-wing's vitriol against Satanist ouiji boards, "Dungeons and Dragons," and New Age witchcrafters with their horoscopes and aroma-therapies, and most recently, against "pagan-earth-worshippers" and "tree hugging idolaters" (environmentalists). In standing tall to "Satan's Kids" and their cravenness, certain neo-Calvinists in Baptist, Presbyterian, and fundamentalist clothing accomplish their own purity and sanctification.

Conspiratorialism

According to Calvin, earthquakes, pestilence, famine, and plague should pose no challenge to faith in God. We petty, self-absorbed creatures have no right to question sovereign reason. But even in Calvin's time, and more frequently later, many Christians have persisted in asking: if God is truly all-powerful, all-knowing, and all-good, then how is evil possible? Why do innocents suffer? One perennial, quasi-theological response is conspiratorialism. In short, there are AIDS epidemics, murderous holocausts, rampant poverty, and floods because counter-poised to God there exists a second hidden force of nearly equal power and omniscience: the Devil and His human consorters—Jews, Jesuits, Hidden Hands, Insiders, Masons, and Bilderbergers.

By conspiratorialism, we are not referring to documented cases of people secretly scheming to destroy co-workers, steal elections, or run competitors out of business. Conspiracies are a common feature of group life. Instead, we mean the attempt to explain the entirety of human history by means of a cosmic Conspiracy, such as that promulgated in the infamous *Protocols of the Learned Elders of Zion*. This purports to account for all modern institutions by attributing them to the designs of twelve or thirteen—one representing each of the tribes of Israel—Jewish elders (Aho 1994, 68–82). *The Protocols* enjoys immense and endless popularity on the right; and has generated numerous spin-offs: *The International Jew, None Dare Call It Conspiracy,* and the *Mystery of [Jewish] Iniquity,* to name three.

To posit the existence of an evil divinity is heresy in orthodox Christianity. But, theological objections aside, it is difficult indeed for some believers to resist the temptation of intellectual certitude conspiratorialism affords. This certainty derives from the fact that conspiratorialism in the cosmic sense can not be falsified. Every historical event can, and often is, taken as further verification of conspiracies. If newspapers report a case of government corruption, this is evidence of government conspiracy; if they do not, this is evidence of news media complicity in the conspiracy. If the media deny involvement in a cover-up, this is still further proof of their guilt; if they admit to having sat on the story, this is surely an admission of what is already known.

Practice

Christianity means more than adhering to a particular doctrine. To be Christian is to live righteously. God-fearing righteousness may either be understood as a *sign* of one's salvation, as in orthodox Christianity or, as in Mormonism, a way to *earn* eternal life in the celestial heavens.

Nor is it sufficient for the faithful merely to display righteousness in their personal lives and businesses, by being honest, hard-working, and reliable. Many Christians also are obligated to witness to, or labor toward, salvation in the political arena; to work with others to remake this charnel-house world after the will of God; to help establish God's kingdom on earth. Occasionally this means becoming involved in liberal causes—abolitionism, civil rights, the peace and ecological movements; often it has entailed supporting causes on the right. In either case it may require that one publicly stand up to evil. For, as Saint Paul said, to love God is to hate what is contrary to God.

Such a mentality may lead to "holy war," the organized effort to eliminate human fetishes of evil (Aho 1994: 23–34). For some, in cleansing the world of putrefaction their identity as Christian is recognized, it is re-known. This is not to argue that holy war is unique to Christianity, or that all Christians participate in holy wars. Most Christians are satisfied to renew their faith through the rites of Christmas, Easter, baptism, marriage, or mass. Furthermore, those who *do* speak of holy war often use it metaphorically to describe a private spiritual battle against temptation, as in "I am a soldier of Christ, therefore I am not permitted to fight" (Sandford 1966). Lastly, even holy war in the political sense does not necessarily imply the use of violence. Although they sometimes have danced tantalizingly close to extremism (in the sense defined earlier), neither Pat Robertson nor Jerry Falwell, for example, have advocated non-democratic means in their "wars" to avert America's decline.

Let us examine the notion of Christian holy war more closely. The sixteenth-century father of Protestant reform, Martin Luther, repudiated the concept of holy war, arguing that there exist two realms: holiness, which is the responsibility of the Church, and warfare, which falls under the State's authority (Luther 1974). Mixing these realms, he says, perverts the former while unnecessarily hamstringing the latter. This does not mean that

Christians may forswear warfare, according to Luther. In his infinite wisdom, God has ordained princes to quell civil unrest and protect nations from invasion. Luther's exhortations to German officials that they spare no means in putting down peasant revolts are well known. Indeed, few theologians have "so highly praised the virtues of the State as Luther," says Ernst Troeltsch. Nevertheless, State violence is at best "sinful power to punish sin" for Luther. It is not a sacred instrument (Troeltsch 1960: 539–544, 656–677). To this day, Lutherans generally are less responsive to calls for holy wars than many other Christians.

John Calvin, on the other hand, rejected Luther's proposal to separate church from State. Instead, his goal was to establish a Christocracy in Geneva along Roman Catholic lines, and to attain this goal through force, if need be, as Catholicism had done. Calvin says that not only is violence to establish God's rule on earth permitted, it is commanded. "Good brother, we must bend unto all means that give furtherance to the holy cause" (Walzer 1965: 17, 38, 68–87, 90–91, 100–109; see Troeltsch 1960: 599–601, 651–652, 921–922 n. 399). This notion profoundly influenced Oliver Cromwell and his English revolutionary army known as the Ironsides, so named because of its righteously cold brutality (Solt 1971). And it was the Calvinist ethic, not that of Luther, that was imported to America by the Puritans, informing the politics of Presbyterians and Congregationalists—the immediate heirs of Calvinism—as well as some Methodists and many Baptists. Hence, it is not surprising that those raised in these denominations are often overrepresented in samples of "saints" on armed crusades to save the world for Christ.

Seminal to the so-called pedagogic or educational function of holy war are two requirements. First, the enemy against whom the saint fights must be portrayed in terms appropriate to his status as a fetish of evil. Second, the campaign against him must be equal to his diabolism. It must be terrifying, bloodthirsty, uncompromising.

"Prepare War!" was issued by the now defunct Covenant, Sword and the Arm of the Lord, a fundamentalist Christian paramilitary commune headquartered in Missouri. A raid on the compound in the late 1980s uncovered one of the largest private arms caches ever in American history. Evidently, this arsenal was to be used to combat what the pamphlet calls "Negro-beasts of the field . . . who eat the flesh of men. . . . This cannibalistic fervor shall cause them to eat the dead *and* the living during" the time of Tribulations, prophesied in The Book of Revelation (CSA n.d.: 19). The weapons were also to be directed against "Sodomite homosexuals waiting in their lusts to rape," "Seed-of-Satan Jews, who are today sacrificing people in darkness," and "do-gooders who've fought for the 'rights' of these groups" (CSA n.d.: 19). When the Lord God has delivered these enemies into our hands, warns the pamphlet quoting the Old Testament, "thou shalt save alive nothing that breatheth: but thou shalt utterly destroy them" (CSA n.d.: 20; see Deuteronomy 20: 10–18).

The 1990s saw a series of State-level initiatives seeking to deny homosexuals civil rights. Although most of these failed by narrow margins, one in Colorado was passed (later to be adjudged unconstitutional), due largely to the efforts of a consortium of fundamentalist Christian churches. One of the most influential of these was the Laporte, Colorado, Church of Christ, America's largest Identity congregation (more on Identity Christianity below). Acknowledging that the title of their pamphlet "Death Penalty for Homosexuals" would bring upon them the wrath of liberals, its authors insist that "such slanderous tactics" will not deter the anti-homosexual campaign. "For truth will ultimately prevail, no matter how many truth-bearers are stoned." And what precisely is this truth? It is that the Lord Himself has declared that "if a man also lie with mankind, as he lieth with a woman, both of them have committed an abomination: they shall surely be put to death; their blood shall be upon them" (Peters 1992: i; see Leviticus 20:13).

Like "Prepare War!," "Death Penalty for Homosexuals" is not satisfied merely to cite biblical references. To justify the extremity of its attack, it must paint the homosexual in luridly terrifying colors. Finding and citing a quote from the most extreme of radical gay activists, their pamphlet warns (CSA n.d.: 19):

> [They] shall sodomize [our] sons. . . . [They] shall seduce them in [our] schools, . . . in [our] locker rooms, . . . in [our] army bunkhouses . . . wherever men are with men together. [Our] sons shall become [their] minions and do [their] bidding. . . . All laws banning homosexual activity will be revoked. Instead, legislation shall be passed which engenders love between men. . . . [They] shall stage plays in which man openly caresses man. . . . The museums of the world will be filled only with paintings of . . . naked lads. . . . Love between men [will become] fashionable and de rigueur. [They] will eliminate heterosexual liaisons. . . . There will be no compromises. . . . Those who oppose [them] will be exiled. [They] shall raise vast private armies . . . to defeat [us]. . . . The family unit . . . will be abolished. . . . All churches who condemn [them] will be closed. . . . The society to emerge will be governed by . . . gay poets. . . . Any heterosexual man will be barred from . . . influence. All males who insist on remaining . . . heterosexual will be tried in homosexual courts of justice."

What should Christians do in the face of this looming specter, asks the pamphlet? "We, today, can and should have God's Law concerning Homosexuality and its judgment of the death penalty." For "they which commit such things," says the apostle Paul, "are worthy of death" (CSA n.d.: 15; see Romans 1:27–32). Extremism fans the flames of extremism.

Organization

Contrary to popular thinking, people rarely join right-wing groups because they have a prior belief in doctrines such as those enumerated above. Rather, they come to believe because they have first joined. That is, people first affiliate with right-wing activists and only then begin altering their intellectual outlooks to sustain and

strengthen these ties. The original ties may develop from their jobs, among neighbors, among prison acquaintances, or through romantic relationships.

Take the case of Cindy Cutler, who was last seen teaching music at the Aryan Nations Church academy (Mauer, 1980). Reflecting on the previous decade she could well wonder at how far she had come in such a short time.

Cindy had been raised Baptist. "I was with the Jesus Christ thing, that Jesus was my savior and God was love. We'd go to the beach up to a perfect stranger and say, 'Are you saved?' " Such was the serene existence of an uncommonly pretty thrice born-again teenager then residing in San Diego—until she met Gary Cutler, a Navy man stationed nearby. Gary was fourteen years Cindy's senior and seemed the "good Christian man" she had been looking for when they met one Sunday at Baptist services.

Gary and Cindy were already dating when he discovered Identity Christianity. Brought up as a Mormon, he had left the church when it began granting priesthood powers to Black members during the 1970s. After several years searching for a new religious home, Gary claims to have first heard the Identity message one evening while randomly spinning the radio dial. An Identity preacher was extolling the white race as God's chosen people. Gary says the sermon gave him "new found pride."

In the meantime, Cindy's fondness for Gary was growing. The only problem was his espousal of Identity beliefs. As part of her faith, Cindy had learned that Jews, not Anglo-Saxons, were from Israel, and that Jesus was Jewish. Both of these notions were in conflict with what Gary was now saying. Perhaps, Cindy feared, she and Gary were incompatible after all. How could she ever find intellectual consensus with her fiance?

Gary and Cindy routinely spent time together in Bible study. One evening Cindy saw the light. She had already learned from church that Jews were supposedly "Christ killers." It was this information that enabled her to overcome what she calls her prideful resistance to Identity. The occasion of her conversion was this passage: "My sheep know me and hear my voice, and follow me" (John 10: 27). "That's how I got into Identity," she later said. "I questioned how they [the Jews] could be God's chosen people if they hate my Christ." Having discovered a shared theological ground upon which to stand, Gary and Cindy could now marry.

The point of this story is the sociological truth that the way in which some people become right-wing extremists is indistinguishable from the way others become vegetarians, peace activists, or members of mainline churches (Lofland and Stark 1965; Aho 1991: 185–211). *Their affiliations are mediated by significant others already in the movement.* It is from these others that they first learn of the cause; sometimes it is through the loaning of a pamphlet or videotape; occasionally it takes the form of an invitation to a meeting or workshop. As the relationship with the other tightens, the recruit's viewpoint begins to change. At this stage old friends, family members, and cohorts, observing the recruit spending inordinate time with "those new people," begin their interrogations: "What's up with you, man?" In answer, the new recruit typically voices shocking things: bizarre theologies, conspiracy theories, manichaeistic worldviews. Either because of conscious "disowning" or unconscious avoidance, the recruit finds the old ties loosening, and as they unbind, the "stupidity" and "backwardness" of prior acquaintances becomes increasingly evident.

Pushed away from old relationships and simultaneously pulled into the waiting arms of new friends, lovers, and comrades, the recruit is absorbed into the movement. Announcements of full conversion to extremism follow. To display commitment to the cause, further steps may be deemed necessary: pulling one's children out of public schools where "secular humanism" is taught; working for radical political candidates to stop America's "moral decline"; refusing to support ZOG with taxes; renouncing one's citizenship and throwing away social security card and driver's license; moving to a rugged wilderness to await the End Times. Occasionally it means donning camouflage, taking up high-

powered weaponry, and confronting the "forces of satan" themselves.

There are two implications to this sociology of recruitment. First and most obviously, involvement in social networks is crucial to being mobilized into right-wing activism. Hence, contrary to the claims of the estrangement theory of extremism mentioned above, those who are truly isolated from their local communities are the last and least likely to become extremists themselves. My research (Aho 1991, 1994) suggests that among the most important of these community ties is membership in independent fundamentalist, Baptist, or Presbyterian congregations.

Secondly, being situated in particular networks is largely a matter of chance. None of us choose our parents. Few choose their co-workers, fellow congregants, or neighbors, and even friendships and marriages are restricted to those available to us by the happenstance of our geography and times. What this means is that almost any person could find themselves in a Christian patriot communications network that would position them for recruitment into right-wing extremism.

As we have already pointed out, American right-wing extremists are neither educationally nor psychologically different from the general population. Nor are they any more status insecure than other Americans. What makes them different is how they are socially positioned. This positioning includes their religious affiliation. Some people find themselves in churches that expose them to the right-wing world. This increases the likelihood of their becoming right-wingers.

Conclusion

Throughout American history, a particular style of Christianity has nurtured right-wing extremism. Espousing doctrines like human depravity, white America as God's elect people, conspiratorialism, Jews as Christ killers, covenant theology and the right to revolt, and millennialism, this brand of Christianity is party rooted in orthodox Calvinism and in the theologically questionable fantasies of popular imagination. Whatever its source, repeatedly during the last two centuries, its doctrines have served to prepare believers cognitively to assume hostile attitudes toward "un-Christian"—hence un-American—individuals, groups, and institutional practices.

This style of Christianity has also given impetus to hatred and violence through its advocacy of armed crusades against evil. Most of all, however, the cults, sects, and denominations wherein this style flourishes have served as mobilization centers for recruitment into right-wing causes. From the time of America's inception, right-wing political leaders in search of supporters have successfully enlisted clergymen who preach these principles to bring their congregations into the fold in "wars" to save America for Christ.

It is a mistake to think that modern Americans are more bigoted and racist than their ancestors were. Every American generation has experienced right-wing extremism, even that occasionally erupting into vigilante violence of the sort witnessed daily on the news today. What is different in our time is the sophistication and availability of communications and weapons technology. Today, mobilizations to right-wing causes has been infinitely enhanced by the availability of personal computer systems capable of storing and retrieving information on millions of potential recruits. Mobilization has also been facilitated by cheap shortwave radio and cable-television access, the telephone tree, desktop publishing, and readily available studio-quality recorders. Small coteries of extremists can now activate supporters across immense distances at the touch of a button. Add to this the modern instrumentality for maiming and killing available to the average American citizen: military-style assault weaponry easily convertible into fully automatic machine guns, powerful explosives manufacturable from substances like diesel oil and fertilizer, harmless in themselves, hence purchasable over-the-counter. Anti-tank and aircraft weapons, together with assault vehicles, have also been uncovered recently in private-arms caches in the Western states.

Because of these technological changes, religious and political leaders today have a greater re-sponsibility to speak and write with care regarding those with whom they disagree. Specifically, they must control the temptation to demonize their opponents, lest, in their declarations of war they bring unforeseen destruction not only on their enemies, but on themselves.

REFERENCES

Aho, J. 1991. *The Politics of Righteousness: Idaho Christian Patriotism.* Seattle: University of Washington Press.

———. 1994. *This Thing of Darkness: A Sociology of the Enemy.* Seattle: University of Washington Press.

Barkun, M. 1994. *Religion and the Racist Right: The Origins of the Christian Identity Movement.* Chapel Hill: North Carolina University Press.

Calvin J. 1966. *On God and Man.* F. W. Strothmann (ed.). New York: Ungar.

Cohn, N. 1967. *The Pursuit of the Millennium.* New York: Oxford University Press.

CSA. n.d. "Prepare War!" Pontiac, Missouri: CSA Bookstore.

Dilling, E. 1952. *The Plot Against Christianity.* n.p.

Flynn, K. and G. Gerhardt. 1989. *The Silent Brotherhood: Inside America's Racist Underground.* New York: Free Press.

Glock, C. 1993. "The Churches and Social Change in Twentieth-Century America." *Annals of the American Academy of Political and Social Science.* 527: 67–83.

Glock, C. and R. Stark. 1966. *Christian Beliefs and Anti-Semitism.* New York: Harper & Row.

Hay, M. 1981 (1950). *The Roots of Christian Anti-Semitism.* New York: Anti-Defamation League of B'nai B'rith.

Lindsey, H. 1970. *The Late Great Planet Earth.* Grand Rapids: Zondervan.

Lipset, S. M. and E. Raab. 1970. *The Politics of Unreason: Right-Wing Extremism in America, 1790–1970.* New York: Harper & Row.

Lofland, J. and R. Stark. 1965. "Becoming a World-Saver: A Theory of Conversation to a Deviant Perspective." *American Sociological Review* 30: 862–875.

Luther, M. 1974. *Luther: Selected Political Writings,* J. M. Porter, ed. Philadelphia: Fortress Press.

Mannheim, K. 1952. "The Problem of Generations," in

Essays in the Sociology of Knowledge. London: Routledge and Kegan Paul.

Mauer, D. 1980. "Couple Finds Answers in Butler's Teachings." *Idaho Statesman.* Sept. 14.

Nisbet, R. 1953. *The Quest for Community.* New York: Harper and Brothers.

Pace, J. O. 1985. *Amendment to the Constitution.* Los Angeles: Johnson, Pace, Simmons and Fennel.

Peters, P. 1992. *Death Penalty for Homosexuals.* LaPorte, Colorado: Scriptures for America. Preamble. 1986. "Preamble to the United States Constitution: Who Are the Posterity?" Oregon City, Oregon: Republic vs. Democracy Redress.

Ring, R. H. 1985. "The Yarbrough's." *The Denver Post.* Jan. 6.

Robison, J. 1967 (1798). *Proofs of a Conspiracy. . . .* Los Angeles: Western Islands.

Ruether, R. 1979. *Faith and Fratricide: The Theological Roots of Anti-Semitism.* New York: Seabury.

Sandford, F. W. 1966. *The Art of War for the Christian Soldier.* Amherst, New Hampshire: Kingdom Press.

Schlesinger, A. 1986. *The Cycles of American History.* Boston: Houghton Mifflin.

Sherwood, "Commander" S. 1995. Quoted in *Idaho State Journal.* May 21.

Shupe, A. and W. Stacey. 1983. "The Moral Majority Constituency" in *The New Christian Right,* R. Liebman and R. Wuthnow, eds. New York: Aldine.

Simpson, J. 1983. "Moral Issues and Status Politics" in *The New Christian Right,* R. Liebman and R. Wuthnow, eds. New York: Aldine.

Solt, L. 1971. *Saints in Arms: Puritanism and Democracy in Cromwell's Army.* New York: AMS Press.

Stark, R. and William Bainbridge. 1985. *The Future of Religion: Secularization, Revival and Cult Formation.* Berkeley: University of California Press.

Stouffer, S. A. 1966. *Communism, Conformity and Civil Liberties.* New York: John Wiley.

Troeltsch, E. 1960. *Social Teachings of the Christian Churches.* Trans. by O. Wyon. New York: Harper & Row.

Walzer, M. 1965. *The Revolution of the Saints.* Cambridge, MA: Harvard University Press.

Wilcox, C. 1992. *God's Warriors: The Christian Right in Twentieth Century America.* Baltimore, MD: Johns Hopkins University Press.

THINKING ABOUT THE READING

Describe the religious doctrines that typically characterize right-wing extremist groups in the United States. After reading Aho's article, do you think that Christianity is a cause of right-wing extremism? If not, how can you account for the religiously inspired rhetoric of such movements? If so, what responsibility do "less extreme" churches have in suppressing extremist groups? In a more general sense, what role do you think religious institutions ought to play in movements for political and social change?

The U.S. Central America Peace Movement

The Individual Activists

Christian Smith

For most of human history, political and military elites have directed the foreign affairs of their tribes, kingdoms, and nations as they have seen fit, largely unencumbered by the concerns of the common people over whom they rule. Generations of ordinary women and men—those who pay the taxes, forge the swords, and watch their sons marched off to battle—have had little say about exactly which wars ought to be fought, which treaties ought to be signed, and which territories ought to be colonized. Common people have paid the costs, and sometimes enjoyed the benefits, of their leaders' ventures in foreign relations. But, with few exceptions, they have been excluded from participating in the decisions about the nature and direction of those ventures.

Recent history, however, has witnessed a difficult, faltering, yet clearly perceptible, upheaval from below. The ideals of human equality and participation that Hebrew prophets and Greek philosophers once proclaimed and subsequent centuries dimmed reemerged from the rubble of medieval Europe. In recent decades, those ideals have been amplified into a "participation revolution" around the world. From Algiers to Prague to Beijing, from Soweto to Santiago to San Francisco, ordinary people are increasingly acting on the idea that all people, and not just elites, ought to participate significantly in shaping the decisions and structures that affect their lives. This "participation revolution" has not left untouched the domain of international relations and foreign policy making—long restricted to the control of elites. In the United States, this recent drive toward greater citizens' participation in matters of foreign policy has expressed itself dramatically in a number of contentious grassroots social move-

ments. These include the anti–Vietnam War, the Free South Africa, and the Nuclear Freeze movements. The importance of many of these social movements has been matched by a plethora of popular and academic literature describing, analyzing, and explaining them.

One of the most interesting and significant of these foreign policy–oriented grassroots movements in the U.S. was the Central America peace movement of the 1980s. In this movement, more than one hundred thousand U.S. citizens mobilized to contest the chief foreign policy initiative of the most popular U.S. president in decades. Ordinary Americans marched in the streets, illegally housed refugees fleeing persecution, traveled to Central American war zones, committed civil disobedience at demonstrations, and hounded their political representatives to stop the U.S.-sponsored war in Central America—all on the assumption . . . that common people can and should shape national foreign policy.

The Individual Activists

. . . Social movements do not consist simply of abstract structures and contexts, of impersonal forces and events. Social movements are, at bottom, real, flesh-and-blood human beings acting together to confront and disrupt. They are the collective expressions of specific people, of concrete men and women struggling together for a cause. . . . Exactly what kinds of people participated in the Central America peace movement? Why did *they* tend to join or become recruited into the movement? What personal characteristics or circumstances may have predisposed them to become activists? And by what processes or mechanisms were those particular people mobilized for activism? . . .

The evidence I use to answer these questions was gathered through two national surveys of and twenty-eight in-depth interviews with Witness for Peace and Sanctuary activists. [Witness for Peace was a politically independent grassroots organization established in the early 1980s to nonviolently challenge U.S. policy and corporate practices in Central America. Sanctuary, established around the same time, was a church-based organization that illegally provided humanitarian aid to Central American refugees in this country.] In 1991, I mailed a six-page, twenty-eight-item questionnaire (closed- and open-ended questions) to a sample of 1,190 former Witness for Peace short-term delegates, randomly drawn from that organization's total list of four thousand former delegates. An almost identical questionnaire was mailed to representatives of all four hundred declared Sanctuary organizations listed in the Chicago Religious Task Force on Central America's 1987 Sanctuary directory. Four hundred and fifty-two Witness for Peace and 129 Sanctuary questionnaires were completed and returned. More than one hundred open-ended follow-up questionnaires, asking for written explanations and interpretations of findings from the first questionnaires, were sent to respondents who had voluntarily waived their anonymity by writing their names and addresses on their original questionnaires. In addition to these surveys, I interviewed twenty-eight movement activists—from seven states representing the northeast, south, southwest, and west coast regions of the country—about their motivations and experiences as participants in the Central America peace movement. By employing these multiple methodologies to examine two very different organizational segments of the Central America peace movement, I hope to capture a fairly accurate picture of those involved in the national movement as a whole.

A Group Portrait of the Activists

What kind of people actually got involved in the Central America peace movement? Table 1 represents a comparison of the characteristics of Central America peace movement activists with those of all adult Americans. Examining this and other tables, we see emerging a distinctive group

TABLE 1 *Comparison of Central America Peace Activists and All Adult Americans, 1985*

Trait	Sanctuary Activists	Witness for Peace Delegates	All Adult Americans
Average age (years)	44***	45***	37
Married (%)	70*	51***	63
Married, without children (%)	65***	77***	50
Caucasian (%)	98***	96***	86
Female (%)	63**	52	52
Median annual household income ($)	31,155***	31,174***	24,986
Completed 4 years of college or more (%)	91***	90***	19
Mean number of prior social movements participated in	7.3***	8***	?<1
Member of one or more political organization (%)	77***	85***	<10
Regularly attend religious services (%)	63***	58***	42
Traveled to Central America before sanctuary (%)	16***	—	<4
Politically leftist in 1979 (%)	23***	25***	7
Postmaterialists (%)	59***	68***	16
Materialists (%)	0***	0***	23
N	(129)	(452)	(239,279,000)

*** = p < .001 ** = p < .01 * = p < .05

profile of the movement activists, one which also sheds light on the issues raised in the literature on differential recruitment to activism.

Attitudes and Values   To begin, we see that both Witness for Peace and Sanctuary activists strongly reflect social and political attitudes and values congruent with and supportive of those of the Central America peace movement. A comparison of the bottom three traits in Table 1 reveals major differences in political ideology and in Inglehart's (1990) scale of "Postmaterialist" values between the activists and all adult Americans. Sanctuary activists were five times more likely and Witness for Peace activists were almost six and one-half times more likely to have been politically leftist in 1979 than the average American. In the context of American politics in the 1980s, such an ideological orientation would clearly predispose one to be very critical of the Reagan administration's military policies and sympathetic to the cause of Nicaragua's Sandinista government and, possibly, El Salvador's FMLN guerrilla insurgency. Table 1 also indicates that more than three and one-half times as many Sanctuary activists and more than four times as many Witness for Peace activists were pure Postmaterialists than were all adult Americans. The activities, in other words, were much less concerned with the values of economic and physical security that informed most of the White House's policies than with the values of social participation and relational fulfillment that are strongly associated with joining in social movement activism (Inglehart 1990). Conversely, while almost one-quarter of adult Americans are pure Materialists, not one of the hundreds of Sanctuary or Witness for Peace activists was. This distribution is even more striking when we consider that Central America activists tended to be older, while Postmaterialist values are strongly associated with youth.

Evidence on the activists' occupational backgrounds seems to corroborate their value-sympathy with the movement. Table 2, which compares the proportion of activists' occupations with that of adult Americans, demonstrates that

Central America peace movement activists were recruited heavily from *human service* occupations. They are religious workers, social workers, clergy, health care administrators, teachers, legislative activists, and nurses. They are not, generally, manual laborers, secretaries, accountants, business managers, technicians, or sales clerks. This data accords with other studies which socially locate political activists as drawn from "new class" backgrounds (McAdam, McCarthy, and Zald 1988: 712). But what might this say about values? When asked to explain this contrast in the follow-up survey, respondents unanimously maintained that the occupational differences reflect value differences. On the whole, they maintained, people gravitate to human service occupations who are more relationally empathetic, who wish to minimize human suffering, and who want to make a positive impact on their social world. By contrast, they asserted, people generally gravitate to business and technical occupations who are less people-oriented, more concerned with making money, and more interested in shaping the material than the social world. This interpretation, which reflects the perspectives and prejudices of human service workers, seems overstated, at least. But it is not entirely implausible. In fact, studies have shown that new-class, human-service occupations do attract or produce people with more liberal or progressive attitudes and values than business people and unskilled operators (among others Brint 1984; Bruce-Briggs 1979; Gouldner 1978).

Interviews with Central America peace movement activists confirm these findings on attitudes. Among Sanctuary activists, for example, according to Jane Guise (1990), "Protestants tended to come from the more liberal end of the spectrum and Catholics were not parish priests but mostly women from religious orders, who tended to be more independently-minded. In the Jewish sector, it was also the more liberal congregations that developed the Jewish sanctuary network."

Witness for Peace delegates also tended to hold sympathetic values and attitudes. Fran Truitt (1990) describes Witness for Peace delegates as most "deeply committed, radical leftist humanists

TABLE 2 *Occupational Ratio of Central America Peace Movement Activist to All Americans, 1985 (Relative frequency of activists employed in occupation vs. Americans employed)*

	Sanctuary	Witness for Peace
Nonclergy religious worker	107[a]	114[a]
Clergy	56[a]	39[a]
Health administrator	24	6.8
Social worker	9.5	17.23
Academic administrator	5.2	2.2
Government/legislative worker	1.8	4.7
Teacher	3.9	4.4
Nurse	2.9	2.8
Attorney	2.2	2.9
Doctor/dentist	1.3	2.3
Science professional[b]	1.4	.23
Medical technician	.61	.65
Business manager	.48	.29
Accountant	.25	.36
Secretary	.16	.24
Sales person	.13	.13
Skilled operator	.12	.09
N	(129)	(452)

Source: Statistical Abstract of the United States 1990, 1987.

Notes: [a]Compared to Americans employed in these fields in 1988. [b]Includes engineers, architects, computer analysts and programmers, chemists, and research scientists.

and Christians." And Mike Clark (1992) affirms, "When I think about the delegations that I led, there were very few people who were in favor of U.S. policy. They were going to be staying with people who had family members killed because of it! The people who went were mostly from the Judeo-Christian community, generally had been involved in social activism, and tended to be politically progressive."

These shared values tended to help to expedite the intended political effects of the Witness for Peace experience. Joe Nangle (1992), for example, observed that "as things moved along people became 'converted' in a very short time. You know? I mean, it took me 8 years working in Latin America before I realized what I was really seeing. Eight years! But it took merely a few weeks for the Witness for Peace folks to get on

track. Now, what would that mean? Were they already there? Liberal, if you will? Or even radical? Perhaps." And, according to Dick Junkin (1991): "Many Christians who came to Central America were already ideologically committed. Sure, we would get some politically uncertain people and a few dyed-in-the-wool Reaganites. But the predominance were people in sympathy with Central American revolutionary movement, or at least open enough to go see for themselves."

Altogether, these survey and interview findings suggest an important, though not surprising, relationship between adherence to values and attitudes that resonated with the Central America peace movement and the likelihood of someone actually joining or being recruited into that movement. But the exact difference these values made is not entirely clear. For the total number of Central American peace activists almost certainly did not exceed one-half of 1 percent of the entire adult American population. If so, this leaves more than 6.5 percent of American leftists and 15.5 percent of American Postmaterialists who did *not* participate in the Central America peace movement—respectively, thirteen and thirty-one times the number who did. This suggests that while compatible attitudes and values may be a necessary condition of recruitment to high-risk activism, they remain an insufficient condition. Sympathetic attitudes and values may have predisposed our activists to participate, but it appears that they alone did not induce participation. Other influences must have also been at work.

Prior Activist Experience   The Central America peace activists studied here exhibit a long history of actual experience in social movements. According to the findings presented in Table 1, the average Sanctuary and Witness for Peace activist had participated in more than seven other distinct social movements before becoming involved in the Central America peace movement. This is a number at least seven times larger than that for all adult Americans. More specifically,

Table 3 shows the percent of Central America peace activists who had previously participated in each of twelve different U.S. social movements. One-third of all Central America activists had prior experience in the women's, anti-apartheid, pro-choice, and anti-nuclear power movements. More than half had participated in civil rights, anti–Vietnam War, environmental, and anti-poverty campaigns. And, two-thirds or more had participated in anti–nuclear weapons work. How deeply were they involved in these movements? Table 4 shows the kinds of protest activities Central America peace movement activists had engaged in before joining in Central America work. Two-thirds or more had participated in lawful forms of disruptive protest, about one-third had joined in illegal forms of political confrontation, and one-fifth to one-quarter had actually been arrested for their prior participation in civil disobedience. In short, the majority of Central America peace movement activists were not political novices, but were quite experienced in prior social movement activism. . . .

Bob Bonthius (1990) observes . . . in Witness for Peace activists: "Many of the people who got involved in Witness for Peace were people who had actually had Central America experience and

TABLE 3   *Prior Social Movement Involvement by Central American Peace Activists (%)*

Prior Movement	Sanctuary	Witness for Peace
Anti-nuclear weapons	66	78
Civil rights	58	56
Anti-Vietnam	54	59
Environmental	53	60
Anti-poverty	51	57
Women's movement	36	46
Anti-apartheid	33	47
Pro-choice	31	30
Anti-nuclear power	28	33
1960s student movement	18	20
Corporate responsibility	17	16
Gay/lesbian rights	13	18
N	(129)	(452)

TABLE 4 *Central America Peace Activists' Prior Protest Experience (%)*

	Sanctuary	Witness for Peace
Previously participated in political protests, demonstrations, marches, sit-ins or vigils	65	77
Previously committed nonviolent civil disobedience or tax resistance	29	37
Previously were arrested for protesting or committing civil disobedience	14	24
N	(129)	(452)

seen a long history of U.S. repression. They had prior experience in church peace and justice work or Third World travel. Many also had come up through the civil rights movement and were pacifists."

According to Betsy Crites (1992), early Witness for Peace recruiting strategies ensured contact with politically experienced people: "We started recruiting and advertising in places that we thought the right kind of people would see it. They were peace and justice people, early on, they had to have been."

This prior experience is significant because it appears to have both radicalized participants and familiarized them with the "script" used to play the "social activist" role. From this perspective, these activists seem to have been engaged in a long-term role-transformation process which had gradually deepened their commitment to and participation in political activism. With each successive social movement involvement, these activists appear both to have become more comfortable with their participation in activism and to have engaged in a broader range of more challenging and disruptive activist tactics. . . . Mobilization into the Central America peace movement . . . typically involved a process of increased political radicalization. Three additional pieces of evidence from the surveys substantiate this. . . . First, as noted above, many participants came to the Central America peace movement already somewhat radicalized (see Table 1). Second, the Central America peace movement clearly helped to advance that process of radical-

ization. A comparison of the reported political stance of survey respondents in 1979 to their stance at the time of their Central America activism shows that 43 percent of Sanctuary and 44 percent of Witness for Peace activists grew more radical in the intervening time period. And of them, 19 percent of Sanctuary and 23 percent of Witness for Peace activists reported undergoing a major radicalization experience, involving a leftward shift at least one-third of the way across the entire ideological spectrum. On the other hand, only 4 percent of all Sanctuary and 7 percent of all Witness for Peace activists grew more politically conservative in the same time span. Betsy Crites (1992) informs us that many of those Witness for Peace delegates with little prior activist experience actually joined with the conscious intent of becoming radicalized: "I would hear people in the training say, 'I want to be transformed. I know I have some changing to do.' And you know, this wasn't supposed to be a group therapy thing, but some people almost seemed to approach it as, 'I need to face something like this, to shape me up and get me active.' And it did."

The third piece of telling evidence is that larger proportions of both Sanctuary and Witness for Peace activities engaged in legal and illegal forms of political protest and were arrested for civil disobedience *during* their Central America activism than beforehand. In other words, the extent of their collective involvement in all types of disruptive protest tactics increased with their participation in this new movement.

Central America peace activists, then, not only held sympathetic values and attitudes, but were also familiar with the processes and techniques of political protest through their considerable prior experience in two decades of social movement activism. And these prior experiences not only helped to shape their political values and attitudes. They also helped to form their personal identities in such a way that these people had come increasingly to think of themselves as "political activists." This meant that when the Central America crisis arose in the early 1980s, these men and women not only felt opposed to the Reagan policy and thought it to be wrong, as did most Americans, who nevertheless did not become mobilized into Central America peace activism. They also had developed personal activist identities which made participation in the movement a natural expression and affirmation of who they thought themselves to be as people. Hence, their familiarity with the role requirements of activism and very sense of "self" helped induce their mobilization into the movement.

Biographical Availability   Reviewing survey and interview evidence, we see that Central America peace activists reflect in their social class and life-cycle statuses a tremendous amount of biographical availability for social movement activism (see Table 1). To begin, as a whole they were significantly older than the population of adult Americans. Being on average middle-aged, rather than in their twenties or thirties, they were largely beyond the exacting tasks of earning educational degrees, establishing new careers, and raising young children, which can compete with the demands of activism. Fran Truitt (1990) describes Witness for Peace delegates as "older people, a lot of older middle class people. Very few were students." And Angela Berryman (1990) recollected:

> What type of people were active in the Central American movement? I'll tell you my small but telling experience from when a number of us did a protest sit-in at the CIA office in the

Federal Building. We were sitting there and someone said, "During the Vietnam war we would have wished that someone with a grey hair was sitting with us. Now we wish that someone without a grey hair were sitting here with us." . . .

. . .

In addition to being older, the Central America peace activists were relatively well-to-do financially, enjoying household incomes about 25 percent higher than that of the average adult American. . . . Central America peace activists were also very well educated, almost five times more likely than the average adult American to have earned a bachelor's degree or more. Indeed, among Witness for Peace and Sanctuary activists, respectively, 44 percent and 46 percent had earned master's degrees and 13 percent and 14 percent had earned doctorates.

Furthermore, Witness for Peace activists, at least, whose involvement took them into dangerous war zones, were much less likely than the average adult American to be married and thus responsible for and accountable to a spouse and possibly children. . . .

Sanctuary activists, on the other hand, were actually *more* likely to be married than the average adult American. However, most importantly, among both groups, the married activists were significantly more free of daily child care responsibilities than the typical married American. Thus, their activism did not place an extra burden on family nurturance on their spouse or hinder or endanger their relationship with their dependent children.

Finally, these peace movement participants were drawn from occupations that facilitated availability for activism. Examining Table 2, we see that, compared to the occupational distribution of all adult Americans, these Central America activists tended to be drawn disproportionally from time-flexible occupations. . . . The typical work schedules of clergy, religious workers, social workers, teachers, legislative workers, and academic and health administrators are much less structurally rigid than the typical nine-to-five-with-coffee-break routines of business people, office workers, and manual operators. Thus, when the refugees in sanctuary need to go clothes shopping, the college professor is able to take them any afternoon after classes. But the secretary can't go until after dinner or on the weekend. Likewise, for a Presbyterian minister, a twenty-day trip to Nicaragua means finding guest preachers for two weeks and postponing the elders' meeting. But for a business accountant, it means spending an entire year's worth of vacation time. . . .

Thus, people involved in the Central America peace movement were those who not only enjoyed relatively high degrees of emotional, relational, and financial freedom to participate, but also those who could expect to generate less friction trying to mesh the demands of activism with those of work.

Relational Links to Activism   Central America peace movement participants also possessed an unusually large number of relational ties to activism. These served both as channels through which the activists were initially recruited into the movement and as social attachments that sustained their involvement over the years of struggle. Table 5 summarizes the sources by which activists were first introduced to Sanctu-

ary and Witness for Peace. It shows that in 70 to 80 percent of cases, knowledge about the Central America peace movement was diffused through personal relationships and organizational memberships (since many personal relationships are formed within the context of formal organizations, such as churches, it is impossible to disaggregate the numbers for the two). Quite clearly, the vast majority of Central America activists were exposed to the movement by friends, family members, fellow political activists, and fellow church and synagogue members.

The activists, however, were not only first introduced to the movement through their relational and organizational ties, most of them—84 percent of Sanctuary and 56 percent of Witness for Peace activists—were also *drawn into* the movement through face-to-face discussions with like-minded people (see Table 6). Hence, making a commitment to activism appears to have been a more relational than private process. Bob Van Denend (1992), for example, recalls the group affirmation he received for his initial desire to do a Witness for Peace trip: "We were involved in a peace group that met in our backyard and also a regular pot-luck dinner with a group of Quakers. We passed the Witness for Peace brochure around at these meetings and everybody said, 'Yes, this is

TABLE 5   *Personal and Organizational vs. Impersonal Sources of Activists' Introduction to Sanctuary and WFP (%)*

Sanctuary			Witness for Peace
Church or synagogue	35	34	Other WFP activists
Prior SMO membership	20	19	Religious publication
Other sanctuary activities	15	16	Family or friends
Religious publications	13	12	Prior SMO membership
Denominational promotion	9	9	Church or synagogue
Secular mass media	8	5	Secular mass media
		5	WFP mailing
Relational/organizational	79	71	Relational/organizational
Impersonal	21	29	Impersonal
Total	(100)	(100)	
N	(129)	(452)	

TABLE 6   *Relational Links to Central American Activism (%)*

	Sanctuary	Witness for Peace
Respondents whose decision to join movement emerged from small group discussions among like-minded people	84	56
Friends on a Witness for Peace trip or in Sanctuary	16	59
Friends involved in Central America peace movement	18	32
N	(129)	(452)

absolutely right.' People communicated that they believed that it was the right thing for me to do."

The importance of relational ties in diffusing knowledge of and evoking commitment to the movement is also clear in the answers survey respondents wrote to open-ended questions about how they became involved in activism, of which the following are representative:

. . .

We knew a priest who was transporting two Salvadoran refugees north and I heard them speak. They asked us for help. On that cold February night, I was dumbstruck, compelled to respond. I thought, "If it were my children, pray God, would someone help them?" (Thirty-eight-year-old, female, Methodist child care worker)

. . .

I was taking a theology course taught by a former Witness for Peace delegate, who shared his experience with the class. I decided I wanted to go too. (Thirty-four-year-old, female, Unitarian Universalist minister)

I was good friends with some strong anti-nuke folk. Their attitude of resistance got me fired up to do Central America work. (Thirty-seven-year-old, male, Catholic teacher)

. . .

We were visiting an old, old friend of ours in Indonesia, a Dutch Jesuit that we worked with years ago organizing labor unions. He talked to us late into the night about liberation theology

and Witness for Peace. (Sixty-two-year-old, female, retired Episcopal)

. . .

My husband was interested in Central America and decided to go on a delegation. I resisted, but finally I decided to go rather than stay home and worry about him. That trip changed my life! (Thirty-seven-year-old, female, Quaker grade school teacher)

A friend of mine told me that a Salvadoran refugee was going to speak in our community. I went to hear him speak and my consciousness was raised and I became involved. (Thirty-seven-year-old, female, Jewish, at-home parent)

A close friend of mine and I were fed up with Reagan's foreign policy. We discussed it a lot and decided to join a peace and justice group, which helped us get more deeply involved. (Twenty-one-year-old, female, Catholic counselor)

Furthermore, beyond the initial introduction and commitment, the activists' ongoing participation itself appears to have been accompanied and reinforced by relational ties to the movement (see Table 6). Among Sanctuary activists, about one out of six friends was also involved in Sanctuary or in the Central America peace movement. Well more than one-half of Witness for Peace delegates traveled to Central America with a friend. And fully one-third of friends of Witness for Peace activists were themselves activists in the Central America peace movement. We see, then, that Central America peace activists were people who possessed extensive relational ties that exposed and recruited them to the movement and offered participation-sustaining companionship during the activism. . . .

Relational Support for Activism Biographical availability and . . . relational ties to activism are clearly important. But a micro-structural explanation that accounts for only these . . . factors still leaves a number of questions unanswered (McAdam and Paulsen 1993). Exactly how do social ties to activism function to mobilize activists? Is the mere *existence* of a tie sufficient? Or does the type or quality of the relationship matter? How do relationships with people *not* tied to activism affect potential activists' decisions about participation? Further, how do social movement recruits negotiate between relationships that support and those that oppose their activism? And what factors might affect the significance of that support and opposition? The identity salience of the supporters and opposers? Geographical distance? Frequency of contact? In what follows, we attempt to begin to answer some of these questions.

In their surveys, Witness for Peace activists were asked to identify the two people who most strongly supported and the two who most strongly opposed their Central America activism. They were asked to specify both the *type* of relationship and the *frequency* of communication they had with each of these people. The results of these questions are striking. To begin, we observe in Table 7 that fully one-half of all Witness for Peace activists had absolutely nobody oppose their Central America activism. They encountered nothing but support for or indifference to their decision to join Witness for Peace, travel to Nicaragua, and fight against U.S. policy in Central America. Comparatively, only 2 percent of Witness for Peace activists had absolutely nobody support their activism. These differences in the absolute amount of support and opposition of any kind are substantial.

Furthermore, we can observe a pattern in the *type* of relationships that tended to support and oppose the activists. Specifically, other than "nobody," the most frequent opponents of activism tended to have been parents and family relatives. Considering that the average Witness for Peace activist was 45 years old in 1985, we can safely suppose that these are mostly relationships of secondary authority and relevance. Indeed, one would almost *expect* elderly parents and family relatives to worry about such involvements. But one would likely not make one's final decision

TABLE 7 *Relationship Offering Witness for Peace Delegates First or Second Strongest Supporter and Opposer (%)*[a]

Relationship	Supporter	Opposer
Friend, Acquaintance, Work Colleague	51	15
Spouse	37	5
Fellow Church/Synagogue Member	24	4
Fellow Member of Political/Social Organization	20	.2
Witness for Peace Spokesperson	17	.2
Clergy	13	1
Children	8	5
Parents	7	26
Family Relatives	4	19
Nobody	2	50
N	(452)	(452)

Note: [a]Percentages do not add to 100 because categories combine percentages of first and second strongest supporter/opposer.

TABLE 8   *Frequency of Communication of Witness for Peace Delegates with Strongest Supporter and Opposer (%)*

Frequency of Communication	Supporter	Opposer
Constantly	13	1
Daily	27	7
Few Times a Week	19	7
Once a Week	18	11
Few Times a Month	13	10
Monthly or Less	10	63
Total	(100)	(99)
N	(452)	(452)

based on their opinions. On the other hand, the most likely supporters of activism were friends, work colleagues, spouses, fellow church and synagogue members, and fellow social activists—all relationships of far greater immediacy and importance. Furthermore, we see in Table 8 that the Witness for Peace activists received support from people with whom they communicated very frequently and encountered opposition from people with whom they interacted very infrequently. Thus, on the whole, the Witness for Peace activists appear to have been supported by people whose opinions were more important, whose presence was more consistent and direct, and whose communications were more frequent than those who opposed them. Thus the identity salience, social proximity, and frequency of communication of supporters and opponents of activism all appear to be important influences in differential recruitment.

To explore more precisely the matter of relational support for activism, I also asked Witness for Peace activists to identify their core "political reference group" (PRG)—that is, the two people whose opinions on social and political issues they most sought out and respected. In this way we moved beyond suppositions about the nature of people's relationships to rely on the respondents' own specific evaluations. Table 9, which shows the PRG members' opinion about the activists' involvement in Witness for Peace, reveals considerable differences in support and opposition. The vast majority of activists had at least one, if not both, members of their PRG supporting their participation in Witness for Peace. Conversely, an equally vast majority had neither of their core PRG opposing their activism. People who actually became mobilized into Central America peace activism, in other words, tended to be those who enjoyed support and encouragement from the

Table 9 Support and Opposition for Witness for Peace Activism from the Two Most Important People in Respondents' Political Reference Group (%)

Two Most Important People	Support	Opposition
Both of two	47	1
One of two	40	11
None	14	88
Total	(101)	(100)
N	(452)	(452)

people whose social and political opinions and judgments they most sought out and respected.

Our evidence confirms the critical influence of all four micro-structural factors in sorting out who became Central America peace activists and who did not. Compared to the population from which they were drawn, our Central America peace activists enjoyed considerably more biographical availability for, relational and organizational ties to, and relational support for social movement activism. These key situational factors, along with people's greater prior activist experience, may account for the fact that, although millions of Americans shared values and attitudes supportive of the Central America peace movement, only a minority of them actually became mobilized into movement activism.

Summary   Forming a composite picture based on our findings thus far, the typical Central America peace activist appears to be a white, forty-five-year-old human service worker— probably a church, health, social-work, or academic professional. He or she—more likely a she—is a person of deep religious faith who actively participates in church or synagogue. Our typical activist possesses a master's degree in their field, possibly even a doctorate, and enjoys a comfortable household income. The structure of their profession affords them the time flexibility to become involved in political activism, an opportunity they take advantage of. Our typical activist is also either unmarried and without children or, if married, childless or with children who are grown and almost out of the house.

Ideologically, our typical Central America activist tends to lean toward the political and cultural left, although they probably dislike thinking in traditional left-right political categories and don't belong to any traditional leftist political parties or organizations. In any case, they are generally suspicious of, if not antagonistic toward, most Reagan administration policies. Indeed, more concerned with issues of human rights, social equality, political participation, and the aesthetic and environmental quality of life than with securing a strong economy and na-

tional defense, they almost certainly voted in 1980 for either Jimmy Carter or John Anderson.

Central America activism is not our typical activist's first experience in extra-electoral politics. Indeed, they have been involved in four or five different political movements during the twenty-five years since their college days—most likely the civil rights movement in the late 1950s and 1960s, the anti-war movement in the late 1960s and early 1970s, environmental and poverty work in the 1970s, and the Freeze campaign in the early 1980s. Before ever particularly knowing much about Central America, they had participated in a few protest marches and demonstrations and perhaps had even committed and been arrested for civil disobedience. For this reason, they don't feel particularly uncomfortable thinking of themselves as political activists.

Finally, most of the social and professional circles in which our typical Central America activist circulates are supportive of their political commitments. Indeed, their Central America activism has been strongly encouraged by an identifiable network of friends, family members, and work colleagues, many of whom are also Central America peace activists. These relationships provide an ongoing reinforcement of our activists' political values and attitudes as well as companionship and support that helps to mitigate the risks and sacrifices inherent in political activism.

Moral Commitments as Motivations

Sympathetic values and attitudes, prior activist experience, biographical availability, and relational . . . ties to and relational support for activism go a long way toward explaining who became Central America peace activists and who did not. But another dimension of the actual process of deciding to become an activist deserves closer attention. In examining how activists actually went about deciding to join the movement and what considerations they took into account in their decision making, we discover a number of curious findings.

For example, the surveys asked Sanctuary and Witness for Peace activists how much they had

TABLE 10   Respondents Calculating the Costs and Benefits of Activism (%)

	Sanctuary	Witness for Peace
Calculated a lot	20	21
Calculated somewhat	23	25
Calculated a little	29	26
Did not calculate	28	28
Total	(100)	(100)
N	(129)	(452)

TABLE 11   Expected Costs of Central American Activism (%)

	Sanctuary	Witness for Peace
Very or extremely costly	14	11
Rather costly	17	19
Somewhat costly	28	27
Hardly costly	32	28
Not at all costly	9	15
Total	(100)	(100)
N	(129)	(452)

calculated the costs and benefits of their potential participation before joining the movement. Table 10 shows that these Central America activists reported more likely than not having calculated the costs and benefits only a little or not calculating them at all. Why would people willfully breaking federal immigration laws and traveling to Third World war zones have done so little reckoning?

Furthermore, the surveys also asked the activists to recall how costly—in time, money, relationships, and lost opportunities—they expected, before becoming involved, their Sanctuary and Witness for Peace activism would be. Table 11 shows that almost one-third of respondents who went on to become activist anticipated beforehand that doing so would be "rather," "very," or "extremely" costly. These numbers are corroborated by many of the comments about the anticipated costliness of activism that respondents wrote on their surveys, including the following:

> When I left for Nicaragua, I thought my marriage was over because my husband said that if I actually went he would divorce me.

> This was 1983 and I expected the worst. I knew full well that any one of us could be badly injured or killed traveling out in the war zones.

> My boss told me that if I went to Central America, there would not be a job waiting for me when I came back.

Did activists like these, who knew that participation could or would be exceedingly costly, merely calculate that the expected rewards of participation would outweigh the high anticipated costs? Or was another dynamic at work?

Two important facts are worth bearing in mind here. First, unlike the case in many social movements, the primary potential beneficiaries of Central America peace movement success would have been the people of Central America, not U.S. movement activists or even U.S. citizens generally. In other words, this is a case of a doubly altruistic motive involving, first, a "*public good*" enjoyed, second, by a public *different* from the one to which the activists themselves belonged. Not only would the good have been consumed by people who did not contribute to providing it, but the good would *not* have been consumed by those who *did* contribute to providing it. The second relevant fact is that Central America peace activists were attempting to reverse the highest-priority foreign policy initiative of one of the most popular, persistent, and ideologically committed U.S. presidents in history. The objective probability of the movement achieving ultimate success was low. Why then would thousands of reasonable decision makers, with an immense variety of potential activities to choose from, commit to engage in one exacting very high personal costs yet holding out little promise of success that, even if achieved, would not primarily be of tangible benefit to themselves or their own society?

A series of additional findings compound the enigma. First, curiously, many of the Sanctuary and Witness for Peace activists claimed that they did not really experience the "costs" of their activism as costs. On many surveys, respondents qualified their answers to questions about the costs of activism by writing in the margins statements like these:

> That's a difficult question to answer because it makes "costs" sound too negative.

> I cannot *not* act on my beliefs, so I didn't think about it in terms of costs and benefits.

> I don't look at the high costs of my work in a negative sense, I just had to spend a lot of time and money.

> I can't describe my experience as costly. It was a gift!

These are intriguing comments. One wonders how to make sense of the notion of "rewarding costs" or "positive costs."

Next, Sanctuary activists who seriously underestimated the costs of activism were no more likely to spend fewer years involved in the movement than were those who correctly estimated or overestimated the costs of activism. One would think that activists who got more trouble than they originally bargained for—that is, who discovered activism to be much more costly than expected—would likely reconsider the cost-benefit ratio and perhaps drop out of the movement earlier than those who didn't. But statistical analyses of the data reveal no relationship whatsoever between people's over- or underestimations of the costs of activism and the number of years of their involvement as activists. . . .

Finally, besides gathering data on activists' calculations and expected costs, the surveys also measured the depth and breadth of each participant's involvement in Central America activism. Respondents reported both the average number of hours they spent on Central America activism per week and the variety of political protest activities in which they participated as a part of their Central America activism. Table 12 shows the correlations between the respondents' expected costs and ability to "free-ride" and their depth and breadth of involvement in activism.

TABLE 12   *Correlation Coefficients for Factors Affecting Differential Levels of Central America Activism*

	Hours Spent in Activism	Breadth of Activist's Political Activities
Greater expected costs of WFP activism	.115*	.121*
Greater expected costs of Sanctuary activism	.040	.257**
Larger Sanctuary core group	.305**	.103
N (Witness for Peace)	(452)	(452)
N (Sanctuary)	(129)	(129)

** = p < .01 * = p < .05

Apparently, the more costly Sanctuary and Witness for Peace activists expected beforehand that their participation would be, the *more* deeply and broadly those activists actually became involved in activism. And the more Sanctuary workers were afforded greater opportunities to free-ride by virtue of working on larger Sanctuary task force committees, the *more* hours they actually spent doing Sanctuary work. Higher expected personal costs and greater opportunities to free-ride did not discourage, but actually promoted greater personal participation in activism.

How are we to make sense of these findings? The most plausible interpretation is that the majority of these activists were motivated primarily by moral commitments that overrode not only the ordinary limits of acceptable action alternatives, but also perhaps the normal process of decision making itself.

Such an interpretation assumes that all human actions are prompted and guided by two irreducible motives: pleasure and morality. On the one hand, people act to satisfy the ubiquitous desire for self-interested pleasure. On the other hand and concurrently, people act to affirm the inescapable imperatives of their moral commitments. These two fundamental motives are irreducible: as sources of valuation they cannot be reconciled or integrated into one all-encompassing utility. Pleasure motives are oriented toward *consequences* of action and the achievement of ends subjectively defined as desirable. Morality motives, on the other hand, are concerned with the *intentions* of actors and the discharging of what are believed to be objectively existing normative obligations. The former revolve around options and interests and seek self-satisfaction, while the latter revolve around imperatives and commitments and strive for identity affirmation. Charles Taylor writes (1989: 4) that moral acts, "involve discriminations of right and wrong, better or worse, higher or lower, which are not rendered valid by our own desires, inclinations, or choices, but rather stand independent of these and offer standards by which they can be judged."

In philosophical language, pleasure is a *teleological* motive—impelling action because of certain desired ends it will achieve—while morality is a *deontological* motive—prompting action because the action is right in and of itself, entirely apart from whatever ends it may produce. In addition to being irreducible, the two motives, are also recurrently in conflict: satisfying one's own pleasure often requires compromising moral commitments, and abiding by moral commitments often requires sacrifices of pleasure.

Human selves, then, are best understood as internally divided, engaged in perpetual, creative inner conflict. People seek to balance their moral commitments and their pleasures, to negotiate a judicious mix of the two, rather than to maximize either. Exactly how they adjudicate between these irreducible and often conflicting motives in choosing courses of action depends largely upon the nature of the actions themselves and the social contexts in which they take place. In some situations—such as choosing vacation destinations—the pleasure motive predominates. In others—such as rescuing one's children from a burning building—moral imperatives largely govern behavior. Most actions and contexts, however, are not that clear-cut and thus involve the significant interplay of both motives. The majority of human activities, in other words, are indeed performed with "mixed motives."

Participation in Central America peace activism, we presume, was prompted by a mix of pleasure-seeking and morality-affirming motives, the exact balance of which probably differed from activist to activist. But given the nature and context of this Central America activism, the motive of abiding by moral commitments appears to have been primary for most of the participants. In other words, the majority of activists became involved more because they believed it was the right and necessary thing for them to do, *whatever the outcome,* and not primarily because they calculated that the probable consequences of their individual participation warranted their involvement and justified the costs it would entail. Thus, engaging in activism represented a response to moral obligations and the dictates of conscience more than the calculated pursuit of either selective incentives or an end-state collective good.

Most of the activists' accounts, gathered in interviews and surveys, confirm this interpretation. The following quotes . . . are representative:

> With regard to motivation, I must say that the moving spirit for Sanctuary was faith in the gospel of Jesus. I had no other choice but to get involved if I was to remain faithful to the Christian Gospel and its option for the poor, the persecuted, and those hungering and thirsting for justice.

> I stayed in the home of a Nicaraguan last January named Manuel Rivera. I promised him then that I would tell his story here in the U.S. I have since learned that he has been killed by the Contras. So I feel even more strongly that I must tell his story. I would rather not get arrested for the first time in my life. But I'm afraid I must. Manuel Rivera is the reason.

> . . .

> As a Jew, I know what it means to be persecuted. If it hadn't been for a few kind people, no Jews would have escaped the Holocaust. Now it was my turn to take risks on behalf of others.

These testimonies are spoken in the language of identity-affirming moral obligation, not ends-oriented rational instrumentalism. Indeed, for these people and the tens of thousands like them, there were, in a sense, ultimately no choices to be made here, no probabilities to weigh or results to consider. They had "no other choice." They "could not have *not* helped in any way possible." In the end, it didn't matter whether they would win or lose. They were simply "chosen." All that remained was to perform faithfully the tasks morality demanded. As John Fife of Southside Presbyterian Church, Tucson, Arizona, explained after his trial about a fifteen-year-old Salvadoran boy who had come to his church for help after his family had been killed (quoted in Tomsho 1987: 206): "The haunting thought that came to me was, if that was my boy, what would I want the church to do? We had no choice. None of us ever had a choice. Our only choice was whether we wanted to sell our souls."

Understanding the participation of activists in the Central America peace movement in these terms makes the curious evidence on calculation and expected costs intelligible. To the extent that the activists' involvements were motivated by moral commitments, many participated *in spite of* the very high expected costs (Table 11), not because some other probable consequences were figured to outweigh those costs. This helps to explain the lack of the participants' calculation of the costs of activism (Table 10). Their primary recognition of the moral obligation to participate tended to render option-evaluating, cost-benefit analyses irrelevant. As the activist cited above stated: "I cannot *not* act on my beliefs, so I didn't think about it in terms of costs and benefits."

This perspective also helps to explain why many activists did not experience "costs" as costs. Spending or losing time, money, energy, and opportunities in order to voluntarily discharge the moral obligations one has internalized can often, in fact, be experienced as affirming and even rewarding. "Costs" as necessary means to ends actually become transubstantiated into integral elements of positively regarded experiences. Thus, survey respondents could claim: "I can't describe my [objectively "costly"] experience as costly. It was a gift!" And Fran Truitt could simultaneously name her calling out of retirement to fight Contra aid a blessing and a burden.

Furthermore, this approach transforms the very meaning of the calculation process itself by reversing the order of the evaluation and the conclusion: "calculating" the costs of activism appears to represent not so much a mechanism for making decisions, but a process of reckoning or coming to terms with the practical implications of what one has *already* decided to do because of other values and commitments. People first realized that they must and would become politically involved, *then* they sorted through the practical implications of what that involvement would entail. This interpretation explains the positive association found between expected costs and the amount of prior calculation. The more costs the already-committed-to participation promised to exact, the more attention the activists had to give to sorting out the implications of those costs. More importantly, this interpretation explains the positive associations found between expected costs and opportunities to "free-ride" and the depth and breadth of the activists' involvements (Table 12). The "expected costs" were, in fact, not factors plugged into a decision-making formula. Rather, they were reflections of an awareness on the part of the incipient activists of just how deeply they were already committed to becoming involved and of the probable costs of that involvement. Moreover, larger Sanctuary task force committees were not viewed as opportunities for free-riding—why would a profoundly morally motivated person wish to free-ride?—but as encouraging and reinforcing resources for accomplishing the tasks people felt responsible to discharge. In other words, for people internally motivated by moral commitments, the effect was one of strength-in-numbers, not shirking-behind-numbers.

So, why would thousands of people, with an immense variety of potential activities to choose from, commit to engage in one exacting very high personal costs yet holding out little promise of success that, even if achieved, would not primarily be of tangible benefit to themselves or their own society? The most plausible answer appears to be: only if they were primarily motivated by moral commitments. But to clarify the implications of this answer . . . we must state that Central America peace movement activists were not necessarily extraordinary saints or ethical virtuosos. Indeed, this view does not require that people become angels before discharging moral obligations in their actions. According to our model, theoretically, most people, given the right experiences and circumstances, should be capable of equivalent expressions of morally driven behavior. What determined that *these* particular people became Central America peace activists, and not some others, was not that they were moral superhumans, but primarily that they possessed the right backgrounds and were found in the right place at the right time. It was this population's unique combination of religious commitments, structural links to Central

America, available organizational capacities, supportive political values and attitudes, prior social movement experiences, biographical availability, relational . . . ties to activism, and relational support for participation coalescing in the context of opening macro-political opportunities that significantly advantaged their chances of recruitment into this particular movement. The activists' differential recruitment, in other words, was just as socially structured as was their moral outrage. . . .

REFERENCES

Berryman, Angela. 1990. Interview, November 26. Philadelphia, Penn.

Bonthius, Bob. 1990. Interview, October 16. Ellsworth, Maine.

Brint, Steven. 1984. "'New Class' and Cumulative Trend Explanations of the Liberal Political Attitudes of Professionals." *American Journal of Sociology* 90: 30-71.

Bruce-Briggs, B. (ed.). 1979. *The New Class.* New York: McGraw-Hill.

Clark, Mike. 1992. Interview, July 28. Washington, DC.

Crites, Betsy. 1992. Interview, August 1. Durham, North Carolina.

Gouldner, Alvin. 1978. "The New Class Project I." *Theory and Society* 6: 153–204.

Guise, Jane. 1990. Interview, August 9. Cambridge, Massachusetts.

Hope, Sam. 1992. Interview, July 28. Washington, DC.

Inglehart, Ronald. 1990. *Cultural Shift in Advanced Industrial Society.* Princeton, NJ: Princeton University Press.

Junkin, Dixon. 1991. Interview, January 7. Pasadena, Calif.

McAdam, Doug, & Ronnelle Paulsen. 1993. "Social Ties and Activism: Toward a Specification of the Relationship." *American Sociological Review.* 99:3 (November).

McAdam, Doug, John McCarthy, & Mayer Zald. 1988. "Social Movements." In Neil Smelser (ed.), *Handbook of Sociology.* Newbury Park: Sage.

Nangle, Joe. 1992. Interview, July 27. Washington, DC.

Pastor, Robert. 1982. "Our Real Interests in Central America." *The Atlantic Monthly* (July): 27–39.

Shumway, Anne. 1990. Interview, December 17. Cambridge, Massachusetts.

Taylor, Charles. 1989. *Sources of the Self: The Making of the Modern Identity.* Cambridge: Harvard University Press.

Tomsho, Robert. 1987. *The American Sanctuary Movement.* Austin: Texas Monthly Press.

Truitt, Fran. 1990. Interview, October 16. Ellsworth, Maine.

Van Denend, Bob. 1992. Interview, August 3. Durham, North Carolina.

THINKING ABOUT THE READING

Describe the typical Central American peace activist. What is the sociological significance of these common traits? Smith writes that these activists were not "moral superhumans, but . . . possessed the right backgrounds and were found in the right place at the right time." What do you suppose he means by this? Unlike social movements that focus on domestic conditions, this one was an attempt to influence foreign policy. Indeed, members of one of the organizations Smith surveyed (Witness for Peace) actually went to Central America to protest U.S. involvement there. What do you think about Americans traveling to foreign countries to protest American policy? Does such activity reinforce American strength on the global stage by showing that the United States can be tolerant of diverse and critical opinions among its citizens, or does it serve as a sign of weakness, disunity, and a potential threat to national safety?